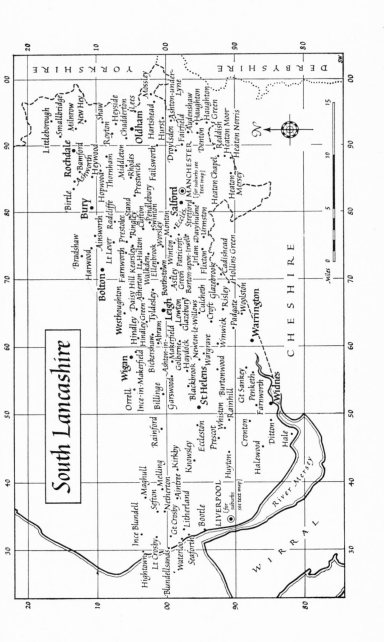

South Lancashire

*The publication of this volume has been made
possible by a grant from*
THE LEVERHULME TRUST
to cover all the necessary research work

THE BUILDINGS OF ENGLAND

Lancashire

I
THE INDUSTRIAL AND COMMERCIAL SOUTH

BY

NIKOLAUS PEVSNER

★

PENGUIN BOOKS

Penguin Books Ltd, Harmondsworth, Middlesex, England
Penguin Books, 625 Madison Avenue, New York, New York 10022, U.S.A.
Penguin Books Australia Ltd, Ringwood, Victoria, Australia
Penguin Books Canada Ltd, 2801 John Street, Markham, Ontario, Canada L3R 1B4
Penguin Books (N.Z.) Ltd, 182–190 Wairau Road, Auckland 10, New Zealand

—

First published 1969
Reprinted 1979

—

ISBN 0 14 0710.36 1

—

Copyright © Nikolaus Pevsner, 1969

—

Made and printed in Great Britain by
Butler & Tanner Ltd, Frome and London
Set in Monotype Plantin

*To all those who
give so generously of their time
and energy to the maintenance and
development of the
VICTORIAN SOCIETY*

CONTENTS

Map References

★

The numbers printed in italic type in the margin against the place names in the gazetteer of the book indicate the position of the place in question on the index map (pages 2–3), which is divided into sections by the 10-kilometre reference lines of the National Grid. The reference given here omits the two initial letters (formerly numbers) which in a full grid reference refer to the 100-kilometre squares into which the country is divided. The first two numbers indicate the *western* boundary, and the last two the *southern* boundary, of the 10-kilometre square in which the place in question is situated. For example Widnes (reference 5080) will be found in the 10-kilometre square bounded by grid lines 50 and 60 on the *west* and 80 and 90 on the *south*; Bolton (reference 7000) in the square bounded by grid lines 70 and 80 on the *west* and 00 and 10 on the *south*.

The map contains all those places, whether towns, villages, or isolated buildings, which are the subject of separate entries in the text.

FOREWORD

Lancashire is published in two volumes: the industrial South and the rural North. The dividing line has been fixed as follows from W to E: Ince Blundell S, Formby N – Maghull S, Lydiate N – Rainford S, Skelmersdale N – Orrell S, Upholland and Shevington N – Wigan S, Standish N – Hindley S, Horwich N – Bolton S, Edgeworth N – Bury S, Tottington and Ramsbottom N – Rochdale and Littleborough S, Whitworth and Wardle N. It is, I am afraid, all rather arbitrary, and if the N volume is called the rural North, that disregards the fact that the industrial towns of Preston, Blackburn, Burnley, Colne, Nelson, Chorley are all in the rural volume. However, it will, I hope, be agreed that they are more incidental to the total scenery than their counterparts in the S, where on even the closest study tour one sees green fields only as a rare reward.

South Lancashire is the most difficult area I have ever had to describe. It is large and it contains Manchester as well as Liverpool, and Bolton and Warrington and Wigan and Rochdale and the rest. I have therefore to begin this foreword by thanking more assistants than is usual in these volumes. Mr Edward Hubbard did the preparing exceptionally fully and wholly impeccably. Moreover he drove me through Liverpool and arranged the drives so that everything was seen in the most practical order, a formidable job of map annotating. And, over and above that, he contributed all the time out of his considerable knowledge of Liverpool and especially of Victorian Liverpool. Not for nothing is he the Secretary of the Liverpool Group of the Victorian Society. Ted Hubbard also drove through most of what might be called the non-countryside. For Manchester Dr Tom Wesley took over, chemist but co-begetter of the best book on the modern architecture of Cambridge. He drove me, and to my surprise enjoyed himself, even his own anger over Manchester housing past and present. Ted Hubbard and Tom Wesley worked every night until late, planning and mapping and making my life generally easier. Seeing the time it took me to visit and to write and them to prepare, my respect for Mrs Wedgwood grew yet greater for having done all this single-handed to describe Birmingham.

Besides Ted Hubbard and Tom Wesley I have to thank my secretary, Mrs J. Tabner, for all the correspondence and filing involved, Miss Dorothy Dorn for once again coping with my abominable writ-

ing and converting it into perfect typescript, Mrs I. Nairn for dealing quietly and faultlessly with all Buildings of England *affairs from the publisher's end – sub-editing, proof reading, and the rest (where would I be without her ?), Mrs and Mr Hubbard for hospitality, Mrs Wesley for resourceful sandwich compositions, Miss E. Jones for making our stay at Rathbone Hall, University of Liverpool, comfortable.*

To these, on the scholarly side, I have to add the following : Donald Buttress for very much unpublished information on Victorian churches, for actually writing descriptive paragraphs on a number of them, and for using his scarce spare time while teaching in America to read my Manchester text and improve it, Ernest Hollowell for providing me with quite a large number of photographs of church interiors which I had not seen myself – never have I been spoiled like that in my whole B. of E. life – John Archer for much material on Edgar Wood, A. W. Sewter for much information on Morris glass, Denis Evinson for information on Catholic churches, Jeffrey Haworth for very much material on Lancashire houses – largely his own research, Ivan Hall for comments on Georgian building in and around Manchester, Dr Quentin Hughes and Frank Jenkins for allowing Mr Hubbard to use theses and similar material in the Liverpool and Manchester Schools of Architecture, J. F. Bradley for material on mills at Bolton and J. B. Howcroft for material on mills at Oldham, and the following librarians who have answered repeated and sometimes difficult questions: Dr G. Chandler, the City Librarian of Liverpool, and Mr. T. Walsh, the Local History Librarian at the Manchester Library, and (in alphabetical order of towns) Mr T. Ashworth, City Librarian of Bolton; Mr P. Chadwick, Borough Librarian of Bury; Mr J. W. Carter, Director of the Oldham Art Gallery; Mr R. E. Birkitt of the Prestwich Area Libraries; Mr P. Sykes, City Librarian of Rochdale; Mr H. Caistor, Chief Librarian of St Helens; Mr G. B. Cotton, City Librarian of Salford; Miss F. Scattergood, Chief Librarian of Stretford; Mr G. A. Carter, Chief Librarian of Warrington; and Mr H. H. G. Arthur, Borough Librarian of Wigan.

I am also greatly indebted to all those incumbents who have answered questions about their churches and read proofs, and to all those owners of houses who have allowed me access. I owe it to them to state here that the description of a house in my gazetteer does not mean that it is open to the public.

The Introduction to Prehistoric Remains and all the gazetteer entries on them are by Derek Simpson. The Introduction to, and the gazetteer entries about, Roman Remains are by Professor Barry Cun-

liffe. The Introduction to Building Materials is written by Alec Clifton-Taylor. The Ministry of Housing and Local Government (here abbreviated M H L G) *have a statutory duty to draw up lists of buildings of architectural or historic interest and have again very kindly put at my disposal the lists compiled by the Chief Investigator and his staff. The National Monuments Record* (N M R) *have as always been helpful and generous. Lancashire is not one of their show counties. There are so far for the whole county only fifty-seven boxes. For Victorian churches my own material was greatly increased by Mr Peter Ferriday's Index of Restorations which he most generously gave on permanent loan to The Buildings of England* (abbreviated PF) *and by the Goodhart-Rendel Index at the Royal Institute of British Architects* (abbreviated G R). *Sir Thomas Kendrick's Index of Stained Glass I have, thanks to his kindness, also had access to* (abbreviated T K).

The principles on which the following gazetteer is founded are the same as in the thirty-five volumes of The Buildings of England which precede it. I have myself seen everything that I describe. Where this is not the case the information obtained by other means is placed in brackets. Information ought to be as complete as the space of the volume permits for churches prior to c.1830 and all town houses, manor houses, and country houses of more than purely local interest. Movable furnishings are not included in secular buildings, though they are in churches. Exceptions to the latter rule are bells, hatchments, chests, chairs, plain fonts, and altar tables. Royal arms, coffin lids with foliate crosses, and brasses of post-Reformation date are mentioned occasionally, church plate of after 1830 only rarely. Crosses are omitted where only a plain base or a stump of the shaft survives. As for churches and chapels of after 1830, I had to make a selection, and this is dictated by significance otherwise in the light of architectural history. The same applies to secular buildings of the C 19 *and* C 20. *The churches of the latter centuries are frequently not orientated. In these cases* W, E, N, *and* S *in my gazetteer are to be understood ritually, i.e. with the altar end called* E.

Finally, as in all previous volumes, it is necessary to end the foreword to this with an appeal to all users to draw my attention to errors and omissions.

INTRODUCTION

THE part of England described in this volume is one of the most densely populated areas of Europe. It comprises less than 500 square miles and had in 1961 a population of about 3½ million: over 13 per cent of England. The result of this in terms of *The Buildings of England* is a unique shortage of buildings before the second half of the C 18, i.e. the beginning of the Industrial Revolution, and a unique wealth of buildings of the C 19. This introduction therefore, in complete contrast to those of any of the volumes so far published, is very largely a Victorian introduction.

If, to keep up the arrangement of all its predecessors, the introduction tries to start with Anglo-Saxon and Norman and Early English, what are their relics? Parts of ANGLO-SAXON crosses at Winwick (which must have been a very large cross), Bolton, Eccles, Childwall (Liverpool), and Walton (Liverpool), a re-set NORMAN chancel arch at Middleton, an Early Norman font with Adam and Eve and Saints at Kirkby, one re-set Norman capital at Childwall (Liverpool), bits of Norman carving at Bolton, and one re-set possibly Norman stone in the E gable of Flixton, the EARLY ENGLISH arcade piers at Rochdale, the E.E. chancel and chancel aisle at Maghull, and the E.E. lower part of the W tower at Wigan, negligible bits of DECORATED work at Deane (Bolton), Farnworth near Widnes, Hale (tower), Radcliffe, Sefton, Winwick (tower and s arcade), and Warrington (the E crypt and the curious variety of reticulated tracery in the chancel). Nothing could expose the insignificance of medieval religious architecture in South Lancashire more dramatically than the total absence of any abbey or indeed proper priory. There was nothing except Kersal (Salford), a Cluniac cell for two monks, and Marland, Rochdale, a grange of the Cistercian Whalley, and, in addition, of houses of friars, the Augustinian (Austin) house at Warrington founded c.1280.

On the other hand manor houses begin to be of more than local interest in the FOURTEENTH CENTURY – manor houses, not castles. For CASTLES are totally absent. The only fortified building in the area is Radcliffe Tower, a pele-tower or tower-house of the North English type with a tunnel-vaulted basement. As for MANOR HOUSES, leaving aside the problems of dating and taking

the c14 with the c15 and the early c16, Bradley Old Hall, Burton-wood has a gatehouse, formerly vaulted, of *c.*1460–5, and Knowsley just one minor part with two flanking turrets (*c.*1500), but the more important houses are all timber-framed. They are Baguley Hall, Wythenshawe (Manchester), early c14, disgracefully treated by the Manchester Corporation, Smithill's Hall, Bolton, also early
14   c14, and Ordsall Hall, Salford, mid c15. They are characterized by the subsidiary timbers of walls and roofs (wind-braces) made
12   into large bold patterns, quatrefoils and others, and by the screen
&   taking the form of the spere truss, i.e. two posts as if dividing
13   aisles from a nave and (originally) a movable screen between.* Also above the high table there were in several cases covings, often called canopies of honour. The hall of Wardley Hall, Worsley originally had an open timber roof, though the room was horizontally divided soon after, the early date being indicated by the moulded beams. The hall of Speke (Liverpool) has moulded beams too. An excellent open timber roof of a hall has recently been discovered by Mr Howarth in what is now a barn at Glaze-
16   bury. The centre of Wythenshawe Hall (Manchester) is early c16. It has symmetrical porch and dais bays and the timbering is largely closely-set studs but also herringbone patterns. Cruck trusses have been found in various places, notably Taunton Hall, Ashton-under-Lyne, Seddon's Fold, Prestolee, and Peel Hall, Ince-in-Makerfield. The c15 roofs are largely preserved in Chetham's Hospital, Manchester, the lucky survival of the c15 premises of the college of priests serving the church which is now
1   Manchester Cathedral. The hall is there with its screen, the kitchen, the gatehouse (rebuilt), and the cloister-walks and doorways to the fellows' rooms. In the centre of Manchester otherwise there is just enough of the timber-framed Wellington Inn in the Old Shambles to make it possible to call it original. Outside the centre c15 and c16 half-timber bits still exist at Clayton Hall, Ashton New Road, Barlow Hall, Chorlton-cum-Hardy, and – as late as *c.*1600 – Hough End Hall, Moston Lane, Chorlton-cum-Hardy. The first and third of these belong to Manchester Corporation and, at the time of writing, are almost as neglected as Baguley Hall. Slade Hall Levenshulme (Manchester) of 1585 on the other hand is in private hands and cared for. Elizabethan (or Jacobean)
17   also is much of the exterior of Speke Hall (Liverpool) and the
&   splendid plasterwork in the Great Chamber. But the best Elizabe-
19

* Stand Old Hall, which does not exist any longer, was of the same type. So was Radcliffe Tower. There are more in the North, and they should really be treated as one.

than timber-framed house is the E part of Hall i't'Wood, Bolton, 18 probably of 1591. This has the gay and busy decorative motifs, such as quatrefoils, which were also applied at about that time to the older timber-framed halls. They make Elizabethan black-and-white so popular. Bolton keeps Hall i't'Wood as a museum, as Manchester does Wythenshawe Hall.

But that does not save the Manchester Corporation's record, especially as it is no better than for timber building when it comes to the brick-built ELIZABETHAN and JACOBEAN HOUSES. Hough End Hall, Chorlton-cum-Hardy, the one Elizabethan brick house of some stature, is falling down, and Peel Hall, Wythenshawe, also brick and C17, is derelict.

But this survey of secular buildings has taken us too far in time too quickly. Nothing has yet been said of PERPENDICULAR CHURCHES, and of those there are at least some. Pride of place must of course be given to Manchester Cathedral, a collegiate 5 church founded in 1421 by Thomas de la Warre and sumptuously endowed. The wardens built from E to W through the C15 and into the early C16. If the result looks as sumptuous as it does, that is due overwhelmingly to the C19 restorers and rebuilders. The W porch, the N porch, the upper parts of the tower, the filigree parapet – all these are C19. Of about the same time as medieval Manchester Cathedral is the Windlesham Chantry at St Helens, a small building founded c. 1435, of which only the W tower and bits of walling remain. In the other surviving Perp churches, mostly also much interfered with, the interesting work is latest Perp, early C16, with the lights of the windows still arched but already uncusped. This bluntness, together with the general North-Country lowness and length and squatness of towers, gives these churches their character. The building histories are not yet sufficiently clear. Deane (Bolton) is the most convincing. Prestwich is larger and puzzling. Others are Middleton and Eccles and Radcliffe. At Farnworth near Widnes and Huyton the towers and chancels are or were Perp. Winwick has a S aisle inscribed 1530 and remarkable for the plaques with the IHS for Jesus Christ in the window tracery. Denton has a timber-framed church of c.1530, but little of the original work is preserved. Sefton is 6, 7, memorable chiefly for its FURNISHINGS – especially the gorge- & 9 ous display of screens.

For other Perp church furnishings Manchester Cathedral is again the place one should go to first of all. The stalls of c.1505–10 10 are among the finest of England. There are also some remains of screens, decidedly minor. There is in addition a screen assigned

to 1527 in Northenden (Manchester) parish church, and others in Rochdale parish church (with bold heraldic patterns in the
8 dado) and Middleton parish church (with stalls and misericords). Both Huyton and Knowsley have screens with Flamboyant tracery of the North Country type more probably developed on recent French patterns than on the English Dec patterns such as the Lancaster stalls. One stall and a few misericords are in Bolton parish church. Add to this the stained glass of c.1500 given by the
11 Asshetons to Ashton-under-Lyne, a display notable in any county, and a bit of early C16 glass at Middleton, and all is said that needs saying.

And as for funerary MONUMENTS, a defaced early C14 Lady at Warrington, a defaced alabaster Priest at Huyton, and four brasses, that in Manchester Cathedral of the first warden of the college (†1458), the two at Winwick (†1495, †1527), and one at Childwall (Liverpool) (†1524) are all that can be scraped together.

That ends the summary of the Middle Ages. The first sign of knowledge of the motifs of the RENAISSANCE is in the Sefton screens. There is no date, but c.1530 is likely. Of about the same time or a few years later must be the panelling in Smithill's Hall, Bolton, partly complicated linenfold, i.e. Late Perp, but partly with heads in medallions, i.e. a typical Early Renaissance motif.

For the ELIZABETHAN STYLE, continued without essential break deep into the C17 and, as we shall see, beyond, there is a little more evidence, but again not much. For Manchester the tally has already been made. The only addition is the foundation of Chetham's Hospital in the college premises in 1653 and the equipping of the Free Library. In Liverpool, except for the two gables of c.1575 with six-light windows at Croxteth Hall, only insignificant C17 bits are preserved.* In the county by far the best Elizabethan survival is the triplet of houses near Wigan: Bispham Hall, Orrell of 1573, Birchley Hall, Billinge of 1594, and Winstanley Hall, Wigan of before 1596. All three have the porch and the hall bay set symmetrically in the re-entrant angles of a façade with recessed centre and wings. For the C17 there are a number of farmhouses in the least urbanized part of South Lancashire, i.e. round Littleborough, and some more ambitious houses of the middle and the later parts of the century. The W part of Hall i't'Wood, Bolton, dated 1648, is the best, with its

---

* Woolton School of 1610, really quite a mean cottage, Tue Brook House of 1615, the Court House at West Derby of 1662 and an undated house close by which is a little better, a gable with mullioned window in Vernon Street, Everton, noticed by Mr Hubbard, and a cottage at Aigburth.

mullioned-and-transomed windows. Others have close affinities to the West Riding of Yorkshire both in motifs and in conservatism. Clegg Hall, Milnrow of *c*.1660 e.g. has a portal with fancy baluster 21 columns which might be at Settle. Fernhill, Rochdale of 1691, has a West Riding lintel, and Alder House, Atherton of 1697 a West Riding stepped three-light window with arched lights. Other contemporary houses are Light Oaks Hall, Glazebury of 1657, a fragment of a bigger house with large mullioned-and-transomed windows, and a brick farmhouse of 1671 at Hindley with letters and date in oversized raised brickwork.* Apart from houses there are four late c16 and c17 SCHOOLS, all of course small: the Middleton Grammar School, built probably in 1586, the Garswood School, founded in 1588, the Merchant Taylors' School at Great Crosby, founded in 1620, and the humble school at Walton (Liverpool).

The dates of the West-Riding-looking houses have shown already how late the change from the Jacobean to the Wren type of house took place. In fact, if you look for dates of cottages with horizontal mullioned windows and not revival but survival cottages, you can find yourself faced with such unlikely results that consideration may be necessary as to whether the dates of the inscriptions can really apply to the windows: 1735 at Haughton Green, 1741 at Lees (Grapes Inn), 1764 at Ashton (Higher Alt Hill Farm), and 1773 at Ainsworth. So the link seems to lead direct to the long mullioned windows on the upper floors of WEAVERS' COTTAGES at Littleborough, Smallbridge, and in those neighbourhoods. Even after 1800 mullions are not necessarily given up, but windows in their general shape are now vertical, not horizontal. The change from survival to revival is imperceptible.

If, on the other hand, one watches for the earliest cottages or farmhouses with vertical, mullion-and-transom-cross windows and strictly symmetrical openings one finds the Vicarage, Astley Green of 1704 (already with a pedimented doorway), Fir Tree House, Billinge of 1704, Laurel House, Hindley of 1714 (with sash windows, it seems), Derbyshire House, Billinge of 1716, and Old Falinge, Rochdale of 1721 – late dates all these. As for symmetry, until then either the doorway had not been in the centre, or the windows l. and r. of it were still differentiated by number of lights so as to indicate – a medieval atavism – where the hall was.

* To these Hale Hall would have had to be added, if it survived. It had a part of 1674 with curious giant arches connecting bay windows high up, and *Nash* took this motif up in his s façade of 1806, which survives, a neglected ruin.

On CHURCHES of the SEVENTEENTH CENTURY a few words
are enough. At Prescot the arcade with octagonal piers and single-
chamfered arches is probably of the same time as the nave roof
which is dated 1610, at Winwick may be some work of c.1600 (N
arcade ?), at Didsbury (Manchester) the W tower is of 1620, and
the unfluted columns of the arcade, though certainly not in their
original shape, may be of 1620 too, in which case they represent an
early turn to classical arcading. At Wigan parish church the N
chapel is also of c.1620 and still has the round-arched lights of the
windows which were the rule a hundred years before. W towers of
the C17 are at Ringley (1625), Bradshaw (1640), and Radcliffe
(1665 – or is this a C17 repair of a Perp tower ?).

CHURCH FURNISHINGS are as few and as unimportant: the
pulpit of 1635 at Sefton with close arabesques, the stalls of 1636
with poppy-heads at St Mary, Prescot and the Laudian communion rail in the same church, one bench end at Childwall (Liverpool), and the interesting Laudian dorsal at Wigan, made at Mortlake after one of the Raphael cartoons. Add to these a few
MONUMENTS, that of a Knight at Farnworth near Widnes which
looks like 1500 but is a deliberate fake of the C17, that of Sir John
Ogle †1612 at Prescot with the effigy with hat and hose standing
upright, that of Sir Nicholas Mosley †1612 and his family in
Didsbury church (Manchester) with kneeling figures, that of
Richard Bold †1635 at Farnworth near Widnes with alabaster
effigies, and that at Winwick of Richard Legh †1687 which, with
its two free-standing busts under a baldacchino, looks forward
already to the C18, and you have exhausted the C17. And add some
brass chandeliers given in 1690 and 1715 to Manchester Cathedral,
a chandelier of 1737 at Childwall (Liverpool), a chandelier of the
same year at Deane (Bolton), and others at Sefton (1773), Prestwich, and Holy Trinity, Warrington (from the House of Commons), add the rich stained glass of 1769 by *W. Peckitt* at St Mary,
Hulme (Manchester), and the splendid wrought-iron screens and
communion rail of 1750–1 in Manchester Cathedral, the part of
the iron communion rail in St Ann, Manchester, and the iron
sword rest in St James, Toxteth (Liverpool), and you have
exhausted C18 church furnishings as well.* As for church monuments not one of the C18 needs a reference.

NONCONFORMIST CHAPELS began to appear just before the
C17 ended: the Quakers at St Helens in 1679–92 with what looks

* The splendid C18 pulpit at St Luke, Cheetham (Manchester) is Flemish,
not English.

just like a cottage with its mullioned, informally set windows, the Unitarians at Land Gate, Wigan in 1697 (entirely altered) and at Dob Lane, Newton Heath (Manchester) in 1698 (entirely altered). At Gateacre (Liverpool) the Unitarian Chapel is of 1700 too, but was enlarged in 1719. The windows here are segment-arched. The Unitarians at Ainsworth built in 1715 (enlarged later), the Presbyterians at Atherton in 1721, the Unitarians at Warrington on quite an ambitious scale in 1744–5.

It is a visible sign of the climate of religion in C18 England that the churches of the GEORGIAN AGE are not essentially different from the Georgian Nonconformist chapels. Both are what the Ecclesiologists of the mid C19 were to call scornfully prattling-boxes, i.e. buildings for worship in which the pulpit mattered more than the communion table and in which the accommodation of a congregation and not the ritual was foremost in the architect's mind. The oblong building with galleries such as Wren's St James Piccadilly is the Georgian standard. The sides nearly always have two tiers of windows, as a rule both round-arched. A good many of them were built, mostly demonstrating the growth of towns. For Liverpool and Manchester the church buildings are linked up with the urban development in the introductions to these cities on pp. 141–50 and pp. 265–72. Here the chronology over the whole of South Lancashire must briefly be looked at. For the early C18 the most enjoyable item is the façade of St Aidan, Billinge of 1718, quite incorrect and full of enterprise. Ellenbrook has a small chapel-like church of 1725, St Mary, Prescot a tower of 1729. St Ann of 1709–12, the first of the new parish churches of Manchester, given by Lady Ann Bland, née Mosley, is a different matter. It is the first example in Lancashire of the new Restoration standard. Round Manchester St Thomas, Ardwick followed in 1741. In and around Liverpool nothing surviving is as early. Rochdale got its second parish church, St Mary, in 1740, Warrington its second parish church, Holy Trinity, in 1760. Lees near Oldham built a new church in 1742. At Salford Holy Trinity has an early C18 tower, and the rest is of 1752. At Flixton the tower is of 1731, the rest of 1756. Village churches of little interest are at Burtonwood (1716), Lowton (1732), Hale (1754), and Great Sankey (1768–9). Astley, large and gutted, is of 1760 and c.1840. From the 1770s onwards much more was built. The dates crowd together now, even if we leave out what Liverpool and Manchester, often senselessly, have destroyed: 1766 Hindley, 1770 St John, Bury, the second parish church of that town (derelict now), 1774 Toxteth Chapel (Liverpool), 1774–5 St

James, Toxteth, memorable for its gallery supports of cast iron,
1781 St George, Wigan, the second parish church there, 1785 the
Moravian Chapel at Fairfield and the whole of that delightfully
orderly and peaceful settlement, 1788 St Peter, the new Catholic
church of Liverpool, 1789 Ashworth and the chapel for the
Countess of Huntingdon's Connexion at Tyldesley, 1790–2 Holy
Trinity, St Ann Street, Liverpool, 1793 the Catholic church at
Netherton – and it should be noted that now Catholic churches
began to come into their own. They usually have the priest's house
attached to them, often under the same roof, and they have altar
walls flat or apsed and emphasized by pilasters or columns. The
series of the C18 churches ends with Wavertree church (Liverpool), 1794 by *John Hope* and more monumental than the others,
and St Mark, Cheetham (Manchester) and St George, Bolton,
also 1794. St George is something special, with its plain seven-bay
brick sides and three-bay pediments, as if they were the façades
of houses. At the first moment one might really be deceived; for
GEORGIAN HOUSES have the same principle of composition and
the same sparingness of ornamental details.

   As Croxteth Hall (Liverpool) is of 1702, this does not yet apply.
23 The w front is quite busy, with decoration composed jerkily.
24 Hale Manor House could well be by the same architect. At Woolton Hall (Liverpool) and Allerton Hall (Liverpool) there is also
some work of about the same time. Sharston Hall, Northenden
(Manchester) is said to be dated 1701. The decoration of the doorway and staircase confirms such a date. The present Lloyds Bank
at Rochdale – to include a town house – is supposed to date from
1708, but does not convince in the form in which we see it. Ince
25 Blundell Hall has a nine-bay brick front of c.1715–20 with giant
columns and pilasters of the type of Buckingham House and the
houses by the Smiths of Warwick. The very long, plain brick
front of Knowsley lacks interest, but the two-storeyed s portico of
28 wooden columns, put up probably in the 1730s, is something entirely exceptional. The wall behind the portico has decoration still
in the early C18 tradition. Striking also first of all by sheer size is the
26 old Bluecoat School at Liverpool, dated 1717. With its far-
projecting wings it is much bigger than the C17 schools in the
county, or indeed the country. The Vanbrugh style of the same
years is represented by Atherton Hall, or rather that one doorway
from it which survives with its cyclopean surround. It is by
William Wakefield, who was in close touch with Vanbrugh in
Yorkshire, and dates from 1723. Foxdenton Hall Chadderton of
c.1710–30 and Alkrington Hall Middleton by *Leoni* of 1735–6 are

of seven and nine bays respectively, brick, and nothing individual.
Finally Rock House Melling. This is still overdecorated in the
early C18 way, but its date is as late as 1744.

By then PALLADIANISM had arrived in Lancashire. It had in
fact arrived with *Leoni*. He has been unfortunate. Bold Hall in
South Lancashire, completed in 1730, and Lathom Hall in
North Lancashire, completed at about the same time, have both
been destroyed during this century. So one has to go to about 1750
to find Palladian work, but then it is first-class work. It is the
Town Hall, or rather the Mansion House, of Liverpool, by *Wood* 30
of Bath, begun in 1749, and the Town Hall of Warrington, built 29
as a house for Thomas Patten in 1750 by *Gibbs*, then aged 68.*
The additions to the Liverpool Town Hall which *Wyatt* made in
1789–92 are in keeping and indeed an improvement. *Wyatt* was 31
responsible also for the infinitely best C18 building of Manchester,
Heaton Park, designed in 1772 and built of ashlar, a building of a 32
refinement and elegance not exceeded in any English house of
these years. The interiors also are worthwhile, and well preserved. 33
They are of course post-Rococo, whereas the two lively stucco ceilings of the mid C18 at Ince Blundell Hall can be called Rococo
still. The one *Adam* building in South Lancashire, the enlargement of Woolton Hall (Liverpool), is a disappointment. Other
later and late C18 houses need only marginal attention. Platt Hall,
Fallowfield (Manchester) of *c*.1764 is the best, also internally.
The façades are of brick, seven bays and lower wings. There are
other houses of this type, brick as well as stone. Brick e.g. are
Newsham House, Anfield (Liverpool), Sandown Hall, Wavertree
(Liverpool), and Woodlands, Crescent Road, Manchester. Stone
are the house in Olive Mount Hospital, Wavertree (Liverpool),
Healey Hall of 1774, Foxholes of 1793, and Mount Falinge, all
three at Rochdale, and Town House of 1798 outside Littleborough.
In the town centres hardly anything is left of the bigger houses.
One of 1736 remains in King Street, Manchester, another of
c.1760 in Long Millgate, Manchester, a third in Dale Street,
Liverpool, and fourth to sixth might be called the houses built for
the famous Dissenters' Academy at Warrington where Priestley
taught and Marat may have taught.

The usual development in towns, especially between *c*.1790 and
c.1830, was brick terraces. Thus e.g. Chorley New Town, Manchester was laid out in 1793–1800, and Rodney Street, Liverpool
was begun in the 1780s. The quarter round Rodney Street, the

* The fine octagonal pavilion in the grounds of Knowsley is dated 1755.

east-end West End of Liverpool, was the finest area in the county, but first the cathedral and then the university have corroded it. The only ones of these terraces reaching out for monumentality are 46 in Percy Street. Gambier Terrace facing St James's Cemetery was left incomplete. Both belong to c.1830. At Manchester even less has remained undisturbed. St John's Street has the best terraces. In many other places one can still see that terraces existed. But only odd houses survive. The same applies to the once handsome Ardwick Green, and also to the towns other than Manchester and Liverpool. At Bury, e.g., off the main street, terraces and fragments of terraces can be sampled. One of them incidentally is dated as late as 1845 and yet still entirely Georgian in style.

So we have entered the NINETEENTH CENTURY, and it is only there that this introduction starts seriously. Up to now all – with very few exceptions – was scarcity. Now all is going to be plenitude. Hardly any areas of England, except of course London, can vie with South Lancashire for wealth and interest of early C19 and Victorian architecture. This is, it need hardly be said, due to the INDUSTRIAL REVOLUTION. A few of the familiar dates just to remind readers. Weaving as well as coal mining had a tradition in Lancashire which goes back to the C13, though not much organized exploitation is reported before the later C16. The chief mining areas were round St Helens, round Wigan, and, further N, Burnley. Cotton was first imported by the Levant Company from Smyrna and Cyprus about 1600. The dampness of Lancashire was an advantage, but weaving of cloth from cotton exclusively was a later C18 innovation and could only flourish after the tax on pure cotton goods had been reduced from 6d. a yard to 3d. a yard. That was in 1774. The famous sequence of inventions were all still made with a view to wool. John Kay's fly-shuttle was invented in 1733, and he came from near Bury, Hargreaves's spinning jenny in c.1765, and he came from near Blackburn, Arkwright's water-frame c.1780, and he came from Preston, Compton's mule c.1780, and he came from and lived at Bolton. Water power was the first means for changing from cottage work to work in factories, coal came after. The first Boulton & Watt steam engines were installed in a Warrington mill in 1787 and a Manchester mill in 1789. After that mills multiplied, though not many of before 1825 survive, and though handloom weaving still remained a going concern till about 1825, and water power was also still widely used. Spinning was the staple industry of Oldham, Bolton, and Manchester. Bleaching and dyeing flourished at Bolton too.

Weaving was concentrated in the North, i.e. Blackburn, Chorley, the Colne Valley, and also Rochdale and Bury in the South. Other industries of course also developed, and the finest C18 factory building to survive is a fragment from the British Plate Glass Company (now Pilkington's) of 1773 at St Helens. Industry needed coal. The Duke of Bridgewater had built his canal in 1759–61 to transport the coal from his Worsley mine to Manchester. It was extended to Runcorn in 1776. The extension became a valuable means of cheap transport for cotton to Manchester, and the canals spread – the Liverpool and Leeds Canal belongs to 1770–4, the Manchester–Bury–Bolton, Manchester–Ashton–Oldham, and Manchester–Rochdale Canals all belong to the years 1790–1805. Some of the early canalscape remains: the basin, steps, and tunnel exist of the Bridgewater Canal at Worsley, the terminal wharf at Manchester with the Canal Office and warehouses, and the gateway and warehouses of the Rochdale Canal terminus. But soon the Liverpool and Manchester Railway (of 1830) was to set the seal on this spectacular development of transport.* Here also the Manchester terminal station is preserved (in Liverpool Road). Better transport, and new manufacturing devices – so South Lancashire attracted ever more of the indigent from the countryside.

A table of population may come in useful here.

	1801	1831	1861	1961
Manchester with Salford and Stretford	c.90,000	c.195,000	c.355,000	c.855,000
Liverpool	c.78,000	c.205,000	c.438,000	c.729,000
Bolton	c.30,000	c.63,000	c.97,000	c.160,000
Oldham	c.12,000	c.32,000	c.72,000	c.113,000
St Helens	c.8,000	c.14,000	c.38,000	c.105,000
Rochdale	c.29,000	c.58,000	c.101,000	c.86,000
Wigan	c.11,000	c.21,000	c.38,000	c.77,000
Warrington	c.11,000	c.18,000	c.24,000	c.75,000

After this table some general remarks as an introduction to the architectural survey of the C19. What the C19 has done to South Lancashire is to crowd out the countryside to the hills E of Oldham and Rochdale towards Yorkshire and a few odd patches otherwise.

* But the Manchester Ship Canal of 1885–94 proved that canals still had life in them. It made Manchester the third port of England – after London and Liverpool – i.e. in terms of tonnage.

All the rest is urban. 'What have you done to Lancashire?' exclaimed Wiliam Morris. 'Were not the brown moors and the meadows, the clear streams and the sunny skies, wealth?'

Administratively speaking there are hardly any Rural Districts in South Lancashire; the districts are Urban Districts, or Metropolitan Boroughs, or County Boroughs. Some of the towns have an ancient origin, Rochdale e.g. and Bolton and Warrington, let alone Manchester and Liverpool, but one cannot see that any longer. Other towns are creations of the C19: Oldham is an example, St Helens is another, and Widnes is yet younger. Visually Liverpool has the immense advantage of a great river; Manchester has no such advantage. Rochdale has parkland right in the middle of the town, with the garden bank reaching up to the church behind the town hall, Bolton has its monumental town hall with its setting, Warrington has attractive Late Georgian terraces quite close to the centre, Widnes has a desperately mean town hall, but it has West Bank, with a superb church, a riverside promenade, and of course two thrilling bridges. Oldham has two streets of some dignity, Bury one, poor Salford one only just. Wigan has nothing of the kind. Nor has St Helens, where even the town hall is a poor job. Bolton and Rochdale are visibly proud of themselves. So are of course Liverpool and Manchester. Liverpool grew by trade, Manchester first by industry and then more and more by trade. The other towns are wholly industrial. Architecturally also there are significant differences, and they will be pointed out when their turn comes.

The turn of one has in fact come. The GRECIAN REVIVAL had, if not a different intensity, a different outlet and a different duration in Liverpool and in Manchester. The start is very much parallel. A cultured upper bourgeois class had grown up, and wanted libraries, clubs, and buildings of the Athenaeum kind, and for them the Grecian style was obviously the only style appropriate. In Liverpool the leader in the endeavour to establish cultural centres was William Roscoe (*see* p. 145). The Lyceum in Broad Street was built already in 1800–2, and the architect was that accomplished Grecian *Thomas Harrison* of Chester. In 1802
35 the same architect was commissioned to build the Portico Library at Manchester. He also built a mansion at Allerton (Liverpool) in 1815, but of that only a fragment remains. As early as the first Grecian public buildings in the two cities, in 1802 Henry Blundell
34 added to Ince Blundell Hall the Pantheon, a free miniature copy of the Pantheon in Rome, to house his collection of ancient statuary.

Roscoe himself added to his house, Allerton Hall (Liverpool), c.1810–12. The Wellington Rooms in Liverpool of 1815–16 (by 36 *E. Aikin*) were built as an assembly room. They have a façade not at all run-of-the-mill. Opposite, the Medical Institution, a professional headquarters, was built in 1836–7 (by *C. Rampling*). At the same time the Mechanics' Institution could afford a substantial Grecian building.* It dates from 1835–7 and is by *A. H. Holme*. While these were all by local architects, *Sir Charles Barry*, then still young and only little known, did the admirable Royal Manchester Institution‡ in 1824–35 and the adjoining Athenaeum in 1837. But the latter is in a different style and will have to come up again later.

The towns built town halls Grecian too. Manchester first, in 1819–34. The architect was *Francis Goodwin*, better known for Gothic churches and not a local man. The building has been pulled down, but part of the façade stands in Heaton Park. Then *Richard Lane* appeared, and he now got most of the Grecian commissions. The Salford Town Hall (1825–7) he did with Goodwin, the Chorlton-on-Medlock (Manchester) Town Hall, almost a replica of the former, alone (1830–1). At Bolton he did the Exchange (1825–9).§ The Oldham Town Hall, as late as 1841, might well be by Lane too. Other Grecian buildings are the screen to the former Botanic Gardens at Stretford of 1828 and the screen to the Jewish Cemetery at Fairfield (Liverpool) of 1836–7. In outer Manchester the Wesleyan Theological Institution built monumental premises in the Grecian style at Didsbury in 1842, but the Lancashire Independent College at Whalley Range in 1840–3 58 in the Gothic style. *Elmes* in exactly the same years built the Liverpool Collegiate High School Gothic,‖ but St George's Hall of 1841–56 is Grecian, even if *Elmes* evolved a highly personal solu- 53 tion in this conventional style. St George's Hall, not the Birmingham Town Hall nor the British Museum, is the climax of the Grecian phase in C19 classical architecture. The way in which Elmes created a unity out of prostyle temple elements and a plan demanding a long, relatively narrow body – entrance hall, court of justice, assembly hall, another court of justice, and at the end *Cockerell's* sumptuous concert hall – could not be bettered. 54

* Now High School for Boys.   ‡ Now Art Gallery.
§ The former Bolton Town Hall in St George's Road is of 1826.
‖ Scholastic Gothic, utilitarian on the whole, had already been used by *Richard Lane* for the Oldham Bluecoat School (seventeen bays long) in 1829–34 and Henshaw's Institution for the Deaf and the Blind at Stretford in 1836–7.

It holds its own in comparison with any classical building of these years in Europe. Externally also the use of pilasters, detached in their upper part, i.e. up there not pilasters but square pillars, was a stroke of genius.

St George's Hall established the classical idiom in Liverpool to a degree incomparable with other English cities, especially Manchester. N of St George's Hall, along William Brown Street, classical façades of public buildings went up in the fifties, sixties, seventies, and eighties, the finest of them the Picton Reading
56 Room of the Library, by *C. Sherlock*, 1875–9, which, with its convex columnar front, marks a break in the frontage of the
57 street. Of about the same years is the Walker Art Gallery. It might be contemporary with Barry's Royal Institution.*

CHURCHES also were done classically in Liverpool, though not exclusively so. But St Patrick, Park Place, Toxteth of 1821–7 with Greek Doric porches, the Methodist Chapel in Upper Stanhope Street, Toxteth of 1827 with Greek Doric columns, St Andrew, Rodney Street of 1823–4, the Doric Mortuary Chapel in St James's Cemetery of *c.*1825–6, St Catherine Abercromby Square of 1829–31 (destroyed), the Husskison Rotunda in St James's Cemetery of 1836 (all these four by *John Foster Jun.*), St Bride,
47 Percy Street of 1830–1 (by *S. Rowland*), St Saviour, Upper Huskisson Street of 1839–40, and the Great George Street Congregational Church of 1840–1 (by *J. Franklin*) are a respectable series.

In the county there is nothing to be set against this except St
37 John (R.C.) at Wigan of 1819 and the superb Catholic church at
48 Rainhill of 1840 with its Ionic portico, giant pilasters on window-
& less walls, and columnar, tunnel-vaulted interior, and in Man-
49 chester it is the same. At Salford *Sir Robert Smirke* of London in
38 1825 built St Philip with the same semicircular porch and round tower as in his St Mary, Bryanston Square, London of 1823–4. In addition the Quakers built a meeting-house in Mosley Street, Manchester in 1828–30.‡ *Lane* was their architect, and so it was Grecian too, and the Presbyterians in Grosvenor Square, Chorlton-on-Medlock (Manchester) built classical also, with giant Corinthian columns and two short towers, in 1849–50 (*Starkey & Cuffley*). § But the Welsh got *Barry* to do their chapel at Chorlton-

---

* Later still is the Harris Museum and Library at Preston, but that is in North Lancashire.

‡ And one at Warrington in the same years.

§ In 1823 the Swedenborgians added a small rotunda to a house at Ancoats (Manchester).

on-Medlock (Manchester), and that, designed in 1837, is
GOTHIC, indeed the first Gothic, seriously Gothic, Nonconformist chapel, it is said, and in 1847–8 *Walters* did the Congregational Church in Cavendish Street, Chorlton-on-Medlock and
that is said (by Professor Hitchcock) to be the first Nonconformist
chapel to look like an Anglican church. Otherwise the Nonconformists all over England made consistent efforts, mostly
right into the sixties and sometimes even the seventies, to appear
demonstratively anti-church, i.e. – an odd contradiction – consistently classical or Italianate. Some instances may be given.
Grandly classical are the Baptists at Everton (Liverpool) in 1847,
and the Methodists at Langsight, Harwood still in 1862,* and the
Brunswick Chapel at Bury even in 1883 – but that is an anachronism. Meanwhile the Italianate, more or less mixed and
more or less debased had appeared in the Welsh Presbyterian
church of 1861 at Liverpool (now University) and the gorgeous
Congregational church at Newton-le-Willows of *c*.1870 (under
demolition at the time of writing). But, once again, by that time
chapels had changed their policy and preferred to look like
Anglican churches.

But Anglican churches themselves looked radically different
then from what they had done in the early C19. They are of the
type one calls Commissioners' Churches after the Church Building Commission appointed in 1818 to provide areas with fast-
growing populations with new churches, as a means of civilizing
the new working class and also, this cannot be overlooked, of
keeping it quiet. The first grant was of £1,000,000 in 1819, the
second of £500,000 in 1825. For all Lancashire the first grant paid
for eighteen churches, the second for sixty-three, but the sums *See p. 479*
allowed for one church were much higher under the first than
under the second grant. St Martin in Liverpool by *Foster* received
£19,948, St George, Hulme (Manchester) by *Goodwin* £15,010,
five churches received between £13,000 and £15,000, and two
more between £11,000 and £13,000. Under the second grant the
highest sums were £7,073 for St Thomas, Pendleton (Salford),
£6,889 for Christ Church, Heaton Norris and £6,612 for St John,
Toxteth Park (Liverpool). Two churches were begun in 1821,
six in 1822, the others under the first grant in 1823–9. They were
all Gothic, except for *Smirke*'s St Philip, Salford. *Rickman* got
six churches to build, *Goodwin* three, *Hardwick* two. Only six
of the first eighteen were in North Lancashire (including two

* And incidentally, and even more contradictorily, the Greek Orthodox
church at Broughton (Salford) in 1860–1.

at Preston). Of the sixty-three under the second grant many more were in the North and in small places. The ones in the South were again all Gothic, except for one classical one (St Matthias, Liverpool, by *Stewart & Picton*, 1832–3*) and two Norman ones (Ancoats (Manchester) 1839–40 and Burnley (North Lancashire), St Paul, 1852–3). *Shellard* was commissioned thirteen times, *Sharpe* five, *Rickman* four, *Vulliamy* four, *Hayley* four. Of younger men *Joseph Clarke* (three) and *George Gilbert Scott* (two) benefited.

But what one tends to call Commissioners' Churches was not always paid for by the Commission. The term has become one for a certain type of very superficially applied Gothic, appearing universally in all parts of England. The type is characterized by general leanness, long lancet windows, single or in pairs or in triplets or equally long windows with Perp tracery, the windows always separated from each other by thin buttresses, often with pinnacles, interiors with three galleries and a thin timber roof or plaster vault.

For South Lancashire the series begins with the Catholic St Nicholas, Liverpool of 1808–12 with a charming tripartite chancel-arch composition. Between 1810 and 1820 I have counted 39 eight: St Luke, Liverpool, begun in 1811 and designed by the two *Fosters*, father and son, the resourceful spire of the Liverpool parish church by *Thomas Harrison*, also of 1811, the W tower of 42 Childwall (Liverpool) of 1810–11, St George, Everton (Liverpool) by *Rickman*, 1812–14, and St Michael-in-the-Hamlet, Toxteth (Liverpool) by the same, 1814–15, both famous and indeed landmarks in that all the tracery in windows and roof and everything else feasible was made of cast iron. The initiative came from John Cragg, an iron-master who induced Rickman to try. Aesthetically the experiment is successful; the two churches look very pretty inside, even if they do not inspire awe. But which of contemporary churches do? Psychologically the Cragg churches are a sign of the adventurous spirit of Lancashire in those decades of the most rapid transformation.‡ Then, going on chronologically, follow St Mary, Edge Hill (Liverpool) of 1812–13, All Saints, Newton Heath (Manchester) of 1814–15, which has two tiers of Gothic windows on the pattern of classical Georgian churches, the naïve

---

* Pulled down.
‡ Cragg also built close to St Michael a number of villas in which as much as possible was made of cast iron. As for cast iron in churches, it has already been mentioned that St Anne, St Anne Street (now replaced) received iron supports for its galleries as early as 1770–2 and St James, Toxteth in 1774–5.

St Thomas, Seaforth of 1815, Holy Trinity, Littleborough by *Thomas Taylor* of Leeds, 1818, St Mary (R.C.), Wigan, also of 1818. Between 1820 and 1830 my tally comes to thirteen, and they include buildings of more than county interest, starting with *Goodwin*'s St Peter at Ashton-under-Lyne of 1821–4 with its unexpectedly transparent w tower appearing at the end of a vista contrived as part of a planned West End development of Ashton by the Earls of Stamford, lords of the manor, and his large St George, Hulme (Manchester) of 1826–8.* Of 1821–4 also is *Smirke*'s St George, Tyldesley, remarkably well-informed for its date on archeological precedent (w tower with a spire à la Louth and octagonal piers inside). Even more seriously concerned with the reality of medieval details is *Philip Hardwick*'s Holy Trinity, Bolton of 1823–5. The very opposite, but just because of that highly enjoyable, is *Barry*'s very first job (recommended by Soane), the church at Stand of 1822 etc. With its crazily high and steep tripartite porch and its ingenious counterpoint of arcade piers and tierceron vaults it is quite a *tour de force*. *Lane*, the Grecian, did St Mary, Oldham in Gothic (1823–7) and, with *Goodwin*, St Thomas, Pendleton (Salford) (1829–31). *Blore* did St Paul, Bewsey Road, Warrington in 1829–30, *Samuel Rowland* St James, Wilderspool Causeway in the same town, in the same years. For the 1830s the total is twenty-two, not including what has already been mentioned in other contexts, and the most memorable is‡ St Luke, Cheetham (Manchester) by *T. W. Atkinson*, again because of the unusual sense of antiquarian responsibility.

So to the 1840s, when this type of church begins to get out of date. Discounting those in the new spirit of which more will be said presently, I make them fourteen, and the only comments called for are on *John Harper*'s All Saints, Elton (Bury) of 1843 because it has its tower not at the w but the E end, on the chancel, and on St Paul, Halliwell, Bolton of 1847 because of its charming setting with rows of cottages l. and r. and two schools, all as one composition. All Saints, Bury incidentally has round-headed windows, and a Norman and more rarely Italian-Early-Christian or Italian-Romanesque fashion did indeed sweep the whole of England in

* His St James, Huddersfield Road, Oldham of 1825–8 on the other hand is poor, but it is interesting for having cast-iron tracery.

‡ Not a late *Rickman*, St John, Lamberhead Green, Wigan of 1830–2 nor two churches with bell-turrets only by *Lewis Vulliamy*, Smallbridge of 1834 and St Clement, Spotland Bridge, Rochdale of 1835, nor *Lane*'s St John, Broughton (Salford) of 1836–9.

the forties. In South Lancashire it is represented by the highly surprising w tower of Ardwick parish church (Manchester) of 1836 (by *William Hayley*), surprising because 1836 is a very early date for an Italian *campanile*, and by the more normally Norman St Anne, Aigburth (Liverpool) of 1836–7 (by *Cunningham & Holme*), All Souls, Ancoats (Manchester) of 1839–40, St Paul, Withington (Manchester) of 1841 (by *Hayley & Brown*), St John, Pendlebury of 1842, St Bartholomew, Ordsall (Salford), also of 1842 (by *Cuffley & Starkey*), and St Mary, the main Catholic church of Manchester, of 1848 (by *Weightman & Hadfield*), with a Norman exterior but a basilican interior.

In looking over the whole series some more characteristics stand out. A w tower can be present or absent, and aisles can also be present or absent. Aisleless naves are usually very wide, aisle piers are without exception thin. Transepts are the rule, especially where there are no aisles. The Commissioners' ground plans died hard. No aisles but transepts still are the scheme at Great Crosby in 1853–4 (*A. & G. Holme*), at St Helens in 1857 (Holy Trinity, Traverse Street by *W. & J. Hay*), Litherland in 1861–3 (by *Gee*), and at St James, Ashton-under-Lyne in 1863–5 (by *G. Shaw*).*

The 1840s are the Great Divide in VICTORIAN ARCHITECTURE, as far as churches were concerned, and *A. W. N. Pugin* was the *deus ex machina*. He for reasons of dedication to Catholicism decreed that architects must not only adhere to the old faith unquestioningly but also accept the architecture of the old faith as their only pattern. This principle alone could not, however, answer what style of the Catholic past should be the pattern. If it was to be the late C13 and early C14 – from Westminster Abbey to Early Dec, i.e. what was called Second Pointed or Middle Pointed – that was a matter of taste. But it was a taste shared by the Cambridge Camden Society and their journal *The Ecclesiologist*. Pugin's combative writings and *The Ecclesiologist*'s praise and criticism shaped English church architecture from the forties to 1870 and beyond.

Manchester has one *Pugin* church of 1842, St Wilfrid, Hulme. There, though on a minor scale, anyone might see at one glance that a Gothic church was now something totally different from say Goodwin's St George, Hulme of only fifteen years before.

* * *

* *George Shaw* of Saddleworth could be tempted into roguery (for the term *see* below). The church at Ashton has two thin w towers with spires, the church at Prestolee of 1863 a very odd tower staircase, and St Paul, Norden, Rochdale of 1860–1 other oddities.

Pugin also did a church at Old Swan (Liverpool), again in 1842, but of that only the correctly Dec tower stands. Moreover, he did the chancel of Winwick in 1847–8 – an Anglican job! *Scott* was so converted at once and preserved through his lifetime his admiration for, and gratitude to, Pugin. His Worsley parish church is of 1846 and stands for Pugin's principles even though illustrated on a scale and with a plenitude of means nearly always unavailable to Pugin.* Also to the new world of archeological respect and knowledge belongs, very surprisingly, *Edmund Sharpe*'s Knowsley of 1843–4; for Sharpe, though a scholar of the Dec style, built as a rule still in a pre-Pugin way, and then *J. E. Gregan*'s St John, Longsight (Manchester) of 1845–6, *J. M. Derick*'s St James, Rusholme (Manchester) of the same years, *Weightman & Hadfield*'s St Mary, Little Crosby of 1845–7, Catholic but in position and style just like an Anglican church, the same architects' St Chad, Cheetham (Manchester) of 1846–7, *William Hayley*'s church of 1846 at Heaton Norris, but only the window and portal treatment (he was more inclined to the Romanesque fashion), and then of 1846–7 and 1848 *W. Young*'s two excellent churches at Leigh and Walkden, both St Paul, and of 1848–9 *J. Harrison*'s St Margaret, Whalley Range (Manchester). It will be noticed that only one Liverpool church is in this series, and it is in fact true that Liverpool remained long in the pre-Pugin state. The churches by *W. & J. Hay* are the best proof of that.

1844 and 1845 are the dates of two of the most remarkable churches of the Victorian Age in Lancashire: St Stephen, Lever Bridge (Bolton) and Holy Trinity, Fallowfield (Manchester). Both are by *Sharpe*, to whom reference has just been made. In these two churches he was certainly not the scholar. The open-work spire of the Bolton church e.g. was a *tour de force* of Gothic fantasy (inspired by Freiburg im Breisgau and alas no longer in existence). But more important than their stylistic position is the fact that they are built as far as could be of terracotta, made by John Fletcher, a colliery owner, and promoted by him for this purpose as a by-product. The facing slabs are even ribbed so as to appear tooled ashlar blocks. All the ornamental parts are terracotta and hence as crisp today as a hundred and twenty years ago. Fletcher with his terracotta is as characteristic of Lancashire resourcefulness in those years of industrial climax as Cragg with his cast iron, and both were no doubt admired for that resourcefulness.

---

* Cheadle, Staffs. is the exception.

But it would not have been the churches which to travellers about 1850, whether they came from the Continent or the Home Counties, would have determined their picture of this new world. It would have been huge mills, five- and six-storeyed, such as Schinkel on his journey to England in 1826 drew with amazement, it would have been the warehouses like Italian *palazzi*, and it would have been the miles upon miles of mean back-to-back brick cottages, if travellers' journeys happened to go through them. The worst they would not have seen as visitors anyway. They would have had to go to Dr Kay's and Friedrich Engels's reports of 1832 and 1844 to get an idea of the scandalous conditions in which the new working class had to live. Those who saw for themselves agreed with Kay and Engels – William Morris, for example, who wrote of 'such monstrosities of haphazard
1 growth as your Manchester-Salford-Oldham etc.'. But the majority of people simply accepted the contrast of new riches and new poverty. Manchester fought for free trade to benefit the new rich, and for the abolition of the corn laws to benefit themselves ultimately too, even if the free import of corn benefited the workers also.

MILLS are the most conspicuous buildings of Lancashire. Yet not many are mentioned in the gazetteer, too few perhaps, now that theses exist dating them and describing their development in certain areas. For the 1830s a specially large and altogether typical one is that by *R. Tattersall* at Golborne, a cotton mill, nineteen bays long.

It is naturally in the smaller places rather than the larger towns that the mills visually dominate, at Leigh, and round Oldham, at Milnrow and Mossley and round Wigan, and at Atherton and Tyldesley. Two of the dozen prominent examples from the 1860s into the C20 must be enough here: the Reddish Mills of Houlds-
67 worth's of 1865, a block forty-five bays long with a street leading axially to it and some housing for the workers, and the Alder Mill of 1907 at Leigh, nearly as large and in the Edwardian style. But style as consciously applied rarely comes into industrial architecture before the later C19, and the Grecian building of the Wigan gas works of 1822 is a great exception.

As the mills dominate vertically, so the housing for the new hundreds of thousands dominates horizontally, and again little is said about it in the gazetteer. Where it is provided by the manufacturer, it may be mentioned (Vulcan Village, Wargrave, close to the foundry, small and humble, of *c.*1840; the Fletchers of Ringley and Prestolee's cottages, close to a paper factory which has been pulled down), otherwise housing is left to its scandalous self. Brick was the material throughout, for reasons of economy, though occasionally from Bolton eastward one comes across stone-built terraces.

The middle class lived, as it did in all England, in terrace houses, or, if more affluent, in villas. Villas go from the Grecian, which can be very fine (e.g. the Mauldeth Home at Heaton Mersey outside Manchester) by way of the Italianate (the house in Victoria Park, St Helens of *c*.1850, John Rylands's house, Longford Hall at Stretford, of 1857, Mossley Town Hall of *c*.1862) to the High Victorian Gothic. Examples of the latter are *Worthington*'s Shirley Institute, Wilmslow Road, Didsbury (Manchester) **68** of 1865, the grandest by far, the only one indeed to deserve being called a mansion; *Pugin*'s house at Childwall (Liverpool), now St Joseph's Home, of 1847 etc., *Waterhouse*'s Xaverian College in Victoria Park (Manchester) of 1874–5, Dunster House, Rochdale by *Joseph Clarke* of 1860,* and Sunny Brow, Archer Park, Middleton of 1864. Some of these villas have become public buildings (Mossley, Radcliffe). They are all large compared with what the affluent would expect now of living space, but they are small compared with Lord Armstrong's Cragside or Sir Titus Salt's decaying Milner Field.

The villas or mansions of the mill-owners were sometimes immediately next to the mills. An example of this is at Buckley, Rochdale where the mill is dated 1863. If they lived less close to the mill, there were of course certain suburbs or areas where their houses gathered: Allerton (Liverpool),‡ Mossley Hill, Woolton (Liverpool), Didsbury (Manchester), and into Cheshire, Upper Broughton at Bolton, Eccles Old Road at Salford, Bury Road at Rochdale.

Villa estates were sometimes laid out as such and even provided with gates and lodges, either simply a street or two such as Grassendale Park (Liverpool) in the forties or in a more complex way with winding streets. Examples are Victoria Park (Manchester), 1836 etc., Broughton Park (Salford), *c*.1840–5, Sandford Park, West Derby (Liverpool), *c*.1850. Desirable sites also were the fringes of public parks, and as a rule an area for villas was set aside when a public park was planned. For these are the years of public parks. *Paxton*'s Prince's Park (Liverpool) was the first,

---

* Now demolished.

‡ At Allerton, to give one example, are or were Allerton Hall where Roscoe lived, Springwood of 1839, Allerton Tower by *Elmes*, Allerton Priory by *Waterhouse*, and houses pulled down by *Scott* and (two) by *Norman Shaw*.

and his first independent job. Its date is 1842. It was immediately followed by Birkenhead Park, which became internationally more important. Sefton Park (Liverpool) came in 1867 etc. (by *André* of Paris and *Hornblower*) and Stanley Park, Anfield (Liverpool) with its bold tower and pavilions in 1867 etc. (by *Kemp*, and for the architecture *E. R. Robson*, who was to go to London soon and become the creator of the Board School style).

So much for the villas and the green suburbs of the prosperous. The mills where they made their money have already received
43 attention. Now to their OFFICE BUILDINGS and WAREHOUSES, as a rule far more palatial than the residences. They still make the centres of Manchester and Liverpool, although they are rapidly and often callously demolished to make way for less solid and less dignified buildings. For solidity and dignity are the hallmarks of Lancashire commercial architecture of the mid century. Stylistically speaking, it could be done Grecian, e.g. in the courtyard of the Queen Insurance at Liverpool (by *S. Rowland*, 1837–9), it could be done as a development from the Grecian, as in the grand
62 Milne Buildings in Mosley Street, Manchester, with its two tiers of giant columns all along the long front, and if an architect of genius was available such as *Cockerell* for the Bank of England,
55 the results are of the highest order internationally (Liverpool, Manchester, both begun 1845). But local architects could work to very high standards too. Such is the case of *Edward Walters* at Manchester, and in a more obscure, less recognized way of *Peter Ellis* at Liverpool. Walters did many of the *palazzo* warehouses of Manchester. The palazzo type had been introduced by *Barry*, fresh from his Travellers' and Reform Clubs in London, at the Manchester Athenaeum in 1837. Walters used it with care for details and considerable panache. Others had their share too. *Travis & Mangnall*'s Watts warehouse of 1851 is the biggest of all, and an example of how the palazzo style was loosened up when the High Victorian moment approached. In Walters's own *œuvre* the most spectacular example of the same increased expansiveness is Williams Deacon's Bank in Mosley Street of 1860. In Liverpool a parallel development is to be seen in *C. R. and F. P. Cockerell*'s Liverpool & London and Globe Insurance, Dale Street of 1855–7, if it is contrasted against the Bank of England building of ten years before. But *Peter Ellis* stands apart. He wanted functionalism obviously, not grandeur, and he believed in the possibility of
64 an original style of the C19. So Oriel Chambers of 1864, famous now, but pretty well totally unknown fifteen years ago, has a facade glazed throughout in the form of angular oriels except for

the stone posts, and even more boldly glazed – curtain-walled
indeed – at the back. Ellis's other office building, No. 16 Cook 65
Street, is as daring but aesthetically less successful. As boldly
glazed but provided with an iron framework were the arcades so
much favoured in those years. The best is in Deansgate, Manches- 66
ter and dates from 1871. Twenty-five years earlier are the fantastic
galleries round the glazed courtyard of the Sailors' Home in 60
Canning Place, Liverpool. But Liverpool also has excellent,
more conventional Italianate office and warehouse buildings
too, for instance two by *J. A. Picton* in Chapel Street, both 63
of 1861, and both more Venetian than Roman. J. A. Picton,
Peter Ellis, and Edward Walters were LOCAL ARCHITECTS, and
it is certainly characteristic of the Victorian Age in Britain and of
Lancashire in particular how leading a role was played by the
locals. Barry, Smirke, Cockerell, Scott, Norman Shaw, Basil
Champneys, it is true, came in from the outside, and the same is
true of church architects from the South, but Waterhouse, who
did so much work in Manchester and Liverpool, was a Liverpool
man by birth, and local also were most of the others who are to be
mentioned, as will be seen.

Local, e.g., are the two who made the most spectacular contribution to what must be called COMMERCIAL PUBLIC ARCHI-
TECTURE: *Thomas Duncan*, who designed the tremendous Everton Water Tower (Liverpool) in 1853, with its two tiers of grand-
iose rusticated arches around, and the great *Jesse Hartley*, who
was Liverpool Dock Engineer from 1824 to 1860. The architecture of the Albert Dock, opened in 1845, and others of his may be 52
inspired by Philip Hardwick's St Katherine's Dock, London –
and *Hardwick* designed the Albert Dock Office himself – but the
cyclopean walls, gatepiers, and lodges with their huge stones
shaped and laid at random have, it seems, no parallel anywhere and are one of Liverpool's most precious architectural
possessions.

As they were built as public buildings, this is perhaps the
moment to move on to PUBLIC BUILDINGS altogether. The
table of population development earlier on must have made it
obvious that new public buildings were needed in large numbers
and of unprecedented size. It is difficult to decide where a survey
should start and how far it should go. We have so far concerned
ourselves only with the Grecian examples and a few Gothic educational foundations. They have taken us to the forties. In the late
forties and early fifties the style might still be classical (*Sydney
Smirke*'s Derby Hall and Athenaeum at Bury or *A. H. Holme*'s

Liverpool School for the Blind (now Police Headquarters) in Hardman Street, both of 1850 etc., or *Dobson*'s restrained and personal Warrington Library of 1855–7), or it might be Italian
61 High Renaissance (*Walters*'s *chef d'œuvre*, the Free Trade Hall at Manchester, monumental and yet amazingly refined), or it may of course be Gothic, and it may also, where evocative reasons
59 suggested it, be Romanesque or Norman (the gargantuan Walton Prison for Liverpool of 1848–55).

For the next decades a survey by types may be the most useful. Town halls of course must take precedence, and town halls now were not complete without a large assembly or concert hall – in fact sometimes this function was kept separate from the utilitarian functions of a town hall. Birmingham had made the start with Hansom's town hall begun in 1832, Liverpool's St George's Hall had followed immediately, in 1836. Then came Leeds, in 1853–8, with a building crowned by a mighty Late Wren kind of dome or tower. The two most splendid town halls in the Lancashire towns other than Liverpool and Manchester were both designed by
70 Leeds architects: Rochdale by *W. H. Crossland* (of Royal Hollo-
69 way College fame) in 1864* and Bolton by *W. Hill* in 1866. Rochdale is Gothic and picturesquely but rather loosely grouped, Bolton is a classical Baroque clearly derived from Leeds, though the dome has become a slender tower. *Waterhouse*'s
71 Manchester Town Hall was begun in 1868. It is grand and symmetrical to Albert Square, highly rationally planned, and full of
72 beautiful spatial intricacies inside. There is plenty of rib-vaulting too.

The number of commissions which fell to *Waterhouse* in and around Manchester is prodigious. He was born in Liverpool in 1830. When he was twenty-nine he went in for the competition for the Manchester Assize Courts, won it, 'and thus established his reputation', as Eastlake writes. The building should never have been destroyed. Between this and the town hall he did some minor ecclesiastical work (Prestwich, Ince-in-Makerfield, Ashton-in-Makerfield, Rusholme (Manchester)), and one major church to be referred to later), some minor public buildings (Educational Institution, Droylsden, Ancoats Library, Manchester), a large private house (Allerton Priory, Liverpool) and the mighty Strangeways Prison (Manchester) of 1866–8, with its minaret chimney. After the town hall there were the original buildings of Manchester and Liverpool Universities (Manchester

* Crossland's tower has been replaced by a less high one designed by *Waterhouse* in 1883.

designed in 1872, but built in 1883–7, Liverpool of 1887–92 and nothing like as successful as Manchester, which can vie with the town hall in its beautiful vaulting), and there were grammar schools at Manchester (Chetham's, 1873–8) and Wigan (demolished), and several hospitals etc. (Park Hospital, Anfield (Liverpool) 1873–4, the Turner Memorial Home at Toxteth (Liverpool) 1881–3, the Liverpool Royal Infirmary 1887–90, St Mary's Hospital, Manchester 1899 etc.), besides another major church, and big commercial buildings such as the Lime Street Hotel at Liverpool (1868–71), the Prudential at Manchester (1881), and the Prudential at Liverpool (1885–6).

Waterhouse's style can't be mistaken, except for that of his imitators.* The Whitworth Gallery at Chorlton-on-Medlock (Manchester) by *J. W. Beaumont* is a typical case of Waterhousism. *Thomas Worthington* of Manchester on the other hand is a parallel to, rather than an imitator of, Waterhouse. His main buildings, usually of brick, are more conventionally High Victorian High Gothic. He was not short of commissions either. It is sufficient to name here the Memorial Hall in Albert Square, Ruskinian Venetian Gothic of 1864–6, the old Magistrates' Courts of 1868–71, and the Nicholls Hospital at Ardwick (Manchester) of 1879. The Manchester Reform Club by *E. Salomons*, also a Manchester architect, is Ruskino-Venetian too and was built in 1870–1. Far more original is *G. T. Redmayne*'s Manchester College of Art at Chorlton-on-Medlock of 1880–1, Gothic in the motifs but stripped of them a building as functional as Mackintosh's Glasgow School of Art and quite probably one of its sources.‡

A building by *Waterhouse* may at first appear impersonally Gothic. In fact it will be found to need close analysis for a full understanding of its creative eclecticism. Waterhouse composed picturesquely but, wherever scale allowed, broadly and boldly. There are never niggly details. His main accents tend to be mature C13 Gothic with simple, easily taken-in geometrical tracery or equally clearly readable Romanesque motifs, a round-headed portal e.g. But wherever no special display had to go on, i.e. in the less stressed parts of a façade, he turned to segment-headed windows or mullioned-and-transomed windows, i.e. forms belonging to quite different styles but suited to their place and function. Brick, often the hot, hard reds of Accrington or Ruabon, suited him as much as stone.

* But one might not recognize Waterhouse in the German Renaissance of his National Provincial Bank in Spring Gardens, Manchester, built in 1888–91.
‡ The extension of 1897 by *J. Gibbens Sankey* is Gothic too and original too.

The two major CHURCHES which *Waterhouse* did in Lancashire show him at his best. St John, Brooklands Road, Wythenshawe (Manchester) dates from 1864–8, St Elisabeth, Reddish from 1882–3. Both are stern, exacting designs. Waterhouse could not have designed pretty had he tried. St John has no tower and no aisles. The interior is faced with yellow brick, the tracery is late C13, i.e. the favourite Second Pointed, but with a preference for bare, uncusped circles. St Elisabeth is of brick, in a style of round arches, of varied derivation, but mostly (and especially in the furnishings) Italian. The church is very high, and architectural motifs are few.

The church was paid for by Sir William Houldsworth, whose giant mill and factory housing has been mentioned some pages back. At Hurst one Whitaker built the church, another the Methodist church, and they built the school too. At Stretford John Rylands, whose chief Manchester benefaction will appear in this survey later, gave the town hall, the public baths, and a coffee tavern. The Heywoods, bankers of Manchester, have been followed in their building activity by the Rev. J. Stanley Leatherbarrow in what is one of the best existing monographs on Victorian architecture and its social setting (*see* Swinton). At Liverpool the Horsfalls did likewise, and they are followed in the account of Sefton Park (*see* p. 234). At Bury is the ambitious Walshaw parish church of 1888 by *L. Booth*, and this was paid for by two Haworths in memory of Jesse Haworth. *Grayson*'s All Hallows, Allerton (Liverpool) of 1872 etc. was built by John Bibby in memory of his first wife, the grand Brookfield Unitarian Church, Gorton (Manchester) was designed in 1869 by *Thomas Worthington* for Richard Peacock of the Gorton 83 Foundry. The outstanding *Austin & Paley* church of St Matthew, Highfield, Wigan was built by Blundells, colliery owners near by (1894). Richard Evans built a sumptuous Congregational church See at Newton-le-Willows, and so on.

See p. 479
In now turning to VICTORIAN ECCLESIASTICAL ARCHITECTURE in more detail, the survey will best be done by architects and in a roughly chronological order of their birth, first national, then local figures. Two Catholic architects, older than Pugin, come into the survey: *J. J. Scoles* (born 1798) for the rather grim, because severely utilitarian, St Francis Xavier, Everton (Liverpool) of 1845–9, with thin E.E. columns,* and *J. A. Hansom* (born 1803) for the two highly idiosyncratic Catholic churches at

* The over-elaborate vaulted Lady Chapel is by *E. Kirby*, 1888.

Leigh of 1855 and Hindley of 1869.* Leigh especially has a gaunt
interior with giant iron columns and confusing roof timbers.
Hansom's Holy Name at Chorlton-on-Medlock (Manchester) 77
on the other hand, though begun in the same year as Hindley, is a
design of the very highest quality and of an originality nowhere
demonstrative. The E solution in particular, with arches thrown
across diagonally, is unexpected in Victorian churches and fully
convincing. The piers are slim and high and thus achieve a spatial
unity from w end to E end. Hansom never again did so
marvellous a church. A Catholic church architect also, though a
full generation younger, was A. W. N. Pugin's son *E. W. Pugin*
(born 1834). He did several Catholic churches, two of them of
national importance, St Francis, Gorton (Manchester) of 1866–72 75
because of its showy façade, and Barton-upon-Irwell of 1867–8, 76
which is the masterpiece of his life without any doubt. The de
Traffords financed the building, and that allowed a lavishness still
rare in Catholic enterprise. The relation of the rib-vaulted
chancel to the rib-vaulted Trafford Chapel is ingenious and intricate, even if perhaps a trifle tricky.‡ *Sir George Gilbert Scott*'s
great estate church at Worsley (for Francis Egerton, Earl of
Ellesmere) has already been introduced. It was built in 1846.
Another equally lavish estate church by Scott is that of the Earls of
Sefton of Croxteth at West Derby (Liverpool) of 1853–6. Two 73
other Scott churches in South Lancashire are of no importance,§
but St Paul, New Cross, Ancoats (Manchester) is both interesting
and puzzling. It was started in 1876 and finished after Scott's
death by his son *John Oldrid Scott*, but it does not feel like either.
The tower and the planning of the available space both seem too
wilful. *Slater & Carpenter*'s Christ Church, Bootle (1866) hardly
deserves a mention, *Joseph Clarke*'s Heywood parish church
1860–2) is large and competent but not more, and *Butterfield*'s
Holy Cross, Clayton (Manchester) of 1863–6 (all three architects
were born in 1819)‖ is recognizably his inside and quite impressive outside by virtue of its height, but it is not one of his major
works. 1817 is the birth-year of *Pearson*. Of his generation he was

---

* But nothing like as idiosyncratic as his phantasmagoric St Werburge at
Preston in North Lancashire.
‡ Other churches by *E. W. Pugin* are at Liverpool (St Vincent de Paul,
1856–7), Victoria Park (Manchester), 1861–2, Stretford, 1862–7.
§ Denton Christ Church 1848–53 and Salford St Luke, Seedley, 1865.
‖ Born in 1819 also was *Henry Clutton*. He is an architect of pronounced
individuality, as comes out very characteristically in the interior, cool and
spacious, of his Catholic church at Ditton of 1876–9. The slender arcade
columns, two deep, with rings round are almost a hallmark of mature Clutton.

infinitely the most sensitive. He, like them, believed in the Second Pointed, i.e. the style of the C13, Franco-Norman as well as Anglo-Norman; for as Scott for St Nicholas at Hamburg (1844) had looked at the German Gothic, as Ruskin in his *Stones of Venice* (1851) had worshipped Venetian Gothic, so now, in the 1850s, French Gothic took its place side by side with English. Pearson's St Agnes, Sefton Park (Liverpool) is as late as 1883–5, and his earlier All Saints, Speke (Liverpool) of 1876 is nothing outstanding. So there is in South Lancashire nothing of his of about the date of Butterfield's Holy Cross. But the style of St Agnes was fully formed already at that time. St Agnes is of brick and vaulted throughout, with a polygonal apse W as well as E, a balcony running all along the walls as something neither triforium nor wall-passage, and the E is wonderfully diversified. This is one of the three most thrilling Victorian churches in the county. Next in order of age comes *Horace Francis* (born in 1821). He and his brother did most of the Warrington parish church in 1859–67, and it is probably the best church they ever did. The soaring spire over the crossing is especially memorable. After Francis *Street*, who was born in 1824, and he is represented in South Lancashire by one of his major works: Swinton of 1869. It looks strong and trustworthy with its bold, flat plate-tracery, but it does not carry you away, as St Agnes does.* *Truefitt* (born 1824 too) did a curiously unorthodox church at Davyhulme (1889–90), and then we come to *Bodley*.

78   His Pendlebury of 1871–4 is one of the English churches of all time. Its sheer brick exterior – no tower, one long roof – and the majestic *sursum* of its interior have never been surpassed in Victorian church building. Inspiration must have come from buildings such as Albi Cathedral and the Blackfriars at Toulouse. The tracery of the windows is Dec in the chancel, Perp in the nave, as if building had gone on for half a century.‡ E.E., the favourite of Scott and his generation, had had an almost absolute command over church building. Now the later Middle Ages returned and

* Other churches by *Street* are that at Whiston of 1864–8, St Margaret, Prince's Road, Toxteth (Liverpool) of 1868–9, Milnrow of 1868–9, and All Saints, Bolton of 1869–71.

‡ St John, Tue Brook (Liverpool) of 1868–70, *Bodley's* other church, is Dec and also very perfect, but in so quiet a way that one hardly notices it. It is only gradually that its great refinement acts on you. *Bodley & Garner's* St Luke, Liverpool Road, Warrington of 1892–3 on the other hand is not at all a success. The attempt at a two-naved church is interesting, but proved unmanageable even in the hands of two men of such competence and experience as Bodley and Garner.

were to be the pattern until period forms were no longer followed at all. Appreciation of the Perp style before 1875 is rare. *Grayson*'s All Hallows, Allerton (Liverpool) is an example, as early as 1872-6.

Grayson was a Liverpool man. So we must now look at the locals. *J. E. Gregan* of Manchester, we have seen, was one of the first to follow in the footsteps of Pugin, Scott, and Ferrey. The contrast between the Commissioners' church of St John Evangelist, Broughton (Salford) by *Lane*, 1836-9, and its choir by *Gregan* of 1846 is illuminating. But at St John, Miles Platting (Manchester) in 1855 Gregan (and *Corson*) produced an Italian Romanesque basilica of brick with a campanile.* *E. H. Shellard* of Manchester was an architect who wavered between the old and the new. St Peter, Blackley (Manchester) of 1844 is still pre-archeological, with paired side lancets and three galleries, the steeples of Audenshaw church of 1845-6 and Failsworth church of the same years are archeologically convincing pieces, and St Thomas, Lees is convincing throughout. But in whatever mood, he never makes a strong impact. *A. H. Holme* of Liverpool in his St Mary, Aigburth of 1853-4 is equally in a quandary. The plan is pre-Pugin, but the exterior looks 1850s all right. Internally it has very curious flying arches of wood in the crossing. The inspiration was probably E. B. Lamb, and E. B. Lamb certainly stands behind *J. Medland & Henry Taylor*'s St Agnes, Levenshulme (Manchester). This is as late as 1884-5, but Medland Taylor can be followed from 1864 onwards. When their *œuvre* is studied, they turn out to be archrogues (the word used in Goodhart-Rendel's sense). Their inventiveness of perversities and their crotchety motifs are unlimited. Yet they were never short of clients. I have counted over twenty-five churches by them (or J. M. alone). St Peter, Parr, St Helens of 1864-5, St James, Waterloo Road, Bolton of 1867-71, St Mary, Haughton Green of 1874-6, St George, Daubhill, Bolton of 1880, St Anne, Haughton of 1882 are the most wilful. Rogue architecture in Liverpool is All Souls, Collingwood Street, Everton of 1870-2 and St Cyprian, Edge Hill of 1879-81. The tracery here has shed all links with the past. Both churches are by *Henry Sumners*. *Thomas Worthington* of Manchester did only one major church, the Brookfield Unitarian Church, Gorton of 1869-71, a building on a grand scale, designed in a competent but not inspired E.E. His son *Percy Worthington* in the Sefton Park Uni-

* Basilica with campanile is also the *parti* of *E. A. Heffer*'s St Bridget, Wavertree (Liverpool). This dates from 1868-72, an even less likely date than 1855 for Romanesque inspiration.

tarian Church (Liverpool) in 1896–9 achieved one of the most
successful groups in the county of church, hall, and other ancillary rooms, but then Gothic was already treated with the freedom
which, as we shall see, Stokes introduced to the North about
1890, exactly when Sedding at Holy Trinity, Sloane Street introduced it to London. *J. S. Crowther* of Manchester, co-author
with Bowman of *Churches of the Middle Ages*, published in 1845–
53, and restorer of Manchester Cathedral was a learned architect and a man of considerable talent. His best churches are of a
nobility that moves immediately. They are high and altogether
beautifully proportioned, and their detail is always of great
finesse. If one tries to make a choice of three or four for this survey, they ought to be St Benedict, Ardwick of 1880 with its soar-
74 ing steeple, St Alban, Cheetham of 1857–64, both at Manchester, the Bury parish church of 1871–6 and St Mary, Hulme
(Manchester) of as early a date as 1856–8. At St Wilfrid, Northenden (Manchester) Crowther chose Perp as early as 1873–6,
but was tied to the style of the predecessor church. Otherwise he
adhered to the Middle Pointed. At the same time *Doyle*, better
known for his Edwardian Baroque secular buildings, did St
Ambrose, Widnes in 1879–83, as a sound, honest red-brick
job.

It is an impressive record of local church building activity. But
of all these Lancashire men only one had genius: Austin of
Paley & Austin. I say Austin; for Paley, born in 1823, the grandson of the theologian, had been first in partnership with Sharpe
and then, from 1851 to 1868, on his own. The churches by him
such as Christ Church, Ince-in-Makerfield (1863–4), Holy
Trinity, Bury (1863–5), St James, Poolstock, Wigan (1866),
St Peter, Hindley (1866) are nothing special, and the ambitious
Bolton parish church of 1867–71 with its vaulted chancel is confident but conventional. So is the Leigh parish church of 1869–73.
H. J. Austin (1841–1915) became Paley's partner in 1868, and then
things began to happen. They must have looked to Bodley, but
their masterpieces are not later than his and often every bit as
exciting, as resourceful and as noble. They are often of brick,
often of red sandstone, and the pinkish mushroom colour of the
sandstone ashlar suits the expensive Late Victorian churches by
them and others. Paley & Austin towers are handled with great
majesty, and their interiors have in all their best designs a completely unexpected, asymmetrical composition of chancel, transepts, and chancel chapels or aisles. Another unexpected effect is
very wide aisleless naves. But even if one can generalize in this way,

Paley & Austin never repeat themselves. It is hard to limit reference here to only a few. Perhaps they ought to be Kirkby of 1869–71, the Mossley Hill parish church (Liverpool) of 1870–5, St Thomas, Halliwell, Bolton of 1875, Daisy Hill of 1879–81, All Souls, Astley Bridge, Bolton of 1880–1, St Peter, Leigh of 1880–1, Prestwich parish church chancel of 1888–9, St Mary, Ince-in-Makerfield of 1887, the Waterloo parish church of 1891–4, and St Matthew, Highfield, Wigan of 1894. All these, though Paley & 83 Austin, whose office was at Lancaster, were local architects, are of the highest European standard of their years. Paley died in 1895, and the firm became *Austin & Paley*. They still did outstanding work in the style early this century (St Margaret, Halliwell, Bolton, 1903, St Mary, West Bank, Widnes, 1908–10), but by 1910 (St Wilfrid, Newton Heath, Manchester) the zest began to flag. St Stephen, Avenue Road, Wigan is as late as 1930–8.

To a certain extent the local Liverpool counterpart of Paley & Austin is *Aldridge & Deacon* with some strikingly good churches to their credit, such as St Benedict, Everton (Liverpool) of 1886–7, St Dunstan, Wavertree (Liverpool), and Rainford (especially the tower of 1903). Other local architects enjoyed this Indian summer of Gothic imitation: *Grayson* in his All Hallows, Allerton (Liverpool) of 1872–6 and St Faith, Waterloo of 1900, *Sinnott & Powell* in their one outstanding church among many more ordinary ones: Sacred Heart, Liverpool Road, Warrington, *John Douglas* of Chester in his Haydock church of 1891–2, timber-framed and strikingly spacious,* and *Demaine & Brierley* of York in their large church at Newton-le-Willows, inspired no doubt by Austin & Paley. This was completed in 1901.

But we are not ready for the C20, nor even for Stokes and Sedding and the changes they brought about; for nothing has yet been said about MONUMENTS in churches and church furnishings altogether. The situation about monuments is curious. There are hardly any in the whole of South Lancashire worth stopping for for more than a moment. The best series is in the Mortuary Chapel of St James's Cemetery in Liverpool, pieces by *Gibson*, by *Chantrey*, by *Joseph Gott*. By Gibson, done when he was appren- 45 ticed with the *Franceys* firm of monumental sculptors, is the tablet to Henry Blundell † 1810 at Sefton; it is like a miniature version of an ambitious monument in Westminster Abbey. Chantrey did a few more monuments, especially the kneeling figure of 1822 on Peter Patten Bold's monument at Farnworth

* Early in his career, in 1866–8, Douglas had done the fully and ruthlessly High Victorian St Anne at Warrington.

near Widnes, and *Westmacott* a monument at Prescot († 1803) and – to bring it in here – the equestrian statue of George III in London Road, Liverpool. *R. J. Wyatt* in Rome did the beautiful

44 relief at Winwick to commemorate Mrs Legh († 1831), and as beautiful is the anonymous relief for Thomas Wilson-Patten († 1819) at Warrington. A large relief also was done by the later famous *Tenerani* of Rome for Princess Sapieha († 1824) at Farnworth near Widnes. Of the mid C19 only one place need be mentioned for monuments, the Dearden Chapel in Rochdale parish church, and that for the disreputable reason that a Dearden *c.*1847 had a number of ancestral stones and brasses faked.

For CHURCH FURNISHING a little more may be of use, and

51 first the complete refitting of the Ashton-under-Lyne parish church in the 1840s, heavily decorated in stone and wood, still with three galleries and with pews facing the pulpit from E as well as w. Then the *Bodley* furnishings of St John, Tue Brook (Liverpool), the reredos signed by *Thomas Woolner* in St John, Walton (Liverpool), and then stained glass, first that designed by *Pugin* for Winwick,* but foremost the *Morris* glass, of which there is much and some outstanding, such as that in St John, Tue Brook (Liverpool) of 1868 and later – Bodley was Morris's first client for glass – All Saints, Wigan of 1868, Halewood of the 1870s, Rochdale St

79 Chad of 1872–4, unusually agitated, Prescot *c.*1879, Emmanuel, Didsbury (Manchester), St Mary, Fairfield (Liverpool), and the magnificent series at All Hallows, Allerton (Liverpool) which extended from 1875 to 1886. *Frederick Shields* designed all the glass for St Ann, Manchester, and *Henry Holiday* glass in a number of churches, e.g. St James, Toxteth (Liverpool) (1881).

Holiday also painted eleven years earlier the 35-ft-long scene of Magna Carta in Rochdale Town Hall. In Manchester Town Hall *Ford Madox Brown* was very busy from 1876 to 1888 painting

80 scenes from the history of Manchester. They are Pre-Raphaelite without any doubt, but they strangely point forward to Stanley Spencer.

SECULAR ARCHITECTURE later than High Victorian has not yet been examined. For domestic designs the paramount influence was *Norman Shaw*. Liverpool had four important houses by him at the end of the Second World War. Now there is only one left; that is the way Liverpool is protecting her architectural heritage.

81 The surviving house is the vicarage of St Agnes, Sefton Park of 1887, and it is an outstandingly composed and detailed job. For

---

* *Pugin* glass is also in the chancel of Warrington parish church.

public buildings and the large commercial palaces the prevalent style of the end of the century was a mixed French Loire and English Elizabethan to Jacobean. Big gables were always insisted on, and the favourite material was red brick with either red or yellow terracotta. Examples are the Midland Hotel, Manchester by *Trubshaw* of 1898, the Refuge Assurance in Manchester by *Paul Waterhouse* of 1891 etc., and the Manchester Institute of Science and Technology by *Spalding & Cross* of 1895 etc. They probably got the job on the strength of their Victoria Square workers' housing at Ancoats (Manchester). This, built in 1889, is a huge block of ranges round an inner courtyard, the façade gabled in the sense just described, though of course less showily. It was a first, much needed slum-clearance endeavour. Liverpool in the nineties also got on to municipally built working-class blocks of flats, and it is interesting to follow their development (*see* introduction to Liverpool, p. 149). Access to the flats by long balconies in tiers was chosen both in Victoria Square and at Liverpool.

All on its own among late C19 public buildings is the John Rylands Library at Manchester, built in 1890–9 to the design of Basil Champneys. It is not a practical building: it is a monument to commercial munificence, and looks, especially internally, as if one of Fred Griggs's Gothic dream drawings had been translated into real stone. It is inventive, extremely pretty, and spatially quite thrilling. Such ornate Perp Gothic was of course the exception, not the rule, in 1890.

The progressive treatment of Gothic was that of *Leonard Stokes*'s St Clare, Sefton Park (Liverpool) completed in the year in which Champneys began, and that of other CHURCHES by Stokes. But Champneys was born in 1842, Stokes in 1858. St Clare is an entirely personal manipulation of Gothic elements into a convincing whole which is of the C19, not of the Middle Ages. The turret in the angle between transept and nave, the sheer E wall, the wall-piers (i.e. really internal buttresses), pierced to allow passages instead of aisles, and the shapes of piers and arches – all this is just Stokes. Gothic remained a stimulus, but it was no longer an authority.

Stokes went further in this than did *Sir Giles Gilbert Scott* in Liverpool Cathedral, which he won in competition in 1901, the first year of the TWENTIETH CENTURY, aged then only twenty-one. He altered his designs radically in 1909–10 and later. The Lady Chapel of 1906–10 was still conventional, the design of 1910 established his peculiar rhythm of sheer walls and small areas of very rich, conventionally Gothic ornament. The outline of the

tower is excellent from wherever one sees it, and such things as the great transept portals, even if functionally hardly justifiable, are very powerful. Yet this is a backward-looking building compared with Scott's own St Paul, Stoneycroft (Liverpool) of 1916, which was inspired by the South-West French Romanesque style, and even more with some churches of the same years by *Temple Moore*, although Temple Moore was born in 1856 and Giles Scott in 1880. Moore's St Anne, Royton of 1908–10 is far more radical than Liverpool Cathedral. With its low, flat-roofed Lady Chapel at the E end separated from the chancel by three arches and its mixture of Dec and C17 windows it is almost excessively inventive. Moore's St Aidan, Manchester Road, Rochdale of 1914 has lancets like a Commissioners' church, but also decidedly personal features such as the different treatment of the chancel N and S walls.*
Comper stands not far from Temple Moore. Both derive from late Bodley. Comper's St Mary, Rochdale of 1909–11 is one of his most interesting buildings. He preserved the N wall of a Georgian church and the N arcade on Tuscan columns, and added a new nave and a new S aisle as wide as his nave. The two are of the same height and of course Perp. So the low Georgian arcade faces a tall Perp arcade of octagonal piers. To one's surprise the juxtaposition comes off. The fitments of course are Comper's too and of the tiresome historicism to which he kept faithful for rood screens and such-like pieces.

But the boldest religious building of the early C20 is without
90 doubt *Edgar Wood*'s Church of Christ Scientist in Victoria Park (Manchester), designed in 1903. It is the only religious building in Lancashire that would be indispensable in a survey of the development of C20 church design in all England. It is pioneer work, internationally speaking, of an Expressionism halfway between Gaudí and Germany about 1920, and it stands entirely on its own in England. Wood's development up to 1903 can be followed. It is almost exclusively domestic, though he had done one major ecclesiastic work in 1899, the Long Street Wesleyan Church at Middleton, Gothic, as free as Stokes, and beautifully grouped with school etc. round a courtyard. The fitments were designed by him too, for he was an Arts and Crafts all-rounder, and they are much more daring than the building. The houses he designed at Middleton in 1895 etc. are of the Voysey kind, broadly speaking. But then another change took place, equally interesting from the international point of view. Wood met *James Henry Sellers*, who
92 in 1906–7 had built a very simple, unassuming office building for a

* *Moore*'s St Cyprian, Gorton (Manchester) is much less interesting.

firm at Oldham, and this was emphatically cubic, as no other building at that moment in England was. And moreover it had a flat roof of reinforced concrete. Wood adopted style and technique and built some equally cubic houses, not in Lancashire, in 1907 and 1908. In partnership Wood and Sellers did the two memorable schools at Middleton, the Durnford Street School and the Elm 91 Street School, both designed in 1908. They have certain C17 and C18 features, but their planning is fresh and convincing, and their general appearance is again strikingly cubic. Here, by experiment, two Lancashire architects of no great renown got as near as any-one in England to the most progressive European and American work of 1900–14.

Meanwhile, in Liverpool the Edwardian Imperial Baroque flourished as nowhere else in the provinces. Exuberant work of a high order such as *Doyle*'s Royal Insurance of 1896–1903, in- 86 spired by *Norman Shaw*'s building for the White Star Line, the Cotton Exchange by *Matear & Simon* of 1905–6,* and *Briggs, Wolstenholme & Thornely*'s Bluecoat School at Wavertree of 89 1903–6 with its spectacular tower of 1915 and its centrally planned and domed chapel, stand side by side with such corny buildings as the Royal Liver of 1908–10 by *W. Aubrey Thomas* and *Thornely*'s 2 Mersey Dock Offices of 1907, buildings one may be impressed by for reason of sheer bulk but can hardly like.

The Edwardian Baroque is at its most likeable in small public buildings such as LIBRARIES. The public libraries of 1890–1910 are indeed all over England a great attraction of suburbs. Liver-pool was particularly lucky with her city architect in those years: *Shelmerdine*'s libraries never fail, though the best are pre-Edwardian. The Bolton architects *Bradshaw & Gass* also did libraries, and incidentally Edwardian public piles as well.

But the finest work of these years in Lancashire in a less radical vein than Wood's and Sellers's was done by *Sir Charles Reilly* in Liverpool. He was ingenious, versatile, and a believer in classicism. Witness are his Students' Union of 1910–13 and his chancel of Wavertree parish church of 1911, both of which grow in stature 93 the more one studies them.‡ Liverpool, we have seen, had had con-sistent classical leanings throughout the C19; so it is not surprising to find it a stronghold of the Classical Re-Revival of the twenties and thirties. *H. J. Rowse* was the centre, and his Martins Bank,

---

* Since demolished.

‡ The only parallel to Reilly one can venture is the Leigh Town Hall of 1904–7 by *J. C. Prestwich*, a building of no great size with a very restrainedly classical façade.

Water Street of 1927–32 is an accomplished piece in a style more
deftly handled as a rule in the United States than in England. But
Rowse's decoration was not classical: it derived from the modernism of the 1925 Exhibition in Paris, and perhaps a little from
Östberg's Stockholm City Hall (see e.g. the details of the Mersey
Tunnel of 1931–4). *E. Vincent Harris* in the Manchester Central
94 Library of 1930–4 used the vocabulary of the Classical Re-
Revival far more conventionally, though his contemporary town
hall extension shows a remarkably original and impressive handling of early C17 elements.

But by 1930–4 in Central Europe progressive architects and
even progressive municipalities were fully committed to a style
totally different from Vincent Harris's. The so-called International
Modern, admittedly by 1930 not yet all that international, had
reached maturity, and in Germany, Switzerland, Austria, Sweden,
Holland was becoming the accepted style for housing, for offices
and factories, for schools, and – with qualifications – even for
churches.

It is only in the field of CHURCH ARCHITECTURE that Lancashire showed itself aware of this development, but there the
industrial south of the county took the lead even over London.
Six churches deserve recording, for varying degrees of appreciation of the new movement. They must be seen against such leading pre-modern buildings of the twenties as *Caröe*'s St Helen at
St Helens of 1926 and the large, weird, byzantinizing Catholic
church of Ashton-in-Makerfield by *J. K. Brocklesby* (1930). The
first of the church architects to look with some understanding to the
Central European style of the twenties was *Bernard A. Miller*.
The blocky exterior and the parabolic arches inside his St
Christopher, Norris Green (Liverpool), begun in 1930, were quite
a bold achievement.* The second name is the more important one
of *Francis Xavier Velarde*. His St Matthew, Clubmoor (Liverpool),
also begun in 1930, is less promising than Miller's St Christopher.
It was to lead into a cul-de-sac; for Velarde here had gone to
the Romanesque of Italy for inspiration, even if nowhere for
imitation. The interior in fact is not without topical interest.

Now the Italian Romanesque in alliance with the Byzantine had
had a certain fascination for English architects, especially Catholic architects, in the mid and the later C19, but Bentley's Westminster Cathedral brought the possibility into the open. So now
we find Corpus Christi, Miles Platting (Manchester) of 1906 by

* His St Christopher at Withington (Manchester) of 1935 is experimental
too, but less so.

E. Gernson adhering to the Italian Romanesque, and *Sir Walter Tapper*, twenty years later, took as his theme the Byzantine one of three domes from w to e in Our Lady of Mercy, Gorton (Manchester), even if the church remained a fragment. From such precedent Catholic architects without much courage or creative ability have gone on with the Italian Romanesque all over England. It is one of the deadest ends in mid-c20 ecclesiastical architecture. Even so, no-one can deny that large domed churches in England have a certain emotional appeal – for rarity, but also for the sheer capabilities of expression of the dome. That applies to St Philip Neri, Catharine Street, Liverpool of 1920 (by *P. S. Gilby*), St John Baptist, Rochdale of 1924 (by *Hill, Sandy & Norris*), even to St Mary at St Helens of 1924–30 (by *Powell*, an ill-advised mixture of Byzantine and Gothic elements), and even more to the church at Ashton-in-Makerfield.

But *Velarde* of course does not have his position in that rank. He moved away from the period imitators with one decisive step when in 1936 he came out with the design for St Monica at Bootle. Even here he remained faithful to round-arched windows, but the rhythm of tier above tier of round-arched openings, something between Henry VIII and Giorgio de Chirico, was in fact inspired by the recent churches of Dominicus Böhm in Germany, modern churches, c20 churches, even if not, like the Swiss Protestant ones, churches directly expressed in the International Modern idiom.*
Links between German churches in that idiom were first established by *Welch, Cachemaille Day & Lander* at St Nicholas, Burnage (Manchester) of 1931–2, a high, square brick building, with typically German raised brick patterns and with enough courage to display a pulpit and lectern as raw brick cubes. The altar is not in the apse, but further w, with bare brick staircases leading up to the Lady Chapel behind it. Liturgically much more radical was Cachemaille Day & Lander's St Michael, Northen- 95 den (Manchester) of 1937; for this has a star-shaped plan, and the altar was intended to stand in the centre. But the bishop would not permit such a thing.

Nowadays it is an arrangement preached with an almost exaggerated zest, and *Sir Frederick Gibberd*'s great Catholic Cathedral 98 of Liverpool, designed in 1959 and consecrated in 1967, makes it its pivot. The history of the cathedral began with the commission given to *Lutyens* in 1930, the design for a vast, centrally planned cathedral by him, classical with Byzantine overtones, and the

* A later church by *Velarde* is St Patrick, Clinkham Wood, St Helens. It dates from 1963–4.

building of the immense crypt. Lutyens's details above ground suffer from the gargantuan jokes to which he was prone in his later years, but the spaces in the crypt cannot fail to impress. Sir Frederick Gibberd ingeniously accepted the crypt without having to depend on it for his design. His is a circle with eight chapels, a conical roof, and a high tapering lantern. The lantern does not compete with Scott's Anglican tower, but holds its own. The central space is very powerful indeed, though externally the motifs of the porch and of every one of the chapels, being different from every other, produce a restlessness and aggressiveness from which church architects in the sixties do not seem capable of escaping. Yet Sir Frederick's chapel of Hopwood Hall of 1963–5, a dress rehearsal for Liverpool, by having no surrounding chapels produces total unity. Mr *G. G. Pace*'s William Temple Memorial Church, Simonsway, Wythenshawe (Manchester) of 1964–5 on the other hand accepts restlessness with fervour and in its interior drives it to extremes. It is a matter of personal character whether one can accept this radicalism at all or for churches, but whatever the emotional reaction, no-one can deny Mr Pace's courage and that of his clients.*

Now churches are springing up everywhere – especially for Catholic worship. Their hyperbolic paraboloid roofs, jabbing at you, their irregular plans, their abstract concrete patterns attack you in nearly all the new housing estates. The best, as history will perhaps confirm, are the ones which allow contemplation and concentration, i.e. which keep quiet. This is true of some by *Weightman & Bullen* (St Margaret Mary, Knotty Ash, Liverpool, and St Ambrose, Speke, Liverpool, and also the chapel of Christ's College of Education, Childwall, Liverpool), some by *Desmond Williams & Associates* (St Augustine, Grosvenor Square, Chorlton-on-Medlock, Manchester), and even more of two small churches by *T. D. Howcroft* which turn inward and have none of the exhibitionism of most of the others (Martin Luther Church, Stretford, Broughton Methodist Church, Salford). Among the best also, and a little older, is *Sir Basil Spence*'s St Francis, Wythenshawe (Manchester) of 1959–61, one of a series of suburban churches which for some years were not at all a mere by-product in their architect's mind.

To SECULAR ARCHITECTURE South Lancashire before the Second World War had very little to contribute. Kennet House, Smedley Road, Strangeways (Manchester) of *c.*1935 by the Cor-

---

* He also did St Mark, Chadderton (in 1962–3), nearly as raw and wild and daring.

poration, a vast block of low-income housing round a courtyard, is inspired directly by Quarry Hill, Leeds and indirectly by Central European housing, with long bands of balconies and horizontal windows. That is derivative stuff, but *Sir Owen Williams*'s Daily Express in Manchester, built in 1939, can hold its own in competition with anything of that date. It has an absolutely smooth façade with a rounded corner, entirely of glass, transparent and opaque, and the printing machinery can be watched day and night. Manchester has not done anything better since.

Yet Manchester has done a great deal and is, at the time of writing, doing more perhaps than any other city in England, especially in the field of council housing (city architect *S. G. Besant Roberts*, director of housing *J. Austen Bent*). The principle is a mixture of high blocks with low terraces, and high blocks are the distinguishing feature in Liverpool and the other towns as well. They are built on industrial systems which – given the speed at which they are needed – is as it should be, though whether flats on the tenth or twentieth floor are what people want, or indeed what it is socially justifiable to give them, is another matter. The decision on this question is not one to be taken by *The Buildings of England*, but it is surely not all that unlikely that in the 2060s these high blocks will be looked at with as much scandalized curiosity as we feel when looking at the low-cost housing of the 1860s. That architects want them is understandable. They provide the necessary vertical accents which in the 1860s would have been the church spires. But their architectural value in the skyline depends on their distribution. A single one, if not lumpy, can make all the difference; so can, on a larger scale, a cluster of them, and where, as at Eccles and Rochdale, a whole group faces the very city centre, the effect may be challenging, and in the future may well be accepted with emotional approval. As a rule, however, the high blocks are scattered all over the suburbs, in which case, even visually, they only disturb.

City architects or borough surveyors are also busy on the renewal of out-of-date centres or, as at Wythenshawe, the provision of a much needed centre. For Wythenshawe, being Manchester's garden suburb (planned by *Barry Parker* and begun in 1931), had made the same mistake as the Hampstead Garden Suburb and left out a commercial centre with shops, pubs, cinema. All this Mr *S. G. Besant Roberts*'s team is now building on a decidedly urban scale.* An example of central renewal on the other hand is

* At Burnage, another Manchester suburb, incidentally, a garden suburb had been begun as early as 1906; but its early growth was very slow.

Oldham, where it is handled quite boldly. Smaller in size because in need is what is being built at Walkden–Worsley, at Bootle, at Ashton-under-Lyne, at Eccles, at Swinton, even at Heywood. As a rule what is built is a combination of new public offices, of civic hall or halls, private offices, and shopping. The quality varies with the architects, *Lyons, Israel & Ellis* (Heywood) having succeeded in civic dignity, where *Leach, Rhodes & Walker* have preferred the gimmicks of the sixties (civic hall etc., Swinton).

This brings us to individual NEW BUILDINGS in other con-
96 texts. We start with Pilkington's new headquarters at St Helens by *Fry, Drew & Partners*, a large group, rationally and admirably managed. Then there is Heinz's new factory near Kitt Green, Wigan, impressive by size and to a certain extent architecturally as well. (It is by *J. Douglass Mathews & Partners* in consultation with *Skidmore, Owings & Merrill* of America.) The other buildings
3 worth a special mention are the Widnes road bridge of 1956–61 (by *Mott, Hay & Anderson*), the warehouse of Geigy's at Trafford Park, Stretford (by *Scherrer & Hicks*), and two hospital enlargements: Great Moss Hospital, Orrell (by *A. Brocklehurst*), and Wythenshawe Hospital (Manchester) (by *Powell & Moya*). Then office buildings. The centre of Manchester has more than that of Liverpool, but few of them deserve comment. The bulk is run-of-the-mill, often now on the Lever House principle of vertical slab on horizontal slab. As a principle there is much to be said for it; but details can still go desperately wrong. This is what has happened in Piccadilly Gardens, Manchester. The three buildings on the common podium – hotel, high office block, diagonally set lower office block – refuse to read as one. The result is visual confusion, a restlessness which, however, at this moment in time, the architects may well have wanted. The best group in Manchester is without doubt that of the C.I.S. (by *G. S. Hay* in consultation with *Sir John Burnet, Tait & Partners*), clean and crisp and responsibly detailed. In addition one ought perhaps to mention *R. Seifert*'s Gateway House by Piccadilly Station.

That leaves the BUILDINGS FOR EDUCATION. Liverpool and Manchester have done and are doing an enormous amount, Liverpool unfortunately on the site of the best Georgian architecture of the city, Manchester on a site which should allow an ultimate co-ordination of the precincts of University, Institute of Science and Technology, and Regional College of Art into one super-precinct. As for the quality of building, Manchester University has been timid, and there are more buildings to be marvelled at for their reactionary style or their readiness to be just utilitarian than buildings to be praised. The best are the University Theatre and the Humanities block by the *Building Design Partnership*. The Institute of Science and Technology suffers from the opposite fault. New buildings are stylistically up-to-the-minute but tend to be gimmicky. The best here may be *Cruickshank & Seward*'s Renold Lecture Theatres Building. The white extension for the Regional College of Art by *S. G. Besant Roberts* can be recommended without reservations. Altogether Mr Besant Roberts's team has done schools, colleges, libraries, etc., which are much to its credit.

Outside the precinct, but near to the university halls of residence, is Hollings College at Fallowfield by *L. C. Howitt*, the then p. 324 City Architect, a whacking big piece of pop architecture which will no doubt, when it is old enough, find its devotees. The Halls of Residence are of no architectural value, except for Owens Village, also at Fallowfield, by the *Building Design Partnership*, with one high block and lower annexes. This is – also socially (cafeteria or restaurant instead of hall with high table; mixed population) – of interest. In Liverpool the best halls of residence are Carnatic Halls, Mossley Hill by *Manning & Clamp* (1965 etc.). As for the academic buildings of Liverpool University, the authorities have certainly had none of the timidity of Manchester. On the other hand no provision for any visual unity has been made. Instead of going to one or a few architects, many have been given a chance, and the result is what has in a similar case, at Yale, been called a zoo of buildings. You stand in admiration or amazement or revulsion in front of one after the other, but no sense of *universitas* results. Were we still in the state of the so-called International Modern of the thirties, that problem would not arise. There was then a common language; now there is not, or if there is, it is spoken with so much savage emphasis that one building shouts down the other and all shout down Georgian Liverpool – none with more self-centred conviction than Mr *Lasdun*'s standing at the corner of Abercromby Square. The best for pure architectural quality are perhaps the Electrical Engineering Building by *Yorke, Rosenberg & Mardall*, a decidedly, deliberately uneventful building, and the Arts, Social Studies, and Law Group by 97 *Westwood, Piet & Partners*, and this because it is a group, i.e. more than one building.

In the later C20 architects must think more and more in terms of groups of buildings, ever larger groups, until architect and planner become one. Whether a renewed Oldham, a Wythenshawe of garden-city housing and a 1960s-centre, will make visual sense depends on the change of forms from the individual building to the ensemble. And so it is unfortunate that South Lancashire had to be surveyed and this introduction written while the new type of housing and the new civic centres and town centres were still in the making. A verdict would have had to be deferred by two years at least.

Finally FURTHER READING. The essential reference book is the Victoria County History in five volumes (1906–14), the essential and indeed admirably detailed old county history is G. Baines: *History of the County Palatine and Duchy of Lancaster* (1836).* In addition one has to consult the *Transactions of the Lancashire and Cheshire Antiquarian Society* (from 1883) and the *Transactions of the Historical Society of Lancashire and Cheshire* (from 1849). A good brief history of Lancashire is that by J. J. Bagley (4th ed., 1967). Peter Fleetwood-Hesketh's *Lancashire Architectural Guide* (1955) is wholly admirable, full, yet readable and extremely well illustrated. R. Millward: *Lancashire* (Making of the English Landscape, 1955) is to be recommended too, and one should also still go to the *Memorials of Old Lancashire*, edited by H. Fishwick and P. H. Ditchfield (1909; 2 vols). Liverpool literature is introduced on p. 150, Manchester literature on p. 272. For Ashton-under-Lyne there is Mrs W. F. Bowman (1951) and for Ashton also G. F. Foster (1947), for Bolton J. C. Scholes (1892), for Eccles F. R. Johnston (1965), for Middleton J. Dean (1907), for Oldham Hartley Bateson (no date), for Preston H. Fishwick (1900), for Rochdale H. Fishwick (1889),‡ for St Helens T. C. Barker and J. R. Harris (1954), for Warrington A. M. Crowe (1947), for Widnes G. E. Diggle (1961).

Then for special types of building there are H. Taylor: *The Old Halls in Lancashire and Cheshire* (1884), and for mills, i.e. factories, four essays of the Manchester University Department of Architecture: R. Bamber for Manchester and Salford (1958), J. F. Bradley for Bolton (1954), J. B. Howcroft for Oldham (1953), and R. C. Kenyon for Oldham too (1957). For the Bridgewater Canal there is now the book by F. Mullineux (1939). On individual architects we have two theses on Rickman (B. A. Jones, R.I.B.A. 1952, and E. D. Colley, Manchester Department of Architecture 1962), on Foster of Liverpool a Manchester Department of Architecture essay (T. Redford 1957), on Sharpe a Manchester M.A. thesis (R. Jolley 1966), on Waterhouse one

---

* One should use the third edition, ed. J. Croston, 1888–93.

‡ H. Fishwick also published the histories of six minor parishes in North Lancashire.

Manchester Department of Architecture thesis (Xenia Norman 1955) and an excellent London Ph.D. thesis not yet completed at the time of writing (Stuart Smith), and on Rowse a special study of the Liverpool School of Architecture (P. Lenssen). Finally Mr J. H. G. Archer has done a Manchester thesis on Edgar Wood and since two papers on him: *J.R.I.B.A.*, 3rd series, vol. 62, 1954, and *T.L.C.A.S.*, vols 73–4, 1963–4.

As for general literature, such sources as the volumes of *Country Life* for country houses, as Mrs M. Wood's new *The English Mediaeval House*, 1965, as H. Colvin's and R. Gunnis's dictionaries of architects and of sculptors, as A. Vallance for church screens, Mill Stephenson for brasses, L. C. Jowett and W. St John Hope for corporation plate, Tristram for medieval wall paintings and so on are a matter of course, and no more need be said about them and similar standard books.

BUILDING MATERIALS*

BY ALEC CLIFTON-TAYLOR

Industrial Lancashire was largely built of brick, for which there is an abundance of locally available clay and shale. The shales from the Coal Measures were brought into service for brick-making about 1800. They make very hard bricks of screaming redness. It is easy to understand why one of the two principal varieties produced by the brickfields at Accrington (N) is known locally as 'Accrington bloods'. All too familiar in this part of Lancashire are these harsh red machine-pressed bricks of uncomfortably large dimensions (a thickness of 3 in. is common), now coated with grime, and anything but enjoyable. In the Victorian period the roofs of these brick buildings were usually of Welsh slate. About the turn of the present century slate began to give place to smooth red or pink tiles which in the hillier parts of the county are even more unwelcome than the brickwork of the walls, for they are wrong in colour, wrong in texture and wrong in scale. Perhaps no English county has suffered more in the past hundred years from the employment of ugly building materials than Lancashire.

Brick was little used, however, before the C17, and then only in the south-western area. Even as late as 1700 brick buildings in Lancashire were by no means common, but during the C18

* This account covers both North (N) and South (S) Lancashire.

the situation gradually changed and some very pleasant bricks were produced, partly owing to the growing scarcity of wood. For in the Middle Ages this had been one of the best wooded counties in England, and until the Georgian period even Manchester (s) still remained predominantly half-timbered. As far north as the Ribble, timber-framed buildings prevailed everywhere away from the Pennines until the end of the C17. Originally the infillings were wattle and daub: that is, clay reinforced with willow-sticks. These infillings were heavily whitewashed, while the timber framework was blackened with pitch. These 'black and white' buildings were often elaborately if somewhat naïvely ornamented; a local characteristic which Lancashire shared with Cheshire was a liking for a shaped cove under an overhanging upper storey.

Considering the extent of Lancashire's industrialization it is remarkable how many half-timbered buildings have survived, including a few really major examples such as Speke Hall (Liverpool; s). Some of the cottages were formerly of the cruck-framed type. The usual roof for the timber-framed house in Lancashire, as so often elsewhere, was thatch, which was of rye-straw wherever this was available, because that was the toughest of the varieties of straw, with an average life of about thirty years. Thatch in Lancashire is to-day rare.

Apart from wood, the traditional building material of Lancashire was stone, with which the county is decidedly well endowed. Some of this stone is, it is true, not of the best quality; much of the New Red sandstone is coarse-textured and friable, and in the south-western parts of the county such medieval churches as have survived have suffered a good deal from patching and re-facing. It is unfortunate too that so much Lancashire stonework has been blackened with soot. Nevertheless the county can still offer considerable pleasures to the lover of stone.

Sandstone plays a much more important part than limestone in the Lancashire picture. Some of the sandstone is Triassic, some Carboniferous. The Triassic (New Red) sandstone underlies the clays of a considerable part of southern and western Lancashire and reappears at the extremities of the Cartmel and Furness peninsulas (N); but usually it is at too great a depth to be quarried. The principal quarries, Woolton and Rainhill, were on the ridges in and near Liverpool (s). Stone from both these quarries is still being used for the Anglican Cathedral at Liverpool; the colour is a somewhat sombre pink, by no means gay despite its comparatively warm hue. Triassic sandstone was also brought into south-west Lancashire from Runcorn and Storeton on the Cheshire side of the Mersey.

The Carboniferous sandstones come partly from the Coal Measures and, outside the coalfields, from the immediately underlying Millstone Grit. These mostly dull buff or grey sandstones, although they lack charm, are much tougher and more reliable than those from the Triassic formation; moreover, they possess the inestimable property, in Lancashire, of being largely resistant to the disintegrating influence of a smoke-laden atmosphere. The sandstones of the Coal Measures are confined to a region well s of the Ribble, well N of the Mersey and well back from the coast, but they make an important contribution to the appearance of such cotton-spinning towns as Oldham (s), Rochdale (s) and Colne (N). The gritstone, often quarried in enormous blocks, is more characteristic of the rural areas; there is plenty of it in the Pennine villages, and everywhere between Morecambe Bay and the Trough of Bowland, not excluding Lancaster itself, which is largely built of pale yellow gritstone (all N).

Despite inevitable losses every year, Lancashire still preserves many thousands of Carboniferous sandstone roofs. In certain places these sedimentary rocks are sufficiently fissile to be split into 'flagstones' at the tap of a hammer, and although by comparison with the famous oolitic slates of the Cotswolds and Northamptonshire these sandstone slates are larger, thicker, darker in tone, more sombre in colour and much heavier, they have a rugged dignity which never fails to impress. Specially sought after were the Rossendale flags quarried in the Forest of Rossendale, between Rochdale (s) and Burnley (N). Their size and weight rendered even a moderately steep pitch unnecessary, and indeed impossible, and the Lancashire roof-builders were not concerned with elegance: their materials alone ruled out any such thoughts. What they achieved was immense sturdiness combined with complete visual harmony, not only with the stone buildings of which they form a part but also with the moorland landscapes in which some of the best preserved of these stone roofs are still to be seen.

Not until we reach the valley of the Ribble (N) does limestone play any part in the Lancashire scene. Carboniferous limestone is in evidence at Clitheroe and at Whalley, and along the valley of the Hodder which marks the boundary with Yorkshire, and finally displaces the gritstone half-way between Lancaster and Carnforth. In North Lancashire, on both sides of Morecambe

Bay, the light grey limestone, usually in rather small, rough pieces, recalls neighbouring Westmorland; and so also at Ulverston and Dalton-in-Furness. One of these limestones, from near Ulverston, will take a polish and so qualifies as a semi-marble, a handsome stone employed in the 1870s at Holker Hall.

Of still more ancient origin is the Silurian stone which characterizes that part of North Lancashire which falls within the Lake District, and which spreads down to the coast at Grange-over-Sands and at Ireleth. This extremely hard, splintery, flaggy material was only normally used as rubble, and its dour colouring, dark greys, blacks and browns for the most part, does not make much aesthetic appeal; but it was a common practice, as can be well seen at Hawkshead, to render with roughcast, and so long as the roughcast is frequently limewashed, this is probably the best method of making use of this intractable stone. There are still a good many whitewashed cottages in the remoter parts of Lancashire, and one is glad of it.

Ordovician and Silurian slate-stone also figures among the building materials of Lake District Lancashire, but the principal role of these slates has been, needless to say, as a roofing material, and in recent years for cladding structures of steel and concrete. Between Kirkby-in-Furness and Little Langdale at least five slate quarries are still working, producing slate varying in colour from lead-pencil grey to the attractive grey-green of the slate from Moss Rigg used for facing parts of Coventry Cathedral. The local slate roofs in this area are a constant pleasure: the best of all this county's roofs. The only trouble is that for most people it requires a real effort to remember that this *is* still Lancashire.

PREHISTORY*

BY DEREK SIMPSON

It was only with the final retreat of the ice at the end of the last glaciation that the region became habitable by man and the earliest penetration by hunting and fishing peoples took place. Scant traces of these settlers have been found at several sites in the vicinity of Bolton (s), on Anglezarke Moor near Rivington (N), and at Radcliffe (s). In these areas have been found microlithic blades and other tools indicating temporary camping sites or flint knapping. Much of the region must have been thickly forested, and an efficient flint axe for forest clearance and wood-

* This account covers both North (N) and South (s) Lancashire.

working was employed by these Mesolithic groups (an example has come from Radcliffe).

The earliest surviving monuments belong to the succeeding period of the introduction of farming and presumably a more settled mode of life. The chambered tomb beneath the long cairn on Anglezarke Moor (N) is related to a series of such monuments to the N, while the remarkable decorated stones, the Calderstones, now housed in Liverpool Museum (s), but formerly elements in a passage grave, show in their art style-links with Ireland. Throughout the prehistory of the region one finds evidence of such contacts across the Irish Sea. Although these two monuments attest to the elaborate nature of burial during this phase, the evidence for domestic activities is slight. A possible settlement site has been located at Storrs Moss, Yealand Conyers (N) where a timber floor consisting of brushwood surmounted by planks was revealed by excavation. The only artefact was the rim of a wooden bowl, but radiocarbon dates suggest that it is to be ascribed to this period. Other evidence for these Neolithic settlers is again provided by flint-knapping sites (e.g. Clitheroe (N); Grange-over-Sands (N); Chorlton-on-Medlock, Manchester (s)), and stray finds of polished stone axes from the axe factories of Great Langdale (e.g. Walney Island, Barrow-in-Furness (N)).

Although the evidence for Neolithic settlement so far recovered is slight, it is the traditions of this period which are predominant in the Early Bronze Age (from c. 1650 B.C.) at a time when adjacent areas were subject to new ideas and new cultural groupings. A cave site, possibly domestic, has been examined at Fairy Holes, near Chipping (N), but the surviving monuments are again largely sepulchral. Many of the cairns in moorland areas of the county must belong to this period, and this supposition is confirmed by the few excavated examples. They have normally produced cremation burials in collared urns, a pottery form which has its origins in Neolithic ceramic traditions, as has the rite of cremation itself. Indigenous too are the platform cairns and embanked cemeteries also generally associated with collared urn burials, and the remarkable funerary and ceremonial timber monument at Bleasdale. The group of free-standing stone circles, again in some cases associated with collared urn burials, in the northern part of the county, could also be considered as part of this surviving Neolithic tradition, although their immediate links are with a group of circles in Cumberland and Westmorland (see The Buildings of England: Cumberland and Westmorland). The Bronze

Age Culture in our region did not develop in complete isolation from the rest of the country, however. It shared, if only peripherally, in the trade in Irish metal products as evidenced by stray finds of flat copper and bronze axes from several localities in the county (e.g. Risley and Rixton, both s, and a decorated example from Read, N). Links with the metal industry of the flourishing Wessex Culture to the s are suggested by a rare bronze tanged spearhead. The lack of datable associations and especially metalwork makes it difficult to estimate how long the collared urn tradition survived in the region. The only material which can be assigned with confidence to the later phases of the Bronze Age is stray finds of metal objects, mostly in river valleys, and hoards of tools and weapons. A number of socketed axes have come from the Ribble, and hoards from Winmarleigh, Walton-le-Dale, and Portfield Camp, Whalley (all N). The latter hoard, deposited in the C7 B.C., consists of two socketed bronze axes of North English type, a socketed gouge, two knife blades, and a bracelet and tress ring of gold. The tress ring is an Irish import and shows the maintenance of Hibernian contacts at this period.

The Portfield Camp hoard was found inside the ramparts of the hillfort of presumed Iron Age and therefore later date. Its possible relationship with a hillfort however emphasizes the problems of conservatism and the survival of earlier traditions in our area which is such a recurring feature of its prehistory. Portfield Camp is one of five hillforts, all in North Lancashire. With the exception of the 15 acres of Warton Crag near Carnforth the forts are small in comparison with the great fortified earthworks of the South and reflect the broken nature of the countryside and a smaller and more scattered population. Few contemporary domestic sites have been excavated. A rectangular embanked enclosure at Urswick containing five round huts produced Iron Age pottery and similar unexcavated sites at Birkrigg Common Urswick, Torver, on Heathwaite Fell near Woodland, and elsewhere probably belong to this or the succeeding Romano-British phase. The native population in Lancashire appears to have been little affected by the Roman occupation, and both the nature and pattern of rural settlement remained unaltered. The only pieces of native Celtic metalwork belong to the latter half of the C1 A.D. – the fine scabbard from Pilling Moss (N), the sword and scabbard from Warton near Carnforth (N), and the beaded torc (lost) from Rochdale (s).

ROMAN LANCASHIRE*

BY BARRY CUNLIFFE

Lancashire is not rich in Roman remains. Six forts, a few unimportant civil settlements, a group of kilns and scattered peasant settlements are all the county can boast. The reasons for this dearth are threefold. In the first place the area was always under military control, and the conditions were therefore not conducive to civil development; secondly large areas of the county were not suited to primitive farming methods; and thirdly, until comparatively recently, competent archeological activity within the county has been negligible. With the growing local interest in the subject, however, it cannot be long before our knowledge of the region is considerably extended.

Even though actual sites and visible remains are thin on the ground, the broad picture of the Roman development is clear enough. The area was finally stabilized by the Roman army at the beginning of Agricola's governorship, but the building of the great legionary base at Chester had been initiated a year or two earlier, and we may suppose that even before Agricola's campaigns some attempt had been made to control the region. The principal line of communications and supply, probably constructed under Agricola, was the road running from Manchester (s), past the forts at Ribchester and Burrow-in-Lonsdale (both N), to link with Hadrian's Wall at Carlisle. Like other military roads of the first century, it cut across important river valley routes, such as the Ribble, the Hodder, the Wenning, and the Greta, enabling the troops to deploy rapidly in the event of the Pennine tribes showing signs of aggressive activity. The encircling roads, as it were, could be used to bottle up dissidents in the hills. Cross-communications were also essential to the efficiency of the system, and both Manchester and Ribchester were joined by trans-Pennine roads to York. A second N–S road was provided nearer to the coast, running from Wilderspool, through Wigan (s) and Walton-le-Dale (N) to Lancaster (N). In all probability this road, too, originated as a military way.

The history of the individual forts has not been worked out in detail, but most show signs of a more-or-less continuous occupation from the C1 to the C4. They would have been required as bases for the troops whose job it was to police the routes from

* This account covers both North (N) and South (s) Lancashire.

Chester to the Wall, as well as to control the tribes in the hills. The fort at Lancaster, on the other hand, may have developed as a semi-naval base in the late c3 or early c4 to guard against pirate raids from the Irish Sea in much the same way as the Saxon shore forts protected the North Sea and Channel coasts, but large-scale excavation will be needed before the nature of the site can be fully understood.

Practically nothing is known of the civilian occupation of the region. Some of the forts developed *vici* outside their gates, and scattered finds from the open country and from caves reflect a generally sparsely populated area. The urban development and villa system of the South East is unknown here.

SOUTH LANCASHIRE

★

ST JOHN EVANGELIST. 1936–7 by *Austin & Paley*. Gothic. A very conservative building, in the style of Sir Giles Gilbert Scott of *c.*1910. Very broad w tower. The ancillary attachments rather square, which spells thirties.

ST NATHANIEL, Platt Bridge. 1905 by *Bradbury & Sons*. Very red brick, with a high s tower. The windows are mostly lancets. Interior with brick arches and white walls.

ACKHURST HALL *see* ORRELL

AGECROFT COLLIERY *see* PENDLEBURY

AIGBURTH *see* LIVERPOOL, p. 207

AINSWORTH

CHRIST CHURCH. 1831–2, according to GR by *Richard Kay*. There was a chapel here in the early C16 for certain. The present church has a w tower and lancets along the sides and was galleried inside, although only the w gallery remains. – PULPIT, LECTERN, and STALLS from Bury parish church, probably of *c.*1840–50. – STOCKS of stone by the gate.

HOLLY PARK, w of the church. 1832. Three bays, porch with columns. At the back a high pointed staircase window.

SCHOOL. 1838. A flat front with pointed windows.

UNITARIAN CHAPEL. 1715, enlarged 1773, repaired 1845. A plain rectangle with three-light mullioned windows in three tiers. Four bays to the sides, two to the front. The pedimented porch heavy, and of 1845 rather than 1773. However, such a neighbourhood as this was extremely conservative. Next to the chapel is a cottage dated 1773, and this still has three-light mullioned windows. They are symmetrically arranged. There is also a house yet closer to the chapel, which is three-storeyed and has mullioned windows. It was built as stables.

(DEARDEN FOLD FARMHOUSE, less than ¼ m. w. The MHLG reports that on the first floor is part of a pointed arch of massive timbers with a carved boss at the apex. This is given a pre-Reformation date.)

AINTREE

3090

ST PETER, Warbeck Moor, really in Liverpool. 1876–7 by *Bell & Roper*. Nothing special. Incomplete at the w end.

ST GILES, Aintree Lane. 1955–6 by *J. G. R. Sheridon* (of *E. Kirby & Sons*). Brick. The N tower has the lower part of the spire surrounded by a rotunda.

RACECOURSE. The first grandstand was by *John Foster*, 1829. It was burnt in 1892, and the present large but unremarkable structure put up.

VALLEY FARM, Wango Lane, ½ m. E of St Giles. C17, brick, with low five-light mullioned windows.

ALKRINGTON HALL *see* MIDDLETON

ALLERTON *see* LIVERPOOL, p. 208

ANCOATS *see* MANCHESTER, p. 298

ANFIELD *see* LIVERPOOL, p. 209

ARDWICK *see* MANCHESTER, p. 302

ASHTON-IN-MAKERFIELD

5090

ST THOMAS. 1891–3 by *Oldham* of Manchester. A good building. Red sandstone with a low w tower. On the N side a transeptal projection set diagonally so as to fit the site. In this projection a rose window with entirely free tracery. Wide aisles, the arches dying into the piers.

HOLY TRINITY, Rectory Road, North Ashton. 1837–8 by *John Palmer*. Yellow ashlar. The sides have the familiar long lancets between buttresses, but the w front is unusual. The w tower is flanked by a kind of rudimentary w transepts. They contain the stairs to the w gallery. The tower top is of 1938 and the chancel of 1914.

ST OSWALD (R.C.), Liverpool Road. 1930 by *J. K. Brocklesby*, and certainly an ambitious building to put up, even if its historicism was totally outdated by 1930. Romanesque exterior, the façade with a r. hand tower with pyramid roof and a l. hand round turret with conical roof. But the interior has two saucer domes and an E apse. The domes are framed to w and E by transverse arches. It is impressive undeniably. – STAINED GLASS. Expressionist figures in deep colours. By *Harry Clark*, 1930–7.

CONGREGATIONAL CHURCH, Gerard Street. By *Waterhouse*, 1865. A poor façade, red brick with blue brick trim. Gothic with an open three-part w porch. No tower.

LIBRARY. By *J. B. & W. Thornely*, 1905–6. In a good position, at a sharp angle. Red brick and stone. Two corner turrets with ogee caps.

ASHTON-UNDER-LYNE*

9090

Ashton-under-Lyne was granted a market in 1284, and its parish church is medieval. But even in 1801 the town still had only 4,800 inhabitants. By 1851 they had grown to c.31,000, and as there are today no more than c.50,000 the main period of growth was clearly the early C19. This growth was due to cotton weaving. Visually the centre of the town was given its characteristic feature somewhat earlier. The Earls of Stamford were lords of the manor, and the fifth earl, after 1768, laid out a new quarter on a grid plan. Bare hills close the views down the streets to the w and N.

ST MICHAEL. The church is large and has an impressively tall and sturdy w tower. But the churchyard on the s side is bleak and barren, and the view to the s is bleak and barren too. And whereas the church authorities cannot help the latter, they can surely raise money for a few trees to be planted in the churchyard. They should not be large trees. The building of the church was begun by Sir John de Assheton early in the C15 and completed under the will of his great-grandson Sir Thomas, who died in 1516. Due to him is the tower. However, it was rebuilt in 1886–8 by *Crowther*, who restored Manchester Cathedral, the N side was rebuilt in 1821 (which the tracery heads of the windows show), and in 1840–4 the church was almost entirely rebuilt. The N porch is a memorial of after the First World War. The interior is an example of rare completeness of the 1840s. Externally, the w tower has openwork battlements and high pinnacles, two two-light bell-openings to each side, and a large w window. The s aisle has four-light windows with Perp tracery, the chancel a seven-light E window. The interior is cram-full with heavily decorated stone- and timber-work. The pieces are Perp, but probably imitation-Perp, with many thin 51

* For Hurst *see* p. 125

mouldings. There are five bays, then the chancel arch, and then two more bays. The spandrels are thickly carved and there is a cresting below the clerestory windows. The spandrels of the chancel arch are carved too. Then there is the ceiling, plastered, with its beams and bosses, and there are three wooden GAL-LERIES, fully carved. The seats are BOX PEWS, equally heavily carved. They face E in the nave, but W in the chancel, i.e. to-wards the PULPIT. This is a Gothic three-decker with an angel of about 1700 at the foot. Heavily carved also is the STAIRCASE in the SE corner. The pulpit incidentally is placed near the middle of the N arcade, four bays W of it, three bays E. This is a Protestant tradition. The chancel is all faced with stone panel-ling. The total effect is singular and not easily forgotten. St Peter at Leeds has the most similar interior. – STAINED GLASS. Ashton has the most complete set of medieval glass in Lanca-shire. It dates from the late C15 and early C16 and consists of eighteen scenes from the Life of St Helena, kneeling members of the Assheton family (all S aisle), and three large figures of saintly Kings (N aisle). There is also some mixed old glass in the aisle W windows and the SE corner. The Asshetons recorded include Sir Thomas, who died in 1454, and Laurence, rector in 1458. So they were probably concerned with the earlier stages in the building of the church. All the ancient glass was in the E window until 1872. – PLATE. Two Patens 1735; two embossed Chalices 1753, large Paten and two Jugs 1755 (all these by *W. Shaw* and *W. Priest*), and two Flagons of 1764. – MONU-MENTS. John Postlethwaite † 1818 by *T. M. Dermott*. Gunnis says that this is the earliest monument displaying emblems of freemasonry. – Edward Brown † 1857 by *Matthew Noble*. Or at least the bust may be by him. Medallion portrait of his wife below and two allegorical figures l. and r.

ST ANN (R.C.), Burlington Street. 1859.

CHRIST CHURCH, Oldham Road. 1847–8 by *Dickson & Break-spear*. A Commissioners' church (cost £2,800). Brick, English bond. A large church, but only with a bellcote. Transepts, chancel, and transept E chapel. The windows are mostly lancets. Interior with octagonal piers.

ST JAMES, Cowhill Lane. 1863–5, according to Mr Buttress by *G. Shaw*. An aisleless church with transepts, still pre-Pugin in plan and emphatically in the curious idea of two W turrets with long spires. Low interior with big open timber roof.

ST MARY (R.C.), Wellington Road. 1869–70. Brick, humble, with a small NW turret.

Sᴛ Pᴇᴛᴇʀ, Manchester Road, the focal point at the w end of Stamford Street. 1821–4 by *Goodwin*. A Commissioners' church, large and ambitious, with pleasantly fanciful motifs. It cost over £14,000. The ᴇ view from Stamford Street is the chancel gable and the chancel aisle roofs continuing it. The chancel window is circular, and below it is a low canted vestry. Four big pinnacles mark aisle and chancel corners. Above the chancel appears the w tower, its bell-stage wide open and indeed fully transparent. The sides of the church have high three-light Perp windows. The interior turns out to be aisleless. But there are of course the three galleries. The roof is of low pitch and ceiled and connected with the walls by a broad ribbed coving. The ᴇ wall, apart from the rose window, is all boldly panelled. The panelling comes from Manchester Cathedral. – High ʙᴏx ᴘᴇᴡs. – ᴘᴀɪɴᴛɪɴɢ. Adoration of the Child in demi-figures. A copy after *Honthorst*? – sᴛᴀɪɴᴇᴅ ɢʟᴀss. The ᴇ window by *Evans* of Shrewsbury, 1853 (ᴛᴋ).

Hᴏʟʏ Tʀɪɴɪᴛʏ, Portland Street. 1876–8 by *J. Medland & Henry Taylor*. Brick, nave and aisles, transept, chancel with wide apse. No tower, only a bellcote. The windows are mostly lancets. Taylor's oddities appear in the low w baptistery and the two big flying buttresses rising above it – all this just for the bellcote – and in the interior, where the arcade piers are short columns of grey granite and the chancel piers of pink granite. The chancel needs piers; for it has a narrow, sunk ambulatory. And in the nave the w bay of the arcades is shorter and lower to link up with the three-bay screen of columns between nave and baptistery. Against all this polished granite the walls are plainly of yellow brick with red-brick patterning.

Aʟʙɪᴏɴ Cᴏɴɢʀᴇɢᴀᴛɪᴏɴᴀʟ Cʜᴜʀᴄʜ, Stamford Street, close to its ᴇ end and in an elevated position. With its size and its spire it places itself in deliberate competition with St Michael, a few hundred yards away. It is by *John Brooke*, 1890–5. A ɴw steeple and a flèche as well. High clerestory; transepts. Dec detail. ɴ and s aisles. Big hammerbeam roof. – (sᴛᴀɪɴᴇᴅ ɢʟᴀss. The ᴇ window by *Morris*, i.e. *Burne-Jones*, the transept windows also but weaker. They are of 1895.)

Mᴇᴛʜᴏᴅɪsᴛ Cʜᴜʀᴄʜ, Stamford Street. 1832. Brick, of four bays, with a four-bay pediment and a porch of two pairs of Greek Doric columns.

Tᴏᴡɴ Hᴀʟʟ, Market Square. 1840 by *Young & Lee*. Seven bays with a five-bay centre. The centre has attached columns and a straight top, the outer bays have end pilasters. An extension on

the l. continues with giant pilasters, although it is as late a
1878, and the WATER BOARD OFFICES at the NW corner of the
Market Place carry on the theme of solid classical ashlar work
The MARKET PLACE was presented to the town by the Earl of
Stamford in 1829, and the N side does indeed do it proud. On
the E side is the brick MARKET HALL, with a prominent tower
The other sides don't count, but at the time of writing a
SHOPPING PRECINCT is being built W of the Market Place
Wellington Street has been widened, and so a less haphazard
character will come to stay. The architects to the precinct are
Bradshaw, Gass & Hope.

HEGINBOTTOM LIBRARY, Old Street and Oldham Road
1891–3 by *John Eaton & Sons.* Gothic, ashlar, with a broad
tower.

ALBION CONGREGATIONAL SCHOOL (former), Cricket'
Lane. 1861–2 by *Paull & Ayliffe.* A large, ill-organized group
of yellow brick with red trim in an institutional Italianate.

GENERAL HOSPITAL, Fountain Street. LAKESIDE, the building
at the SE end of the site, was the WORKHOUSE. It dates from
1850–1 and is a long stone range with a broad pedimented centre

PUBLIC BATHS, Henry Square. 1870 by *Paull & Robinson.* An
amazing performance. Brick, Italianate – or is it Transitional
between Norman and E.E. ? Anyway it has a slender tower à la
Siena Town Hall, with machicolations but adapted as a chim
ney. Even the swimming hall has medieval columns (in pairs
set two-deep) and a hammerbeam roof.

PERAMBULATION. The Earl of Stamford's plan for a West End
has not materialized well. The grid of streets is there, but little
to grace it. The only street worth walking along is Stamford
Street. To its S nearly all is desolation at the time of writing
and to the N there is hardly anything of interest. STAMFORD
STREET from the E end by the Congregational Church has thi
of noteworthy buildings. First No. 95 of three bays with giant
pilasters and an unusually pretty doorway, then E of the church
approach the former PARISH OFFICES of 1870 by Mr *Eaton*
of brick, Gothic, then W of the church approach another
Georgian house with a nice doorway. After that OLD SQUARE
a polygonal circus which has not come off, and MARKET
AVENUE, dated 1847, a pedestrian way which has come off
Minor Georgian doorways extend into WARRINGTON
STREET. The ODDFELLOWS' HALL is dated 1855; it is three
storeyed and pre-classical. BARCLAYS BANK next door i
dated 1900 and has chosen the Loire Renaissance. Then on th

N side is CROFT HOUSE (now Westminster Bank), Samuel Heginbottom's house of 1812, brick, of two storeys and five bays with a three-bay pediment and a stone porch. One more Georgian doorway on No. 234, and a few more in SHAW STREET.*

OXFORD MILLS, Oxford Street. 1845, a very large block with a plan incorporating l. and r. of the centre deep and rather narrow courtyards open to the street. This was the mill of the Mason family of Groby Hall, a villa no longer in existence. It can be assumed that the terraces of COTTAGES close by were provided by them as well. One of them displays a lot of blank arcading towards Stockport Road.

N of Ashton is a rural area, with bare hills and the valley of the river Medlock. There are still quite a number of farmhouses. The most remarkable are these:

TAUNTON HALL, now in the suburban Newmarket Road, very remarkable indeed for a tremendous cruck-truss inside the back wing. The GATEPIERS are probably Jacobean.

HIGHER ALT HILL FARMHOUSE, Alt Hill Road. Dated 1764 and yet still with mullioned windows and even a greater number of lights to mark the hall, i.e. no Georgian symmetry yet. Can it really be so late?

More farmhouses are listed by the MHLG.

ASHWORTH

8010

ST JAMES. In the hills, surprisingly secluded, considering the proximity to Rochdale. 1789, but the successor of a church in existence in 1514. The chancel remained in the C16 form until 1837. A rectangle of two by five bays with arched windows. The windows have wooden Y-tracery. – PLATE. Chalice and Paten inscribed 1808.

ASHWORTH HALL. C17 gatehouse and some C17 windows. However, there is more to the building than this, it seems.

ASTLEY BRIDGE see BOLTON, p. 84

ASTLEY

7090

ST STEPHEN. Burnt out in 1961 and recently demolished. It was a large brick church, evidently Georgian. It was indeed built

---

* Off the w end of Stamford Street by MARGARET STREET new housing by F. Jones & Son and Denis Harper.

with its w tower in 1760, but the wide N aisle which made the total plan almost square was an addition of 1834 or 1841 or 1847. So the building had four arched side windows and four arched E windows.

VICARAGE. 1704. Brick, of five bays with two later front gables. The front windows have wooden mullion-and-transom crosses, but there are small mullioned stone windows round the corner. Fine doorway with stone pediment.

DAM HOUSE (Astley Hospital). Dated 1650 (not in original numerals). The doorway is late C18, the low mullioned six-light windows to its r. will be original, the other front windows look Victorian, and the pebbledash is a great pity.

6000   ATHERTON

Atherton, being a small town, seems more dominated by its mills than are the larger towns.

ST JOHN BAPTIST. 1879 by *Paley & Austin*. A monumental church with a SW tower with polygonal buttresses outside the S aisle. Also a two-storeyed vestry attachment. Long aisles with square-headed Dec windows. There are five bays of nave and a sixth E of the chancel arch. The clerestory windows are round, two to each bay. Six-light E window with a chequer-board pattern of square fleurons below outside. – STAINED GLASS. The E window by *Kempe*, 1896. – PLATE. Flagon, given in 1723; Chalice and two Patens, undated.

ST ANNE, Tyldesley Road. 1898–1901 by *Austin & Paley*. NE tower, low, with a higher stair-turret, and w of it the N transept. Dec details. The church has aisles and a fine NE group of spaces with a chapel under the tower accessible from the transept.

ST MICHAEL, Howe Bridge. By *Paley & Austin*, 1875–7. Unified roof for nave and chancel. The line of demarcation indicated by the position of a high, turret-like flèche. Well-considered window details, but of course a minor church, compared with *Paley & Austin*'s other two.

UNITARIAN CHURCH, Bolton Old Road. Built in 1721 as a Presbyterian chapel. Enlarged in 1901. Brick, with arched windows in two tiers. Nice open cupola. Bulgy stone gatepiers.

COUNCIL OFFICES, Bolton Road. 1898–1900 by *J. C. Prestwich* of Leigh. Red brick and stone. Only six bays with a tower with cupola. Swags over the doorway.

LIBRARY, York Street. Brick. 1904–5 by *Bradshaw & Gass*. With gables and mullioned-and-transomed windows.

s of the church is an OBELISK, erected in 1781.

In Leigh Road is a terrace of cottages dated 1873 on the centre-piece, which has a half-hipped roof. They were for workers of the Atherton Colliery (Fletcher, Burrows Ltd).*

ALDER HOUSE, Alder Street, off High Street. Dated 1697 on the very naïvely carved heavy canopy on big brackets. The house has three gables. The window with the three stepped round-arched lights and the stepped hood-mould over is a West Riding motif. Georgian staircase.

CHANTERS, Tyldesley Old Road. 1678. Only a little more than half of the original front remains. Most of the mullioned windows are of five lights. The porch gable has a circular opening.

ATHERTON HALL, 1⅛ m. SW. The centre of the house is of 1930. The wings are older, but of the Atherton Hall illustrated in *Vitruvius Britannicus*, vol. 3, i.e. in 1725, as by *William Wakefield*, 1723, there is just one doorway with a very heavily rusticated surround.

AUDENSHAW

909?

ST STEPHEN, by Guide Bridge Station. 1845–6 by *E. H. Shellard*, and typical of him. Essentially this is still of the Commissioners' type, i.e. paired lancets along the sides, quatrefoil piers with fat shaft-rings, three galleries with Gothic parapet, but the w tower with broach spire and two tiers of lucarnes already recognizes the new principle of archeological accuracy. The church was in fact paid for by the Commissioners (£2,900). The chancel was rebuilt in 1900.

RYECROFT HALL (Council Offices). Originally the house of Abel Buckley, owner of the Ryecroft cotton mills at Ashton-under-Lyne. Gabled Tudor with an asymmetrical front. Gothic porch, but Elizabethan windows. In the middle of the house a skylight visible above an octagonal gallery – all small in scale.

BAGULEY HALL *see* WYTHENSHAWE, MANCHESTER, p. 344

BALDERSTONE *see* ROCHDALE, p. 380

BAMFORD

8010

ST MICHAEL. 1885 by *H. C. Charlewood*.

BAMFORD HALL, a grand early C19 mansion, has been demolished. Opposite the lodge is a Tudor Gothic house.

* I am told that they built the very first Pithead Baths.

BAMFORD CONGREGATIONAL CHURCH. 1801 (or is it 1841 ?).
Thin and very tight lancet front, with three steep gables.

BARDSLEY see OLDHAM, p. 360

BARLOW HALL see CHORLTON-CUM-HARDY, MANCHESTER, p. 305

BARROW BRIDGE see BOLTON, p. 85

BARTON-UPON-IRWELL

7090

Although Barton itself, N of the Ship Canal, is just extended Eccles, the place where the two churches stand, which is now administratively just across the boundary of Urmston, is something quite of its own and in its setting will not be forgotten. The churches, Church of England and Catholic, stand so close together that the churchyard of the former runs to the fence of the latter. Look W and you see a few pylons and then the splendid group of the BRIDGE of the M62 MOTORWAY over the Ship Canal. Look E and you have a POWER STATION with one of the two chimneys rising from an open concrete frame. Look S and you have an unenclosed TRANSFORMER STATION, and look N, and there is the SHIP CANAL itself with the SWING BRIDGE carrying the Bridgewater Canal across the Ship Canal and opening when one of the improbably large ships wants to pass. The swing bridge replaces *Brindley*'s aqueduct which went across here.

So much for the setting. Of the churches the Catholic one is far more eventful.

ST CATHERINE. 1843 by *E. Welch*, the chancel, deliberately in keeping with the church, by *Preston*, 1893. Red stone, weathered. Lancets, buttresses and pinnacles. W tower deprived of its spire. The interior has only one gallery. The big roof timbers are oddly unorthodox, with their imitation-Jacobean pendants.

CHURCH OF THE CITY OF MARY IMMACULATE* (R.C.). By *E. W. Pugin*, 1867–8, and his masterwork. Given by the de Trafford family. The cost was over £25,000. Nave and aisles. No tower, but a high and just a little projecting bell-turret. No chancel, but a high polygonal apse, with cross-gables and a N chapel also with cross-gables and its own shrine-like roof. This is the de Trafford Chapel, and their coat of arms is over the W entrance into it. The W wall below the bell-turret has a very

---

* Better known as All Saints.

large rose-window, rather fussy in its details. Fussiness was of
course the curse of E. W. Pugin, and one can blame the interior
on that score as well. Yet it is undeniably splendid. The nave   76
is of seven bays. The stonework is striped. The capitals are
sumptuously carved with naturalistic foliage. The very high
roof has scissor-crossed braces. In the chancel the pitch is much
higher. The windows are shafted, and shafts carry a rib-vault.
Moreover, the N chapel, three bays long, is rib-vaulted too, and
on the chancel side the vault does not spring from the piers of the
arcade, but from extra piers, very thin, inside the chapel. The
effect is confusing but exhilarating. – The PAINTING on the
chancel S wall is of c.1868. On it Pugin with the plan of the
church can be found. – The REREDOS is very elaborate, with
highly competent figure carving. In addition the figure of
Christ, dead, below the altar table. The sculptor's name has
not yet been found out.

BEDFORD HALL *see* LEIGH

BELFIELD *see* ROCHDALE, p. 379

BESWICK *see* MANCHESTER, p. 303

BEWSEY OLD HALL *see* WARRINGTON

BICKERSHAW   *6000*

1¾ m. SE of Hindley

ST JAMES. 1905 by *F. R. Freeman*. Brown stone with red stone
dressings. Nave and chancel, the bellcote on the E gable of the
nave.

BILLINGE   *5000*

ST AIDAN (not so called originally). The church was first established in the early C16, rebuilt in 1718, and enlarged in 1908 by
Sir T. G. Jackson. The building of 1718 survives entirely. The
apse was set back beyond Jackson's additions. Jackson added
very tactfully, if perhaps a little too grandly, the transepts
and a new apse. The old building has large round-headed
side windows with reticulation units in the three-light tracery.
The window bays are separated by pilasters. The façade is
a piece of remarkable originality. There are pairs of angle   27
pilasters with a piece of triglyph frieze. The centre bay has

a doorway with two detached Tuscan columns, and they
carry a projection with a small square-headed Gothic three-
light window and an open columnar rotunda on top. The
interior has four-bay arcades of Tuscan columns on high square
bases (which box pews would of course have hidden) and round
arches. The ceiling is tunnel-vaulted, and the small Gothic
window throws light into that vault. The church has a west
gallery only. – Against the s wall a small brass inscription
TABLET originally marking the pew of James Scarisbrick, a
Liverpool merchant, who initiated the rebuilding of the church.
– MONUMENTS. Thomas Snape † 1801. With a small group of
Charity by *W. Spence*. – Meyrick Bankes † 1827. Signed by
Franceys & Spence of Liverpool.

ST MARY (R.C.), s of St Aidan and opposite Birchley Hall. 1828.
Ashlar, with a wide, decidedly Nonconformist three-bay front
and three-bay pediment. Arched windows and a porch of two
pairs of Tuscan columns. Apse.

METHODIST CHURCH. 1845. Italianate, with arched doorway
and windows.

BILLINGE BEACON. A sea-mark erected in 1788 on a hill 589 ft
above sea level. It was originally a summer house of Winstanley
Hall and had a pyramid roof. This is now missing.

BIRCHLEY HALL. A mystery house, dated 1594, mysterious not
only because it has priest-holes in the wing projecting from the
s end of the main range and formerly containing the chapel and
another priest-hole at the back of the main range, and not only
because a secret printing press operated in the house, but also
architecturally. The house has two wings and a recessed centre
with shallower square projections in the re-entrant angles.
The doorway in the r. one of these is new. The original doorway
was in the l. one, but clearly on the first floor. The remains of
seats in the closed porch or lobby remain. That means the first
floor was the main floor, but the remains of mullioned windows
– not many of the house survive in a complete form – on the
ground floor are by no means as if that had been a kind of basement. The wings have large gables, the centre three smaller
ones.

MALTHOUSE, in the main street, just s of St Aidan. 1674, with
some mullioned windows.

FIR TREE HOUSE, Pimbo Road, 1¾ m. WNW. 1704. A symmetrical
five-bay front of two storeys with windows which must formerly
have had mullion-and-transom crosses. Plain doorway.

DERBYSHIRE HOUSE, French Road, 1⅝ m. WNW. 1716. A

symmetrical front of five bays and two storeys with stone mullion-and-transom-cross windows and a pedimented doorway.

BIRCHLEY HALL *see* BILLINGE

BIRTLE

8010

ST JOHN BAPTIST. On the hillside, up Castle Hill. Nave with bellcote and chancel. By *G. Shaw* of Saddleworth, 1845. A Commissioners' church (cost £1,350 only). Fine view of hills and chimneys.

BISPHAM HALL *see* ORRELL

BLACKBROOK

5090

ST MARK, really Haydock. 1910 by *E. H. Barker*. Red stone, rock-faced, no tower.

CONGREGATIONAL CHURCH. 1891–2 by *T. W. Cubbon*. Dec, with a NW steeple.

BLACK LANE *see* RADCLIFFE

BLACKLEY *see* MANCHESTER, p. 315

BLUNDELLSANDS

3090

ST NICHOLAS, Bridge Road. 1873–4 by *T. D. Barry & Sons*. Dec, no tower, only a flèche, high polygonal apse with gables above the windows. The W end is by *W. D. Caröe*, 1894, and much more interesting, with a low polygonal baptistery projection open to the church by tripartite arcading. – STAINED GLASS. N aisle W, by *Kempe*, early.

ST JOSEPH (R.C.), Warren Road. 1885–6 by *A. E. Purdie*. Odd W front with a turret on the l., a diagonal porch and attached apsed chapel on the r. The church is in the E.E. style and quite large.

PRESBYTERIAN CHURCH, Warren Road. 1898–1905 by *W. G. Fraser* and *A. Thornely*. Large, with a SW tower; in free-Perp forms.

In WARREN ROAD a Gothic terrace, probably of c.1870, with its own Gothic archway. No. 78 Warren Road is called REDCOT. This is by *F. Atkinson*, 1913. It is in the neo-William-and-Mary style, with a big hipped roof. Five bays; semicircular porch, with a half-dome.

In Osbert Road is a house called Glencaple with a Beaux-
Arts-Grec Conservatory by *Rowse*.
(West Lancashire Golf Club, N of Hall Road West.
The club has a sensible clubhouse by *Tripe & Wakeham*, built
in 1961.)

BOLD HALL *see* ST HELENS, p. 387

BOLTON

7000

INTRODUCTION

Bolton with 160,000 inhabitants is the third largest city of Lancashire. But in 1901 there were 168,000, and that illustrates the
situation in a city which had to adjust itself to the shrinkage of the
textile industries. Indeed, in and around Bolton one sees time and
again large cotton mills converted to other industrial purposes.
Apart from spinning, the chief industries of Bolton were cotton
bleaching, dyeing, and printing. Yet Bolton is not a town created
by the Industrial Revolution. It received its charter for a market in
1251, and Leland mentions it as a textile market. Cotton began to
replace wool in the late c17. Crompton invented the spinning mule
at Bolton and derived no material benefit from it, Arkwright was
a barber at Bolton and died a rich man. The first power mill was
set up in the 1780s. But the town still had only 17,000 inhabitants
in 1801. In 1851 there were 61,000, in 1901, as has already been
said, 168,000. Bolton has been much maligned. It has in fact a
centre of some dignity, a proud town hall, a number of good c18
buildings, several highly interesting timber-framed halls in the
outer suburbs, and above all the moors in the distance and a hilly
site with a valley right in the centre bridged only in 1874–7. From
Bolton into the hills cottages and farms change from brick to
stone, and that also is a visual asset.*

INNER BOLTON

Inner Bolton is here used for the area approximately between a
little north of St George's Road N, Marsden Road and Moor Lane
W, Crook Street and Trinity Station S, and Bridgeman Place and
Bradford Street S.

CHURCHES

St Peter. Fragments of Norman carving establish the age of a

---

* The MILLS mentioned in brackets on the following pages were kindly
contributed by Mr J. F. Bradley.

church preceding this which is entirely of 1867–71. It was largely paid for by Peter Ormrod of cotton-spinning wealth. His father had started spinning by water power in the 1790s. The architect was *E. G. Paley*, and it is a confident if conventional piece of work, not as enterprising as Paley & Austin were going to be. Late C13 to early C14 style. Big N W tower outside the N aisle. Large W and E windows. Aisles and transepts. Five-bay arcades, and narrow three-bay chancel arcades. The piers of the latter have naturalistic capitals, and the chancel is stone-vaulted, with tierceron ribs. – STALLS (S aisle W). Perp. One end with angels and a shield, and a big poppyhead. Three MISERICORDS, with the bust of an angel, a bird in its nest, and an acorn with two leaves. – SCULPTURAL FRAGMENTS. Part of an Anglo-Saxon cross with the head. It is similar to the Whalley Cross. – Adam and Eve, under an arch, Norman. – STAINED GLASS. The N window in the N transept is older than the church; it must be mid-C19. – PLATE. Chalice and Paten of 1648; two Patens of 1710 by *R. Richardson* of Chester; two Chalices, 1711, Chester-made; Paten, 1713 by *J. Edwards*; two Flagons, 1716 by *John Fawdery*. – MONUMENTS. John Taylor † 1824. By *Chantrey*. Profile on a draped base (tower porch). – Samuel Crompton † 1827. Absolutely plain grey granite chest (churchyard). – Ralph Fletcher † 1832. Mourning woman by an urn. – Benjamin Hick, the mason-architect, † 1842. A kneeling youth and a standing woman unveiling the portrait of the deceased.

ALL SAINTS, All Saints Street. First built in 1726–43. Rebuilt in 1869–71 by *Street*. An inexpensive job. Nave and chancel and a flèche. Bold, large-scaled plate tracery.*

ST GEORGE, St George's Road. 1794–6. Brick, with a surprising side along the street – and the N side as well. They are just like house façades. Seven bays, two storeys, with arched windows and a three-bay pediment. Only the W tower behind tells what this is, and the chancel and S chapel, the latter two by *James L. Simpson*, 1907. He also remodelled the interior and built the baptistry at the E end of the N aisle. The interior has three galleries; the columns between it and the segmental ceiling are unfluted Ionic. The chancel W columns of 1907 are effective. The tower doorway of 1794–6 is broad and has no pediment. The W window alone has an ogee arch. – Again of 1907 are the PULPIT (high up) and the STALLS etc. – FONT.

---

* I was unable to see the interior. The church is disused.

A Gothick baluster and basin. – FONT COVER. Concave-sided. It looks c.1700. – MONUMENTS. Alice Ainsworth † 1802. Small pensive male figure by a pillar. – William Wright † 1814. By *S. & T. Franceys* of Liverpool. Kneeling woman by an urn with military trophies. – Richard Ainsworth, 1834. Sarcophagus and palm-frond. – Rev. William Thistlethwaite † 1838. Draped urn.

ST PATRICK (R.C.), Great Moor Street. 1861 by *Charles Holt*. An asymmetrical front with a SW turret. The presbytery composes well with the church.

ST PAUL, facing the W end of Deansgate. 1862–5 by *J. Murray*.*
A picturesque composition, as seen both from the W and the N, with the school immediately adjacent. The style is late C13. The aisles are cross-gabled and those to the S have rose windows. SW steeple.

41 HOLY TRINITY, Trinity Street. By *Philip Hardwick*, 1823–5. A Commissioners' church and an expensive one. The cost was nearly £14,000. The church is of the Commissioners' type too, but handled with uncommon earnestness. A comparison with Barry's church at Stand is illuminating. Barry is inventive, Hardwick tries – within the limits of the Commissioners' scheme – to be correct. His tower is substantial, his long side windows have convincing Perp tracery. The piers of the seven-bay arcades have no capitals. The nave ceiling has depressed-pointed transverse arches of wood, the aisles are given octopartite plaster rib-vaults.

BANK STREET CHAPEL, Bank Street Manor. Founded in 1696. The present building of 1856. With a lancet front.

BRIDGE STREET METHODIST CHURCH, Bridge Street. 1803. Brick, five by five bays, with arched windows. Three W doorways, the middle one with a pediment. The whole front has a pediment too, with a quatrefoil (a Gothick motif) and a modest garland below.

CLAREMONT BAPTIST CHURCH, Great George Road. 1868–9. Brick, Italianate, with a big pediment.

ST GEORGE'S ROAD CONGREGATIONAL CHURCH. 1862–3. By *Oliver & Lamb*. Early C14 tracery; SW steeple. The building cost c.£6,500 (GS).

NEW CHURCH (New Jerusalem Church), Bridge Street. 1844. Three bays, brick, modest, with arched windows and a pediment across.

* I owe the name to Mr Buttress.

PRESBYTERIAN CHURCH, Bowkers Row. 1845–6. An attractive
Gothic front with an asymmetrically placed bell-turret and
lancets.

WESLEYAN CHURCH, Castle Street and Bradford Street. By
Bradshaw & Gass, 1905. Brick, red and yellow terracotta. The
window treatment is turning original. Some tracery has Art
Nouveau touches. The w window is crossed vertically by two
huge projecting mullions. Also the parts tend to go cubic.

PUBLIC BUILDINGS

TOWN HALL. A first suggestion was made in 1863. A competition
was held and adjudicated by Professor Donaldson. Gothic designs were ruled out – which is interesting as illustrating the
tensions between Lancashire towns. *William Hill* of Leeds was
in the end appointed. Donaldson praised his plan for its four
good entrances, spacious lobbies and staircases, and simple,
clear corridors. The building was begun in 1866 and completed
in 1873. Hill was a Leeds man, and Leeds obviously stood
behind the wish of Bolton to have a town hall on that scale and
behind Hill's design. But the Bolton town hall is not an imitation of that of Leeds. The tower with its French cap makes that 69
clear at once. Otherwise, it is true, it is a composition of columns,
detached and attached, like Leeds. The Bolton town hall has a
six-column portico of Corinthian columns reached majestically
up a wide staircase. The ends of the front of four columns each,
the sides of the building two projections each with four columns.
The scale is grand throughout, and there is nothing of the
showiness which so often mars such buildings. Inside the
portico is Renaissance decoration. The great hall is disappointing after the exterior. The organ gallery has Baroque atlantes
like that of St George's Hall Liverpool.

MUNICIPAL BUILDINGS, behind the town hall. A quadrant,
classical, with very creditable detail. They are by *Bradshaw,
Gass & Hope* and with a completion date 1939 mark indeed the
end of a period. But there is, surprisingly enough, no tiredness.
The panache is kept up.

Former TOWN HALL (now LIBRARY), at the E end of Great
George Road. 1826. Three wide bays and two storeys. Rusticated door surround. Pilaster strips with sunk panels. One-bay
pediment.

Former EXCHANGE, Victoria Square, by the town hall. By *Lane*,
1825–9. Grecian, of five bays, with two unfluted Ionic columns

in antis. Panels with the caduceus (sign of Hermes and Commerce) and wreaths.

EDUCATION OFFICES, Nelson Square. Designed* as the Dispensary in 1825 by *Benjamin Hick* and altered for the new purpose. The pretty medallion with a boy studying must be a sign of the change of purpose. Five bays with a Greek Doric porch and the main windows tripartite and pedimented. A very satisfying ensemble.

COUNTY COURT, Mawdsey Road. 1869 by the County Surveyor, *Thomas Charles Sorby*. Ten bays with Italian Renaissance upper windows. Below, the keystones have all flowers and the VR.

TECHNICAL COLLEGE (County Grammar School), Great Moor Street. Red brick and red terracotta, gabled and symmetrical.

TECHNICAL COLLEGE, Silverwell Street, s of the parish church. A picturesquely Gothic building.

ST PETER'S SCHOOL (former), Silverwell Street. A detached two-storeyed building of nine bays, dated 1819. The windows have Y- and intersecting tracery.

ST GEORGE'S SCHOOL, at the top of Bath Street. 1847. Jacobean. Five bays with a big shaped gable all across.

MARKET, Knowsley Street. 1853–5 by *G. T. Robinson*, originally *c*. 300 by 220 ft in size but later enlarged. The front is Robinson's, with a giant portico of paired Corinthian columns and outer pillars with a big pediment. Inside, iron and glass with a nave and aisles and transepts.

OCTAGON THEATRE, Howell Croft South, close to the town hall. By *Geoffrey H. Brooks*, the borough architect, 1966–7. A small, modern theatre, for only 420, neatly and crisply done. The auditorium-cum-stage is a hexagon which rises above the amply glazed additional parts. The auditorium is flexible and can be but need not be used for 'theatre-in-the-round'.

QUEEN'S PARK. Laid out in 1866 by *William Henderson* of Birkenhead. In it STATUES of Disraeli by *John Morris* 1887, John T. Fielding by *William Bowden* 1896, Dr J. Dorrian by *Cassidy* 1898.

PERAMBULATION

The perambulation is short, as the area is small, and will be mostly devoted to the churches and public buildings. What there is otherwise can be arranged in Georgian and post-Georgian.

* So Mr Haworth tells me.

Georgian, i.e. terrace houses of brick with columnar doorways, all late Georgian or even post-Georgian in date, are a terrace in GREAT GEORGE ROAD, some houses in BACK STREET, a specially good four-bay house in MAWDSEY STREET (No. 20), and one opposite (No. 23), the SWAN HOTEL in CHURCH-GATE with two bows – the doorway has Tuscan columns and so have the bows – some more houses in WOOD STREET, off Bradshawgate, and the COMMERCIAL HOTEL in Victoria Square with a Tuscan porch and a three-bay pediment.

Starting in VICTORIA SQUARE the following Victorian items can be put down: the two STATUES in the square: Chadwick, 1873 by *C. B. Birch*, and Sir Benjamin Dobson by *John Cassidy*, 1900, and the much better Crompton STATUE in NELSON SQUARE, 1862 by *Calder Marshall*, a seated bronze figure and two reliefs – Hall i't'Wood and Crompton contemplating the spinning mule. At the corner of BRADSHAWGATE and Nelson Square is the PRUDENTIAL ASSURANCE of 1889 in the unmistakable Prudential style derived from Waterhouse, red brick, red terra-cotta, and Gothic touches. In WOOD STREET is the HALIFAX BUILDING SOCIETY, apparently of shortly before 1849. This is in the style of Barry's Travellers' Club, i.e. Italian Renaissance of a gentle kind. In KNOWSLEY STREET is VICTORIA HALL (Methodist Central Hall), the high tower of 1900 by *Bradshaw & Gass*, octagonal top and copper cap, and in DEANSGATE the EMPIRE AND HIPPODROME of 1908, rather formidable with its stone façade and its Baroque motifs.

Finally, earlier than anything else and a reminder of the existence of a larger, outer part of Bolton – larger than has so far been contemplated – is HAULGH HALL in HILDEN STREET just N of the School of Art. It is partly of *c.*1600 but very small fry. (BRADSHAWGATE MILL, Bollings Yard, dates from 1797. A part was demolished to allow the construction of the railway, but some of the original structure can still be seen today. It is four storeys in height.)

INNER SUBURBS

They have no identity of their own, but are just outside the perambulating area.

ST BARNABAS, Chorley Old Road (NW). 1911 by *F. R. Freeman*.

EMMANUEL, Cannon Street (SW). 1837–8 by *E. Welch*. Thin W tower with recessed spire. The sides have stepped triple lancets. The S porch is placed far E. No aisles. The chancel is of 1848 by *Gregan*.

ST JAMES, Waterloo Road (N). 1867–71 by *J. Medland Taylor*. The church is to be demolished. It has all the oddity of Taylor. Octagonal central tower and apse and a gable on the S side of the crossing tower.

ST JOHN, Latimer Street, off Folds Road (NE). 1849 by *Shellard*, and typical of him. Largish, Perp, with a tower and almost genuine-looking in its details, but the long side windows and the transepts harking back to the early C19 Gothicism. Also still a short chancel.

ST MARK, Fletcher Street (S). 1868–71 by *Cunliffe & Freeman*.

ST MATTHEW, Thomasson Park (N). 1876 by *T. D. Barry*. Quite large, with many gables. No tower. At the NE corner is an octagonal vestry like a miniature chapter house.

ST PETER AND ST PAUL (R.C.), Pilkington Street (SW). 1897 by *Sinnott, Sinnott & Powell*. Brick, with a high NW tower with pyramid roof. The windows are mostly lancets. Thin granite arcade columns with shaft-rings.

ST SAVIOUR, Deane Road. By *Paley & Austin*, 1882–5, and one of their noblest churches. Brick, with Dec detail, but not at all in the Dec spirit. Solid and high W tower, high N porch, solemn in mood. High four-light windows, high twin-windowed transepts. The church, to one's surprise, has no aisles. The very wide nave faces the chancel with two-bay side chapels on each side. They are also two bays deep, the outer ones issuing from the transepts, the inner from the transepts and of course the chancel. After the width of the nave the very high piers separating the chancel from the chapels and the chapels from one another make a poignant contrast.

DERBY STREET CONGREGATIONAL CHURCH (SW). Brick and terracotta, with florid decoration.

ST PETER'S METHODIST CHURCH, Derby Street (SW). Italianate, with a big pediment.

MERE HALL MUSEUM, Thomasson Place. Mere Hall was a private house. It is of red brick, quite substantial and four-square, with a porch of four columns and round the corner a big bow. The house was built *c.*1837 by Benjamin Dobson.

OUTER SUBURBS

ASTLEY BRIDGE

ALL SOULS, Astley Street. 1880–1 by *Paley & Austin*. A very impressive exterior, brick with a W tower and a 'rood turret' on the N side. The side otherwise is just high three-light Dec side windows above a dado terminated with a blank arch. The inspiration is Bodley. The nave is to one's intense surprise aisleless (but cf. St Saviour, p. 84 above). For the E end is tripartite in plan, a shallow chancel and polygonal apse and two side chapels, and they are separated by two-bay arcades of high and noble piers, giving a hall effect. The SCHOOL to the E is no doubt also Paley & Austin's.

ST PAUL, Holland Street. 1848 and 1869. To the earlier date belongs the wide nave, to the latter (*J. Medland Taylor*) no doubt the tacked-on aisles. The CHURCH HALL is a charming building of *c*.1900 with two big Voysey gables and between them the doorway and an oriel with flèche above it.

CONGREGATIONAL CHURCH, Blackburn Road. 1895 by *Jonathan Simpson* at the expense of W. H. Lever (Lord Leverhulme). A proud church with a SW steeple and a high but shallow polygonal apse. Perp style. The MANSE groups with the church. Wide and spacious interior* with richly panelled arcade piers and capitals.

LIBRARY. 1912 by *Bradshaw & Gass*. In the brick-and-much-stone-trim style of Edwardian libraries all over the country. They are very often the most handsome jobs of their date in a suburb.

(SIR JOHN HOLDENS MILL, Blackburn Road, Sharples. 1925–6 by *Bradshaw, Gass & Hope*. At the time of building, this mill was considered revolutionary, as the motive power was all-electric. This omitted the chimney, boiler house, and rope race elements previously always required. The exterior is of pressed red facing brick incorporating a certain amount of terracotta and a considerable amount of decoration, e.g. caps, exterior pilasters, cornices, roof balustrading, etc.)

BARROW BRIDGE

DEAN MILL. Robert Gardner in 1830 built two six-storeyed mills and a high chimney ¼ m. away. Both mills and the chimney have gone, but he also built a model estate, and this survives, off Bazley Street. It consists of five rows of six houses each, the sixth of each row with its entrance in the return wall. The houses are of three bays and two storeys with front gardens and backyards. Thus there is plenty of space between the rows. Another row is by the stream, six houses arranged as 3–6–3–6 bays. The doorways here are still arched.

* So Mr Buttress tells me.

BRIGHTMET *see* TONGE FOLD

DARCY LEVER *see* TONGE FOLD

DAUBHILL *see* GREAT LEVER

DEANE

St Mary. A village church still, and a proud one. We have no dates for it, but it is evident that all is Perp, mostly Late Perp, except for the w tower and the N doorways with simple continuous early c14 mouldings. The upper aisle windows and the clerestory date from 1833.* Was all this done in connexion with the provision of galleries? But galleries, according to the VCH, came only in 1849. The church is long and low and embattled – a typical North Country sight. The windows not yet mentioned have uncusped arched lights, a Henry VIII motif. The interior is Late Perp. It has five bays with low octagonal piers, plain capitals, and double-chamfered arches. Capitals at the w end have a little elementary motif of decoration, including shields (cf. Eccles). Three of the arches on the N side further E have their chamfers hollow. That indicates gradual growth, as the VCH suggests. The chancel E wall was pushed forward by 10 ft in 1884. – PULPIT. Mid-c17, but with the back plate and some trimmings of *c.*1700. – SCULPTURE. A stone bust outside the s wall, and two wooden bust corbels (from an aisle roof) in the s aisle at the E end. – CHANDELIER. Large, of brass. Commissioned in 1737 from *George Tarlington* for the brass, *John Pearson* for the iron. The former received £12, the latter £5 15s. 6d.‡ – STAINED GLASS. The E window is by *Warrington* (TK). – PLATE. Chalice 1607; Chalice and Cover Paten 1655; Credence Paten by *William Atkinson*, 1729; two Plates by *D. Smith* and *Robert Sharpe* 1782; two small Flagons 1801. – MONUMENT. Roger Holland † 1828. Mourning woman bent over a double profile medallion, and a single medallion on a sarcophagus above.

(DOVE MILL, Deane Church Lane. An excellent example of early c20 mill architecture. Seven storeys. Architects: *Stott & Sons* of Manchester.)

(CROAL MILL, Callis Road, E of Haslam Park. By *Bradshaw, Gass & Hope*. Also of seven storeys and also an excellent example.)

* So Mr R. Walmsley tells me.
‡ I owe this information too to Mr. Walmsley.

GREAT LEVER AND DAUBHILL

ST GEORGE, Roseberry Street, Daubhill. 1880 by *J. M. & H. Taylor*. Brick, a typical Taylor contraption of w baptistery and buttresses for the bell-turret. The interior shows Taylor at his trickiest. The transepts are two bays (of the arcade) deep, and then the walls cant in towards the chancel. The woodwork takes care to stress this irregularity.

ST MICHAEL, Manchester Road, Great Lever. 1851 by *Dickson & Breakspear*.

ST SIMON AND ST JUDE, Rishton Lane, Great Lever. 1900–1 by *R. Knill Freeman*. Red brick and red terracotta. Dec style. Small s w tower.

LIBRARY, Bradfield Road, Great Lever. 1912 by *Bradshaw & Gass*. Very red brick and much stone. Symmetrical. One main floor. Baroque motifs.

(BEEHIVE MILLS, Crescent Road. Two almost identical early c 20 mills side by side with a dual engine house as the link element. Six storeys in height.)

(SWAN LANE MILLS, Higher Swan Lane. 1904–5 by *Stott & Sons* of Manchester. An excellent example of brick arch floor construction. Seven storeys high, and said to have been once the largest spinning mill under one roof in the world.)

HALLIWELL

ST LUKE, Chorley Old Road. 1869–75 by *J. Medland Taylor*. The walls of dark brown stone, laid crazy-paving-wise. Three E apses, one of them polygonal.

ST MARGARET, St Margaret's Road. By *Austin & Paley*, 1903. Stone, without a tower. Nave and chancel under one roof. Free Dec tracery. Attractive s E entrance and chapel. The chancel is a grand climax. Two-bay arcade, very high, to the organ chamber on the N side, lower arcade of three bays to the s chapel.

ST PAUL, Halliwell Road. 1847. Small, with a bellcote. The windows have Y-tracery, but with solid tympana. Short chancel. No aisles. What makes the church worthwhile architecturally is its setting: two rows of cottages, ST PAUL'S PLACE, also dated 1847, flank it and are flanked by two SCHOOLS, dated 1847 and 1856. Cottages and schools have windows with four-centred arches and hood-moulds. The architect, according to Mr Buttress, was *James Greenhalgh*.

ST PETER, Halliwell. 1840. The clumsy pinnacles indicate the date at once. Long lancet windows and buttresses between. W tower, transepts, one-bay chancel, no aisles. The roof beams have broad and summary tracery over. The arches to transepts and chancel are decorated with dogtooth.

ST THOMAS, Eskrith Street. By *Paley & Austin*, 1875, and in its brick simplicity sensational for the date. It is for ever a pity that the N tower was not completed. The brick walls of the church are unadorned, the aisles have just seven small lancets, the clerestory fourteen. The entrance arch of the N porch is brick. The arcade arches are brick, and brick is exposed above them. Only the W and E walls have a more elaborate fenestration, that of the E side entirely original, with its one long middle lancet and the flanking smaller lancets. The whole group incidentally is placed high up to allow for the reredos. SEDILIA and PISCINA in all this insistence on lancets have round arches. The arcades are of five bays with round piers and very simplified E.E. leaf and crocket capitals. The source of Paley & Austin's inspiration was probably the Bodley of Pendlebury.

METHODIST CHURCH, Chorley Old Road. 1902–3. Brick and stone. A symmetrical façade with columns in two orders, and at the back a dome with a lantern – something quite exceptional in Methodist architecture.

LIBRARY, Chorley Old Road. 1910 by *Henderson & Brown*.

(HALLIWELL LODGE, now a hotel. Built by the Ormrods – *see* St Peter, i.e. Bolton parish church, and Scorton, North Lancashire.)

(ATLAS MILLS, Chorley Old Road and Mornington Road, NE of the Grammar School. A good example of a mill of the second half of the C19.)

(UNION MILL, Davenport Street, is a little N of St George's Road. No. 2 is of the second half of the C19, No. 3 of the first years of the C20. No. 3 is five storeys high and very well constructed with the employment of steel beams, cast-iron columns, and concrete filler joist floors. Roof reservoir and twin windows with cast-iron centre mullions. The mill is an early example of pressed red facing bricks used for all external walls.)

(FALCON MILL, Handel Street. By *G. Temperly*, 1903–4. One of the first mills to be equipped with concrete filler joist floors. Pressed red facing brick exterior with bands of yellow glazed bricks. Six storeys in height.)

HALL I'T' WOOD *see* TONGE MOOR

HEATON

CHRIST CHURCH, Chorley New Road. 1895–6 by *R. Knill Freeman*. A nice, relaxed composition, with a turret with wooden top by the transept. The transept is two arcade bays in width, and the arcade takes no notice of it.

GRAMMAR SCHOOL, Chorley New Road. A very large building, consisting of a court open to the S and with the main major rooms around it and two long wings continuing the ends of the three sides at r. angles. The building was won in competition by *Charles T. Adshead* of Manchester in 1919. It is of red sandstone in a Tudor style with gables as occasional accents and no ornate decoration. Entry from the road to the court is by a gatehouse in the Tudor way. Lord Leverhulme (W. H. Lever) gave several of the other buildings to the school, e.g. the swimming bath in 1901.

CHORLEY NEW ROAD. Along the S ridge of the hills rich Boltonians built their mansions and villas. Many of them survive, the most picturesque being WOODSIDE with its towers, 1877–80 for J. P. Thomasson.

Further W yet are LOSTOCK HALL and LOWER HOUSE. For these *see* Horwich in the *North Lancashire* volume.

SMITHILLS HALL
Smithills Dean Road

The impression is still of a country house, although suburban housing is very near. The house is large, but that is due to Victorian W extensions. What is older than that is substantial enough. It consists of three ranges E, N, and W of an open court. It is very likely that a S range also existed; for the gatehouse was at the S end of the present W range, a position implying that the house went on, and Nathaniel Hawthorne in 1855 says so on good authority. The oldest part is the great hall in the N range. This is assigned to the early C15 and has its screens passage complete with four doors to the service sand the spere truss to the hall. The W wall has big timbers and bold elongated quatrefoil bracing. The same appears between the speres and the N and S walls. And the same appears all up the E wall, i.e. the high-table wall. There are here also horizontally halved quatrefoils. If a coving over the high table existed, it is no longer there. The roof has three tiers of boldly quatrefoil wind-braces. It is a room as impressive as the hall at Ordsall (Salford), and as that at Baguley (Manchester) must have been. The N and S walls

were rebuilt of stone in the C16 or C17, and perhaps at the time
when the W range was extended in stone to the W. That work is
dated 1579 on one of the gables. Seen from the S, the addition
consists of the gatehouse end and a W–E range with three small
even gables. Beyond this is Victorian extension; first of stone,
then with half-timbering more ornate than the original work.
This is of c.1875 or later and by *Devey*.* But on the E side the
rooms beyond the hall are of the date of the hall. The chamber
and solar have a big, heavily timbered gable to the S and inside
moulded beams. There is also a big fireplace in good condition.
It is to the E and externally not easily seen. In the E wing itself is
the drawing room, with a large square timber-framed bay
window to the E. The room has panelling of c.1535, the best of
that moment in Lancashire. Most of it is complicated linenfold
stuff, but there are also the characteristic panels with small
heads in profile in small medallions. At the S end of the E range
is the chapel, rebuilt in 1858. The timber-framed two-storeyed
corridor W of the drawing room and leading to the chapel is
supposed to be a C17 addition, with the ground floor yet later.
The C17 work has prettily fanciful patterns.

The STABLES and COACH HOUSE are very probably also by
Devey and also of c.1875.

TONGE FOLD, BRIGHTMET, AND DARCY LEVER

The centre is LEVERHULME PARK, given to Bolton by Lord
Leverhulme in 1917 and opened in 1939. It was laid out by
T. H. Mawson.

ST CHAD, Tonge Fold. 1937 by *Richard Nickson*.

ST JAMES, Brightmet. 1855–6 by *W. R. Corson*. A Commissioners'
church (cost £3,195).

ST STEPHEN, Lever Bridge, Halgh. The church, with the
SCHOOL and the recently demolished vicarage, made a most
interesting group – loose, with plenty of trees in the middle.
They are by *Edmund Sharpe* and the first of his churches built of
terracotta – what disrespectfully was called his pot-churches.
It was built in 1842–5. Holy Trinity, Fallowfield, Manchester
followed. The idea came to John Fletcher in 1841. He owned
the Hollins Colliery and manufactured fire-bricks from the
colliery clay.‡ He invited Sharpe to design the church in

---

* The VCH in 1911 says 'within the last 25 years'.

‡ He died in 1876 and has nothing to do with the John Fletcher of Prestolee
and Ringley who died in 1889.

such a way as to demonstrate the wide possibilities of terra-cotta. Indeed all except the rubble infilling of the walls and of course the foundations is terracotta. The total cost was less than £3,000. It is a great shame that the church has lost most of its tower, and particularly its delightful openwork spire suggested by that of Freiburg-im-Breisgau. The walls are terracotta-faced, with even the tooling marks of the mason reproduced. And all the finely carved details are in terracotta, the openwork canopy, the elaborate surround of the w doorway, the foliage mouldings of the windows, the inscription frieze all round, the blank arcading, and the fanciful canopies of the chancel. *The Ecclesiologist** objected violently, calling such buildings not 'a worthy offering to the glory of GOD' and 'subversive of the variety and originality necessary for true art'. The nave E, chancel E, and the transept arches have ballflower decoration. Considering that Sharpe was the greatest connoisseur of flowing tracery of his age, it is curious that he did not introduce it anywhere. – BENCHES. The ends and backs are of terracotta – so is the ORGAN CASE. – STAINED GLASS. One N window has glass by *Holiday*, of 1884, the figures rather pale and posturing.

METHODIST CHURCH, Radcliffe Road, Darcy Lever. 1846. With a funny stepping-up front and two oversized pinnacles.

At the junction of RADCLIFFE ROAD and Castle Street is a charming cottage, dated 1834, stuccoed, with two gables and hood-moulds over the windows.

TONGE MOOR

ST AUGUSTINE, Thicketford Road. 1880–6 by *R. Knill Freeman*. Stone, towerless, Dec. Interesting N porch arrangement.

CROMPTON'S BIRTHPLACE. At the foot of Firwood Lane, where it has stopped being a street, is this stone cottage of the late C16 or early C17, with its gable and mullioned windows.

HALL I'T'WOOD. The house as it appears now owes much to Lord Leverhulme, who bought it in 1899 and had it carefully restored by *Jonathan Simpson* and *Grayson & Ould*. It had come down in the world, and when Crompton, the inventor of the spinning mule, spent his childhood in the house, it was divided into tenements, and his father had a few rooms on the upper floor. Hall i't'Wood is the most rewarding C16 and C17

---

* Vol. 111, February 1844. So Mr R. Jolley writes in his as yet unpublished paper on the pot-churches (*The Architectural Review*).

house around Bolton. The front faces s and consists of a timber-framed E and a stone w part. The timber-framed part contains the former hall running s–N, and followed originally probably by the kitchen etc. to its N, i.e. in the NE corner. Whatever the date of the structure of this part – and it has been ascribed to c.1500 – its external appearance is all Elizabethan and could be yet a little later. It has the familiar patterns of ogee braces, cusped concave-sided lozenges, and cusped St Andrew's crosses. One gable-end is to the s, another to the E at the NE corner. Underneath this is an eight-light window. Then to the N, immediately round the corner, is a back range of stone with mullioned windows, which could, but need not, be older than the timber-framed part. This back range is dated 1591 in a room on the upper floor. The w part of the front range is dated 1648 and fully characteristic of such a date. It is far more monumental than the older parts. It has typical mid-C17 baluster pinnacles ending in steep cones, a square porch, and a round-arched entrance and a transomed five-light window over. To the w of the porch are two more five-light transomed windows on the lower and two on the upper floor. To the w the range has a canted bay window. Then follows a small recessed courtyard and then the back range already referred to. After entering the range of 1648 one is at once faced with the staircase, oddly small and in an odd position. The main room on the ground floor has an overmantel with figures and panelling from Buntingford in Hertfordshire and a plaster ceiling copied from a house in Deansgate. The main room on the first floor has panelling from Ashford in Kent and a plaster ceiling copied from Chastleton in Oxfordshire.

BOOTHSTOWN

2 m. w of Worsley

(ST JOHN, Mosley Common. Consecrated in 1895. Designed by *F. H. Oldham.**)

BOOTLE

Bootle was a bathing resort in the early C19; now it is docks, commerce, and industry.

ST ANDREW, Linacre Road. 1903 by *Willink & Thicknesse*. Not large. Red brick and yellow terracotta. No tower. Free Perp tracery. Altogether a Nonconformist type.

* According to Mr Buttress.

CHRIST CHURCH, Breeze Hill. By *Slater & Carpenter*, 1866. Unimpressive exterior with a w tower with broach spire; pinnacles on the broaches. Nave and aisles, twin lancets in the aisles, single lancets in the clerestory; apse. The interior looks polychrome brick and stone, but both the black and the red are merely painted on.

ST JAMES (R.C.), Chesnut Grove. 1884–6 by *C. Hadfield*. Very large, but badly placed in a side street. Red stone, sw tower, geometrical tracery. High nave, unfortunately proportioned.

ST MATTHEW, Stanley Road. 1890–1 by *Aldridge & Deacon* and not up to their best work, yet serious and without any tricks. Red brick. The façade with a porch to the w on the l. of the w window and a turret on its r. Quiet interior.

ST MONICA (R.C.), Fernhill Road. By *F. X. Velarde*, 1936. An epoch-making church for England, though of course not for Europe. The inspiration came clearly from Dominikus Böhm's churches of 1928–30 (St Joseph Hindenburg, Caritas Institute Cologne-Hohenlind, St Camillus Mönchen-Gladbach). Pale brick, broad w tower opening to the full width towards the nave. Normal s aisle, but the N aisle only a passage. The aisles are taken through wall piers, i.e. internal buttresses. They reach above the roof and are pierced there each by an arch, like flying buttresses. Yet the nave has a flat ceiling. The distinguishing and indeed unforgettable feature of the church is the windows, of mullions and transoms, and a stark round arch to every light. In the chancel N and s walls they are seven-light windows with two transoms. The tower w wall has three two-light ones with three transoms. This in particular is a Böhm motif. A great pity that the altar wall is so prettified. The sculpture here is by *W. L. Stevenson*; the angels of the façade are by *H. Tyson-Smith*.

ST PAUL AND HOLY TRINITY PRESBYTERIAN CHURCH, Trinity Road. 1887. A big church with a NW tower.

WELSH PRESBYTERIAN CHURCH, Stanley Road. By *Noel Woodall* of *Richard Owen & Son*, 1951. Quite an original design. NW tower with spire. One composition, with the hall to the E.

THE CIVIC CENTRE. Yes – Bootle has a civic centre, even if it is not at all imaginative in layout – simply a chain of buildings in two streets. It establishes Bootle's identity, which would otherwise not appear to the eye, as there is no break whatever between Liverpool and Bootle. Everton has no civic centre, Toxteth has none, and both have no identity either. The

Bootle Civic Centre starts in ORIEL ROAD with the TOWN
HALL, 1882 by *John Johnson* of London, with a tower and a
mildly Baroque hall range to its l.* Then follow the municipal
offices, then the LIBRARY, 1887, also by *Johnson*, low and of
five bays, the POLICE, 1890 by *C. J. Anderson*, the POST
OFFICE, a little more Baroque, at the corner of BALLIOL
ROAD, 1905. Then in Balliol Road the BATHS, 1888 by *George
Heaton*, and finally the buildings of the TECHNICAL COLLEGE.
They are by *Best & Callon*, 1900, and by *Grayson & Ould*,
1909, and consequently of brick, one symmetrical of seven
bays with cupola, the other asymmetrical.

COLLEGE OF FURTHER EDUCATION, Stanley and Balliol Roads,
1966–8 by *Thomas Finlay*, the Borough Architect.

MUNICIPAL OFFICES, Stanley Road Precinct. *See* below.

INLAND REVENUE, Stanley Road Precinct. *See* below.

GIRO HEADQUARTERS, Southport Road. By the *Ministry of
Public Building and Works*, 1966–8. Very large. It consists of a
ten-storey block and spreading three-storey parts.

DOCKS. *See* Liverpool, p. 164.

No perambulation is possible. The most interesting development
in the centre is the STANLEY ROAD PRECINCT, N of Balliol
Road, twenty acres of new offices. By *Gunton & Gunton*. The
first to be completed was ST HUGH'S HOUSE (1964) for the
Inland Revenue. MAGDALEN HOUSE for the same, SE of the
former, followed (1966), and then BALLIOL HOUSE W of Magdalen House, for the Municipal Offices (1967). E of this is ST
PETER'S HOUSE for government departments (1967). The
next two buildings after that will be W of Stanley Road. What
has so far been built is gratifyingly unmannered.

Between Stanley Road and Jersey Street is NEW STRAND, with
a new high block of over twenty floors and a long, low super-
market. Its centre is octagonal and raised and has a folded roof.
Architects *T. P. Bennett & Son*. The scheme is only begun
at the time of writing.

Of Bootle before the C19 no more can be sought out than one
cottage in MERTON ROAD, by the roundabout. It has two
window bays only and looks later C18. It belonged to a shooting
box of the Earls of Derby, lords of the manor. They laid out
the centre of Bootle as a fairly regular grid S from Balliol Road
with Oxford and Cambridge street names and a recreation
ground.

* INSIGNIA. Chain and Badge 1874–5; Mace 1889.

BRADFORD *see* MANCHESTER, p. 303

BRADLEY OLD HALL *see* BURTONWOOD

BRADSHAW

7010

ᴛ Maxentius. Immediately by the Riding Gate Brook, which seems here quite a respectable river. In the churchyard is the tower of the preceding church, dated by the vch 1640. The church was rebuilt in 1775 and again by *E. G. Paley* in 1872 (after Sharpe and before Austin). The bell-openings of the old tower are just small arched single-light windows. Paley's church is not impressive. It has a bellcote, transepts, and a vestry with a cross-gable. The tracery is geometrical.

ᴏf Bradshaw Hall only the porch survives, ½ m. n. It has a round-arched entrance, Roman Doric columns l. and r., and baluster pinnacles with conical tops exactly like Hall i't'Wood, Bolton.

ᴀ new shopping area has recently been built. It has a vertical concrete feature.*

BRIGHTMET *see* BOLTON, p. 90

BRINDLE HEATH *see* SALFORD, p. 394

BROAD OAK *see* ST HELENS, p. 386

BROUGHTON *see* SALFORD, p. 393

BUCKLEY *see* ROCHDALE, p. 379

BUCKLEY MILL *see* DROYLSDEN

BURNAGE, *see* MANCHESTER, p. 304

BURTONWOOD

5090

ᴛ Michael. Founded in 1606, rebuilt in 1716. The s aisle with its arcade of Tuscan columns is by *E. J. Dod*, 1939. The c18 building is of brick with stone dressings. sw tower with a pretty wind-vane. Arched windows. The apse has two of them. – bench end from the former church. With the date 1610 and the name of Sir Thomas Bold (of Bold Hall). – (Also an Elizabethan overmantel.)

* I asked a passer-by what it signified, and the answer was: 'It's just some ᴀrchitecture of some sort'.

BRADLEY OLD HALL, ¾ m. NNE. The ruined gatehouse is c
*c.*1460–5. Yellow stone with red stone buttresses. Four-centre
arch framed by a former giant blank arch reaching up highe
Springers of the former vault. The house is C18, but the fror
door is a re-used C16 piece.

8010

BURY

INTRODUCTION

Bury is a cotton-weaving and a cotton-printing town. John Kay
the inventor of the fly-shuttle, was born at Bury, and Robert Pee
father of Sir Robert, helped to establish the leading firr
of calico printers here in 1773 (cf. also Blackburn, Nort
Lancashire). Sir Robert was the first Prime Minister to come fror
a commercial family. The town is not too big for the open countr
and the hills to play a part in the visual scene, even in the triangl
in front of the town hall. Bury has a medieval past, though ver
little of it is visible. There was a castle at Bury (licence to crenellat
was given in 1465), but in Leland's time it was already ruinous
From the C16 the Stanleys, Earls of Derby, were lords of th
manor. Expansion beyond the area round church and marke
place began in the second half of the C18. The town had 7,00
inhabitants in 1801, 30,000 in 1861, 60,000 in 1961.

INNER BURY

CHURCHES

ST MARY. The origin is medieval, but the building is Victorian
The rather mean W tower with broach spire is of 1844–5, bu
the rest is by *Crowther*, of 1871–6, and hence of considerabl
dignity. The style chosen is still that of the late C13; ten year
later it would probably have been Perp. Long nave with aisles
clerestory, chancel, and polygonal apse. N rood-turret with
flèche, baptistery with polygonal apse projecting to the N a
the W end. The interior is high, with four wide arcade arches,
high, solemn apse, and a two-bay S chancel chapel. Three-arcl
W screen just E of the W entrance. – SCREEN. Of iron, high and
thin-membered. – STAINED GLASS. In the apse and S chape
apparently by *Hardman*. – MONUMENT. Lieutenants Rober
and George Hood † 1821 and † 1823. Relief at the foot with
female figure and also an elephant and a seal.
ST JOHN, The Rock. Consecrated in 1770 and now alas derelict
Of stone with a five-bay side and a three-bay front. The fron

has a truncated gable and two entrances with pediment. The windows are all round-arched and in two tiers. The E end is a shallow apse with a Venetian window. The interior has thin Tuscan giant columns and galleries.

ST MARIE (R.C.), Manchester Road. 1841 by *J. Harper* of York. w front with porch, five-light Perp window, and a high octagonal entirely transparent bell-turret perched precariously on top. The sides have high two-light Perp windows. The church is aisleless. – STAINED GLASS. The E glass could well be of the forties.

ST MARK, Brookshaw Street. 1882–3 by *J. W. Connon* of Leeds and *James Demaine*.

ST PAUL, Church Street. At the end of an axial approach. 1838–42. Is this the church at Freetown mentioned by Mr Colvin as by *Harper*? The w tower is rather clumsy and very incorrect. The aisles have just one w lancet. To the N and s paired lancets and buttresses. Short chancel. Arcade of decidedly awkward piers. Of the three galleries only the w gallery remains. The PARSONAGE of the church is much more informal and inventive. Can it be as early as *c.*1890–5?

ST THOMAS, Rochdale Road. 1866 by *Laurence Booth*. w tower, nave and aisles, chancel. Grouped lancets with colonnettes.

HOLY TRINITY, Spring Street. 1863–5 by *Paley*. Nave and chancel and a N aisle as wide as the nave. The arcade is of round piers with naturalistic capitals. Above are brick arches and brick walls, unfortunately whitened at the time of writing. The N aisle ends in a three-bay arcade, two into a chapel, the third into a passage. The exterior of the church is of stone with heavy plate tracery, and all the details which were to be carved have been left undone.

BRUNSWICK CHAPEL, North Street. 1883, but still grandly classical, with Ionic giant pilasters and a pediment. Only the rock-faced sides and their windows get one near the real date.

BANK STREET UNITARIAN CHURCH. 1852 by *Bowman & Crowther* of Manchester. Perp; no tower.

PUBLIC BUILDINGS

TOWN HALL. 1936–54 by *Reginald Edmunds* (of *Jackson & Edmunds* of Birmingham). Sir Hubert Worthington was the assessor of the competition. Very large and square, of good stone, with little in the way of decoration but little individuality either. In front – separated by the sunk railway line – the

4—S.L.

CLOCK TOWER in memory of Walter Whitehead, a Manchester surgeon. It is by *Maxwell & Tuke* and of 1914 – a square stone structure with an ogee cap and four keep-like turrets around it. It has bits of Arts-and-Crafts-Gothic decoration.

ART GALLERY AND LIBRARY, Silver Street. 1899–1901 by *Woodhouse & Willoughby*. Probably the best building in Bury. In a decidedly 'artistic' style, suitable for its purpose. Two frontispieces l. and r. with columns in three orders and a three-bay centre between with an arched screen. The columns are Ionic above Doric. To the side a four-column portico. The columns otherwise projecting carry their own pieces of entablature.

SCHOOL OF ARTS AND CRAFTS (former Technical Schools), Broad Street. 1894 by *Maxwell & Tuke*. Also 'artistic', with panels with appropriate reliefs above the four ground-floor windows and the portal.

CASTLE ARMOURY (now Drill Hall), Castle Street. As late as 1868, yet still of an early C19 picturesqueness. Very Norman, with battlements and turrets, totally asymmetrical. The building stands on the site of the medieval castle, whose centre was a keep. The architects were *Henry Styan* of Manchester and the Borough Surveyor *James Farrar*. In 1906–7 the building was doubled in size.

PERAMBULATION

If one does not look at the public buildings, it is uneventful. In any case it only pays to walk from the Town Hall to the Market Place and back by Market Street.

At the junction of Manchester Road and Manchester Old Road are the FOUNTAIN GARDENS. The FOUNTAIN, in debased Renaissance forms with four granite columns, was designed by *T. R. Kitsell* of Plymouth and erected in 1897.

Quite a few remains of Late Georgian brick terrace housing can still be seen, right N of the Town Hall in MANCHESTER ROAD (Nos 1 etc., Nos 12 etc.), then in the street W of it, where incidentally ST MARY'S PLACE carries a date 1845 (which is a warning that Late Georgian does not always mean Late Georgian), then to the E in BANK STREET, and so to the Market Place. But first there is MARTINS BANK, built as the Bury Banking Company, probably in 1868,* in a free Renaissance, quite lavish, though only of five bays and two storeys.

* Dates on the building 1836 and 1868.

The ROYAL HOTEL, in a sort of French Renaissance, by *Maxwell & Tuke*, 1892.

In the MARKET PLACE is the STATUE of Sir Robert Peel by *E. Baily*, 1852. The reliefs on the plinth are of a sailor and of Commerce. N of the church is a detached three-bay brick house of the late C18 with a doorway flanked by columns.

MARKET STREET has the excellent group of Derby Hall and the Athenaeum, both by *Sydney Smirke*, the former intended as the town house, the latter built as the Mechanics' Institute. An adjoining hotel has been pulled down. DERBY HALL is classically Italian, of seven bays, with a Venetian window in the middle. At the s end is, as a separate unit, a pedimented upper portico of four attached columns. The ATHENAEUM is of seven bays too. The doorway has alternately blocked columns and the ground-floor windows rusticated surrounds of alternate size. Derby Hall dates from 1850, the Athenaeum followed immediately.

At the s end of Market Street is a triangular open space and on it the MONUMENT to John Kay, a kind of solid pavilion with a stone dome. A bronze Fame on the top.

Outside this core only one old house can be said to belong to Inner Bury. It is CHESHAM OLD HALL in Chesham Crescent. It is dated 1719, but still entirely C17 in style. Also, it is only half the original house. It has mullioned-and-transomed windows below, mullioned windows above.

OUTER BURY

ELTON, to the W

ALL SAINTS, Walsham Road. 1843 by *John Harper*. This is a most remarkable conceit. The big square tower is on the square chancel. This was no doubt done because the church lies on a hill to the w, and only an E tower could dominate the scene as this one does. The windows are round-headed and along the sides are placed in pairs. There are no aisles, but transepts. The ceilings are flat. Norman SCHOOL and gatepiers.

ST STEPHEN, Bolton Road. 1881–2 by *G. T. Redmayne*. A very picturesque group towards the street. Two cross-gables to the s, two to the N, polygonal E apse. The w side is unfinished. Inside, the walls are of exposed brick.

WELLINGTON BARRACKS. Opened in 1859. A number of long, two-storeyed stone ranges. The centre is a gateway, then an archway through a range, and in the distance a range with pediment in the middle.

ELTON SQUARE. This was originally the Militia Barracks and was opened in 1859 too. Wall with angle bastions and in the middle a gateway and two oriels.

HEAP BRIDGE, to the E

ST GEORGE. 1891 by *J. Lowe*. The chancel was consecrated only in 1912. Nave and chancel in one. NW turret; low baptistery; S aisle. – The circular STONE PULPIT looks High rather than Late Victorian.

REDVALES, to the S

ST PETER, Manchester Road. 1871–2, remodelled or rebuilt by *Medland Taylor* in 1899–1900. High round apse.

CEMETERY. 1866–9. The chapels by *Henry Styan* (and the Borough Surveyor, *J. Farrar*). It is curious how Victorian architects, when faced with the job of designing cemetery chapels, lost all restraint and indulged in levity. The three chapels are as different from each other as possible, and roguish details abound.

EARL OF DERBY'S ESTATE WORKSHOPS, Manchester Road. 1866 by *James Green*. They cost £10,000 to build (GS). The prominent part that remains is the gatehouse with its Italianate tower. The buildings are of brick.

Next to them is a new MOTOR SHOWROOM, uncommonly crisp, of glass and steel painted black. It is by the *Northern Design Group*, 1963.

A little further N, on the E side of the Manchester Road, is STARKIES, a very curious group of C18 brick houses. Why should the most prominent one have three oval windows one above the other, and circular windows in the gable? The house is dated 1717.

UNSWORTH, to the SE

ST GEORGE. 1843 by *Mills & Butterworth*. Brick, with lancets and a bellcote.

METHODIST CHURCH. 1846. Classical, of brick with stone dressings. Four-column Ionic portico.

WALMERSLEY, to the N

CHRIST CHURCH. 1883 by *Maxwell & Tuke*. Large, with transepts and a SW tower with a nice rounded corner where the

staircase goes up. The details of *c*.1300; the interior uninteresting.

WOOLFOLD AND WALSHAW, to the NW

CHRIST CHURCH, Walshaw. Named prominently on the w
front the Jesse Haworth Memorial Church. The Haworths
were cotton spinners and fustian makers, and two of them
paid for the church. The church is indeed a demonstration
of liberality. *Laurence Booth* designed it in 1888, and he rose to
the occasion. He also rose to the capabilities of the site on the
hill and composed an admirable steeple for the SE end of the
church to be visible from the town below to the E. The church
is large and the nave as wide as in the preaching houses of
Nonconformists. Jesse Haworth indeed held evangelical
views. The aisles are mere passages, the arcade piers just
granite columns with shaft-rings. There are broad transepts
the width of two arcade arches. The arcade continues, but instead of one column there are two set in depth, both with rings.
To the outside the aisles have four small cross-gables. The
windows are Gothic but have un-Gothic transoms. – FONT.
Circular and encrusted with stiff-leaf.

ST JAMES, Woolfold. 1931 by *R. Martin*.*

BYROM HALL see LOWTON

CADISHEAD   7090

ST MARY, Liverpool Road. 1891 by *J. Lowe*. No tower. The w
end is incomplete.
WESLEYAN CHAPEL, Liverpool Road. 1873–4. Red brick with
a pedimental gable. Italianate, if anything.
On the w side of the road is one three-bay Georgian house with a
column-porch.

CALDERBROOK see LITTLEBOROUGH

CASTLETON see ROCHDALE, p. 380

CHADDERTON   9000

CHRIST CHURCH, Black Lane. 1870 by *H. Ainley*.‡
CORPUS CHRISTI, Derby Street. Brick, with white terracotta

---

* I owe the name of the architect to Mr Buttress.
‡ So Mr Buttress tells me.

tracery and a bellcote with concave-sided gable. That alo[ne]
demonstrates 1904, the date of the church.

EMMANUEL, Chestnut Street. Very red brick. Perp details, [a]
tower. 1911 by *A. J. Howcroft*.

ST LUKE, Buckley Street, above Broadway. No tower, geomet[ri]
cal tracery. The flying buttresses do not support a vault, bu[t a]
kingpost roof of uncommon span (34 ft).

ST MARK, Ogden Street. By *G. G. Pace*, 1962–3. One must lea[ve]
it to Mr Pace – he is always fresh and never afraid of exper[i]
ment, and he does not follow all the latest fashions. This is a[n]
interesting church, with the forked timber supports of t[he]
roof inside, with the windows of many lights with broad flu[sh]
unmoulded mullions and broad flush transoms in rando[m]
places, and the tower with its steep saddleback roof. T[he]
gables have small windows in five tiers. – The FONT perha[ps]
has really too odd a shape, but, once again, Mr Pace is capab[le]
of convincing his clients that they should let him have his wa[y].

ST MATTHEW, Chadderton Hall Road. Of *c*.1849–57 by *Shella[rd]*.
sw steeple with pinnacles round the octagonal top stage a[nd]
with a short spire. Dec window details, very simple. – STAIN[ED]
GLASS. In one s window glass by *Kempe & Tower*.

ST SAVIOUR, Denton Lane. 1960–2 by *Taylor, Roberts & Bo[w]
man*. Square, of brick, with in the w wall a low round arch as t[he]
portal, asymmetrically placed, and at the E end a higher bri[ck]
semi-cylinder, glazed in the front, i.e. to the w, to focus light [on]
the altar.

TOWN HALL, Middleton Road. 1912–13 by *Taylor & Simist[er]*.
Red brick and much stone. The centre is a semicircul[ar]
columned porch and a stone dome at the top with a lanter[n].
Three bays l., three bays r.

FOXDENTON HALL, Foxdenton Lane. Externally a beautif[ul]
early C18 brick house with stone quoins, the front of seven ba[ys]
with a recessed three-bay centre and a big hipped roof. Doo[r]
way with pediment. The opposite side is flush. Staircase wi[th]
moulded balusters and still a string.

FOXDENTON FARM, opposite. The house has a cruck truss insid[e].

CHARLESTOWN *see* SALFORD, p. 395

CHEETHAM *see* MANCHESTER, p. 338

CHILDWALL *see* LIVERPOOL, p. 214

CHORLTON-CUM-HARDY *see* MANCHESTER, p. 305

CHORLTON-ON-MEDLOCK *see* MANCHESTER, p. 306

CLAYTON *see* MANCHESTER, p. 336

CLEGG HALL *see* MILNROW

CLIFTON 7000

ST ANNE. 1874 by *E. M. Barry*. Not a run-of-the-mill design, though in the Middle Pointed of the High Victorians and with geometrical tracery. The W rose is uncommonly prominent, and so are the transept fronts. There is no tower; only a bellcote on the nave E gable. The chancel arch below stands on stiff-leaf corbels.

CLOCK FACE *see* ST HELENS, p. 387

CLUBMOOR *see* LIVERPOOL, p. 216

COLLYHURST *see* MANCHESTER, p. 315

CROFT 6090

CHRIST CHURCH, Lady Lane. 1832–3 by *Blore*, a Commissioners' church. It cost £1,457. Red sandstone, s w steeple with wholly incorrect spire of quite an enterprising design. Lancet windows and short chancel. The galleries have been removed.
ST LEWIS (R.C.), Little Town. 1826–7. Brick, to the E the church, to the W and flush with it the priest's house. The latter has a chequer front and a doorway with recessed columns, the former arched windows and a W pediment and pedimented W porch. The E wall inside is distinguished by pilasters, as the Catholics liked it.

CROMPTON *see* SHAW

CRONTON 4080

HOLY FAMILY (R.C.). 1910 by *Fogarty*.
CRONTON HALL, Hall Lane. Five bays; the façade was treated in Early Victorian days, but the house itself must be early C18. This is patent from the excellent staircase running through from

basement to upper floor. It has twisted balusters, the twist starting only above an urn shape, and a handrail curving up to the newel-posts. Fine GATEPIERS in front of the façade, with big vases and, to the outside, paired Tuscan columns.

CROSBY *see* GREAT CROSBY *and* LITTLE CROSBY

CROXTETH HALL *see* LIVERPOOL, p. 216

CRUMPSALL *see* MANCHESTER, p. 315

CULCHETH

6090

HOLY TRINITY, Newchurch. 1904–5 by *Travers & Ramsden*. Incredibly retardataire. This brand of neo-Norman might be 1850. – BRASS. A brass inscription to Elizabeth Egerton † 1646 is signed *John Sale sculpsit* – an oddity of the first order.

LITTLE WOOLDEN HALL, 1½ m. WSW. Brick, c.1800. A seven-bay front with the three middle bays a little recessed. Niches l. and r. of the doorway.

DAISY HILL

6000

ST JAMES. 1879–81 by *Paley & Austin* and one of their most masterly performances. Stock brick, red brick, and red terracotta. A wide aisleless nave with large Perp windows. A transept is added only on the N side, and in addition a two-bay organ chamber. On the S side instead, on a projection, rises a tower-like bellcote for three bells – two and a third above them. In the chancel are two two-light windows on the sides. They have to the inside detached blunt polygonal shafts like the wall-passages of English C12 and C13 churches. The window in the bellcote projection is larger and the shafts are stouter in consideration of what they have to carry. – STAINED GLASS. The E window is by *Morris & Co.*, of 1897–8.

DARCY LEVER *see* BOLTON, p. 90

DAUBHILL *see* BOLTON, p. 86

DAVYHULME

7090

ST MARY, Davyhulme Road. Davyhulme is indistinguishable from Urmston. The church is by *Truefitt*, 1889–90, and a building of considerable character. Short aisleless nave, transepts chancel, and an octagonal crossing tower with paired lancet windows and a pyramid roof. Other windows have plate tracery. The chancel E end has a high reredos, and consequently the five E windows are arranged so that the outer two are placed much lower than the stepped inner three. The capitals of the crossing have deliberately simplified E.E. caps. The string-course all around has no other purpose than to hide a pipe. Goodhart-Rendel calls it 'a filthy sham'.

DEANE see BOLTON, p. 86

DEARNLEY see LITTLEBOROUGH

DEEPLISH see ROCHDALE, p. 380

DENTON

9090

ST LAWRENCE, Stockport Road. Built c.1530. Of that time however there is no more than the timber posts of the nave and some of the roof timbers with the cusped wind-braces. The rest is Victorian. Chancel and transepts date from 1872. The gay external black and white patterns are painted on. – FONT. An C18 baluster. – PEW BACK. C18, under the W gallery. – BENCH ENDS. In the stall a number of well-traceried bench-end panels. – STAINED GLASS. C15 or early C16 fragments including figures in the chancel N and S windows and on smaller bits in others. – PLATE. Two C17 Chalices. – MONUMENT. Edward Holland † 1655. Oval inscription plate between two lumpy columns. Top achievement.

CHRIST CHURCH, Manchester Road. Paid for by the Commissioners (£4,500). By G. G. Scott, 1848–53. A plain, honest piece, not exciting. NW tower with broach spire. Nave and S aisle under separate roofs. The windows are widely spaced. Their details belong to c.1300. – The SCHOOL opposite is of 1846–8 (MHLG) and could well be by Scott too.

ST MARY (R.C.), Duke Street. 1962 by Walter Stirrup & Son. With wildly neo-Expressionist roofs over a square body.

HOPE CONGREGATIONAL CHURCH, Stockport Road. 1877. Brick, debased Italianate.

DENTON HALL, Windmill Lane. The great hall of the C15, still described by Mrs Wood, has entirely disappeared. Only a brick-faced range remains which has medieval timbers inside. According to the MHLG (1963) they are of the C16, four trusses, one with Gothic moulded posts rising from the ground and one with heavy cross-framing against a bay, E, with doorway on the first floor. The sides of the main tie-beams have incised Gothic panels. Two posts have carved heads with leaves. Will this last remnant of Denton Hall also be allowed to be broken up?

HYDE HALL, Love Lane, c. ¼ m. SE of the former. The oldest part is the hall, built of stone, with a buttress to N and S. On the S side a timber-framed bay with overhang and a corresponding stone projection. On the N side a porch with the date 1625. Mullioned-and-transomed windows. Opposite large Georgian STABLES with round-arched windows but round the archway some ogee detail too.

(Manchester is building a HOUSING ESTATE of 1,472 dwellings here. Director of Housing *J. A. Bent*.)

DERBYSHIRE HOUSE *see* BILLINGE

DIDSBURY *see* MANCHESTER, p. 317

4080

DITTON

ST MICHAEL, Ditchfield Road, Hough Green. 1870–1 by *Grayson*. Aisleless.

ST MICHAEL (R.C.), St Michael's Road. 1876–9 by *Clutton*. The church is strikingly big for its surroundings, but it must be remembered that it was built in connexion with the settling-down here of a community of Jesuits expelled from Germany. Red brick with an assertive W tower with steep saddleback roof. The bell-stage of three lancets framed by shafts with shaft-rings. Lancet windows and several rose-windows, as *Clutton* liked them. Very Cluttonian also the E wall with two windows separated by a big shaft, and the interior. Slender columns coupled in depth and with shaft-rings and French Early Gothic crocket capitals. The arcade runs through from W to E, with eight bays. The chancel projects beyond by only some 8 ft. There are transepts, but the arcade takes no notice of them. The interior is spacious and airy, cool and as self-confident as the tower.

HOUGH GREEN STATION. Of the type of Widnes North (*see* p. 423).

8090

DROYLSDEN

ST MARY. 1846–7 by *Shellard*. A Commissioners' church. It cost *c*.£3,500. No tower, only a bellcote. Mostly lancets, but the clerestory windows spherical triangles. Six-bay arcades with quatrefoil piers, thin shafts in the diagonals, and stiff-leaf capitals. Yet the church has a w gallery and no doubt had N and S galleries too. High hammerbeam roof, the hammers on short E.E. shafts resting on head stops. Long chancel.

CEMETERY. The Mortuary Chapel of 1896 (?) is quite sizeable and has a s steeple.

COUNCIL OFFICES, at the corner of Manchester Road and Market Street. Built as the Educational Institute by *Waterhouse* in 1858, but not to his credit. Plain oblong with a big roof with dormers. Red and yellow brick, two storeys, segment-headed windows.

BUCKLEY MILL FARMHOUSE, Cross Lane, ⅞ m. NE. An interesting C17 brick house with two gables, windows under hood-moulds and very flat, summarily shaped relieving arches, and plenty of lozenges, single and more than single, formed of raised bricks.

EARLESTOWN *see* NEWTON-LE-WILLOWS

ECCLES

Eccles is a small town. It has 42,000 inhabitants, only 6,000 more than it had in 1891. The boom years were the twenty years before 1891. The figure for 1871 was only 19,000. The staple industry used to be textiles, cotton and silk. Hand-looms were still in operation a great deal as late as the 1830s, and as for employment, in 1836 the silk industry employed 779 hands, 218 of them under twelve years of age and 371 between twelve and eighteen. But the only nationally famous factory was Nasmyth's iron foundry, and that is in Patricroft.

ST MARY. The first mention of the church is of 1180. The present building is large, of red sandstone, and behind it now are lawn and some new high blocks of flats. The church was built in the C15 and early C16, though early C19 finds have proved the existence of a Norman predecessor building. The short w tower has straight-headed three-light bell-openings. Nave and aisles are all embattled. The aisle windows have panel tracery, but entirely uncusped. That is a sign of the early C16. But at the w end of the N aisle is a half-uncovered earlier three-light window close to the nave. The E end was rebuilt by *Holden* in 1862–3. Most of the rest was refaced in 1907–8. Inside is the earliest evidence, the arch to the s transept, which must be C14 and not too late. A chantry was founded by Thomas Booth of Barton Hall in 1368, two others by William Booth, Archbishop of York († 1464). The high tower arch was filled in by a w porch in 1862–3 and the upper part converted into a sham window. The tower is earlier than the arcades. When they and the aisles were built, they were made wider, so that the tower is now not in axis. The four-bay arches have four chamfered projections and thin hollows in the diagonals. The capitals are elementary and have shields as their only decoration. The chancel has two-bay arcades of the same type. – SCULPTURE. At the E end of the N arcade part of an Anglo-Saxon cross-shaft with knot-work and part of the head of a C15 lantern cross with the Trinity. – STAINED GLASS. In the s aisle w window early C16 Flemish glass: the Entry of Christ into Jerusalem. This comes from St John, off Deansgate, Manchester. – PLATE. Two Chalices 1618; Paten 1681; two Flagons 1723 and 1724; Almsdish 1777. – MONUMENT. Richard Brereton † 1600 and wife, recumbent stone effigies, by her side a baby. The tomb-chest has square angle balusters and otherwise only shields.

ST ANDREW, Monton Road. 1879 by *Herbert J. Tijou*. Big, with a good s tower and a polygonal apse. Geometrical tracery, but the capitals of the round piers of the seven-bay arcade have knobbly leaves in the C14 fashion. – STAINED GLASS. All the E end by *Kempe*.

ST MARY (R.C.). 1897–8 by *W. H. Rowle*. Stock brick and red brick. No tower.

TOWN HALL, Church Street. 1880–1 by *John Lowe*. Arched main windows, but a pavilion roof.

LIBRARY, Church Street. 1907 by *Edward Potts*. Brick with much stone. The main windows are Venetian under a super-arch, with sculpture in the spandrels. Baroque portal and spacious reading room with a stucco tunnel-vault.

MONK'S HALL, Monk's Hall Grove. The front is roughcast, Tudor of *c*.1840, with hood-moulds over the windows. At the back timber-framed work of *c*.1600.

The only other secular building to be noted is HALLS BUILD-INGS, Church Street, a small timber-framed building of two storeys with brick infill in a backyard opposite the War Memorial. Its roof trusses are preserved. It was a hall-house with a hall only one storey high and a back-to-back fireplace between hall and parlour.

A new SHOPPING AREA is going up w of the church and N of the Market Place. This was designed by *Leach, Rhodes & Walker*.

N of the railway and W of the station, along the canal, is the BRIDGEWATER FOUNDRY. For this *see* Patricroft.

ECCLESTON

4090

Eccleston is today really a western part of St Helen's.

CHRIST CHURCH, Church Road. 1838. Paid for by *Samuel Taylor*, the Lord of the Manor, to whom Mr Fleetwood-Hesketh also attributes the design. He was a cotton manufacturer. Red stone, rock-faced. Lancet windows mainly. W tower with recessed spire, short transepts, and a short chancel. – FONT. Alabaster, in the Arts and Crafts taste, probably *c*.1900. – The WEST GALLERY and the COMMUNION RAIL come from St Peter in Liverpool. They have Rococo decoration and religious reliefs and are, it looks, Flemish or French C18 work.

EDGE HILL *see* LIVERPOOL, p. 217

ELLENBROOK

7000

1¼ m. NW of Worsley

ST MARY. Brick, 1725, on the site of an older building. Apparently enlarged later to the E. Also, in 1842 the Norman N porch and the chancel were added. The Georgian work is simple with large, wide segment-headed windows with two wooden mullions. The windows may not even be of 1725.

ELTON *see* BURY, p. 99

EVERTON *see* LIVERPOOL, p. 220

FAILSWORTH

9000

The typical place in this part of the county, neither town nor village, the direct, unnoticeable continuation of the Oldham Road, Manchester, through Newton Heath, yet with one area, by Daisy Nook, still totally rural and of Pennine character.

ST JOHN, Oldham Road. 1845–6 by *Shellard*. W tower with broach spire, nave and aisles, paired lancets and spherical triangles for clerestory windows; galleries. The church was built by the Commissioners. It cost £3,200.

HOLY TRINITY, Oldham Road and Broadway. 1909 by *F. R. Freeman*. Yellow stone with red stone dressings. Perp style. Incomplete at the E end.

METHODIST CHURCH, Oldham Road. 1866. Red brick, round-arched windows. Characteristic of a late date of the type is the triple opening above the doorway and the heavy detailing of the latter.

DOB LANE CHAPEL, *see* Newton Heath, Manchester, p. 336.

COUNCIL OFFICES and former LIBRARY, Oldham Road. 188c by *J. N. Firth*, the Library and the whole façade 1909 by *E. Ogden & P. Cartwright*. Brick with stone dressings and patterns. A very pretty composition.

THE FIRS, Oldham Road. Now a clinic, but originally a manufacturer's house; probably of *c.*1850. Red brick and stone dressings. Two storeys. Three widely spaced bays. One-bay pediment. Still in the classical tradition.

FAILSWORTH LODGE, close to the s end of Broadway. A simple, red-brick house of five bays, with a doorway with broken pediment and two-bay lower wings. (Nice chimneypiece and plasterwork inside. D. Buttress) The house has the date 1770.

MEDLOCK HALL, just w of the Daisy Nook bridge, i.e. at the w end of Newmarket Street, Ashton-under-Lyne. Timber-framed in a rural setting – that is all that needs saying.

FAIRFIELD

Fairfield is the earliest Moravian settlement in England. It was established in 1785 under the direction of Benjamin Latrobe, father of the great architect. It was intended to be a self-contained community with its own crafts, and it is still an oasis of neatness and order in this industrial waste-land. The centre is the CHAPEL with wings l. and r. forming the focal point. In front of it is a garden with an avenue of trees leading to it. It was the graveyard originally. The centre is of five bays with a pediment across, the wings are of three lower and then towards the middle two higher bays. They were for the sisters E, the brothers w. The doorways have stone surrounds and pediments. On the roof of the chapel is a cupola. The interior of the chapel is orientated, and since the whole front range faces s, that means an unexpected and awkward turn of direction. Behind that range is a square of cottages facing outward on to nicely cobbled streets and some tree planting. The cottages grew in number in the C19. Everything is brick.

Along an outer periphery to the s and E, in BROADWAY and BROADWAY NORTH, *Wood & Sellers* in 1914 built forty-six houses. They seem at first the standard neo-Georgian semi-detacheds coming into fashion just before the First World

War, but then one notices such features as the severely cubic shape of the projecting part of each house, and also some odd details such as the pediment raised some distance above the doorway. But even so, there is nothing of the radicalism here which Edgar Wood's and Henry Sellers's earlier work was fired by.

FAIRFIELD *see* LIVERPOOL, p. 225

FALINGE *see* ROCHDALE, p. 378

FALLOWFIELD· *see* MANCHESTER, p. 320

FARNWORTH
3 m. SE of Bolton

7000

There is no break between Bolton and Farnworth.

ST JOHN. *See* Kearsley.

ST GREGORY (R.C.), Preston Street. 1873–5, yet all lancets, as if it were 1825.

CONGREGATIONAL CHURCH, Church Road. Perp, no tower but the church groups with the hall, which has its little tower.

METHODIST CHURCH, Church Street. 1860–1. Big, Italianate, of brick, with a pediment across.

In MARKET STREET is a group of three buildings which manage to convey for a moment a sense of civic identity. All three are of brick with ample stone work. The TOWN HALL is of 1908 and by *W. J. Lomax* of Bolton. It is symmetrical, of nine bays and two storeys, with a steep, i.e. C17, pediment and porch with columns which is more than semicircular, and a cupola. The LIBRARY, also by *Lomax*, was built in 1910. It has columns, a semicircular (i.e. C17) pediment, and a dome. The BAPTIST CHAPEL came first. It was designed by *Bradshaw & Gass* and dates from 1906. It has less conventional motifs.

Bradshaw & Gass also did the THEATRE in PEEL STREET, with its big pediment. This is of 1901.

ST JAMES, St James's Street, New Bury, 1 m. WSW of St John. 1862–5 by *Isaac Holden & Sons*.

(FISHPOOL WORKHOUSE, 1 m. WNW. 1858. By *George Woodhouse* and *Leigh Hall* of Bolton. Now part of the Bolton General Hospital.)

FARNWORTH
N of Widnes

5080

ST LUKE. This is evidently a church of some antiquity. But what features belong to an early date ? The w wall is partly late c12, says the vch, on the strength of walling below the floor. But some of the stonework above is of typically Norman shape too. To this w wall a tower was added in the c14. Towards the nave this is now 6 ft out of axis; and the suggestion of the vch is that after the tower had been built, the arcades were both moved n. It is hard to see why, but the details of the octagonal piers are indeed pre-Perp c14, and so is the s doorway with its broad, continuous mouldings. The e end on the other hand is late c15 Perp. But the c17 seems to have been at work too – see the s porch entrance and some of the windows of the e end with their uncusped round arches to the lights. The n arcade of the nave and n aisle, including the Bold Chapel, were rebuilt in 1855. More and better restoration in 1892–5. An interesting detail of the c15 or (probably) the c17 is the timber-framed gables of transept and chancel, as they appear behind the battlements. Handsome panelled c15 chancel roof with the griffin of the Bold family. The s transept was a family chapel too – see its separate entrance from the w. It was built by Bishop Smith of Lincoln for the inhabitants of Cuerdley. Rough original roof. – ALTAR. With linenfold panelling from the screen to the s transept. – SCREEN. Under the tower arch; c17; with balusters. – WALL PANELLING, in the aisles; c17 and later (one date is 1705). It was originally pew ends. – PEW. Nave, w end, dated 1602. Plain. – BREAD SHELF behind the former. Dated 1724, but still entirely in the Jacobean tradition. – BOOK DOOR, i.e. with dummy books. From Bold Hall (*see* St Helens, p. 387). – STAINED GLASS. By *Morris & Co.* the three white figures in flames (s aisle). The date is 1875. – MONUMENTS. Nearly all in the Bold Chapel. Effigy of a Knight holding a book. Meant to look *c.*1500, but very probably a c17 fake. – Richard Bold † 1635. Two alabaster effigies, formerly no doubt on a tomb-chest. – Peter Bold † 1762. Fine, large tablet. – Also a number of other tablets. – Peter Patten Bold. Signed by *Chantrey* and dated 1822. White marble. Mourning young woman kneeling over a pedestal. – Mary Bold, Princess Sapieha (a Polish family), † 1824. By *Pietro Tenerani*, made in Rome. Tenerani was a pupil of Thorwaldsen. Large relief, with the young woman on a couch, her sorrowful husband standing by her head, an angel by her feet. Sentimental of course, but very competently done. – Alice Houghton † 1852. White effigy; asleep. – Also, but in the chancel, John Atherton † 1820. Fine, large, simple sarcophagus in relief.

In the SE corner of the churchyard the LOCKUP, marked Bridewell 1827. It is just a plain oblong.

FAZAKERLEY see LIVERPOOL, p. 226

FIR TREE HOUSE see BILLINGE

FLIXTON   7090

ST MICHAEL. The existence of a Norman church is proved by one stone built into the chancel E gable. The chancel E wall is of the C15. The N chancel aisle is Victorian; the rest is C18. It is an enjoyable church, and it has the rare distinction in this part of Lancashire of having a free view to the S over green fields. The W tower was rebuilt in 1731, the nave and aisles in 1756. The S chapel was then obviously still C15 throughout. Now only the E respond is. The piers may date from 1815, when the chancel was partly rebuilt. The E respond of the S aisle arcade shows that the intention must have existed to continue the C18 rebuilding to the E. The nave arcades are Tuscan columns, the aisle windows arched on pilasters. The same is true of the tower, but the bell-openings have been victorianized. Inside the neo-Georgian porch is a splendid doorway with pilasters and pediment. – STAINED GLASS. S aisle E and SE by *R. B. Edmondson*, 1858 (TK). – PLATE. Flagon of 1776. – MONUMENTS. Brass plaque to Richard Radcliffe † 1602 and family (S aisle), kneeling figures, one group facing the other. – Ralph Wright † 1831. Tablet with urn on sarcophagus.

STATION. Opened in 1873. Red brick with prettily bargeboarded gables. One of a number of almost identical stations.

In THE VILLAGE, a street no longer villagey, a pair of timber-framed cottages. Further N, beyond the railway, FLIXTON HOUSE, four bays, yellow and red brick chequer, with a handsome doorway.

A similar three-bay HOUSE is on the S side of the Irlam Road, ⅝ m. from the (not vehicular) ferry.

FOXDENTON HALL see CHADDERTON

GARSTON see LIVERPOOL, p. 227

GARSWOOD   5090

SCHOOL, School Lane. Founded in 1588. An oblong building of two storeys, three bays long, with cross windows and middle doorway and three low two-light windows over. The fenestration looks C17 rather than C16.

GARSWOOD HALL has been demolished. However, the very odd LODGE remains, with a doorway with thick, heavy, Tuscan columns but straight-headed broad windows with round-arched lights – a combination of the French Revolution with Henry VIII. (The MHLG also mentions the ICE HOUSE circular, of brick, formerly domed.)

GATEACRE see LIVERPOOL, p. 228

6090

GLAZEBROOK

STATION. With gables with divers patterns to the bargeboards. The water basin with dock leaf is dated 1872.

6090

GLAZEBURY

ALL SAINTS. 1851 by *E. H. Shellard*.

HURST HALL. Mr Jeffrey Howarth allowed me to mention the barn, which must have been the hall of a house and seems to date from the C15. It has heavy timbers: tie-beams on arched braces, cusped kingposts and cusped raking queenposts, and three tiers of quatrefoiled wind-braces.

LIGHT OAKS HALL. The E side is spectacular, evidently possible only if the house was originally much larger. It consists of a five-plus-five-light transomed window on the ground floor with the doorway close to it, a window of the same size above the other, and five-light windows with transoms further on on the r. There is a date 1657 inside, and that suits the façade fragment.

GLODWICK see OLDHAM, p. 359

6090

GOLBORNE

ST THOMAS. 1850 and 1860 by *Joseph Clarke*. A well-known name, but a church of little interest.

ALL SAINTS (R.C.). 1927 by *Philip Clarke*. Red brick and lancets.

COTTON MILL. Built by *Richard Tattersall* for Samuel Brewis. Brick, nineteen bays long. A date-stone says 1839.

(LIGHTSHAW HALL, Lightshaw Lane, 1½ m. N. Inside two moulded beams, one on uprights which support the roof truss with cusped members. MHLG)

GORTON see MANCHESTER, p. 326

GRASSENDALE, see AIGBURTH, LIVERPOOL, p. 207

GREAT CROSBY

3090

ST FAITH. *See* Waterloo, p. 419.

ST LUKE, Liverpool Road. 1853–4 by *A. & G. Holme*. Still the aisleless early C19 type with transepts and apse. Modest W tower with broach spire. Dec features. – BOX PEWS with Gothic detail. – STAINED GLASS. In both transepts all by *Capronnier*, between 1860 and 1881. – PLATE. Paten of 1724; Chalice C18, though Elizabethan in style.

ST PETER AND ST PAUL (R.C.), Liverpool Road. 1892–4 by *Sinnott, Sinnott & Powell*. Yellow and red stone. The church front and the presbytery form a good group. Six-light W window with tracery of a geometrical-cum-Perp variety. The interior, as so often with this firm of architects, is thoroughly reactionary.

CONGREGATIONAL CHURCH, Eshe Road North. 1898 by *Douglas & Fordham*. Substantial and good. Free geometrical tracery; flèche.

WESLEYAN CHAPEL, Mersey Road. Really Blundellsands. 1890–2 by *Doyle*.

LIBRARY, College Road. By *G. R. Mason*, 1964–7. Red brick and stone with Baroque touches. Big stone lantern.

MERCHANT TAYLORS' SCHOOL FOR BOYS, Liverpool Road. 1878 by *Lockwood & Mawson*. Red brick, large, with central tower. The centre is symmetrical, but the end pavilions differ; one is gabled, the other has a hipped roof. The style is of course Gothic. The tower top has four thin tourelles, between them a truncated pyramid, and it ends in a pyramid.

MERCHANT TAYLORS' SCHOOL FOR GIRLS. Inside the premises is the original boys' school, founded in 1620 by John Harrison. Stone, large for an early C17 school. Two-storeyed, with a two-storeyed porch. Mullion-and-transom-cross windows with hollow-chamfered mullions. Where two are close together they form a unit with a nicely profiled middle mullion. Round-arched porch entrance. Pretty frieze of paterae on the façade string-course. At the back a staircase projection with a three-light window and a late C18 doorway.

In LIVERPOOL ROAD as part of NAZARETH HOUSE is CROSBY HOUSE, a stuccoed five-bay house with two pediments and a

Tuscan porch. Nearly in Liverpool Road are also a few Late Georgian houses with enriched doorways of types familiar from Liverpool.

In MOOR LANE, opposite Fairfield Lane, is a brick tower MILL with cap, but without sails.

GREAT LEVER see BOLTON, p. 87

5080

GREAT SANKEY

ST MARY. 1768–9. The chancel rebuilt by *W. Owen*, 1834. The little bell-turret dates from 1865, but the body of the church, including, it appears, the polygonal w end for the font, is Georgian; only the window details must be changed. The church is of brick and aisleless. – MONUMENT. Tablet to the Rev. Edward Lloyd, 1815. Putto by an urn on a pedestal.

SANKEY STATION. Of the type of Widnes North (*see* p. 423).

GREENLANE END FARMHOUSE see LEIGH

GUILDHALL FARMHOUSE see RAINFORD

4080

HALE

ST MARY. C14 w tower, much smoothed over. The rest of 1754, though inside only the WEST GALLERY remains of that date, and the other furnishings belong to the restoration of 1875. The windows have keyed-in arches, except for the w wall, where there are two circular windows, one on top of the other. There is no separate chancel at all. The altar place is simply marked by a Venetian window. – MONUMENT. Pretty tablet to Ireland Aspinwalle † 1733, and other tablets.

MANOR HOUSE, Church End, NW of the church. Not originally the manor house. At the time the house was given its lively, attractive, and mysterious features, i.e. about 1700–10, it was the parsonage. The façade is of five bays, red sandstone and brick, two storeys with dummy oval windows at the top. These windows are part of a remarkably lavish scheme of decoration, with giant rusticated pilasters marking the angles and the angles of the middle bay. This bay has a broad doorway with fluted columns and a curly open pediment, the window above it has long pilasters on big brackets of dubious correctness, and on top is a pediment with odd decoration. Round the corner to the r. is a shallow giant arched recess and the start of another

motif yet higher. What can the intention have been? Hale
Manor House has a fine panelled entrance hall with fluted
pilasters, a staircase with twisted and columnar balusters, and
a secondary staircase with flat balusters of wavy outline. They
are in the C17 tradition but need not be older than the other
features.

HALE HALL, some distance w of the church. The drive starts in
the centre of the village. The house is in ruins, and only the
s facade still makes sense. It is known from illustrations and
documents that a Tudor or Early Stuart house with irregularly
spaced bays and gables was regularized in 1674 by Sir Gilbert
Ireland. What he did was to connect the existing bay windows
with arches high up on which he could put an even parapet.
This had the horizontally placed ovals characteristic of the
later C17. This side of the house faced N. In 1806 *John Nash* designed a new s façade and gave it bays and arches high up as well,
though more monumentally and more uniformly.

In the HIGH STREET (No. 22 has crucks; MHLG), No. 4, called
OLD SCHOOL HOUSE, a brick façade of three bays with a
square porch in the middle. There is a date 1739 and an open
cupola.

LIGHTHOUSE. Handsome, white, early C20.

HALEWOOD

ST NICHOLAS. 1839, enlarged 1847. No architect is recorded.
What is the enlargement? The church is aisleless, but has
transepts and a shallow polygonal apse. The tower is an addition
of 1882. It is on the s side, and its lowest stage is treated as a
porch. Inside the church, as so often, the transepts cause complicated timber arrangements in the roof. – The BOX PEWS are
preserved. – But the pride of the church is its STAINED GLASS,
by *Morris & Co.*, mostly, it seems, of the 70s. In the apse are
nine large single figures. – More in the s and also the N windows.
– The transept windows are both by *W. H. Sullivan* of Liverpool, 1871. Both are poor, compared with Morris. It is curious
that one has (still) a large pictorial scene, though the other has
small scenes in medallions.

To the E nice group of SCHOOL and SCHOOL HOUSE, probably
also of the 1840s. Of the same time the RECTORY, N of the
church.

SECONDARY MODERN SCHOOL, Wood Road. By *Weightman
& Bullen*, 1963–4; good.

HALLIWELL see BOLTON, p. 87

HARPURPHEY see MANCHESTER, p. 315

9000   HARTSHEAD

(St Augustine, Hartshead Green. 1823. Or must it not b
mid C19? Small, with coupled lancets and apse. By the B619
road (Lees New Road). Information kindly provided by Mr 1
Bolton.)

Heartshead Tower. A memorial which, though – as suc
objects go – it is small, appears prominently against the sk
from many places. It is circular with a conical roof and com
memorates the marriage of the Prince of Wales in 1863. It wa
intended to be 85 ft high.

7010   HARWOOD

Christ Church, Stitch Mi Lane. 1840–1. w tower thin, wit
short spire. High round-headed windows. Transepts, sho
chancel with stubby blank arcading, and a second upper tie
opening into auxiliary rooms. The LYCHGATE is dated 1840 an
has mullioned windows. – (ALTAR TABLE. Elaborately carved
Dated 1561 and said to be Nuremberg work.) – PULPI
Cheetham says 1660, from the Chapel Royal, St James
Palace. Plain late-C17-looking panels. – WOODWORK. Muc
has been brought in, figure work and ornamental worl
most of it probably Netherlandish. – STALLS. The faces an
foliage of the MISERICORDS look genuine and English. –
ORGAN. This is said to come from Edgware, i.e. the Chandos
Handel neighbourhood. However, the case is Victorian min
mum-Gothic. – LECTERN. A very animated eagle, qui
probably Flemish Baroque. – MONUMENT. John Loma
† 1827, yet still a totally asymmetrical Rococo cartouche. Or
would expect a date seventy-five years earlier.

Langsight Methodist Church. 1862. Of stone, and sti
classical.

9090   HAUGHTON

St Anne. 1882 by J. M. & H. Taylor.* Red brick with an asser
tive crossing tower, no aisles, but transepts and a straight-ende
chancel. Everything is odd about the church. The tower has

* According to Mr Donald Buttress.

truncated pyramid roof and ends in a pyramid roof. The stair-turret is separate in the angle between nave and s transept. At the w end is a baptistery projecting triangularly. The s transept rose-window has tracery with mullions as if it were not a rose. The interior is faced with yellow brick. In the crossing are timber ribs making an octopartite vault. But the weirdest thing is the E angles of the crossing. They are short fat granite columns, and behind them the angle is chamfered off so as to form a kind of squints.

The RECTORY is of 1882 and without any doubt by *Taylor* too. It is exactly as strange.

HAUGHTON GREEN

9090

ST MARY. 1874–6 by *Medland & Henry Taylor*. Timber-framed, but with a funny polygonal N tower, containing the baptistery below. The idea to do a timber-framed church came of course from Denton. As it is, the interior is as idiosyncratic as those of the neighbouring Taylor churches. The nave is very wide, the s aisle cross-gabled, and the weirdest traceried openings are set between the nave roof and the aisle bay roofs. The arcade has timber posts, the roof tie-beams and raking queenposts, and the chancel arch is cusped.

MANOR FARM, Haughton Green. A two-storeyed cottage dated 1735. The window details are all altered, but what is certain is that, although the façade is symmetrical, the windows were low and of two lights, i.e. pre-classical.

Haughton Green is not a pleasure to look at, and the three high slabs immediately N of the church do not help.

METHODIST CHURCH, Two Trees Lane. 1810. Very plain, brick, of three bays, with a (plastered) pediment. Arched windows.

HAWKLEY HALL FARMHOUSE *see* WIGAN, p. 430

HAYDOCK

5090

ST JAMES. The church is by *Douglas & Fordham* and was built in 1891–2, but it is an addition to the older church of 1866, now the N aisle. This is by *W. & J. Hay*. The church of 1891–2 is timber-framed, yet large and very spacious inside. Wide nave and low s aisle; clerestory; narrower chancel. The exterior with brick infilling is hardly more than an envelope. It had a spire originally, but this was taken down in 1930.

St Mark. *See* Blackbrook.

Haydock Lodge, 1¾ m. NE. Late C18. Two-storeyed, of ashlar.
Quite a noble façade. The centre is a bow; l. and r. are three plain
bays and then a wider one with, on the ground floor, a tripartite
window under a blank arch. Substantial additions.

HEALEY *see* ROCHDALE, pp. 378, 379

HEAP BRIDGE *see* BURY, p. 100

HEATON *see* BOLTON, p. 89

8090

HEATON CHAPEL

St Thomas. An odd sight. A humble nave, rendered white, and
a square brick thirtyish chancel and w porch. The core is of
1765 and had arched windows. About 1875 tracery was put into
these windows and the Gothic w windows were made. Then
Bernard A. Miller came along in 1937 and did the rest. –
Monuments. Several tablets, classical and Gothic.

8090

HEATON MERSEY

St John Baptist, Didsbury Road. A Commissioners' church
(£3,950), 1846–50 by *P. Walker*. The architect went in for
excessively steep lancets for his side windows, still with buttresses between, after the Commissioners' fashion, and also for
his porch entrance. Thin w tower with spire. Aisleless nave.
The chancel is by *Preston & Vaughan* (PF) of 1891, and well in
keeping with the rest. The stone Lychgate is of 1927 by
Taylor & Young.

Congregational Church, Didsbury and Mersey Roads.
Grand stone façade with a three-gabled porch. But round the
corner it looks domestic, in spite of the wooden church windows.

Sunday School, by St John's. 1822, red brick, two-storeyed,
with arched windows, two by six bays.

Barnes Industrial Home, Didsbury Road. Originally for
neglected and destitute boys. A forbidding-looking Gothic
front of red brick with brick polychromy. Symmetrical, with
steep lancets and steep gables.

Mauldeth Home, Mauldeth Road. The centre is Mauldeth
Hall, an exceptionally fine ashlar-faced late Grecian villa.
Its main front unfortunately is half-covered by an extension.
One can still see the giant portico of unfluted Ionic columns
and pediment. The entrance side is seven bays long, with a one-

storey porch of four Greek Doric columns. Round the corner a segmental bow. Good entrance hall, now subdivided. The most likely date is *c.*1830.

HEATON MOOR

8090

ST PAUL, Heaton Moor Road. 1876–7 by *Bird & Whittenbury*. Large, with a SE tower, its top stage octagonal. Lancets and geometrical tracery. The interior is nothing special.

CONGREGATIONAL CHURCH, Heaton Moor Road. 1896 by *Darbyshire & Smith*. SW steeple and geometrical tracery.

METHODIST CHURCH, Heaton Moor Road. 1873 by *T. H. Allen*. Gothic with a fancy SW turret. It cost £5,000 to build.

HEATON NORRIS

8090

Views, grim but splendid, over Stockport with its factories, viaduct, and parish church.

ALL SAINTS, Manchester Road. 1886–8 by *Preston & Vaughan*. Mathematical tiles and terracotta. No tower. Motifs of *c.*1300. The E end appears with three gables.

ST MARY (R.C.), on a bank just W of the Teviot Dale Station. Small, of brick, with a bellcote and a W rose window. By *Pugin & Pugin*, 1897.

TEVIOT DALE METHODIST CHAPEL, Lancashire Hill. 1824 by *Richard Lane*. Classical ashlar front of three bays, with one-bay porch attachments. No pediment, just a big parapet. The main porch is in the middle and has four unfluted Ionic columns.

CHRIST CHURCH, Church Road. 1846 by *W. Hayley*. Cost nearly £7,000. Built with a Commissioners' contribution. Large, with a W tower with recessed spire. Nave and aisles. Paired lancets. Transepts and a short lower chancel. The interesting thing is the W tower with its E.E. portal and its W window with plate tracery. This for 1846 and Hayley is very early. The church otherwise is decidedly pre-Pugin and pre-Scott in character. Or are these motifs a later alteration?

STOCKPORT COLLEGE OF ART, former PENDLEBURY MEMORIAL HALL AND ORPHANAGE, Old Road and Lancashire Hill. Built in 1880–2 by *J. W. Beaumont*. Red brick; a high tower with domed cap. See p. 479

HEATON PARK see MANCHESTER, p. 328

HEYSIDE

9000

ST MARK. 1878 by *Wild & Collins*. No tower, only a bellcote.

HEYWOOD

St Luke. 1860–2 by *Joseph Clarke*. A large church in the centre of the town. It has a NW steeple outside the N aisle, with a broach spire. The rest is of even outline, without attempts at picturesqueness. Seven-light E window, six-light w window. Five bays. Thin quatrefoil piers. – High, very thin iron SCREEN.

The VICARAGE is N of the church, a three-bay brick house with a recessed doorway.

ALL SOULS, Rochdale Road. 1898–9 by *Frank P. Oakley*. The tower was the gift of the vicar, Rathbone Hartley, in 1908. It is a large church with a noble N porch tower, a polygonal apse, and tracery of *c.*1300.

St JAMES, St James's Street. 1838. w tower, aisleless nave with lancet windows with Y-tracery, and a short chancel. Timber roof with fanciful tracery. Three GALLERIES. – The STAINED GLASS of the later five-light E window seems to be by *Hardman*. The SCHOOL, w of the church, is dated 1835 and has a flat, five-bay front. Pointed windows with Y-tracery.

NEW (i.e. Swedenborgian) CHURCH, Church Street. 1828 and 1838. Three bays, arched windows. The doorway and the window above it are Victorian.

MUNICIPAL BUILDING, Longford Street. A humble, stuccoed three-bay building of 1850. It was built as the Mechanics' Institute.

CIVIC HALL, Church Street, E of the Library. By *Lyons, Israel & Ellis*. Engineering bricks. Well done, up-to-date, unshowy and yet dignified.

LIBRARY, Market Place. 1905–6 by *S. V. North & C. Collas Robin*. Stone, symmetrical, with a Baroque portal but an Elizabethan gable and Elizabethan canted bay windows.

GRAMMAR SCHOOL, Hind Hill Street. Built as the Technical School. By *Woodhouse & Willoughby*, 1894. Red brick and red terracotta. Only the portal is of stone. The front is successfully asymmetrical.

(ASHWORTH FOLD. An attractive group, mainly C17–18, with low mullioned windows, but also 'a late Gothic doorway'. MHLG)

RYECROFT, Bury Road. On the estate *Peter Womersley* in 1960 built two attractive small houses.

(EDGECROFT, Manchester Road. 1921 by *Edgar Wood*, his last building before he retired. Tudor, brick, of simple shapes and few mouldings.)

DARN HILL ESTATE. Housing for Manchester.

HIGHER HURST see HURST

HIGHFIELD see WIGAN, p. 428

HIGHTOWN

2000

Between ALT ROAD and the foreshore a HOUSING scheme by *Eric Thomson & Associates* is under construction. It is in the end to consist of about 1,000 dwellings and school, library, and shops. Traffic segregation is provided. Work began in 1965. It consists all of single-family houses.

HINDLEY

6000

ALL SAINTS. This delightful brick chapel started life as a chapel of ease to Wigan parish church. After the Civil War it became Presbyterian and remained so until 1690. It then reverted to the established church and was rebuilt in 1766. This is the building we see. Two by four bays, with a doorless front with two large arched windows, a small lunette window over, and a pedimental gable. The arched windows have their glazing bars as three stepped pointed lights. The w gallery is of 1776, the N and S galleries are later Georgian.

ST BENEDICT (R.C.), Market Street. 1869 by *Joseph Hansom*. Without architectural interest outside, but very odd, architecturally poor stuff inside. Round apse. Narrow aisle passages. The Lady Chapel was added by *Velarde* in 1954.* It is a small circular room with a conical roof, connected with the S aisle by a rectangular space. The windows are rather 1925- than 1955-looking.

ST PETER, Atherton Street. 1866 by *E. G. Paley*. A sizeable church with a SW steeple with broach spire. The tracery is Dec. The interior has no thrills – it is very much a pre-Paley & Austin church.

ST JOHN'S METHODIST CHURCH, Market Street. 1900–1 by *Waddington & Son* of Manchester. With a thin octagonal NW steeple and all round-headed windows.

UNITARIAN CHAPEL. The chapel, although as old as 1788, was pulled down in 1966.

LIBRARY. 1886 by *Thomas Worthington*. Free-Elizabethan and asymmetrical. Except for the tower roof, very acceptable.

LEYLAND FARMHOUSE, Lord Street. Brick house with a square porch and I A 1671 in very large raised brick lettering across the r. side of the front.

* This I was told by Mr D. Evinson.

LAUREL HOUSE, Atherton Road. Dated 1714 and apparently from the start of five bays with sash-windows with moulded surrounds, which would be very early for Lancashire.

(HINDLEY HALL. It looks Late Georgian, and the MHLG says indeed c.1807. But Mr J. Haworth suggests 1767 instead. Seven bays, three storeys. The parapet sweeps up to the middle three bays.)

(A good recent HOUSE by *A. Grimshaw* is in Hindley Mill Lane, close to the cemetery. It is of buff bricks and has relatively narrow vertical windows.)

HINDLEY GREEN
6000

1½ m. SE of Hindley

ST JOHN EVANGELIST. 1895–1903 (1893–9 ?) by *C. E. Deacon*. Stock brick and red brick dressings. Elaborate bell-turret on the E end of the nave. Strange windows, their lights round-headed and yet cusped.

BRUNSWICK METHODIST CHURCH. 1905 by *Gilbert Ackroyd Potts*. Red brick and yellow terracotta. Free tracery configurations. NW tower with copper cap.

HOLLINGWORTH *see* LITTLEBOROUGH

HOLLINS GREEN
6090

ST HELEN. 1735 the body of the church, and perhaps the cupola. All other detail 1882.

(OLDHAM GARDEN SUBURB. 1906–13. Ebenezer Howard was present at the opening in 1909. The total, according to Miss Tims, is 156 houses.)

HOLLINWOOD *see* OLDHAM, pp. 360, 361

HOPWOOD
8000

ST JOHN EVANGELIST. 1903–5 by *F. P. Oakley*. Dec, with a NW turret. Inside the aisles differ considerably: S wall-piers and low aisle passages. The brick arches of the passage and the wall-piers towards the nave are of brick. N is a more orthodox aisle: elongated octagonal piers and arches dying into them. Yet both aisles are part of the original design.

HOPWOOD HALL (De la Salle College). Hopwood Hall itself is a house of brick, of four ranges round a small courtyard. It has inside, at the E end of the hall, a medieval roof-truss, and in one room a Jacobean overmantel. The great canted bay-window with three transoms is original too. So are two staircases, one with sturdy turned balusters whose centre member is a square, the other late C17 with twisted balusters and still a string. But most of the details s of the hall over the brow of a hill are the college buildings, one group utilitarian, the other earlier and more ambitious, i.e. higher and gabled. The former is of 1961–3, the latter of 1952 and 1956 (by *Reynolds & Scott*).

On the brow *Sir Frederick Gibberd* (in association with *Reynolds & Scott*) built his thrilling chapel, evidently a dress rehearsal for the new Liverpool Cathedral, and purer than this by the absence of all the variously shaped outer chapels. At Hopwood Sir Frederick just placed an octagon with solid walls of purple concrete blocks below and a band of forcefully detailed concrete above. Between them is just a slit-like long band of glass. Then follows the high and prominent octagonal lead roof and a high glazed lantern of tapering sides. This, with its rather crude oblong panes of coloured glass (by *D. Atkins*), throws all the light on the altar, which stands in the middle of the room with seats facing it on five sides of the octagon. The structure which is invisible outside is clear inside: eight concrete members connected by concrete ring-beams. The walls are again absolutely plain. Opposite the entrance behind the altar is the organ, its decoration hardly Sir Frederick's work.

On the approach from the w one passes two impressive open BARNS, with square brick pillars and in the end walls large bare pointed arches. What is their date ?

HOUGH END *see* CHORLTON-CUM-HARDY, MANCHESTER, p. 305

HOUGH GREEN *see* DITTON

HOWE BRIDGE *see* ATHERTON

HULME *see* MANCHESTER, p. 330

HURST

9000

ST JOHN EVANGELIST, King's Road. A Commissioners' church (cost £2,200). 1847–9 by *Shellard* (transepts and tower 1862 etc. by *G. Shaw*). Nave and aisles, long transepts and square chancel. Side lancets and, inside, quatrefoil piers. The tower with boldly done octagonal top parts and spire is set w of the s aisle and visually independent of it. It was added in 1862, as were also the transepts. The church was built by the munificence of Oldham Whitaker, a member of the great mill-owner family of Hurst. The founder John I was a Methodist and gave the first Methodist chapel. Of his two sons John II and Oldham, the former was Methodist, the latter joined the established church. They lived, first John II, then Oldham in Springfield House, later called Hurst Hall, demolished c.1955–60. The first mill was built in 1808. By 1840 there were 1,000 employees. The MILL is that now of Mackison's in QUEEN'S ROAD, with a front of six storeys and thirty-three bays.

The NEW CONNEXION METHODIST CHURCH is also in Queen's Road. It is by *W. Hayley* and of 1846 (enlarged 1857). It has lancets and a turret in the angle to the s transept. In it MONUMENT by *Foley* to John Whitaker I, † 1840, a group of figures, some or all portraits, called Charity. An uncommonly fine, tender piece.

The SCHOOL opposite is of 1860 and is also a Whitaker gift.

LADYSMITH BARRACKS, Mossley Road. 1841–3. An impressive group. To the street a long range behind a heavily classical gateway with two pedestrian entrances. Behind a large yard with three independent ranges; in the centre of the far range, pedimented, the officers' mess.

HURST HALL *see* GLAZEBURY

4090

HUYTON

ST MICHAEL. In its appearance mostly C19, but in fact a medieval church. The material is red ashlar. The tower is Perp, but the obelisk pinnacles look C17 or early C18. The very wide s aisle and the narrower N aisle were rebuilt in 1815–22, and the N arcade dates from that time too. But the s arcade is C14, with octagonal piers and double-chamfered arches. The s doorway is of the same time. The chancel is Perp; original the priest's doorway. The hammerbeam roof in the chancel is mostly probably of the C17. – FONTS. One is Early Norman, the other Perp. The Norman one is tub-shaped and has extremely primitive heads in arcading, and a frieze of rosettes above. The Perp one has the usual pointed quatrefoils with shields. – SCREEN. A fine, typically Northern piece of c.1500 with single-light divisions and dainty Flamboyant tracery. An inscription no longer preserved, told of pulling the screen down 'in time of rebellion 1647' and repairing it and setting it up again in

1663. The Jacobean-style repairs are worth seeking out. – WOODWORK in the chancel, c.1700 and probably Flemish. – STAINED GLASS. In the s aisle two windows by *Holiday*, 1883 and 1885. – PLATE. Cup and Cover Paten 1695; two Plates by *Benjamin Branker* of Liverpool; Breadholder 1714; Flagon 1719; Strainer 1799. – MONUMENT. Defaced effigy of a Priest, alabaster; C14 or C15.

ST AGNES, St Mary's Road. 1964–5 by *L. A. G. Prichard*.

ST BARTHOLOMEW, Roby Church Road. 1875 by *Ewan Christian*. Competent, conventional, and quite large. w tower with broach spire, round apse, prominent clerestory. The style is c.1300. Can the timber with its 'rogue' details be by Christian too? Dull interior. – STAINED GLASS. s aisle w by *Kempe*, 1899.

CONGREGATIONAL CHURCH, Victoria Road. 1889–90 by *W. G. Caröe*. With a prominent steeple. C13 details, derived, it is said, from Truro Cathedral (by Pearson).

Huyton has more than one character. Of the villagey past hardly anything remains round Derby Road. By the church is a pretty GREEN with a tall CROSS. This dates from 1897, but replaces one by *Rickman* of 1820 and looks in its proportions as if it were a copy after Rickman. The little green has very much an estate-village character, and Huyton is indeed very close to Knowsley. Then there are a large number of Victorian villas amid leafage, and extending beyond that are Liverpool housing estates of 1932 etc. (Huyton Farm Estate, Knowsley Estate), 1937 etc. (Longview Farm), and 1946 etc. (Brookhouse Estate).

Of individual buildings the following qualify for mention:

INFANT SCHOOL, Derby Road. Small, Gothic, and probably of c.1830.

SHOPPING CENTRE, Derby Road. 1962–6 by *Chapman, Taylor & Partners* of London. A successful new-townish design.

HURST HOUSE (Golf Club), Huyton Road. The house in its present form looks c.1830. It is of red ashlar: five bays and two storeys with a porch of coupled Roman Doric columns. Behind in the 1870s a huge red-brick excrescence developed, with a high slender tower, a big broad tower dated 1877, and turrets on the stables as well. This Victorian work was done for Jacob Atherton, one of the founders of what is now British Insulated Callenders. Victorian work has recently been demolished.

C. F. MOTT COLLEGE, Liverpool Road. The core is THE HAZELS, a brick house of 1764. The façade is rather bleak. The brickwork is smooth, there are three storeys to the five bays, and a three-bay pediment is awkwardly framed by a five-bay pedi-

ment. But inside are cross-vaulted corridors running across on
the ground floor and the upper floor, and a spacious staircase
starting in one flight and returning in two. On the intermediate
landing is a Venetian window. Another and a canted bay window
at the back. Many additions for the college, most recently two
hostel blocks which are prominent from afar. They are by
R. Bradbury, the Liverpool City Architect, and date from
1964–6.

HYDE HALL *see* DENTON

INCE BLUNDELL

3000

INCE BLUNDELL HALL. The Blundells settled here during the
C13 at the latest. S of the Hall is a fragment of their OLD HALL,
C16, of brick, with long, low, mullioned windows. The new Hall
was built in the Early Georgian decades, probably *c.*1715–20.
25 The main, i.e. now garden, front is of nine bays, brick with
stone dressings, and of two storeys, with an attic storey above
the cornice. The three-bay centre has two giant pilasters and
two giant demi-columns, all Corinthian. There are also giant
angle pilasters. The ground-floor windows l. and r. of the centre
have pediments, those of the centre are segment-headed. It is
all of the type of Buckingham House London, some Shropshire
houses, and the houses of the Smiths of Warwick, but coarsely
handled. Some Victorian interference is possible. On the back
of the house this is obvious. To this house in 1802 Henry
Blundell added the PANTHEON, an independent building with
a portico of four unfluted Ionic columns and a dome without
drum. It was built to house Henry Blundell's collection of
antique statuary. His collection was inspired by that of his
neighbour Charles Townley. The exterior of the Pantheon
has still some ancient work, but the sculpture inside has been
sold to Liverpool Corporation. The Pantheon was joined to
the house by a passage with an octagonal vestibule and by a
34 big dining room in 1860. The Pantheon has a coffered dome with
sky-lit centre and giant pilasters. Four shallow niches with
marble columns carrying arches. The Dining Room was decorated by *Crace*, who also did the Picture Gallery and the wall
panels of the Drawing Room. All this dates from 1847–50 and
is pretty, very light Raphaelesque stuff. The Drawing Room
on the other hand has a splendid Rococo stucco ceiling of
*c.*1750. Another in another room. The staircase has a chaste
metal railing.

In the garden a MONUMENT consisting of a Tuscan column with one eagle, and a TEMPLE with a portico of four Tuscan columns and some antique reliefs. This is probably of *c*.1780, by *William Everard* of Liverpool, and was built to house Henry Blundell's first antiques. Originally a greenhouse was behind. It is to this that the inscription refers. Between the house and the chapel is the C18 SERVICE WING, of seven bays, brick, with a central lunette window, a pediment, and a lantern.

The STABLES are of nine bays, brick, with a pedimental gable and keyed-in round, above the oblong, windows. Archway in the outermost bays.

The LION GATE, on the Southport road, is an ambitious affair. Centre with Tuscan demi-columns flanking an arch and carrying a wide open pediment with an urn. Rusticated pedestrian entrances l. and r. and above them lions.

The SE GATES have coupled Corinthian pilasters and garlands in the frieze.

CHAPEL. 1858 by *J. J. Scoles*. Oblong, with clerestory windows and an apse. Flat ceiling. The detail outside and inside a modest Quattrocento. The painted decoration may well be by *Crace*.

SCHOOL. 1843, with mullioned windows and inscription in black letter on scrolls. An asymmetrical front.

PRIEST'S HOUSE, on the Southport road, s of the Hall, opposite the Victorian Gate to the estate. Circular, with the main sides flattened. Circular chimney.

INCE-IN-MAKERFIELD

5000

CHRIST CHURCH, Ince Green Lane. 1863–4 by *E. G. Paley*. An aisleless church with geometrical tracery, with nothing yet of the Paley & Austin qualities. Transepts and polygonal apse; N transept turret; open three-bay w porch.

ST MARY, Lower Ince. 1887 by *Paley & Austin*. A grand church, yet a church built of stock brick with red-brick trimmings. John Pearson and Thomas Knowles, managers of the local colliery, contributed £5,000 each. Long roof with a flèche on a broad wood-shingled substructure. There are no aisles proper, only a low aisle passage and above it a cornice running through, above which are plain, internally deeply splayed single lancets. The crossing is all brick, responds and arches, and there are transepts and single-bay chancel chapels. To the outside transepts and chapels appear as pairs of cross-gabled projections. The chancel is rib-vaulted.

CEMETERY. The chapels were won in competition by *Waterhouse*.

5—S.L.

He was commissioned in 1855, and they were completed i
1857, an early Waterhouse date. One is simple Gothic with
bellcote, but the other is Norman with an apse, which is ur
expected.

COUNCIL OFFICES. 1903, by *Heaton, Ralph & Heaton*. Re
and red terracotta. The typical Edwardian motif of alternatel
blocked columns. Cross-windows and fancy gables.

POWER STATION. 1948–51. *Robert Atkinson* was consultant.

(PEEL HALL, Holt Street, N of Manchester Road. The MHL
reports cruck timbers.)

DOWER HOUSE FARMHOUSE, Moss Lane, nearly at Platt Bridge
Not large. Brick, two-storeyed, asymmetrical, with mullione
windows below thick raised brick relieving arches.

7090

IRLAM

ST JOHN BAPTIST, Liverpool Road, Jenny Green, Higher Irlan
1865–6 by *J. Medland Taylor*. Small, with a crossing tower wit
broach spire, very short transepts, and an apse. The W wall ha
a most unorthodox rose-window. Internally the Taylor touc
is the crossing arches of voussoirs of alternating thickness – ju
as in certain Georgian door surrounds. And whereas this mot
is used simply and straightforwardly in the arches of the
windows, in the crossing arches it is done in two orders. Insid
the roof timbers start very low, and the church is made lighte
by dormers in the roof.

ST TERESA (R.C.), Liverpool and Astley Roads. 1903 by *Oswal
Hill*.

7000

KEARSLEY

ST JOHN EVANGELIST, Church Street, S of Farnworth Statio
1826. Ashlar, the W tower with polygonal buttresses, the side
with two-light windows, not too narrow. Three galleries; fl
ceiling. The chancel is of 1871.

ST STEPHEN, Manchester Road. 1870–1 by *J. M. & H. Taylo*
Dec. The crotchetty side of the Taylors' *œuvre* comes out le
in the church (bell-openings of the tower) than in the PARSON
AGE. One ought to look at the gable, its shape and its rose
window, but there are plenty of other roguish touches.

KEMPNOUGH HALL *see* WORSLEY

KERSAL MOOR *see* SALFORD, p. 395

KIRKBY

4090

ST CHAD. By *Paley & Austin*, 1869–71, replacing a Georgian chapel, which replaced a much older chapel of ease. The church is one of Paley & Austin's most powerful, externally by virtue of its high, slender central tower with the blunt saddleback roof which Bodley had introduced in the 1860s, and internally by the superb excelsior of the tall high tower arches and the rib-vault inside it high up. All this is Gothic, but details are Norman, and the rich. rather conventional S doorway is ornately Norman. The church is of red stone and has windows mostly lancets and a short square-ended chancel. The buttressing of the tower on the S side deserves special attention. The nave, once one has entered, strikes one as long and very high. The chancel has arcading some way up the wall. – FONT. Early Norman, tub-shaped. On the bowl seven Saints, Adam and Eve with the tree and the serpent, the Angel of the Expulsion, and St Michael spearing a serpent. The serpent creeps round the underside of the bowl like a rope-moulding, and the short stem and the base have indeed fat roll-mouldings. – STAINED GLASS. By *Holiday*, from 1872 over a long period. The W windows e.g. of 1897. He is recognizable everywhere, though the style and the intensity of the colour change. – ALTAR WALL. Last Supper in mosaic, and angels and virtues in *opus sectile* stone mosaic, also by *Holiday*; the Last Supper 1899.

VICARAGE. 1848, and typical of the date. Red stone.

WHITEFIELD HOUSE, Whitefield Drive, ⅝ m. SW. A three-bay Georgian house with lower one-bay wings right in the middle of a housing estate. One is glad to see it preserved. Opposite the highly curious DOVECOTE of 1703, a square red stone pillar or short tower.

SIMONSWOOD HALL, 1½ m. NNW. Dated 1687. Stone, asymmetrical, with a cross-gable on the r. side. Only in this gable is a transomed window; the others are lower and have mullions only. The door surround of ashlar of alternating sizes is the only indication of a late C17 date.

KIRKBY INDUSTRIAL ESTATE. The only factory worth two lines is YORKSHIRE IMPERIAL METALS, with good W and E terminal blocks. This is by *Sir Percy Thomas & Son* and of c.1950.

KIRKDALE *see* LIVERPOOL, p. 228

KNOTTY ASH *see* LIVERPOOL, p. 229

KNOWSLEY

ST MARY. A large church, the work of *Sharpe*, and then of *Paley*.
Sharpe did the nave and the W tower in 1843–4, Paley the
transepts in 1860 and the Derby Chapel in 1871. Sharpe was
archeologically correct here and exhibits great dignity, both in
the tower with its broach spire and in the long arcades of quatrefoil piers with stylized foliage capitals. The stone vault in the
tower is unexpected and impressive. Sharpe's church has lancet
windows, Paley introduces bar tracery, especially in the Derby
Chapel. – STALLS. From Knowsley Hall. Flamboyant decoration, i.e. early C16 and C18 oval scenes, probably Flemish. –
MONUMENT. Fourteenth Earl of Derby, 1872 by *Matthew
Noble*. White, recumbent effigy.

SCHOOL, N of the church. 1845. Red stone, nicely symmetrical.

KNOWSLEY HALL. The device of the Stanleys, Earls of Derby, is
Sans changer. It has not prevented the successive earls from
changing Knowsley Hall more often and more drastically
than most of their fellow noblemen have changed their mansions. The result is confusing and also confused. It does not
flow together into one coherent whole. The estate became
Stanley property by marriage in 1385, and it is Stanley property
to this day. The chief seat of the family, however, was Lathom
House until this was destroyed in the Civil War. So there is
little at Knowsley earlier than the second half of the C17.

The house is L-shaped. The older and more drastically
altered wing runs W, i.e. with fronts to N and S. To its E is the
later, more unified wing, and this runs N, i.e. has its fronts to
W and E. They are for convenience's sake to be called here
the W and the E range. The W range is of stone, the E range
of brick. The oldest part is about the centre of the W range.
It is known as the Royal Lodging and has two rounded turrets,
one with a spiral stair, and faces N. It probably dates from
c. 1500. What surrounds it is part of a nine-bay range with
windows of a type of *c.*1700 and castellation of 1820 by *John
Foster* (*see* below).

Also of about 1500 are minor fragments of two piers in the
courtyard and by the now isolated W tower. Otherwise all
around here is C19. But the latest C19 work has been demolished
in the last Knowsley change, which is that effected by *Clau
Phillimore* in 1953–4.

The E range looks all of a piece to the W with its 5–6–5 rhythm
of fenestration and its two-and-a-half-storey centre and two-
storey wings. One would call it Early Georgian. But that also is

not intact. A painting of *c.*1730 in the house shows it with a pediment over the whole middle seven bays and a cupola behind. This is no longer so, and the present W porch is *Phillimore*'s. The range received a library extension in the 1880s, and that has been pulled down. The E side of the E range is very long – in 1937 it was still a full 415 ft – and consists of two parts, both apparently C18. The r. part is of four bays and two storeys and plain. Then follows the centre of 2–5–2 bays and three storeys with an ornate portal by *Romaine-Walker* of 1910, and after that a continuation of 5–6–5 bays, all two and a half storeys high. Until the eighties however there were only two storeys and a parapet, and in Tillemans' painting there are here still a variety of gabled parts, some half-timbered, some of stone, some of brick. Tillemans means *c.*1710–20, the other painting *c.*1730. So that dates the E range.

The S end of the E range is the climax of the C18 house, a 28 five-bay portico or veranda of two storeys, made of wood. It has paired Tuscan columns below, paired fluted Ionic columns above. Behind it, the wall of the house itself has niches on both floors and on the upper floor also pediments to the windows and much stucco decoration. Dates are not certain, but all this work seems to have been completed by 1736. The wall of the portico side may well be some ten or fifteen years earlier than the wooden verandas.

To continue along the S front to the W, past the verandas, the range now jumps back by six bays. There is here a link of three bays with coupled Tuscan columns of wood on the ground floor. Then follows the medievalizing C19 part, i.e. that designed by *John Foster* in 1820. The State Dining Room of 1820 lies behind the Royal Lodging. Then there is another recession, this with a nine-bay Gothic arcade. But all this part was heightened in effect in the 1840s by *William Burn*. His are the details and the Flag Tower, and also the now isolated Dynamo Tower at the end of the range. Among other destroyed items was the replacement of the cupola of the E range by a whacking big square tower with a steep saddleback pavilion roof, as if it were a public building. This had been put on in the eighties.

INTERIOR. There is not as much of interest inside Knowsley Hall as the exterior would make one expect. The main staircase in the E range of the lushest late C17 forms is by *Romaine-Walker*. By the same is the Walnut Drawing Room, at the S end of the E range behind the upper veranda. The *boiseries* however are supposed to be original French C18 work. Other principal rooms in the E range are the Gallery with a gorgeous Rocc doorcase dated 1733 (*ex situ*) and the Stucco Room betweer and S range and in the latter, with three windows to the S, th to the N, and a small bow window to the N. In the S range is t State Dining Room with a carved ceiling with lantern lighti and elaborate woodwork of 1890. The fireplace however loc as if it went back to *Foster* and 1820.

Many SUBSIDIARY BUILDINGS. The GATES W of the W fa of the E range are of *c.*1730. The STABLES are a large quad of r brick and have a cupola recently brought in. In the park to t NE of the mansion is the NEW HOUSE, by *Claud Phillimo* plainly neo-Georgian.

ORCHARD LODGE, NW of the stables, is Victorian, with jol very florid bargeboards.

BOAT HOUSE, on White Man's Dam, by the lake. The hou was built in 1837. It has deep eaves and bargeboards w pendants. The LAKE was made *c.*1720–30 and enlarged *c.*17

THE NEST, NW of the Boat House. The entrance side is gabl and looks 1830s, the garden side is Georgian with a bow windc The house was the centre of the thirteenth earl's menagerie a aviaries.

On the other side of White Man's Dam is a TOWER, squ and bleak. In Tillemans' time it was round and white. Near is the WHITE MAN, a lead statue on a pedestal.

Finally BRIDGE LODGE, NE of the Octagon (*see* belov picturesque and asymmetrical. The bridge goes across t Octagon Pond. The OCTAGON is a summer house of 17. built also to be an eye-catcher, E of the house. It is of buff stc and has stucco decoration inside.

Of the LODGES the best is the LIVERPOOL LODGE, SW the house, red stone, asymmetrical and embattled. The otl lodges are minor. The CROXTETH LODGE (W) is also red sto but has shaped gables.

LAMBERHEAD GREEN *see* WIGAN, p. 428

LEE HALL *see* GATEACRE, LIVERPOOL, p. 228

9000

LEES

Visually this is all part of Oldham.

ST JOHN BAPTIST, N of the High Street, at the end of St Jo Street. Built in 1742. Stone, with the windows in two tiers. T two E bays were added in 1772. Unfortunately made respectal in 1865 by *H. Cockburn*. But he left the pretty, open octagonal cupola, and what he did inside is attractive. He renewed the three galleries (the iron columns must be Victorian) and made a chancel by inserting two-bay piers so as to create a 'hall'-type space. Dog-tooth in the arches. The E window has flowing tracery. – STAINED GLASS. *Capronnier* was busy here, in recognition probably of what he had done in the other church. The dates are 1884–96 (signed in 1896 by *Comère & Capronnier*). – (PLATE. Two Chalices, 1742.)

f the church is the GRAPES INN, dated 1741, and yet still with mullioned windows.

THOMAS, s of the High Street. 1848 by *Shellard*, and remark-able in that it is no longer of the Commissioners' type. The w tower has no longer tight proportions, the s porch of two storeys is archeologically perfectly convincing, and the Perp tracery is correct. Octagonal arcade piers and a proper chancel. Hammerbeam roofs and dormers. Only a w gallery. The pro-gressiveness is felt everywhere. Yet the church was built with a contribution from the Commissioners (total cost £3,815). – BOX PEWS. – STAINED GLASS. By *Capronnier* quite a number of windows, dating from 1874–98. The Good Samaritan of 1888 is the popular favourite.

HEARTSHEAD STREET is WELLFIELD HOUSE, a mid-C19 stone villa of five bays with an elaborate iron trellis porch.

THENS MILL. 1905 by *F. Dixon*. A good example of the plain Accrington brick type. J. B. Hawcroft)

OME MILL, Springhead, E of Lees. 1907 by *Joseph Stott & Son* of Oldham. Mr Hawcroft writes: 'The modifications treatment in brickwork, particularly in the top storey, make it one of the best-designed mills in Lancashire.')

LEIGH   6000

:igh has little to show for its 46,000 inhabitants, except for the arket place with the church immediately adjoining it and the wn hall facing the church across the open space. There are wnscape possibilities here which ought to be guarded. Other-se, and especially at a distance, the town is more dominated by xtile mills than most.

MARY. The tower is Perp, but it is refaced and looks the same date as the rest – which is 1869–73. The architects were *Paley & Austin*. The church is of red sandstone and Perp in all motifs. The clerestory runs through for nave and chancel and is em-

battled. So is the square-topped tower. There is a more pictu
esque corner to the SE with the vestry doorway set diagonal
The choir vestry is a special N attachment, well done in 19
to suit the church (by *Austin & Paley*). Six-bay interior wi
octagonal piers and double-chamfered arches, none yet of t
spatial thrills of which Paley & Austin were capable later. T
tower arch is evidently true Perp, and the roof-line of t
previous church appears above it. – STAINED GLASS. In the
window by *Kempe*, c.1905. – PLATE. Elizabethan Cup; C
of 1650; Set of 1723–4.

CHRIST CHURCH, St Helen's Road, Pennington. 1850–4
Shellard. Big, rather dull Perp church. W tower, nave and aisl
chancel. Octagonal piers inside, but still a W gallery.

ST JOSEPH (R.C.), Chapel Street. 1855 by *Joseph Hansom*.
odd façade and an odder interior. The façade is tight, with bu
resses with many set-offs appearing in profile and the top
steep gable between two buttresses. But inside one wou
forget that one is in a church if it were not for the *bondieuseri*
It is a wide room with iron columns carrying timber arch
from column to column, i.e. W to E, and at the same time bear
sticking out of the wall like hammerbeams, i.e. N–S and S–
The result is very matter-of-fact.

ST PAUL, Pickley Green, Westleigh. 1846–7 by *W. Young*. Bu
by the Commissioners. (It cost £3,100.) Surprisingly pos
Commissioners in style. Nave and S aisle, S tower outside t
aisle, and chancel. Octagonal piers. Dec style, i.e. in cognizan
of the Pugin–Scott revolution.

ST PETER, Firs Lane, Westleigh. 1880–1 by *Paley & Austin* ar
one of their most thrilling churches in Lancashire. Brick wi
red sandstone dressings. Central tower with pyramid roof ar
a stone frieze below the top. The aisle windows are straigh
headed. The details are Dec throughout. Inside, the nave ar
chancel impress by their big timbers – hammerbeams in t
chancel, tie-beams in the nave, but the central tower stands
responds and arches built up (without any capitals) of bri
entirely, and a vault of brick ribs closes the view into the tow

ST THOMAS, Chapel Street. 1906–10 by *R. B. Preston*. A lar
church with a S tower. Very red brick. Dec details. Five-b
arcades with a transeptal widening of the fourth and fifth bay

KING STREET METHODIST CHURCH. 1870–1 by *C. O. Ellis*
of Liverpool. With a steeple and geometrical tracery.

TOWN HALL. 1904–7 by *J. C. Prestwich*. An exceptionally go
building, representational yet not showy. To the Market Pla

it has a front of seven bays with upper giant columns alternately blocked, a hipped roof, and a cupola. The portal has a big, almost semicircular pediment. In addition there is a separate l. angle bay with rather more Baroque decoration, and this leads to the side frontage, which is longer, in itself symmetrical, and, with shops to the street, less stately. N of the town hall, in the Market Place is an OBELISK with sunk panels which looks Georgian but dates from 1859.

LIBRARY and former Municipal College, Railway Road. 1894 by *J. C. Prestwich* and *J. H. Stephen*. Red brick and asymmetrical. A turret on the l., a big gable on the r., otherwise dormers. Cross-windows.

Mills close the views along many streets. The most monumental is ALDER MILL, just N of Chapel Street, a block of five storeys, of red and yellow brick and yellow terracotta. The date of the building is 1907; the architect was *Henthorn Scott*. There is a gatehouse with a parapet typical of the date, and a high tower with an adventurous top and a copper cupola.

BEDFORD HALL, at the s end of Hooton Lane. C17. Symmetrical, of stone, with two gables and the same number of lights to the windows l. and r. But the centre has the doorway not in the middle.

(GREENLANE END FARMHOUSE, Green Lane. C18 brick with a five-window front. Plaster ceiling in the hall. MHLG)

LEVENSHULME *see* MANCHESTER, p. 332

LIGHT OAKS HALL *see* GLAZEBURY

LIGHTSHAW HALL *see* GOLBORNE

LITHERLAND

3090

N of Bootle and indistinguishable from it.

ST PHILIP, Church Road. 1861–3 by *Gee*. Of small yellow stones. Still unaisled and with a transept – the tradition of the pre-archaeological decades of the early C19. The detail also is singularly ignorant. The way the spire starts as low as the ridge of the nave roof is but one example.

ENGLISH MARTYRS (R.C.), School Lane. 1935 by *L. A. G. Prichard*, brick, Romanesque, with a SW campanile.

LITTLEBOROUGH

9010

As the old houses in the hills are focused on Littleborough, so the churches in the hills are listed under Littleborough too.

HOLY TRINITY. 1818–20 by *Thomas Taylor* of Leeds. w tower with a spire recessed behind four not steep gables. Low l. and r. attachments with battlemented lean-to roofs. The side windows are high and of three lights, with intersecting tracery. The chancel is a different story. It has a higher roof and competently done Perp details. It is evidently the work of a major architect, and it is indeed by *Crowther*. It dates from 1889. Inside the nave three poor galleries.

CONGREGATIONAL CHAPEL, Victoria Street. 1876. Five bays with a pediment across. Doorway with Doric pilasters. A triple-arched opening above.

ST ANDREW, Dearnley. 1894. Chancel and chapel 1912 by *F. P. Oakley*.

ST BARNABAS, Shore. 1901 by *R. B. Preston*, and stone, not brick as he mostly used, and hence of greater dignity. Big s tower and ancillary rooms around its base. It is in its variety a successful group.

ST JAMES, Calderbrook. 1870 by *G. Shaw* of Saddleworth.* Square s steeple linked by broaches to an upper octagon, an unorthodox procedure. A two-bay s chapel E of the tower.

ST MARY (R.C.), Featherstall Road. 1863 by *Clegg & Knowles*.

In the little town and its environs stone predominates throughout. Many WEAVERS' COTTAGES will be noticed, recognizable by the long, many-mullioned upper windows. They are a feature specially characteristic of this area of Lancashire and the West Riding of Yorkshire.

TOWN HOUSE (N). 1798. A fine Georgian stone front of five bays with a three-bay pediment. The doorway has columns and a broken pediment, and the window above it some decoration. Elizabethan additions of 1915. Behind a WAREHOUSE with a wide loading-opening in the middle of each floor. The attachment on the l. is dated 1752, and the windows are still all mullioned.

OLD BENT HOUSE, off the Halifax Road (NE). Two dates: 1691 and 1620. A flat front with mullioned windows with thick glazing bars. They are of 4–4–2–4 lights above, of 6–6–6 below, with the doorway between the first and the second. It is this doorway which is dated 1691.

WINDY BANK FARMHOUSE, S of Old Bent House, at the start of Blackstone Edge Old Road. A fine front with two equal gables and one different. Mullioned windows. A more irregular back. On the façade the date 1635, at the back 1611.

* So Mr Buttress informs me.

STUBLEY OLD HALL, Stubley Brow (which is part of the road to Rochdale). A fine C17 house with two cross-gables at the end of the façade. The façade is interestingly windowed. The doorway is still in the medieval position. To its r. under the cross-gable is one window of five lights with two transoms, to its l., marking the hall, is a four-light window and then (for the high table) a six-light two-transomed one. The parlour under the other cross-gable has five lights and only one transom. Above, all smaller windows.

DEARNLEY OLD HALL, New Road, SE of the hospital. Flat, asymmetrical front with mullioned windows. Again the largest (six lights) is on the r. of the doorway marking the hall space.

SHORE HALL, NW of Shore, up Higher Shore Brow (WNW of Littleborough). The date is 1605. Again the doorway is in the old position, and again the hall space is made obvious, here by the only two-transomed windows, one of three lights, that for the high table end of five.

LITTLE CROSBY   3000

ST MARY (R.C.). 1845–7 by *Weightman & Hadfield* – not by Pugin. Just like an Anglican village parish church – a sign of the strength of Catholicism in this part of the country. A simple, straightforward building, already archaeologically accurate. The architects had been quick in learning the Pugin lesson. W tower with broach spire. Nave and aisle. Dec tracery. – MONUMENTS. William Blundell † 1854. With recumbent stone effigy in a tomb recess in the chancel. – Nicholas and Agnes Blundell † 1894 and 1890. Copper plaque in the Arts and Crafts style; in the porch. – Pleasant PRESBYTERY dated 1850.

CROSBY HALL. The house has recently been much reduced in size and is now as it was made to look in 1784–6. Stone with mid-pediment and a lunette and a Venetian window under. On the entrance side this seems interfered with in the Victorian period. The portico on one side of the house was brought in in 1955 from Claughton Hall near Garstang (North Lancashire). On the garden side is a wide, asymmetrically placed canted bay window. This corresponds to the handsome library inside and dates from 1815. SSE of the house is the chapel known as HARKIRK. It was built in 1889. In it a decorated STOUP dated 1668. To the house belongs a Late Classical LODGE of probably *c.* 1850 and another in the Tudor style probably of about the same time.

In the village street a COTTAGE dated 1669 with some mullioned windows.

LITTLE HULTON see WALKDEN

7000
LITTLE LEVER

ST MATTHEW. The former church was of 1791, the present one is by *Paley*,[*] 1865. Nave with a big roof. W porch and a big rose-window over. SE tower. Aisleless nave of wide span. All the tracery is of the plate variety and heavily detailed. All decoration – capitals, hood-mould stops, etc. – has been left undone.

LITTLE TOWN see CROFT

LITTLE WOOLDEN HALL see CULCHETH

LIVERPOOL

[*] Information kindly given me by Mr Buttress.

INTRODUCTION*

From the point of view of visual thrills Liverpool has one not shared by any of the major cities of England, the position on a really wide river – the Mersey at the tunnel is nearly three-quarters of a mile wide. On the other hand, compared with these other major cities the centre of Liverpool has proved unable to make the most of its position. It only occasionally gives you a sense of historical growth or of streets running with a visual purpose, and its centre, round St George's Hall, and the tunnel entrance, is confusing. Moreover, its past, stretching over centuries, appears hardly anywhere.

* Although it has already been said in the Foreword to this volume, it must be repeated here and with specific application to Liverpool. Without Mr Edward Hubbard's knowledge and help these pages on Liverpool would contain far less information and far more errors.

For, though there is in the whole present municipal area only one medieval church – at Childwall, still in a villagey setting – and only one manor house – the splendid timber-framed Speke Hall of the C15 to early C17 – Liverpool's development goes back to the Middle Ages.* The town grew on the peninsula between the river and the Pool of Liverpool, a tidal creek, now Canning Place. The first mention is c.1192, the first charter including a gild merchant 1229, the earliest evidence of a mayor 1352. About 1235 a castle was built, where there is now Derby Square. A little earlier the streets of the town had been laid out. The seven original streets are Dale Street and Water Street, Tithebarn Street and Chapel Street, and, running across, Old Hall Street, Exchange Flags, High Street, and Castle Street ending at the castle. At the river end of Water Street Sir John Stanley built himself a tower in 1406. So the Stanleys, now Lords Derby, were great already in the C15; so were the Molyneuxs, now Lords Sefton. Near the tower was the parish church of St Nicholas, a building of c.1360, still existing but totally altered. The chapel or church of St Mary-at-Kay was earlier (it seems, of the C13) but not a trace of it is left. In any case Liverpool became a parish only at the end of the C17, in 1699. Until then the churches had been chapels of ease of Walton. The so-called seven ancient streets made a perfectly comprehensible pattern, but growth after the Middle Ages has not extended that pattern materially.

Liverpool's growth began seriously only in the later C17. Population in the early C17 is calculated as about 2,000, in 1700 as about 6,000, in 1801 it was nearly 80,000. The first cargo from America is recorded for 1648. The trade was especially with the West Indies and Virginia and dealt with sugar, tobacco, and cotton. To this, early in the C18, came the slave trade which flourished in the later C18 and came to an end in 1807. Already in 1698 Celia Fiennes speaks of 'London in miniature' and of 'houses high and even' and people 'very well dressed and of good fashion'. In c.1709–21 the first dock was built, in the creek. The upper

---

* Of prehistoric remains we have THE CALDERSTONES, now housed in the City Museum. Six of the stones had previously been set up in a circle in a small enclosure outside the Menlove entrance to Calderstones Park, after the destruction of the original monument to which they belonged in the C19. The six stones appear to have formed components in a megalithic passage grave covered by a round barrow. The surviving stones are of interest chiefly for the art which is pecked on their surfaces and includes cup and ring motifs, spirals, representations of human feet, and a possible representation of a bronze or copper halberd. These designs link the Calderstones with art on passage graves in Ireland and Brittany.

reaches of the creek were thereby put out of operation. They became Paradise Street and Whitechapel. In the course of the C18 the number of ships using the port in a year rose from 102 to 4,746.

But the C19 and early C20 became the Golden Age for Liverpool. It was only then that it established itself as England's prime Atlantic port. Further docks were built in 1734, 1753, 1767, 1773, 1784, c.1785, 1796, and so on, into the C19. The latest and largest of the Liverpool docks is actually outside Liverpool, at Bootle, just as Trafford Park is outside Manchester at Stretford. The prosperity of the C18 found its official expression in the Bluecoat School of 1716–17, very large for Early Georgian schools, and 26 in *John Wood*'s Town Hall of 1749–54. For ecclesiastical archi- 30 tecture Liverpool has managed to destroy all traces of the four new churches of 1700–75: St Peter Church Street of 1700, St George Derby Square of c.1730, St Paul St Paul's Square of 1763, and St John next to St George's Hall of 1775. For private architecture one has to go to what is now the suburbs and was then in the country. C17 survivals are rare. Besides the latest parts of Speke Hall there are only a small part of Croxteth Hall, of c.1575, Tue Brook House of 1615, two houses at West Derby, a cottage in Aigburth Hall Road, and Toxteth Chapel of c.1618 but visually nearly all 1774. For the early C18 Croxteth Hall is large, and its façade of 1702 is curiously restless and 23 crowded. Woolton Hall must once have been similar in character, and the Unitarian Chapel at Gateacre of 1700 precisely is so modest that it has no architectural features.

More spectacular developments had to wait for the last thirty or forty years of the Georgian era. Now a new 'west end' was built E of the centre, starting in brick in the 1780s with Rodney Street and ending in ashlar in Percy Street and Gambier Terrace. Con- 46 currently villas were built outside the town, in the C18 especially on the Everton ridge, but also in other parts. At Everton there are now only traces, but 'Allerton' by *Thomas Harrison*, Allerton Hall, Sandown Hall Wavertree, the house which is the core of the Mount Olive Hospital, and *Robert Adam*'s part of Woolton Hall are (more or less) surviving examples. New churches became neces- sary too, near the centre and far away from the centre, the former represented by St James Toxteth of 1774–5, the Catholic St Peter of 1788, and Holy Trinity St Anne Street of 1790–2, and the latter by Wavertree parish church of 1794. But of these decades also, i.e. of before 1820, more was destroyed than kept: Christ Church Hunter Street of 1797, the Newington Chapel of 1799, St Mark

Upper Duke Street of 1808, the Brunswick Methodist Chapel of 1810, and St Andrew Renshaw Street of 1815* – it is a disgraceful record, and (to anticipate) the demolition of churches goes on. An interesting sign of religious needs or their absence is the fact that proportionately so many more Catholic churches survive and remain in use than Anglican.

For the years from *c*.1810 to *c*.1830 the tally of survival and disappearance of church buildings in or near the centre is particularly poignant. The following six remain: St Nicholas, the Catholic church, of 1808–12, St Patrick Park Place Toxteth (Catholic) of 1821–7, St Luke St Luke's Place of 1811–31, St Andrew Rodney Street (Presbyterian) of 1823–4, the mortuary chapel in the cemetery by the cathedral of *c*.1825–6, the latter three by the younger *John Foster*, Corporation Surveyor and the leading Liverpool architect of those years, and St Bride Percy Street of 1830–1.‡ But *Rickman*'s St Philip Hardman Street of 1816, St Martin Blenheim Street of 1825, St David Brownlow Hill of 1826, the Presbyterian Church on Mount Pleasant, *Foster*'s St Catherine Abercromby Square of 1829–31, and *Rickman*'s St Jude Hardwick Street of 1831 have been allowed to disappear – the last-named only in 1966 and St Catherine just as recently and especially scandalously.§

In what is now the suburbs churches now multiplied. Everton received St George, a grand Gothic church by *Rickman*, in 1812–14, and the same architect built St Michael-in-the-Hamlet Toxteth in 1814–15. Their importance will be pointed out presently. St Mary Walton, the former parish church of Liverpool, received a new tower in 1828–32, St John Knotty Ash and St Mary Kirkdale are both of 1835 and both Gothic. The Wesleyan Chapel in Upper Stanhope Street, Toxteth of 1827 is Doric, the former Methodist Chapel at Everton of *c*. 1839–40 is Doric too.

Rickman's two surviving churches are of much more than local interest, because they are built with as many cast-iron parts as could possibly be introduced. This was due to John Cragg, the

* St Michael Upper Pitt Street of 1816 was the victim of wartime bombing.
‡ The following is the LIST OF CORPORATION SURVEYORS after Foster: *Joseph Franklin* 1835, *John Weightman* 1848, *E. R. Robson* 1865, *Thomas Shelmerdine* 1871. He retired in 1914 and was succeeded by *Albert D. Jenkins*, with the new job of Director of Housing given to Shelmerdine's deputy for housing, *T. Fletcher Turton*. Turton was followed by *E. G. Badger* in 1919 and (*Sir*) *Lancelot Keay* in 1925. Keay became City Architect as well, in 1938. Keay's successor is *Ronald Bradbury* (since 1948). To these names must be added that of *John Brodie*, City Engineer from 1898 to 1926.
§ *Foster*'s finest secular building, the Custom House of 1829–31, is a war loss.

on-master who made the suggestion and insisted, not wholly to Rickman's delight. Round St Michael he built some houses too, again using cast iron everywhere. Rickman complied but was critical. He said: 'His ironwork is too stiff in his head to bend to any beauty.'

Yet the cast-iron tracery, especially in St George Everton, is extremely pretty, though of course Georgian-pretty rather than 15-pretty. Rickman may have felt this more and more strongly as he grew older. For he developed into an architectural scholar – his *Attempt to Discriminate the Styles of English Architecture* of 1817 is a milestone, and we owe it the terms Early English, Decorated, and Perpendicular – and some of his late churches are archeologically more accurate and serious than those of other architects. In fact Liverpool was blamed more than once by *The Ecclesiologist* for the reactionary, un-ritualistic layout of its churches in the second third of the century.

Liverpool, as we have seen, had about 80,000 inhabitants in 1801. In 1821 there were 118,972, in 1831 205,572, in 1841 286,487. Prosperity grew by leaps and bounds, as Liverpool supplied the cotton for Lancashire. In addition passenger traffic grew, with liners coming into operation in the forties. With population increase and spatial expansion went a new phenomenon: an ambition to civilize the town, to make it culturally worth while. The centre in these endeavours was William Roscoe, co-founder of the Liverpool Society for the Promotion of Painting and Design, the Botanic Garden, and the Liverpool Royal Institution. He was the son of a publican and market gardener, himself an attorney and later an unsuccessful banker. He also was Unitarian. He established the possibility of a man of international reputation in letters belonging to a provincial city. His book on Lorenzo the Magnificent came out in 1795. Translations into German, French, and Italian were published in 1796–9. His book on Leo X bears the date 1805, and translations into the same three languages were at once undertaken.

The Lyceum Club was built in 1800–2, the architect being that arch-Grecian *Thomas Harrison* of Chester (who, however, also did the delightful fancy-Gothic spire of St Nicholas, the parish church, in 1811–15). Then, in 1815–16, the Wellington Rooms followed, in 1835–7 the Mechanics Institution (now Liverpool Institution High School for Boys) by *A. H. Holme*, in 1836–7 the Medical Institution by *C. Rampling*, and in 1841, after winning the competition in 1839, young *Harvey Lonsdale Elmes* submitted his revised plans for St George's Hall. In 1836 Liverpool had

needed new Assize Courts and wanted a Civic Hall, after Birming
53 ham had begun hers in 1832. St George's Hall, as finally completed
after Elmes's death by *C. R. Cockerell* in 1856, combines both
functions and remains the most powerful and original monument
of the Grecian mode in all England. The plan is most ingenious
in its perfect simplicity and the use of Grecian motifs very bold
for a building so far from the straightforward Grecian temple plan
54 adopted by Hansom at Birmingham. Cockerell's Concert Room
with its cast caryatids is superb, as is his other Liverpool work
55 the branch building for the Bank of England in Castle Street
(1845–8). No-one in England could to the same extent be
Cockerell both classical and personal.

Jesse Hartley on the other hand, as great a man in his own way
as Cockerell, managed to endow the Grecian with a sense of the
cyclopean, the primeval, which is also unparalleled. His Albert
52 Dock, with its squat Tuscan columns, may be inspired by Hardwick's St Katherine's Dock in London (and *Hardwick* designed
the Albert Dock Office himself), but the walls, the gatepiers, the
gate lodges are entirely Hartley's and one of the finest examples
anywhere in Europe of romantic *architecture parlante*, i.e. of
expressing the strength of resistance to water and the bulk of
ships. To pull down the Albert Dock would be a black disgrace.
The same sense of the cyclopean imposed itself on the Everton
Water Tower of 1853 etc., and the result is the most imposing of
59 its kind in England. Walton Prison of 1848–55 was no doubt
designed with a similar aim in view, but the use of Norman with
its Keep associations is a much more naïve kind of *architecture
parlante* than that of Hartley and *Thomas Duncan*, the engineer
of the water works. The commercial warehouses round Bath
Street are impressive too, though more by bulk than by any
architectural finesse.

St George's Hall established the classical style so firmly in
Liverpool that to its N the whole series of public buildings – the
one attempt at giving dignity to the setting of St George's Hall –
is classical, even as late as the seventies (Art Gallery) and the
56 eighties (Sessions House). The best of the group is the Picton
Reading Room of 1875–9 by *Cornelius Sherlock*. But the Gothic
could not be excluded entirely, and the same *Elmes* to whom we
owe St George's Hall, in 1840–3 did the Liverpool Collegiate High
School at Everton in Gothic. But Gothic never assumed the same
importance at Liverpool as it did at Manchester, although one
57 might well argue that the most memorable of the office buildings
in Liverpool, Oriel Chambers by *Peter Ellis* (1864), is designed

on the Gothic principle of slender stone mullions and large expanses of glass. Oriel Chambers belongs to the small number of buildings pioneering the principles of the modern office building. Architecturally among the finest of the office buildings are those in an Italian Gothic to Quattrocento such as Hargreaves Building and Richmond Buildings in Chapel Street (the latter now de- 63 molished), both of 1861 and both by *Picton*.

It is right and proper that office buildings come first in a conspectus of Victorian architecture in Liverpool; for this is where the money was made. It was spent on houses in the suburbs, and it is a great shame that Liverpool has allowed three houses by *Shaw* and one by *Scott* to disappear. By *Shaw* there is now only the vicarage of St Agnes, Sefton Park, one of his best houses and 81 hence one to be preserved at all costs. St Agnes itself is by far the most beautiful Victorian church of Liverpool. It is by *Pearson* and shows him at his very best. It is of brick, in the C13 style, vaulted throughout, and has one of those E ends of complex grouping and spatial interplay in which Pearson excelled. St Agnes, which dates from 1883–5, is an epitome of Late Victorian nobility in church design. The change from the grosser High Victorian, as illustrated in an extreme form by *Henry Sumners*'s demonstratively unbeautiful All Souls Collingwood Street Everton of 1870–2 and Prince's Gate Baptist Church Toxteth of 1879– 81, to the restraint of the Late Victorian can be observed very early at Liverpool: in *Bodley*'s St John Tue Brook, which is as early as 1868–70. Close by Pearson's St Agnes is the Sefton Park Unitarian Church by the Manchester architect *Percy Worthington*, and perhaps his best work, specially successful in the composition of church, hall, and ancillary building, and again not far is *Leonard Stokes*'s St Clare Sefton Park. The Unitarian Church is of 1896–9, St Clare of 1888–90, an amazingly early date for what it is. How- 85 ever, Stokes was born in 1858, and that explains the profound difference between St Clare and, say, St Agnes. St Agnes is the climax of the faith in the motifs and elements of the C13, even if they are handled freely; for Stokes the Gothic ensemble was no longer a commitment. His ensemble is entirely his and what motifs come in, both externally and internally, such as the round arches of the aisle passages, the balconies or boxes over them, the sheer E wall with the broad window high up, the fenestration on the S side, are admitted exclusively for the sake of that ensemble.*

The three churches just discussed all have Sefton Park as

---

* The best local firm of architects of these years is *Aldridge & Deacon*, inspired by Pearson and a parallel to Paley & Austin in other parts of Lancashire.

their eponym. Sefton Park is one of the three most important public parks made in the mid C19. Prince's Park was the first. It is by *Paxton* and was his first independent job. Birkenhead Park across the Mersey followed immediately and more than Prince's Park made his international fame as a designer of parks. Sefton Park is of 1867–72 by the Parisian *André*, with *L. Hornblower* of Liverpool. Stanley Park Anfield with its bold architectural features by *E. R. Robson* (who later designed the London board schools) is by *Kemp* and was also begun in 1867.

The late C19 and early C20 were a period of boom for Liverpool. Its population was 685,000 in 1901, and its port was the largest in England except for London. The architectural expression is
2 the Pierhead, built on a covered-up dock. The Dock Offices Building (1907) and the Royal Liver Building (1908–10) are swagger though coarse. *W. Aubrey Thomas*, the architect of the Royal Liver, is as corny in the Tower Building opposite, but *Arnold Thornely*, the architect of the dock offices, in the Bluecoat
89 School at Wavertree in 1903–6 (*Briggs, Wolstenholme & Thornely*) has shown a much more discriminating sense of display. These three and *Matear & Simon*'s Cotton Exchange of 1905–6 have few Edwardian parallels outside London. *Norman Shaw* also did an office building in those years, for the White Star Line, and *John Francis Doyle*, a disciple of Shaw and his collaborator
86 on the Pacific Steam Building, did the excellent Royal Insurance in Dale Street in 1896–1903. In this style, though of course in a minor key, are several branch banks for Martins Bank. But for the small-scale public building of Late Victorian and Edwardian style the libraries by *Thomas Shelmerdine*, city surveyor from 1871 to 1912, are exemplary – lively and varied. Subtlety one must not expect; for subtlety in Edwardian terms, guided by Parisian classicism, one has to go to the few buildings by *Sir Charles Reilly*, the Students' Union of 1910–13 and the chancel of
93 Wavertree church of 1911, with its exquisite management of the vestry etc.

Quite apart from the demonstrations of prosperity and the
87 blandishments of classicism stands Liverpool's most famous
& C20 building, *Sir Giles Gilbert Scott*'s Anglican Cathedral, won
88 in competition in 1901 and largely re-designed in 1909–10. It is a masterpiece of its own kind, but that kind is still essentially late C19 not C20. It is Gothic, and Gothic treated as freely as Stokes had done. Major elements such as the tower and the transept portals are very effective indeed – the tower especially is a great asset to the skyline of the city. Functionally much can be

ojected to, and the fitments and the furnishings are on the whole
eak.

Lutyens's Catholic Cathedral was initiated in 1930 and stopped
hen the Second World War came. It was to be enormous in size,
d the crypt which was built is indeed enormous. The style
ould have been a personal, rather capricious, blend of classicism
th Byzantine allusions. It is however undoubtedly the greatest
onument of the inter-war years, in its unjustified optimism and
refusal to accept the new style of architecture. *H.J. Rowse*, who
signed the architectural appurtenances of the Mersey Tunnel
1925–34 and whose *chef d'œuvre* is Martins Bank of 1927–32,
so believed in Classicism, of an École des Beaux Arts kind
bibed in America rather than Paris, but in all the decorative
ements of his buildings shows himself indebted to the modern-
ic features of the Paris Exhibition of 1925.

The International Modern of the 1930s found its way into
verpool by means of the municipal blocks of flats built under
e direction of the Director of Housing and later City Architect
r *Lancelot Keay*. He followed; he did not lead. The L.C.C. had
ne before, in the use of long sweeping balconies and long bands
windows. Liverpool has a highly interesting record of muni-
al flats from the end of the C19 onwards, incidentally with
ncrete introduced in the Eldon Street flats in 1905 by the City
gineer *J. A. Brodie*.* This will have to be pieced together on
rambulations. Brodie was a remarkable man in other respects
well. His was the conception of Queen's Drive, a ring road for
verpool, and the wide roads radiating from it. The beginnings
te from 1904.

As for the total acceptance of the style of the C20, Liverpool had
wait long. Only in the last ten years has a transformation taken
ace, and no longer in the direction of the International Modern
the 1930s but in that of the new individualism and the new
pressionism of the 1960s. The major monument is *Frederick
bberd*'s Catholic Cathedral, circular, with a ring of chapels and 98
trances and a high tapering lantern, fully successful in its main
ace but aggressive and restless in the contrasting forms of
apels and entrances. The treatment of the Lutyens fragment and
e ancillary buildings is very successful again, ingenious and well
aled down from the bulk of the cathedral itself. The university
s been the principal client for modern architecture. They
fused to accept one architect and hence one style and preferred –

* They exist no longer. The technique was most interesting. Each room had
lls, floor, and ceiling consisting of one pre-cast slab.

like e.g. Yale – to provide themselves with the maximum variet
of effects – from *Yorke, Rosenberg & Mardall*'s impeccable an
neutral Electrical Engineering Building and *Sir Basil Spence*
interestingly planned and un-gimmicky Physics Building to th
deliberately outrageous Sports Building by *Denys Lasdun*, doub
painful because it refuses to blend not only with the designs
its contemporaries but also with the Georgian square at whos
corner it stands. It is true, it was unfortunate that the Universi
of Liverpool should have been started in the Georgian 'west en
– really east end – of Liverpool and by its growth was bound
destroy the best domestic quarter of the town, but where pr
servation had been decreed, such as in Abercromby Squar
architects could have been expected to show some regard for th
past. Meanwhile of course the university itself has behaved
badly as some of the architects and has decided to pull down f
its new Senate House the side of the square with *Foster*'s porti
of St Catherine. The most successful of the new buildings f
the university are those which appear as a group and not
97 separate items (Arts, Social Studies, and Law by *B. & N. Wes*
wood, Piet & Partners). Equally successful, because again a grou
is Carnatic Halls, the new halls of residence, at Mossley Hill, l
Manning & Clamp.

Modern architecture is as much a matter of visual planning
of detailing, and where planning is not done on a sufficient scal
fragmentation is the result, especially at present, when mo
architects, if left to themselves, contrive sculptural monumen
too strong in their display of personality to be acceptable neigl
bours.

The emphasis on planning must stand as the end of this intr
duction, also in its importance for Liverpool as a whole. Liverpo
in the fifteen years after the war could have laid foundations for
city both better-looking and better-working. Many opportuniti
have been lost. Finally in 1961 *Walter Bor* was appointed planni
officer and *Graeme Shankland* planning consultant. What of the
schemes may come to fruition remains to be seen. Beginning
have been made.

FURTHER READING

The main book is J. A. Picton's *Memorials of Liverpool*, 2nd ed
1875, but the book which users of this volume are recommende
to buy, look at, and read, because it is well written and we
illustrated, is Quentin Hughes's *Seaport*, 1964. It is also st
worth while to browse in Sir Charles Reilly's *Some Liverpo*

Streets and Buildings, 1921, with much shrewd criticism. As for
the history of Liverpool, *The Story of Liverpool*, à propos an
exhibition in 1951, is only a brochure, but it is excellently done
and quite adequate for most users of *The Buildings of England*. If
a larger book is preferred, there is Ramsey Muir, *A History of
Liverpool*, 1907. Peter Fleetwood-Hesketh's *Lancashire Architectural Guide* is as excellent for Liverpool's buildings as it is for
the whole of Lancashire.

THE CENTRE

CHURCHES

OUR LADY AND ST NICHOLAS, Pierhead. The parish church
of Liverpool. It was originally built c.1360 as a chapel of ease
to Walton. Liverpool became a parish only in 1699. Before 1360
there was however a chapel at Liverpool, called St Mary-at-Kay.
Nothing is left of this, nor is there anything left of the St Nicholas of the c14. The oldest part of the church is the steeple, which
dates from 1811–15 and is by *Thomas Harrison* of Chester.
Square substructure with panelled buttresses. Delightful spire
on an open recessed octagonal lower stage. Flying buttresses
connect it to angle pinnacles. The church itself was destroyed
in the Second World War and replaced by a sadly conventional
Gothic building, by *Edward C. Butler*, completed in 1952. –
PLATE. Flagon of 1729. – MONUMENT. Robert Hawkinson
† 1829. By *W. Spence*. Bust on a pillar in relief. On the base fine
relief with the three Cardinal Virtues.

ST LUKE, St Luke's Place. Designed in 1802 by *John Foster Sen.*
and built by his son, *John Foster Jun.*, in 1811–31. He made
certain alterations in 1827. A stately, ashlar-faced building
with w tower, broad nave, and lower chancel of four bays, a
liturgical anomaly at a date earlier than the propaganda of the
Ecclesiological Society. The style is Perp, with very large
windows, separated by buttresses carrying big pinnacles. The
w tower is amply decorated and also with big pinnacles. L. and
r. of it low porches, lower than the nave. The church is excellently placed at the end of Bold Street. It was gutted during the
Second World War and is now open to the sky. Originally it
had a plaster vault.

ST MARY (R.C.), Highfield Street. 1948–53 by *Weightman &
Bullen*, replacing a war-damaged church by *A. W. N. Pugin*.
Brick, square, without a tower. Square interior with a coffered

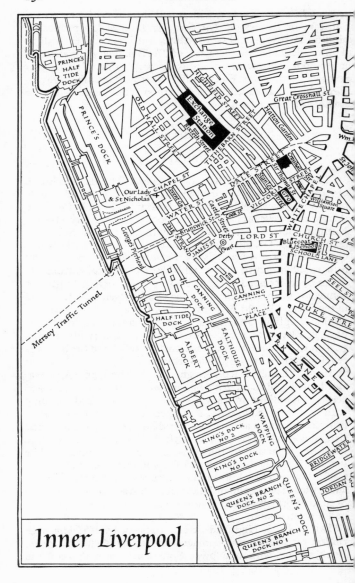

Inner Liverpool

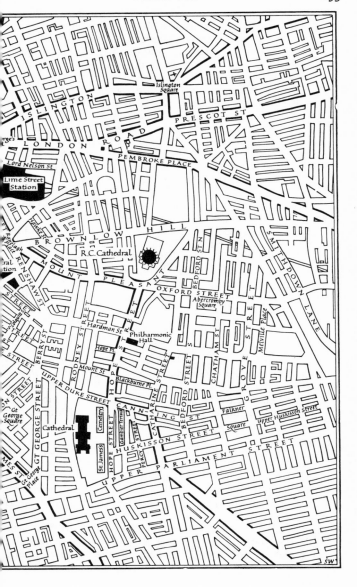

concrete ceiling and plain arched arcades. Chancel with high lighting from the w, sanctuary with tall side windows.

ST NICHOLAS (R.C.), Hawke Street. 1808–12 by *John Bird*. Brick. The front with two staircases into a one-storeyed porch. The long side clumsy, with high three-light Perp windows. The five-light E window may be a remodelling. Battlements and pinnacles. The interior is much more rewarding, especially the delightful two w galleries, accessible by two staircases and the upper one far recessed. All this is very thin and fragile-looking. The nave is wide and the chancel shallow and separated from the nave by a tripartite arch with pendants. Thin ribs on the chancel vault. – MONUMENTS. William White † 1832. Tablet with portrait in profile. – Thomas Pensick † 1836. Tablet with Faith by an altar. Signed by *Peter Turnerelli*.

ST PETER (R.C.), Seel Street. 1788, with the sanctuary enlarged in 1843. White rendered exterior with arched windows and a handsome, wholly domestic doorway in the N transept. It has recessed slim Greek Doric columns. The chancel is hidden behind a brick house-front. The interior has a flat ceiling and three wooden galleries. The giant pilasters and shallow tunnel-vault of the chancel with its skylight may be of 1843. – PAINTING. Altarpiece with the Nations of the World doing homage to St Peter. By *Edward du Jardin*, 1845. – MONUMENTS. Rev. Archibald McDonald † 1814 and Rev. William Tarleton † 1816, both tablets with an urn, and both by *S. Gibson*. – Rev. Thomas Robinson † 1837 by *C. M. Seddon*. Tablet with kneeling Faith. – Rev. Vincent Glover † 1840. Tablet with frontally kneeling female figure by an urn. Also by *Seddon*. – Rev. James Appleton † 1847. Relief with a priest anointing a sick person.

ST VINCENT DE PAUL (R.C.), St James's Street. 1856–7 by *E. W. Pugin*. Front with an eight-light window and the oddest little open bell-turret. Uninteresting interior with aisle and large clerestory. Short chancel with a nine-light window. Early C14 detail.

GUSTAF ADOLFS KYRKA (Swedish Seamen's Church), Park Lane. 1883–4 by *W. D. Caröe*. Brick, a modest but lively asymmetrical façade. Stepped gables. The centre of the church is octagonal. Inside it has been divided horizontally (the church itself is now on the upper floor) and the exposed brickwork is painted.

GREAT GEORGE STREET CONGREGATIONAL CHURCH, excellently placed at the sharp corner of Great George Street and Nelson Street. 1840–1 by *Joseph Franklin*, the younger Foster's successor as Corporation Surveyor. Late Classical, with a semicircular porch of Corinthian columns and a dome on a windowless drum. The sides have giant pilasters and arched windows in two tiers.

METHODIST CENTRAL HALL, Renshaw Street. 1904–5 by *Bradshaw & Gass*. Red brick and yellow terracotta with a big domed corner tower. Touches of the Byzantine. Art Nouveau detail, especially in the long wing along Renshaw Street. Reilly calls it all 'gim-crackery'.

PUBLIC BUILDINGS

ST GEORGE'S HALL. The new town hall in Birmingham had 53 been begun in 1832. In 1836 Liverpool decided to do likewise. A competition was held in 1839 and *Harvey Lonsdale Elmes*, aged only 25, won. It was for a concert hall to be built by public subscription. In 1840 a competition was held for assize courts, and Elmes came first. The concert hall did not receive subscriptions as easily as expected, and so the city took it over and decided to build one building for both functions. *Franklin*, the corporation surveyor, was to build it, but Elmes protested, and Franklin backed his claims. Elmes's finally revised plans are of 1841. Elmes died in 1847 and *C. R. Cockerell* and the engineer *Sir Robert Rawlinson* finished the building. It was completed in 1856. So, while the brief for the Birmingham town hall was extremely simple, that for St George's Hall was complex, and the way Elmes has fulfilled it is superb. Thanks to the challenge he produced the freest neo-Grecian building in England and one of the finest in the world. As complex and yet as simple as the plan – the great concert hall with the two assize courts to its N and S and long corridors along the E and W sides – is the elevation. It is Grecian, but not as basic as say the British Museum with its even columniation hiding what goes on behind. Elmes went to Berlin and Munich to study Schinkel and Klenze, but his result is all his – a varying of external features according to internal uses. As one faces the great S portico one expects a building of Grecian proportions and nothing as long and relatively narrow as St George's Hall is. The S portico has eight Corinthian columns and is two columns deep. The pediment sculpture, representing Britannia with Commerce and the Arts, was designed by *Cockerell* with help from *Alfred Stevens* and was executed by *W. G. Nicholl*. It has unfortunately been removed, the stonework having become

unsafe. But the s portico is not the main entrance. This, with
the main portico, is in the middle of one of the long sides, the E
side. This portico is of thirteen bays with giant Corinthian
columns and an attic, not a pediment. To the l. and r. are
windowless recessed parts with relief panels on the high plinth.
The panels are by *Stirling Lee*, *Conrad Dressler*, and *Charles J.
Allen* (1894). They are framed by the lowest parts of giant
pilasters, which above this zone become free-standing square
pillars. The outer bays are blank and solid. Behind the portico
are three doorways, one large and two small. All the details are
Grecian, but very restrained. For statues see St George's
Plateau. The portico doorways lead into a narrow corridor,
and then directly into the Great Hall. The opposite, W, side is
clearly the back. It came very close to St John's church, which
exists no longer. Yet, though flatter, it is as dignified as the E
façade. It is twenty-nine bays wide. The angle bays and the
whole fifteen-bay centre have giant pilasters. In the centre, as
in the side parts of the façade, they turn into free-standing
pillars, but here only on the second floor. Behind is the clerestory of the hall. Above rises a high, long attic.

The N side has a generous apse with attached columns. This
belongs to the Concert Room. The interior should be approached from the grand portico on the E side. One has then
on the l. and r. a vista along one of the two tunnel-vaulted
corridors which accompany the whole of both long sides of the
building and, crossing the corridor, is at once in the Great Hall.
This is flanked by red granite columns which carry a mighty
tunnel-vault inspired by Blouet's reconstruction of the Baths
of Caracalla, published in 1828. This is made of hollow blocks,
a structural device introduced by *Sir Robert Rawlinson*, the
engineer. Between the columns are arches, and from them to
the outside walls run short transverse tunnel-vaults. The niches
thus created, five E and five W, are filled in by the corridor in
their lowest part, but there are balconies or a gallery above the
corridors. The colouring of the decoration is somewhat sombre,
but that only adds to the grandeur of the hall. The floor is of
Minton's tiles, mostly brown and strong blue, and the design
especially of the figure panels owes something to *Alfred Stevens*.
But it is said that Prince Albert's mentor, *Gruner* of Dresden,
also had something to do with the floor. Between the columns
are STATUES of worthies. They are (chronologically) William
Roscoe by *Chantrey*, seated; George Stephenson by *John Gibson*, 1851, also seated, but in Roman garb and much less easy

in the drapery and animated in the head than Chantrey's; Sir Robert Peel by *Noble*, 1852; Archdeacon Brooks by *Benjamin Spence*, 1856; Sir W. Brown by *MacDowell*, 1858; Joseph Mayer by *G. Fontana*, 1869; Dean McNeile by *G. G. Adams*, 1871; S. R. Graves by *Fontana*, 1875; E. Whitley by *A. Bruce Joy*, 1895. Of the time of the completion of the hall by *Cockerell* are the BRONZE DOORS, the CHANDELIERS, and the ORGAN, on granite columns and two Baroque atlantes. The organ was placed by Cockerell in such a way that it interrupts the view from the hall to the adjoining room, a view deemed important by Elmes. The S end of the hall opens in a Robert Adam way, tripartite with architrave and open lunette, to the adjoining CROWN COURT. Beyond the organ at the N end is the CIVIL COURT. The two courts are of the same size but differ in design. The Civil Court has a coved ceiling, whereas its counterpart is tunnel-vaulted and has fewer granite columns. Beyond the courts are the two ENTRANCE HALLS, S decidedly disappointing, as it leads from the temple portico dead against a blank wall. There are however columns in the corners, two in each of them. The N entrance is more spacious and has Greek Doric columns on the landing level and a Greek Doric ambulatory at that level round the semicircle. In the axis STATUE of Henry Booth, engineer and inventor of the Booth coupling, by *W. Theed*. The coupling is duly carved and a scroll with a locomotive drawn on. Of other rooms the GRAND JURY ROOM above the S entrance hall has a fine ceiling, but the best of the whole interior is still to come, the CONCERT ROOM, above the 54 N entrance. It is internally wholly by *Cockerell* – circular with a balcony carried by maidens. The material they are made of is still unrecognized. They are hollow and cast; for there are only two types repeating. They carry a balcony which curves forward between each pair. Beautiful cast-iron trellis railing. The walls are wood-panelled, the friezes etc. of papier-mâché. The ceiling is arranged with radial panels. Attached columns on the platform. The cresting of the platform front is cast-iron too. In the frieze are medallions with names of the most deserving composers. They are a remarkable selection: Handel and Haydn on the platform, Mozart and Beethoven immediately adjoining, and Mendelssohn in the axis of the semicircle. Among the others are Bishop and Wilby, Arne and Spohr.

ST GEORGE'S PLATEAU and ST JOHN'S GARDEN. The gardens to the W were terraced by *Shelmerdine* following the demolition of St John's church. Several MONUMENTS are placed here, in the centre Gladstone by *Sir Thomas Brock*, 1904, bronze with two allegorical bronze figures below. Below this monument that to the King's Liverpool Regiment, Britannia and soldiers, 1905 by *Sir W. Goscombe John*. Also statues of William Rathbone 1899, Sir Arthur Bower Forwood 1903, and Canon T. Major Lester 1907, all by *George Frampton*, and Alexander Balfour 1889 by *A. Bruce Joy* and Monsignor James Nugent 1905 by *F. W. Pomeroy*.

The plateau to the E has in its middle the CENOTAPH, 1930 by *Lionel Budden*; the bronze sculpture, especially the long reliefs, one with marching soldiers, the other with mourners, is by *H. Tyson Smith*. To the l. and r. are two pairs of recumbent bronze lions by *Nicholl*, 1855. The principal MONUMENTS are two equestrian statues, Queen Victoria and Prince Albert by *Thomas Thorneycroft*, 1870 and 1866. In the centre of the wide steps of St George's Hall is a statue of Disraeli, 1886 by *C. B. Birch*, moved to its present position in 1927 to make way for the Cenotaph. At the corner of the building Major General Earle, 1887 by *Birch*. To the N is the MONUMENT to Wellington, a Tuscan column with the figure on a little top cupola much as the Duke of York's column in London. It is by *G. A. Lawson* of Glasgow and was completed as late as 1863. The base has battle-scenes in relief, also by Lawson. To the w of the column is the STEBLE FOUNTAIN with bronze figures of the four seasons. This is of 1879 by *W. Cunliffe*.

THE WILLIAM BROWN STREET GROUP. This was a highly commendable civic enterprise. It was for once felt that *noblesse oblige*, and that buildings had to be created here to form an appropriate foil for St George's Hall. They are consequently mostly classical and remarkably correct and restrained for their dates and are from E to w as follows:

SESSIONS HOUSE. 1882–4 by *F. & G. Holme*. Free classic style. Portico of paired columns. The two frontal atlantes l. and r. of the window above the doorway show up the real date. Charming Italian Renaissance staircase hall with a series of little saucer-domes. The room on the l. has panelling and rich stucco in the late C17 style.

WALKER ART GALLERY. 1874–7 by *Sherlock & Vale*. Not large, and with a single-storey façade. So Grecian that it could easily be mistaken for contemporary with Barry's early Manchester Art Gallery. Portico with Corinthian columns and pediment. To the l. and r. stone STATUES of Raphael and Michelangelo, poor, by *Warrington Wood*. The building w extended at the back by *C. Sherlock* in 1882–4 and again in 1931–3 by *Sir Arnold Thornely (Briggs & Thornely)*, when also the entrance hall and staircase were remodelled.

PICTON READING ROOM. 1875–9 by *Cornelius Sherlock*. 56 Semicircular front with detached Corinthian columns. The semicircle was chosen to hide the fact that the axis of the row of buildings here breaks. It is an ingenious and completely successful device. Behind the semicircle is a domed rotunda. The Hornby Library at the back, with Edwardian Imperial interior decoration, is by *Shelmerdine*. The façade is attached on the r. to the art gallery, on the l. to the William Brown Library.

WILLIAM BROWN LIBRARY AND MUSEUM. 1857–60. Designed by *Thomas Allom*, but modified by the Corporation Architect *John Weightman*. Seventeen bays wide with a six-column Corinthian portico with pediment, modelled on St George's Hall. The entrance is up a wide staircase. The building was gutted in the Second World War and reconstructed by *R. Bradbury*, the City Architect. He also alas added on top of the building and thereby abolished the fine skyline.

COLLEGE OF TECHNOLOGY AND MUSEUM EXTENSION, the front to Byrom Street. This alone is not classical, but Edwardian Imperial. *E. W. Mountford* was the architect, and the building took from 1896 to 1902. The façade is convex in plan and has on the second floor coupled attached columns. The doorway is flanked by the typical Liverpool alternatingly blocked columns. These appear again, huge in scale, in the end bays towards St George's Hall, high up and flanking recesses semicircular in plan with windows, a splendid motif. Edwardian Baroque interiors with Art Nouveau touches.

TOWN HALL, at the N end of Castle Street. 1749–54 by the elder 30 *John Wood* of Bath. An ornate building of ashlar stone, nine by nine bays. In 1789–92 *James Wyatt* designed additions. They were carried out by the elder *John Foster* and included a large block to the N containing a ballroom. In 1795 the building was gutted by fire, and reconstruction within the surviving shell was carried out by Foster, his designs being approved by Wyatt. The dome on its high drum is datable to 1802, and the S portico was added in 1811, but the state apartments do not seem to have been finally completed till *c*.1820. The original building was erected as an Exchange, just like Wood's building at Bristol. It is now the Mansion House rather than the Town Hall. As an exchange it had a central courtyard. There was a dome on

the s side instead of the present dome. The building as it now
is has a rusticated ground floor with arched windows, originally
open for exchange purposes, giant pilasters on the upper floor,
arched windows with pilasters, and a sumptuously carved
frieze. To the E is a pedimented three-bay centre. This i
Wood's, but the almost (though not quite) identical w façade
dates from 1792 and was designed by Wyatt, following the
demolition of adjoining property. Wyatt's N side has an upper
loggia with coupled columns. Four statues on the parapet, taken
over from the Irish Houses of Parliament at Dublin. The
entrance hall has a *Minton* tile floor, mostly brown and strong
blue, paintings in the lunettes of the wall by *J. H. Amschewitz*
1909, and a gorgeous wooden fireplace, made up lushly in the
C19 from Flemish C17 bits and pieces. The staircase rises under
the dome. Statue of Canning by *Chantrey*, 1832. There are also
Doric iron stoves, and the pendentives were painted by *Furse*
c.1900. The interior of the Council Chamber is by *Shelmerdine.*
Coade-stone statue of Britannia by *Rossi*.

On the first floor in the s range to Castle Street are three
reception rooms, the middle one with shallow lunettes and far
spandrels and again iron stoves, the other two with segmental
tunnel-vaults. Fine decoration of the Wyatt period. Along the
E side the Small Ballroom with another segmental tunnel-vault
and shallow apses at both ends. Then towards the N the Large
Ballroom, 89 ft long, also with a segmental tunnel-vault. Giant
pilasters. In the s wall is a niche for the band with a handsomely
coffered apse. Panels by *Romaine-Walker & Jenkins* of c.1905.
To the w the Dining Room again with giant pilasters. Beautiful
porphyry vases and more iron stoves. There are small rooms
inside, behind the staircase. The whole is an exceptionally
complete example of Late Georgian decoration and one of the
best civic ensembles in the country.* In front of the N façade
in Exchange Flags the Nelson MONUMENT, completed in 1813.
Bronze. By *M. Cotes Wyatt*. (Gunnis adds that much of the
modelling was done by *Westmacott*.) Battle scene at the top,
four chained prisoners and relief panels below.

MUNICIPAL BUILDINGS, Dale Street. 1860–6 by *John Weightman*, Corporation Surveyor, completed by his successor *E. R.
Robson*. Large and symmetrical with at the ends French pavilions

___

*INSIGNIA. Jacobean Mace of copper. – Silver-gilt Mace 1667. – Sword
of 1702. – Silver-plated and gilt Mace of 1746. – Silver-gilt Mace of 1763.
Sword of 1763 (London-made). – Sergeant's Mace and Oar 1785 (by *James
Young*, London-made). – Mace of 1785.

roofs and in the middle a tower with a freely shaped spire or steep pyramid roof. Giant pilasters and attached giant columns. The whole is in the mixed Italianate-cum-French, not stylistically definable. The Corinthian capitals of pilasters and columns are all carved differently – a Gothic, not a Renaissance ambition. The top of the pyramid spire is also a Corinthian capital. The ANNEXE was built as the CONSERVATIVE CLUB in 1882–3 by *F. & G. Holme*. This is more sweepingly French and has an iron balcony on the first floor.

CITY EDUCATION OFFICES, No. 14 Sir Thomas Street. Narrow with high dormers. 1898 by *Charles E. Deacon*.

CITY TRANSPORT OFFICES, Hatton Garden. 1905–7 by *Thomas Shelmerdine*, the Corporation Surveyor. Good; of nine bays and four storeys with Edwardian Imperial features including architectural sculpture.

SESSIONS HOUSE. *See p. 158.*

MAGISTRATES' COURT, Nos. 111 etc. Dale Street. Three-storeyed, long and dignified, with a middle pediment. By *J. Weightman*, the Corporation Surveyor, 1857–9.

JUVENILE COURT, Crosshall Street, former Wesleyan (Victoria) Chapel. Of small rusticated stones. In the style of c.1210 and quite original. 1878–80 by *Picton Jun*.

FIRE STATION, Hatton Garden. 1898 by *Thomas Shelmerdine*. Brick, long and low, and an imaginative design with Jacobean windows and nice other motifs.

GENERAL POST OFFICE, Victoria Street. 1894–9 by *Tanner*. The tops had to be taken down after the Second World War.

TELEPHONE EXCHANGE, Old Hall Street. By *David Thomson*, 1939.

WALKER ART GALLERY. *See p. 158.*

WILLIAM BROWN LIBRARY AND MUSEUM. *See p. 159.*

PICTON READING ROOM. *See p. 159.*

UNIVERSITY. *See p. 197.*

COLLEGE OF TECHNOLOGY. *See p. 159.*

NAUTICAL CATERING COLLEGE, Canning Place. 1965–6 by *Herbert Thearle & Partners*. An attractive little job.

BLUECOAT SCHOOL, School Lane, at the end of Church Alley 26 as seen from Church Street. The school was founded in 1709 and built in 1716–17. The building is of brick and consists of a centre, formerly with chapel and hall, and two long wings. The centre is of five bays and two storeys and has close-set high windows with arches in arched surrounds on pilasters. Three-bay pediment and small cupola. The back has a convex centre.

The wings are also two-storeyed. They are eleven bays long, articulated 5–1–5. At the top attic with ovals to reach the height of the centre. All the windows have cherubs in the keystone. The ends of the wings have just one window of the type of those of the centre. Three doorways each in the long inner sides of the wings. Nothing original is left inside. When the school moved to its new premises in Wavertree (*see* p. 256) the building was saved from demolition by the generosity of the first Viscount Leverhulme.

COTTON EXCHANGE, Old Hall Street. The front by *Matear & Simon*, 1905–6, was demolished in 1967, yet another act of civic vandalism. The front was the architectural expression of the tremendous power of the cotton trade, a design of superbly self-confident grandeur. Two Edwardian Imperial angle turrets with boldly Baroque tops. Ground floor with a long colonnade of Tuscan columns between two projecting one-storeyed pavilions. They had banded rustication, and so had the windowless ground floor of the centre behind and above the colonnade. Upper colonnade too, taller and more elegant, with ten fluted Ionic columns. The exchange court has also been destroyed. What remains is the side elevation to Edmund Street. This is iron-framed, with iron spandrel panels and large areas of plate glass rising through several storeys. All the iron work has classical detailing.

LIME STREET STATION. The monumental building which is now offices was built as a hotel. It is by *Waterhouse*, 1868–71, large and symmetrical except for the differing oriels in the end pavilions. Five storeys plus dormers. The windows are mostly round-arched or with straight tops on quadrant curves. Inside is a staircase with open well and cast-iron handrail leading visibly right up to the top floor. The iron shed adjoining on the E was begun in 1867 by *Baker & Stevenson* and had then the largest span in the world, though it was almost at once outstripped by the shed of St Pancras Station. The span is of 200 ft (St Pancras 240 ft), but too low to be impressive. An extension to the S (the almost identical parallel shed) dates from 1874–9. The present station had two predecessors. The first, opened in 1836 (previously the Liverpool and Manchester Railway), terminated at Crown Street and was by *John Cunningham* with an entrance screen by the younger *Foster*. This was replaced in 1846–51 with a shed by *Richard Turner* and *Sir William Fairbairn* and buildings by *Sir William Tite*, but with Foster's screen surviving. Part of Tite's building still remains in the ground floor of the block to the N, between the sheds and Lord Nelson Street.

EXCHANGE STATION, Tithebarn Street. 1884–6 by *H. Shelmerdine*, son of Thomas. Long front with columns to all windows. The style is a free Renaissance. Pretty iron porte-cochère for the hotel.

CENTRAL STATION, Ranelagh Street. Opened 1874. Quite an impressive roof space (engineers *John Fowler* and *W. M. Brydone*).

MIDLAND RAILWAY GOODS OFFICES, Victoria Street, Peter Street, and Crosshall Street. An impressive brick block with the windows set in giant arches. Reilly called it 'one of the best buildings in the town'.* Architect and date could not be ascertained.

MERSEY TUNNEL. 1925–34, by the engineers *Sir Basil Mott* and *J. A. Brodie. Herbert J. Rowse* was appointed architect in 1931. The following buildings belong to the tunnel: ENTRANCE from St George's Plateau. Lodges with French–1925–*moderne* details, with Egyptian touches, especially the fluted column-like buttresses. Behind the entrance STATUES of George V and Queen Mary by *Sir W. Goscombe John*.‡ The GEORGE'S DOCK VENTILATION STATION was rebuilt by *Rowse* after war damage in 1951–2. The NORTH JOHN STREET VENTILATION STATION is entirely windowless, but with reeded giant blank windows. It has a square tower. The NEW QUAY VENTILATION STATION has two towers. All these buildings are characterized by the squareness of the towers and the stress on cubic blocks and the verticals of mullions etc. There is also some geometrical brick ornamentation. The tunnel itself is 2.13 miles long. For the buildings of the tunnel on the Birkenhead side see *The Buildings of England: Cheshire*.

PLAYHOUSE, Williamson Square. Built in 1865 as the Star Music Hall. The handsome Beaux-Arts–classical interior is a remodelling of 1912–13 by Professor *Adshead*. Particularly notable is the foyer, in the Reilly neo-Grec manner, with curved end wall, heavily enriched Doric columns, and trellis and leaf motifs. Extensions to the building by *Hall, O'Donahue & Wilson* are at present under construction. See p. 479

---

* Strange he could not appreciate Oriel Chambers – *see* p. 178.
‡ Mr Hubbard points out that the original buildings and layout have been much altered.

THE DOCKS

INTRODUCTION

As a sign of the growth of shipping at Liverpool the first dock w.
built *c.*1709–21 by *Thomas Steers*, who was appointed dockmast
in 1717. It filled part of the creek, the Pool of Liverpool, ar
is now Canning Place (*see* p. 169). Then followed, along the rive
in chronological order the Salthouse Dock 1734 etc., the Cannir
(originally Dry) Dock 1753, the George's Dock 1767, the Duke
Dock 1773 (i.e. the Duke of Bridgewater's as the terminal of h
canal),* the King's Dock 1784 etc., the Manchester Dock *c.*178
etc. More was added about and after 1800, but the greatest activi
belongs to the years when *Jesse Hartley* was dock engineer, i.
between 1824 and 1860. During these years the acreage of th
docks grew from 51 to 212. Hartley was the son of the bridg
master of the West Riding and grew up with, and started h
professional life in, bridge work. For the Liverpool Docks h
changed from sandstone, used until then, to granite, although th
material was far more costly. But he had a vision of infinite du
ability by means of mass as well as material. This is what Picto
wrote about him: 'For thirty-six years [he] guided with a despot
sway the construction of some of the mightiest works of their kin
ever executed. . . . He had grand ideas and carried them int
execution with a strength, solidity and skill which have nev
been exceeded. Granite was the material in which he delighte
to work. His walls are built with rough Cyclopean masses . .
cemented together with a hydraulic lime of a consistency as har
as the granite itself.' The RIVER WALL which he built is 11
thick and about 40 ft high, the DOCK WALL towards the town 18
high. Granite was first used by Hartley in ashlar blocks, but soc
he changed to a cyclopean technique of large and smaller irregu
larly-shaped blocks fitted together like a jigsaw puzzle. The gate
piers, which had been Grecian at first, were now round, of coloss
girth, and gatekeepers' lodges and the like are equally massiv
It is an architecture for giants, and this is how Hartley must hav
felt about his harbour.

Hartley late in the thirties got involved in the struggle fo
warehouses as a part of docks and surrounding them. It was
struggle between ownership by the town and ownership by privat
people who were building warehouses near, but not in, the dock

---

* The magnificent, classical warehouse of 1811, one of the oldest preserve
examples of the type at Liverpool, was senselessly destroyed in 1966.

ae private owners sat on the council and made the change
possible, although a Royal Commission had recommended it
1821, saying that warehouses ought to be 'insulated from
aces of public access'. Hartley pleaded for enclosure, won in
37, met with cancellation of the plans in 1838, and finally won
1841. The result is the Albert Dock.

Apart from what is described below, swing-bridges, bollards
d the like must also be observed. The docks are here described
om N to S, including those at the N end which are outside what
in this book called the centre. Except for Stanley they are all w
the dock road.

PERAMBULATION

LADSTONE DOCK was completed in 1927. S of this follow
HORNBY DOCK opened in 1884,* ALEXANDRA DOCK opened
in 1880, LANGTON DOCK opened in 1879, and BROCKLEBANK
(originally CANADA HALF-TIDE) DOCK opened in 1862, all at
Bootle. The Liverpool docks proper start with CANADA DOCK
opened in 1858‡ and continue with HUSKISSON DOCK opened
in 1852 and SANDON DOCK opened in 1851. This is where we
first meet *Jesse Hartley*. His are the round gatepiers. More is to
be said about them later. WELLINGTON DOCK was opened in
1850 and SANDON HALF-TIDE DOCK in 1903, being a reconstruction of two earlier docks. The next, BRAMLEY MOOR
and NELSON DOCKS, were both opened in 1848.

COLLINGWOOD and SALISBURY DOCKS opened in 1848.
To them belongs the ornamental VICTORIA TOWER, dated
1848, round below, octagonal above, of the large irregular,
cyclopean blocks of granite that Hartley favoured. Machicolated balcony and machicolated embattled top. It is all ham,
but it tells of the commercial pride of the decades. The Dock
Master's Office is an exception in Hartley's *œuvre* in that it has
Gothic windows, minimum of course. It is embattled too.

STANLEY DOCK. Opened in 1848 but half filled in when the
large Tobacco Warehouse was built. This was completed in
1900 and has the typical free Renaissance decoration only
right up, attached to the top storey – what Osbert Lancaster
once called 'above the snow-line'. Hartley's warehouses of
1825–6 still stand, however. They are five-storeyed and have

---

* In many instances, docks have undergone alteration and enlargement since
ir first opening.
‡ The Canada Dock hydraulic tower, no longer existing, was the weirdest
all Hartley's medieval-inspired buildings.

the Doric columns of cast iron slightly concave (the oppos
of entasis) which we shall find again (Wapping Dock). T
colonnades for unloading are interrupted by three ellipti
arches. There is also an octagonal hydraulic tower, castella
of course. The Stanley Dock lies further inland than the othe
as it was built at the terminus of the Liverpool and Leeds Car
The last four locks are immediately to its E. Good examples
this area of Hartley's entrance gates (including four to Stan
Dock itself) with the central pier forming the keeper's hut a
with the gates sliding back through the side piers.

After that earlier docks. But Hartley's really early perio
now only represented by the GATEPIERS, which are Greci
of smooth ashlar, i.e. in the pre-cyclopean style. The CLAREN
DOCK (for steamers!) was indeed opened in 1830, the TRAFA
GAR DOCK in 1836, the VICTORIA DOCK (also for steamers)
1836, the WATERLOO DOCK in 1834. The CORN WAREHOUS
were built in 1867. They are two huge ranges, six-storeyed, w
rusticated segmental arches on the ground level and small tv
round-arched windows above. They have higher erections
two places each. The designer was *George Fosbery Lyster*, t
then dock engineer.

The next docks were begun earlier still, but little of t
original work survives: Prince's Dock 1816–21, Georg
Dock begun 1767 (on the site of today's Pierhead and
buildings), Manchester Dock c.1785. Other docks, earlier st
follow further s.

CANNING DOCK. Constructed by *Steers* as a dry d
adjoining the Old Dock (i.e. the present Canning Place) t
converted to a wet dock by *Hartley* in 1829.

CANNING HALF-TIDE DOCK was opened in 1844. This
at the river-side three of Hartley's watchmen's huts by the d
gates, octagonal, and two with an odd baluster on the roof.

52   ALBERT DOCK was begun shortly before 1841 and opened
1845. It is the unquestionable climax of Liverpool do
architecture, and the fact that at the time of writing its preser
tion is in jeopardy is disgraceful. The architect was of cou
again *Hartley*, but *Philip Hardwick* was consulted, and it is
known whether or how much he had to do with the desi
Hardwick certainly is the architect of the DOCK TRAFF
OFFICE (1846–7; top storey by Hartley, 1848), with its power
portico of giant Tuscan columns and its pediment like t
columns of cast iron. The galleried office interior unfortunat
is derelict. If Hardwick was consulted for the warehouses

well, the reason was that he had been architect of the St Katherine's Dock in London, begun in 1827 and undoubtedly the source of inspiration for the Albert Dock. The Albert Dock has indeed warehouses on all four sides. They are of five storeys, the ground floor being open in a Doric colonnade. This is interrupted every so often by an elliptical arch. The pattern is regular and the columns not concave-sided. For sheer punch there is little in the early commercial architecture of Europe to emulate the Albert Dock.

SALTHOUSE DOCK. Originally built in 1734–53. Begun by *Steers*, completed by *Henry Berry*. The very long, all-granite shed is probably from the time of the enlargement, i.e. 1855.

DUKE'S DOCK. Built by the Duke of Bridgewater in 1773.

WAPPING DOCK. Opened in 1855. This is the other major *Hartley* dock. It is here that one can but admire his entrances with enormous round piers and gatekeepers' lodges, even more enormous and elliptical. The gates slid out of the side piers. The lodges have conical roofs ending in the chimney. The warehouse is of four storeys, and the details are much like those of Stanley and Albert, though Albert is always a little more accomplished. Wapping Dock has a hydraulic tower with machicolation and battlements, dated 1856.

KING'S DOCK was first opened in 1788, but is now entirely reconstructed. QUEEN'S DOCK opened in 1796. A dock on the site of COBURG DOCK dated back to 1816, but it underwent three reconstructions by *Hartley*, the last in 1858. BRUNSWICK DOCK, opened in 1832, was *Hartley*'s first, and has a tower of 1889, common brick and red brick with a picturesque skyline. TOXTETH DOCK, opened in 1842, and HARRINGTON DOCK, opened in 1844, were later rebuilt. HERCULANEUM DOCK was first opened in 1866.

PERAMBULATIONS

he Centre is here demarcated by the following: The Mersey, ing Edward Street, Leeds Street, a short length of Vauxhall ʾad, Great Crosshall Street, Byrom Street, William Brown reet, Lime Street, Ranelagh Place, Renshaw Street, Berry reet, Great George Street, Parliament Street.

Streets are in alphabetical order, but the note below is a guide ʿ those who have the stamina for a complete perambulation.*

* St George's Plateau with the streets surrounding it, especially William ʾown Street, Dale Street, off into Hatton Garden, Water Street, off into ʾvent Garden, George's Dock Gates, The Strand, Pierhead, New Quay,

BERRY STREET. Some decaying Late Georgian houses.

BIXTETH STREET. LOMBARD CHAMBERS of *c*.1855 is Got
and brick, the larger building at the corner of George Stree
stone, classical, and dignified, with large windows and in
columns as mullions. – (On the corner of Edmund Str
ORLEANS HOUSE by *Matear & Simon*, the iron fram
similar to that of the side of their Cotton Exchange.)

BOLD STREET. Laid out *c*.1780, and still called by Reilly in 19
'reserved and intimate'. At the w end the LYCEUM CL
1800–2 by *Thomas Harrison*. Ashlar-faced and one of the fin
early buildings of Liverpool. The façade is to Ranelagh Stre
It is of five bays, with four demi-columns. Large pediment
windows, one l., one r. No upper floor appears, but above
columns of the centre are reliefs. No main pediment. To B
Street the five-bay centre is recessed and has unfluted Io
columns. Behind them the upper floor is visible, but the si
bays have again only one large window each. They are tripart
under segmental arches. The Lyceum was built to house
Liverpool Library.* This was in a domed room. – No. 7 is
PALATINE CLUB. It is a *palazzo* of three bays and four store
freely detailed. It is by *G. O. Parnell* and of *c*.1854. – Then
the other side No. 52, the former Music (i.e. Concert) H
though it is inscribed *Halle des Modes*. This is characteristica
Early Victorian, i.e. latest classical, and stuccoed. It was rebu
in 1853 by *Holme*.‡ – No. 58, minor, has on its upper flo
details typical of *c*.1900, especially the three oriels and the ba
of small upright windows without any mouldings. – Nos 43–
back on the N side, is another *palazzo*, of stone, five bays wi

Chapel Street with Lancelot's Hey, Old Hall Street with Queen Street
Union Street, Tithebarn Street, off into Bixteth Street, off into Highfi
Street, Great Crosshall Street, back to the Town Hall by way of Excha
Flags, Castle Street, Brunswick Street, James Street, Derby Square, C
Street, North John Street with Mathew Street, Victoria Street with Tem
Court, off into Stanley Street, off into Sir Thomas Street, off into Cross
Street, Whitechapel, Lord Street, Church Street, by way of Church Alley
School Lane, by way of Williamson Square and St John's Lane to Lime Str
Ranelagh Place, Ranelagh Street, Renshaw Street, St Luke's Place, Bold St
with Colquitt Street and Parr Street and back, Berry Street, Seel Str
Gradwell Street, Duke Street, Great George Street, Great George Place, G
George Square, St James's Street for Bridgewater Street and Jordan Str
Sparling Street, Park Lane, Canning Place, South Castle Street.
   * This, founded in 1758, was the first gentlemen's subscription library
England.
   ‡ Mr Hubbard suggests that the colonnade at the back may belong to
old building.

with a big pediment to the former doorway. It looks 1850s. – No. 55 has a somewhat Soanian stucco front with some incised decoration. – Then Nos 65–7 has modernistic quartzite facing. It was built in 1937–8 to designs by *Quiggin & Gee*. – After that Nos 77–79, Grecian, stuccoed, ambitious and good. It is of five bays, bays one, three, and five being pedimented. Bays one and three have absurdly thin pilasters, bay three a pair of set-in attached columns. – Finally the LIVERPOOL SAVINGS BANK, 1861 etc. by *Culshaw*, of six bays with two entrances. Ashlar-faced, late classical, i.e. the upper windows with alternatingly shaped pediments, but e.g. the tops of the lower windows already incorrectly detailed. At the end, across, the tower of St Luke's.

BRIDGEWATER STREET, off St James's Street. Some early WAREHOUSES.

BRUNSWICK STREET. HALIFAX HOUSE is a good quiet five-bay *palazzo* with aedicule windows on the main floor. A panel records the date 1835, but that must be too early.

CANNING PLACE. Canning Place is on the site of Liverpool's first dock. This was built by *Thomas Steers c.* 1715. In the centre, until the Second World War, was *Foster*'s grand CUSTOMS HOUSE, begun in 1828 and finished in 1839.* – SAILORS' HOME. 1846–8 by *John Cunningham*. Large, Jacobean, but treated in a very cavalier fashion. Square corner turrets with ogee caps, large mullioned-and-transomed windows, odd, flat window surrounds, and a completely free, very large portal. The shaped top gables exist no longer. Inside on the first floor a long glazed court with tapering sides and iron galleries on five 60 levels. The iron pillars are fancy Jacobean too. The whole is an amazing sight. – For the Nautical Catering College *see* p. 161. – The N side of Canning Place has classical buildings typical of the 1840s, stucco and also ashlar. – ALBION BUILDINGS are at the corner of South Castle Street, continued into that street. Nice contemporary shop at the rounded corner. The l. neighbour of Albion Buildings (REVENUE CHAMBERS) has a pub at the rounded corner.

CASTLE STREET. This is one of Liverpool's seven ancient streets. At its s end, in the present Derby Square, was the castle. The street was widened in 1786. It is indeed one of the widest streets in the centre of Liverpool. At the N end across is the town hall, but just off axis. – On the E side No. 5 is by *Grayson & Ould*,

* The buildings now going up are by *Kingham Knight Associates* and *Hall, O'Donahue & Wilson*.

c. 1889.* – On the other side at the corner of Water Street (*se*
there) the District Bank, in the Loire style. – Then the WEST
MINSTER BANK, by *Norman Shaw*, 1901–2. This is not
specially striking building. Its façade is quiet, the principa
motif being the large portal with alternate blocking in the sur
round. Low, circular banking hall, the wall piers horizontall
striped, as Shaw liked it. – Then the Loire style takes over agair
It appears in various forms in Nos 30–32 (WESTMINSTE
BANK), and Nos 34–6 (MIDLAND BANK, by *Grayson & Oula*
and MARTINS BANK both at the corner of Brunswick Stree
The last-named is by *Caröe*, 1892–4 and is the best of them
busier than the others, but also more inventive. Brown and re
stone. Marble-faced banking hall with pretty plaster ceiling
Bronze doors by *Stirling Lee*. – Opposite No. 22, the HUDDERS
FIELD BUILDING SOCIETY, of three bays only, classical, wit
a portico of attached columns and a pediment. – Its neighbou
is *Cockerell*'s famous BANK OF ENGLAND Liverpool branch
built in 1845–8. This also has three bays, but appears in spit
of that majestic, thanks to the scale of the motifs. They ar
classical, but in Cockerell's inimitable way turn every so ofter
to completely free motifs. On the front, ground floor and firs
floor are tied together by attached Roman Doric columns. Th
second floor is recessed and has an Ionic aedicule window unde
a blank arch reaching up into a pediment broken wide open. T
Cook Street the centre of the elevation has three tripartite giar
windows under arches. Inside only the middle one counts. Th
other two have mezzanines behind the arches. But the middl
arch marks a bold tunnel-vault across the building. Inside, th
centre of this room has four columns. It is a compositio
characteristic of Cockerell in the proportions and the spatia
resourcefulness. The interior recently mutilated. On the oppo
site side, Nos 40–44, with three gables, is by *Grayson*. – *Picton*
Nos 48–50 of 1864 is sandwiched between what must be frag
ments of the late C18 rebuilding of Castle Street. – Finally th
exuberant MIDLAND BANK, 1868–9 by *Lucy & Littler*.

CHAPEL STREET. One of Liverpool's seven ancient streets. I
LANCELOTS HEY off Chapel Street an early warehouse. – I
Chapel Street two important commercial buildings: No. 5
HARGREAVES BUILDING, by *J. A. Picton*, 1861, a dignifie
Venetian five-bay *palazzo*, and, opposite, No. 26, RICHMON

---

* *Grayson* and *Grayson & Ould* designed some eight or nine mor
buildings in Castle Street.

BUILDINGS, even finer, also a *palazzo*, also by *Picton*, and also 63
1861.* – For EXCHANGE BUILDINGS, *see* Exchange Flags.
CHURCH STREET. No. 17, formerly LLOYDS BANK, by *H. J.
Rowse*, 1929. Brick and stone; neo-Romanesque. The original
ground floor is not preserved.)

COLQUITT STREET. Off Bold Street to the s. The only interesting
building is the ROYAL INSTITUTION (now University Extra-
Mural Department), originally the private house of Thomas
Parr. It was built *c*.1799, with office and warehouse still at the
back in the medieval way. Five bays, two and a half storeys,
brick, without a centre pediment. Later Greek Doric porch.
Two one-and-a-half-storey wings of one bay connected
with the centre by wings. The Royal Institution was created
by William Roscoe for the cultivation of literature, science,
and the arts. It opened its doors in 1817.

COOK STREET. No. 16 is by *Peter Ellis*, 1866, a narrow, high,
three-bay front, as original as that of Oriel Chambers, but less
disciplined. The three giant bays end boldly, but not strongly,
in a triplet of stepped arched tops. But there is here also an
amazing amount of plate glass. The courtyard is from the point
of view of the Modern Movement even more amazing. A whole
wall and a tight spiral staircase are almost entirely of glass, with 65
only the thinnest iron mullions. But it is of course all entirely
utilitarian here. – Almost opposite No. 16 was *C. R. Cockerell*'s
BANK CHAMBERS. This was demolished in 1959.

COVENT GARDEN, off Water Street. On the w side the flank of
Oriel Chambers and then a new extension replacing a bombed
part of the building. 1959–61 by *James & Bywaters*, very
sensitively adjusted to its distinguished neighbour. Opposite
the two the flank of No. 10 Water Street, with large tripartite
windows separated by thin iron columns.

DALE STREET, from w to E. One of Liverpool's seven ancient
streets. At the corner of the town hall is the LIVERPOOL &
LONDON AND GLOBE INSURANCE, 1855–7 by *C. R.* and *F. P.
Cockerell*, a fine classical building of seven bays with attached
columns on the second floor and an impressive, very original
doorway. It is pedimented and set in a French niche of banded
rustication. French also are the thick garlands l. and r. The long
side is towards the town hall. Note the curious treatment of the
staircase à la Chambord, set back behind one of the portals. –

* Richmond Buildings, to the disgrace of Liverpool, was demolished in
967. In spite of its *palazzo parti* it had wide areas of glazing and subtle
hythm of windows and excellent stone carving.

Then on the other side the MIDLAND BANK, on the corner o
Castle Street. The brick portion, with carved brick ornament, i
by *Salomons* of Manchester, for Agnew's as an art gallery. Th
stone portion is of *c*.1863–4 by *Sir James Picton*, with muc]
variety in the carving. Although High Victorian in feeling, i
illustrates (almost as well as did the same architect's Richmon(
Buildings) Liverpool's steadfast refusal to go Gothic. Then th
QUEEN INSURANCE BUILDING (Nos 8–10), grand, wit]
upper giant columns and a big top balustrade. Behind, at th
end of the narrow courtyard, is an exquisite building of 1837–(
by *Samuel Rowland*. Ashlar, five bays, with a three-bay projec
tion. Attached Greek Doric columns on the ground floor, talle
attached Ionic columns on the upper floor. Three-bay pedi
ment. Main hall with four columns near the corners. Gorge
ously rich classical stucco. – After that the STATE INSURANC
BUILDING (No. 14), 1906 by *W. Aubrey Thomas*, in the playfu
Gothic typical of *c.* 1900.* The offices placed round a gallerie(
court with a glass tunnel-vault. – Again on the N side No. 11 b
Picton, then RIGBY'S BUILDINGS, the shallower, less drama
tic, stuccoed type of *c.* 1850. – On the S, at the corner of Nort]
John Street, STATE HOUSE, recent, by *Edmund Kirby & Sons*
– On the opposite corner of North John Street the ROYA]
INSURANCE, a splendid Edwardian-Imperial piece by *J. Franci*
Doyle, 1896–1903. Long front to North John Street, narrow bu
high, crowded front to Dale Street. The motifs of the towe
with cupola and the alternately blocked columns are inspired b
Shaw (who was assessor for the competition). The frieze o
sculpture (on the second floor) by *Allen* is a much-favoure(
Arts and Crafts motif. The rocky base of the façade ought to b
specially noted. The building is steel-framed, an early case
The main hall along North John Street has neo-late-C17 stucco
so has the plaster tunnel-vault of the Board Room. In the boar(
room replicas of Dutch chandeliers. The originals which be
longed to the company came from Utrecht Cathedral and wer(
given back by the company to the cathedral. In return th
company received the splendid Dutch cupboard now in th
board room. – Next (S) THE TEMPLE, Italianate, with a centra
turret, 1864–5 by *J. A. Picton & Son*. – Then the PRUDENTIA]
ASSURANCE, 1885–6 by *Waterhouse*, the same type as th
London head offices. Red brick and red terracotta, with spar
ingly used Late Gothic motifs, 'red, hard and forbidding
(Reilly). The tower and the bay E of it were added in 1904–6

* Originally the façade was symmetrical about the turret (E. Hubbard)

– Nos 48–54, the former JUNIOR REFORM CLUB, is more
determinedly Gothic, and No. 62, IMPERIAL CHAMBERS, is
Gothic too. – The former CONSERVATIVE CLUB is now the
annex to the Municipal Buildings (*see* p. 161). – Opposite is
PRINCES BUILDINGS, high, and roughly in a Loire style. –
No. 127 at the corner of North Street is HIGSON'S BREWERY
OFFICES, 1964–5 by *Ormrod & Partners* (*D. H. Mills*), and
well done. Much granite – black below, green above – and
glass and stainless steel. – Finally No. 139, at the corner
of Trueman Street, is one of the very few a little more ambitious Georgian houses left in the centre of Liverpool. Brick,
with a three-bay pediment and behind it a Venetian window
with some Adamish decoration and a tripartite doorway.
The date is probably the late c18.

DERBY SQUARE. Where Derby Square now is, stood the
CASTLE. It was built before 1235 and belonged to the Welsh
type with angle towers, but it was not regular in plan. The gatehouse was not in the middle of one side. Also, it had only three
towers. A sw tower was added in 1442. The castle was demolished in 1720 and St George's church built in its place. This
in its turn was rebuilt in 1819–25 by the younger *Foster* and
demolished in 1897. In the centre is now the QUEEN VICTORIA
MONUMENT, 1902–6 by *F. M. Simpson*, with *Willink & Thicknesse*. The sculpture is by *Charles J. Allen*. Domed baldacchino
on four clusters of diagonally set columns. The statue is under
the baldacchino, and the enclosure has groups meant to represent Education, Industry, Commerce, and Agriculture. Only
one building in Derby Square needs a mention, CASTLE MOAT
HOUSE, probably 1841, three bays with giant angle pilasters
and a pediment. Originally there were columns instead of the
pilasters (Peter Fleetwood-Hesketh). Below is an undercroft
with shallow vaults. It has an interesting plan and lay inside the
moat, but outside the square castle.

EXCHANGE FLAGS. The quadrangle was formed when new
Exchange Buildings were erected in 1803–9, probably by
James Wyatt or the elder *Foster*. They were rebuilt in 1863–7
by *T. H. Wyatt* and again from 1937 by *Gunton & Gunton*. For
the Nelson Monument *see* Town Hall, p. 160.

GEORGE'S PIER GATES. TOWER BUILDING. This is on the site
of the Tower of Liverpool, built by Sir John Stanley in 1406.
It is of 1908, by *W. Aubrey Thomas*, steel-framed and with
white terracotta facing. Large and symmetrical, with polygonal
buttress features also on the turrets. Reilly's judgement is:

'One would think it would be impossible to achieve a more clumsily detailed building than the Liver Building [*see* Pierhead, p. 175], yet the same architect has beaten his own record.' To the l. of Tower Building the gateway to the parish church. (GRADWELL STREET. On the E side two early C19 warehouses.)

GREAT CROSSHALL STREET. Near to its E end a neo-E.E. building of quite good elevation, the former St John's School. The first-floor windows are set in an arcade. The top centre window breaks through into a gable. Further w the School and Presbytery of Holy Cross – *see* p. 203.

GREAT GEORGE PLACE. DAVID LEWIS HOTEL FOR MEN, built in 1902 (to *J. Francis Doyle*'s design) as a hostel for single men. Large, of red and yellow brick, with angle cupolas and Dutch gables.

GREAT GEORGE SQUARE. Now mostly surrounded by recent houses, but on three sides still a few early C19 houses. Before the war it was one of the best of Liverpool's squares.

HATTON GARDEN. KINGSWAY HOUSE, 1965–7 by *Derek Stephenson & Partners*, has a long front and is going to be extended to Dale Street. It is a satisfying design and interesting in that it provides for future pedestrian circulation on the first-floor level as it is planned for this whole area. For the Fire Station and the City Transport Offices *see* p. 161.

JAMES STREET. ALEXANDRA BUILDINGS (No. 19) by *Grayson*, dated 1864, a dignified seven-bay *palazzo* with columns on the ground floor carrying arches. For the Pacific Steam Navigation Building *see* The Strand.

JORDAN STREET, off St James's Street. Some of the most impressive WAREHOUSES are here. – Also three-storeyed municipal housing of 1916.

LANCELOTS HEY. *See* Chapel Street.

LIME STREET. Just S of the station is the CROWN pub, 1905 with shallow bow windows and large florid decoration, a pleasant start to the street as a street proper, though the decoration is conservative for its date. – Further down, at the corner of Ranelagh Place is THE VINES, 1907 by *Walter Thomas*, a large, loosely classical building with florid gables and a turret. On the ground floor one of the two best Liverpool pubs of *c.*1900. Chimneypiece with caryatids, entertaining putti frieze etc.

LORD STREET. At the corner of North John Street a long, latest classical, building, stuccoed and still in shallow relief. The centre has a portico with attached columns and pediment.

(MATHEW STREET. A fireproof warehouse of the 1840s by *A. H. Holme.**)

NEW QUAY. *See* p. 203.

NORTH JOHN STREET. No. 41, CENTRAL BUILDINGS, is of twenty bays, with granite columns on the ground floor. For the Royal Insurance Building *see* Dale Street.

OLD HALL STREET. One of Liverpool's seven ancient streets. It was then the High Street. The present name derives from the hall, i.e. house, of the Moore family. – NUMBER ONE is a new building, 1966–7 by *E. Kirby & Sons*. It is a pleasing design, with the ground floor of blue bricks and the shops with shallow segmental arches.‡ – On the corner of Fazakerley Street is CITY BUILDINGS, the spectacular glass and iron frontage of which results from a remodelling, *c.*1906, by *Frederick G. Fraser*. – Opposite THE ALBANY, *c.*1850 by *J. K. Colling*, eleven bays, brick on a stone ground floor. 'A very free treatment of the Renaissance with Arabesque variations' (*The Builder*, 1853). Good iron gates and thin iron balconies in the long courtyard behind. – For the Cotton Exchange *see* p. 162. – Further on LITTLEWOOD'S, by *W. L. Stevenson* of Littlewood's, an acceptable curtain-walling job, 1965–6. The building is 320 ft high. A substantial extension is being built at the time of writing.

PARK LANE, so called because it once led to the royal park of Toxteth. No. 168, KEAN'S HOTEL, is a riotous piece, the ground floor juicily decorated, the skyline quite fantastic.

PARR STREET, at the foot of Colquitt Street. There are some early WAREHOUSES here, especially No. 33, of only three bays, but with a pediment across. It originally had a date 1808.

PIERHEAD. Facing the Mersey on the land gained by covering the 2 George's Dock are three extremely ambitious buildings. They represent the great Edwardian Imperial optimism and might indeed stand at Durban or Hongkong just as naturally as at Liverpool. The grandest of the three is the ROYAL LIVER BUILDING, 1908–10 by *W. Aubrey Thomas*. It is of reinforced concrete (an early use) and showy in the extreme but, it can't be denied, also impressive. It is eight storeys high with two more in the roof and has to W and E an identical middle tower ending in a free, entirely un-period top or domed cap with the legendary Liver Bird, perhaps in its motifs faintly Byzantine.

* This is a discovery of Mr W. Sutherland.

‡ (Warehouses in UNION STREET and QUEEN STREET, off Old Hall Street.)

The corners have, in the same spirit, small stone domes. To the river, at the foot of the tower, is an ample semicircular porch. – The CUNARD BUILDING is a less demonstrative, square block with the sculptural features kept well in. It is agreeably proportioned. The frame is reinforced concrete. The building was begun in 1913. Neo-Grec detailing. The architects are *Willink & Thicknesse* with *Arthur Davis* (of *Mewès & Davis*) as a consultant. – MERSEY DOCKS AND HARBOUR BOARD OFFICES. 1907 by *Thornely* (with *Briggs & Wolstenholme* and *F. B. Hobbs*). The façade has eleven bays with three steep pediments, two semicircular, the middle one triangular. The four angle bays of the buildings are polygonal and carry cupolas, formerly with high lanterns. The top storey of the building is post-war. Over the centre a big copper-covered dome on a high drum. The centre is an octagonal hall reaching up to the dome. It has arched galleries on four levels, the second and third pulled together. The building, taking it all in all, is more conventional than the Royal Liver and the buildings by Doyle. – MONU-MENTS. Edward VII by *Sir W. Goscombe John*; equestrian. – Sir Alfred Jones by *Frampton*, bronze, with a young woman on top. – Engine Room Heroes, by *Sir W. Goscombe John*. – Merchant Navy (s w corner), by *Stanley H. Smith* and *C. F. Blythin*. Round pillar with a top beacon in a rounded walled area.

QUEEN STREET. *See* Old Hall Street.

RANELAGH PLACE. The ADELPHI HOTEL, big, stone-faced, and stodgy, is by *F. Atkinson*, 1912. It was originally intended to enclose an inner courtyard, but the back was not built. – Opposite is LEWIS'S with a giant figure and reliefs by *Epstein*.

ST GEORGE'S PLATEAU and ST JOHN'S GARDENS. This is described on p. 157. The N side is William Brown Street, *see* p. 158. Unfortunately this is the only side which tries to match St George's Hall in distinction. The Lime Street Hotel (*see* p. 162) is monumental too, and the new St John's Precinct (*see* St John's Lane, below) may turn out monumental too, but to the w there is a sad tailing off.

ST JOHN'S LANE. This faces the s portico of St George's Hall. A precinct with a new MARKET and a hotel had just been begun at the time of writing. The architect is *James A. Roberts* of Birmingham. The area is 6 acres, and the buildings are to include the Retail Market which was on part of the site, a 150-bedroom hotel, a car-park for more than 500 cars, an underground service road, shops on the two levels of two adjoining streets, and a beacon of concrete, 335 ft high, rather like the recent post-office towers. It will have a revolving restaurant and serve as a vent and flue for the precinct. – No. 12, the former PEARL ASSURANCE, is by *Waterhouse*.

EL STREET. Some HOUSES with Late Georgian doorways.

OUTH CASTLE STREET *see* Canning Place.

PARLING STREET. Enormous warehouses of the 1860s.)

ANLEY STREET. Nos 8–12 is a very remarkable building, severe and original. It has large tripartite windows with pink granite columns and three low-pitched gables with stepped tripartite windows. One may even be reminded a little of Lethaby. The date is supposed to be 1888.

HE STRAND. For the three majestic buildings on the w side *see* Pierhead. On the E side is WILBERFORCE HOUSE and MERSEY HOUSE by *Gotch & Partners*, 1965–7, a lively modern composition. In the courtyard ingenious fountain by *Richard Huws* Then the PACIFIC STEAM NAVIGATION OFFICES, formerly White Star Line, at the corner of James Street. By *R. Norman Shaw*, with *J. Francis Doyle*; 1896. Striped brick on a stone ground floor. Gable (before the war with a top aedicule) and angle cupolas.*

NION STREET. *See* Old Hall Street.

ICTORIA STREET. Formed in 1867–8.‡

ATER STREET. One of Liverpool's seven ancient streets. At the corner of Castle Street the DISTRICT BANK, pretty French-Early-Renaissance. – Opposite the national head-quarters of MARTINS BANK, large, French-classical, seen through American eyes. 1927–32 by *Herbert J. Rowse*, who had travelled extensively in America. It is a very adroitly done job. Low banking hall, with glass ceiling. On all four sides arcading on columns. In the four corners small rotundas for four different purposes. The internal decoration is of the jagged Paris-1925 type. – After that No. 14, ORIEL CHAMBERS. This [64] is by the almost unknown *Peter Ellis* and was built in 1864. It is one of the most remarkable buildings of its date in Europe. Its façades – basement and three and a half storeys – are mostly of glass, the tall oblong windows boxed out as so many oriels and separated by very slender stone mullions with a kind of nailhead decoration. The mullions, as Reilly rightly observed, are 'designed to look like cast iron'. The top has uncouth pinnacles and an uncouth middle gable. The doorway is very narrow, not symmetrically placed and provided with an elon-

* s of this in SEABROW some early warehouses.
‡ TEMPLE COURT to the s has a plain early warehouse.

gated octagonal window above. The top windows have cham
fered upper corners too. It is all deliberately incorrect an
wilful, but the aim is that of the Chicago skyscrapers of twenty
five years later. *The Builder* hated it. It speaks of a 'vas
abortion' and an 'agglomeration of protruding plate glas
bubbles', and even Reilly did not like it. He called it 'logica
and disagreeable' and a 'cellular habitation for the huma
insect'. We all know what he means. Only we appreciate th
honesty of admitting that this is what such a building function
ally means, and he does not. The iron framing of the orie
windows themselves is of the thinnest section. The front t
Water Street is seven bays wide, but to Covent Garden ar
twelve bays. The extension replacing a war-damaged part i
by *James & Bywaters*, 1959 etc., and done with full appreciation
of Ellis's work. Ellis's courtyard is from the point of view o
prophecy of the C20 even more amazing than the façades. T
the S the walls are almost entirely of glass, i.e. cantilevered i
front of the frame. The frame is of cast iron with shallow bric
arches. – Opposite Oriel Chambers INDIA BUILDING, b
Herbert J. Rowse, 1924–32, with an impressive tunnel-vaulte
corridor through to Brunswick Street.* The building is face
in Portland stone and cost £1,250,000. It was built for th
Holts' Blue Funnel Line. – Nothing of note after that. Towe
Building is in George's Pier Gates.

WILLIAM BROWN STREET. *See* Public Buildings, p. 158.

WILLIAMSON SQUARE. For the Playhouse *see* p. 163. – Th
premises of the UNION COLD STORAGE COMPANY wit
their noble convex side to Williamson Square were originall
the THEATRE ROYAL. This dated from 1772, but the sym
metrical façade is of 1803, either by the elder *Foster* or b
Harrison. Projecting three-bay centre. Rusticated ground floor
ashlar above with four pairs of unfluted Ionic pilasters. Panel
representing drama.

THE CATHEDRALS, UNIVERSITY, AND

GEORGIAN AREA

INTRODUCTION

Between the 1780s and the 1840s Liverpool expanded vigorousl
in all directions. To the E the 'west end' was built – streets o
sober and well-proportioned brick terraces. It became one of th

---

* Rowse won this in competition. Sir Giles Scott was the assessor.

best west ends in England, and such streets as Rodney Street and Percy Street still are perfect examples of the kind. Churches so were provided, and certain public buildings: the Wellington Rooms, the Medical Institution, and the (former) Mechanics Institution.

Of the churches St Andrew (Presbyterian), St Bride, and St Saviour, besides the St James's Cemetery Chapel, remain. St Mark Upper Duke Street, St David Brownlow Hill, St Catherine Abercromby Square, the Brunswick Methodist Chapel, and the Presbyterian Church in Mount Pleasant have been pulled down without replacement. Equally whole terraces of Georgian houses have been demolished. These losses were caused by the interference of a new function for the area, and this function is by now busy altering the N half radically. But the first interference, of scale more than anything, was not the university but the cathedral.

So now the area can be looked at on three different levels: the east-end west end, the cathedrals – for the new Catholic cathedral is also in the area – and the university.

The area is defined here as follows: s of London Road (and excluding it), w of Boundary Place, the w end of West Derby Street and Smithdown Lane, N of Upper Parliament Street (and including it), E of Great George Place, Great George Street, Berry Street, Renshaw Street, and Lime Street (and excluding all these).

THE EAST-END WEST END

The area was known as Mosslake Fields. Building started with Rodney Street and Mount Pleasant in the 1780s, but a unified layout was only drawn up by the elder *John Foster* in 1800, and most of what was built dates from the 1820s and 1830s.

CHURCHES

For the cathedrals *see* p. 187.

ST BRIDE, Percy Street. 1830–1 by *Samuel Rowland*. Straight- 47
forward parallelepiped but with a monumental portico of six unfluted columns and a pediment. The sides have six high windows with fine architraves on brackets. Bays one and six are flanked by giant Doric pilasters. The E end has the slightly projecting chancel with a large tripartite and pedimented window and low one-bay attachments. The frieze below the pediment has wreaths as decoration. Inside, the three galleries on cast-iron columns are connected by sweeping quadrant

curves. Flat ceiling. The E window has columns inside. – Carved ROYAL ARMS. – MONUMENTS. Rev. J. H. Stewart † 1854. With an urn. – W. M. Fallcon † 1891. Is the top with the urn from an older monument ?

ST NATHANIEL, Dinorben Street. 1905 by *George Bradbury & Son*, except for the W tower which remained from the preceding church. This was by *David Walker*, of 1868. The new church is of hot Ruabon brick, with an apse and lancet windows.

ST PHILIP NERI (R.C.), Catharine Street. 1914–20 by *P. S. Gilby*. Neo-Byzantine, with a low dome and tiny corner domes close to it instead of pinnacles. Portal with sculpture and above it a fully carved Last Supper by *T. Murphy*. Narthex with mosaics. The nave is tunnel-vaulted in its W part, but has a shallow dome in its E part. Both are of stone blocks, and there is no convincing division between them. The arcade piers with their heavy, blocky capitals run through regardless of them.

ST SAVIOUR, Upper Huskisson Street. 1839–40, and a very handsome classical building. The long side to the street has elegant giant pilasters and arched windows. The E wall is barer, and above it is a low polygonal dome. One tripartite window tells in a loud voice of work of *c*.1900. The church was indeed gutted by fire in 1900 and reconstructed by *Willink & Thicknesse*. The nave has a shallow segmental vault. The apse certainly is of 1900. Until then the orientation was the opposite way. Where the low baptistery now is, was the altar space.

ST STEPHEN, Grove Street, replacing St Stephen, Edge Hill, by *G. G. Scott* (1850–1), demolished because of railway works. 1881 by *T. D. Barry & Son*. Red stone. Lancets and geometrical tracery.

SYNAGOGUE, Hope Place. 1856–60 by *T. Wylie*, the dome by *J. A. Picton*. The front arcade has been bricked up.

ST ANDREW PRESBYTERIAN CHURCH, Rodney Street. 1823–4 by *John Foster Jun.* and his best remaining building. Classical ashlar-faced front with two short towers and a three-bay loggia with fluted Ionic columns between. The sides have two tiers of arched windows. Inside three galleries supported by thin columns and carrying thin columns. Flat ceiling. The building in the churchyard with its Venetian end window is of 1872. In the churchyard MONUMENT to William Mackenzie, railway contractor, † 1851. It is a severely plain granite pyramid and was erected in 1868.

CATHOLIC APOSTOLIC CHURCH, Catharine Street. Apparently of 1840–56. The completion by *G. B. Nicholls* and *E. T*

Owen (GS). The nave with Dec tracery, rather flat, the transept tall and tight. Asymmetrical bell-turret.* The chancel, built before the nave, is quite different, with flying buttresses, an ambulatory, and an apse. The ambulatory is vaulted, the chancel was no doubt meant to be vaulted too. *The Ecclesiologist* (December 1853) reports that 'the plan was revealed to the minister by revelation'. – STAINED GLASS. Nelson reports some C15 Flemish roundels. *See p. 480*

JAMES'S CEMETERY. So named after the church of St James, which is just across the Toxteth border. The cemetery was made in 1825–9 inside an abandoned quarry. The choice was a stroke of genius. It makes the cemetery the most romantic in England and forms an ideal foil for the cathedral next to it. Rock walls to the E, ramps with family vaults to the w. The monuments are crowded and enjoy a happy neglect. Only two buildings stand out – the HUSKISSON MONUMENT of 1836 by *John Foster* and the mortuary chapel by the same. Huskisson, the liberal politician and M.P. for Liverpool, had been killed during the opening ceremony of the Liverpool–Manchester Railway in 1830. The building is a domed rotunda of Corinthian columns with the walls between filled in, except for square grilles at the top. Inside the STATUE of Huskisson by *John Gibson*, 1831–3. Splendid entrance arch and lodge at the SW corner. The MORTUARY CHAPEL is at the far NW end of the cemetery on the level of the present cathedral's future façade. It is oblong, with porticoes of six Greek Doric columns to both ends. Inside four fluted Ionic monolith columns on either side, and ridged skylighting – a noble exterior and a noble interior. – MONUMENTS. They are mostly of *c.*1830–40. Emily Robinson † 1829. By *John Gibson*. Tablet with a woman holding a book and seated by a shaft with an urn. – William Ewart † 1832. By *J. Gott*. Seated, amiably expounding something. Free-standing monument. – William Hammerton † 1832. By *Gibson*, 1832. Large relief, the figures in Roman dress. He offers food and drink to an exhausted woman with a child in her lap and a young girl standing behind her. – William Nicholson. By *Chantrey*, 1834. Standing monument with a mourning husband and wife. She kneels, he bends over an urn. – Rev. Ralph Nicholson and wife † 1794 and 1801. With medallion with double profile portraits. – William Earle † 1839. By *Gibson*. Tablet with large relief of a seated man. – John Gore † 1830. Large tablet with mourning woman by an urn.

45

* The design included a steeple.

PUBLIC BUILDINGS

POLICE HEADQUARTERS, Hardman Street. Long, symmetrica
late classical front of ashlar. Built as the School for the Blin
by *A. H. Holme* in 1850–1. A new building with its long sid
to Hope Street was built in 1931–2. It is strictly classica
with fluted giant pilasters, and rather forbidding. Th
architects are *Minoprio & Spencely*. Bronze DOORS by *Jam*
Woodford.

COLLEGE OF ART, Mount Street. 1882 by *Thomas Cook* (
Liverpool, and debased Victorian. An extension to Hope Stree
on the other hand, by *Willink & Thicknesse* of 1910, is remark
ably elegant in the Liverpool neo-Grec way, see especially th
details of the two bows. A yet more recent extension is differen
It is by the City Architect's Department (*R. Bradbury*). Curtai
walling to Hope Street, a blank brick wall to the cathedral. Th
latest extension was completed in 1961.

LIVERPOOL INSTITUTION HIGH SCHOOL FOR BOYS, Moun
Street. Built as the Mechanics' Institution in 1835–7 by *A. F.
Holme*. Ashlar-faced and of remarkable dignity for what it wa
Nine bays and two storeys with a portico of two pairs of un
fluted Ionic giant columns. No pediment.

LIVERPOOL INSTITUTION HIGH SCHOOL FOR GIRLS. Four
ded in 1844 by the generosity of George Holt. The core i
Blackburn House, a house existing on the site. The larg
symmetrical, Italianate main building with its big French pav
lion roof is of 1874.

SCHOOL FOR THE DEAF, Melville Place. A three-bay, ashlar
faced house with a spacious porch. The date is 1840.

ROYAL INFIRMARY, Pembroke Place. By *Waterhouse*, 1887–9
Common brick and red brick, like the Victoria Building of th
University characteristic Waterhouse, with big dormers an
gables, but also round arches to windows. The chapel has aisle
a three-sided apse, and also both pointed and round-heade
arches. Typical Waterhouse tiling with predominant cool blu
and green.

MEDICAL TEACHING CENTRE. *See* p. 218.

MEDICAL INSTITUTION. *See* p. 186.

PHILHARMONIC HALL, Hope Street. 1937–9 by *Rowse*. Larg
of brick, with a façade in the Dutch Dudok style. Interior wit
corrugated walls and ceiling for acoustic purposes. The decora
tive details are modernistic in the Paris-1925 way.

WELLINGTON ROOMS. *See* p. 185.

PERAMBULATION

ı the following pages streets are listed alphabetically, but for
ɔse who feel up to a walk of several miles a sequence is suggested
the footnote in which all streets can be visited.*

ʙERCROMBY SQUARE. Laid out *c.* 1815 and built mostly in
ɪ825–35. A ROTUNDA in the centre whose original function
ɜeems to be unknown. The three surviving sides are all single
ɔompositions, each with a Greek Doric porch in the middle and
ɯost of the other doorways with Doric pilasters and heavy
ɪintels. On the N side the E end (No. 19) is different. It is of
ɔ.1860, classical and well-mannered, but a separate unit. It was
built for C. K. Prioleau, a merchant, and became the Bishop's
Palace. It has a rather fine galleried staircase hall. On the same
ɜide No. 22 and former adjoining houses was given lavish late
ɔ17 style interiors for the SCHOOL OF EDUCATION of the
ɯniversity *c.* 1921 by *Ronald P. Jones.* In the SW corner the
Department of Civic Design. For this *see* p. 201. The climax
ɔf the square was the portico of St Catherine (by *Foster,*
ɪ829–31), but this the university has ruthlessly destroyed.
How well it could have been incorporated into a design for the
ɲew Senate House!

ᴅFORD STREET NORTH. At the N end all is university. The
ɪively group of stuccoed houses on the W side has recently been
ɗemolished by the University. On the E side all is minor.
Finally on the W side, very major and, as we shall see, very
ɔbjectionable, the University Sports Centre.

ᴅFORD STREET SOUTH. Largely university, but on the W side
ɑ very attractive stuccoed group, especially the nine-bay begin-
ɲing. Further S houses with porches of unfluted Ionic columns
(cf. Huskisson Street).

ᴀCKBURNE PLACE. Blackburne Terrace is dated 1826.

ᴀNNING STREET. Mostly porches with unfluted Ionic columns,

* Start from the Adelphi Hotel and walk up Mount Pleasant to the end,
ɲ Bedford Street to the S, including Abercromby Square, Chatham Street
the N, Grove Street to the S with a turn E by Blanche Street to
ɪithdown Lane for one item, then Upper Huskisson Street to the W,
kner Square, Huskisson Street, the S end of Hope Street, Upper Parlia-
ɲt Street to the E, again by Falkner Square to Canning Street, Catharine
ɜeet, Blackburne Place, Percy Street, Gambier Terrace, Upper Duke
ɜeet, Rodney Street, E a stretch of Mount Pleasant again, and Hope Street
the S with turns into Hardman Street and Mount Street. That leaves
ɑrate Lord Nelson Street, just N of Lime Street Station, and St
ɗrew's Gardens.

i.e. c.1835–45, but towards the corner of Percy Street a terrace (Nos 2–16) which is ashlar-faced. Between Catharine and Bedford Streets a terrace with two pediments.

CATHARINE STREET. Nos 44–50 have porches with fluted Ionic columns and honeysuckle in the friezes. Nos 47–57 are a similar terrace, also with fluted columns. They are of three, two, two, three columns for the six houses. Further s (59–63) Greek Doric porches.

CHATHAM STREET. From N first the debased former Welsh Presbyterian Chapel (*see* University p. 202), then on the w side Late Georgian terraces, even s of Myrtle Street.

CLARENCE STREET. *See* Mount Pleasant.

DUKE STREET. Some early C19 brick houses, each with a pediment all across. On the corner of Slater Street the former UNION NEWS ROOM by the elder *Foster*, 1800.

FALKNER SQUARE. Planted in 1835. Stuccoed houses mostly with porches. They have Tuscan or unfluted Ionic columns.

GAMBIER TERRACE. 1830–c.37 the w half. The E half is mid Victorian. The older part consists of the following. A grand beginning of seven bays, ashlar-faced, with unfluted upper giant Ionic columns and, round the corner, an enclosed Greek Doric porch, then twenty-one bays with a long Greek Doric colonnade in front, and then six bays with giant Doric pilasters. As a composition it is not particularly successful, but then it is no doubt incomplete.

GROVE STREET. At the time of writing the remaining houses of c.1830 with their Greek Doric porches are in utter decay.

HOPE PLACE. *See* Hope Street.

HOPE STREET. This is a very mixed street, and of the former Georgian terraces only bits survive here and there. The most prominent individual building is FEDERATION HOUSE, for the Building Trades Employers, 1965–6 by *Gilling, Dod & Partners*. Curtain walling, but on the ground floor a wildly ornamental concrete feature by *W. G. Mitchell*. Whom of the members of the Federation or the passers-by can this please? The building occupies the site of Hope Street Unitarian Church of 1848–9 by *T. D. Barry* and *W. Raffles Brown*, which was one of the first instances anywhere of a Nonconformist chapel completely adopting the form (including the chancel) of a Gothic parish church. – Opposite is HOPE PLACE with some Late Georgian doorways, and further N, at the corner of Hardman Street, is the PHILHARMONIC HOTEL, 1898–1900 by *Walter Thomas*. The building has stepped gables and to Hope Street central feature with a double-curved balcony and two turrets. Sumptuous iron gates by *H. Blomfield Bare*. Splendid interior with much plasterwork, also repoussé copper panels by *Blomfield Bare* and plaster caryatids by *C. J. Allen*. The interior work was supervised by *G. Hall Neale* and *Arthur Stratton*. The (then) School of Architecture and Applied Art of the University had much to do with it.

HUSKISSON STREET. Largely terraces of *c*.1830–40. The porches have unfluted Ionic columns.

LORD NELSON STREET, immediately N of Lime Street Station. Former premises of Cope Brothers, by *Douglas*. Very Gothic and very picturesque. Stock brick and red brick with very steep roofs, a turret, and an attached gateway. The building is only three bays wide and at the time of writing derelict. – (Further down, on the opposite side, the former OWENITE HALL OF SCIENCE, 1840.)

MOUNT PLEASANT. No. 2 is the UNIVERSITY CLUB by *Willink & Thicknesse*. Neo-Grec interior. – On the N side much minor Late Georgian, on the S side a five-bay brick house with a very unusual doorway. It has a broken pediment, which is three-dimensional and rests on brackets turned outwards. – Then the Y.M.C.A. BUILDING, brick, Gothic in a C13 version, and asymmetrical. It is of 1875–7, by *H. H. Vale*. – No. 68 is another five-bay house. Three-bay broken pediment. Charming doorway with carved frieze. This is hardly later than 1800. – No. 70 was built as the Consumption Hospital. It is by *Grayson & Ould*, 1904, red brick and terracotta, tripartite, with two pediments. – On the N in CLARENCE STREET some more Georgian terrace houses. – Again on the S side NOTRE DAME CONVENT, a motley group of buildings, the nucleus of which is a Late Georgian five-bay house (No. 96) with inside a good staircase. Enlargements 1857 by *Charles Hansom** and the chapel 1865–7 by *M. E. Hadfield & Son*. This is on the first floor, its flèche visible from the street. Apse semicircular outside but polygonal inside. Interior vaulted. Originally a rich and splendid example of High Victorian decorative art, but now emasculated almost out of recognition. The convent was several times further enlarged in the C19. – Opposite the WELLINGTON ROOMS, built as a subscription assembly room. 1815–16 by *Edmund Aikin*. A very fine reticent front. Semicircular mid-projection with attached Corinthian columns, but originally detached. L. and r. bare walls, just with one finely carved panel.

* Information from Denis Evinson.

The end bays are also blank. They are framed by Corinthian pilasters. The shape of the rooms inside survives and the decoration of the ballroom, which however looks partly Early Victorian. The ballroom was lengthened by *Doyle* in 1893. – Then on the s side at the corner of Hope Street the MEDICAL INSTITUTION, 1836–7 by *C. Rampling*, ashlar, classical with a portico of six unfluted Ionic columns developing round the rounded corner. Then three bays l. in Mount Pleasant and three r. in Hope Street. Staircase with convex landing. On the first floor three rooms with circular skylights. – MONUMENT from St Peter's church. John Rutter † 1838, tablet with a sarcophagus. – At the top of Mount Pleasant all is now University and Catholic Cathedral.

PERCY STREET. This is the grandest street in the area, though it is not long. Why was ashlar stone used here consistently ? Next to St Bride a terrace (Nos 3–17) with three projections and a Greek Doric colonnade in front of the recessed parts. Opposite two terraces occupying nearly the whole length of the street. The style makes building *c.*1825–30 probable.

RODNEY STREET. Built up at the end of the C18 and in the early C19. All brick and with handsome doorcases, mostly recessed with columns, slender Ionic or slender Greek Doric, also normal doorcases with Tuscan columns. The heavy Greek Doric stone porch of No. 29 must be an addition of *c.*1820–30. No. 35 is a five-bay house with a five-bay pediment. The doorway has swags in the frieze. No. 62 of 1796 (Gladstone's birthplace) is of five bays with a three-bay pediment and a more than usually ornate doorway. Nos 84–88 have a pretty Gothick balcony; Nos 51–75 are one composition with a five-bay centre pediment.

(ST ANDREW'S GARDENS. Corporation flats of 1936 – post-Georgian. They are built round a semicircular courtyard.)

SANDON STREET. *See* Upper Parliament Street.

SMITHDOWN LANE. On the E side a big, strange, bottle-shaped railway ventilation shaft.

UPPER DUKE STREET. Facing the cathedral a group of four houses called MORNINGTON TERRACE, with a three-bay pediment. The group is plainer than Rodney Street round the corner.

UPPER HUSKISSON STREET. In its E part wide, tree-planted, and of even architecture, though not special in quality.

UPPER PARLIAMENT STREET. Between Grove Street and Bloom Street a complete terrace of *c.*1830. It is called MONT-

PELIER TERRACE and has three Ionic porches of three columns
each. Further E on the Toxteth side a stuccoed group also of
c.1830. Work of c.1830 also in SANDON STREET. On the N side
at the very top, in Dinorben Street, a new high block of flats.

THE CATHEDRAL

The diocese of Liverpool was established in 1880. At first the
church of St Peter did service for a cathedral. A competition
for the site of St John was held in 1887. It was abandoned in
1888. The final site was selected in 1901. It was ideal from the
point of view of the cathedral dominating the city and the river
views as it should do, but it made nonsense of the Georgian
terraces around. Still in 1901 architects were asked to submit
portfolios of work. At first it was stipulated that designs must be
Gothic, but after objections, raised particularly by *The Architectural Review*, this condition was abandoned. The assessors
were Bodley and Norman Shaw. They chose five out of 103.
The five were, apart from *Giles Gilbert Scott*, Austin & Paley,
C. A. Nicholson, Malcolm Stark, and W. J. Tapper. Among
those not selected were e.g. Lethaby, Mackintosh, and Reilly.
The design by Scott accepted in 1903 was different in many
ways from that executed. It was cruciform with a six-bay nave
and twin towers over the transepts. As Scott was only twenty-
one when he was chosen, Bodley was nominated joint architect.
This, however, did not work well, and when Bodley died in
1907 Scott took over as sole architect. Work started in 1904,
after certain alterations had been made to the design, and work
on the superstructure started in 1906.

The Lady Chapel came first, in 1906–10. Then, in 1909–10
Scott made sweeping changes. The central tower replaced the
twin towers, two sets of transepts were designed to frame it,
and the nave was shortened drastically to match the choir. It
became an entirely different, but spatially equally convincing
composition. Liturgically this is hardly so. The transepts, the
major portals between them, and the tower space are useless,
functionally speaking; and that has remained a worrying fact
about the cathedral. Under the new scheme choir and E transepts were built in 1910–24,* the tower to a once again revised
design in 1924–42. The W transepts were completed in 1941,
the tower in 1942, and the nave was begun in 1948. Scott made
a revised design for the W front in 1942, an elaborate affair with

* E, W, N, and S, are here used ritually. In fact my W is really N, my N is E, etc.

an angular w porch. The w front now intended to be the end of the building's long history is by *F. G. Thomas* of Sir Giles Scott, Son & Partner. When Scott died in 1960, he had been connected with the cathedral for fifty-nine years, against Wren's thirty-four years at St Paul's. But Scott, though younger than Wren, was more tired towards the end, and the style of his building has worn worse than Wren's. In 1715 there were few who would have had a right to call St Paul's old-fashioned; Liverpool Cathedral in 1942, let alone today, is desperately of a past that can never be recovered.

The cathedral is built of red sandstone. It will be *c*.600 ft long when the nave is finished, and the tower is 331 ft high. It is this height which remains in one's memory and which succeeds in 'sending' one.* The earliest part of the building is the LADY CHAPEL, and that is still conventionally, though very competently, Gothic of the Late Bodley kind, high, with buttresses with many set-offs and tall two-light Dec windows. Only the s porch is freer in the details, with Arts and Crafts touches. Two-light balcony with sculpture (designed by Miss *Reed*). The CHAPTER HOUSE followed. It was begun in 1906. It is octagonal and connected with the choir by a passage which continues as an ambulatory behind the sanctuary, and also by a bridge higher up, the sort of romantic feature one can find in Beresford Pite's or Fred Griggs's dream drawings. The CHOIR was started in 1910. The e wall has two very long two-light windows, also Dec in detail – Scott was partial to these dualities – and two turrets with oddly short spires or polygonal pyramid roofs. What distinguishes the choir, and especially its n and s sides, from the Lady Chapel is what distinguishes the whole of the rest of the building – a style no longer dependent on Bodley. Scott now uses very large, bare, smooth surfaces, and contrasts them with small, prettily detailed and highly ornamental areas, all Gothic, all Dec, but tending to the Flamboyant rather than the English Dec. The choir has a smaller outer gallery of little arches right at the top, a motif inspired by e.g. Albi. The windows are not Dec, but in a rather bald late c13 Geometrical. Highly original and bold is the composition of two TRANSEPTS flanking the tower and the main portal. This is known as the RANKIN PORCH and it is matched by the WELSFORD PORCH, utterly useless, because leading straight into the abyss of the cemetery. But it had to be there, because n must match s. The

* I use this term, because I used it when describing Coventry Cathedral for *The Buildings of England* some years ago.

portals themselves are preceded by a deep niche or porch
opening to outside by a large round arch. The whole is power-
fully framed by the transepts. Low entrances outside the
transept fronts to W and E lead into the undercroft. The arches
die into the imposts. This is another of Scott's favourite motifs,
and another derived from the best Gothicists of the late C19.
Inside the porch are three identical portals, their details in an
ornate Late Gothic evidently influenced by the Spanish style
of the Reyes Catolicos, i.e. the period about 1500. Spain
altogether must have impressed Scott most. The TOWER is
magnificent seen at a distance from anywhere. The slightly
leaning four angle turrets are most sensitively detailed; again
there is much bare wall and much busy little decoration,
especially at the top. The pinnacles seem tiny. Of the NAVE
little can as yet be said. May it not be curtailed. From far away
too short a nave would be disastrous.

Entering by the Rankin Porch one finds oneself in a narrowly
confined space, with another set of two identical Spanish
portals and a figured rib-vault. The building is then entered
straight into the space of the TOWER, a height which seems
immense. The figured rib-vault seems far away. The height is
the greatest asset of the cathedral, though the management of
the spaces is exciting too, and much of the older detail con-
vinces in the historical setting of 1900–10.

The LADY CHAPEL came first. It is an impressive interior,
very Bodleyish, with elongatedly polygonal piers, their arches
dying into the imposts, a transparent triforium or passage half
below the clerestory windows. The triforium has a florid Arts
and Crafts cresting and at its sill an equally florid inscription.
The vault has curved ribs such as they occur in Spain, but
hardly in England. Triple-arcaded W gallery with organ above.
The black and white marble flooring has asymmetrical patterns.
The Lady Chapel is reached from the S chancel aisle. The
CHOIR has a much simpler vault. Just two narrow quadripartite 88
bays for each bay below. The choir aisles are really not aisles
but ample passages through side spaces with transverse ribbed
vaults, the type of Albi and Catalonia. The aisles are continued
behind the altar by a low passage which continues to the N as
the passage by which the chapter house is reached. The transepts have no gallery nor triforium, but just a long balcony.
The part of the central space under the tower is carried to a
greater height. Construction of the chancel and E transepts had
been begun before Scott's redesigning of 1909–10, and this

explains the enormous transept columns (which, when started
were intended to carry the twin towers) and the curious vaultin
devised to overcome the difficulty of the central space bein
wider than the chancel. For the sake of balance these feature
were repeated westwards. Scott constantly continued to chang
and revise his designs in minor as well as in more fundamenta
ways – see, e.g., the varying designs of balcony balustrade
throughout or the mouldings and treatment of the piers in th
E and W transepts. Even the pier shafts of the E and W towe
arches are different.

The nave is cut off from the W transepts by a cross balcon
on a round arch, a strange device. In the first bay of the nav
two long staircases lead up to this balcony.

FURNISHINGS. Much of the decoration suffers from an eas
sentimentality – what the French call *bondieuserie*. Little re
quires more than factual information. – FONT. Marble, wit
relief figures by *E. Carter Preston*. – The CANOPY designed b
Scott, square, with flamboyant top. – REREDOS. A Spanis
retablo in style. Designed by *Scott* and made by *Walter Gilber*
and *L. Weingartner*. – COMMUNION RAIL. By *Gilbert* an
Weingartner too, with few, widely spaced uprights. – CHOI
STALLS. By *Waring & Gillow*. Feeble. – ORGAN CAS
Designed by *Scott*. – ALTARPIECE in the Lady Chape
Designed by *Bodley* and *Scott*. Again entirely un-English.
SCULPTURE. Pietà by *E. Carter Preston*. – Holy Family b
Josephina de Vasconcellos. A fibre-glass moulding after th
original in St Martin in the Fields in London. Another mould
ing is in Gloucester Cathedral. – STAINED GLASS. Mostl
by *Powell & Sons*, and nothing worth commenting on.
In the chapter house all by *Morris & Co.*, but only a sign of th
total decay of the firm before its liquidation. – On the chapte
house staircase by *Kempe*, 1916, i.e. also too late to be goo
– PLATE. Chalice, C14, probably French. – Principal Set 188
silver-gilt. Designed by *W. C. Goodman* and made by *Elking
ton*'s. – Much designed by *Scott* and carried out by *W. Bain
bridge Reynolds*. – After the Second World War much by *Lesl
Durbin*. – NEEDLEWORK. Some (e.g. Lady Chapel frontals
designed by *Bodley*. – MONUMENTS. In the Lady Chapel Mr
Neilson † 1945 by *E. Carter Preston*. – Also Nurses' Memori
by *David Evans*. – In the S choir aisle Bishop Chavanne † 193
By *Evans*. – Bishop Ryle † 1900. By *Carter Preston*. – Dea
Dwelly † 1957. By the same. – In the SE transept sixteenth Ea
of Derby. Designed by *Scott* and made by *Farmer & Brindley*.

CATHOLIC CATHEDRAL OF CHRIST THE KING

MOUNT PLEASANT

Liverpool became a Catholic diocese in 1850. In 1853 a cathedral was begun in the grounds of St Domingo House at Everton, where the bishop lived. The architect appointed was *E. W. Pugin*, and no more was built than the Lady Chapel.* Then, nearly eighty years later, in 1930, the diocese, fortified by the strong and lively Irish–Catholic contingent of Merseyside, decided on building a cathedral such as Britain had never seen and such as few churches in the world would emulate.

Sir Edwin Lutyens was commissioned. The design was exhibited in the Royal Academy in 1932. Christopher Hussey called it 'English renaissance of Wren, but with his baroque idiom modified by what may be termed a fusion of Roman precedent with twentieth-century austerity'. The area to be covered by the cathedral was 233,000 sq ft, the length was to be 680 ft, the width 400 ft, the height to the top of the dome 510 ft. These figures compare with 715, 450, and 450 for St Peter's in Rome, 510, 250, and 366 for St Paul's in London, and Lutyens's central dome was to have a diameter of 168 ft, larger than existed anywhere (St Peter's 137, St Paul's 112). The plan was for a longitudinal but very compact building. It was to consist of a short nave and double aisles, the dome to the diameter of nave and inner aisles, transepts of nave and double aisles, and a short chancel with an apse and the circular chapter house behind it. But that was not all. The nave was to start‡ at its 'w' (i.e. s) end with a narthex and 'N' and 's' chapels, the 's' chapel being the baptistery. The transept ends were to have angle chapels too, four of them. Moreover, the apse was to be flanked by large apsed chapels, and 'N' and 's' of these were to be sacristies.

The exterior was to be of buff brick with much of granite dressings. The walls, in the model, look severe, with small, arbitrarily placed windows. The 'w' (i.e. s) front was to have four huge piers, sheer, except for decorative aedicules high up. The piers were to carry three arches, the middle one wider and much higher, forming three deep recesses, a Lincoln motif

* See p. 222

‡ The cathedral was (and is) not orientated. Ritual E is in fact N. This is ̶ue also of the cathedral as built, and in the whole of this description 'E' will ̶ean factual N, but E factual E.

much enlarged. The stone-work, all already detailed meti-
culously by Lutyens, was to be the supreme example of his late
passion for modular relations between all ashlar blocks. The
major proportions were equally rationalized into simple relations.

Work began in 1933 but was abandoned in 1940. Only the
CRYPT had been built, but what a crypt! For a comparison one
can only think of that of St Peter's, and in addition of the substructure of such a Roman palace as that on the Palatine, or
better still Diocletian's at Spalato. The crypt covers no more
than the choir area of the cathedral, i.e. its 'E' (=N) end. The
plan is very complex and hard to understand, as one wanders
under these vaults which seem to stretch into infinity. Entry is
from the South Court (i.e. from the E). The room one enters is
called the Chapel of Our Lady of Dolours. It has aisles, really
double aisles of different widths. The chapel ends in three
apses. They are scooped into the mighty substructures of the
organ wall and chapter house above. To them correspond two
circular rooms below. But outside the aisles of the Chapel of
the Dolours are a further aisle to the N ('E') and the S ('W').
They run all the length of the crypt, i.e. the width of the
sanctuary. They differ in details: one has the two amply-scaled
circular staircases and a narthex between, the other has the
two ends with columns so as to create three-naved fragments
of the type which Romanesque crypts favoured. Moreover, 'N'
of the two circular rooms, the whole of the Chapel of the
Dolours repeats as the Chapel of the Crucifixion, and 'W' of
the two circular rooms, beneath the future high altar, is the
large Archbishop's Chapel.

The crypt was built to a height of 12 ft above ground. It is
entered from the South Crypt Court (i.e. the E) by two doorways. These and the large window between have all the exasperating whimsy of late Lutyens, exasperating not *per se*, but in
such a building and on this monumental scale. No-one can
afford to be a joker when it comes to a cathedral and its colossal
architectural members. Take the leaning blocking of a large
part of the tapering doorway pillars, or the hole through to
expose a circular motif. However, once this shock is got over
– and its repetition in such internal motifs as the 'Rolling
Stone', which is the entry to the Archbishop's Chapel, a
circular piece weighing six tons and swinging round – the
spatial effects inside are superb. The brickwork is superb too –
exposed by Sir Frederick Gibberd, against Lutyens's intention

– especially in the tunnel-vaults and groin-vaults without transverse arches. The staircases are wide and of the newel type, with wide flights interrupted by intermediate landings and a wide open well. Each flight has steps carefully detailed so as to start with convex and end with concave steps. The balustrade was to have no raised posts or knobs of any kind which would have prevented choristers from sliding down it – a typical Lutyens touch.* Where columns appear in the crypt they are of the Tuscan order and have *no* entasis.

The Lutyens cathedral, having been stopped in 1940 and being obviously far too large ever to be completed, was finally abandoned when a competition was held in 1959.‡ The greatest problem was what to do with the crypt. *Sir Frederick Gibberd* won the competition in 1960, and the stroke of genius which alone made him deserve his victory is to finish the crypt off with a large platform for open-air services, continue that platform to the S, and build his cathedral on that S half of the site, which was unimpeded by Lutyens. It was the stroke of genius corresponding to Sir Basil Spence's of keeping the Perp walls of St Michael's as the forecourt to his Coventry Cathedral.

Otherwise the change of architectural mood, from 1951, the year of the Coventry competition, to 1959 is overwhelming. In 1951 it was a matter of course that the winning design would be longitudinal and that a central design with the altar in the middle such as the growing Liturgical Movement demanded would have no chance of prize and execution. So Sir Basil Spence had to work to this traditional scheme, and believed in it. The Liverpool competition insisted on a close association of the congregation with the celebrant, i.e. the central importance of the high altar, and on perfect visibility for all 2,000 for whom accommodation had to be found. This clearly meant that only a central plan could win. That there are functional *cons* in part of the congregation following mass from half behind the priest's back is at present too easily forgotten. Acoustic problems of course also arise.

Sir Frederick Gibberd's plan is convincingly simple. He gave it a dress rehearsal in his chapel for Hopwood Training College. It is a circle of 194 ft diameter surrounded by thirteen chapels, the main entrance hall, and two side porches. The entrance is from the S ('w'), the N ('E') chapel projects further than the others. So an axial system is firmly established. The

---

* Not apocryphal, as far as I know.
‡ So was a scaled-down version by *Adrian Gilbert Scott*.

structure is sixteen reinforced concrete trusses of boomeran
shape held together by a concrete ring at the height of the ber
of the boomerang members and again at their top. On the upp
ring stands the high, fully glazed lantern, weighing 2,000 ton
It ends in pinnacles and is to their tops 290 ft high. The con
crete boomerangs are helped in their function by flying but
tresses which reach them at the lower ring. They alone, thoug
they were an afterthought, are extremely prominent.

98   The cathedral stands at the N end of Hope Street, and as th
Anglican cathedral stands near the S end of the same street,
relation between the two cathedrals is at once established.
will be more obvious when the direct approach to the ma
portal is built. Up to the present one arrives on a ramp fro
the E and has to turn 90 degrees to enter. Sir Frederick's lanter
is in recognition of the special relation to Scott's cathedral.
does not compete, yet it responds. It is with its pinnacles
the same tribe, but where Sir Giles is solid, Sir Frederick
details are thin and delicate. The Liverpool skyline has at on
taken to this newcomer.

For the rest of the exterior doubts cannot be silenced. Th
chapels and porches surrounding the cylinder are each differe
in shape from the next, and nearly all deliberately uncouth
The source of this uncouthness is of course late Le Corbusie
and the skylight funnels on some of them, round and square, a
only too clearly derivative. Their aggressiveness, and especial
that of the jagged main portal, contradicts the serene simplici
of the main space, and the barbaric concrete relief above th
main entrance (by *William Mitchell*) is even more aggressiv
The symbolism of the three crosses can just be detected, b
the forms are of a painful primeval cruelty. Whom will, who
can this appeal to, among those who visit the cathedral to pr
or for services ?‡ The bell-holes above the relief are equal
blunt and ruthless. The nearest architectural parallel is Breuer
St John Collegeville, as the nearest parallel of the who
scheme of the cathedral is Niemeyer's Brasilia Cathedral.

Sir Frederick denies that there was direct inspiration. H
pronounced himself 'infuriated' by that comparison and poin
out that it is only superficial, because his structural membe
are vertical below the lower band, or if you include the flyin

   * Nicholas Taylor, belonging to a different generation, calls it 'appeali
clumsiness'.
   ‡ Professor Gardner Medwin in *The Times* calls it 'a striking artefact whi
could be taken for some obscure symbol of an ancient cult'.

buttresses, delta-shaped, whereas Niemeyer's trusses slant from the start. But the flying buttresses of Liverpool, even if they are only additional support, are the most prominent feature, especially as they are distinguished by white mosaic facing set against the greyish-white Portland stone of the rest and the truncated cone of the aluminium roof.

The interior is easier on the eye and the mind. The entrance hall is low, and beyond it there is at once the wide, single space under the funnel-shaped roof. It is splendidly spacious and appeared even more so before the benches and the altar canopy were *in situ*. Its diameter is 194 ft (Aia Sophia Istanbul 107 ft). The structural members appear here in full clarity. They are of exposed concrete poured into smooth shuttering. The chapels and porches are – a brilliant conceit – treated as independent buildings not only because they are of brick, stone-faced, but visually even more convincingly, because they are framed l., r., and top by small strips of dark blue glass.* The irregularity of the shapes of the chapels is much more easily accepted inside than outside. What they have in common is that they are all very high in relation especially to their depth. Lighting is diverse too, and so are the wall surfaces. Some are wide open to the centre, others are all but closed, and the small arched entrance of one is a clear indication that Sir Frederick is not lacking in sympathy with the Lutyens of the crypt. As for shapes of chapels, the baptistery for instance is horseshoe-shaped to the inside, the 'E' chapel (of the Blessed Sacrament) is oblong with tapering sides and has a monopitch roof rising to the 'E' wall. The 'E' wall is of pitted stone. The 'N' and 's' chapels with the subsidiary entrances have balconies low down. The chapel following clockwise after the 'N' chapel (St Joseph) has wood slatting and a steep pyramid ceiling. The chapels l. and r. of the 'E' chapel are the only ones treated symmetrically. Following after the chapel to the r. of the 'E' chapel is the one with the Lutyens arch. The chapel r. of the 's' chapel receives light through an oculus in the roof of a kind of tight, high apse. But on the whole the variety of shapes appears less dominant inside than outside. Instead it is the fenestration and the colouring of the glass which tell, e.g. red in the chapel immediately l. of the main entrance, white and light brown in the Lady Chapel, green and yellow in that with the bishop's throne, etc. -

* The STAINED GLASS is by *John Piper* and *Patrick Reyntiens*. The danger of the dark blue is that in certain light it makes the altar look all blue and not white, as it is surely meant to appear.

The HIGH ALTAR stands right in the centre of the rotunda. I
is a slab of pure white marble quarried at Skopje, 10 ft b
3 ft 6 in. by 3 ft 6 in. in size and weighing nineteen tons. Abov
is a circular CANOPY, designed by *Sir Frederick Gibberd* an
consisting of vertical tubes of various lengths. It is a doubtfu
blessing. From some viewpoints it links the altar to the lantern
from others it confuses the S–N ('W'–'E') axis. – The CRUCIFI
high up is by *Elizabeth Frink*, the ALTAR CROSS and CANDLE
STICKS by *R. Y. Gooden*. – The FLOOR pattern (and also th
BAPTISTERY GATES) are designed by *David Atkins*. – Th
BENCHES are by *Frank Knight*. They are low and simple an
do not detract from the spatial unity. – In the Chapel of th
Blessed Sacrament REREDOS and STAINED GLASS are by *Ce*
Richards, in the Lady Chapel and the Chapel of St Paul th
glass is by *Margaret Traherne*. – The STATUE of the Virgin i
by *Robert Brumby*. – By *R. D. Russell* is the BISHOP'S THRON
with its simple canopy, by *William Mitchell* the main DOOI
again decidedly frightening. It might be the introduction t
some cruel Mexican ritual.* – The climax of the interior is th
STAINED GLASS of the lantern. It is abstract and moves from
yellow (N, i.e. 'E') to red (SW) and blue (SE). It was designed b
John Piper and made by *Patrick Reyntiens*. – PLATE. Baroqu
silver-gilt Chalice. – Processional Cross, also not recent. – Gol
Chalice with embossed figure of Christ by *Dunstan Pruden*
1959. – Crucifix and Candlesticks by *R. Y. Gooden*, 1967, th
bronze figure of Christ by *Elizabeth Frink*.

Sir Frederick's cathedral stands on a podium which is th
continuation of that levelling off the top of the Lutyens crypt
The Lutyens part Sir Frederick simply made into an area fo
open-air services. The N ('E') end of the church has an open-ai
altar, and the Lutyens staircases are delightfully finished b
concrete pyramids as Gibberd as they are Lutyens. The podiun
part below the Gibberd building is used for car parking –
service road runs through it – sacristies, storage, lavatories, an
even a tea room, accessible direct from the entrance hall.

Finally, E of the podium and mostly of the Lutyens part ar
some accessory buildings: a small CONVENT, the PRESBYTERY
and the UNIVERSITY CHAPLAINCY. They are all ashlar-faced
and they are extremely well scaled and prettily landscaped
Their simplicity is the right foil for the main building. Th

---

* And it is no good trying to justify this ferocity by saying that Romanesqu
sculpture can be ferocious; for the twentieth century just isn't the twelfth
and, balancing one thing against another, that is perhaps just as well.

convent has an internal courtyard, and there is a garden between presbytery and podium. The presbytery contains flats for the administrator and six priests, the convent is for nuns attached to the cathedral. It took five years to build the cathedral. Consecration took place in May 1967. The total cost was something like £1½ million.

THE UNIVERSITY

Liverpool University has the great advantage over others of the English universities that its buildings are within walking distance of the city centre. The advantage was bought dearly at the expense of the total of visual attractions of Liverpool; for the university has rooted itself as a parasite in the finest domestic part of the city.

Liverpool University started as University College in 1881. It became a member of the Victoria University (with Manchester) in 1884 and the University of Liverpool in 1903. In the following account the beginning will be the oldest buildings, and a perambulation will be attempted after that. The majority of the buildings are of after the Second World War. Some are distinguished, some acceptable, some objectionable, but as a whole the university suffers from a nimiety of architects. The whole is not a whole but a zoo, with species after species represented. If only such a client resisted one architect more! This does not mean pleading for the uniformity of Mies van der Rohe's work at the Illinois College of Technology, but at a moment when architects are inclined to show off anyway and to shock rather than please, a variety of architects can be fatal. I (if the author may speak as a person) find it difficult to describe much that has grown in this period recently without using negative terms all the time. There will therefore in the perambulation be much factual information and little criticism.

VICTORIA BUILDING. By *Waterhouse* 1887–92. Common brick, red brick, and red terracotta. In Waterhouse's typical free Gothic, with motifs from the C13 and the C15 and much that was simply useful. The main accents are the tower, to its r. the large windows, characterized as those of the staircase, and the angle turret. Entrance hall opening in two levels to the staircase. Much faience. On the second floor the Tate Hall, originally the Library, with a large open timber roof. To the l. of this building ENGINEERING LABORATORIES of 1887–9 also by *Waterhouse*, and rightly with less features. Into the back court looks the back façade of the former FACULTY OF ARTS, 1913 by

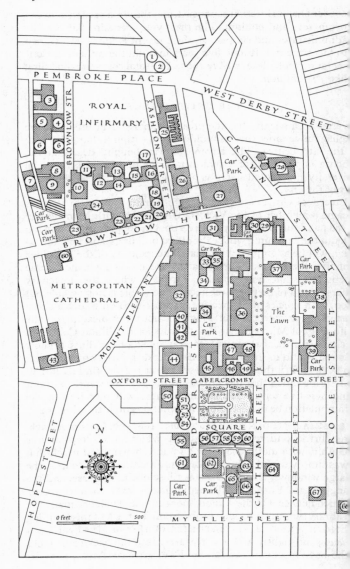

Briggs, Wolstenholme & Thornely, red brick and much stone, with giant pilasters and some Baroque sculpture in the centre (*see* below for the front). Also towards the same courtyard is CIVIL ENGINEERING by *E. Maxwell Fry* with one blank wall used for the display of the names of great engineers. The building faces into BROWNLOW STREET.

Brownlow Street opposite, from s to n MECHANICAL ENGINEERING, recent, by *Courtauld's Technical Services*, then ZOOLOGY, 1905 by *Willink & Thicknesse*, then BOTANY, 1905 by *F. W. Dixon*, and then Geology. GEOLOGY, 1929 by *Arnold Thornely*, is of brick with stone dressings and exhibits the nice Neo-Classical derived from Reilly. VETERINARY MEDICINE behind, also Reilly-ish, is by *Budden & Marshall*, 1929. Finally TROPICAL MEDICINE.

Turning into PEMBROKE PLACE there is on the s side the Royal Infirmary (*see* p. 182), then on the n the DENTAL SCHOOL AND HOSPITAL, 1909 by *G. de C. Fraser*, and on the s the MEDICAL SCHOOL by *Weightman & Bullen*, 1953–8, the main block long and indifferent, but at the n end a separate, canted-forward lecture theatre. A new wing at the rear, by the same architects. Ground floor open, except for the heavy supports of the upper storeys. Restless window pattern.

Along ASHTON STREET s of the Medical School is the HAROLD COHEN LIBRARY, of 1936–8, by *Harold E. Dod* of *Willink & Dod*, Portland-stone-faced, with a seven-bay centre, a little à la R.I.B.A. Building. Opposite is the building which used to be the FACULTY OF ARTS (*see* above), with a centre with six giant pilasters and a pediment, entirely conventional.

At the corner of BROWNLOW HILL, next to the Cohen Library, *Yorke, Rosenberg & Mardall*, in 1963–5, erected their excellent ELECTRICAL ENGINEERING BUILDING. It consists of a six-storeyed and a three-storeyed block with single- and double-storeyed extensions of the latter at its back and is faced with this firm's unmistakable unbonded white tiles. No tile had to be cut. The detail is indeed impeccable (and undevelopable). E of Electrical Engineering is LIFE SCIENCES, under construction at the time of writing. It is by *Robertson Young & Partners*. Also under construction the COMPUTER LABORATORY by *Yorke, Rosenberg & Mardall*.

E of Electrical Engineering VETERINARY MEDICINE by *E. Maxwell Fry*, disappointing towards the street and really facing s. The building does no credit to a pioneer architect such as Maxwell Fry was. The ALSOP BUILDING, w of the former,

is also still building while this is written. It is two-storeyed and
contains university shops etc. It is by *Tom Mellor & Partner*
So to the STUDENTS' UNION in Bedford Street, but entere
usually from MOUNT PLEASANT. The oldest part is that by
Sir Charles Reilly, of 1910–13. The Mount Pleasant entranc
was originally for girls, the Bedford Street entrance for boy
This is supposed to explain the different mood of the two, an
also something of the rather intricate planning. The female sid
small and dainty, in spite of the attached Greek Doric columr
of the ground floor which include the bow window. The uppe
floor of the bow has attenuated baluster-like columns in pair
To Bedford Street the front is standard, of six bays with
massive Beaux Arts balcony along the first floor, bluntly ped
mented French windows on that floor, and round window
over. The top cornice is unbroken. To the N is a largely window
less brick wall with two bowed staircase projections and
portion with brick columns and pediment high up. It must b
remembered that here the railway originally ran open belo
the building. The Gilmour Hall inside is Reilly all over wit
its dark sturdy columns and heavy Beaux-Arts-Grecian decora
tion. The other Reilly interiors also deserve a glance. In 193
the Union received an indifferent, tentatively modern bric
extension by *Reilly, L. B. Budden*, and *J. E. Marshall*. Recentl
a further brick extension, this one up-to-date but tactful, b
Bridgewater, Shepheard & Epstein in 1961–3. The two opposin
monopitch roofs towards the Catholic Cathedral media
between the Union and that new neighbour.

In BEDFORD STREET opposite the Union, s of the Alsop Buildin
is OCEANOGRAPHY and NUMERICAL ANALYSIS (strang
bedfellows) in the front and the higher slab for MATHEMATIC
behind. They are all three by *Bryan & Norman Westwoo*
1959–61, the computer room with an enterprising hyperboli
paraboloid roof, its jabbing shape rather arbitrarily re-echoe
on part of the roof of the Mathematics block. Windowle
concrete walls have diamond-cut blocks or patterned panels.

Behind, i.e. E of, this group is *Sir Basil Spence*'s PHYSICS, on
of the visually best new buildings of the university. It dates fror
1958–60 and consists of a nine-storey block, largely on stilt
teaching laboratories, and lecture theatres, lined up with grea
clarity l. and r. of a spine corridor. The lecture theatres hav
exposed rising floors and are faced with Derbydene stone. Th
sill zones of the high block have bluish-grey mosaic facing. T
the E the building faces THE LAWN, at last an attempt at seein

new university buildings together and not merely as isolated specimens.

of The Lawn is the block of the SCIENCE LECTURE ROOMS by *Saunders, Boston & Brock* (associated with *Robert Gardner-Medwin*), concrete, rather overpowering with its raw shuttering, concrete reliefs by the entrance, and two of the four lecture theatres sticking out. The windowless part of the building has brick panels in concrete frames. Towards The Lawn an outer staircase projects free of the building. How much is it used ?

of The Lawn is CHEMISTRY by *Stephenson, Young & Partners*, the N part 1955–8, U-shaped, brick, and so reasonable that it is quite a relief. The S part is of 1961–3, largely with curtain walls. of The Lawn, facing on Oxford Street, the OLIVER LODGE PHYSICS LABORATORY is being built at the time of writing. Architects: *Tom Mellor & Partners*.

o to ABERCROMBY SQUARE.* At its NW corner the SCHOOL OF ARCHITECTURE. The extension of 1932–3 by *Reilly, L. B. Budden* and *J. E. Marshall* obviously endeavours to harmonize with the square and yet be modern of a kind still rare in England by 1932. Note the horizontal window band. The SPORTS CENTRE by *Denys Lasdun*, 1965–6, endeavours just as patently to be rude to the square. Nothing could be more demonstratively anti-Georgian than these concrete posts rising diagonally with equally slanting glass walls between. Rectangularity is the ground work of the Georgian century. Mr Lasdun fully realizes this, and so the building must be meant as an affront. So is, though perhaps less so, the bare concrete wall to Bedford Street. Inside to the E the swimming pool, to the W the gymnasium with a glorious climbing wall of blue brick.

he STAFF CLUB is opposite in OXFORD STREET, a pleasant, modest, glass-fronted building by *Gerald R. Beech*.

he E side of the square is to be the SENATE BUILDING (only started at the time of writing). The architects are *Tom Mellor & Partners*.

he SE corner is CIVIC DESIGN by *Gordon Stephenson*, 1950–1, in the style of the thirties, i.e. brick with, on the first floor, a long window band. The second floor is recessed and has a canopy, set asymmetrically – a Maxwell Fry motif. This was the first university building after the Second World War.

pposite is the ARTS FACULTY, forming the major part of a block, together with SOCIAL STUDIES and LAW. The whole is by *Bryan & Norman Westwood, Piet & Partners*, 1962–4,

* Cf. also p. 183.

and, being all one group by one architect, is the most successfu
part of the new university to date. It is true that much of th
detail is overdone – the besetting sin of the sixties – but th
unity of conception wins. The happiest part is the Arts Librar
in Bedford Street, forbidding to the street, but opener inwards
Rough concrete and dark brick. The concrete slabs are onl
approximately vertical. They deviate slightly, but at differin
angles, and this results in a kind of seasick feeling not suite
to a library. The library has its own small turfed courtyarc
and one passes through this to reach the irregular courtyar
between. As for the higher buildings, Social Studies is of te
storeys, Law, to Chatham Street, has the motif of vertical fins
The general colouring of the buildings is sombre.

In CHATHAM STREET is the EXAMINATION SCHOOL, for
merly a Welsh Presbyterian Chapel. With its giant pilasters
broken pediment, and grotesque bellcote it is typical of Non
conformist architecture of c. 1860. Architects: *Oliver & Lamb*
Cf. p. 184.

In MOUNT PLEASANT, opposite the Medical Institution an
away from the other buildings, is *Sir William Holford*
NUCLEAR PHYSICS.

CARNATIC HALLS, *see* p. 231.

DERBY HALL, RATHBONE HALL, ROSCOE HALL, GLAD
STONE HALL, *see* p. 239.

EXTRA-MURAL DEPARTMENTS, *see* Colquitt Street, p. 171.

WYNCOTE SPORTS GROUND, *see* p. 209.

INNER DISTRICTS NORTH

The area is N of the centre, W of Byrom Street and Scotland Roac
and E of the Docks.

CHURCHES

ST ALBAN (R.C.), Athol Street. 1849 by *Weightman & Hadfield*
The style is of c.1300. The only impressive thing is the ver
high and narrow proportions of the nave.

ST ANTHONY (R.C.), Scotland Road. 1833 by *John Broadbent*
Ashlar, without a tower. The sides with high coupled lancet
between buttresses, the W and E with a triplet of stepped lancets
At the E end low vestries below them. The W front is quit
ambitious, with its lancets and pinnacles. The interior has th
charming motif of a shallow chancel and shallow chapels l. an
r. of it, the three as one tripartite group with pointed arches t

the w. No N and S galleries are preserved, yet the width of the nave proves that they must have been there.

ST AUGUSTINE (R.C.), Great Howard Street. 1848–9. A very wilful façade with a bellcote. E.E. to early C14 details. Small.

ST BRIGID (R.C.), Bevington Hill. 1894. Built of common brick and red brick with a NW tower of the oddest shape. It has very high blank arches and a bell-stage boxed out. The church had lancet windows. Interior with short granite columns and big, square, stiff-leaf capitals. The church was pulled down in 1967 in connexion with work on the approach to the new Mersey Tunnel.

HOLY CROSS (R.C.), Standish Street. 1859–60 by *E. W. Pugin*, the chancel of 1875. The church was blitzed in 1941 and rebuilt in 1955. The plaster-vaulted apse looks 1859, but apparently is also of the rebuilding. – The PRESBYTERY faces Great Crosshall Street and is of 1859 (GS).

OUR LADY OF RECONCILIATION (R.C.), Eldon Street. 1859–60 by *E. W. Pugin*. Of stone, along the street. Clerestory with sex-foiled circular windows. E apse. Poor interior.

ST SYLVESTER (R.C.), Silvester Street. 1888–9 by *Pugin & Pugin*. Fiery red Ruabon brick. Quite a large church. Dec detail. The prominent tower with pyramid roof stands to the S connected by a passage to the church. Interior of little interest.

Former WELSH CALVINISTIC METHODIST CHAPEL, Burlington Street. Ashlar-faced, of five bays, upper attached Ionic columns. A fine, noble façade, probably of *c.*1830.

PUBLIC BUILDINGS

For the DOCKS, *see* p. 164.

SCHOOL, Great Crosshall Street, *see* Holy Cross, above.

ARCHBISHOP WHITESIDE SECONDARY SCHOOL, Silvester Street. A good group. By *Weightman & Bullen*, 1961–3.

PERAMBULATION

Two types of building must be followed, warehouses and municipal blocks of flats.

WAREHOUSES. These towering, severely utilitarian buildings are the *basso continuo* of our particular area. Immediately N of the centre they start in NEW QUAY with five pediments. Then in BATH STREET, at its N end, is one which must be specially early. It has three equal pediments and classical trim on the ground floor. Otherwise, most of the interesting warehouses will

be found between GREAT HOWARD STREET and WATERLOO
ROAD and in Gibraltar Row and the streets N of it: Denison
Street, Roberts Street, Barton Street, etc. The warehouse in
Formby Street is, according to Mr William Sutherland, the
earliest surviving fireproof building in Liverpool. It was erected
in 1836. Two enormous blocks between Vaudries Street and
Vulcan Street (1842–3) and between Dickson Street and Dublin
Street are also fireproof. They have cast-iron frames and were
designed by *A. H. Holme*. The big later warehouse by the top of
Waterloo Road belongs to Stanley Dock (*see* p. 165). A ware-
house dated 1847 is in VAUXHALL ROAD opposite Blenheim
Street.

As for FLATS, the earliest blocks are ST MARTIN'S COTTAGES,
Vauxhall Road and Silvester Street. They were put up in
1868–9. Two ranges of four storeys, brick, with the open staircases which had become an accepted hygienic device in London
from about 1850. They were built by the corporation as an
example to private enterprise, which failed to take the hint,
and it was not until 1885, with the building of Victoria Square
and the slightly later Juvenal Dwellings (no longer existing),
that a further attempt at municipal housing was made. For the
new early C20 friendliness excellent examples are first ST
ANNE STREET and BIRKETT STREET of 1914, still with the
open balconies in two tiers, as they had been usual in the late
C19, but with plastered gables and pretty stucco garlands. At
the S end of LIMEKILN LANE are three-storeyed, gabled brick
blocks dated 1911. Rather more utilitarian blocks further up
Limekiln Lane, but SUMMERSEAT has two-storey houses, and in
ELDON GROVE, BEVINGTON STREET, ELDON STREET,
and BOND STREET are three-storeyed blocks dated 1911, with
half-timbered gables and again with balconies. This type has
diagonally planned staircases projecting at the rear.* At the E
end of BURLINGTON STREET and in MILE END are blocks
of 1910, with a canted-back plan, gables, two tiers of balconies,
and big semicircular porches. In HORNBY STREET a large
number of very unusual blocks with free-standing pyramid-
roofed staircase towers and yellow terracotta trim. They date
from 1905 to 1913. All this early C20 housing is by the then city
surveyor, *Thomas Shelmerdine*, or rather by *T. Fletcher Turton*,
his deputy responsible for housing.

More neo-Georgian in TITCHFIELD STREET and BOND

* At the foot of Eldon Street were *Brodie's* pre-cast concrete flats. *See* Introduction, p. 149.

STREET, at the foot of which are later blocks with long horizontal strip balconies. Finally, to the w, another three-storeyed block with two tiers of balconies in SALTNEY STREET, next to Stanley Dock. This is of 1911.

INNER DISTRICTS, NORTH-EAST

The area is N E of the centre and N of the University area. It includes London Road and goes to Islington Square and then follows the jagged boundary of Everton and on the w side runs along Byrom Street.

CHURCHES

ST ANNE, St Anne Street. By *E. R. Robson*, 1870–1, replacing a church of 1770–2 which had, according to Mr Sutherland, the earliest cast-iron gallery columns in any English church. Red brick with a big NW tower with pyramid roof and higher crocketed stair-turret. Low aisles and a high clerestory, lower chancel than nave. Simplified Dec tracery; rather a blunt building. Disappointing interior.

HOLY TRINITY, St Anne Street. Built in 1790–2. Classical, ashlar-faced. w tower, the top stage with concave angles. The sides have two tiers of windows, segment-arched and round-arched. Short chancel with Venetian window and low one-bay attachments. The interior has little to offer. Flat ceiling and three plain galleries.

PUBLIC BUILDINGS

TECHNICAL COLLEGE, Byrom Street. 1960 and 1965. Mostly curtain walling. No architectural interest.

MONUMENT, Monument Place, London Road. George III, an equestrian figure of bronze in Roman dress, of very good quality. The inspiration came from Marcus Aurelius. By *Sir R. Westmacott*, 1822.

PERAMBULATION

The only street worth a consistent walk is ISLINGTON. Starting from the E end of William Brown Street, there is first MESSRS BRADSHAW'S premises, dated 1897, with nice brick decoration, then No. 47 with a Georgian doorway and another more ambitiously decorated doorway in CLARE STREET. Opposite is the side elevation of a very remarkable office building of

Liverpool Suburbs

0   1/4   1/2 mile

----- Administrative Boundary

c.1900. Seven bays and three storeys, brick piers, the main windows of stone with completely flat mullions and transoms, and the middle bay gently convex. Opposite, in FRASER STREET, the SHAKESPEARE THEATRE, 1887–8, probably by *H. Havelock Sutton*. Its very ornate auditorium has recently been entirely and faithfully reconstructed after a fire. Then in ST ANNE STREET a store of OWEN OWEN, late 1850s, formerly the showroom and offices of a coach works. A fine cast-iron front, with columns on three floors, those on the ground floor being longer than the others. The house is of five bays with the middle three projecting considerably. The building itself is not iron-framed. Immediately N of Holy Trinity church, neo-Georgian flats of 1931 etc., axially planned about QUEEN ANNE STREET. For municipal housing further N *see* above, p. 204. Back into Islington and past some more Late Georgian terraces to ISLINGTON SQUARE, which has two good houses of *c*. 1830 on its N side, one of five bays and two and a half storeys, brick, with a five-bay pediment and a substantial Greek Doric porch, the other stuccoed and (at the time of writing) neglected. This is of two storeys and has rather coarse details somewhat reminiscent of Soane. It was originally a musical academy.

N from Islington Square is Shaw Street, *see* p. 224.

LIVERPOOL SUBURBS

AIGBURTH

ST ANNE, Aigburth Road. 1836–7 by *Cunningham & Holme*. Chancel and transepts 1853. Neo-Norman, and an early case of that revival. Red sandstone, with a squat w tower ('laughable' says *The Ecclesiologist*) and the early C19 plan type with no aisles, but transepts and a square chancel. Round-arched lancets and in the chancel round-arched triplets. Strikingly many corbel-heads and head-stops inside as well as out. Even the gatepiers are Norman.

ST AUSTIN (R.C.), Aigburth Road. 1838. Red stone façade. Plain rectangle with big w pinnacles and small steep-gabled w porch. The sides are brick with lancets and buttresses. There is only the shallowest chancel. It is flanked by low side chapels. Over their entrances gables, and over them blank arches to match the chancel arch.

ST MARY, Aigburth Road, Grassendale. 1853–4 by *A. H. Holme*. In spite of its late date still of the same plan as St Anne. The aisle must be later (1880 ?). The exterior, however, is a decided step in advance of St Anne. Dec, with a N W steeple. Inside, the most interesting thing is the laminated beams of the timber roof, forming a cross of flying arches over the central space between the transepts.

AIGBURTH METHODIST CHURCH, Aigburth Road, opposite St Anne. Brick with stone dressings, a N W tower, and the typical free Perp motifs of the Edwardian Methodists. Yet the date is 1926–8. Architect: *A. Brocklehurst* of Manchester.

There is little else to report. At the N end of the Aigburth part of Aigburth Road, at the corner of Ashfield Road, is one of the typical MARTINS BANK buildings, red brick and stone dressings, free Baroque, rather playful details, including a corner cupola. In AIGBURTH HALL ROAD, where Aigburth Hall Avenue forks off, is a cottage with a three-light mullioned window. This is said to be a survival of STANLAWE GRANGE, a grange of the Cistercian Abbey of Stanlaw in Cheshire. (The MHLG reports in addition a cruck-framed part which they assign to the late C 13.)

N W of St Mary Grassendale at the end of Grassendale Road is the entrance to GRASSENDALE PARK. Two streets and a riverside promenade laid out as a private venture. In South Road and North Road are a number of uncommonly attractive stuccoed houses belonging to the 1840s. The features are still entirely classical, but the heaviness e.g. of the cast-iron balconies shows that the date can't be earlier. Immediately by St Mary is the entrance to another such development, CRESSINGTON PARK, obviously a little later. The entrance lodge is worth a glance.

ALLERTON

ALL HALLOWS. Built for John Bibby of Hart Hill in memory of his first wife, daughter of Jesse Hartley – hence the size and the care taken. The architect is *G. E. Grayson*, the date 1872–6. Red sandstone. Mighty Perp w tower of Somerset type. Perp also the rest, an early case of the return to Perp. Ashlar-faced interior. The arcade of alternating pier shapes. – STAINED GLASS. All* by *Morris & Co.*, and all figure-work designed by *Burne-Jones*. The best are w and e, the latter the Adoration of the Lamb. The aisle windows are more routine, it seems. The E and W windows were done in 1875–6. They are in an exceptional and exquisite colouring of predominant white and brown.

* Except N transept E, which is by *Heaton, Butler & Bayne*.

They as well as the transept windows (of 1877 ? s and 1880 N) incorporate small panels with stories, all remarkably easily readable – more so, undeniably, than C13 glass. The chancel N windows (angels) followed in 1881. The glazing of the aisles was done in 1882–6. The colours are stronger and darker, and also unusual, deep rose and pink, pale mauve, much dark blue, etc., the latter chiefly in small pieces in the backgrounds. – MONUMENT. Mrs Bibby by *Federigo Fabiani*, who did several of the monuments in the Staglieno Cemetery outside Genoa. Free-standing figures. She is rising heavenward and an angel with spread wings hovers over her.

LL SOULS, Mather Avenue. 1927 by *D. A. Campbell & E. H. Honeybourne*. Pale brick, Romanesque, with a campanile.

CEMETERY, Woolton Road. Opened in 1909.

LIBRARY, ⅜ m. NNW. 1964–5 by *R. Bradbury*, the City Architect. Good and straightforward, but why this coarse, restless all-over concrete pattern in the one bare wall ?

QUARRY BANK SCHOOL. *See* below.

NEW HAYS GRAMMAR SCHOOL. *See* below.

WYNCOTE SPORTS PAVILION, ¼ m. W of the church. By *Gerald Beech*, 1961–2. An excellent plan and excellent details. The centre is the all-glass pavilion. A corridor runs through it and continues axially as a glass passage to the changing rooms on one side, a very long viewing platform on the other. If the pavilion is all glass, the changing rooms are mostly blank walling.

Allerton has kept more merchants' mansions and grounds of merchants' mansions than any other Liverpool suburb, in spite of the fact that here also the ruthlessness of the Corporation has done much damage. One area is round Allerton Hall, the other round Calderstones. Originally of course Allerton was not a suburb, and the mansions were in the country.

ALLERTON HALL, Clarke's Gardens, Woolton Road. This is William Roscoe's house, but he only added to it, or rather completed a previously begun rebuilding of an C18 house. Standing in front of Allerton Hall, the r. side is Early to Mid Georgian. This part includes the upper giant portico of unfluted Ionic columns and pediment and the four bays to its r., the last two a little projecting. It also includes the return side of course, where the windows have surrounds of stones of alternating size. Inside, here is a room with a stucco ceiling with thin Rococo decoration and Kentian overdoors. Roscoe completed the house *c.*1810–12, but had to sell in 1816. His is the room with the back screen of fluted Ionic columns.

SPRINGWOOD lies just w of the grounds of Allerton Hall. It
dated 1839 and eminently characteristic of that date, i.e. whol
classical, but very heavy in such motifs as balustrades, volute
etc. It is a five-bay ashlar-faced house with broad giant pilaste
at the angles of the front and an enclosed porch. Garden from
with bow windows. Noble staircase hall with skylight. Th
LODGE is of the same date. The house was begun by Willia
Shand, plantation owner, but completed by the shipowne
Sir Thomas Brocklebank. Part of the former grounds to the
covered by typical inter-war neo-Georgian housing.

ALLERTON PRIORY, Allerton Road, $\frac{1}{2}$ m. N of Allerton Hal
1867–70 by *Waterhouse*. A large mansion built for J. Gra
Morris, a colliery owner. The house has a typical Waterhou
tower. The top is a steep truncated pyramid. Gothic vaulte
porch, Gothic colonnade to the garden. Gothic entran
hall and staircase. The leading motifs are C13, but Wate
house was sensible in using motifs from other phases
Gothic or other periods as well, where usefulness pointed
them.

ALLERTON TOWER, Woolton Road, $\frac{1}{4}$ m. E of Allerton Prior
1847 by *Elmes*. The house has been demolished, but the lo
orangery, the stables, and the lodge remain. The orangery is
fourteen bays with Tuscan columns and an asymmetric
Tuscan porch (NMR). The lodge is a painful mixture of debase
Early Victorian and classical motifs.

NEW HAYS, Allerton Road. The New Hays Grammar School t
Herbert Thearle and the City Architect *Ronald Bradbury* is
good building, essentially L-shaped, with a three-storey clas
room block and a lower area with assembly hall, dining ha
and gymnasium. Much glass and much patterned brickwor
The school stands in the grounds of a steep-gabled bri
mansion of the 1860s.

ALLERTON ROAD is a document of senseless destruction. T
enumerate the losses from s to N: CLEVELEY was by *Sir G.*
Scott for Joseph Leather, a cotton merchant, 1865, and on
the lodge and stables remain on either side of the mode
Cleveley Road. ALLERTON in the middle of the golf club w
by *Harrison* of Chester. It was built in 1815 for Jacob Fletche
son of a highly successful privateer. Just enough stands to ma
one mourn over the fire which gutted the house – a colonna
of eight Greek Doric columns and round the corner a front wi
a wide shallow bow and attached Greek Doric columns and o
tripartite window l., one r. The OBELISK is earlier and was

eye-catcher from Allerton Hall. Next CALDERSTONES* in a large municipal park. The house is of 1828, painted ashlar with a one-storeyed Greek Doric four-column porch and a segmental bow round the corner. The staircase is top-lit. The stables are of red sandstone with lunette windows and an interesting centre feature.‡ Opposite the Allerton Road entrance of Calderstones the stables of *Norman Shaw's* destroyed ALLERTON BEECHES, brick, with characteristic tile-hanging and a timber-framed gable. To its N was another *Shaw* house: Greenhill. Both were of 1884 and for members of the Tate family, sugar refiners. In Hart Hill Road QUARRY BANK, a Gothic mansion of 1866, now a school. Rich Gothic interior with galleried entrance hall. Steep-roofed lodge. Finally the entrance to John Bibby's HART HILL, sumptuous, with two gigantic atlantes, and statues of the four seasons, brought from Brown's Buildings in the city centre (1861–3 by *Picton*) when this was demolished. Also a lodge with big bargeboards. The former is at the corner of Harthill Road and Calderstones Road, the latter in Harthill Road.

To these houses can be added THE GABLES, Gothic, of 1882, in Menlove Avenue, ½ m. SE of Calderstones, and DRUIDS CROSS, ⅜ m. NE of Calderstones. For this *see* Woolton.

ANFIELD

ALL SAINTS (R.C.), Oakfield. 1888–9 by *J. & B. Sinnott*. Rock-faced; without a tower. Dec details. Quite varied in the exterior. Interior with a rose-window high up above the altar.

ST CHAD, Walton Breck Road, at its W end. 1884–5 by *John Sulman*. A conscientiously designed church in a bad position. Brick, with lancet windows and no tower. Inside, the brickwork is showing, but the round piers are stone. Pretty aisle windows.

ST COLUMBA, Pinehurst Road. 1932 by *Bernard A. Miller*. Pale brick, and impressively blocky, rising from nave to chancel and from chancel to sanctuary. Small round-headed windows, long only in the sanctuary. Bellcote on the chancel facing N. Interior with three low bays of arcades, completely unmoulded. Chancel with big W and E arches. – ROOD by *B. Copnall*. – REREDOS in the SE chapel by *Mary Adshead*.

ST DAVID, Hampstead Road. 1910 by *George Bradbury & Son*. Stock brick with red-brick dressings. Free Dec tracery, NW tower.

---

* For the Calderstones themselves see Introduction, p. 142n.
‡ Mr Hubbard told me about the interior.

ST MARGARET, Belmont Road. The very powerful church of
1873 by *W. & J. Audsley* in a fully convincing High Victorian
Gothic and with structural polychromy outside and inside has
been replaced after a fire of 1961 by a modish building by
Bruxby & Evans, thin, and with the almost unavoidable 'col-
lapsing roof'. The timber construction inside is interesting
perhaps, but what a restless place for worship! – SCULPTURE.
A statue of St Margaret from the old church stands outside. –
Over the altar a bronze Crucifix by *Sean Rice*. – Next to the
new church the SCHOOL of 1877.

ST MARY, Walton Road, is the parish church of Kirkdale. Hence
see p. 229.

ST PHILIP, Sheil Road. *See* Fairfield, p. 225.

ST SIMON AND ST JUDE, Anfield Road. 1893–6 by *T. C. Ebdy*.
The estimate was £6,650 (GS). Brick, without a tower.

HOLY TRINITY, Breck Road. 1847 by *J. Hay*. Gothic, and
typical of its date in several ways. The W steeple in its details,
with an octagonal bell-stage rising into eight steep gables behind
coupled pinnacles and its spire, is far from archeologically
justifiable, and the body of the church is still smooth, with tall
windows. Also there are still broad transepts. Aisleless interior,
also an early feature. Low apse.

OAKFIELD METHODIST CHURCH, Oakfield Road. Red brick,
with the typically playful 1900-Gothic details. No tower.

STANLEY PARK. One of the best mid-Victorian parks not only
of Liverpool but of the whole North. 1867–70 by *Kemp*, the
architectural features by *E. R. Robson*, then Corporation Surveyor. Robson's principal glory is the very long screen wall with
Gothic details, a Gothic mid-pavilion, and two open octagonal
Gothic end-pavilions. Terracing below and originally an unobstructed view towards the picturesque lake. May it soon be
unobstructed once more! The lake has undulating banks, and
there is a sunk part of the park near it which has undulating
beds too. Stone BRIDGE across the lake to a Gothic GAZEBO.
All this is small in scale, yet the bridge has proper projecting
balconies or platforms like respectable medieval bridges. Also
in the park a CONSERVATORY, all glass and iron. This is still
in the Paxton tradition but dates from 1899. It is signed by
Mackenzie & Moncur of Edinburgh. Inside STATUE of Flora
Macdonald by *Benjamin E. Spence*.

LIVERPOOL CEMETERY, Walton Lane. The competition for
the layout was won by *T. D. Barry*, but the layout was done by
Kemp. The work took from 1856 to 1863. The buildings are

by *Lucy & Littler*. They are amazingly ambitious and also resourceful in the plans and details, none more than the main GATES with two lodges and an entrance screen culminating in a fanciful Gothic clock-tower. Outstanding iron gates. From there a straight avenue to the middle one of the three chapels. This is long, with a w and an E apse and the steeple in the middle of the broad side facing the avenue. The details here and in the following buildings are all E.E. To reach the N and the s chapels one passes a range each of what is called the Catacombs, low, E.E., with buttresses. The halls stretching out l. and r. from the middle passage though have stone transverse arches. The North Chapel and the South Chapel, axially placed, differ deliberately in most details yet balance one another well. Both have a steeple on the side towards the middle avenue from gatehouse to central chapel, and both have a polygonal apse. The E entrance is combined with a railway bridge. Heavy Gothic arches and a tourelle at one corner. Again excellent iron GATES, as they are in the other entrances as well. The CREMATORIUM was built later, in 1894–6, which is still remarkably early for a crematorium. The architect was probably *James Rhind*. It is in a free Perp with a big square tower, a successfully irregular composition.

RK HOSPITAL, Orphan Drive, Newsham Park. Built in 1871–4 by *Waterhouse* as the Seamen's Orphan Institution. Brick with stone dressings, in Waterhouse's sparing Gothic, with a bold angle tower with steep pavilion roof. The w front is quite irregular, the s range (girls originally) plain and regular and very Waterhousish. The chapel was at the N end (beyond the boys' range), but has been pulled down. Dining hall with straight-topped Gothic two-light windows and a heavy wooden minstrels' gallery.

FIELD ROAD SCHOOL. 1895 by *Thomas Shelmerdine*, the then City Surveyor. Stock brick and red brick, with an extremely odd tower, turning circular in the top parts, behaving as if it were a bobbin, and ending in a conical spire. A large range recessed to the s.

WSHAM PARK was laid out *c.*1870. Part of the area was used for houses, and they are easily recognizable. In the park is NEWSHAM HOUSE, late C18, of five bays and two and a half storeys, brick, with a three-bay pediment. Some discreet stone decoration round the middle window. The porch is later.*

* For the adjoining parts to the w and s *see* Fairfield, p. 226.

CHILDWALL

Childwall is the only suburb of Liverpool which has kept a villag
character, at least in its centre. It is true that even at Childwall th
after-the-war years have done their best to ruin it, partly by dire
interference and partly by spoiling the view over the wide valle
This is now largely covered with housing and studded – witho
system, it seems – with high blocks of flats.

ALL SAINTS. Here, in the only remaining Liverpool village,
also the only remaining medieval church in the whole of th
metropolitan area. It has externally its C14 masonry and simp
straight-headed two-light windows in the chancel and Pe
masonry and equally simple features in the S aisle wall and th
S porch. The family pew (or Salisbury Chapel) E of the porc
on the other hand is of 1739–40, the W tower of 1810–11, ar
the N widening and N wall (by *Doyle*) of 1905–6. The tower h
a spire recessed behind a typical Gothick openwork parapet ar
a large window with Y-tracery. The chancel E window look
early C19 too. The interior has arcades of plain octagonal pie
with double-chamfered arches, but they are interrupted c
both sides by a round arch of double the size. This is due to th
removal of one pier to clear the view from the family pew.
Outside the chancel is the head of a Perp window, and attache
to the porch W wall a fragment of a Saxon CROSS SHAFT wi
basket ornament. – Inside, in the chancel E wall, is a Norma
multi-scalloped CAPITAL set horizontally. – Used as a W galle
support, moreover, is part of a C13 shaft with base. – FONT. A
C18 baluster. – BENCH END. One, coarsely carved, with
poppyhead, C17. It is under the chancel arch. – BOX PEW
They are Victorian, from the restoration by *Raffles Brown*
1851–3, and yet, in spite of the late date, still box pews. –
CHANDELIER. Of brass, dated 1737, rich and elaborate, al
in the ironwork of the support. – STAINED GLASS. In the
chapel one window by *William Warrington*, others in the chanc
S. They look *c.*1853 and are poor. – S aisle E by *Kempe*, *c.*1900–
–PLATE. Set of 1772. – MONUMENTS. In the S aisle two roun
arched funerary recesses. – Also in the S aisle brass to Hen
Norris of Speke † 1524 and wife (?). 31 in. figures. – Major V
Pitcairn Campbell † 1855. A large painted board, all Gothi
with leaf decorations etc. and small figures; very unusual as
memorial.

In the churchyard an early C19 castellated HEARSE HOUS

Opposite it the CHILDWALL ABBEY HOTEL, a Gothick house of the early C19 with all its windows ogee-headed. Two canted bays to the E and between a tripartite doorway and a tripartite window. Their middle arches are ogee, the side arches plainly pointed. Side elevation of seven bays. This looks into the large grounds of CHILDWALL HALL, a castellated mansion by *Nash* gone long ago and now replaced by a County College of depressingly undistinguished appearance. Also in the grounds facing E is the new SCHOOL FOR DEAF CHILDREN, 1965–7 by *Herbert Thearle*, extensive, and with plenty of monopitch roofs. It faces ELM HOUSE, an early C19 three-bay house with battlements.

In the area of today's Childwall, ½ m. SW from the church in WOOLTON ROAD, is an interesting group of Catholic institutions.

BISHOP ETON MONASTERY (Redemptorists). 1858 by *E. W. Pugin*, with a wing of 1889 by *Sinnott, Sinnott & Powell*. The church (OUR LADY OF THE ANNUNCIATION) was begun earlier, in 1851, and by the great *A. W. N. Pugin*.* His son completed it in 1858. How much is by the father? The simple exterior could be: features of *c*.1300 and an open timber crossing turret. Polygonal apse and side chapels facing into the church with different fronts. – STAINED GLASS. Some apparently by *Hardman*, the large w window by *Kempe*.

To the W of this is ST JOSEPH'S HOME, built as a private house by *A. W. N. Pugin*. It was begun in 1845 and finished in 1847.‡ It has a blunt exterior to the street, but is more elaborate to the garden, with two cross-gables, one with an oriel on a buttress. This, however, is dated 1866. Embattled chimneystacks. Inside remains of typical Pugin decoration. Later work (presumably of 1866) looks *E. W. Pugin* and includes an elaborate fireplace. Attached to one side is a recent enlargement by *Weightman & Bullen* with a monopitch roof. The LODGE is characteristic Pugin work.

CHRIST'S COLLEGE OF EDUCATION, opposite the two former. A large, new establishment. By *Weightman & Bullen*, 1964–6. The most interesting part is the CHAPEL. In plan it is a square overlaid by a diagonally set square. In the diagonal corners are chapels. The roof rises towards the middle, in unequal pitches so that a slit of glazing is contrived, throwing light on the altar. Interior with low ambulatory and timber-boarded roof.

* Information from Mrs Stanton.
‡ These dates were found by Mrs Stanton.

CLUBMOOR

St Matthew (R.C.), Townsend Avenue. By *F. X. Velarde*, 1930. Built of brick. The exterior is not up to the reputation of the church. The NE campanile is high, but the top stage with its stubby Romanesque angle columns and its copper cupola is decidedly embarrassing, and the body of the church with small round windows is without distinction. But inside, the very low five-bay arcades to the passage aisles, arches rising from the ground, are impressive, and so are the short chancel and short sanctuary, the segmental ceiling, and the pair of transverse brick arches separating the S transept, one behind the other. The distance between them corresponds to the width of the passage aisle which they continue.

The church is at the corner of Queen's Drive, *Brodie*'s ring road, begun in 1904. Townsend Avenue is one of his radial roads, though a minor one. The central reservations between the carriageways of his roads were originally hedged-off tram tracks. To the SW in Townsend Lane and beyond the railway is the Clubmoor Hotel, one of a number of 'Moderne' Georgian pubs of the thirties in Liverpool by *Harold E. & H. Hinchcliffe Davies*.

CROXTETH HALL

Croxteth Hall was built by Sir Richard Molyneux about 1575. Of that house no more is visible externally than two gables with six-light mullioned windows on the S side, w of the gatehouse, and internally no more than one studded door, marking the entrance to the C17 house. In 1702 Richard Molyneux, the second Viscount, added the spectacular w front, and in 1874–7 the fourth Earl of Sefton the E range and the S range as far as the gatehouse. In 1902–4 the whole N range was done. The design is by *J. McVicar Anderson* (R.I.B.A. drawings). The parts are easily distinguished from each other. The w front of 1702, the showpiece of the house, is eleven bays wide, of brick with stone dressings such as quoins to the angles and the angles of the three middle bays. The whole front has a very curious composition. First of all the main floor stands on a terrace, and the terrace has big circular and oval windows. Then the windows of the main floor have pediments alternately triangular and segmental, but that does not read as one composition, because the outer two windows are squeezed close together, whereas the inner have normal spacing. The portal, undeniably splendid, is 23 too big for all this, if one wants to apply correct criteria. It has coupled Corinthian columns, a carved frieze, and an open segmental pediment with trophies. Above it is a very large vertical panel again with trophies. The parapet is evenly spaced and does contradict the windows. Large outer staircase to the portal.

The N front is larger and, though entirely of 1902, consists of two parts. The pattern for both was the style of 1702, but it has been rationalized and simplified. In the NE corner it meets the work of 1874 which is gabled Tudor. Where the genuine C17 work meets 1702 at the SW corner, McVicar Anderson threw out an extension containing the dining room. This has some imitation late C17 stucco. Otherwise the house has little of architectural interest inside, as much behind the W front was destroyed in a fire in 1952. In the W entrance hall is an arched doorway with leaf spandrels and the client's cypher. It now leads to the grand staircase of 1902, a very successful piece.

The STABLES have dates 1676 and 1706. They are irregular. Towards the house a pair of fine GATEPIERS.

The DAIRY is by *Eden Nesfield*, of 1861–70, nicely tiled inside and with nicely painted Gothic ceiling beams. The painting was done by *Albert Moore*. Originally a fountain was in the middle. The adjoining house has a two-light Gothic window and a round chimneystack by Nesfield. Eastlake calls the dairy 'admirably conceived and executed with great refinement and artistic skill'.

A little away to the E are the KENNELS. They are by *J. Douglas*.

EDGE HILL

T ANNE (R.C.), Overbury Street. By *Charles Hansom*, 1845–6, with chancel, apse, and two transepts by *Pugin & Pugin*, 1888–9. A big church. Prominent W tower. The chancel opens in arcades of columns paired in depth to the organ chamber on the l., and to one of two chapels E of the S transept on the r.

T ANNE'S HALL (former Congregational Chapel), Marmaduke Street. Rock-faced, the W front with two open quadrant-shaped porches. Dec features. Built in 1877–8.

T CATHERINE, Tunnel Road. 1862–3 by *John Denison Jee*. Rather poverty-stricken-looking and now roughcast. The features are of *c.*1300. Flèche on the E gable of the nave.

CHRIST CHURCH, Kensington. 1870 by *W. & G. Audsley*. Common brick with red and blue brick decoration. Tall sheer N W tower, formerly with a steep pyramid roof. The W doorway is in it with free Romanesque stone decoration. All windows round-headed. Much structural polychromy – stone and red and black brick (actually this is painted, but almost certainly represents the natural colours). Nave arcade with round arches and polished granite shafts. Chunky Romanesque capitals, all different of course, and similar ornament elsewhere. – REREDOS. A continuous arcade.

ST CYPRIAN, Durning Road. 1879–81 by *Henry Sumners*. A very remarkable church, highly original in its details, such as the windows. The tracery is of no period at all. Rock-faced with a prominent W tower with higher stair-turret. Broad nave with narrow passage aisles. Round-arched arcades, the capitals in a free Romanesque with Arts and Crafts touches. They date, according to Goodhart-Rendel, from 1898 (by *Willink & Thicknesse*). The roof was reconstructed in 1896, and the clerestory windows could be of that date too.

ST MARK, Edge Lane. 1925–7 by *Frank Rimmington*. Low and cottagey. Brick with much timber and a flèche on the big roof.

ST MARY, Irvine Street. 1812–13. Brick, with a slender square W tower, a broad aisleless nave with pointed windows in two tiers, and a short, never lengthened chancel. Nave and chancel are thinly embattled. The interior still has its three wooden galleries on very thin supports and with pretty Gothic decoration. – STAINED GLASS. In the N wall two *Morris* windows, one with a date of death 1870, the other, it seems, later. – MONUMENT. Edward Mason † 1814. Tablet with a winged genius on clouds. Drapery cascades down and is lifted by two putti to reveal the inscription.

SACRED HEART (R.C.), Mount Vernon Street and Hall Lane. 1886, possibly by *Pugin & Pugin*. Rock-faced. Dec apse and S W turret.

CONVENT OF THE SISTERS OF MERCY, Mount Vernon Street. Extensive buildings in a simple Puginesque style, mostly invisible from the street. Apparently 1857 by *Goldie*.

LIBRARY, Kensington. By *T. Shelmerdine*, 1890, enlarged 1897 Pretty and asymmetrical. Brick and stone. Entrance with a semicircular hood. White, wooden cupola. The design is full of little inventions.

MEDICAL TEACHING CENTRE, Prescot Street. By *W. Holford & Associates*. Under construction at the time of writing. A very large scheme with buildings varied in bulk, height, and shapes. The principal range is two-storeyed on a podium. Round concrete chimney as high as a Post Office Tower, set on a heavy concrete substructure along the street.

BOTANIC GARDENS, Edge Lane. Founded in 1800 by William Roscoe, in Mosslake Fields, moved to Edge Hill in 1835, built in 1836–7, and acquired by the Corporation in 1846. Substantial ashlar lodge with giant pilasters and top acroteria. Forbidding front to the street.

BUS DEPOT, Edge Lane. By the architects in the office of *A. D. Jenkins*, the Corporation Surveyor. Large, neo-Georgian, of brick and stone. Completed in 1927.

EDGE HILL STATION. Of the original Liverpool–Manchester Railway of 1830. The station building is low down in a cutting. It is of ashlar, small, and classical in an appropriately massive way. The building consists of two low ranges, along the two platforms. A later block rises higher than the rest and has arched windows. The entrance to the TUNNEL has a surround of vermiculated rustication. It dates from 1847.

(PADDINGTON COMPREHENSIVE SCHOOL. By *R. Bradbury*, 1967–8. Purple brick and curtain walling.)

QUEENSLAND SCHOOL, Queensland Road. 1883 by *T. Melland Reade*. A very unusual building for its date, elegant and civilized. Brick and stone, small, with a pediment. The centre has large two-light windows.

PERAMBULATION. In IRVINE STREET, W of St Mary, a terrace of early C19 brick houses with nice doorways with recessed columns, the type of the Rodney Street neighbourhood. E of the church in MARMADUKE STREET is CLARE TERRACE of *c.*1830, long and stuccoed, with pedimented accents, originally three, but now only two. In OVERTON STREET S of Marmaduke Street is one short brick terrace. S of this, and just S of SMITHDOWN LANE, is ENTWISTLE HEIGHTS, a twenty-two-storey block of reinforced concrete, by *R. Bradbury*, the City Architect. For the Ventilating Shaft *see* p. 186.

A short separate walk might be further N along PRESCOT STREET to the W. There is the ROYAL LIVER BUILDING, ashlar, Latest Classical, with a turret, and then, at the corner of MOSS STREET, MARTINS BANK by *Doyle*, 1905. Ashlar with plenty of Baroque motifs. The entrance is at the corner, with giant columns above and a turret. Opposite (and outside the boundary of Edge Hill) the PRINCE OF WALES HOTEL, Victorian Gothic.

Facing Wavertree Park off Edge Lane is the very large, symmetrical building of LITTLEWOOD'S, all square, yet still classically committed. High central tower. The building is by *G. de C. Fraser;* 1938.

EVERTON

INTRODUCTION

Everton was a village on the brow of a hill with spectacular views to the w. Of the village a shadow remains. Then, in the C18, Everton became a favourite area for rich merchants' houses – St Domingo House, Mere Bank, and others – but of them even less is in existence now. Baines in 1829 still called it 'a very favourite residence of the gentry of Liverpool'. It is now all densely built over, just amorphous Liverpool. A new pattern of high blocks of flats is, however, emerging, a visual shock, and in the end not as a rule architecturally rewarding.

CHURCHES

ALL SOULS (R.C.), Collingwood Street. 1870–2 by *Henry Sumners* (of *Culshaw & Sumners*). A wild, low façade, asymmetrical of course. The chief motif is a broad window into which cuts the steep gable of the former main entrance. The tracery is elaborately and complicatedly Dec. No tower or turret. The interior is surprising but has its explanation in the fact that the church was built as a mortuary chapel. All the same, it is highly ingenious, though – like the façade – overdone. Nave of two bays only plus polygonal apse, all with granite columns. The nave has a timbered ceiling, the aisles lean-to roofs and an ambulatory. This is lit by three large pointed lunette windows, again with the most complicated flowing tracery.*

ST BENEDICT, Heyworth Street. 1886–7 by *Aldridge & Deacon*. Of brick, quite exceptionally good and very similar to St Dunstan, Wavertree. A splendid tall front to the street, with three high lancets, their surrounds continued to the bottom by flat buttress-strips. Above the heads of the lancets some brick decoration and three little gablets. The church has all lancet windows, low in triplets in the aisles, higher and in pairs in the clerestory. A w tower has not yet been built. The interior has round stone piers, but brick arches and brick all exposed higher up. A decorative brick band runs along the N, S, and W sides. Good substantial timber nave roof.

* The church has alas been demolished.

CHRYSOSTOM, Aubrey Street. 1852–3 by *W. Raffles Brown*.
With w steeple and flowing tracery. Galleries in the transepts.
The church displeased *The Ecclesiologist*.

CUTHBERT, Robson Street. 1875–7 by *T. D. Barry & Sons*.
Stone, Dec style, sw steeple.

MMANUEL, West Derby Road. 1866–7 by *G. E. Grayson*. Stone,
with a polygonal apse, a N transept, and a steeple, fussy in the
details of the upper parts. Late c13 style.

FRANCIS XAVIER (R.C.), Salisbury Street. 1845–9 by *J. J.
Scoles*. An uncommonly interesting interior, though more
sensible than sensitive. The exterior is of stone, with geometrical tracery. The sw tower with recessed spire, dull in the details
('below criticism', *The Ecclesiologist*, 1853), stands outside the
s aisle. The interior is dominated by the strikingly thin limestone columns with their poor stiff-leaf capitals and their gargantuan bases. The arcade is eight bays long. Large aisle
windows. Polygonal apse. The single-mindedness of Scoles is
completely upset by the showmanship of *E. Kirby* in adding
the Lady Chapel in 1888. The exterior shows it to have an
elongated polygonal centre and low, asymmetrical additions
including a portal by the E end. This leads into a most curiously
planned ambulatory. The centre is indeed an elongated octagon
and has a plaster rib-vault, a bad lapse in 1888. The style is E.E.
throughout, and there are plenty of Purbeck marble shafts. To
the E follows a two-bay chancel with clerestory and a polygonal
apse and aisles and ambulatory, to the w a nave of one double
bay with aisles and another polygonal apse. The lowish entries
into the aisles are in the short diagonal sides of the polygon.
That is the description. For most visitors, however, the whole
will remain a confusion.

A little further s in Salisbury Street are the COLLEGIATE
BUILDINGS. Something is said by the MHLG to be by *Clutton*,
and something is said to have been completed in 1856, but the
most interesting building must be later. It is of brick and red
terracotta, nine bays long, with even buttresses and even
dormers. They are oddly set back behind an openwork balustrade. The doorway is round-arched, the rest of the motifs are
in a stripped Gothic, a little like Waterhouse. This is supposed to be of 1877 and may be by *Scoles*.

T GEORGE, Heyworth Street. The parish church of Everton.
1812–14 by *Rickman*, with the so-called Commissioners' con-
vention outside but an exceptionally delightful interior, thanks ⁴²
to the use of cast iron for nearly all the decoration. The idea

came from John Cragg, owner of the Mersey Iron Foundry
Rickman had already begun to work for him at St Michael-in-
the-Hamlet when the Everton church turned up. Rickman was
not entirely happy with Cragg's passion (*see* p. 243). The style
of St George's is Perp. Big w tower facing the view down from
the ridge. The w tower has plenty of solid walling. Three-light
bell-openings, crown of prettily decorated battlements. Large
Perp three-light windows along the sides, framed by buttresses
with pinnacles. Six-light E window in the short embattled
chancel. The tracery of all the windows is of iron. So are the
galleries with their thin columns, and so are the arches with
their open tracery across aisles and nave and between nave and
aisles. Even the exceedingly pretty ribbed panelling of the flat
aisle and the canted nave ceilings is of iron. Well decorated
recently (by *Dewi Prys Thomas*).

ST JOHN EVANGELIST, Breck Road. 1890. By *F. C. Clarke* of
Liverpool. Conservative for its date. Square NW tower. Perp
w window and a low baptistery under. Brick-exposed interior.
Wide nave and apse, low aisles, and large clerestory.

ST JOSEPH (R.C.), Grosvenor Street. 1878 by *J. O'Byrne*. Red
brick, all round-arched windows. NE bellcote. Interior with
thin granite columns with shaft-rings and Norman block capitals. Round arcade arches of course.

ST MICHAEL (R.C.), West Derby Road. 1861–5 by *E. W. Pugin*.
Brick, the w front with a big rose-window. No aisle windows.
Quatrefoil piers and above them large stops as if they were
corbels for vaulting-shafts. They have plenty of naturalistic
foliage, à la Exeter. Polygonal apse with lancets high up.

OUR LADY IMMACULATE (R.C.), St Domingo Road. 1856 by
E. W. Pugin; enlarged 1885. This is the Lady Chapel and
chancel chapels of the Catholic cathedral planned to be built
here, in the grounds of the former St Domingo House which
was then the residence of the bishop. Straight E end; style of
*c.*1300.‡

ST POLYCARP, Netherfield Road. Built in 1886. Common
brick and red brick. Short, and without a visible chancel.
Odd s aisle with gabled doorway as part of the aisle. The
interior is to one's surprise faced with white glazed bricks; also
some coloured brickwork.

* The VCH says 'later practically rebuilt'.
‡ Mr E. Hubbard has recently discovered that E. W. Pugin's greater father
A. W. N. Pugin, is reported to have submitted designs in 1845. St Domingo
House was acquired by the Catholic church in that year.

St Saviour, Breckfield Road North. 1868–9 by *Gordon M. Hills*. Stone, in the late C13 style. No tower.

St Timothy, Rokeby Street. 1861–2 by *W. H. Gee*. Estimated cost £2,600 (GS).

St Domingo Methodist Church, Breckfield Road North. 1870–1 by *Hill* of Leeds. Ornate, fanciful, asymmetrical façade with spirelet. The sides rather Mary Anne.

Rydal Youth Centre (former Methodist Chapel), Great Homer Street. 1839–40. Stone, of seven bays, with seven arched upper windows. Below a porch with Greek Doric columns *in antis*. Five-bay pediment. A dignified composition.

(Richmond Baptist Church, Breck Road. 1864–5 by *J. A. Picton & Son*.)

Particular Baptist Church, Shaw Street. 1847. Brick and stone dressings. Three bays with a three-bay pediment. The entrance with two unfluted giant Ionic columns *in antis*.

Welsh Methodist Chapel (former), Shaw Street. Classical, with an upper portico of coupled columns and a pediment. Recessed end bays. 1866, by *John Denison Jee* (GS).

PUBLIC BUILDINGS

Liverpool Collegiate High School, Shaw Street. By *Elmes*. Founded in 1840 and opened in 1843. Elmes won the competition which was held for it. Scott & Moffatt came second. Elmes quarrelled with the committee and was not allowed to supervise the construction. Tudor Gothic. A thirteen-bay front, with a centre and end motifs and the rest with high Perp windows almost unnoticeably divided for the purpose of the floor between the two main storeys. Below, a low ground floor. In the middle a kind of gatehouse motif, but treated with great originality. The entrance is only on the ground floor, above is a giant niche with another of the high windows. In the end bays two-storeyed oriels. At the back, placed centrally, an octagonal lecture hall. (In the headmaster's study a very elaborate chimneypiece; so Mr Hubbard tells me.)

Water Works, Aubrey Street. 1853 etc. by *Thomas Duncan*. The water tower is a tremendous piece, round, with two tiers of grand rusticated open arches. Concentric with them to support the tank are two more rings of arcading. The scale is much larger than one would expect. The original short top bit is unfortunately no longer there. There are also two pumping houses, the earlier one in a very monumental, big-boned

Italianate, and the retaining walls of a large underground reservoir.

LIBRARY, St Domingo Road. 1895–6 by *Thomas Shelmerdine*, and unusually excellent. Red brick and much stone. To the street three identical gables, but the treatment below differs entirely. In the middle the recessed entrance with short bulgy columns, on the l. one long mullioned-and-transomed window, on the r. a two-storey treatment and a small corner entrance, also with bulgy columns, under a turret. Much carved relief decoration.

ST FRANCIS XAVIER COLLEGE, Salisbury Street. *See* St Francis Xavier, p. 221.

PERAMBULATION

One should start by the former GREEN at the E end of EVERTON BROW. On the green the round stone LOCKUP of 1787 with a conical roof. This was the village centre, and the Village Cross was here. Turning S one ought to walk SHAW STREET, which was laid out in 1826–9. There are some terraces of *c*.1830 left, all on the w side, first from 93 upward, then from 37 upward (with good cast-iron balconies), and then on the E side Nos 6–10. This links up directly with Islington Square (*see* p. 207).

To the N from the village green all along NETHERFIELD ROAD is (to date) the most consistent high-rise housing of Liverpool, quite a number of blocks, on the whole of little architectural interest. The best is the sheerest. It stands directly N of the N end of EVERTON TERRACE. Of older building in Everton Terrace is a house of brick with stone dressings with a two-bay pediment and a doorway with Doric columns. Opposite the former stables. The house is now a POLICE STATION. A little further N, higher up the bank, a pair of houses with canted bay windows l. and r. of the entrance.

Now, a N–S line further E, starting with ST DOMINGO ROAD. S of the Lady Chapel of the intended cathedral on the site of St Domingo House are typical blocks of municipal flats, of 1938–9 with the sweeping balconies and the Dudok inspiration. Then S, to what is the visual centre of Everton now, the group of St George, the Library, and the MERE BANK pub, a piece of exuberant black and white, built *c.* 1882. This is at the N end of HEYWORTH STREET.

From the s end of Heyworth Street one can return to the village green by RUPERT LANE, with a Late Georgian terrace. In

. Salford, air view

2. (above) Liverpool, Pierhead
3. (below) Widnes, road bridge, by Mott, Hay & Anderson, 1956–6

(left) Winwick church, arches fourteenth century, piers
perpendicular or *c.*1600
(above) Manchester Cathedral, *c.*1420–*c.*1520, engraving

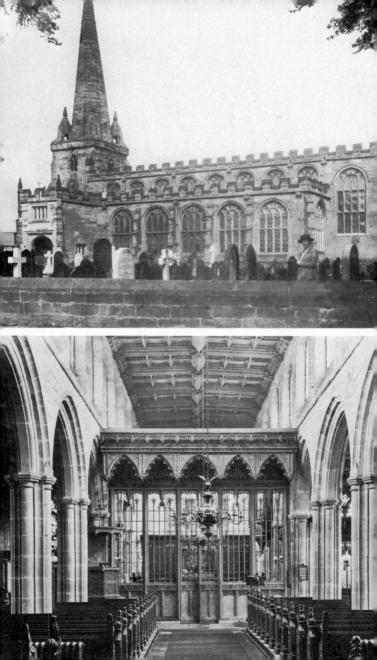

6. (above left) Sefton church, Perpendicular
7. (left) Sefton church, Perpendicular
8. (top) Middleton, St Leonard, rood screen, Late Perpendicular
9. (above) Sefton church, screen, early–mid sixteenth century

10. (left) Manchester Cathedral, stall canopies, c.1505–10

11. (below left) Ashton-under-Lyne, St Michael, stained glass, late fifteenth–early sixteenth century

12. (left)
Manchester
(Wythenshawe),
Baguley Hall, hall,
fourteenth century

13. (below left)
Salford, Ordsall
Hall, hall, fifteenth
century (*Copyright
Country Life*)

14. (left) Salford, Ordsall Hall, south front, fifteenth century
(*Copyright Country Life*)

15. (above) Manchester, Chetham's Hospital, hall, screens passage,
fifteenth century

16. (above) Manchester, Wythenshawe Hall, early sixteenth century
17. (above right) Liverpool, Speke Hall, Elizabethan
18. (right) Bolton (Tonge Moor), Hall i't'Wood, Elizabethan

19. Liverpool, Speke Hall, great chamber, ceiling, Jacobean

20. (right) Manchester (Didsbury), St James, monument to Sir Nicholas Mosley †1612

21. (below right) Milnrow, Clegg Hall, c.1660, doorway

22. (left) Manchester (Cheetham), St Luke, pulpit, Flemish, eighteenth century

23. (right) Liverpool, Croxteth Hall, west portal, 1702

24. (below) Hale, Manor House, c.1700–10 (*Copyright Country Life*)

25. (left) Ince Blundell Hall, *c.*1715–20 (*Copyright Country Life*)
26. (below left) Liverpool, Old Bluecoat School, 1716–17
27. (below) Billinge church, 1718
28. (bottom) Knowsley Hall, south end of east range, complete by 1736(?)

29. (above left) Warrington Town Hall, by James Gibbs, 1750
30. (below left) Liverpool Town Hall, by John Wood the elder,
1749–54
31. (above) Liverpool Town Hall, small ballroom, by James Wyatt,
1789–92

32. (top) Manchester, Heaton Park, by James Wyatt, designed 1772 (*Copyright Country Life*)

33. (above) Manchester, Heaton Park, by James Wyatt, designed 1772, room above the Saloon, paintings by Biagio Rebecca (*Copyright Country Life*)

34. (right) Ince Blundell Hall, Pantheon, 1802 (before removal of statues) (*Copyright Country Life*)

35. (top) Manchester, Portico Library, Mosley Street, by Thomas
Harrison, 1802–6
36. (above) Liverpool, Wellington Rooms, Mount Pleasant, by
Edmund Aikin, 1815–16
37. (above right) Wigan, St John, 1819
38. (right) Salford, St Philip, by Sir Robert Smirke, 1825

39. (above) Liverpool, St Luke, St Luke's Place, designed by John Foster Sen., 1802, built by John Foster Jun., 1811–31

40. (below) Stand church, by Sir Charles Barry, begun 1822

41. Bolton, Holy Trinity, by Philip Hardwick, 1823–5

2. (left) Liverpool (Everton), St George, by Thomas Rickman, 1812–14

3. (right) Liverpool, warehouses in New Quay

4. (below right) Winwick church, monument to Ellen Legh †1831, by R. J. Wyatt

45. (above) Liverpool, St James's Cemetery, monument to William Nicholson, by Sir Francis Chantrey, 1834

46. (below) Liverpool, Gambier Terrace, 1830–c.37

Liverpool, St Bride, Percy Street, by Samuel Rowland, 1830–1

8 and 49. Rainhill, St Bartholomew, 1840

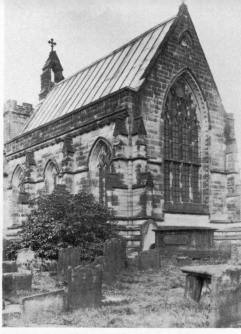

50. (above)
Winwick church,
chancel, by
A. W. N. Pugin,
1847–8

51. (below) Ashton
under-Lyne, St
Michael, rebuilt in
1840–4

Liverpool, Albert Dock, by Jesse Hartley and Philip Hardwick, 841–5

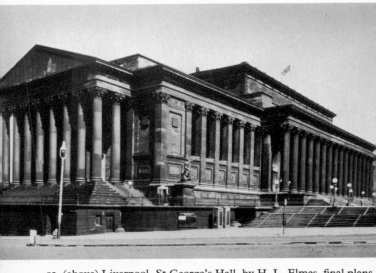

53. (above) Liverpool, St George's Hall, by H. L. Elmes, final plans 1841, completed by C. R. Cockerell, 1856
54. (right) Liverpool, St George's Hall, Concert Room, by C. R. Cockerell, 1847–56

55. (left) Liverpool, Bank of England Castle Street, by C. Cockerell, 1845–

56. (below) Liverpool, Picton Reading Room, by Cornelius Sherlock, 1875–9

57. (right) Liverpool, Walker Art Gallery, by Sherlock & Vale, 1874–7

58. (below right) Manchester (Whalley Range), Lancashire Independent College, Irwin & Chester, 1840–3

(above left) Liverpool, Walton Prison, by John Weightman,
48–55
(left) Liverpool, Sailors' Home, Canning Place, by John
inningham, 1846–8
. (above) Manchester, Free Trade Hall, by Edward Walters, 1853–6

62. (top) Manchester, Milne Buildings, Mosley Street, *c.*1845
63. (above) Liverpool, Richmond Buildings (demolished), Chapel Street, by J. A. Picton, 1861
64. (right) Liverpool, Oriel Chambers, Water Street, by Peter Ellis, 1864

65. (left) Liverpool, 16 Cook Street, by Peter Ellis, 1866, courtyard

66. (below) Manchester, Barton's Building, Deansgate, by Corbett, Raby & Sawyer, 1871, arcade

67. (right) Reddish, Mills, 1865

68. (below right) Manchester (Didsbury), Shirley Institute, by Thomas Worthington, 1865

. (left) Bolton Town Hall, by William Hill, 1866–73
. (below left) Rochdale Town Hall, by W. H. Crossland, 1866–71
. (below) Manchester Town Hall, by Alfred Waterhouse, begun
868

a. (left) Bolton Town Hall, by William Hill, 1866–73
b. (below left) Rochdale Town Hall, by W. H. Crossland, 1866–71
c. (below) Manchester Town Hall, by Alfred Waterhouse, begun 1868

72. (left) Manchester Town Hall
by Alfred Water-
house, begun 1868,
staircase

73. (below left)
Liverpool (West
Derby), St Mary,
by Sir George
Gilbert Scott,
1853–6

74. (right) Man-
chester (Cheetham),
St Alban, by J. S.
Crowther, 1857–60

75. (left) Manchester (Gorton), St Francis, by E. W. Pugin, 1866–72

76. (below left) Barton-upon-Irwell, Church of the City of Mary Immaculate (All Saints), by E. W. Pugin, 1867–8

77. (left) Manchester (Chorlton-on-Medlock), Holy Name of Jesus, by J. A. Hansom, 1869–71

78. (below left) Pendlebury, St Augustine, by G. F. Bodley, 1871–4

79. (left) Man-
chester (Didsbury),
Emanuel, stained
glass by William
Morris, 1889

80. (right) Man-
chester Town Hall,
Great Hall, paint-
ing by Ford Madox
Brown, 1876–88

81. (below right)
Liverpool (Sefton
Park), St Agnes'
Vicarage, by
Norman Shaw,
1887

82. (left) Manchester (Levenshulme), St Agnes, by J. Medland & Henry Taylor, 1884–5

83. (below left) Wigan, St Matthew, Highfield, by Austin & Paley, 1894

84. (right) Manchester, John Rylands Library, by Basil Champneys, 1890–9

85. (below right) Liverpool (Sefton Park), St Clare, by Leonard Stokes, 1888–90

86. (left) Liverpool, Royal Insurance, Dale Street, by J. Francis Doyle, 1896–1903

87 and 88. (below left and right) Liverpool Cathedral, by Sir Giles Gilbert Scott, begun 1904

89. (left) Liverpool (Wavertree), Blue-coat School, by Briggs, Wolstenholme & Thornely 1903–6

90. (below left) Manchester (Victoria Park), First Church of Christ Scientist, by Edgar Wood, 1903

91. (right) Middleton, Durnford Street School, by Edgar Wood & J. Sellers, 1908–10

92. (below right) Oldham, Dronsfield's Offices, by J. H. Sellers, 1906–7

93. (left) Liverpool (Wavertree), Holy Trinity, east end, by Sir Charles Reilly, 1911

94. (below left) Manchester, Central Library and Town Hall extension, by E. Vincent Harris, designed 1925, completed 1930–4 and 1938

95. (right) Manchester (Northenden), St Michael, by Cachemaille Day & Lander, 1937

(above left) St Helens, Pilkington Glass Works, by Fry, Drew &
rtners, 1956–65

(left) Liverpool University, Arts Library, Social Studies,
l Law, by Bryan & Norman Westwood, Piet & Partners, 1962–4

(above) Liverpool, Catholic Cathedral of Christ the King,
Sir Frederick Gibberd, designed in 1959

99. Manchester (Wythenshawe), William Temple Memorial Churc[h]
by G. G. Pace, 1964-5

VILLAGE STREET also a few Late Georgian survivals. EAST-
BOURNE STREET leading s has a more complete and even
terrace. At the N end of EVERTON ROAD is a remarkable
survival,* a genuine C17 fragment, ashlar-built, with mullioned
windows and a gable. It is at the corner of BRECK ROAD. In
Breck Road some Late Georgian terrace houses too.‡ At the
corner of Everton Road and Village Street is a stuccoed house
with giant pilasters. A little further s in Everton Road a detached
three-bay house with a Greek Doric porch. Then a long terrace
(Nos 47–65).

of the s end of Everton Road is WEST DERBY ROAD, and at the
w end of this is yet another terrace (Nos 34 etc.)§ and the
LOCARNO, former OLYMPIA (by *Frank Matcham*, 1903 – not
as opulent as he can be). s of the West Derby Road, in GLOU-
CESTER PLACE, a row of working-class cottages called ALEX-
ANDRA TERRACE. It is of *c.*1880 and is interesting in that it
already consists of lower two-storey maisonettes and upper
one-and-a-half-storey maisonettes accessible by two open end-
staircases and a balcony.

uite separate from all this is ST DOMINGO GROVE, off Breckfield Road North. This is a long street, and, together with the
parallel (less well preserved) St Domingo Vale, it was built as a
private venture (with its own lodges), the Grove in 1845 etc.,
the Vale in 1860 etc. The houses are mostly gabled, often
bargeboarded, but some Italianate too. In BEACON LANE the
former Boys' Catholic Orphanage, 1861 by *E. W. Pugin*.

FAIRFIELD

T JOHN THE DIVINE, Holly Road. 1851–3 by *W. Raffles Brown*.
Dec, with a sw steeple and flowing tracery. The aisle windows
curious in that they are traceried nearly all over.

T PHILIP, Sheil Road. 1885–90 by *J. Bevan*. Red stone. Lancet
windows and windows with geometrical tracery. Long row of
clerestory lancets in threes. No tower. – Much of the STAINED
GLASS is older than the church. It comes from St Philip
Hardman Street by *Rickman* and looks mid-C19.

* Spotted by Mr Hubbard.
‡ Much farther out Breck Road and s by WOODVILLE TERRACE (actually
Whitefield Road) to the factory of BARKER & DOBSON, 1922 by *Wallis,
lbert & Partners*, a straightforward concrete job with large windows, a type
t at all usual in England yet about 1920. (Parallel to Woodville Terrace is
CHMOND TERRACE, *c.* 1849, with semi-detached houses.)
§ Mr Hubbard also considers BROUGHAM TERRACE worth including. It
of *c.* 1832 by *Picton*.

8—S.L.

FAIRFIELD PRESBYTERIAN CHURCH, Beech Road. 1863–4 by
W. J. Mason (GS). Of stone, Dec, with a NW spirelet.

JEWISH CEMETERY, Deane Road. 1836–7. The entrance
screen is splendid, though not Palestinian or Israelite, with it
doorway with Greek Doric columns and pediments in the
centre.

LUNDIE MEMORIAL, Beech Road. Symmetrical, of brick, with
a central bell-turret, the whole like a school.

PERAMBULATION. N of St Philip is SHEIL PARK, where recently
the Corporation has built three twenty-two-storey blocks of
flats. They are designed by *R. Bradbury*, the City Architect.
The Camus system of precast concrete was used, and the blocks
are very sheer and impressive, especially from a distance. s of
Newsham Park is an area of Early Victorian villas, classical
also bargeboarded and also Tudor. Some are in ELM VALE
some in PRESCOT ROAD, some in FAIRFIELD CRESCENT and
PROSPECT VALE. s of Prescot Road there are some Early Victorian houses, e.g. in HOLLY ROAD (one Gothic, one Italianate), in BEECH STREET, and in DEANE ROAD opposite the
Jewish Cemetery (Tudor). At the corner of Deane Road and
KENSINGTON* an entertaining branch of MARTINS BANK,
riotously Edwardian Baroque, especially in the top chimney.
It is of brick with much stone and was designed in 1898 by
James Rhind.

FAZAKERLEY

EMMANUEL, Longmoor Lane. Brick, large, by *W. G. Ward &
W. G. Cogswell.* Consecrated in 1908.

HOLY NAME (R.C.), Longmoor Lane. 1964–5 by *P. S. Gilby &
Associates.* A mannered exterior with a concrete tower and
exposed portal frames for the body of the church. The interior
is calmer but suffers from restlessness in the multitude of
surfaces.

ST OSWALD, Netherton. *See* Netherton, p. 353.

ST PETER, Aintree. *See* Aintree, p. 66.

LONGMOOR LANE METHODIST CHURCH. Jacobean, near the
s end of the street.

EVERTON CEMETERY, Higher Lane. 1879. The chapels are, as
so often in cemeteries, deliberately different from one another. One has a SE, the other a NW steeple, and so on.

KIRKDALE CEMETERY, Longmoor Lane. Opened in 1881. The

* For Kensington *see* p. 218.

main chapel is really two, though they are connected and only one has a steeple. The w fronts are self-consciously different one from the other. On the other sides they are similar. The third chapel is humbler.

ᴇw Hᴀʟʟ, Longmoor Lane (Home for the Mentally Deficient). Built in 1887–9 by *Charles H. Lancaster* as cottage homes for the upbringing of deprived children. The whole colony was to be independent as regards day-to-day provisions. The clients were the Poor Law Guardians. A very interesting layout of individual gabled houses with two-bay fronts, along a long internal street, interrupted by the dining hall with a tower with fancy top.

ᴀʀᴛʟᴇʏ's Fᴀᴄᴛᴏʀʏ. A grand brick mass, dated on the detached gateway 1886. The dining hall to the l. is dated 1895. Such a building indicates care for the working staff, and there is indeed a factory village (Hᴀʀᴛʟᴇʏ Vɪʟʟᴀɢᴇ) or housing estate immediately next door, gabled brick houses, semidetached, or four or six together. It does not add up to much but is socially notable. It was begun in 1888.*

ᴏ perambulation is possible or necessary. Fazakerley is mostly housing estates of between the wars and after.

ɴe more hint. In Hɪɢʜᴇʀ Lᴀɴᴇ between Longmoor Lane and Everton Cemetery, when driving, one has for a minute or two the illusion of being in the country.

GARSTON

ᴛ Mɪᴄʜᴀᴇʟ. 1876–7 by *T. D. Barry & Son*. Large, with a ɴw porch tower and an apse. Dec style. In the churchyard a shaft, perhaps ᴄ17 and perhaps for a sundial.

ɪʀ Aʟꜰʀᴇᴅ Jᴏɴᴇs Hᴏsᴘɪᴛᴀʟ, Church Road. 1914–15 by *C. T. Anderson* and *R. S. Crawford*. A handsome nine-bay neo-Queen Anne house with hipped roof.

ᴛᴀᴛɪᴏɴ. Opened in 1873. The exterior, in spite of stepped gables, is inconspicuous, but inside is an unusually spacious staircase with fancy iron railing and a tricky timber roof.

of the church is a planned ᴇsᴛᴀᴛᴇ of dreary cottages, quite extensive.

ɴ Speke Road is Sᴘᴇᴋᴇ Rᴏᴀᴅ Gᴀʀᴅᴇɴs, municipal housing completed in 1933 and unusual in that it consists of blocks of flats linked by two-storey houses.

* Information kindly given me by Miss Margaret Tims.

GATEACRE

OUR LADY OF THE ASSUMPTION (R.C.), Hedgefield Road. By
L. A. G. Prichard & Son.

ST STEPHEN, Belle Vale. 1872–4 by *Cornelius Sherlock*. Red
sandstone, in the style of *c.*1300, with a NW steeple. – STAINED
GLASS. W window by *Morris & Co.*, of the 1880s.

UNITARIAN CHAPEL, Gateacre Brow. Licensed in 1700, enlarged in 1719. Plain rectangle, pitched roof with a lantern,
segment-headed windows except for the round-headed one
above the round-headed doorway. – (PULPIT. C18. Panelled.)

The centre of Gateacre is not the church but the chapel. Opposite
it the excellent new MIDLAND BANK by *Weightman & Bullen,*
*c.*1965, E of it the PRUDENTIAL ASSURANCE in a black-and-
white house probably of *c.*1875. It has plenty of pargetting, the
panels apparently cast from Flemish C17 panels with scenes
from the Bible. In the same place the DRINKING FOUNTAIN
of 1883, under an octagonal sandstone canopy, the type of
ancient market crosses.

In HALEWOOD ROAD, ¼ m. SE, the GATEACRE HALL HOTEL
has a garden gateway probably of the later C17, broad, with a
pediment on pilasters with alternate blocking.

LEE HALL, ¾ m. ENE, called by Mr Fleetwood-Hesketh 'one of
the most perfect smaller Georgian houses in Lancashire', was
demolished less than ten years ago. There is in the grounds now
the Lee Park Estate. At its E end in KING'S DRIVE impressive
high slabs.

But if you want to see housing in 1967 at its wildest go to HARTS-
BOURNE WALK, Hartsbourne Avenue, at the end of Craighurst
Road, *c.* ¾ m. NNW of the chapel. This new scheme of pedestrian
shopping with flats and maisonettes to emulate Habitat at
Expo 67 in Montreal is by *Gerald R. Beech*. It is tricky, it is
intricate, but is it competitive in cost, and is it practical in
use? Also, is it an attractive environment? The young must
decide.

GRASSENDALE *see* AIGBURTH

KIRKDALE

ST ALEXANDER (R.C.), St John's Road. 1955–7 by *F. X. Velarde*
– PLATE. Molyneux Chalice, presented in 1695 to St Swithun
West Derby.

ATHANASIUS, Fountains Road. 1954–7 by *Herbert Thearle*. Really a disastrous design, with the joke roof of the tower and the mean cast-concrete side windows so totally different in spirit.

JOHN EVANGELIST (R.C.), Fountains Road. 1885 by *J. & B. Sinnott*. Rock-faced, in the geometrical style of tracery. No tower. Big seven-light E window, five-light w window. Aisles. No structural division between nave and chancel.

MARY, Walton Road, the Kirkdale parish church. 1835, with the front and E wall of 1841–3 by *A. H. Holme*. The original church is of brick with minimum lancet windows. The front is stone, with Dec details, thin but quite sweet.

PAUL, Brasenose Road. 1868 by *Culshaw & Sumners* and 1905 by *Henry Sumners*. Small. Restless stone front with asymmetrical spire. The body of the church is of brick with plain lancet windows.

ION PRESBYTERIAN CHURCH, Fountains Road. 1876–81 by *J. Wainwright & Sons*. With a NW tower. In the late C13 style.

ANLEY HOSPITAL. 1870 etc. by *Duckworth & Metcalfe*. A long, symmetrical brick front with minor Gothic detailing and some brick decoration. Later additions.

PERAMBULATION. In BOUNDARY STREET is the big square HUSKISSON (Railway Goods) WAREHOUSE, five-storeyed, of common brick and red-brick dressings. Part of the ground floor is open with iron columns. The date seems to be 1880. The front to DERBY ROAD is thirty bays long. In Derby Road early warehouses as well as modern ones. Among the latter Messrs Huskisson Transit Co. is specially impressive because of its size and its closely set parabolic concrete arches much like those of a hangar. The building was completed in 1957, and its design is credited to *Cementation Ltd* and the *Technical Department of Tate & Lyle*. *See* p. 480

KNOTTY ASH

JOHN EVANGELIST, Thomas Lane. 1835–6 by an unknown architect. Red stone, thin w tower with a recessed spire and thin polygonal buttresses. The sides of the church high, with three-light Perp windows and thin buttresses. The chancel with s chapel is an addition of 1890 by *Aldridge & Deacon*. Nave arcade of slender columns and four-centred arches. w gallery. Chancel and chapel in sympathetic Perp, though naturally

more 'correct'. – STAINED GLASS. The centre window on
N side, 1872 by *Morris*, includes a representation of Absalom.
Opposite the small SCHOOL, dated 1837.

ST MARGARET MARY (R.C.), Pilch Lane. By *Weightman*
Bullen, 1962–4. One of the best recent churches in Liverpo
Square concrete tower, square plan of the church. Flat ceili
except for the light-giving erection over the altar, with
folded roof. The side walls are of brick below, of stone abo
and the light comes in high up from gabled windows. Narr
N and S passage aisles. The baptistery is convincingly plac
in the tower.

Dovecot House has disappeared, but its former STABLES rem;
in THINGWALL LANE, of eight bays, stuccoed, with a cent
pediment and broad pointed windows, i.e. early C19.

DOVECOT ESTATE was developed in the grounds of Dove
House from 1930 onwards. In 1933 came the SHOPPI:
CENTRE with LIBRARY nicely done by *Sir Lancelot Keay* o:
curve with a three-bay centre with the large round-head
library windows, below them an axial passage through into
estate, and on the top a cupola. The shops have a rather narr
continuous canopy.

MOSSLEY HILL

ST MATTHEW AND ST JAMES, Rose Lane. This is one of
best Victorian churches of Liverpool. It is by *Paley & Aus*
and was built in 1870–5. It is uncommonly large, of red sto:
and has a truly monumental crossing tower. The style is l
C13. Attached to the E end on the S is a polygonal vest
attached to the W end, i.e. projecting N from the W bay of
N aisle, is the porch. This unusual device results in a W faça
not symmetrical. Six-bay nave, two-light clerestory, the
terior of the tower open to the inside with a narrow wall-pass;
behind high, noble, transomed two-light openings. The cro
ing arches have four stepped chamfers each and no capitals
all. – STALLS. Though they are mostly C19, it looks as if p
of the back stalls might be Perp. Nothing is known of prov
ance. – STAINED GLASS. All the glass, including work
Morris and by *Holiday*, was destroyed in the war. – SOU
AFRICAN WAR MEMORIAL. In the vestry porch. Copper;
Nouveau.

The VICARAGE, immediately E of the church, is dated 18
and presumably by *Paley & Austin*. A very free desi;

.-shaped, with large tower, traceried staircase windows, and a
int of Philip Webb in the simple domesticity of the l.-hand
wing.

ANTHONY OF PADUA (R.C.), Queen's Drive. By *Anthony
Ellis*, 1931–2.

BARNABAS, Allerton Road. By *Doyle*, 1900–14. The exterior
brick-faced, in a very odd pattern, bricks, half-bricks, and big
brick slabs like ashlar. Perp style, with W tower, aisles and
transepts. Cool, dignified interior, ashlar-faced. The arcade
between chancel and S chapel finer and more ornate than the
nave arcades. It is a serious, sober piece of work.

OSSLEY HILL BAPTIST CHURCH, Dovedale Road. Opened
n 1906. Exceptionally ambitious and in the free forms then
favoured by the Nonconformists. Flint and red brick, with a
high tower with fancy top. Perp details, handled with a roguish
touch.

OSSLEY HILL HOSPITAL, $\frac{1}{2}$ m. NW, includes a Gothic mansion of 1868–9.

OVEDALE TOWERS, Dovedale Road. This was the house of
A. G. Kurtz, a chemist and art collector. It was called Grove
House and seems to date from *c*.1850. The style is indeed Early
Victorian. The features and especially the tower are what one
now calls 'debased'. The tower was originally higher and
wilder.

DLEY (Art Gallery), Mossley Hill Road, $\frac{1}{4}$ m. S. The house of
Emma Holt, who left it and her pictures to the Corporation.
Ashlar-built and sensible. Of *c*.1830, it seems, including the
fine staircase, but with additions and alterations of the 1880s.

M. MARSH COLLEGE OF PHYSICAL EDUCATION, S of Sud-
ey, also in Mossley Hill Road. The centre is a stuccoed villa
of *c*.1830. To the garden it has a porch of pairs of Greek Doric
columns, to the entrance a semicircular bow, with the porch
ncluded. The bow has Doric pilasters. To this house additions
were made, first also stuccoed, then a neo-Georgian range of
1954 (by the then County Architect), and now a hall, a twelve-
storey block (with one of the inescapable, though meaningless
long concrete reliefs), and a separate games hall of hangar
construction. It is by *Roger Booth*, the County Architect, and
entirely satisfying.

ARNATIC HALLS, NW of the church. On the site of a house the
name of which commemorated one of Liverpool's greatest
prizes of privateering, the French East Indiaman Carnatic,
brought into Liverpool in 1778, laden with spices and diamonds.

Now Carnatic Halls is a growing group of halls of residence
the university. The architects are *Manning & Clamp*. The fi▮
phase was built in 1965–7. It is of purple brick, three store▮
and less in height. Apart from the study-bedrooms there is t▮
canteen building, awkwardly called Catering Building. It
covered with one of those arched concrete roofs which Sir Ba▮
Spence's University of Sussex has made fashionable. (He h▮
them from Le Corbusier's Maisons Jaoul.) The building
L-shaped, with the main dining hall in the shorter arm on t▮
ground floor, and smaller dining halls on the upper floor of t▮
longer arm. This longer arm has a terrace and faces a lo▮
formal pool. The concrete shuttering is exposed in the ru▮
way popularized by Le Corbusier. The residential parts ha▮
an odd rhythm of windows, oblong and with a thin glazed s▮
sticking out at the top on one floor to the l., on the next to t▮
r. Would it really have done harm to keep to a regularity whi▮
is after all that of the shapes of the rooms inside ?

See
p.
480 N of the church is THE HOLMSTEAD, now St Saviour's Conve▮
Early Victorian Tudor (possibly by *Cunningham & Holm▮*
with a High Victorian addition. Interiors of both period▮
Lodge and outbuildings of the earlier.

NORRIS GREEN

CHRIST CHURCH, Sedgmoor Road. 1931–2 by *Quiggin & G▮*
Brick with round-headed lancets. Just a touch of the Swed▮
of the 1920s in the W lancet.

ST CHRISTOPHER, Lorenzo Drive. 1930–2 by *B. A. Mill▮*
Brick, with a broad, low, blocky crossing tower. The ma▮
windows and the W portal are parabolic, quite an enterprisi▮
thing to do in 1930. The original colouring is probably re▮
resented by the ceiling of the tower. The rest in its new pa▮
Wedgwood blue and cream is unpardonable. Originally it w▮
in strong red, orange, and purple, with the stalls red and blac▮
Terrible also the chi-chi decoration of the E wall, but that
original. – The FONT is star-shaped in plan and straight ▮
elevation and all faced with mirror-glass, this also a chi-c▮
touch.

ST TERESA (R.C.), Utting Avenue East. 1937 by *F. E. G. Badg▮*
Rarely has there been such a haphazard assortment of styl▮
in one church. The columns are Romanesque, the arches Per▮
the high clerestory windows a 1920s 'Moderne', the flute▮
pilaster strips between them classical anyway, and on top ▮

the whole is a Gothic timber rib-vault. It is a high and long church of brick with two short façade towers.

ANKIN MEMORIAL PRESBYTERIAN CHURCH, Lorenzo Drive. 1930–1 by *George Downie*. Italian Romanesque with a campanile – an odd choice for Presbyterians. Large, of brick, the campanile octagonal.

IBRARY, Utting Avenue East. By *Sir Lancelot Keay*, the City Architect, 1937–8. Square, i.e. modern, but with a three-bay entrance which shows that this is only a paring off of decoration and mouldings from a basically neo-Georgian composition.

AIG MEMORIAL HOMES, Muirhead Avenue. By *Grey Wornum & Louis de Soissons* with *Harris & Hobson*, 1929. Three sides of a quadrangle, brick, neo-Georgian, and much like the surrounding housing.

he NORRIS GREEN ESTATE was begun in 1926. In BROAD-WAY is the SHOPPING CENTRE, completed in 1929. It is two-storeyed, on a curve, and punctuated with gables. Poor detail of the shopping canopy.

OLD SWAN *see* TUE BROOK

PRINCE'S PARK *see* SEFTON PARK

IN AND AROUND SEFTON PARK AND PRINCE'S PARK

RINCE'S PARK was laid out as a public park for Richard Vaughan Yates by *Paxton* in 1842.* It was Paxton's first independent job and was immediately followed by Birkenhead Park in 1843, a much more influential piece of work. Paxton established the pattern for the Victorian public park, valid for France as much as for America. Prince's Park has the houses and terraces immediately surrounding the park on the pattern of Regent's Park, and the drive around and the lake with island and bridge. The main entrance is perhaps by *Pennethorne*, with handsome classical gatepiers and ironwork of radial pattern, and formerly with a Doric lodge. Dr G. F. Chadwick suggests that the picturesque rustic boat house may be by *John Robertson*. The housing around the park took some time to build and does not adhere exactly to Paxton's plan. For St Paul's church and the housing, *see* below.

EFTON PARK followed later. The design was won in competition in 1867 by *Édouard André* of Paris and *Lewis Hornblower* of

* In the early stages of the project the name of *James Pennethorne* was associated with Paxton's, but his contribution is not likely to have been great.

Liverpool. The making of the park was completed in 1872. It is much larger: 387 acres, of which 120 were reserved for the building of houses. The accepted plans were more ambitious than the execution, but even the execution has many more features than Prince's Park. Foremost is the PALM HOUSE, opened in 1896, and made by *Mackenzie & Moncur* of Edinburgh and Glasgow. It is octagonal, with an ambulatory and an octagonal lantern. In it the STATUE of Highland Mary by *B. E. Spence*, and around it eight statues by *L. C. Chavillaud*, curiously four of stone and four of bronze, the latter much livelier. Below is the lake and facing it a STATUE of William Rathbone, by *Foley*, 1874-7.* Smaller pools follow to the N; at their end is a grotto. N of the main lake copies of *Alfred Gilbert*'s Shaftesbury Memorial (Eros) in Piccadilly Circus (1932) and of the Peter Pan statue in Kensington Gardens (1928). Mossley Hill Drive is carried across a dingle by a cast-iron BRIDGE. The SOUTH LODGE is typical of its date: red brick and half-timber painted green; fussy detail. – At the NW corner is the Samuel Smith OBELISK, with bronze reliefs on the base. It is of 1909, by *Willink & Thicknesse*, with sculpture by *Charles J. Allen*. – The NORTH-WEST LODGE is similar to the other, but the GATES have in the middle a short tower in the E.E. style, debased with relish. Note the top with the shaft with shaft-ring and the two fat granite columns nudging it, all three supporting the roof.

The area round Sefton Park developed into a favourite one for the villas of the affluent, not the mansions of the richest. Those were at Allerton, Woolton, West Derby.

CHURCHES

ST AGNES, Ullet Road. St Agnes was built at the expense of Douglas Horsfall, a wealthy stockbroker, whose house, Merebank by *Norman Shaw*, has recently been demolished. He was a benefactor of churches and member of a family of benefactors of churches.‡ The architect of St Agnes was *Pearson*, and the dates are 1883-5. It is the noblest Victorian church in Liverpool.

---

* Reliefs by *Brock*.

‡ Mr Hubbard gave me much information on the Horsfalls. Christ Church Everton was built in 1848 as a memorial to Charles, a merchant, by his children but the church does not exist any longer. Robert, Douglas's father, built S Margaret, Princes Road, *see* below, p. 244, George built Christ Church, Sefton Park, *see* below, p. 236, and Douglas himself founded St Chad's Theological College at Durham besides building several Liverpool churches.

erect and vigorous, and not in the least humbled by being of red brick. The style is that of the C13, English with French touches, combined to achieve perfect unity. This was of course Pearson's favourite style, and he knew how to handle it with ease and without ever stooping to imitation. The church is high, with aisles and clerestory, a polygonal apse, E transepts, and – a surprising feature – W transepts. The apse has outer blank arcading high up, and there are two turrets in the re-entrant angles of E transepts and chancel. Windows are lancets or have plate tracery. They differ from one another when it comes to the end walls of the transepts. Two porches flank the short bay W of the W transept and open to the W. There is no tower. The interior is ashlar-faced and stone-vaulted, with the quadri-partite rib-vaults of French cathedrals. Pearson uses no gallery, but a balcony all along, with the high single lancets of the clerestory above it. The W bay has a tripartite arcade to mark a lobby space. The nave is of four bays. At the E end Pearson intensified his effects by subsidiary structures, low and them-selves vaulted. An octagon in the NE transept with mid-pier to carry the organ, a Lady Chapel off the SE transept with its own aisles, and the N aisle continued to form a very narrow ambulatory round the apse. The feature is almost identical with that used by Pearson before at St Michael in Croydon (1871). – REREDOS in the Lady Chapel. By *Bodley*, 1904. – Lady Chapel SCREEN. By *Bodley*, 1903. – SCULPTURE. In the apse by *Hitch*, 1893–5. – Also many playful corbel-heads and grotesques done *c*.1910, including a falling horse for Horsfall. – STAINED GLASS. Several windows by *Kempe*.

The VICARAGE is by *Norman Shaw*, 1887, and one of his 81 best domestic works. It was built originally as a clergy house and the cost was defrayed by Douglas Horsfall's mother. Red brick, with stone dressings, quite asymmetrically composed and yet strictly disciplined. To the street a gable with a shallow canted oriel. (Here is the chapel.) To the apse of the church more complicated composition with a pointed-arched doorway, the flat chimneybreast to the r., its l. angle caught on a stone corbel and a differently canted oriel under a different gable to the r. of the chimney. (The interior is classical in its elements.) Simple PARISH HALL by *Shaw* behind, connected with the church by a short, conventionally Gothic passage, also by *Shaw*.

ALL SAINTS, Bentley Road. 1882–4 by *Gordon M. Hills*.

ST BEDE, Hartington Road. 1883 by *J. E. K. Cutts* and *A. H. Mackmurdo*. Stock brick and red brick. Nave and chancel, two w porches with baptistery between. The roof, probably with the fancy turret of 1891, by *Habershon & Fawckner*, but this might be as late as 1924, when rebuilding took place after a fire. Of the brilliance and daring of Mackmurdo nothing is noticeable outside. – The VICARAGE is dated 1891.

CHRIST CHURCH, Linnett Lane. Built at the expense of George Horsfall. 1870–1 by *Culshaw & Sumners*. Highly original, with many touches of roguery. w front with two porches set diagonally. E front with NE steeple, the broaches of the spire convex in outline. E porch N of the steeple, chancel apse S of it. The aisles are cross-gabled so that the clerestory windows have only enough space to be window-heads. The tracery is geometrical. The interior is ashlar-faced and more orthodox. Six-bay arcades, tall piers, naturalistic capitals. – STAINED GLASS. By *Hardman* probably the glass in the apse.

ST CLARE (R.C.), Arundel Avenue. By *Stokes*, 1888–90, and a memorable building. The development in the three years from Pearson's St Agnes is striking. Stokes handles his Gothic with much more individuality, so that the ensemble is far away from any period precedent. Common brick and stone dressings. Long and high nave and no tower, but a turret with spire in the re-entrant angle of N transept and nave. Sheer E wall, with the window broad and high up. Characteristic parapet, not embattled, but with occasional rises. On the S side the confessionals project beyond the aisle and are given irregular fenestration as though they were designed today, and l. and r. of the chancel are long side chapels. The interior is determined by what in German Late Gothic and some Baroque churches is called *Wandpfeiler*, i.e. wall-piers, really deep buttresses drawn inside to separate chapels. It is the system of Albi too and of Bodley's Pendlebury of 1874. But Stokes pierces the wall-piers to create aisles and gives the aisles a low arcade to the nave – with round arches on piers of elongated lozenge-shape placed transverse to the nave – so as to create a balcony or boxes over. This arcade system is not interrupted for the chancel side chapels. The front parts of the lozenge-shaped piers are carried up as triangular shafts till they meet a chamfered horizontal band at the top of the wall. The chamfering is exactly one side of the triangle, so that each bay seems to be framed l., r., and top by a boldly bevelled frame. It is a pity the interior is all plastered cream-colour and not ashlar-faced. Goodhart-Rendel complained about this too, but sums up: 'Probably Stokes's best work.'

The PRESBYTERY adjoins immediately and is as free in

composition. The hood-mould stops of the doorway are amazing for their date – fully Art Nouveau.

St Paul, Belvedere Road. 1846–8 by *A. H. Holme*. The church has a very dominating steeple, with incorrect detail, e.g. the extremely long transomed three-light bell-openings and the prominent pinnacles. In spite of its date the plan of the church is also pre-archeological, without aisles, but with transepts. The end-bays of the transepts incidentally are internally used for staircases. The windows are all still as long and lean as those of the Commissioners' churches, and the tracery is still Perp. *The Ecclesiologist* (December 1853) was outraged by the church. It wrote: 'It is an immensely broad cross church, without aisles; the windows of the most vulgar churchwarden's Gothic; the roof, a portentous erection, with hammer-beam, and collar, and king and queen-post (if we may use the expression) all in one. The transepts have actually three windows, both in breadth and depth; their extremities are screened off for staircases to their galleries, and the skylights have been opened into them. We should not, however, have noticed this building as one of the best specimens we ever saw of the pepper-box style, had it not been for some arrangements, to which we will beg the reader's attention. The altar stands at a distance from the east wall, behind the mountain of pulpit and reading desk. Observing a mat at the east end of the altar, we enquired its use. "Why, sir," was the reply, "Dr M'Neile reads the *Communion* at the north side of the table; but at the *Sacrament* he stands facing the congregation." So we have the old Basilican arrangement restored! The pulpit is unique. A kind of iron crane, padded at the end, is attached to the back: when the preacher has mounted his elevation, an official pushes this instrument forward, the divine bestrides it, and is ready for his task. In fact, he must present a very tolerable representation of a martyr on the *equleus*; with the one exception, that in former ages the actor on that instrument was tortured for the amusement of the spectators; here the spectators must be tortured for the amusement of the actor. The pulpitolatory of another arrangement is almost incredible. Suspended in the air, at some distance in front of, and higher than, the preacher's head, is a gas reflector with seven burners. On the Sunday morning the gas is lighted but kept low. Should the day be foggy, it is turned on in full power; and thus, while the rest of the church is in mist and obscurity, the preacher's head is encircled by a nimbus of glory. We doubt whether ecclesiology

can present a more ludicrous spectacle than that of a man
preaching on a padded horse, and with the effulgence of seven
lamps streaming, at mid-day, on his face. Were the Pope,
instead of Dr M'Neile, concerned, would not the arrangement
be called, by all good Protestants, a vile parody of Moses on
the Mount, and of a still more solemn passage in the Apo-
calypse ?' Needless to say, not all the arrangements here described survived the Victorian era, and a chancel (with good
Minton tiling) was added in 1886. According to Mr Hubbard,
a far more ecclesiologically correct 'Middle Pointed' design was
earlier made by *Elmes*. It was intended to carry this out much
further back in Prince's Park itself, isolated in the landscape.

St Columba Presbyterian Church, Smithdown Road.
1896–7. Red brick with a big, almost wholly transparent w
tower. Saddleback roof. The church has free-Perp tracery of
yellow terracotta.

Unitarian Church, Ullet Road. 1896–9 by *Thomas Worthington*, but in fact by his son *Percy Worthington*. They were
Manchester Unitarians. The Unitarian church was very strong
at that time and indeed throughout the c19 in Liverpool, as
such names as Roscoe, Rathbone, Holt, Booth, Brunner, Tate
show. The church therefore is one of the most ambitious
Unitarian churches in the country, and it happens to be an
excellent design, grouping delightfully with the hall added in
1902 and the Memorial Passage to it. The buildings are of red
brick, and the church is quite simple in its elements. Dec
features, a bellcote and no tower. But the HALL is as original
and as picturesquely composed as if it were by Stokes, with the
shallow, canted stone bay to the main road and a semicircular
bow to the side street by the entrance. The interior is stone-
faced, has aisles of seven bays, more conventionally done, and
a broad, shallow canted apse. Between nave and façade is a
large lobby. – The library and the vestry have impressive
frescoes by *Gerald Moira*, 1902. The subject in the library is
the Pursuit of Truth, in the vestry the Cardinal Virtues. –
LIGHT FITTINGS. Art Nouveau. – STAINED GLASS. Mostly
by *Morris & Co.*, that in the apse the earliest (1897–8) and the
best. – WEST DOORS. Of beaten copper. By *Richard Rathbone*. –
MONUMENTS. Roscoe by *Gibson*, a bust. – Edward Roscoe
† 1834. An angel in profile looking up. – W. Rathbone † 1868
By *Foley*, 1874. Large relief with the deceased on a sarcophagus
and two groups of mourners l. and r.

Toxteth Park Cemetery, Smithdown Road. 1856.

PUBLIC BUILDINGS

SEFTON GENERAL HOSPITAL, Smithdown Road. A former WORKHOUSE, 1858 etc. by *Culshaw*. Very similar to the Walton Hospital, i.e. a very long brick block with projecting wings and a central tower, with more stone trim, the motifs being debased.

THE UNIVERSITY HALLS. Built in the grounds of the Rathbone property immediately E of Sefton Park with frontages to Greenbank Lane and North Mossley Hill Road. GREENBANK itself is a delightful, small Gothick house of *c.*1800 with later additions. The original house is of three bays with a tripartite porch and tripartite loggia over, both vaulted in plaster. L. and r. are castellated ground-floor bay windows. Round the corner the most charming two-storeyed iron veranda. Incidentally, whereas the former side is of ashlar, the latter is stuccoed. Inside a plaster-vaulted entrance passage with a large boss traceried as a mouchette wheel. The university halls are DERBY HALL, 1937–9 by *Willink & Dod*, neo-Georgian, in red brick, RATHBONE HALL, 1958–9 by *Gilling, Dod & Partners*, the architecturally least successful of them, then the excellent utilitarian extensions in yellow brick to both, 1960–1 by *M. G. Gilling*, and GLADSTONE HALL and ROSCOE HALL, 1962–4 by *David Roberts*, good and unruffled, yet not unaware of the change in taste of the last few years. The landscaping of the whole precinct is exquisite.

PERAMBULATION

The following areas deserve a visit.

PRINCE'S PARK. The park itself has been described. PRINCE'S PARK TERRACE, at the junction of Croxteth and Sefton Park Roads, is a long, four-storeyed stucco terrace by *Wyatt Papworth*, won in competition in 1843, yet really very drab, especially to the park. Near by in Sefton Park Road is a house called PARK LODGE, memorable only in so far as it is supposed to contain some masonry from one of the lodges of Toxteth Deer Park (*see* p. 242). Behind this is WINDERMERE TERRACE, a part of the park where houses were built inside the drive as well as outside. Windermere Terrace has two bows to the park. Next to it is a handsome three-bay house with four Ionic columns. On the opposite (w) side of the park is CAVENDISH GARDENS with giant Corinthian pilasters to the park and SUNNYSIDE, next to it, a little later, hence with *palazzo* motifs. These two terraces are off DEVONSHIRE ROAD, and here, as was discovered by Mr Hubbard, is a house by *Waterhouse*, Gothic and asymmetrical. It was built for Lyster, the dock engineer, in 1863.

N of the NW gates of Sefton Park, off Sefton Park Road, is GROVE PARK, started in 1852. It has mostly semi-detached, stuccoed houses, Late Classical or Italianate.

Due S from Sefton Park and stretching to the river is FULWOOD PARK, laid out about 1840. It is only a street, but has its own lodge. The houses are stuccoed and Italianate.

SPEKE

ALL SAINTS. By *Pearson*, 1876, but not on a level with St Agnes, Sefton Park. All Saints is simple, reasonable, and serious, but devoid of Pearson's great enthusiasms. Red stone with a moderate S steeple with broach spire. Dec details, but five-light geometrical E window. N aisle and N transept only. The arch between chancel and organ chamber is treated as a two-light opening with geometrical tracery, as the mid C19 liked it.

ST AMBROSE (R.C.), Heathgate Avenue. By *Weightman & Bullen*, 1959–61. Plain rectangle of ten by seven bays, concrete structure, brick infilling, and at the top windows on all sides under shallow concrete arches. On the entrance side is a three-bay narthex, and beyond this the square tower with baptistery and the entries l. and r. of it. The interior of the church has a narrow ambulatory all the way round. This again has concrete piers and shallow arches. They connect with the outer arch by tunnel-vault. The spacious centre has a flat ceiling, disappointingly treated.

LIVERPOOL AIRPORT. 1931–7. The buildings by *Sir Alan J. Cobham* with *Sir John Burnet & Partners*.

The SPEKE HOUSING ESTATE was planned by *Sir Lancelot Keay* in 1936, begun in 1937, and continued into the 1950s. It is a depressing affair, with all the monotony and none of the freshness of earlier estates such as Norris Green.

17 SPEKE HALL. When Christopher Hussey wrote about Speke Hall in 1922, he could still grow lyrical over the 'windswept firs', the 'broad grassy glade', the 'fairy arabesque of leaves', the 'sweet scent', the stillness and distance from the 'ever-growing city'. Now the trees between the house and the river have given way to a runway of Speke Airport, and the *Hinterland* has become all industry. Yet the house remains as one of the finest examples of timber-framing in the county. It was built by the

Norris family, but no-one has proved yet who built what. The house has an inner courtyard and is surrounded by a moat, now dry. It is fully preserved, without Victorian alterations. Its external appearance is Elizabethan, and the only dates are indeed Late Elizabethan and Jacobean, 1598, 1605, 1612. But the authors who have written on Speke Hall insist that pre-Elizabethan work remains. The truth of this is evident in only one place outside, the kitchen window, and only one place inside, the hall. The kitchen window is of seven lights with a transom and uncusped round heads to the lights at the top and below the transom. The whole is smaller than it sounds here, and one would date it Henry VIII (certainly not C15). The hall goes through two storeys and has a ceiling with moulded beams, and the low screens passage also has moulded beams. That could be *c.*1500 but need not be. 1500 would mean Sir William Norris I, Henry VIII means Henry Norris or Sir William II, 1598 and 1605 means Edward, and 1612 Sir William III.

It is not necessary to describe the exterior in detail. There is a base of red sandstone and occasionally red sandstone walling (E) or red sandstone chimneybreasts (W). The latter have cornices definitely Elizabethan. Of stone also is the bridge from the N and the main porch with its sides crowned by a typically Jacobean heavy cresting and also the small S porch dated 1612 and a small garden gateway dated 1605. The rest is black and white. There is none of the close studding which one would expect of the C15, but there is big, bold herringbone bracing, and in selected places are decorative features, mostly quatrefoils. Over the main entrance is a date 1598 and an inscription referring to the building of 25 yards of something – probably the N range E of the N return of the W range. On the N side also occur elaborate bargeboards, square panels with four spurs to create the effect of diagonally placed quatrefoiling and the familiar concave-sided lozenges, i.e. Elizabethan motifs. The ensemble is extremely picturesque, especially the S front and the court-yard with its two yew trees. Along the W and N sides of the courtyard runs a passage or corridor on both floors. That must be an Elizabethan alteration, especially as it has been pointed out that the ridge of the W range roof is in the middle of the range minus the corridor. Towards the courtyard is again quatrefoil decoration. In the rooms at the corner of W and N ranges are three Elizabethan chimneypieces, two on the ground floor, one on the first. They are all of the same type, with flat summary foliage decoration on imposts and lintel. Much more ambitious is the chimneypiece in the Great Chamber, but also much less acceptable. The wooden overmantel represents three generations of Norrises, Henry on the l., Sir William with two wives and many children in the middle, and Edward on the r. The carving is ludicrous. That is all the more remarkable as the plasterwork in the same room is so accomplished: large panels of vine-trails, rose-trails and others, between the beams. Mr Lees Milne compares the work with Gawthorpe. In the adjoining hall the inner bay has fragments of C15 STAINED GLASS. The outer bay is the size of a room and has its own big fireplace. The hall fireplace is in the wall towards the screens passage. It is obviously a later insertion, and as it has the initials of Sir William who died in 1567 or 1568 that proves the greater age of the structure. Elaborate plaster battlements etc. over the fireplace. Fine panelling along the upper end of the hall, obviously *ex situ*.

A special attraction of Speke Hall are the hiding-places and observation holes. The Norrises were recusant Catholics. Haward refers to recesses in the chimneys of the chapel and the room above, a closet with observation hole above the main door in the courtyard, a watching gap in the panelling of the great hall, a whole system of hiding-places, and a main escape shaft in the N wing. It is entered through a cupboard in the Priest's Room in the N wing. A further hiding-place is in the Haunted Room.

Speke Hall was rented by F. R. Leyland, the shipping magnate, and Whistler, who painted the Peacock Room in Leyland's London house, stayed at Speke for long periods.

STANLEY *see* TUE BROOK

STONEYCROFT *see* TUE BROOK

TOXTETH

Exclusive of the Sefton Park and Prince's Park areas Toxteth in the Middle Ages was a deer park. It was disafforested about 1600. There never developed a Toxteth village, though the Jacobean Toxteth Chapel must have had a congregation.

CHURCHES

ST MICHAEL-IN-THE-HAMLET. *Thomas Rickman* met John Cragg, owner of the Mersey Iron Foundry, in 1812. Cragg was a fanatic of cast iron for all purposes and was at that time busy designing St Michael and a group of houses by the church (*see* below, p. 248). Rickman helped him, and was no doubt responsible for much that we see now. St Michael was built in 1814–15, i.e. after St George Everton, though it was designed before that church. Rickman was not wholly satisfied. He wrote of Cragg: 'His ironwork is too stiff in his head to bend to any beauty.' St George Everton, more Rickman's own, is indeed, though very similar, more beautiful, especially externally. At St Michael everything that could be made of iron, has been made of iron, even the stone-looking high plinth which is in reality iron plates, the cladding of the clerestory, and of course all the window tracery, door and window surrounds, crestings, churchyard fence, churchyard gates, etc. The church has a w tower, aisles, and a clerestory. The style is Perp. Inside there is only one gallery, in the tower. The E window is of six lights, and its tracery is exactly like that of the Everton E window. Iron arches on slim iron shafts divide nave from aisles, run across the aisles, and help to carry the roof with its pretty iron tracery panels.

t ANDREW, Aigburth Road. 1893 by *George Bradbury & Sons*. A brick interior very much better than the outside leads one to expect.

t CHARLES BORROMEO (R.C.), Aigburth Road. By *Sinnott, Sinnott & Powell*, 1900. Dec style, w tower, nothing remarkable outside. But inside this ought to be 1845 and not 1900: aisleless nave, open timber roof, tripartite opening into chancel and side chapels.

t CLEMENT, Beaumont Street. 1840–1. The usual Commissioners' type, i.e. oblong with lancet windows. But there is one weird feature: the w bell-turret is placed over a narrow w bay higher and with a steeper roof than the rest. Inside, the ALTAR is placed in a shallow polygonal recess. GALLERIES on three sides, carried on cast-iron columns. 'Hammerbeam' roof with the hammerbeams supported by a further set of iron columns. The original arrangement and furnishings remain intact, even the two-decker pulpit in front of the altar. – PULPIT. Particularly ungainly and rendered asymmetrical by its stairs. Top deck on four iron columns and approached by a separate spiral stair. Classical iron balusters, but Gothic iron trefoils here and on other furnishings and fittings. – BOX PEWS. – This rare survival of an Early Victorian church should be carefully safe-guarded.*

* Thanks are due to Mr John Vaughan for drawing attention to this re-markable interior.

St Cleopas, Mill Street. 1865–7 by *J. D. Jee.*

St Finbar, Dingle Mount. 1963–4 by *L. A. G. Prichard Son & Partners.*

St Gabriel, Beaufort Street. 1883–4 by *H. & A. P. Fry.*

St James, St James's Place. 1774–5. Built and perhaps designed by *Cuthbert Bisbrowne*, a builder. The design is certainly elementary enough for a builder. Red brick, blunt w tower, side windows round-arched in two tiers. The chancel similar but of 1900 (by *H. Havelock Sutton*). The interior is spatially not of interest, and it is – who would be surprised? – poorly maintained. Three galleries, open roof. What is, however, highly memorable is that the supports of the galleries are of cast iron, a very early example of the structural use of that material.* – Sword rest. Of iron, c18, the only one in a Liverpool church. – Stained glass. In the e window, by *Henry Holiday*, 1881, very characteristic of him, and very good as well. – Monuments. George Pemberton † 1795. With a kneeling figure by an urn. – Moses Benson † 1806. With a mourning figure by a sarcophagus. – J. E. Irving † 1821. With a seated figure.

Our Lady of Lourdes (R.C.), Kingsley Road. 1901 by *Pugin & Pugin*. Perp, without a tower, but with a successful w front widened by placing outside the aisles the two porches open to the w. An odd feature is the e window, which is really just a large traceried window head.

Our Lady of Mount Carmel (R.C.), High Park Street. 1876–8 by *James O'Byrne*. Red brick, no tower, geometrical tracery. Nothing seems special until one notices the details of the three w doorways. They have quadrant jambs and arches dying into them, a motif typical of the most progressive work during the last quarter of the c19.

St Margaret, Prince's Road. Paid for by Robert Horsfall, a stockbroker.‡ 1868–9 by *Street*, but not especially impressive. Red brick, the façade with two three-light windows. Wide aisles, no clerestory. Bell-turret at the e end of the nave. The interior lacks distinguishing features, except perhaps for the single arch between chancel and side chapels, much smaller than the arcade arches. Very extensive stencilled decorations on walls, roofs, etc., by *Maddox & Pearce* are being restored at the time of writing, though not strictly to the original design. – Stained glass. Much by *Clayton & Bell*. – (Needlework. Two Frontals designed by *Street* and made by *Mrs Horsfall*.) –

---

* But cf. St Anne of 1770–2 on p. 205.

‡ On the Horsfalls *see* note on p. 234.

MONUMENT. Robert Horsfall † 1881. Brass in the chancel floor, worth looking at. It was made by *Barkentin & Krall*. At the foot is Horsfall, seated, holding a drawing of the church.

T PATRICK (R.C.), Park Place. 1821-7 by *John Slater*. An interesting and very unusual plan. It is a Latin cross, but the long arm is the body of the church, the short arm only a w extension, and the two cross arms are staircase halls. The porches are attached to them, one-storeyed Greek Doric colonnades of four columns. Inside three galleries plus an upper w gallery and a segmental ceiling. Enormous ALTARPIECE of 1953 with two giant Corinthian columns. The altar itself is by *Bentley* and of 1867. The PAINTING, also enormous, is inspired by Rubens. It is by the famous *Nicaise de Keyser* of Antwerp and dates from 1834. Next to the church is the CHURCH SCHOOL, dated 1835. Seven bays with a three-bay pediment. Two storeys, the lower with arched windows.

T PHILEMON, Windsor Street. 1872-4 by *Culshaw & Sumners*. The dedication is the most remarkable thing.

BENEZER CHAPEL (former), Beaufort Street. Stuccoed. Five bays with a five-bay pediment. The ground-floor windows with alternatingly triangular and segmental pediments.

REEK ORTHODOX CHURCH, Berkley Street. 1865-70 by *Henry Sumners*. A large church. Red brick and stone dressings, faithfully keeping to the Russo-Byzantine style.

T PETER'S METHODIST CHURCH, High Park Street. 1877-8. Common brick and red brick. E.E. Gothic, an asymmetrical façade of the 'rogue' kind. There is no tower, but a turret between nave and N aisle on the façade rising from an elaborate bracket and supported from the w by a flying buttress.

RINCE'S GATE BAPTIST CHURCH, Prince's Gate, by Prince's Park. 1879-81 by *Henry Sumners*. An astonishing performance, reactionary and at the same time furiously idiosyncratic. The style can be called a debased Italianate. Stock brick and stone. The façade incorporates two staircases up and one down, and a rose-window at a level so low that the two arched entrances frame it. Gable to this composition and gable higher up to the rest of the building. The circular windows along the side should not be missed, and the rounded corners of the façade noted.

YNAGOGUE, Prince's Road. By *W. & G. Audsley*. Opened in 1874.* Common brick and red brick, the w portal in the early C13 style, but the lobes of the arch Moorish – remember the ancient synagogues of medieval Spain. The rose-window of

* But illustrated in the *Building News* in 1882 as 'new'.

course carries you firmly back to the north of Europe. Ver
lavish interior with low aisles and gallery, painted with muc
black and gold in the original scheme. The nave is tunne
vaulted in plaster. The Ark of the Torah Rolls is formed like
Byzantine church, with its five domes. The two reading pla
forms are richly detailed too, but again neither Spanish nc
Byzantine.

TOXTETH CHAPEL, Unitarian, but originally Presbyterian, Par
Road. 1774, though the masonry probably of the Jacobea
predecessor. Small, oblong, with three galleries and the pulpi
all in a very limited space. The present porch is of 1841, th
former porch was on the opposite side. – BOX PEWS. One en
below is dated 1650, one end above 1700. – There were in th
C17 only two galleries, the third, connecting one, dates fror
the C18 rebuilding.

TOXTETH BAPTIST TABERNACLE, Park Road. 1870–1. Italiar
ate. Brick and much yellow brick. Round-arched twin window
but the arches in the centre pointed and yet a pediment ove
The loss of discipline belonging to these years is patent.

(TOXTETH CONGREGATIONAL CHURCH, Aigburth Roac
1870–2 by *H. H. Vale*.)

TRINITY PRESBYTERIAN CHURCH, Prince's Road. 1879.* Re
brick; no tower. Façade with two turrets, a rose-window, an
an elaborately but not very well carved triple portal.

WELSH PRESBYTERIAN CHURCH, Prince's Road. 1865–7 b
W. & G. Audsley and fully churchy, with s w steeple, the spir
surrounded by four pinnacles, transepts, a big E rose, and gec
metrical tracery in the other windows.

WESLEYAN CHAPEL, Upper Stanhope Street. 1827. Tw
storeys, five bays. Three-bay pediment and below it the thre
doorways close together, but each flanked by Greek Dori
columns, a strange effect. The upper windows are arched.

PUBLIC BUILDINGS

TOXTETH PUBLIC OFFICES (Ministry of Social Security), Hig
Park Street. 1865–6 by *Layland* (estimate £5,788; GS). Ashla
with a three-bay centre. Heavy fenestration.

TOXTETH LIBRARY, Windsor Street, behind cathedral an
cemetery. 1902 by *Shelmerdine* and typical of his régime. Re
brick and stone trim. Symmetrical, with two big Venetia
windows beneath two gables with obelisks, and in the middle

* Or 1865?

doorway with far-projecting segmental hood. Small cupola above.

TURNER MEMORIAL HOME, Dingle Lane. By *Waterhouse*, 1881–3. Red ashlar, with a façade as varied as Waterhouse liked to make them for such a purpose. Large Perp E window of the chapel, but also a little round turret with a conical roof and mullioned-and-transomed windows. The chapel has aisles and a high timber roof. In the entrance hall group of Charles Turner and his son, white marble by *Hamo Thornycroft*. Seated figures looking at the plan of the building.

DEAF AND DUMB INSTITUTE, Prince's Avenue, Prince's Road. 1887. A curious design, octagonal like a Waterhouse Congregational church. Also as red, in brick and terracotta.

FLORENCE INSTITUTE FOR BOYS, Mill Street. 1889. Red brick and red terracotta with big shaped gables and a plain (unfinished?) angle turret. The windows are mullioned-and-transomed and cant forward. It is an attractive design.

LIVERPOOL DOMESTIC MISSION, Mill Street. 1892. Brick, painted white. Asymmetrical, with two big Gothic windows under two differing gables. Other windows mullioned-and-transomed.

BRUNSWICK GOODS STATION, Park Street. Built as the terminus of the line later extended to Liverpool Central. Front with three pediments. Simple iron roof inside. Next to it a building with the inscription CHESHIRE LINES. This is of 1864. It is three-storeyed with the huge inscription attic over. Red brick and rusticated elliptical arches on the ground floor.

RESERVOIR, High Park Street. 1855. Retaining wall and one round angle tower. Nothing like the Everton Reservoir.

PERAMBULATION

Instead of a perambulation only a few hints need be (and can be) given. At the N end of PARK ROAD and the surrounding streets remains of Late Georgian terraces still exist, much as to the w beyond Upper Parliament Street. In STANHOPE STREET, just s of Upper Parliament Street, is HIGSON'S BREWERY, a lively brick and terracotta façade of *c*.1880 with a big tower. A good deal further E in Park Road is the LIVERPOOL SAVINGS BANK by *Grayson*, 1881. It is of ashlar, four bays only, the first floor with pilasters, the windows with mullions and transoms, i.e. a kind of free mid-c17.

Until recently much municipal housing, dating from the regime of *Shelmerdine*, remained W of Park Road. Now there is only one block of flats of 1913 in NORTHUMBERLAND STREET Along CARYL STREET blocks of 1936–8 by *Sir Lancelot Keay* marking his change from Neo-Georgian to a Dudok-inspired Modern.

PRINCE'S ROAD was designed as a monumental avenue to approach Prince's Park (*see* p. 239). But the park and its surroundings were built up earlier than the road. Two STATUES in Prince's Road: Huskisson by *John Gibson*, 1847, made for the Customs House in Canning Place, and Hugh Stowell Brown, by *F. J. Williamson*, 1889. At the N end monument to Florence Nightingale designed by *Willink & Thicknesse*, the sculpture by *C. J. Allen*.

Only one more nucleus – ST MICHAEL'S HAMLET, S of the W end of Aigburth Road. Here John Cragg, the iron-master built five houses close to his church of St Michael and put as much of iron features in as he could. The houses are CARFAX (formerly The Nunnery – note the romantic names) at the corner of St Michael's Road and St Michael's Church Road, then in the latter THE HERMITAGE and opposite THE FRIARY, and in St Michael's Road HOLLYBANK, Cragg's own house, and THE CLOISTERS. The houses are stuccoed and the features are in a minimum Tudor, but windows, fireplaces, door-frames, etc., are of iron. Behind The Cloisters hostel buildings for NOTRE DAME COLLEGE OF EDUCATION 1960 by *Edmund Kirby & Sons*.

TUE BROOK, OLD SWAN, STANLEY, STONEYCROFT

CHURCHES

ST JOHN BAPTIST, West Derby Road, Tue Brook. 1868–70 by *Bodley*. It is a plain, unshowy, but dignified and sensitive building, and it lies back parallel to the road. It is of red stone and has a W steeple, long nave and aisles, a clerestory, and a lower chancel. The spire is bluntly recessed. Only to the S by the E end there is more liveliness, with the little forecourt of the vestry. The features are of a restrained Dec. The interior is architecturally very simple too – in fact it would hardly be noticed if it were not for the resplendent fittings. This turn to simplicity is indeed one aspect of the turn from High to Late Victorian. High nave of five bays with octagonal piers. The clerestory windows are over the spandrels not the apexes of the arcade arches. Eastlake in 1873 wrote as follows: 'For correctness of design, refined workmanship, and artistic decoration, this church may take foremost rank among examples of the Revival.' – PAINTING. Fine STENCILLING of the clerestory walls. – Wall paintings by *C. E. Kempe* on the E and W walls of the nave. – The panelled canted roofs are painted too. – REREDOS. High and gilt, with the E window high up above it, as Bodley liked it. – PULPIT. Also no doubt by Bodley. – SCREENS. The rood screen with coving and a loft parapet painted with flower panels and scenes. – Screens also to the chancel chapels, the one on the r. one composition with the ORGAN prospect.* – STAINED GLASS. By *Morris & Co.* the E window, not too well preserved, and the more impressive chancel S window with musicians in two tiers on blue clouds. The glass was made in 1868 (A. C. Sewter). – The VICARAGE with its mullioned and transomed windows is said to be by *Bodley* too.

ALL SAINTS, Broad Green Road, Stoneycroft. 1872–5 by *T. D. Barry & Son*. Rock-faced, in the Dec style, without a tower, but with transepts. A satisfying exterior, but the interior is unimpressive.

ST ANNE, Prescot Road, Old Swan. 1889–91 by *Aldridge & Deacon*. An impressive church. Rock-faced, with a square, strong S tower. Lancet windows and windows with plate tracery. Nave, aisles, clerestory. Spacious interior, ashlar-faced, with quatrefoil piers. W screen of columns for a shallow (too shallow) low baptistery. The clerestory has detached arcading of chamfered shafts without capitals and pointed arches towards the inside.‡

ST PAUL, Derby Lane, Stoneycroft.§ By *Sir Giles Gilbert Scott*, 1916, i.e. an early work, and outstandingly original and good, as Giles Scott's early churches can be. Pale brick with a mighty central tower crowned by a pyramid roof. The plan consists of three high square groin-vaulted bays separated and framed on the N and S sides (ritually speaking) by short pointed tunnel-vaults. They stand on big square internal piers pierced by low passages, the motif of St Front at Périgueux. This and other churches of that part of France must have inspired the architect, but to the outside his solution is entirely original. The three sets of short tunnel-vaulted bays to S and N appear as transeptal

---

* The church also possesses at present the *Bodley* SCREEN from Dunstable Priory Church in Bedfordshire.
‡ The church has recently been partitioned.
§ Built at the expense of Douglas Horsfall.

projections, each in its end wall with a group of three very tall lancets under a blank arch and each (of all things) with a half-hipped roof. It all comes off beautifully. To the s between the three projections are tiny doorways in low masonry blocks. It is unfortunate that the colours of the interior are so unsympathetic.

ST OSWALD (R.C.), St Oswald's Street, Old Swan. Of the church of 1842 by *A. W. N. Pugin* only the w steeple remains. It is Dec and has a broach spire and fine carved detail. The church itself was totally rebuilt in 1951–7 by *Adrian Gilbert Scott*. Red ashlar below, concrete above. The concrete includes big parabolic arches across the nave, across the aisles, and between nave and aisles. Four-light conventional Perp windows in the aisles. – The SCHOOL s of the church is dated by Kelly 1855 and attributed (not convincingly) by Goodhart-Rendel to *A. W. N. Pugin*.

PUBLIC BUILDINGS

POWER STATION, Lister Drive, Stanley. The old building, large and of brick, is by *Shelmerdine*, c.1902. The most recent building is of 1966–7.

SLAUGHTERHOUSE, Prescot Road, Stanley. 1929–31 by the architects in the office of the City Surveyor *A. D. Jenkins*. Very large, in a Baroque neo-Georgian, brick and stone, with a middle tower.

POLICE SPORTS PAVILION, Prescot Road, Stanley. By *Robin Clayton*, 1965–6. A good job in today's idiom.

GREEN LANE CARNEGIE LIBRARY, Stanley. 1904–5 by *Shelmerdine*. A corner composition with a pretty little turret and C17 windows. Red brick and stone dressings.

MILLBANK COLLEGE OF COMMERCE, Bankfield Road. By *Gilling, Dod & Partners* in collaboration with the City Architect. A good, straightforward job completed in 1963.

PERAMBULATION

Hardly a perambulation. At Tue Brook, at the extreme E end of WEST DERBY ROAD, is TUE BROOK HOUSE, dated 1615, and thus the oldest dated house in Liverpool. It is a modest farmhouse now set closely between suburban houses. Centre and two cross gables. All front windows low and mullioned, of five lights, symmetrically arranged, except in the centre, where the plain, unmoulded doorway is set to the r. to allow for the five-light hall window. The mullions are perfectly plain too. Inside a priest-hole reached by a trapdoor.

At Old Swan, in PRESCOT ROAD, two banks side by side which make an entertaining comparison. MARTINS BANK is gay and stripy and probably of *c.*1905 and by *Grayson & Ould*, the MIDLAND BANK is straightforward neo-Georgian of one storey, but has a new top storey, boldly put on in an unmistakably 1960s style.

In BROAD GREEN ROAD, near the Prescot Road end, the CONVENT OF ST VINCENT. The centre is a late C19 red-brick house of five bays with a three-bay pediment and some sparing decoration of the middle window. The house was later heightened and enlarged. Amusing gatepiers in the form of bulgy Tuscan columns. To the r. of this an Early Victorian three-bay villa with a delightfully ornate cast-iron veranda. (Also Early Victorian stucco terraces in DERWENT ROAD.)

WALTON

CHURCHES

ST MARY, County Road. The parish church of Walton. An ancient foundation, though no ancient architectural features survive. This was until 1699 the parish church for Liverpool. The w tower is of 1828–32 by *John Broadbent*. The quatrefoiled-circle windows show that date. The N side was remodelled in 1840, and the close buttresses and perhaps the windows suit that date. The s chapel is of 1911, the s aisle probably remodelled, and inside all is post-war by *Quiggin & Gee*, without aisles, with concrete arches, in a discreet and feeble Gothic. – FONT. Originally Norman, but cruelly hacked about. The top moulding is now an impossible coarse egg-and-dart, and below are the Flight into Egypt, St John Baptist, and Adam and Eve. – CROSS SHAFT. Anglo-Saxon fragment (in the room behind the altar), with interlace panels and a panel with a running scroll.

At the entrance to the churchyard the old SCHOOL HOUSE, humble, C17, with mullioned windows and an extension at the back. The school was established in or about 1613.

BLESSED SACRAMENT (R.C.), Walton Vale. 1876–8 by *Edmund Kirby*. A plain rectangle in plan, and no tower. At the w end the lancets, at the E end a rose-window high up. The interior in no way remarkable.

ST FRANCIS DE SALES (R.C.), Hale Road. 1887 by *J. & B.*

Sinnott. Rock-faced; Dec; no tower. The odd arcade and its odd external consequence are the distinguishing feature of the church. They are highly original, but the architects were not up to them. The arcade consists of normal low arches, interrupted by three wide and high arches. To these correspond outside three cross-gables, their tops rising dormer-wise out of a pitched roof. The principle is really that of de Keyser's Amsterdam churches, but translated into an indifferent Gothic.

ST JOHN EVANGELIST, Rice Lane. Begun 1875 by *Aldridge & Deacon*, completed 1897 by *Deacon*. Rock-faced, with lancet windows and, in the aisles, plate tracery. Good w front with porch open to the w at the w end of the s aisle. Flèche awkwardly close to the front. – REREDOS. Signed by *Thomas Woolner*. Crucifixus and kneeling Virgin and St John, richly sentimental. Said to be designed by *Street* (Kelly).

ST LAWRENCE, Barlow Lane. 1878–81 by *Henry Sumners*. The church is of brick, but the E end and the s transept, which is the main feature, are stone-faced. This transept front has an outer arcade of five open arches, the r. hand two in front of the base of a steeple. The transept window has a head only, i.e. is a pointed lunette. It has fancy late-geometrical tracery and a blank frieze of panels below.

ST LUKE, Goodison Road. By *J. F. Doyle*. 1898 (VCH 1892); consecrated 1901. Stock brick and red brick, all windows round-arched. No tower. The chancel seems to bless the Everton Football Ground.

HOLY TRINITY PRESBYTERIAN CHURCH, Rice Lane. 1897–8. No tower, but the w porch with a spire à la Edinburgh and Newcastle Cathedrals.

PUBLIC BUILDINGS

ARNOT STREET SCHOOLS. The contrast ought to be noted between 1953–4 by *Willink & Dod*, modern, with a minimum of façade features, and the original Victorian building with odd dormers, hipped and half-hipped and plenty of other freely Gothic features.

ALSOP HIGH SCHOOL, Queen's Drive, just E of the parish church. The main building is of 1923–6 (by the City Surveyor *A. D. Jenkins* and his architects). It looks much earlier. Seven bays, two storeys, symmetrical, with free Gothic motifs, a central porch tower with a lively skyline, and sensibly large and plain classroom windows. Behind and even part of the school a

Gothic house in WALTON VILLAGE, part of what used to be the village. It was the rectory, is of stone, and consists of two parts, the E part c.1800, the W part c.1830. The windows and a general thinness characterize the earlier part, the three broad, open porch arches across the W front and a general heaviness the later part.

WALTON HOSPITAL, Rice Lane. The original building dates from 1868 and was the West Derby Union Workhouse. One long block of stock brick with a largely stone-faced central tower with a steep pavilion roof and twenty-three bays of windows plus projecting wings on either side. (In the former chapel, now a warehouse, MONUMENT to Agnes E. Jones by *Pietro Tenerani*, 1869. Large, frontally seated white angel on a big base.) A rebuilding programme, designed in 1960, was begun in 1962. It is by *W. E. Tatton Brown* of the Ministry of Housing and Local Government in association with *T. Noel Mitchell*.

WALTON PRISON, Hornby Road. Begun 1848 by *John Weightman*, Borough Surveyor, and completed in 1855. The prison has a grossly colossal gatehouse and an even more colossal 59 centre of the main range behind. They are of brick with much stone trim and Norman in style. The gatehouse has a giant, strictly Norman two-storeyed recess. In the range behind, the arrow-slits or rather cruciform gun-ports will be noticed. To the l. and r. of the gatehouse are two perfectly harmless and unperturbed late-classical villas with a big bow. In Hornby Road two terraces of prison-staff housing. *See* p. 480

LIBRARY, Rice Lane. 1910–11 by *Briggs, Wolstenholme & Thornely*. C20-classical corner building, one storey high. On the top three heavy crowning features.

PERAMBULATION

The centre is of course by St Mary, with the Gothic house already mentioned. Queen's Drive cuts off from this centre the former WALTON HALL. QUEEN'S DRIVE (*see* also p. 216) is a remarkably early example of a ring road. It was begun by the then City Engineer, *J. A. Brodie*, in 1904. The Walton section was done in 1909, and there are terraces of cottages there which go with that date. A little further along begins neo-Georgian municipal housing, characteristic of *Sir Lancelot Keay*'s inter-war régime. Brodie also proposed radial arteries, and WALTON HALL AVENUE is one of them.*

* Radial arteries in other directions are Prescot Road and Menlove Avenue.

RICE LANE is the chief street N of the church. At its N end
MARTINS BANK, by *Willink & Thicknesse*, 1898, and directl
inspired by Shaw, with its big gables with obelisks and i
circular angular tourelles.

WAVERTREE

Wavertree was still rural when Picton published his book in 187
Wavertree Park was made in 1856, after the Corporation ha
bought the grounds of Wavertree Hall, a mansion of *c.*1715.

CHURCHES

HOLY TRINITY, Church Road. The Wavertree parish churcl
1794 by *John Hope*, the E end by *Sir Charles Reilly*, 191
Ashlar-faced, with a w tower alas deprived of its upper stag
and lantern. The buttressing of very odd obelisk shape
Reilly's. The body of the church is five bays long with two tie
of windows, the smaller, lower ones segment-headed, the larg
upper ones round-headed. Entries with pediments on bracket
in the w bays. At the top a balustrade. Reilly added the E ba
and the apse with three very close-set slender round-heade
windows with straight architraves on brackets. To the l. and
of the apse low attachments. But where Reilly's work is trul
remarkable is inside. A chancel is created by square pilla
which stand free above low enclosed spaces, one of them th
vestry, the other the organ chamber. The pillars here of cours
appear as pilasters. This, it will be noticed, is a St George
Hall motif. The w entrances to the low enclosed spaces hav
pediments on brackets, and above them are, again free-stand
ing, urns. The apse has a kind of white trellis in its vault. Th
old church has a flat ceiling and on the window walls swag
below the main windows. The church has lost its N and
galleries but has a w gallery. Under the tower Reilly created
circular vaulted baptistery. – PULPIT. Square and typical of th
late C18. – LECTERN. Also late C18. The shaft is a Doric co
umn. – STALLS. The two main seats are characteristic
Reilly. – Many TABLETS, none noteworthy.

ST BRIDGET, Bagot Street. 1868–72 by *E. A. Heffer*. This is
very exceptional conceit for its date – a real basilica, even if
common brick with red and purple brick, i.e. of nave and aisl
with an apse and a high NW campanile. All windows of cours
are round-headed. The w entrance niche alone is freer, wit
a gable crowned by a medallion with the head of God. Th

inside is basilican too, even to a free-standing altar in the apse. The nave arcade of nine bays has round arches and returns on the w wall as a three-bay blank arcade. Foliated capitals of varied design. Coffered and heavily enriched ceiling. – REREDOS, a mosaic Last Supper, 1886 by *Salviati*. – PULPIT. Huge, rectangular, and of stone and marble. The only place in the church where Gothic detailing is to be seen. – LECTERN. On a simple marble column.

CHRIST THE KING (R.C.), Queen's Drive. By *Prichard, Son & Partners*, 1966–7. Large, of brick, with a pyramid roof and brick slab walls. It is their best work, more forceful and less gimmicky than most others.

ST DUNSTAN, Earl Road. 1886–9 by *Aldridge & Deacon*. Very similar to their St Benedict, Everton. Very red Ruabon brick. w front with two angle turrets and a group of five stepped lancets. Above them brick-carved angels and Christ. Low baptistery below, opening into the nave in three arches. A flèche sits uncomfortably just E of the w front. The side windows are all lancets, small stepped triplets below, singles in the clerestory. The interior has round stone piers, but all the rest is brick. A brick frieze runs along above the arcade arches and also round three sides of the chancel. The chancel E window of three stepped lancets high up. – LECTERN. Very rich wrought iron, with a small figure between the uprights of the shaft.

ST MARY, Victoria Park. The original church in Sandown Park (*see below*) was destroyed by bombing. The present building is a former Methodist chapel of 1872.

OUR LADY OF GOOD HELP (R.C.), Chesnut Grove. 1885–7 by *J. & B. Sinnott*. The porch was meant to carry a tower.

ST THOMAS, Ashfield. 1896. Common brick and red brick with a very long, thin, rather funny turret near the E end. It has a needle spire. The fenestration of the church is by lancet windows.

PUBLIC BUILDINGS

TOWN HALL, High Street. 1872 by *John Elliot Reeve*. Very conservative for its date. Ashlar-faced and Latish Classical. Porch and balcony over, flanked by two tiers of paired columns.

LIBRARY, Picton Road. 1902–3 by *Shelmerdine*. Red brick and much stone. A symmetrical façade, the details C17 to C18. Gabled wings with big windows, tripartite with a tripartite lunette above. The lower part has alternately blocked pilasters.

Recessed centre with semicircular gable, porch with segmenta
hood. A very enjoyable little building.

TECHNICAL INSTITUTE (now part of the Regional College o
Art), Picton Road. 1898–9 by *Shelmerdine*. In a free C17 styl
with mullioned-and-transomed windows and l. of the entranc
a wide, shallowly canted bay window. The doorway has alter
nately blocked columns.

OLIVE MOUNT HOSPITAL, Mill Lane. The hospital incorpor
ates a fine late C18 house, ashlar-faced, of five bays and tw
storeys. The windows have no mouldings at all. Porch wit
Adam-style columns. Cast-iron honeysuckle balcony. Abov
the first-floor windows are garlands. Top parapet. The hous
belonged to Sir James Picton and the heavy plasterwork of hal
and staircase are probably his. Bang in front of it now are thre
of the more awkward Liverpool skyscrapers.

MABEL FLETCHER TECHNICAL COLLEGE, Sandown Road
Long, flat, curtain-walling fronts with an asymmetrically place
tank on the top. One of the good Liverpool schools, complete
in 1962.

BLUECOAT SCHOOL, Church Road. This is without any doub
the most spectacular building in Wavertree and one of the mos
spectacular half-dozen of its date in Lancashire. It is by *Briggs
Wolstenholme & Thornely* and dates from 1903–6. It is of re
brick with stone dressings, less or more conspicuous. Toward
Church Road the effect is rousing. Coming from the churc
there is first the entrance range with its tower and then th
chapel. The entrance range is one-storeyed, of nine bays, wit
89 C18 Baroque details, and the tower is *c*.105 ft high and sheer
of brick, but the whole top stage, with four aedicules and a
ogee cap, is of stone. The tower was given by Sir Charles Nall
Cain in 1915. To the l. is the Board Room with a segmenta
ceiling. Under the tower one enters the spine corridor, and thi
leads straight to the hall, with a tunnel-vaulted ceiling. Sym
metrically arranged courtyards l. and r. and long ranges beyon
with cupolas. The CHAPEL is entered by a narthex and has
Greek-cross shape with short arms and an ample though lov
domed centre. To the street is the apse. In the diagonals ar
smaller apses, not visible outside. The cross-arms have Venetia
windows, the centre pilasters, the lantern columns set inside.
MONUMENTS. John Harrocks, 1823. Tablet with an urn on
pillar and two mourners l. and r. – Richard Dobson † 1835
Very Grecian and rather too ornate.

THE HOLT GRAMMAR SCHOOL, Queen's Drive and Childwa

Road. 1937 by *Albert D. Jenkins*, the then City Surveyor. Neo-Georgian with cupola.

PEKELAND ROAD GOODS DEPOT. 620 ft long and 104 ft wide. Completed in 1958. The architects were the *Architect's Department, Midland Region*, the engineers *A. J. & J. D. Harris*.

PERAMBULATION

he natural start is the CLOCK TOWER, of 1884. It is thoroughly debased, in the so-called Mixed Renaissance, and not an appropriate commemoration for so discriminating a man as Sir James Picton.

o the w is the HIGH STREET with brick houses of the early C19, including a stuccoed group and with decent neo-Georgian flats of 1935. Go N along Sandown Lane and you come to the SANDOWN PARK area, laid out picturesquely about 1850, with winding streets. Typically Early Victorian villas. Originally a church, ST MARY, belonged to this. It was built *c.*1850 and has been pulled down. The Mabel Fletcher Technical College stands on the site. Along Long Lane to OLIVE LANE and to SANDOWN HALL, early C19, of two storeys and five bays, stuccoed. Three-bay pediment, porch of paired unfluted Ionic columns. On the side elevations two tripartite windows with columns – a handsome job. To the NW of the Clock Tower the LAMB HOTEL, quite a fine nine-bay composition of the late C18 with a recessed centre of two and a half storeys and pedimented side parts. The entrance and the windows l. and r. are of course Victorian. A little to the E of the Clock Tower is the LOCKUP, stone, octagonal, with four gables and a steep later roof. Most of the openings are blank. The doorway has a thinnish portcullis.

of the Clock Tower is MILL LANE, and at the N end of this OLIVE MOUNT VILLAS, stuccoed Early Victorian, and one red-stone villa which is dated 1847. This is Jacobean, with gables, a turret, and a curious octagonal annex with hardly any windows. The composition is totally asymmetrical and quite impressive.

ow back to the Lockup and E to MOSSFIELD, at the corner of CHILDWALL ROAD and Thingwall Road, an Early Victorian villa. The elements of the s front typical of the way details go fussy about 1850. Thingwall Road and then Southway take you to the LIVERPOOL GARDEN SUBURB, the fragment of something intended to be much larger. What was built is of

1910 etc., the layout typical, especially Nook Rise with it
cul-de-sacs. The layout was won in competition by a student
J. N. Dixon (adjudicator Sir Raymond Unwin). The architec
in 1914 and perhaps earlier was *G. L. Sutcliffe*. The houses ar
roughcast and gabled, characteristic of the most advance
housing of that moment.*

Finally s of the Clock Tower first the COFFEE HOUSE TAVERN
Early Victorian and stuccoed, but with a jolly ground floor b
Walter Thomas (of Philharmonic Hotel fame). Then i
CHURCH ROAD two Georgian five-bay houses of brick, th
better-preserved now the Liberal Jewish Congregation. Thi
has a pedimented doorway.‡

WEST DERBY

West Derby has an ancient identity. There was a castle her
in the late C12 and C13. It was ruinous by 1327. Absolutel
nothing remains of it, or of anything prior to the C17.

ST MARY, West Derby Village. The parish church, but in scal
and lavishness and uniformity wholly an estate church. Th
building lies indeed just inside the Croxteth estate, facing th
w lodge. Lord Sefton chose *George Gilbert Scott* to be his architect. Work began in 1853 and was completed in 1856. Th
preceding church had been built in 1793. Scott's is of red stone
with a proud crossing tower,§ a nave with clerestory and aisles
high transepts, the fenestration of their end walls deliberatel
different one from the other, and a polygonal apse. The style i
Scott's beloved Second Pointed, i.e. late C13 to early C14.‖ Th
interior inspires awe at once, by height and nobility. Th
capitals are elaborately and competently carved with naturalistic foliage. – STAINED GLASS. Much evidently by *Hardman*
– In one s aisle window poor glass by *Charles Gibbs* (date o
death commemorated 1859).

The church is by the lodge, and the lodge gates are open to th
village centre. The CROSS stands here, very, very Gothic, with
a shaft of five detached shafts, like the shaft of a font, and with
a seated figure of Christ at the top, in the C13 style, and to

---

* My attention was drawn to this garden suburb by Miss Margaret Tims
‡ The other has meanwhile been demolished.
§ Insisted on by the Committee and not approved by the ecclesiologists
See The Ecclesiologist, 1853.
‖ *The Ecclesiologist* called it 'a great improvement on any church now
existing at Liverpool'.

large for its tabernacle. The cross is by *Eden Nesfield*, 1861–70, the carving by *Forsyth*. W of it is the COURT HOUSE, 1662, a tiny cottage with just a doorway and one mullioned window to the front. A little to the N another house of about the same date, with two five-light windows below and two three-light windows above. The doorway is not yet central, which helps in the dating. Opposite the HARE AND HOUNDS, early C19, stuccoed, with two pediments and an unpedimented centre. N of the church in Meadow Lane is the SCHOOL, Gothic of 1860, with a short tower with stone pyramid roof.

For other public buildings *see* below.

GOOD SHEPHERD, Carr Lane. 1902–3 by *J. Oldrid Scott*, left unfinished and completed in 1931–7. Of the later date the top of the central tower with its lively parapet and the whole W part of the nave. Scott's work is rather conventional, with lancet windows in the aisleless nave and a polygonal apse. The capitals of the E parts remained uncarved.

ST JAMES, Mill Lane. By *Welch*, 1845–6 and still pre-archeological, i.e. with a thin W tower, its bell-stage battered, a thin tall broach spire, the broaches very low, a nave with lancets between buttresses, transepts, and originally a short chancel. The present chancel is by *W. & J. Hay*, of 1876–9. Interior with broad nave, W gallery, and extremely clumsy roof trusses.

OUR LADY QUEEN OF MARTYRS (R.C.), Stonebridge Lane. 1966–7 by *L. A. G. Prichard & Son*.

ST PAUL (R.C.), Town Row. By *Pugin & Pugin*, 1880. Rock-faced, with a SE tower with a depressing, slated, steep pyramid roof. The aisles each have four cross-gables. There is an apse too. The interior is more convincing than in most of the P. & P. churches.

ST SWITHUN (R.C.), Gill Moss. By *L. A. G. Prichard & Son*, completed in 1959. – PLATE. Molyneux Chalice given in 1738.

WEST DERBY CEMETERY, Lower House Lane. Opened in 1884. The lodge has a tower, the chapel is brand-new, 1965 by *Ronald Bradbury*, the City Architect; central, with a jagged roof.

The other areas of interest at West Derby are these.

1m. SE from the church in YEW TREE LANE and GREEN LANE are two wealthy houses. The latter, called LEYFIELD HOUSE, is of *c*.1830–40, of three bays, stuccoed, with a porch, the former belongs to the Broughton Hall High School and is High Victorian Gothic, rock-faced, on an E-plan with the details of the wings significantly differing, the l. with an oriel on an awkwardly long bracket. Altogether the architectural quality is poor. On

the l. a glass and iron conservatory. The house is said to hav
been built about 1856.

West Derby has not retained its character as an area of mansion
and villas. One of the vanished houses was DEYSBROOK, wher
in 1847 three rooms were decorated by *Alfred Stevens*.

SANDFORD PARK, ½ m. s of the church, is an estate with a pic
turesque Victorian layout, probably of the mid century. It ha
its own walls and lodges. The estate was developed out of th
grounds of OLD HALL, an C18 brick house of five bays almos
entirely transmogrified. The winding roads have villas in thei
ample gardens. The styles are divers, from Italianate with
tower to bargeboarded. Much poor infill and replacement.

LIBRARY, Queen's Drive. By *Ronald Bradbury*, the city architect
Completed in 1964. Glass and a baffle wall of ornamental con
crete. It is a pleasing building, but how could Liverpool fo
its sake pull down LARKHILL HOUSE, a good C18 house o
five bays with wings and colonnades?

WEST DERBY SECONDARY TECHNICAL SCHOOL, Queen'
Drive. 1956–8 by *H. E. Davies & Son* with the city architect.

BLESSED AMBROSE BARLOW SECONDARY SCHOOL, Queen'
Drive. Next door to the preceding school, and a satisfying
design, completed in 1961. The architects were *Weightman &
Bullen*.

WOOLTON

ST PETER. 1886–7 by *Grayson & Ould*. Red sandstone, large
Perp, with a SE tower. Substantial interior with a five-bay
arcade. – Very complete furnishings, with alabaster FONT an
alabaster PULPIT, thin iron SCREEN, and STAINED GLASS
mostly by *Kempe*. But there are also two *Morris* windows,
aisle SE and baptistery S. – Ornate timber-framed LYCHGATE
typical *Edward Ould*.

ST MARY (R.C.), SW of St Peter. 1860 by *R. W. Hughes* o
Preston, the PRESBYTERY by *E. W. Pugin*, 1864. Mr Hubbar
suggests that the REREDOSES may be by *E. W. Pugin*. -
STAINED GLASS. The E window typical *Capronnier*, date
1878. – PLATE. Chalice of 1694.

LIVERPOOL CONVALESCENT HOME, Allerton Road, but look
ing out across Hillfoot Road. Large, Gothic, of 1873.

The village centre of Woolton is still recognizable, with the step
and part of the shaft of the VILLAGE CROSS and a few cottage
in the winding street s along the wall of the Hall grounds. Tur

v off that street into SCHOOL LANE to find the most miserable
of ancient grammar schools. The SCHOOL was founded in 1610,
and the almost featureless cottage may well be of that date. To
ts N are again the Hall grounds.

OOLTON HALL is a disappointing building, if one visits it
knowing that one part of it is of 1704, built by the son of the
Molyneux who built Croxteth Hall, and that the other part is
by *Robert Adam* (1774–80). Externally the older part is hardly
recognizable. Only the pediment with trophies is convincing.
But are the windows in order? Is even the fact that below the
pediment there are two not three windows to be trusted? If
original, the triglyph frieze is noteworthy. Just one triglyph at
the top of the angle quoins and just with one metope in the
middle. The apsidal end of the range is in any case very probably
mid-C19. The Adam front is not more rewarding. Seven bays
with two two-bay pediments. In these outer parts medallions
between lower and upper windows, in the centre paterae in the
top frieze. The small semicircular porch has been replaced by
a big porte-cochère of *c.*1865. Inside, of Adam's time is the
Octagon Room and one room each on ground floor and upper
floor. They have characteristic but not outstanding stucco
ceilings. Of the early C18 a panelled room with fine fluted
pilasters.

CHURCH ROAD, N of St Peter, Early Victorian sandstone
villas (and one stuccoed, E of the church). (REYNOLDS PARK
has at the N end a small disused quarry, with a house with
Gothick windows in a crevice of the rock. P. Fleetwood-
Hesketh) At the N end of the street KNOLL PARK. The LODGE
has Greek Doric columns *in antis*. The house is of painted
ashlar, of six bays, with a slight middle projection and broad
giant pilasters. Four-column porch of Corinthian columns *in
antis*. Entrance hall, not in axis, with four columns and a little
dome. Good stucco. Staircase with apsidal landing. It all points
to *c.*1840. Good STABLES fronting on Church Road.

BEACONSFIELD ROAD round the corner of Knoll Park is
CEDARWOOD, the Woman's Journal House of the Year 1960,
by *Dewi Prys Thomas* and *Gerald R. Beech.* Cantilevered timber
upper storey with shallow pyramid roof. Immaculately detailed.
Several other houses by *G. R. Beech* in this neighbourhood, e.g.
COURT HOUSE, Beaconsfield Road, 1961, and THE GREY
BUNGALOW, Quarry Street, 1963. Also in Beaconsfield Road
sandstone villas, and at the w end two mansions, ABBOTS LEA
and then STRAWBERRY FIELD, Gothic of probably *c.*1870.

Finally, parallel to Beaconsfield Road further N in DRUII
CROSS ROAD, the house called DRUIDS CROSS, 1847 I
Elmes and a bitter disappointment, as nearly all his building
other than St George's Hall, are. Five bays, painted ashl:
heavy doorway with columns with alternate blocking and
massive lintel. Garden side with tripartite part-pediment
windows l. and r. and a broad canted bay in the middle wi
Ionic aedicule windows. Top-lit staircase hall, heavily arcade
STABLES with Italianate turret.

LONGFORD HALL *see* STRETFORD

LONGSIGHT *see* MANCHESTER, p. 326

LOSTOCK

See North Lancashire under Horwich.

LOWER INCE *see* INCE-IN-MAKERFIELD

LOWER KERSAL *see* SALFORD, p. 396

LOWER MOOR *see* OLDHAM, p. 360

LOWTON

6090

ST LUKE. 1732. Of brick with keyed-in arched windows wi
Y-tracery. Transepts, that to the S with two lunette window
The chancel has elementary Venetian windows. There are
and transept galleries. The W tower is of 1863 and turns tl
Georgian round arches to a Norman purpose. – FONT.
primitive baluster. – BOX PEWS.

ST MARY, Lowton Common. 1861 by *E. G. Paley*. Mode
Aisleless. The best feature is the W front with its double be:
cote.

ST CATHERINE, Lane Head. By *Weightman & Bullen*, 1957–
Octagon plus a detached openwork concrete façade tower ov
the baptistery. Fussy in all details.

ANDERTON HOUSE (National Coal Board). 1965 by *Young*
Purves (with *J. H. Bourne* of the National Coal Board). Co:
crete-framed block.

BYROM HALL, 1 m. NE of St Luke. Three-bay front, rendere
Inside a handsome staircase with twisted balusters. The hou
has a date 1713.

MAGHULL

ᴋ ANDREW. 1878–80 by *J. F. Doyle*. Sizeable, rock-faced, with a w tower. Late c13 style. Not of special merit. The interior in particular lacks interest. – MONUMENT. In the churchyard truncated pyramid to members of the Harrison family. The first burial, † 1835, marks the date – see the heavy Grecian palmettes at the top.

ʟᴅ Sᴛ ANDREW. Of the medieval church only the chancel and the N chapel were left standing. They are late c13. The arcade is of two bays and has round piers and double-chamfered arches. The chapel E window is small, with intersecting tracery. The prettily placed turret was the bell-turret of the former nave, which dated from *c.*1830. The w doorway is clearly re-used material.

ᴴAPEL HOUSE, NE of the church, in Dyes Lane. Stone, c17, with mullioned and transomed windows, dormers, and an asymmetrically placed porch.

ANOR HOUSE, Sefton Lane, ⅝ m. w. A handsome c18 house. The façade is of basement and two storeys, with two canted bay windows, provided with columns. Nice doorway up an outer stair. Top parapet. At the back of the house is a re-erected arch from the old church. It is part of an arcade of at least three bays. Round late c13 piers, double-chamfered arches.

MANCHESTER

INTRODUCTION

Manchester was the site of the Roman fort of Mamucium, occupied from the C1, which originally lay on the spur of land known as Castlefield, partly flanked by the river Medlock. Now it is crossed by the Rochdale Canal and two railway arches, and one insignificant fragment of Roman walling remains in Collier Street, off Liverpool Road. At the time of the Domesday Survey the town had two churches.* After the Conquest the manor came to the Greslet family, and from them by heritage in the early C14 to the de la Warres. In 1422 Thomas, the last de la Warre and rector of the parish, founded the college whose church became the cathedral and whose residential parts Chetham's Hospital. With that the two medieval buildings of Manchester are named. The medieval town lay on the bluff of sandstone at the junction of Irwell and Irk. No houses whatever remain. Nor is much left of Tudor and Early Stuart building, and what there is has been treated scandalously by the Corporation. To see house after house decaying, neglected, pulled down, or beyond repair leaves one speechless with incomprehension and anger: Baguley Hall with its immensely interesting C14 hall timbers, Hough End Hall, the only Elizabethan brick mansion in Manchester, Hough Hall, Clayton Hall – all timber-framed – and Peel Hall again of brick.‡ In the centre of Manchester only the littlest bit of timber-framing survives in the Old Shambles N of Market Street.

The prosperity of Manchester in the late Middle Ages and the Tudor period was already weaving. About 1375 Edward III settled a colony of Flemish weavers. The materials used were wool and linen, though import of cotton from Smyrna and Cyprus had already begun on a very small scale. Leland praised Manchester as 'the fairest, best builded, quikkest and most

---

* But it is possible that the second church of the entry is the church of Ashton-under-Lyne (Donald Buttress).

‡ Against this must in fairness be set Wythenshawe Hall, Platt Hall, and Heaton Park, which are kept up excellently.

populus tounne of al Lancastreshire'. In 1595 Sir Nicholas
Mosley, a cloth merchant and Lord Mayor of London, bought
the manor. It remained in the Mosley family till 1845. The c 17
saw much increase. The main streets at that time were Market
Street, Deansgate, and Long Millgate. By 1750 the area between
Deansgate and Market Street as far as Brazennose Street, Tib
Lane, and Spring Gardens was developed. Defoe speaks of
the spread about 1700, Celia Fiennes writes: 'This is a thriving
place.' The population is estimated at about 10,000. In 1721
the Irwell was made navigable, in 1759 the Duke of Bridgewater's Canal was begun by *Brindley* to carry coal from his
Worsley mine to Manchester, and in 1776 it was extended to
Runcorn, and that meant that raw cotton could come to Manchester by water. The Manchester–Bury–Bolton, Manchester-
Ashton–Oldham, and Manchester–Rochdale Canals followed
between 1790 and 1805. It marks the beginning of the Industrial
Revolution. Cotton now fully replaced wool as the product
woven, but principally traded, by Manchester. For Manchester
is as much a city of merchants as of manufacturers. It is the
towns around – Bolton, Bury, Oldham, Rochdale, Stockport –
that manufactured wholly. The story of the inventions of the
c 18 which made the Industrial Revolution possible is familiar
and it is repeated in the general introduction to this volume on
p. 24. Industry changed the appearance of Manchester. Lord
Torrington in 1790 called the town nasty, Richard Holden in
1808 'abominably filthy'. The population in 1801 was ap-
proaching 70,000.

The first third of the c 19 saw an unprecedentedly rapid
growth of industry and trade, but legislation was still focused
on the greatest benefit to the land-owning nobility and gentry
Hence the Corn Laws of 1815, hence the absurdly inadequate
representation of the new cities in Parliament. Manchester
became the centre of the fight for the abolition of the Corn
Laws and for Free Trade. The Free Trade Hall is the great
architectural monument of the struggle won. But free trade
also implied opposition to efforts made by legislators to improve
the conditions of the new class of workmen, work-women,
work-children in factories. And whereas the abolition of the
Corn Laws benefited these new poor, the mill-owners and
merchants of Manchester by and large approved of the Government sending troops and dispersing demonstrations of the
labouring classes. Their fight also had Manchester as its centre
And as the Free Trade Hall is a monument to a deserved victory

so St Peter's Square perpetuates the name of St Peter's Field, which is for ever shamefully connected with Peterloo. Improvements of the conditions of the working men were left in the hands of some humane and far-seeing manufacturers and of the pamphleteers: Dr Kay's *The Moral and Physical Condition of the Working Classes* of 1832 and Engels' *The Condition of the Working Classes* of 1844 were both based on Manchester, and Chadwick of the *Report on the Sanitary Condition of the Labouring Population* of 1842 was Manchester-born.

If Manchester at the time of writing this is engaged in one of the largest slum-clearance enterprises of all time, if one walks and drives in many places through areas of total desolation, that is the heritage of John Bright, M.P. for Manchester, as much as the Free Trade Hall. Manchester in the C 19 was very rich, but the riches were concentrated in the hands of one class, and its members were munificent or mean, humane or callous. It is all expressed in architectural terms for those with eyes to see.

Other than architectural terms do not concern us here, but for historical completeness' sake it must at least be recorded that Manchester became the see of an Anglican bishop in 1847, Salford the see of a Catholic bishop in 1855, that the city finally became administratively a city in 1853, and that at the end of the century the commerce of Manchester received a much needed fillip by the far-sighted provision of the Manchester Ship Canal (1885–94) and the development at Stretford of the Trafford Park Industrial Estate. Few realize that Manchester is the third largest port of England (in tonnage).*

But to return to architectural terms, and the earlier C 19, the buildings erected for the making of the money had, needless to say, no architectural ambitions. The early mills, preserved around Manchester rather than in Manchester, were high and bare and bleak. Schinkel, the greatest architect of the moment on the Continent and a Grecian as far as style was concerned, visited England in 1826 and wrote in amazement: 'At Manchester since the war 400 large new factories for cotton spinning have been built, several of them of the size of the Royal Palace in Berlin, and thousands of smoking obelisks of the steam engines 80 to 180 ft high destroy all impression of church

---

* That Stretford and Salford to this day are not administratively one with Manchester is one of the most curious anomalies of England. Taking them together, as they are socially and visually one, Manchester would have a population of about 875,000, which is the only true figure.

steeples.' He also sketched this totally new type of building ('vaulted and fireproof'), and there can be no question that he was impressed, even if with a shudder. So was Carlyle in 1843, when he wrote in *Past and Present* that Manchester was 'every whit as wonderful, as fearful, as unimaginable as the oldest Salem', and so was Disraeli, who in 1844 called Manchester 'the most wonderful city of modern times'.

By the time of *Coningsby* the railway had arrived – the famous Liverpool–Manchester railway of 1830 – and the population had gone up to 243,000 (1841). The growth of Manchester in the C18 and up to the time when Queen Victoria came to the throne can visually be observed in the streets and by plotting churches and watching public buildings.

Streets first. The medieval nucleus began to show signs of growth to the s of Market Street. St Ann's church was consecrated in 1712 and the square to its N laid out in 1720. In King Street is a house of 1736. SW of this area and beyond Deansgate the terraces of St John's Street are the best preserved Georgian sequence in Manchester. Of the second half of the C18 also is the Mosley-Street–Portland-Street development. Chorley New Town was laid out in 1793–4, and bits and pieces, mostly Late Georgian, can still be picked out in Oxford Road, Lloyd Street, and also on Ardwick Green. The Crescent at Salford is the most impressive stretch of Late Georgian domestic building around Manchester. The best individual house is Sharston Hall, Wythenshawe, of 1701, and this was of course miles out of Manchester. The major Georgian mansions of Manchester were also right out in the country and in their own grounds, the first being Platt Hall Fallowfield of *c*.1764 and – this alone of the highest national standard – *James Wyatt*'s Heaton Park of 1772.

32 & 33

As for churches, the villages had their medieval churches, but they didn't survive. St Wilfred at Northenden is of 1873–6 but supposed to be a copy of the Perp building preceding it. Of dates we have 1573 for Newton Heath and 1595 for Rusholme, and the parish church of Didsbury still has its w tower of 1620 and something like the columns (no longer Gothic piers) of the nave arcade, even if vaguely remodelled. In the centre, after St Ann, came St Mary E of Deansgate in 1753, St Paul in Turner Street in 1765, St John in St John's Square in 1769, St James in George Street in 1787, St Peter in St Peter's Square in 1788–94. Not one of them has been allowed to remain. In addition, the Nonconformists built the Cross

Street Chapel in 1698, the Quakers their Meeting House in 1828–30 – this alone survives – the Methodists a chapel in Oldham Street in 1780, and the Catholics their first church in Mulberry Street in 1794. Outside the centre the list would be the Dob Lane Chapel of 1698 on the very boundary of Manchester and Failsworth, St Thomas at Ardwick 1741 (since enlarged), St Clement at Chorlton-cum-Hardy 1779 (demolished in 1949), the Unitarian Chapel at Fallowfield 1790, and St Mark, Cheetham Hill 1794.

St Mark represents the standard plan for the Late Georgian church, as long as it did not go Gothic: an oblong building with two tiers of round-headed windows and three galleries inside. The type is even more frequent in and around Liverpool. All Saints Chorlton was classical too, and is of 1820, but in Manchester after 1820 Gothic was preferred. All Saints Newton Heath is of before 1820 and Gothic, and then followed in quick succession *Barry*'s St Matthew Campfield (1822; demolished), *Goodwin*'s St George Hulme (1826 etc.), *Atkinson & Sharpe*'s St Andrew Travis Street (1829–31; demolished), *Atkinson*'s St Luke Cheetham Hill (1836 etc.),* the Welsh Chapel at Chorlton-on-Medlock by *Barry* (1837 etc.), Christ Church Harpurhey by *Welch* (1838–41), All Souls Ancoats by *Hayley* (1839) – this one Norman – *Pugin*'s St Wilfrid Hulme (1842), *Shellard*'s St Peter Blackley (1844), and so on.

Public buildings after 1800 tell the story of growing cultural ambitions and a growing civic pride. It is typical that the first building to be mentioned is a subscription library, the Portico Library by *Thomas Harrison* of Chester (1802–6) – Chetham's 35 Library in the College buildings was established in 1653 as a free library – and the second the Royal Manchester Institution (now Art Gallery) by *Barry* (1824–35), and that they are both severely classical. So was *Goodwin*'s old Town Hall in King Street (1819–34; the façade partly re-erected in Heaton Park) and so were the town halls of Chorlton-on-Medlock and Salford (1830–1 and 1825–7) by *Richard Lane* and *Lane & Goodwin*.‡

The Wesleyan Theological Institution Didsbury of 1842 was still Grecian, but the Lancashire Independent College Whalley 58 Range of 1840–3 (by *Irwin & Chester*) is Gothic, and *Barry*'s

* St Saviour Plymouth Grove of 1836 was classical. It was demolished some five years ago.

‡ Mr Buttress is of the opinion that the best Grecian work in Manchester was the gateway, chapel, etc. of the Harpurhey Cemetery, of *c.*1840, destroyed a few years ago.

Athenaeum next to the Art Gallery is an Italian *palazzo*. The
latter two heralded the future. Gothic and Italianate dominated
the Manchester of the High Victorian decades, Gothic in such
public buildings as *Waterhouse*'s masterly Assize Courts (1859),
71&   which should not have been destroyed, his equally masterly
72   Town Hall (1868 etc.), and his University (1883–7), and still
in *Basil Champneys*'s far more fanciful, more inventive, but a
84   trifle less high-minded John Rylands Library (1890–9), Italian
in a more or (later) less restrained form in the great warehouses
and office buildings of the centre, the best of them by *Edward*
61   *Walters*. He also is the architect of the Free Trade Hall, perhaps
the noblest monument in the Cinquecento style in England.

The villas which the merchants and manufacturers built for
themselves have been sadly depleted. The only one deserving
68   the name mansion is the Shirley Institute Didsbury, designed
in 1865 by *Thomas Worthington* in a florid Gothic style. For
villas one must look to such areas as Victoria Park or Upper
Broughton, Salford.

Meanwhile the slums and the dreary streets of brick cottages
were growing apace. No serious efforts of alleviation were made
municipally before *Spalding & Cross*'s Victoria Square Ancoats
of 1889, large, with a spacious inner courtyard, with balcony
access to the flats in several tiers and with Jacobean gables on the
façade. Gabled façades, part Jacobean, part French Renaissance
were indeed the favourite style of the ending C19 – see the
Institute of Science and Technology of 1895 by the same
Spalding & Cross or the Whitworth Gallery by *J. W. Beaumont*
of 1895 or *Paul Waterhouse*'s Refuge Assurance of 1891.

Paul Waterhouse was the son of Alfred, and Alfred Waterhouse was a Lancashire man. So, although his main office was
transferred to London as early as 1865, he must be counted as
a local architect. And it is indeed interesting to observe how
much of C19 architecture in a city like Manchester was still
commissioned from local firms. Walters has been mentioned
already. So has *Thomas Worthington*, who also did the Magistrates' Court (brick, Gothic) and much else. *Edward Salomons*
built the Venetian Gothic (Ruskinian) Reform Club, *G. T.*
Redmayne the excellently functional College of Art (1880–1).
In churches at the same time *E. H. Shellard* still stood at the
watershed between Commissioners' Gothic and Puginesque
Gothic and could not make up his mind, *J. Medland & Henry*
Taylor produced church after church with features of as roguish
a wilfulness as any by E. B. Lamb or Teulon (St Stephen Hulme

1868, St Agnes Levenshulme 1884–5), and *J. S. Crowther* 82 restored the cathedral and built such high and noble churches as St Benedict Ardwick (1880) and St Alban Cheetham (1857– 74 64).

Indeed, even in the twentieth century the preference given to local firms over London firms survives. The university shows that, and, especially after the Second World War, much to its disadvantage. What local firms have provided is mostly tame and featureless. It is true that in these sixties of ours features can be overdone, and *Cruickshank & Seward*, another Manchester firm, in the buildings for the Institute of Science and Technology are overdoing them, but there are plenty of possibilities between these extremes. The buildings by the *Building Design Partnership* for the university, and especially the theatre, prove that, as does the Examination Board Building by *Playne & Lacey*, built in the university precinct though not for the university.

While for university architecture the thirties were sadly uneventful, for the city two events of more than local interest are to be recorded: the buildings of the garden suburb of Wythenshawe, begun in 1931 to the designs of *Barry Parker*,* and the building of the Daily Express in 1939 to the designs of *Sir Owen Williams*. This, with its absolutely smooth façades of bands of transparent and opaque glass, is as good as anything in England of those years or anything of today.

The best of the commercial buildings of today is unquestionably the group of C.I.S. and C.W.S. buildings in Miller Street (by *G. S. Hay* and *Sir John Burnet, Tait & Partners*). It is a group of three – twenty-five storeys, one-storeyed conference hall, fourteen storeys – and has curtain walling, but with a fine mosaic-clad services tower attached to the highest of the three, and it is detailed as carefully and crisply as a good American job. The interiors are by the *Design Research Unit* and also carefully done to the last detail. Moreover, the group of three succeeds in being a group. This is more than one can say of the Piccadilly group of three which, in spite of a common architect and a common podium, seems to be done by three different people not in sympathy with each other. Most of the many new office buildings use curtain walling, and yet curtain walling is not helpful in preserving and developing the specific Manchester

---

* But the first attempt at a Manchester garden suburb is much earlier, very early indeed, nationally speaking – Burnage in 1906 etc.; but little was built.

character of the centre, which is a character of the dour solidity of good ashlar stone. Today where so much is done in concrete it ought to be possible by spending money on concrete finish or facing materials to produce something modern and yet in harmony with that tradition.

The same problem arises in the suburbs, where new housing replaces old. The City Architect, Mr *S. G. Besant Roberts*, is doing excellent work. His schools, his branch libraries, such a major building as the extension to the Regional College of Art fill one with confidence,* but industrial housing under Mr *J. Austen Bent*, the Director of Housing, remains visually indifferent, and, even where much care has been taken on the designing of the façades, socially dubious. Do we really want these towers of flats everywhere? Do tenants want them? Should they be accepted as living conditions by any but bachelors, spinsters, young couples without children, and old people? Will they not be the slums of fifty years hence?

With these fundamental questions of life and environment unanswered we must leave this survey of the development of Manchester.‡

FURTHER READING

On the history of Manchester the handiest book is N. J. Frangopulo: *Rich Inheritance*, 1962.§ On the architecture of Manchester there is now the well illustrated and inexpensive special number of *Architecture North West* (No. 19), called *Manchester Buildings*. This came out in 1966, || and one can only express the hope that other cities will do likewise. For Georgian buildings one should try to consult Ivan Hall: *The*

---

* Mr Besant Roberts provided me with a list of seven schools, as a sample of the work of his department. Those I have not looked at myself are placed in brackets.

‡ As this introduction goes to the printer, it must in fairness be added that Mr Bent's department, together with the *Manchester Housing Development Group* (Stones, Pearlman, Kennedy, Millard, Zadzink, Bennett, etc.), have for some time been working on schemes of a socially far more acceptable kind, but nothing belonging to this new deal can yet be seen. The areas illustrated from plans and models are Longsight (Gibson Street), Harpurhey (Turkey Lane), and Beswick–Bradford (Wellington Street). The areas are of 430, 1,000, and 300 acres respectively. Architecturally the schemes are intended to be enlivened by the restless and aggressive motifs of the 1960s. See *The Architectural Review*, CXLII, 1967, 355 etc.

§ W. H. Thompson: *History of Manchester to 1852* came too late for consultation.

|| Expanded edition, London 1968, as a book.

Classical Architecture of Manchester, Ph.D. thesis, Manchester
University, 1965, for iron framing in mills, warehouses, etc.
R. Bamber: *Cast Iron in Manchester and Salford*, Undergradu-
ate Thesis, Department of Architecture, Manchester Univer-
sity, 1958.* The specialist on Victorian architecture in Man-
chester was the late Cecil Stewart. His *The Stones of Manchester*,
London, 1956, is indispensable, but the following gazetteer also
leans heavily on his *Index to the Buildings and Architects of
Manchester*, published by the Manchester Central Reference
Library, with an annotated copy in the University Library.

THE CENTRE

The boundaries are as follows: N and E of Victoria Station – Miller
Street – Swan Street – Great Ancoats Street – Pin Mill Brow –
Fairfield Street – Fairfields – West Whitworth Street – Whitworth Street – Bridgewater Viaduct – Dawson Street – along the
river Irwell to Victoria and Victoria Station.

THE CATHEDRAL

In 1421 Henry V granted a licence to Thomas de la Warre, rector 5
of Manchester, to refound his parish church as a collegiate
establishment with a warden, eight priests, four clerks, and six
lay-choristers. It was essentially a chantry college, as masses
were to be said every day for Henry V, the Bishop of Coventry
and Lichfield, Thomas de la Warre, and their progenitors. The
domestic premises are by some good fortune preserved. They
became the Chetham Hospital in the C17 (*see* p. 285). The first
warden John Huntington (1422–58) rebuilt the choir of the
church, the third warden Ralph Langley (1465–81) the nave,
and the fifth warden John Stanley (1485–1509), Bishop of Ely,
i.e. John Stanley the younger (for his uncle John Stanley had
been warden before him) adjusted and altered some of the
earlier work. What precisely he did do, is not known. The VCH
seems too confident in its report of the history of the building
between *c.*1420 and *c.*1520. All that can be said with assurance
is that nothing in the church is pre-Perp, and that there is no
stylistic argument to place one detail before another. This
applies also to the chantry chapels which grew around the core
of nave and aisles and choir and aisles and give the church its

* No effort has been made to visit iron-framed mills for inclusion in the
gazetteer. So anyone wanting to study this particular aspect will have to study
Mr Bamber's thesis.

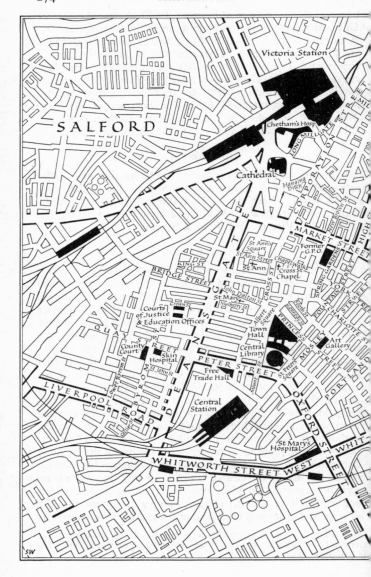

Inner Manchester

present character. Externally they create the impression of an outer N aisle and choir aisle (the Derby Chapel, begun by Bishop Stanley c.1513) and an outer S aisle and outer S chapels (the Jesus and the Fraser Chapels, the latter a newcomer of 1886, the former endowed as a guild chapel in 1506). Between the two is the tiny octagonal chapter house. The Lady Chapel is small too, and projects to the E only a little. It was rebuilt after war damage by *Sir Hubert Worthington*. The W porch and vestries are by *Basil Champneys*, of 1898, as is the large S annex (1902–3). As one would expect, they are excellent, the porch as ornate as the church, the annexes subdued, yet charmingly varied in the grouping and with felicitous decorative passages such as the two S oriels to the S. Other, earlier, C19 work concerned restorations, first a disastrous one in 1814–15, then much refacing and the rebuilding of the tower by *J. P. Holden* in 1862–8, and then the more scholarly restoration of 1885–6 by *J. S. Crowther*. *Sir Hubert Worthington*, after the Second World War, restored and rebuilt what was necessary. The C19 restorers determine much of the external appearance of the building. Thus Holden heightened the W tower by nearly 20 ft and decorated it and entirely rebuilt the Jesus Chapel, and Crowther put on all the pretty pierced parapets. He also built the N porch. Internally Crowther rebuilt the inner as well as the outer arcades. However, the original details seem to have been respected.*

The church is 172 ft long, i.e. the length of a parish church of the first order, and ornament is lavished on its exterior – more by the C19 than by the C15. The W tower is sheer below but richly appointed at the top. On each side are two two-light bell-openings with transom, and there is panelling over. The battlements are openwork, as all battlements of the church are. The buttresses are recessed and decorated with a niche. The two porches are two-storeyed. The outer S aisle has four-light windows of two different designs, and the Jesus Chapel has again a different design. The E view is impressive, thanks chiefly to *Worthington*'s bare E wall. Above it is the seven-light choir E window. The N outer aisle has four-light windows, but to the E five and to the W seven.‡ The clerestory windows are

* Mr Buttress comments: Most of the inner part of the choir is medieval. The inner faces of the tower N and S walls retain the plastering done by *Palmer c.1815.*

‡ The Ely Chapel which projected N from the Derby Chapel was not rebuilt after the Second World War.

of five lights, and there are open battlements too. Here and everywhere, below the battlements is a frieze of square fleurons. At the junction of nave and choir are two prominent rood-stair turrets, differing in details.

The interior is of six bays to the choir arch and of six bays for the choir. The piers and arches are of seven different designs, but it must be said once again that no sequence of building can be deduced from them. The VCH e.g. dates the choir E responds and the Lady Chapel arch *c.*1330, but bases and capitals are polygonal, and so the date seems too early. The others – choir arcades, chapter-house entrance, Derby Chapel arcade, nave arcade, outer N aisle arcade, outer S aisle arcade – are worth some study and record. There certainly was no endeavour to keep in keeping. Points of special interest are the portal to the chapter house with its panelled arch and panelling above the doorway, the very high tower arch, and the excellent roofs, that of the nave with angel-busts and bosses and that of the choir with tracery enrichment. The W beam of the choir roof has Hartington's rebus in the spandrels – a proof that he did and finished the work in the choir. The choir arch with traceried spandrels and cresting is attributed to Stanley.

FURNISHINGS. They are described topographically from E to W. In the Lady Chapel TAPESTRIES designed by *Austin Wright* and made by *Theo Moorman* in 1957, with attractive figures and scenes. – The SCREEN is partly original, and the statuettes are a specially welcome survival. The strip below the canopies has entertaining grotesques. – The choir E part has wrought-iron SCREENS, with Gothic pinnacles, and a wrought-iron COMMUNION RAIL, both delightful. They date from 1750-1. – Above the screens the upper parts of Perp wooden SCREENS, just one large ogee arch per bay and very big panel tracery. – The STALLS are of course the most famous thing in the cathedral. They are without any doubt the finest in the North of England. They were installed by Bishop Stanley *c.*1505–10. Above the exquisite canopies is another tier of simpler canopies and then a cresting with segmental arches on pendants. The stalls have a full set of MISERCORDS, on the S side with the Stanley Arms, on the N side with the merchant's mark of Richard Beswicke. The N side is a little later than the S side. On the S side from E to W Rabbit cooking the Hunter, Unicorn, Cock and Cockatrice fighting, Venerer and Stag, Stag and Hound, the Fox's Triumph, Men playing Back-gammon, Child fighting Dragon, Winged Lion, Man having

broken his wife's Cooking Pot, Dragon, two Monsters fighting
Pelican, Angel Bust. On the N side E to W Gryphon, Antelope
Sow playing Bagpipes and Pigs dancing, Wild Men and Dragon
fighting, Lion and Dragon fighting, Lion passant, Bear-baiting
Man robbed by Monkeys, Fox stealing Goose, Men on Camel
fighting Unicorn, Elephant and Castle, Shield, Dragon, Eagle
Eagle and Child. The front stalls have poppyheads, and animal
and grotesques on the front curve up to the poppyheads.

SCULPTURE. A beautiful relief panel of the Christ Child with
St Mary, St Denys, and St George, by *Eric Gill*, 1933, is ove
the entrance to the auxiliary buildings to the S of the church.
CHANDELIERS of brass in the chancel, given in 1690 and 1715
– BRASS in the chancel floor to Warden Huntington † 1458
The figure is 3 ft 3 in. long and has a canopy surround.
MONUMENT to Bishop Fraser † 1885 by *Forsyth*. White marbl
recumbent effigy. – The SCREEN to the chapel is partly original
– So is the SCREEN from the Jesus Chapel to the N. – PAINTIN
over the entrance to the chapter house: The Teachings o
Christ, by *Carel Weight*, 1963. – MONUMENT to Thoma
Ogden † 1766. Tablet with an obelisk on top. – MONUMENT
to Hugh Birley, M.P., alabaster effigy recumbent, 1886; whon
by? – In the Derby, i.e. N, chapel BRASS to Bishop Stanle
† 1515, fragmentary and now 29 in. long. – Against the W wal
of the chapel MONUMENT to Charles Lawson, 1810 by th
younger *Bacon*. Tablet with the headmaster and two boys,
bust of Homer on the ground. – Also in the chapel is the C1
FONT of the cathedral, a partly fluted octagonal bowl on
baluster stem. – The SCREEN to the choir aisle is only ver
partly original. – The nave is divided from the choir by a ROO
SCREEN, a broadly treated piece with a four-light opening l
and r. of the doorway. It was erected by Bishop Stanley. Th
lower parts in their present form are made up of old fragments
The screen was restored and altered by *Scott*, to whom th
parapet is due. – In the E respond of the N arcade is a re-se
piece of Anglo-Saxon SCULPTURE, the small relief figure o
an angel with the wings spread in two different directions. – I
the S aisle STATUE of Thomas Fleming, by *Baily*, 1851. – A
the W end of the aisle MONUMENT to Dauntsey Hume † 1828
tablet with the Good Samaritan. – At the W end of the N aisl
seated figure of Chetham, by *W. Theed*, 1853, a schoolboy a
the foot of the base.

PLATE. Two Chalices of 1584–5 by *A.B.* – Two Chalices o
1626. – Three Patens and one Almsdish (by *W.S.*) of 1676–7.

Small Flagon by *Peter Harracke*, 1697–8. – Pitcher Flagon by *John Ruslem*, 1701. – Four large Flagons and two Patens by *Nathaniel Lock*, 1707–8. – Almsdish 1715. – Also four Beaker Cups made in 1620 for the Church of the Scots Factors at Campvere, i.e. Veere, in Holland. This was not really a church, but one aisle of the church of Veere.

CHURCHES

t ANN, St Ann's Square. 1709–12. The square was laid out and the church founded by Lady Ann Bland née Mosley. Red stone. The w tower looks blunt, but it had originally a three-stage cupola. Six-bay sides with two tiers of round-headed windows and coupled pilasters below, coupled strips above. Apse with giant Corinthian pilasters. The church was restored in 1886–91 by *Waterhouse*. He created the choir in the nave. The interior has kept its three galleries. The short Tuscan columns below them are not original, but the slim upper columns are. – PULPIT. Fragment of a three-decker with angle columns. – PULPIT RAIL. Part of the original communion rail. Wrought iron. – FONT. Octagonal bowl on a baluster stem. – BOX PEWS. – STAINED GLASS. All designed by *Frederick Shields* and made by *Heaton, Butler & Bayne*. Figures in rich Germano-Swiss architectural surrounds, much too obtrusive for the church. – PLATE. Set of 1697 by *John Bathe*; Tankard of 1701; Plate and two Tankards of 1716; small Cup of 1743; Set of 1756.

t MARY (R.C.), Mulberry Street. 1848 by *Weightman & Hadfield*. A bad site and an uncouth façade. Red brick, Norman, with a richly carved portal and a s w tower with Rhenish spire. In contrast to this the interior is basilican, with six bays of green-marble columns and round-arched clerestory windows. Pugin wrote that the building 'shows to what depth of error even good men fall, when they go whoring after strange styles'.

CONGREGATIONAL CHURCH, Pin Mill Brow. Derelict. Red and yellow brick, geometrical tracery. An interesting plan to cope with the essentially triangular plot. The church is by *Waterhouse*. A signed drawing is preserved.*

ALBERT HALL (Methodist). *See* Peter Street, p. 295.

CROSS STREET CHAPEL (Unitarian). Founded in 1698. 1958–9 by *F. Leslie Halliday*. From the style and especially the attenuated Grec detail one would guess 1928.

* So Mr Buttress tells me.

FRIENDS' MEETING HOUSE, Mount Street. 1828–30 by *Richard Lane*. Ashlar stone. Five bays with a three-bay portico of un fluted Ionic columns and a pediment. The interior is altered.

PUBLIC BUILDINGS

TOWN HALL. In 1867 George Godwin, editor of *The Builder* was asked to inspect the designs which would be sent in for the new town hall to be built at Manchester. 136 were received and Godwin set aside ten designs by eight architects. They were then passed on to Professor Donaldson and to Street, and the result was that Speakman & Charlesworth of Manchester came first, J. Oldrid Scott second, Thomas Worthington third, and Alfred Waterhouse fourth.* *Waterhouse* was however specially recommended for convenience of plan and economic soundness and so, in the end, he was commissioned. In 1868, when building began, he was thirty-eight years old. He came from a Liverpool Quaker family and had been a pupil of Richard Lane. His first jobs were a church at Hulme and a warehouse for Benyon & Fryer on a site close by. Both have been demolished. Then, in 1859, he won the competition for the assize courts, and they proved a masterpiece in Gothic composition as well as in plan. They also proved already the architect's accuracy of estimates and general reliability. The demolition of this building, a milestone in the history of the Gothic Revival, is unforgivable.

71   The town hall is built of brick with stone facing. The style chosen is E.E. The façade towards Albert Square is – as against that of the Law Courts – symmetrical, the one feature in which the town hall is perhaps inferior to the law courts Victorian architects were at their best in asymmetrical compositions – but then the Natural History Museum and the Prudential prove perhaps that Waterhouse's orderly mind liked symmetry. The centre is a high tower with octagonal top stage and spire 286 ft high. A large portal in the tower is the main entry The principal windows on the upper floor are of two lights with a sexfoil in a circle.

One enters and finds oneself in a low, vaulted ENTRANCE HALL‡ and proceeds into another lying across and being three-naved. From this the two staircases rise. The r. part of the

* Among the others were T. H. Wyatt and Cuthbert Brodrick.
‡ SCULPTURE. Statue of Sir William Fairbairn by *E. E. Geflowski* (1878 and seated figures of Dalton by *Chantrey* (1837) and Joule by *Alfred Gilbert* (1893).

front next to the tower is the STATUARY HALL, again vaulted in three vessels. The intermediate landing of the staircases has a quadrant-curved wall. Behind the staircases are less ceremonial but visually more thrilling spiral stairs in open 72 shafted cages. On one of them a STATUE of John Bright by *W. Theed Jun.*, 1877. The main staircases lead to the lobby of the great hall, which has a skylight.

The GREAT HALL itself has a hammerbeam roof, seven bays of windows with geometrical tracery, fully shafted, an apse filled by the organ, and a w window of six lights. Below the side windows are the WALL PAINTINGS by *Ford Madox Brown*, 80 done in 1876–88. They represent the Romans building their Manchester fort, the Baptism of King Edward, the Expulsion of the Danes from Manchester, the Establishment of Flemish weavers, the Trial of John Wyclif, the Proclamation on Weights and Measures in 1556, Crabtree watching the transit of Venus, Chetham's Life Dream, Bradshaw's Defence of Manchester in 1642, John Kay, the Opening of the Bridgewater Canal, and Dalton collecting Marsh Gas. They are, in spite of their late date, entirely Pre-Raphaelite, with ample italianisms and well characterized. Certain motifs of unexpected foreshortenings point forward unmistakably to Stanley Spencer. In the hall also STATUES of Villiers and Gladstone by *W. Theed Jun.*, 1876 and 1878.

Along part of the Albert Square front is the LORD MAYOR'S SUITE. Its centre is the Parlour, with a panelled ceiling and a sumptuous Gothic chimneypiece. To the s follows an anteroom and then the former Council Chamber, surprisingly small. It has another Gothic chimneypiece and galleries of cast iron on two sides. To the N are the Tower Room and the Reception Room. The main corridors are vaulted, which allows the sense of medieval civic dignity and pride to be kept up beyond the entrance hall and staircase hall. Manchester of course was very specially in need to establish by this building its claim to be second to no Hanseatic city. *The Builder* in 1896 wrote: 'In after years it will probably be accounted one of the most excellent works which the nineteenth century has bequeathed to its successors.' We of the later twentieth century have no hesitation in subscribing to this statement.

The side towards Princess Street is more varied than the façade. It has for example a turret near the r. end, but a recessed tower near the l.

The EXTENSION is *Vincent Harris*'s best job, infinitely

superior to the Library, though the two buildings were designed
together and sent in for the same competition in 1925. The
building was opened in 1938. The front part, connected to the
old building by two picturesque bridges, is very high, with a
perfectly sheer steep gable to the N, a bare wall with one high
staircase window with French-1925 decoration to the Library,
and to the W round-arched arcading absolutely plain and above
it three tiers of high mullioned-and-transomed windows looking
as if they were each one enormously high giant window. Inside
behind this front range is the long low curved hall with all the
counters, following the line of the Library. The range to St
Peter's Square is entirely utilitarian, but thanks to its steep
roof impressive too.

INSIGNIA. A seventy-four-piece service of 1877; designed
by *M. Willens*, Gothic with Byzantine ornaments, and made
by *Elkington*. – Chain and Badge of 1851 by *John Hall & Co.*
of Manchester. – Silver-gilt Mace of 1895.

61 FREE TRADE HALL, Peter Street. By *Walters*, 1853–6, and the
façade very well restored after disastrous war damage by *L. C.
Howitt* in 1950–1. The interior, including the hall, is his, but
the façade has come out once again as a monument of which
Manchester can be as proud, both architecturally and civicly,
as of the town hall. It is in a Renaissance style, as restrained and
as refined as McKim, Mead & White's forty years later. Nine
bays, the ground floor arcaded on strong rectangular piers.
Carved spandrels. The upper floor has arches also, on coupled
columns and with allegorical SCULPTURE by *John Thomas*
in the tympana. Below them pedimented windows. Broad
cornice with thick garlands and top balustrade. The system
continues into South Street for three bays, and then follows
Howitt's work, very severely and very sympathetically.

ALBERT BRIDGE HOUSE, Bridge Street. For about 800 tax
officials. By *E. H. Banks* (Ministry of Works), 1958–9. Eighteen
storeys high. Set at an angle to the street. More low blocks are
to come behind to form a group. The high block has concrete
framing, Portland stone cladding, and sill panels of grey glass.

EDUCATION OFFICES, Crown Square. By *Leach, Rhodes &
Walker*, 1965–7. Part of the scheme of public buildings round
Crown Square (*see* Courts of Justice, below). A very large,
good building, the windows boxed out as all-glass oriels of
rectangular plan.

COURTS OF JUSTICE, Crown Square. 1960–2 by *Leonard C.
Howitt*. Symmetrical and feebly playful. What a come-down

after Waterhouse's brilliant early work, demolished so recently. The new building has a façade 289 ft long* and will later be flanked by the County Court and the new MAGISTRATES' COURT (by *Yorke, Rosenberg & Mardall*). The latter is to stand on a podium used for car parking. It is to be an oblong block with a recessed top storey but otherwise without any projections or recessions. In plan it is to be tripartite, with offices and the magistrates', solicitors', and barristers' suites running along the short sides and the court rooms in the middle. The structure will be of concrete members with the posts set outside the actual building. The court rooms will be further recessed behind the frames so that there will be ample entrance loggias to them, a sensible and crisp solution. The framing has the wide module favoured by Yorke, Rosenberg & Mardall.

COUNTY COURT, Quay Street. Built *c.*1770 as a private house (for the banker William Allen). It became the County Court in 1878. It is a sober classical house, five bays wide. Doorway with Tuscan pilasters and a heavy lintel.‡

MAGISTRATES' COURT, Bloom Street and Minshull Street. 1868–71 by *Thomas Worthington*. Brick with stone dressings. E.E. with a tower, an asymmetrical composition, not well placed.

POLICE AND FIRE STATION, Whitworth Street and London Road. By *Woodhouse, Willoughby & Langham*, 1901–6. Red brick and yellow terracotta with a tower characteristic of the date. The building fills a whole triangular block.

GENERAL POST OFFICE SORTING OFFICE, Lever Street. 1965–8 by *H. G. Swann* of the Ministry of Public Building and Works. A large, even block, except for the more dramatic l. corner and back.

GENERAL POST OFFICE (former), Spring Gardens. Former – as it is doomed to disappear. It was a tremendous *palazzaccio*, like a Ministry building in Rome. Central upper giant portico. The architect was *J. Williams*, the date 1881–7.

PARCEL POST OFFICE, St Andrew's Street and Fairfield Street. 1966–8 by *H. G. Swann* of the Ministry of Public Building and Works. Concrete, large, compositionally in two parts plus a low canteen annex.

* Mr Buttress tells me that some of *Woolner*'s statues from Waterhouse's demolished building stand against a low wall at the w end.

‡ Mr Buttress and Mr R. R. Emmanuel told me about the early history of the house.

TELEPHONE HOUSE, Portland Street. 1959–61. Curtain-wall
slab by *E. Norman Bailey & Partners*.

ART GALLERY, Mosley Street. Built as the Royal Manchester
Institution by *Sir Charles Barry*. The dates are 1824–35, i.e.
Barry was only twenty-nine years old when he won the competition for the building. It is Grecian, but as a composition
remarkably original. Portico of six unfluted Ionic columns with
pediment, then three recessed bays with two columns *in antis*,
and then three-bay solid ends. Fine entrance and staircase hall
with skylight, a Greek Doric colonnade on three sides, and
parts of the Parthenon frieze over. The gallery uses as an
annexe the former ATHENAEUM, in Princess Street. This is
also by *Barry*, but it dates from 1837, the year of the Reform
Club in London. So it is a stone *palazzo* of nine bays. Pedimented *piano nobile* windows, portal with Tuscan columns.

JOHN RYLANDS LIBRARY, Deansgate. The library was built
and endowed by Enriqueta Augustina Rylands in memory of
her husband. He had been a textile manufacturer. The building
is by *Basil Champneys*, who was commissioned on the strength
of his Mansfield College at Oxford. Building started in 1890
and was completed in 1899. It is in the Gothic style, in spite
of that style's 'recent unpopularity', as Champneys himself
said in 1900. Champneys's Gothic is still Victorian Dec, but his
freedom of composition, his playing with spaces, and his wealth
of motifs are all the equivalent to the Arts and Crafts events
of the nineties. The façade is symmetrical and reveals nothing
of the intricacies of the interior. It is a tripartite façade, the
centre a portal with *trumeau*, two oriels over, and above,
recessed, the reading-room E window. L. and r. two-bay blocks
ending in octagons, and behind them tower-like eminences
flanking the reading-room window. The ornamental detail is
lacy and elaborate. Along the sides, not meant to be seen,
except in extreme foreshortening, upper two-storey oriels. We
must see what they do inside.

One enters a vaulted entrance hall with slim shafts and turns
to a sumptuous vaulted staircase. The intermediate landings
are below the octagon, and one looks up into this through a
circular opening with a balcony round. Moreover, the tower is
simply above the top landing. It is a cavalier throwing-away
of whole large parts of the building to spatial extravagance
pure and simple. The top landing has also a small picturesque
balcony to connect with a room not otherwise attainable. The
reading room is 125 ft long and arranged college-wise with

bays l. and r. and an upper gallery. The centre is high and tier-ceron-vaulted. The bays are divided off by the vaulting piers. Between them the bays below have a busy arcading with two openings to one vaulting pier. On the gallery level there is only one arch and one clerestory window to each vaulting bay. Each bay has to the outside an oriel, below as well as above. Only the w and the E bay are treated differently, one might say transept-wise. The end windows (giving much too little light) are of ten and eleven lights and have *Kempe* STAINED GLASS. There is a lending library on the ground floor with a separate entrance, and also on the ground floor are a conference room and committee rooms. – The METALWORK details by *Singer* of Frome are enjoyably Arts and Crafts. – SCULPTURE. Statue of John Rylands by *J. Cassidy*, c.1893 (price asked £1,325). – Statue of Mrs Rylands by *Cassidy*, 1907. – By the same the group of Theology, Science, and Art. – A back EXTENSION of 1912 etc. is also by *Champneys*. The library incidentally had electric lighting from the start, produced by its own dynamos.

CENTRAL LIBRARY. 1930–4 by *E. Vincent Harris*. Portland stone. Circular, with a five-bay Corinthian portico and an upper 94 order of giant Tuscan columns. The reading room has a dome and a skylight and Tuscan columns in four blocks round the perimeter, to the centre a bewildering kind of cinema fountain, a baldacchino of green marble columns and a scrolly metal top. The utilitarian rooms are well distributed all around. The library ought to be judged as part of the general scheme of town-hall extensions.

UNIVERSITY. *See* Chorlton-on-Medlock, p. 309.

INSTITUTE OF SCIENCE AND TECHNOLOGY (*see* also Chorlton-on-Medlock, p. 312). The old buildings are in Whitworth Street and Sackville Street. The front, with its façade to Sackville Street, is a grand composition in the Loire style, with a gabled gatehouse-type centre. It is by *Spalding & Cross*, 1895–1912. The other building was designed in 1927, by *Bradshaw, Gass & Hope*, but only completed in 1957, a gross anachronism then. Red brick and much yellow terracotta, Norman-Shaw gables, and a high set-back top at r. angles to the façade.

COLLEGE OF COMMERCE, Aytoun Street. 1962 by *S. G. Besant Roberts*, the City Architect.

CHETHAM'S HOSPITAL, Long Millgate. On the foundation of the college *see* cathedral, p. 275. The college was dissolved in 1547. The buildings were bought by the Earl of Derby in 1557 for his town house. They were fortified in the Civil War, and

Humphrey Chetham, textile manufacturer and merchant
bought them in 1653 to found his school for forty boys. A
library, public from the beginning, was attached. It is inter
esting to note that the premises cost £400, but the books fo
the library, got together in London, £1,000. For the MAN
CHESTER GRAMMAR SCHOOL, to cope with its C19 growth
Waterhouse erected a brick building along Long Millgate i
1873–8. It is not very ambitious, but has a high gatehouse moti
in the centre with a high chimney towards the school yard. Th
building s of the college rectangle which looks like a chape
was put up for additional school accommodation in 1878 (b
Waterhouse – which one would not recognize).

The college premises were erected N of the church and a
some distance from it. What use was made of this space ? Th
survival of so complete a set of medieval collegiate buildings i
rare. They are red sandstone, irregular, a rectangle with a clois
ter and then a long E wing and with a short SE extension endin
in the GATEHOUSE. The gatehouse was rebuilt in 1816. It i
not vaulted. It has a spacious upper room with an open timbe
roof, and this is of the type of all the others, with arched brace
to collar-beams and in addition the distinguishing feature of
longitudinal beam below the ridge, at the level of the colla
beams. The E range with its SE hook was quarters for servant
and guests. The roofs are of the same type as the gatehous
roof. The upper floor is reached by an outer staircase next t
the gatehouse. Below about midway to the W was the BAKE
HOUSE. To the W of this is a passage, leading out to the N an
the River Steps, and then the kitchen. In the angle between th
kitchen and the rectangular main block is the entrance porc
not at all prominent. It leads into the hall screens passage. Th
SCREEN is of the spere type with two entrances. It is origin
C15 work except for the cresting. The HALL has three tran
somed two-light windows. They have cusped heads to th
lights, as have all the C15 windows of the college. The hall roo
is again of the type found before. The high table has a panelle
coving over. The fireplace is now in the W ingle formed b
E. J. Haywood, who restored the hospital. The fireplace was i
the place where the ingle now is. The bay window towards th
cloister is one bay N of the high-table bay and is followed i
that direction by a doorway. This connects with the cloiste
and the Audit Room, former Chamber. The AUDIT ROOM ha
a square bay window and a ceiling with moulded beams an
bosses and a plaster frieze of trails of *c.*1600. The cloister

QUADRANGLE has a cloister walk with three-light openings to only three sides. Along it lay the eight fellows' sets, much as in Cambridge or Oxford colleges, except that the cloister walks themselves are two-storeyed. The doorways to the sets are preserved. The N range of the cloister continues straight to the screens passage and entrance porch. From the screens passage, as usual, doorways led into buttery and pantry; the KITCHEN however was not approached between them but lies to their E. It is the height of the full two storeys and has its enormous fireplace in the N wall. On the upper floor, above the Audit Room, is in the solar position what must have been the WARDEN'S CHAMBER. It was converted by Chetham and received at that time a plaster tunnel-vault, which has since been removed. But the splendid tympanum in the N wall remains. It is of the time of Charles II and has a coat of arms, two wreathed obelisks standing on books and carrying lamps of knowledge, a pelican, and a cock, all carved in wood. At its NW end a doorway leads to a small room with small Henry VIII windows to the cloister and two tiny quatrefoil openings into the hall. However, originally the room was open to the hall. Chetham's LIBRARY is on the upper floor of the S and W ranges. The roof is that of the college. When this was still fellows' quarters, of course, cross-walls divided set from set. The library presses were heightened in the C18, and the gates are C18 too. Parts of a late C17 RAIL with twisted balusters may connect with the date of the tympanum in the solar or the tradition that the Derbys had a chapel here, or they may simply be *ex situ.* – In the W window at the N end some minor C14 STAINED GLASS. – Of the time of the library also is the STAIRCASE in the NE angle of the cloister, with flat, cut-out balusters.

ST MARY'S HOSPITAL, Whitworth Street West. 1899–1904 by *Waterhouse & Son.* Recognizable as the firm's, though no longer Gothic. The style has turned quite nondescript.

HOSPITAL FOR SKIN DISEASES, Quay Street. 1903–5 by *T. Worthington & Son*, i.e. *Percy Worthington.* In the Edwardian Baroque. Note the pair of turrets to Byrom Street.

MARKET HALL, Liverpool Road. Iron and glass; nothing special. Completed in 1880.

SMITHFIELD MARKET, Goadsby Street. From Shude Hill a Gothic opening leads to one of the main entrances. It is dated 1854 and has classical detail. Inside iron and glass, not particularly interesting.

PICCADILLY STATION. 1862, with a new high office block of

neutral appearance. It is oblong. The middle of the short sid
to the town has a higher tower with horizontal slit windows i
groups of two. The long sides have long bands of white an
glass. Architects: Midland Region Architect's Office, *R. L
Moorcroft*; date 1959–64. The GOODS DEPOT in Ducie Stree
is a seven-storeyed brick block with small segment-heade
windows. (It has cast-iron columns and wrought-iron jack-arc
floors.)

CENTRAL STATION. The facade is despicable,* but th
train shed with its 210 ft span is only 30 ft less than St Pancras
It is 10 ft more than Lime Street Station at Liverpool. Th
shed was designed by *Sir John Fowler*. The building was pu
up in 1876–9. Below the ground is a vast undercroft vaulted i
brick with intersecting tunnel-vaults. This and the shed ough
to be preserved.

VICTORIA STATION. The platform roof of 1844 by *Georg
Stephenson* survives and is 700 ft long.

LIVERPOOL AND MANCHESTER RAILWAY STATION (former)
See Liverpool Road, p. 293.

HANGING BRIDGE. Half an arch of the medieval bridge at the v
end of Hanging Ditch is exposed w of Highland House (*se
p. 290), and sw of the s porch of the cathedral, deep down,
railed-off rectangular pit.

VICTORIA BRIDGE. *See* Deansgate, p. 290.

STREETS

The streets are arranged alphabetically; for those who take thei
walking seriously, a map of the centre is provided on pp. 274–5
To suggest a consecutive perambulation taking in all streets, as
have done for Liverpool, has defeated me. The street pattern i
too much a grid, and hence too much repetition would be involved

ALBERT SQUARE. Only the s side can make any claim to be
worthy foil for the town hall. The l. corner is quite ornat
Gothic (St Andrew's Chambers); then Bridgewater Buildings
also Gothic; Albert Chambers, Italianate with giant uppe
pilasters, and the MEMORIAL HALL of 1864–6 by *Thoma
Worthington*, brick and stone and decidedly Venetian Gothic
Its longer side is to South Street. The other sides of the squar
have nothing much to offer. In the square the ALBERT MEM
ORIAL, the statue under a canopy. The design is by *Worthington*

* Mr Buttress says that the intended office building was never built.

the statue by *Matthew Noble*. The Albert Memorial was designed in 1862,* i.e. a little earlier than Scott's in London.‡ Other STATUES: Oliver Heywood by *Albert Bruce Joy*, 1894. stone. – John Bright by *W. Theed*, 1891, stone. – Gladstone by *Theed* too, 1879, bronze. – Bishop Fraser by *Woolner*, 1888, bronze, with reliefs.

LOOM STREET. Between Minshull and Chorlton Streets a whole block treated as one vaguely Italianate composition. Brick, twenty-four twin bays.

OOTH STREET. No. 10 is the SAVINGS BANK by *Salomons*, 1872, a debased *palazzo*, Nos 22–6 to the corner of Cooper Street a long four-storeyed *palazzo* with three florid doorways.

RIDGE STREET. SCOTTISH LIFE HOUSE. High block on a podium. 1965 by *Leach, Rhodes & Walker*.

YROM STREET. Facing the former church of St John a group of Late Georgian houses with Gothick door surrounds. *See* p. 480

HANCERY PLACE. Note No. 1, brick, Gothic, with gables and a traceried doorway, and the street name carved in a stone scroll.

HAPEL WALKS. TUDOR HOUSE is brick below and elaborate half-timbering above.

HARLOTTE STREET. Nos 10, 12, and 34 are by *Walters*, 1857, 1860, and 1855. No. 10 is the most ambitious, with its nine bays, stone below and brick above. But what matters in all three is the conscientious and discriminating detailing.

OLLIER STREET. *See* Liverpool Road.

ORPORATION STREET. At the top on the E side NEW CENTURY HOUSE, the new building of the C.W.S., a curtain-walled slab of fourteen storeys, part of the C.I.S. group in Miller Street (*see* p. 294). By *G. S. Hay* and *Sir John Burnet, Tait & Partners*. Abstract stone relief by *John McCarthy* on a screen wall at r. angles. – Then the old COOPERATIVE WHOLESALE SOCIETY, two large blocks of the same design, in a weak Baroque. By *F. E. L. Harris*, begun in 1905. – Nothing else of note. Corporation Street will be affected by the big new development N of Market Street.

ROSS STREET. At the corner of Market Street is the ROYAL EXCHANGE, 1914–21 by *Bradshaw, Gass & Hope*, a big block with giant columns and pilasters and a round angle tower on the NW corner. The hall inside has giant demi-columns and three glass domes. The first Manchester Royal Exchange was

* The design was published in *The Builder* on 27 September 1862.
‡ Gilbert Scott's design for the London Memorial was accepted on 22 April 1863.

10—S.L.

erected by Sir Oswald Mosley in 1729. It was in Market Stree
It was rebuilt by *Thomas Harrison* in 1806–9, enlarged by *Ale*:
Mills in 1847–9, and rebuilt by *Mills & Murgatroyd* in 1869–7.
DEANSGATE. An uneventful street, especially in its N stretche
– with one exception. Between Deansgate and Exchang
Station is HIGHLAND HOUSE, 1966 by *Leach, Rhodes &
Walker*, a normal high-rise block made abnormal by funne
like holes sticking out at regular intervals. I made it 198 on th
N façade only. – Just w of Highland House is VICTORI
BRIDGE, 1837–9, with a heavy stone parapet and in the middl
of one parapet the queen's orb on a massive Grecian scroll.
Deansgate proper starts with the GROSVENOR HOTEL, larg
and dated 1879, a mixture of giant columns and Gothic detail
– Then MAWSON BUILDINGS, three bays only, Gothic.
Opposite these at the N corner of the public garden STATUE (
Cromwell, bronze, by *M. Noble*, 1875. – Then buildings sta
on the E side, first SPEAKERS HOUSE, concrete, by *Dougla
Stephen & Partners*, 1963. – Then BARTON'S BUILDING (
1871 by *Corbett, Raby & Sawyer*, a long and thoroughl
ignorant façade – the ground-floor pilasters must be seen to b
believed – but behind a gorgeous glass and iron shopping an
office arcade with two glass domes and balconies in two an
three tiers. – No. 66 (w), HAYWARD'S BUILDING, is fre
Renaissance with three large twin-arched first-floor window
but six smaller ones above. – KENDAL MILNE'S STORE i
by *J. S. Beaumont*, 1939, in the German type of store archi
tecture created by Messel early in the century. – At th
corner of St Ann's Street NATIONAL HOUSE of 1875–6, i
free Renaissance moving away from the *palazzo* type. – At th
corner of John Dalton Street a Gothic office building, 1876 b
Pennington & Brigden, Gothic – but no longer High Victoria
Gothic. The portal may still be that, but on the façade there i
too much bare wall, and the rhythm is already turning Lat
Victorian.

FOUNTAIN STREET. No. 68 is brick, Gothic, with steppe
window arches giving a saw-tooth effect. – The PHOENI
INSURANCE is a good example of functional Victorian Gothic
– BARNETT HOUSE by *Cruickshank & Seward*, 1959–61.

GREAT ANCOATS STREET. DAILY EXPRESS. By *Sir Owe
Williams*, 1939, following the example of his Daily Express i
London. An all-glass front, absolutely flush, with rounde
corners and translucent glass and black glass. The top floor
are stepped back. A little turret at the l. corner. It is the bes

Manchester building of between the wars. – Further E a large WAREHOUSE of *c.*1830. – Opposite this one can reach the area of the ROCHDALE CANAL WHARVES, with another large warehouse in LEECH STREET. This one has small round-headed windows.

HIGH STREET. At the corner of Church Street is an impressive new building. Concrete podium with only a narrow horizontal slit of window. Four storeys above, recessed from Church Street. The architects are *Leach, Rhodes & Walker*.

JOHN DALTON STREET. ST JAMES'S HOUSE by *Leach, Rhodes & Walker*, 1965, is a high block on a podium. – No. 16, PRINCE'S CHAMBERS, by *Salomons*, 1865, is five-storeyed, of brick, with tripartite windows, their arches of stepped brick-work in a kind of sawtooth fashion. – DALTON BUILDINGS at the corner of Deansgate is classical, with Doric pilasters, but a florid portal.

KENNEDY STREET. Note the LAW SOCIETY, 1885 by *Thomas Hontas*, Venetian Gothic, of only three bays.

KING STREET. In King Street was the old TOWN HALL of Manchester. It was by *F. Goodwin*, 1819–34, and the centre of its façade has been re-erected in Heaton Park. – The King of King Street is *Lutyens*'s MIDLAND BANK, built in 1929. It is a nearly square block and treated as such, with the upper motifs identical on all four sides. The two angle porches are in King Street. The elevation steps back and contracts, and the tops of the centre motifs have French pavilion roofs. The pro-portions are ingeniously calculated, as Lutyens in his later years adored to do. The top stage is two-thirds of the stage from the obelisks to the next set-back, and that middle stage is two-thirds of the bottom stage. Also the walls above the first-floor sill have a very slight batter: 1 in. in every 11 ft. The banking hall could not be sky-lit, so Lutyens gave it arcading on all four sides and wooden galleries much as in Wren churches. The galleries have large arched windows to let enough light in. The building was designed in collaboration with *Whinney, Son & Austen Hall*. – Opposite the REFORM CLUB by *Edward Salomons*, 1870–1, a very good example of the Venetian Gothic. Two angle turrets, fanciful portal. (The interior is of two periods, one contemporary with the exterior, the other of the 1890s. To the first belong a fine staircase running up the full height of the building, with even the longcase clock built into the linenfold panelling, the grand main dining room two storeys high on the piano nobile, and an enormous billiard

room, running the whole length of the house, in the roof – a
very complete. Also on the top floor are the kitchens. Of th
second phase, the best rooms are the magnificent lavatorie
with much fretwork and marble panels in the ceiling. On th
top floor, in the same style, the card room with painted pane
and stained-glass windows.[*] – Nos 84–8 is of ashlar, classica
with giant pilasters and wreaths in the frieze. – Its neigh
bour is the BANK OF ENGLAND, by *Cockerell*, 1845–6, on
five bays, but almost overpowering with its giant attache
Tuscan columns and its crowning motif of an aedicule windo
in an arch which pushes up into the pediment. The pedimer
is three bays wide, and in this part the lower windows are larg
and arched with a recessed tripartite arrangement with lunett
over. They correspond to the banking hall, but only the middl
one is carried on as a tunnel-vault leading to a saucer dome an
continuing in another tunnel-vault. The dome stands on fou
Tuscan columns with pierced capitals (what for ?). – Opposit
the headquarters of the DISTRICT BANK by *Casson, Conde
& Partners*, 1966–9. It is only six storeys high, which is a reli
after all the tower lumps around. Secondly it is entirely face
in granite, vertically ribbed, and that also is a relief after all th
raw concrete and the tinny curtain-walling. The general shap
is a slab set back from the streets and at its two ends irregula
octagons elongated in the directions at r. angles to the slab. O
the ground floor the areas between slab and streets are filled ir
and there are here also canted projections, just as the roof i
canted too. The banking hall inside is elevated by a few step
above the concourse. – Then *Waterhouse*'s minor but un
mistakable PRUDENTIAL ASSURANCE building of 1881.
w of Cross Street the EAGLE INSURANCE by *Charles Heathcot
& Sons*, 1911, not large, with a rounded corner and nic
Edwardian Baroque motifs. – No. 35, a five-bay brick hous
with short lower wings, is of 1736. It is the only one of its kin
and date in Inner Manchester. The doorway has a pedimer
on brackets. – Opposite two modest buildings with cast-iro
window arcading, then again on the N side JAEGERS, high an
elaborate, all in half-timbering.

LEECH STREET. *See* Great Ancoats Street.

LENA STREET. *See* London Road.

LIVERPOOL ROAD. Opposite the Market Hall is GUNN HOUSE
brick, of three bays, modestly Gothick.‡ – In COLLIE

* This description of the interior is by Roderick Gradidge.
‡ Mr Buttress thinks that it once had a plaque with the date 1821.

STREET is a fragment, 3 by 3 ft, of the E wall of the ROMAN FORT. It is preserved in a timber yard under a blocked railway arch.* – At the W end of Liverpool Road, on the N side, is the original TERMINAL STATION of the Liverpool–Manchester Railway. It was built in 1829–30. The front to the street is stuccoed. It has five bays and two storeys, with a tripartite entrance and a tripartite window over. To the r. the building goes on with a long row of doorways and windows all with segmental arches. Part of the platform canopy and ticket office also remain (D. Buttress).

LONDON ROAD. Down LENA STREET is the castellated gateway to the ROCHDALE CANAL BASIN. – At the corner of Lena Street an OFFICE BLOCK (actually No. 107 Piccadilly) in the typical Edwardian Baroque with gable and round angle turret, and with alternatingly blocked columns. The architect was *Charles Heathcote*, and the date is 1898. – Opposite, at the corner of Auburn Street, another of the same time, this red with yellow terracotta. It is by *J. W. Beaumont* and dates from c.1905. – Along the approach to Piccadilly Station *R. Seifert & Partners* are building GATEWAY HOUSE, with a very impressive long, sweeping, undulating façade, the horizontals stressed throughout. Window frames and window panels and the casing of the concrete floor slabs is all in aluminium differently anodized.

LONG MILLGATE. The MANCHESTER ARMS is a five-bay mid-Georgian house. The doorway has carved palm fronds below the pediment.

LOWER BYROM STREET. One Georgian house still carries on. It has the best doorway remaining from Georgian Manchester. Tuscan columns with leaf capitals, triglyph frieze, and pediment.

MAJOR STREET. No. 55 is YORK HOUSE, a building of great and unexpected interest. It is by *H. S. Fairhurst* and was built in 1911 as a cotton-goods warehouse. The façade is of no value but the back is unique. The preservation of the building is uncertain, and its importance can be measured by the fact that Walter Gropius made an appeal for it by a personal letter. It is all glazed and stepped up and back, much like James Stirling's History Library of 1966–7 at Cambridge, i.e. each floor has vertical glazing and then lean-to glazing. This repeats seven times. The two end gables, sheer and windowless, run up in one sweeping diagonal.

* An extensive cemetery lay to the E.

MARKET STREET. Little worth watching for; and much of t
N side will be demolished for a big development which is
stretch as far NW as Corporation Street. – Nos 70 and 34
the s side are dignified five-bay stone premises still in t
classical tradition. No. 70 has upper giant unfluted Ion
columns. – No. 62 at the corner of Brown Street is Wat
housish Gothic (STEPHENS BUILDINGS). – On the N side
the corner of Romford Court is a Saracen joke. – At the E e
on the s side is the very big block of the ROYAL EXCHANG
For this see Cross Street.

MILLER STREET. Arkwright's Mill was here, the first cotto
mill in Manchester. – The COOPERATIVE INSURAN
SOCIETY has the highest building in Manchester. It is a
the best of the new high office blocks, done with a discipli
and consistency inspired no doubt by the achievements
Skidmore, Owings & Merrill. Steel frame and a window
service tower of reinforced concrete clad with mosaic and risi
to 400 ft. The architects were *G. S. Hay* of the C.W.S. a
Sir John Burnet, Tait & Partners. The building during the d
time houses a staff of 2,500. It consists of a twenty-five-stor
tower, a five-storey lower part, and the fourteen-storey N
Century House in Corporation Street for the C.W.S. (*see*
289). Between the two is a conference hall for 1,000. This
glass and black steel. Black steel also are the sill panels of t
C.I.S. building itself. The details round the entrance are t
only weakness. The entrance hall itself is excellent. T
MURAL by *George Mitchell* is one of the few of this fashionab
aggressive kind which come off. The interior of the conferer
hall by the *Design Research Unit* is exemplary.* The who
group was completed in 1962.

MOSLEY STREET. For the beginning *see* Piccadilly. – T
WILLIAMS DEACON'S BANK has two buildings connect
by a big portal. They are of 1860, by *Walters*, his last gre
work. Two-storeyed rusticated giant pilasters below so th
the pedimented *piano nobile* windows are on the second floor

35 Next the former PORTICO LIBRARY, 1802–6 by *Thom*
Harrison of Chester. Centre loggia with four unfluted Ion
columns. Pediment. On the side to York Street attach
columns. A noble, yet unassuming design. Interior with
saucer-dome and segmental tunnel-vaults to E and w. It is
pity that a ceiling was put in between them and the grou
floor. – Opposite is a fifteen-bay warehouse by *Walters* of 185

* (The sculptured panels in the Conference Hall are by *Stephen Syke*

brick, with five portals, four with attached upper windows, all these features very wildly detailed. – MILNE BUILDINGS are the most startling warehouse of Manchester. Twenty-one **62** bays, in two giant orders one on top of the other. The angle five bays have columns and pediments, the centre pilasters. The capitals are Graeco-Egyptian. The most likely date is c.1845. The architect seems unrecorded. – Opposite the COMMERCIAL UNION ASSURANCE, 1964–6 by *H. A. J. Darlow* of *Watney, Eiloart, Inman & Nunn*. Portland stone with boxed-out windows in a chequer pattern.

MOUNT STREET. The corner to Albert Square has two ornate Gothic buildings. – At the corner of St Peter's Street is the ABC TELEVISION BUILDING, a straight curtain-walling job. By *J. E. Beardshaw & Partners*, 1959–60.

NEW BROWN STREET. Nos 18–20 is a large five-storeyed brick house, but the stuccoed ground floor has Doric pilasters and a doorway with set-in Greek Doric columns. In the frieze in three places are wreaths.

OLD SHAMBLES (Market Place). The WELLINGTON INN has some claims to be the only ancient timber-framed building in Inner Manchester.

OXFORD STREET. The offices of the CALICO PRINTERS' ASSOCIATION were built in 1912. They are by *Charles Clegg & Son* and *Fryer & Penman*, high and broad and all stone; Baroque. – Their neighbour is a humble five-bay house with an iron and glass front. – TOOTAL BROADHURST LEE & CO. are large too, red brick and yellow terracotta, but comparatively classical, with giant columns. 1898 by *J. Sankey Gibbons*. – The REFUGE ASSURANCE is also very large, and of red brick. High tower with Baroque yellow-terracotta top. The rest of the decoration is of North Italian early c16 type. The architect was *Paul Waterhouse*, and the building dates from 1891–1912.

PARKER STREET. *See* Piccadilly Garden.

PETER STREET. For the Midland Hotel *see* St Peter's Square. – Then the Y.M.C.A. by *Woodhouse, Corbett & Dean*, 1909. This is a reinforced concrete structure and externally terracotta with nice detailing and very shallow projections. – The THEATRE ROYAL is of 1844, by *Irwin & Chester*, altered by *Salomons* in 1875. It is stuccoed, with giant Corinthian columns, a big cornice, and a pedimental gable. – The ALBERT HALL is a Methodist Hall, 1910 by *W. J. Morley* of Bradford, large and just approximately churchy in some details. Yellow terracotta; angle tower.

PICCADILLY. *See* Piccadilly Garden.

PICCADILLY GARDEN. The garden is on the site of the firs
Royal Infirmary. The following description takes in the top
of PORTLAND STREET and MOSLEY STREET and the whol
of PARKER STREET. On the Parker Street side the 1984
Manchester has gone to town. The three buildings, mor
exciting than architecturally valuable, are by *Covell, Matthew
& Partners*, 1959–65, and part of one and the same design. Thi
includes a podium uniting the three parts and a first-floo
shopping piazza. The hotel is a high slab parallel to Piccadilly
The slab is cantilevered out on a sloping underside. The lo
restaurant projects towards Piccadilly and has three funn
little roofs. The slab is stressed horizontally. The high offic
slab, twenty-four storeys high, SUNLEY HOUSE, has not go
that horizontal emphasis. Also it stands at r. angles to Piccadill
and has towards it a bare wall with just one long window slo
Thirdly at the corner of Mosley Street, EAGLE STAR HOUSE
a lower office block placed at an angle and with a stabbing-ou
roof. One can see what was in the minds of the architects: onl
it has not come off, and the group, instead of reading together
looks desperately disparate. – On the w, i.e. the Mosley Stree
side, a good classical three-bay house of 1836 with a three-ba
pediment on giant Corinthian pilasters. – The N side, Piccadill
proper, has nothing of interest. – On the E side, in Portlan
Street, is first the QUEEN'S HOTEL, 1845 by *Walters*, stuccoed
Italianate, simple, but with an ornate porch. – Then No. 3
a six-bay warehouse with quiet motifs, arched windows o
the ground floor, segment-headed on the first, with segmenta
pediments on the second. – Then two more warehouses. No.
is dated 1863. No. 9 by *Walters*, 1851, is specially lavish. – I
the public gardens STATUES of Sir Robert Peel by *Marshall*
1853, bronze with two bronze allegories below, of Wellingto
by *M. Noble*, 1856, with four allegories, of James Watt b
Theed Jun., 1857, and the Queen Victoria Memorial by *Onslow
Ford*, 1901, with seated figure, in bronze against a Baroqu
architectural background. Also 'Adrift', a group by *John
Cassidy*, 1907. The husband and father raises a piece of cloth
the wife and children lie below. – Piccadilly itself carries on
little to the SE and continues as London Road. Next to th
Queen's Hotel two more stuccoed buildings of the same style
– Opposite, No. 75 is Italian round-arched Gothic, No. 7
Northern Gothic. – The RODWELL TOWER is of 1963–6 b
Douglas Stephen & Partners, concrete, with an eighteen-store

tower and a lower part. The constructional interest lies in the fact that the building had to span the canal. Visually the building belongs to the Louis Kahn succession (Medical Research Building, Philadelphia).

ᴘORT STREET. At the fork of Newton and Port Streets BRADLEY HOUSE, a late classical warehouse (five storeys, brick on a stone ground floor). To the junction still a tripartite window with pilasters. – N of this building two Late Georgian HOUSES with pedimented doorways are left.

ᴘORTLAND STREET. For the first houses *see* Piccadilly. – Then the COOK AND WATTS WAREHOUSE, the largest of Manchester; 1851 by *Travis & Mangnall*, with its four roof erections breaking the *cornicione* principle of the *palazzo* warehouses. The style is Italianate still, the length is twenty-three bays or *c.*300 ft, the height nearly 100 ft. – ST ANDREW'S HOUSE, a twenty-one storey slab with a multi-storey garage behind, is by *Leach, Rhodes & Walker*, a straightforward job. So is Telephone House opposite (*see* p. 284). – Nos 129–31 has a long brick front with giant blank upper arches.

ᴘRINCESS STREET. From W to E. Behind the town hall some Late Georgian HOUSES. – At the corner of Cooper Street an OFFICE BUILDING with Gothic giant blank arches. – No. 103 (N), 1854 by *J. E. Gregan*, is a brick *palazzo*, No. 109 typical debased Italian Gothic. The segmental arches stilted on vertical pieces ought to be noted. The building is by *Clegg & Knowles*, 1863. – CENTRAL HOUSE, No. 74 (S), is Gothic with angle tourelles. It was built in 1884.

ǫUAY STREET. The OPERA HOUSE began life in 1912 as the New Theatre. The design is by *Richardson & Gill* with *Farquharson*. – Farther W QUAY HOUSE, large, concrete, by *H. S. Fairhurst & Son*, 1964–5. – Yet farther W GRANADA HOUSE by *Ralph Tubbs*, 1960–2.

ᴛ ANN'S SQUARE. STATUE of Cobden, by *Marshall Wood*, 1867.

ᴛ ANN STREET. The building of WILLIAMS DEACON'S BANK at the corner of St Ann's Square is a free version of the *palazzo* style, widely spaced. It is by *J. E. Gregan*, of *c.*1848.

ᴛ JOHN STREET. The church was pulled down in 1928. The street which led to it has two fairly complete Georgian terraces, that on the N side with the better doorways. Tuscan columns and broken pediments.

ᴛ PETER'S SQUARE. The MIDLAND HOTEL, 1898 by *Charles Trubshaw*, is a vast and varied affair, red brick and brown

terracotta, with the French touches of e.g. the Russell Hotel i
London. – The CENOTAPH is by *Lutyens*, 1924, similar to th
Whitehall one.

SPRING GARDENS. For the Midland Bank and the Refor
Club *see* King Street. – For the Phoenix Insurance *see* Fountai
Street. – The NATIONAL PROVINCIAL BANK is by *Alfre
Waterhouse*, 1888–91, and not at all Gothic. The style migl
be called a free German Renaissance, with its variety of gable
The stone front curves round and has a thick relief, thank
chiefly to very prominent brackets for balconies and pediment
– The WESTMINSTER BANK is Edwardian Baroque, red bric
and much stone with an angle dome (corner of York Street
The building is by *Charles Heathcote* and was begun (for Parr'
Bank) in 1902.

WHITWORTH STREET. From Oxford Street first the Refug
Assurance, *see* Oxford Street, and opposite it Nos 58–6c
BRIDGEWATER HOUSE, typical ambitious business archi
tecture of the teens, stone below, faience above. – LANCASTE
HOUSE is at the corner of Princess Street, two different design
both Edwardian Baroque. High angle turret. By *H. S. Fairhur
& Son*, 1912–15. – Then the old buildings of the Institute c
Science and Technology (*see* p. 285).

YORK STREET. BARCLAYS BANK is by *Green, Lloyd & Son
1962–4. It is an agreeable composition with a high pre-cas
concrete slab, its short side between two low stone ranges, a
three running N–S. The low ones have long vertical windows
i.e. a touch of the classical deliberately conjured up. – For th
Westminster Bank *see* Spring Gardens.

MANCHESTER SUBURBS

ANCOATS AND MILES PLATTING

The boundary is on the N side of the railway from Cheetham Hi
Road to the Philips Park triangle, on the E and SE sides the railway
a short stretch of Ashton New Road, and then Palmerston Stree
and on the SW side the boundary of the Centre to Cheetham Hi
Road.

ALL SOULS, Every Street. A Commissioners' church (cos
£4,818).* 1839–40 by *William Hayley*. Neo-Norman, vaguel
Red brick, a plain rectangle with uncouth pinnacles. Th
façade has a mid-projection also be-pinnacled. Tall round

* According to Mr M. H. Port.

Manchester
Suburbs

headed windows. Round-headed portal with a frieze of intersecting arches over. Very short chancel. Two galleries inside.

St Anne (R.C.), Carruthers Street. 1847–8 by *Weightman &
Hadfield*.

Corpus Christi (R.C.), Varley Street. 1906 by *Ernest Gernson*.
Large, of red brick, in the Italian Romanesque style. Broad
façade with an incomplete s w tower and an apsidal baptistery
projecting from it. The w portal has a tympanum with tracery
of no known shapes, of course not Italian Romanesque, but not
Northern either. The same is true of the large lunette window.
Interior with columns and ornamented block capitals. The
arches slightly horseshoe. Ceiling of the type of S. Zeno at
Verona. Tunnel-vaulted chancel and apse.

St George, Oldham Road. 1877 by *W. H. Lord*, replacing a
late c18 brick church. The spire added in 1880. Red brick. The
spire crowns a very high tower. A high clerestory too.

St John Evangelist, Oldham Road, Miles Platting. 1855 by
J. E. Gregan, completed after his death by *W. R. Corson*. The
land belonged to Sir Benjamin Heywood (*see* Swinton, p. 406),
and he paid for the church and also for a school, baths, and a
mechanics' institution. The church was notoriously ritualistic.
In style it is Italian Romanesque, and it has a n w campanile.
Red brick. Italian portal with a rose window above. Apse.

St Luke, Alburn Street, Miles Platting. 1875 by *J. M. & H.
Taylor*. At the time of writing in the middle of vast demolition.
But the church holds out, and the RECTORY, next door and
obviously contemporary, keeps its trimness too. Nave and
aisles, transepts with three-light end windows with plate
tracery, and apse with apsidal side chapels. Five-light clerestory of stepped lancet lights. On the w front a baptistery
projects in the middle, and on the l. of this is a thin turret.

St Mark, Holland Street, Miles Platting. 1884 by *Tate &
Popplewell*. Smallish, red brick, without a tower. Lancets and
plate tracery; apse. – E of the church is St Mark's House,
the former rectory, by *Mackmurdo & Hornblower*, 1892. A
plain square brick building, but with the coved top cornice
below the roof which became characteristic of Voysey. The
unusual thing is the tripartite ground-floor windows, with a
big bulgy frieze and an architrave rising into a semicircle in
the middle. The doorway on the N side is tripartite too, and on
this side there is only one window; it is above the doorway.

St Patrick (R.C.), Livesey Street. 1936 by *H. Greenhalgh*.
Large, Romanesque. With yellow marble columns and an apse.

ST PAUL, Oldham Road, New Cross. 1876–8 by *Sir George Gilbert Scott* and after his death continued by his son *John Oldrid Scott*. The church replaced St Paul, Turner Street, which was built in 1765. A strange building for the father as much as the son. High, with a short nave and SE steeple with, at the top, four gables and a flèche. Also the tracery is far from conventional – see e.g. the use of the Star of David in the W rose-window. Moreover, to link the church with the street, a very narrow S aisle is provided, running at an angle, but rising higher close to the S transept. Inside, the surprise is that the N aisle is perfectly normal and very wide – so wide indeed that it has two W windows. Why did the Scotts then not shift the axis of the nave to the N to allow for more normal aisles ?

ST PETER, Blossom Street. 1859–60 by *Isaac Holden & Son*. Red and yellow brick. Romanesque in style. Nave and aisles and apse. Big NW campanile with a concave-sided roof. The interior (DB) has five lofty bays with thin cast-iron columns and semicircular brick arches. Superb roof; segmental plaster vault with slight coffers divided into bays by four elegant cast-iron trusses with enriched spandrels. The BENCH ENDS are in cast iron too. The PULPIT may be older than the church.

ST PHILIP, Ridgway Street. 1850 by *E. H. Shellard*.

BUTLER STREET METHODIST CHURCH. By *J. C. Prestwich & Sons* of Leigh. Consecrated in 1964.

CONGREGATIONAL CHURCH, Oldham Road. Brick, Romanesque, with three arches into a narthex.

SWEDENBORGIAN CHURCH (former), No. 20 Every Street. A perfectly harmless Georgian three-bay brick house with a pretty doorway, but behind it the rotunda of the church, with round-arched windows. It was built in 1823.

BRANCH LIBRARY, Every Street. 1866 by *Waterhouse*, and worthy of his name. Just two bays with a hipped roof, but the two large front windows (and one round the corner) have three stepped lights under one pointed arch and are crossed instead of a transom by a broad inscription bar, saying in the front Manchester Free Library Ancoats Branch.

ANCOATS HOSPITAL, formerly Dispensary, Mill Street. By *Lewis & Crowcroft*, 1873. Gothic, symmetrical, with a tower with saddleback roof. Brick with black brick and stone trim. There are projections and recessions and dormers – all a little crowded.

GIRLS' INSTITUTE, Mill Street. By *Alfred Darbyshire*, 1890–2. Brick. Nice, and quite delicately done. In a kind of modest

Italianate. The main windows are on the top floor. They are of the cross type.

VICTORIA SQUARE, Oldham Road. A vast slum replacement of 1889. The Corporation, moved by public complaints about the sanitary conditions round Oldham Road and Portland Street, sponsored a competition, and this was won by *Spalding & Cross*. The result is a vast five-storeyed block with an inner courtyard or square round which balconies run on four levels. The iron railings show at once that the architects wanted to do more than the strictly necessary without at all going elaborate. The eighteen-bay front to Oldham Road has indeed good brickwork, a middle gable with some terracotta and Dutch side-gables. The sides of the block are stock brick with large segment-headed windows in pairs alternating with small round windows in pairs.

(In CANNEL STREET is the famous FAIRBAIRN FOUNDRY. According to the NMR it has a date 1832.)

BUTLER STREET and GUNTON STREET DEVELOPMENT. A large area is being developed. Work started in 1965, and the architectural standard is higher than in most of the other recent Manchester housing. The City Housing Director *J. Austen Bent* is in charge. There are five thirteen-storey blocks and three four-storeyed terraces of maisonettes.

ARDWICK

The boundary is on the N side (not including) Fairfield Street and Ashton Old Road, on the E side (not including) Pottery Lane, on the W and S sides (including) London Road, Downing Street, Ardwick Green South, Stockport Road, Devonshire Street, Hyde Road, Bennett Street, Vaughan Street, and Gorton Road. Ardwick in 1830 was described as 'a fashionable residential quarter for Manchester merchants' (so Mr Fleetwood-Hesketh reports). It certainly is not that now.

ST ALOYSIUS (R.C.), Park Place. 1884–5 by *Healey*. Brick, with a SW steeple.

ST BENEDICT, Bennett Street. 1880 by *J. S. Crowther*. A remarkably large church, done with panache. The costs were met by John Marsland Bennett, a timber-merchant. Brick and E.E. in style, except for the excessively high NW tower with pyramid roof and pinnacles. The nave has a large rose-window above big blank arcading. Inside, brick is exposed. Only the quatrefoi piers are stone. Five-bay nave, four-light windows, very high chancel arch, and very rich seven-light E window.

ST MATTHEW, Hyde Road and Devonshire Street. 1866–8 by *J. M. Taylor.*

ST STEPHEN, Milton Street. 1853–4 by *E. H. Shellard,* the chancel 1862 by *John Lowe.* Sizeable, with a NW steeple and tracery of *c.*1300.

ST THOMAS, Ardwick Green North. Built in 1741 on a small scale, widened in 1777, lengthened by two bays to the E in 1831, and provided with its W tower in 1836. The tower is the one really remarkable feature of the church; for it is of the Italian campanile type, and that would not be expected before the 1840s. The architect was *Hayley.* Otherwise the church is true to type. Brick, with an absolutely plain, flat side to the Green. Two tiers of arched windows with Y-casements. The interior has its three galleries and flat, deeply coffered ceiling. – PAINTING. Adoration of the Shepherds; Flemish C17; good.

(ARMITAGE PRIMARY SCHOOL, Rostron Street. By *S. G. Besant Roberts,* the City Architect, 1966–7. Built in the CLASP system for 310 children.)

NICHOLLS HOSPITAL, Hyde Road. 1879 by *Thomas Worthington.* Brick, of eleven bays, symmetrical, with a tower with very steep saddleback roof, four tourelles, and a two-storey oriel. Cross-windows and dormers.

TERRITORIAL ARMY OFFICES, Ardwick Green. 1886 by *Laurence Booth.* Symmetrical, stone, Norman details.

ARDWICK GREEN is a shadow of its pleasant former self. Not an old house remains on the S side, and a total of about half a dozen on the N. And as for HIGHER ARDWICK, the MHLG listed in 1947–8 and graded as II seventeen houses. There are three left. The lodges and mortuary chapel of the Ardwick Cemetery also were Grade II, and yet they also have disappeared.

BAGULEY HALL *see* WYTHENSHAWE

BARLOW HALL *see* CHORLTON-CUM-HARDY

BESWICK AND BRADFORD

The boundary is on the N side the railway from Clayton Street to Ashton New Road, on the E side Clayton Street, Clayton Lane, and Clayton Lane South, on the S side (including) Ashton Old

Road and Pottery Lane, on the w side Pin Mill Brow and Palmerston Street.

ST BRIGID (R.C.), Mill Street. 1878–9. Stock brick and red brick, with a short NW tower with pyramid roof. Long round-headed windows. The W front promises aisles, but there are none, and the interior with its open roof and its chancel arch and two chapel arches l. and r. of the chancel arch looks 1830 rather than 1880.

ST JEROME, Barlen Street. 1913 by *E. Lingen Barker*.

ST PAUL, Philips Park. 1908 by *E. Lingen Barker*.

PHILIPS PARK CEMETERY. Opened in 1866. The chapels and gates with lodge are by *Paull & Ayliffe*, typical of cemetery architecture in that they all differ in composition from each other as much as could be done.

ABATTOIR. The new Manchester Abattoir is N of the cemetery, a vast enterprise ingeniously planned and equipped. By the City Architect *S. G. Besant Roberts*'s Department.

PHILIPS PARK was made in 1846 out of the grounds of the former Bradford Hall.

On the future housing round WELLINGTON STREET *see* p. 272n.

BLACKLEY *see* COLLYHURST

BRADFORD *see* BESWICK

BURNAGE

The boundary is on the N side Kingswood Road and Burnage Hall Road and a straight line to the NE corner of Cringle Fields Park, on the E side the Manchester boundary, on the S side (not including) Parrswood Lane, on the w side Parrswood Road South, Parrswood Road, Parrswood Road North, and Ladybarn Lane.

ST MARGARET, Burnage Lane. 1874–5 by *Paley & Austin*, but not worthy of special notice. Red sandstone, with only a bell-cote. Tracery of *c.*1300 treated fairly freely.

ST NICHOLAS, Kingsway, by Burnage Station. 1931–2 by *Welch, Cachemaille Day & Lander*. A milestone in the history of modern church architecture in England. Of brick, high and square, with a German-inspired passion for raised brick stripes, vertical (near the top) and horizontal. High apse to the street, as high as the rest of the church. Slender, long windows in the chancel, tight between buttresses. To the S another apse holding the font. White walls inside and a flat ceiling. Very low aisle passages. The altar is not in the apse, but further w. It is flanked by two staircases which lead up to the apse at a higher level, and it is here that the Lady Chapel is placed. The altar wall is brick-faced, and PULPIT and LECTERN are simple cubes of brick. – The other FITMENTS, especially the font cover, are of the modernistic-kind of the Stockholm City Hall and the Paris Exhibition of 1925. The w bay was added in 1964.

BURNAGE GARDEN VILLAGE was begun in 1906 to the designs of *J. Horner Hargreaves.** The original part is that N of Mauldeth Road and between Kingsway and Burnage Lane. It consisted of 136 houses and dates from 1907–10. Now it has become part of a much larger layout of Wythenshawe type.

CHEETHAM *see* STRANGEWAYS

CHORLTON-CUM-HARDY

The boundary is on the N side (including) Wilbraham Road, on the E side (including) Princess Road, on the s side the river Mersey, on the w side the Manchester boundary and s along Egerton Road North to Wilbraham Road.

Chorlton-cum-Hardy still has its village centre, CHORLTON GREEN, but how dismal it has been allowed to become. Just trees along the border of what was once grass, and just the arched GATEWAY with a timber-framed turret to the church-yard and the former church of St CLEMENT, built in 1779. Not a stone remains of this now. It was demolished in 1949. And as for the mansion which lay ¾ m. E, in MAULDETH ROAD, i.e. HOUGH END HALL, the Corporation has not done anything to preserve it. Yet it is, or was, the best, the only major, Elizabethan mansion of Manchester, red brick, on an E-plan, with mullioned and transomed windows and gables. It is an act of unpardonable callousness. At the time of writing the roof is open to the skies, and the porch has collapsed. The staircase has been taken to Tatton Lodge.

Another C16 to C17 house, BARLOW HALL, in Barlow Hall Road, is a golf club house and well looked after, but alas very little of original work has survived. The great hall was in the w range and was burnt in 1879, but the original NW bay window belonged to it. This is timber-framed, and there is also some old timber-framing in the N range. In the N range also is the former porch with gable and some timber decoration. A sundial

* Information supplied by Miss Margaret Tims.

has the date 1574. An interesting point is the existence of corridors along the ranges towards the quadrangle (cf. Smithills Hall, Bolton, p. 89).

ST AMBROSE (R.C.), Princess Road. 1958 by *Reynolds & Scott*

CHRIST CHURCH, Barlow Moor Road. 1881–2 by *H. Littler*, the gift of Mr Roberts, a brewer. Large, in the style of *c.*1300.

ST CLEMENT, St Clement's Road. 1861–6 by *Pennington & Brigden*. S transept and chapel by *W. Higginbottom*, 1895.

ST JOHN (R.C.), High Lane. Opened in 1927. Red brick and yellow terracotta. Dec and Perp tracery. No tower. The interior wide and aisleless with three parallel E chapels, an early rather than a late C19 *parti*.

ST WERBURGH, Wilbraham Road. 1899–1902 by *R. B. Preston*. Stock brick and red terracotta, the W view with three parallel gables; flèche.

MACLAREN MEMORIAL BAPTIST CHURCH, Wilbraham Road. 1906 by *William Waddington & Son*. Large, of red brick and yellow terracotta, with a big octagonal NW tower carrying a short spire. Free, very simple tracery in round arches.

METHODIST CHURCH, Manchester Road. 1873 by *H. J. Paull*. With a SE turret and geometrical tracery.

(RIVERSIDE SCHOOL, Barlow Hall Road. 1963–5 by *S. G. Besant Roberts*, the City Architect. For 120 children. Load-bearing brick walls.)

(CHORLTON PARK SECONDARY SCHOOL, Mauldeth Road West. The extensions of 1957–9 are by *L. C. Howitt*, the then City Architect. Load-bearing brick walls.)

CHORLTON-ON-MEDLOCK

The boundary is on the N side the centre, on the E side (not including) London Road, Downing Street, Ardwick Green South, Stockport Road, on the S side (not including) Moss Lane East, on the W side (including) Cambridge Street, Lower Cambridge Street, Higher Cambridge Street, Lloyd Street North.

CHURCHES

ST AMBROSE, Higher Chetham Street. 1884 by *H. C. Charlewood*. To be demolished.

(ST AUGUSTINE (R.C.), Grosvenor Square. By *Desmond Williams & Associates*. Under construction in 1967.)

CHRIST CHURCH, Lloyd Street. 1899–1904 by *W. Cecil Hardisty* on the site of an C18 proprietary chapel.* Red brick, with the bellcote sitting roguishly on one shank of the gable. Perp tracery with over-much cusping.

HOLY NAME OF JESUS (R.C.), Oxford Road. 1869–71 by *Joseph Aloysius Hansom*, and his finest or one of his two finest churches (after or side by side with Arundel). His design had a steeple 240 ft high. The present octagonal top part of the tower is by *Adrian Gilbert Scott* and was completed in 1928. It could not be better suited for its task. Hansom's tower is much broader than it is deep. The façade is deliberately not identical to the l. and r. of the tower. The sides of the church have flying butt-resses, and along the S side low outer chapels are expressed by small gables and small windows. The E end consists of transepts, a short chancel, and a high polygonal apse with a narrow ambulatory and cross gables. Two E turrets rise where the chancel sets in. The interior is overwhelming in airiness, 77 because all the piers are extremely slim so that space can flow freely. The nave has four bays, the transepts are entered by a high arch continuing the nave arcade. The chancel is very high too, but as its width equals that of the nave only by adding to it the ambulatory entrances, Hansom had the original idea of connecting the transept and the chancel arches by an arch struck diagonally, an arch yet higher than the transept arches. It is a little like what Wren had done in classical terms at St Paul's. E of either transept is a pair of chapels. They are rib-vaulted, and indeed the whole church is rib-vaulted. Hansom achieved this by the ingenious device of using polygonal terra-cotta blocks instead of stone, thus lightening the weight con-siderably. Terracotta is also used as a facing material, in some places ornamented. Of individual motifs it may be said that the chancel and apse piers are of the French type of Chartres, Reims, and Amiens, and that Hansom favoured rose-windows and windows of the so-called spherical triangle shape. The low S chapels are spatially unnoticeable because behind stone screens. – REREDOS. 1890 by *J. S. Hansom*.

Behind the church to the N is the CHURCH HALL, a crisp brick job by *Edmund Kirby*, 1892. – The new CHAPLAINCY in Oxford Road by *Mather & Nutter* is a rather mannered design with a saw-tooth roof.

ST JOSEPH (R.C.), Plymouth Grove. By *Lowther & Rigby*, 1914–15. Red brick, with a NW tower with pyramid roof,

* So Mr Buttress informs me.

fancy tracery, and Art Nouveau mouldings round the doors. The arcade piers are elongated, chamfered lozenges, and the depressed pointed arches die into them. Very high clerestory.

ST PAUL, Brunswick Street. 1862–3 by *Clegg & Knowles*.

CONGREGATIONAL CHURCH, Cavendish Street. 1847–8 by *Walters*. Henry-Russell Hitchcock says: 'Perhaps the first dissenting church to appear like a contemporary Anglican church', though – he adds – it lacks of course a chancel. In this church appearance lies the importance of the building, but it is dignified and substantial as well: E.E. with a SW steeple. The interior has four-bay arcades with quatrefoil piers and taller arches to the transepts. Thin open timber roofs. – Steeply banked GALLERIES, with arcaded fronts, look down on to a richly furnished PULPIT group, all in a convincing E.E. An elegant matching ORGAN CASE sits over the choir loft on top of a fine, pulpitum-like SCREEN with two entrances l. and r. giving into the low eastern vestries beyond the apse, where one would expect the chancel in a fully developed church (DB).

PLYMOUTH GROVE METHODIST CHURCH. Dec, with a NW tower.

PRESBYTERIAN CHURCH (former), Grosvenor Square. 1849–50 by *Starkey & Cuffley*. A very fine façade, the two end bays with giant pilasters and banded rustication, the centre recessed behind two giant Corinthian columns. The centre has a pediment, and l. and r. there are two short recessed towers, quite Baroque in outline and detail.

WELSH CHAPEL, Upper Brook Street. 1837–9 by *Barry*, and much less accomplished than his contemporary secular work. Lancets separated by buttresses along the sides in the accepted Commissioners' fashion. E rose-window. Only the W side with a giant niche with much shafting is more personal. The interior has a pointed plaster ceiling divided into six compartments by bold ribs. The arrangement with three moulded arches opening into the westernmost bay, similarly vaulted, is extremely elegant. Three galleries; the lancet windows begin at gallery level. A simple ORGAN CASE (extended sideways) dominates an impressive PULPIT and platform on the east wall (DB). This is said to be the first Gothic Nonconformist chapel.

WESLEYAN CHAPEL (former), Grosvenor Street. 1820. Red brick with a flat roof and battlements. Pointed windows in two tiers. Five-bay façade with lower one-bay appendages.

PUBLIC BUILDINGS

Chorlton is the see of the majority of the ACADEMIC INSTITU-
TIONS of Manchester: the University, the Institute of Science
and Technology, the Municipal College of Technology, and the
College of Art. Each of them has so far developed in its own way,
and there are few places where one feels that one's movements
are directed by a plan. Recently *Sir Hugh Wilson* and *Lewis
Womersley* have been working on a grand design to connect the
premises of the four institutions and create one campus, more or
less on the scale of Berkeley. May something come of this.

THE UNIVERSITY. The university started as Owens College in
1851 under the will of John Owens. It was reorganized in 1870
and moved to the present site in 1873. It became the first college
of the new Victoria University in 1880, with Liverpool joining
in 1884 and Leeds in 1887. In 1903 it became a separate university.

Waterhouse was appointed architect in 1869. Building began
in 1870, and the plan of the whole quad was, though different
from today in many ways, exhibited at the Royal Academy in
1872. The first building is the w range, quite low and intimate
in scale. It is symmetrical in its centre, but the wings differ.
The outline with projections and recessions and the skyline
are nicely varied. Then Waterhouse moved on to the E range
along Oxford Road, and this was built in 1883–7. Now this
was building for a new university, and so everything had to be
grand. Waterhouse was equal to the challenge. The façade is
asymmetrical, with a high tower crowned with one of Waterhouse's steep pyramid roofs. There is a bay window to its r.
with geometrical tracery, housing the staircase, the archway
into the quad on the l. To the r. of the bay all is firmly utilitarian,
with tripartite windows of no period character whatever. To
the l. is the Whitworth Hall, added later and completed by
Paul Waterhouse in 1902. It has high Perp windows. Waterhouse
had never sold himself to any one brand of Gothic. The hall
ends with a porch and a tower to the s. You enter, and at once
find yourself in vaulted spaces of E.E. character, much as in
the town hall. The staircase is fascinating, with its glimpses
into subsidiary upper caged-in staircases. The Whitworth Hall
is six bays long and has a mighty hammerbeam roof and a six-
light end window.

The quad was completed in 1888, when *Waterhouse* built the

N range (Zoology) and the N half of the E range, the latter fo
the MANCHESTER MUSEUM. This was extended northward i
1912 by *Paul Waterhouse* and again in 1927. The extension
are Gothic too. The S range of the quad, the CHRISTI
LIBRARY, is by *Alfred Waterhouse* and dates from 1897–8.

Other early buildings are as follows: the yellow brick Chem
istry and Medical Schools to the W of the quad, begun in 187
(ROSCOE LABORATORIES) and continued in 1895 (SCHOR
LEMER LABORATORIES), in 1904 (PERKINS and SCHUNC
LABORATORIES), and in 1908 (MORLEY LABORATORIES)
To the N of the Museum and along Bridgeford Street is th
pretty METALLURGY BUILDING by *Charles Heathcote & Son*
of 1908, brick with much stone, of five bays only, Edwardia
Baroque, and a semicircular half-domed porch, and N of Coup
land Street, behind the Museum (whose back incidentally i
very different from its front: brick with a charming flèche
the former PHYSICS DEPARTMENT of 1900 (SCHUSTE
BUILDING), red brick, with transomed windows and gables
then the WHITWORTH LABORATORY, 1909 by *J. W. Beau
mont*, red brick, with two orders of pilasters, and the TURNE
DENTAL SCHOOL, built in 1939–40 (by *Sir Hubert Worthing
ton*) and quite featureless. It was completed by a fourth rang
in 1951–2.

So to the development of the university in the last fifty year
Architecturally it is a sad record. If the University of Liverpoo
has asked too many architects to design their buildings and th
result is lack of unity, the University of Manchester has show
too little initiative, too easy a sense of satisfaction, and the resul
is lack of architectural interest. Denys Lasdun's building fo
Liverpool may be an outrage, but Manchester University ha
too much that is just run-of-the-mill. This is the justificatio
for the following perambulation giving for many buildings n
more than architect and date.

The university area goes from Cambridge Street on the
to Upper Brook Street on the E. Oxford Road bisects the pre
cinct, which is therefore not a precinct. Roughly speaking,
the W are the Arts, to the E the Sciences. We have already looke
at the W part N of Burlington Street. S of Burlington Street wa
the first major extension; towards Oxford Road the UNIO
1953–6 by *J. S. Beaumont*, stone-faced and stodgy, behind i
facing N the FACULTY OF ARTS, red brick, symmetrical, wit
a classical stone portico, 1911–19 by *Percy Worthington*, an
to the W of this the ARTS LIBRARY, 1935–7 by *Sir Hube*

Worthington, symmetrical again, and stone below and brick above. The area s to Spa Street has moreover a concrete extension to the Arts Faculty by *H. S. Fairhurst & Son*, 1957–8, and in its NE corner the group of REFECTORY, MOBBERLY TOWER (a hall of residence), and STAFF HOUSE by *J. S. Beaumont*, 1960–5, deplorably unsubstantial next to Waterhouse.

s of Spa Street is the HUMANITIES BUILDING, 1961–7 by the *Building Design Partnership*, at last a building of some power. It is of brown concrete bush-hammered, with the verticals of the frame projecting in front of the wall. Low l. addition with one of the abstract concrete reliefs which are so much overdone at present. A pretty inner court between the high and the low part. What is so far built is only Phase One. In an angle of this building is the UNIVERSITY THEATRE, also by the *Building Design Partnership*, and also a convincing job, windowless, except for the foyers.

To the w of this group is the JOINT EXAMINATION BOARD, not strictly a building put up by the University of Manchester. It is by *Playne & Lacey*, lower than its neighbour, octagonal, and with a pointed roof ending in a nice lantern. Altogether it is a more intimate building, as befits its function. The octagonal shape was first suggested by the course of the future s ring road, but it suited the fact that the core of the building had to be one large packing room for examination papers. The middle pier of the octagonal room carries the flue.

Now E of Oxford Road. It is there that one gets weary of so many big buildings of so little character. We start at the N end with the most interesting: *Scherrer & Hicks*'s MATHEMATICS BUILDING, 1967–8. This is concrete-framed, the lower part with brick facing. The tower is assertively composed of free cubic shapes stepping vertically and horizontally. Then follows a group designed round a monumental W–E axis (Brunswick Street) which Worthington had proposed. On the N the WILLIAMSON BUILDING, on the s the SIMON ENGINEERING LABORATORIES, both by *H. S. Fairhurst & Son*, 1957–66, and then on the s ELECTRICAL ENGINEERING by *J. S. Beaumont*, 1953, frankly neo-Georgian at this late hour, but on the N a breath of fresh air, the ROSCOE BUILDING, chiefly of lecture theatres, by *Cruickshank & Seward*, 1964, concrete with a six-floor glass façade, not a building of great individuality but easily the best in the area. The E end is two big buildings by *H. S. Fairhurst & Son*, PHYSICS and CHEMISTRY, with much brick.

s of Dover Street is the former HIGH SCHOOL FOR GIRLS, red brick by *Mills & Murgatroyd*, 1881–6, and next to it the new SOCIAL SCIENCE AND ECONOMICS BUILDING by *Cruickshank & Seward*, 1966–7, concrete, with the windows boxed out in canted surrounds.

INSTITUTE OF SCIENCE AND TECHNOLOGY. This is part of the university, but an autonomous body dealing direct with the University Grants Committee. It started as a municipal college, but its successor as such is the John Dalton College (*see* below). The precinct of the Institute is cut by the railway, and the old buildings face on Whitworth Street. They are therefore in this volume treated as part of the centre of Manchester (p. 285), although one walks no longer than two minutes from them to the new buildings. The centre of the new area is the JACKSON STREET MILL, a utilitarian brick building converted well by *H. S. Fairhurst & Son*. Of new buildings the following deserve notice: the RENOLD BUILDING by *Cruickshank & Seward*, a building of lecture theatres with one for 500, two for 300, six for 160, and twelve smaller ones. It is a perfectly reasonable, sensibly planned building, but why must it have this horizontally folded wall to the E? The same kind of objection arises to the same architects' (in charge *W. A. Gibbon*) STUDENTS' UNION with the WRIGHT ROBINSON HALL, a tower of residence. The vertically stabbing erections and the funnel giving skylight to the staircase have no sufficient *raison d'être*. CHANDOS HALL, across the railway but s of the old buildings, is again by the same architects (in charge *W. A. Gibbon*) and has ribbed concrete walls. It is for 160 students, and each floor has nine single and two double rooms and a common room with kitchen. Along one side rises a glass staircase tower. The windows of the rooms are units, not parts of bands, and they are not over-large. s of the Union and the Renold Building is a turfed precinct reached by a handsome flying staircase descending in two arms. The large CIVIL ENGINEERING BUILDING is by *H. S. Fairhurst & Son*. E of the old mill is the CHEMICAL ENGINEERING PILOT PLANT by *Fairhurst*, engineering brick s, glass N. s of this MATHEMATICS AND SOCIAL SCIENCES, by *Cruickshank & Seward*, 1966–8, a tower block, and E of that CHEMISTRY by the same architects, concrete and quite extensive, with a high slab, a bridge across Sackville Street, and a four-storeyed part. The irregular abstract patterning of large concrete surfaces helps rarely.

JOHN DALTON COLLEGE OF TECHNOLOGY, Oxford Street. By *S. G. Besant Roberts*, 1961–4, a sensible job with the low so-called communal facilities (offices, common rooms, refectory, library) to the E of a high block and the low workshops with an attractive roof-line to the w. The bronze STATUE of John Dalton (seated) is by *W. Theed Jun.*, 1854.

REGIONAL COLLEGE OF ART, Cavendish Street, really in Grosvenor Square. The original building is of 1880–1, by *G. Tunstall Redmayne*, and a remarkable building it is. It is Gothic and symmetrical, with a central entrance, but take the period details away and you have Mackintosh's Glasgow School of Art of 1898, i.e. an ornate treatment of the centre, but otherwise all frankly large studio windows. At the back is an excellent extension of red brick, dated 1897. It is by *J. Gibbens Sankey* and has three plain gables and one tier of E.E. two-light windows with angels in the tympana. A bridge of unexpected geometrical shapes connects this building diagonally with a new nine-storeyed block by the City Architect's Department (*S. G. Besant Roberts*), straightforward bands of glass and white mosaic and a lower part to the w, well composed.

The former Chorlton TOWN HALL, also facing Grosvenor Square, is now part of the college. It is by *Richard Lane*, 1830–1, nine bays wide, with a severely Greek Doric portico and pediment. Wreaths in the frieze.*

(COLLEGE OF MUSIC, Oxford Road and Booth Street West. By *Bickerdike, Allen, Rich & Partners*. To be begun in 1968. A concrete rectangle, only two storeys high. Auditoria, offices, etc., below, practice rooms above. The model looks promising.)

TOWN HALL (former) *see* Regional College of Art, above.

ROYAL INFIRMARY, Oxford Road. 1905–8 by *E. T. Hall* and *John Brooke*. Vast and in the Greenwich Baroque. Brick and much stone. Monumental centre with a stone cupola, two prominent towers further out.‡ Upper giant columns and pilasters.

ROYAL EYE HOSPITAL, Oxford Road. 1886 by *Pennington & Brigden*. Symmetrical, brick, in the style popularized by Norman Shaw a decade or so before.

ST MARY'S HOSPITAL, Oxford Road. 1909 by *John Ely*. Red

---

* Mr Buttress tells me that behind the former town hall is a splendid pilastered mid-c19 hall with a coved plaster ceiling.

‡ The building was symmetrical, but one part of it was bombed in the Second World War.

brick and red terracotta, symmetrical and mildly Edwardian.
Behind is a new concrete extension by *Watkins Grey Associates*.

WHITWORTH GALLERY, Whitworth Park. The park was
opened in 1890, and in it is a STATUE of Edward VII by *J.
Cassidy*, 1911–13. The gallery building was won in competition
by *J. W. Beaumont* in 1895. Waterhouse was the assessor, and
that explains the building nearly completely. All red terracotta.
Symmetrical, with two low towers, cross-windows, and polygonal buttresses on the angle parts. Semicircular columned
entrance porch.

VICTORIA BATHS, Hathersage Road. 1905–6. A rich façade, red
brick and yellow terracotta, symmetrical, with steep gables and
a clock cupola.

PERAMBULATION

Instead of a perambulation only a few indications need be given.
Chorlton New Town was laid out in 1793–4, but the Napoleonic
wars prevented development. What survives of terrace houses
looks mostly early c19 to the 1830s – but how little survives!
Whole areas in the N of the district are laid waste, and the big
and greedy institutions will eat it all up. May the result look as
happy as the streets of Georgian terraces did.

In Oxford Road Georgian housing can be followed: Nos 88–100,
and still Nos 323–9 and the handsome STUDENTS' HEALTH
CENTRE, a detached house with three pretty doorways.

Parallel with Oxford Road to the E is UPPER BROOK STREET
with bits such as Nos 48 (with a semicircular porch) and 54,
and s of Lorne Street an Early Victorian stuccoed pair. RUS-
HOLME STREET crosses Upper Brook Street further N. The
houses of interest are Nos 96–116. It is doubtful, however, how
far this listing serves any purpose; for this whole area is one of
projected comprehensive development.

The centre of Georgian Chorlton was GROSVENOR SQUARE. On
it stood ALL SAINTS, built in 1820 and bombed and demolished. The town hall has been described (p. 313). One house
only remains to look out for: the EAR HOSPITAL, three bays,
the doorway with Tuscan columns and a pedimented window
over. In GROSVENOR STREET No. 98 has a Georgian doorway.
Then, now w of Oxford Road, in LLOYD STREET occasional
houses up to about No. 100, i.e. nearly to Denmark Street.*

* One more specially attractive survival must be picked out: No. 84
PLYMOUTH GROVE, three bays, stucco, giant pilasters, and a closed-in
porch, the capitals with egyptianizing detail.

CLAYTON *see* OPENSHAW

COLLYHURST, HARPURHEY, BLACKLEY, AND CRUMPSALL

The boundary is on the N side the Manchester boundary, on the E side (excluding) Moston Lane and (including) Ashley Lane, Norman Road, Church Lane, and Thorp Road to the railway, on the S side the railway to Cheetham Hill Road, on the W side the river Irk and (excluding) Smedley Road, Woodlands Road, Greenhill Road, Crescent Road.

ALBERT MEMORIAL CHURCH, Queens Road, Collyhurst. 1864 by *John Lowe*. Red brick with some polychromy in the arches. NW tower with a blunt spire. Two cross gables on the N side by the E end. Geometrical tracery. Gaunt, barn-like interior with open timber roof (DB).

ST ANDREW, Crab Lane, Blackley. 1864–5 by *J. Medland Taylor*. On a hill and in Crab Lane still accompanied by villagey cottages.

ST ANNE (R.C.), Crescent Road, Crumpsall. By *Greenhalgh & Williams* of Bolton, 1957.

CHRIST CHURCH, Church Lane, Harpurhey. 1838–41 by *Edward Welch*. Still of the Commissioners' type and uncouth in the handling. W tower with spire and big pinnacles. The bell-openings are a stepped triplet of lancets. So are the side windows of the church, placed between close-set buttresses. Aisleless interior with three galleries. Open roof with heavy tracery.

w of the church is YORK PLACE, a minor terrace of about 1840–5.

ST CLARE (R.C.), Victoria Avenue, Blackley. By *Weightman & Bullen*, completed in 1958.

ST EDMUND (R.C.), Monsall Street, Collyhurst. 1894 by *P. P. Pugin*.

ST JAMES, Teignmouth Street, Collyhurst. 1874 by *Lowe*. Large, with a SW steeple balanced by a NW porch, and a polygonal apse. Geometrical tracery.

ST JOHN, Ashley Lane, Harpurhey. 1908 by *R. B. Preston*. Pale grey brick with a bellcote at the NW corner of the nave facing N.

ST MARY, St Mary's Road, Crumpsall. 1875 by *Crowther*. The tower is earlier (by *Travis & Mangnall*). Large, with a high W tower with broach spire. Geometrical tracery. Five-bay arcades, quatrefoil piers, but brick facing above. High chancel arch, two-light chapel openings with a sexfoil in a circle in the tympanum and angels to the l. and r. of the circle. Five-light E window. Blank arcading in the chancel.

ST MATTHEW, Delaunays Road, Crumpsall. 1908–10 by *Isaac Taylor*. A large church with a NW tower. Conventional Gothic, but with some early C20 touches, e.g. piers without normal capitals and arches with one broad hollow chamfer. The chancel has short diagonal side walls with one-light windows. The interior is brick-faced.

ST OSWALD, Rochdale Road, Collyhurst. Derelict at the time of writing. 1855 by *Shellard*, the NE steeple by *Lowe*. Insignificant nave, but a spectacularly picturesque E end towards the road, with the group of E gables and the steeple. The style is late C13.

OUR LADY OF MOUNT CARMEL (R.C.), Old Road, Blackley. 1908. Red brick, Perp, with NE turret.

ST PAUL, Victoria Avenue, Blackley. Incomplete, elementarized neo-Georgian. By *Taylor & Young*, 1933. Mr Anson says: 'The architects let themselves go on the furniture.'

ST PETER, Old Market Street, Blackley. The village centre was here. A Commissioners' church (£3,162). 1844 by *E. H. Shellard*, and still pre-Puginist. W tower with E.E. bell-openings, the sides with twin lancets and buttresses. Short chancel. Aisled interior, quatrefoil piers, three galleries, and Gothic BOX PEWS.

ST THOMAS, Hazelbottom Road, Crumpsall. 1863 by *G. & J. R. Shaw*.

HOLY TRINITY, Cobden Street, Harpurhey. By *Basil Champneys*, 1908, and a tired interior, in spite of the bold motif of transverse pointed stone arches. Dull, low aisle passages. But the exterior has life. Red brick, with big buttresses. The W buttresses are particularly aggressive. A SW tower has never been built. The windows on the sides are set in broad blank arches. E bellcote.

CHEETHAM HILL METHODIST CHURCH, Bury Old Road, Crumpsall. 1894–6 by *W. Waddington & Son*. An oddly detailed building. For example the staircase in the SW steeple projects into a domestic-looking canted bay and the baptistery projects triangularly from the middle of the W front. Interior very wide with aisle passages and galleried transepts. Fancy Dec tracery.

CRUMPSALL METHODIST CHURCH, Oak Road. 1909 by *A. E. Lambert* of Nottingham. Red brick and yellow terracotta. Large, with a SW steeple and a flèche. Typically free Dec details.

HARPURHEY METHODIST CHURCH, Rochdale Road. 1884. Brick, sumptuously Italianate, with a NW tower carrying a domed cap.

UNION CHAPEL, Queen's Park, Collyhurst. 1855 by *R. Moffat Smith*. Weird details, especially the low NW tower with higher stair-turret.

BLACKLEY CREMATORIUM. 1959 by *L. C. Howitt*, the Corporation Architect. The crematorium has a long, convex, symmetrical façade, the centre with closely set mullions and two transoms high up. In it are three chapels. Opposite is the dodecagon of the Chapel of Remembrance with its concrete framing exposed and ending gallows-wise above the roof.

HARPURHEY CEMETERY. *See* p. 269n.

SPRINGFIELD HOSPITAL, Crumpsall. The SE part is the former Manchester Union Workhouse and as such recognizable. It is of 1854–5, by *Mills & Murgatroyd*. At the N end of the whole extensive group is DELAUNAY'S HOSPITAL, and this was the Prestwich Union Workhouse. The date of this is 1869. The long building between with its spurs to both sides was built as the Manchester Union Infirmary *c.*1863.

WOODLANDS, Crescent Road. A handsome brick five-bay country house, of *c.*1800, still entirely on its own. The shallow porch with Adamish columns and the window above it are set in a blank giant arch. Three-bay pediment.

QUEEN'S PARK MUSEUM, Harpurhey. 1883–4 by *J. Allison*, the City Surveyor. Red brick with a gabled porch and otherwise just an even series of ground-floor windows and no upper windows at all. The upper rooms have sky-lighting.

BLACKLEY LIBRARY, Rochdale Road and Tudor Avenue. Built in 1900–1 and designed by *J. Gibbons*. Red brick and yellow terracotta, quite a gay little building.

Round TURKEY LANE in Harpurhey is one of the areas for which the *Manchester Housing Development Group* has made comprehensive plans (*see* p. 272). They are certainly bold, but, if one can rely on illustrations before the event, they look rather frightening, with the long snaking line and the snaking-off branches, all with angular details and six storeys high.

CRUMPSALL *see* COLLYHURST

DIDSBURY AND WITHINGTON

The boundary is on the N side (including) Wilbraham Road to Yew Tree Road and (not including) Wilbraham Road E of Yew

Tree Road and then Moseley Road, on the E side (not including
Ladyburn Lane, Parrswood Road North, Parrswood Road, an
Parrswood Road South, on the S side the river Mersey, and on th
W side (not including) Princess Road.

St BERNADETTE (R.C.), Princess Road, Withington. By A
Walmsley of *Greenhalgh & Williams*, 1960–3.
St CATHERINE OF SIENA (R.C.), School Lane, Didsbur
1928–9 by *Arthur Fairbrother & Partner*.
St CHAD, Mauldeth Road, Withington. 1907 by *W. C. Hardist*
St CHRISTOPHER, Minehead Avenue, Withington. In th
middle of a housing estate. 1935 by *B. A. Miller*. Brick. *
square W tower in the middle and l. and r. of it, symmetricall
arranged, three slim windows. Their stepping-forward tops ar
typical of the Östberg and Paris-1925 moment. The plan is nc
what one would expect. As you enter, the altar space is nc
facing you. The apse holds the baptistery instead, and th
altar is at the l. end, the nave filling the r. part – a disturbin
change of direction. Low passages instead of aisles run alon
l. and r. of nave and chancel. – REREDOS. By *Mary Adshea*
with large Crucifixus and many small scenes.
St CUTHBERT (R.C.), Palatine Road, Withington. 1880–1,
completed 1902 by *W. T. Gunson*.
EMMANUEL, Barlow Moor Road, Didsbury. 1858 by *Starkey &
Cuffley*. Thin W tower, the upper parts polygonal. No aisle
but a S transept – still in the tradition of 1840. Arcade of roun
piers. The geometrical tracery of the windows is probably a
alteration of 1872. – STAINED GLASS. The transept S windov
79 is a gorgeous piece of *William Morris* glass. It dates from 1889.
The three figures fill only the upper part of the lights, the lowe
is entirely large, bold leaf-scrolls. Leaf-work also in the tracer
head. It makes all the other glass in the church look despicabl
including *Capronnier*'s S aisle E window of 1874.
St JAMES, Skinner Lane, the parish church of Didsbury and a
least very partly pre-Georgian. The W tower is of 1620, whe
the church was rebuilt. The parapet with the openwork loop
and the obelisk pinnacles is unmistakable. W doorway and v
window are Victorian. So is the whole rest of the exterior – c
1855, 1871 (chancel), and 1895 (S aisle E part). Inside, th
columns between nave and aisles look unconvincing for an
age, but in 1620 there just existed in England the possibilit

---

* GR says by Messrs *Goldie*.
‡ Letter from Mr A. C. Sewter.

of using unfluted columns instead of piers. So maybe they have only been badly treated later. The position of the chancel arch shows that the part with the columns was once the whole nave, and that the present chancel was built E of the original chancel. – PLATE. Small Paten given in 1741; small Chalice 1743; Paten given in 1748; Flagon given in 1753; undated Chalice; Chalice given in 1813. – MONUMENTS. Sir Nicholas Mosley † 1612 and two wives and children. Kneeling figures flanked by columns, he on top, the rest below. Alabaster. – Sir John Bland † 1715 and Ann Dowager Lady Bland, 1736, two tablets.*

ST PAUL, Wilmslow Road, Withington. 1841 by *Hayley & Brown*. Stock brick, the W tower with square pinnacles and a neo-Norman portal, the sides with round-headed lancets. Barn-like interior with the chancel flanked by side chapels. The detail here is Victorian, especially the three-bay chancel S arcade. That will be the enlargement of 1864 by *Lowe*. – MONUMENT. Robert Tebbutt † 1842 by *Patterson & Co.* of Manchester. Urn at the top.

ST PAUL METHODIST CHURCH, Wilmslow Road, Didsbury. A proud church with a SW steeple. Free treatment of late C13 motifs, the aisles e.g. simply five arched lights per bay. The clerestory has dormers. The church was designed by *E. T. Barry & Sons* in 1875.

LIBRARY, Wilmslow Road, Didsbury. 1915 by *Henry Price*, the City Architect. Gothic, of brick and stone, centrally planned. Polygonal porch. Didsbury has an uncommon number of educational institutions. Pride of place must go to the WESLEYAN THEOLOGICAL INSTITUTION, Wilmslow Road, now the DIDSBURY COLLEGE OF EDUCATION. The old building dates from 1842 and has – like the exactly contemporary Lancashire Independent College – a long ashlar front. But the style chosen by the Methodists was Grecian. The façade is eleven bays long and of two storeys with a three-storeyed five-bay centre. The giant pilasters here are placed up the first and second floors, in the end pavilions up the ground floor and first floor. The end pavilions have tripartite windows, the centre has a pediment. The centre was originally the Governor's residence. Fine staircase with iron railing curving up behind the entrance hall separated by a screen of two columns. Long lower ashlar-faced wings behind, leaving a courtyard formerly

---

* Mr Buttress suggests a mention of the old PARSONAGE, a rambling early C19 cottage with modest Gothic trimmings. The gateway has re-used bits from a city warehouse.

open. A large extension by *Francis Jones & Son* is being buil
behind.

COLLEGE OF EDUCATION HOSTEL, Wilmslow Road. Opposit
the above. A seven-storey block by *S. G. Besant Roberts*, th
City Architect, 1963.

GREYSTOKE, hostel for the Elizabeth Gaskell College, Merse
Road. 1961–2. Also by *S. G. Besant Roberts* and his team.

DIDSBURY COLLEGE OF FURTHER EDUCATION, Barlow Moo
Road. 1966–8, again by *S. G. Besant Roberts*'s department.

PARRS WOOD. Parrs Wood is an area once the gardens of PARR
WOOD, a stuccoed house of the early C19 with a long shallov
bow and a porch, the columns of which Mr I. Hall calls a late
addition. In the grounds are the PARRS WOOD HIGH SCHOOL
by *S. G. Besant Roberts*, the City Architect, built in 1964–5 o
the CLASP system (650 children) and the ROYAL FORI
HOSTEL of 1964–5. This is a fourteen-storey tower built o
the Bison System of industrial construction. The design come
from *S. G. Besant Roberts*, the City Architect.

68 SHIRLEY INSTITUTE, Wilmslow Road. This is the Cotton an
Man-made Fibre Research Institute, and its centre is th
grandest of all Manchester mansions. It was designed b
Thomas Worthington in 1865 for John Edward Taylor, pro
prietor and editor of the *Manchester Guardian*, and is grossl
picturesque, in red brick and yellow terracotta, with an asym
metrically placed porch tower and, at the r. corner, a polygona
oriel with spire. The doorway is E.E., the windows and especi
ally the dormers are derived from the Loire. From the entranc
hall, now subdivided, rises the staircase behind a screen o
granite shafts. The house is supposed to have cost £50,000
Opposite, No. 809 WILMSLOW ROAD is a stuccoed hous
with giant pilasters and a recessed centre. But little of that tim
survives, and what survives is as poor as BROOME HOUSE i
Wilmslow Road by Sandhurst Road, with a bow and a probabl
re-set pretty doorway. Didsbury is rather a hunting ground fo
Victorian villas. In MERSEY ROAD are a number of large ones
THE CEDARS, Wilmslow Road, NE of the Shirley Institute, i
nothing special, although by *Walters* (1857).

FALLOWFIELD, RUSHOLME, AND VICTORIA PARK

The boundary is on the N side (not including) Hathersage Roa
and Plymouth Grove, on the E side (not including) Birch Lane
Dickinson Road, Birchfields Road, on the S side (including

Moseley Road and Wilbraham Road, on the w side (including)
Yew Tree Road, Claremont Road, Parkfield Street, Moss Lane
East.

T CHRYSOSTOM, Oxford Place, Victoria Park. 1874–7 by *G. T.
Redmayne*. Some rebuilding after a fire in 1904, e.g. the doorways. The church has a thin SE tower. Polygonal apse, lancet
windows. – FONT. Square, of black marble, with E.E. decoration.

ST EDWARD (R.C.), Thurloe Street, Victoria Park. 1861–2 by
E. W. Pugin. Small, a sober exterior, with an apse. Details of
*c.*1300. A SW tower has not been built. Inside, short, polished
granite columns with summary capitals typical of E. W. Pugin.

HOLY INNOCENTS, Wilbraham Road, Fallowfield. 1870–2 by
Price & Linklater, with a NE steeple and a rounded apse. Geometrical tracery. The details of the steeple are personal and
effective. The interior is not interesting. Behind is the SCHOOL,
no doubt by the same architects.

ST JAMES, Danes Road, Rusholme. 1845–6 by *J. M. Derick*,
Pusey's architect. The church is a building with archeological
ambition. SW tower with broach spire, windows with plate
tracery, five-bay arcades with round piers. Chancel arch and
proper chancel. Rose-window, and below three pointed tre-
foiled lancets with a detached inner shafting. The exterior is
dignified, with much bare wall, even if it is not exciting. The
church cost £4,300 and is the replacement of a chapel of
1595. To the SW is the little BIRCH SCHOOL, 1841, of brick,
with Jacobean gables.

HOLY TRINITY, Platt Lane, Fallowfield. 1845–6 by *Edmund
Sharpe*. Considering his unrivalled connoisseurship of the Dec
style, he is here curiously loose in his use of historical authority.
The majority of the motifs he employs are of *c.*1300, but there
are ogee details too, and the bell-openings of the SW steeple
have geometrical tracery. The most interesting thing for us
nowadays is the fact that Sharpe used yellow terracotta as his
facing material, throughout and inside as well as outside. Holy
Trinity was the second of Sharpe's terracotta churches. On the
story of the 'pot churches', as they were disrespectfully called,
see St Stephen, Lever Bridge, Bolton, p. 90. The terracotta
blocks at Holy Trinity are done in such a way as to simulate the
mason's tooling. Ruskin's *Seven Lamps* was not to come out
for another three years. The top of the tower is handsomely if
playfully made an octagon, and the octagon is held up by flying
buttresses. The spire follows. The church has a w and a tower

11—S.L.

s porch, both, capitals and all, of terracotta. Inside even th
piers are terracotta. They are quatrefoils, and the bays are wid
so that two clerestory windows correspond to one bay. Th
chancel is two bays long and has a five-light E window.
STAINED GLASS. In the chancel of *c.*1849–50. – At the tim
of writing a CHURCH HALL is being built E of the church. It i
strictly up-to-date in style. It will be low but will block th
view of the church from Platt Hall.

SYNAGOGUE, Wilbraham Road, Fallowfield. 1912–13 by *Josep.
Sunlight.* Central plan with a low dome. But also a dome
tower with four angle tabernacles à la Salamanca and Zamora

CONGREGATIONAL CHURCH, Wilmslow Road, Rusholme (dis
used). 1863–4 by *Waterhouse.* Heavily Gothic, of darkene
brick, with a high NW tower. The tower has four steep gable
and a short spire. The windows are all round-arched, but witl
a meaning of conveying the transition to E.E.

FIRST CHURCH OF CHRIST SCIENTIST, Daisy Bank, Victori
Park. 1903 by *Edgar Wood,* and one of the most original
buildings of that time in England or indeed anywhere. On
would be tempted to call the style Expressionist, if the dat
were 1923 and not 1903. Brick and white rendering. Th
church has a steep gable with a stone chimneystack up the to
and beyond it. Below the place where that stack starts is ai
extremely long round-headed window, extending l. and r
below the springing of the arch into two very small oblon;
two-light windows. The portal is of cut bricks, round-arched
Two wings project diagonally from that centre, a motif Woo
had learned from E. S. Prior (The Barn, Exmouth). One o
them is the reading room, the other the hall. The reading roon
has to the forecourt and on the opposite side a canted ba
window which is gabled in such a way that the gable rises
broken round the angles of the canted sides. Between the hal
range and the church front finally is a fat, short round towe
with a conical roof, lower than the church gable. One cai
hardly drive originality and wilfulness farther, unless one i
called Gaudí. Along the w side of the church is a porte-cochèr
with a little dome.

UNITARIAN CHAPEL, Wilmslow Road, Fallowfield. 1790.
Brick, of three bays, with arched windows set in blank arches
The Romanesque porch is of 1874.

Fallowfield is a suburb of park, playing fields, and private gardens

---

* *Carr* of York has been suggested as the architect, comments Mr Buttres

of university hostels, schools, and villas. The Wilmslow Road cuts it in two.

OWENS PARK VILLAGE, Wilmslow Road. Of all the Halls of Residence of the University, to use that silly genteel term, Owens Park is the only one of architectural interest. It is also the only one of social interest in that it is for women as well as men students and in that it has no hall with high table but a cafeteria or restaurant or canteen. Once the equally silly name Village has been forgotten, one can appreciate the architecture. The buildings are by the *Building Design Partnership*, 1964–6, of yellow brick, with a square nineteen-storey tower and a high, prominent tank on top. In the tower are sets for 388 boys. It has a core and four splaying-out wings. There are six sets on each floor, and a small kitchen serves every twelve sets. Grouped around to E and S are the courts for the girls. They are of three and four storeys. To Wilmslow Road are the hall, library, offices, etc. Another tower (of fourteen storeys) is to come to the S and another court to the SE.*

WOOLTON HALL, Carrill Drive, S of the above, is by *Sir Hubert Worthington*. It was opened in 1959 and looks 1929. Pitched roofs with pedimental gables. The hall windows with heads convex–concave–convex in an Italian Baroque tradition and thinly neo-Georgian doorways.

ALLEN HALL, N of Owens Park (for R.C. students). 1960–1 by *Reynolds & Scott*.

ASHBURNE HALL, Wilmslow Road. Victorian buildings, one the house of the Behrens family, and additions of 1910, 1922, and 1932. Of the latter date the neo-Georgian hall and the expensive neo-Georgian gates by *Sir Hubert Worthington*.

HULME HALL, Oxford Place, Victoria Park, yet another University Hall of Residence. Good recent extension by *Bernard Taylor & Partners*, 1966 etc.

HOLLINGS COLLEGE, Wilmslow Road, Fallowfield. By the City Architect, *L. C. Howitt*, 1957–60. Here is a piece of pop architecture if ever there was one. The people have indeed found it a nickname: they call it the toast-rack, for its visible construction by means of a large number of very closely set very steep parabolic concrete arches. The floors, owing to this, decrease in depth from bottom to top: seven, six, five, four, three windows. The staircase windows slant like the arches. Workshop extension at the back, circular hall etc. to the road.

* The overall plan did not make it necessary to wipe out *Waterhouse*'s BARCOMBE COTTAGE.

Hollings College, by L. C. Howitt, 1957–60

DALTON HALL, Upper Park Road, Victoria Park. 1881–2 b
   G. T. Redmayne. A Quaker Hall of Residence for members o
   the Society of Friends to attend Owens College. Stock bric
   and red brick, gabled.
MANCHESTER GRAMMAR SCHOOL, Old Hall Lane. The cor
   1931 by *Francis Jones* and *Percy Worthington*. Brick, neo
   Georgian, and strictly axial. The premises consist of a larg
   quadrangle entered by a tripartite archway under a cupola, th
   hall at the N end of the quadrangle, lushly panelled library an
   museum l. and r. of the archway, a second quad to the E wit
   the lecture theatre on its N side, the dining hall on its E side, t

the NE a yet smaller quad for science rooms set diagonally, and a large gymnasium SE of the dining hall. The STATUE of the founder, Bishop Oldham, is placed outside the lecture theatre. It is of bronze and was done by *William McMillan.*

ЁGERTON SCHOOL, Clifton Avenue. 1964–5 by *S. G. Besant Roberts*'s Department. Built on the CLASP system. Small; for sub-normal children.)

USHOLME LIBRARY, Dickinson Road. 1860. Stone, gabled front with a short castellated tower on the l. Portal and main upper window are Gothic, the others have mullions and transoms.

LATT HALL, Platt Lane, Fallowfield. After Heaton Park the best Georgian building in Manchester. It was built *c.*1764 for John and Deborah Carill Worsley. It is of red brick, only seven bays long, and with two and a half storeys. Links connect the block with lower wings. The centre has a three-bay pediment, and the mid-window a pediment too. Porch of two pairs of unfluted Ionic columns. At the back the centre is a decidedly awkwardly placed Venetian window. The architect is not known; *Lightoler* is the most probable name. Inside, the entrance hall leads by two screens of two columns to the very handsome staircase, starting in one flight and curving back in two. Iron balustrade of lyre-shapes. Lovely plaster ceiling with vine motifs. Between the staircase and the front rooms on the upper floor runs a short corridor of one oblong bay flanked by two small groin-vaulted ones. A Venetian opening between the staircase and this corridor. The dining room is in the centre on the upper floor. It has a plain ceiling but Rococo stucco panels on the walls. – In the park s of the Hall STATUE of Abraham Lincoln by *George Grey Barnard*, 1919.

ſ other domestic architecture in this area the most interesting is VICTORIA PARK, an estate of large villas laid out in 1836 by *Richard Lane*, the architect, in the hope that he would be asked to design the villas. There are in fact some of about 1840, but most of the houses are later, say of 1850–60. The estate was surrounded by a wall with gates closed at night. None of the lodges have been preserved. The oldest houses are stuccoed and still classical, e.g. one in Lower Park Road with the inscription Concordia res parvae crescunt, another in Upper Park Road with two bow windows, and Egerton House in the same street. In Oxford Place opposite Upper Park Road is a stuccoed Tudor house, Sherwood House in Upper Park Road is very large and Italianate, and then there are the Gothic ones:

Marylands (Regent House) in Lower Park Road, yellow bri
with tricky details, Gartness in Upper Park Road, and Milve
ton Lodge in Anson Road, small and symmetrical. Tl
XAVERIAN COLLEGE in Lower Park Road started as a maj
Gothic villa too. It was built in 1874–5 by *Waterhouse* for tl
Hetherington family, whose wealth came from blast furnace
In Daisy Bank, i.e. E of Anson Road, developments in the san
style, e.g. Addison Terrace in the Tudor style, stuccoed.

Of domestic architecture at FALLOWFIELD little need be sai
THE FIRS, E of Woolton Hall, is Early Victorian, stuccoed ar
informal. It was built by *Walters* for Sir Joseph Whitworth
1851. In Wilmslow Road, N of Brighton Grove, is the LIVER
POOL VICTORIA INSURANCE, a stuccoed five-bay pair
about 1840, with two tiers of attached columns set back belo
the string courses. N of this some recent high housing, a tow
and a slab, both satisfactory. It was completed in 1967 and
by *J. Austen Bent*, the Director of Housing.

At RUSHOLME nothing to report except two detached three-ba
brick houses with columned porches N of Holy Trinity, Pla
Lane, and, like the church, probably of the 1840s.

VICTORIA PARK SECONDARY SCHOOL, Daisy Bank. By tl
Building Design Partnership, with the City Architect's Depar
ment, 1960–2. Good, in the 1960s way, with brick walls risi
above the roof-line and some monopitch roofs and tile-hur
sills.

GORTON AND LONGSIGHT

The boundary is on the N side the railway lines, on the E side tl
Manchester boundary, on the S side the Stockport boundary ar
(including) Hemsworth Road, Mellard Road, Mount Roa
Stanley Grove, on the W side (including) Stockport Road ar
(excluding) Devonshire Street, Hyde Road, Bennett Street, ar
Vaughan Street.

ST BENEDICT, Bennett Street. *See* Ardwick, p. 302.

ST CLEMENT, Dillon Street. 1874–6 by *J. M. Taylor*. Brick, E.E
with a thin square turret at the NE end.

ST CYPRIAN, Stanley Grove and Rushford Street. By *Temp*
Moore, 1908–16. Not one of his more interesting building
Chequered brick, with a square, plain SW tower. Dec window
the E arrangement being one, three, one, all starting quite lo
down. S aisle only, uncommonly wide.

ST FRANCIS (R.C.), Gorton Lane. The Franciscans returned

Manchester in 1861. Their house, to the r. of the church, was begun in 1863 or 1864 to the design of *E. W. Pugin*. In 1866 the church was begun, also by Pugin. It was consecrated in 1872. It was meant to be a demonstration, and it has remained a showpiece. No-one could deny that it is over-detailed. It is of red brick with generous stone dressing. The style is late c13. The façade is four bays wide and has four portals into a narthex. Behind, the sloping roof-lines of the aisles appear, and their fronts have rose-windows. The centre rises high, with two tall two-light windows and three buttresses, oddly connected with the wall behind by tracery. Out of the middle buttress grows a stepping-out panel with the Crucifixus, and on top of the gable over this is a high bell-turret. It looks as if it were made of icing sugar from a distance. The E end is a very high polygonal apse. The interior is dull and has typical E. W. Pugin capitals and other details.

T GEORGE, Abbey Hey Lane. 1903 by *C. K. & T. C. Mayor* (D. Buttress). Brick and red terracotta, no tower, Perp in style, a type more usual for the Nonconformists.

T JAMES, Wellington Street. 1871 by *G. & R. Shaw*. Dec, with a NW broach spire.

T JOHN, St John's Street, Longsight. 1845–6 by *John Edgar Gregan*. Large, with a SW broach spire. Nave and aisles, transepts. E.E. style, the transept ends with three high lancets. This is an exterior of archeological ambitions, only a few years after Pugin's conversion to archeological faithfulness. The interior unfortunately is dull. – STAINED GLASS. Sir Thomas Kendrick reports glass by *Willement*. It could be that in the N transept.

T MARK, Clowes Street. 1864–5 by *Isaac Holden*. Red and blue brick, coarse window detail; bellcote.

UR LADY WITH ST THOMAS OF CANTERBURY, Mount Road. 1927 by *Tapper*. Only a stump of the intended building. Two bays. The intention was to have three bays and cover them with saucer domes connected by short tunnel-vaults and extended towards the outer walls by short tunnel-vaults as well. The aisles would be low and run through the piers between these latter transverse tunnels and continue below them.

T PHILIP, Brookhurst Road. 1908–9 by *W. Cecil Hardisty*. Yellow and red brick, round-arched windows, no tower.

ACRED HEART (R.C.), Levenshulme Road, Longsight. By *Reynolds & Scott*, 1962. It looks c.1930.

ROOKFIELD UNITARIAN CHURCH, Hyde Road. By *Thomas*

Worthington, 1869–71. A very large and strikingly prosperous looking church. It was built at the expense of Richard Peacock of the Gorton Foundry. His villa used to be s of the church E.E. style, with a NW steeple. The church has a bold, simple and perfect Tractarian interior, with high quality fittings adapted for Puritan worship. Six-bay arcade of dark sandstone on pink granite columns which contrast well with the plastered walls. Impressive painted TYMPANUM of the early C20 – angel chorus, all wings, ribbons, and clouds (DB). – MONUMENT. of the church is the Mausoleum of Richard Peacock † 1875, three-bay shrine of white stone. – The church has a setting exceptional for Manchester. To its s and w there is a land-scaped dip and the Sunny Brow Park. Moreover, FAR LANE, skirting it, is clearly a village lane and still has some cottages.

(ST PETER AND ST PAUL'S SECONDARY SCHOOL (R.C.), Holmcroft Road. 1965–6 by *Mather & Nutter*. For 400 children.)

Round GIBSON STREET, Longsight, 430 acres make up one of the areas of intended comprehensive development. The interesting plans are by the *Manchester Housing Development Group* (cf. p. 272).

HARPURHEY *see* COLLYHURST

HEATON PARK

The house was built for Sir Thomas Egerton, seventh Baronet and later first Earl of Wilton. *James Wyatt* exhibited a drawing for it at the Royal Academy in 1772. In that year Egerton was twenty-three, Wyatt twenty-six. It is the finest house of its period in Lancashire, and one of the finest in the country. is not large, and it is the remodelling of a mid-C18 brick house which was seven bays long with a three-bay projection and pediment. This older house is fully preserved on the N side and Wyatt only added a portico of four Tuscan columns with Adamish capitals and a straight entablature. There are lower wings l. and r.; Wyatt built these and gave them four giant central pilasters. The splendid blocks of chimneys formed as Doric pillars and connected by a joint entablature at the top look an early C19 alteration. For the s side Wyatt was wholly responsible. It is ashlar-faced and exquisite in composition as well as details. There are one and a half storeys, and the articulation of centre, links, and end pavilions is perfect. The centre is a broad bow with demi-columns and three relief panels, and l. and r. are just one large Venetian window, of the type contained under a blank arch. Giant pilasters and a guilloche string-course. Then follow the links, each with a colonnade of five bays with Tuscan columns. The end pavilions have canted fronts. The fronts of these have again a contained Venetian window, the canted sides garland panels. The giant pilasters here carry a fluted frieze. The capitals of these and of the columns are of *Coade* stone.

The l. pavilion contains the KITCHEN, an unusual arrangement. The r. pavilion is the LIBRARY, an octagonal room with a screen of two Ionic columns to separate it from an apsed back bay. The chimneypiece has Ionic columns. This is followed by the MUSIC ROOM with a coved ceiling and an ORGAN by *Samuel Green*, made in 1790 and painted in grisaille on a greyish-green ground with putti and two winged genii holding the portrait of probably Handel. The mechanism of the organ is of great interest as being in several ways extremely progressive. The room has an exquisite chimneypiece, as have most of the other rooms. The next room is the BILLIARD ROOM. It has a beautifully dainty stucco ceiling, the first of a number of such ceilings, and the walls are reserved for rather anaemic mythological paintings by *Biagio Rebecca*. The Venetian window has to the inside scagliola columns and fine details. The SALOON has in front of its end wall a screen of two scagliola columns. The space between them and the end wall is segmentally tunnel-vaulted. In either of the side walls are two statues in niches and a chimneypiece. W of the Saloon is the DINING ROOM, with an apsed end wall, containing the original sideboard, and again scagliola columns for the Venetian window. N of the Saloon are the staircase and the entrance hall. The ENTRANCE HALL has apsed ends and simple, but elegant Regency decoration.* The STAIRCASE is splendid, rising in one flight and returning in two. Simple iron balustrade. On the upper floor along the N and S sides are brown scagliola columns. There is a coved ceiling and in its centre a glazed cupola. The room above the Saloon is one of the most ornate of the house, an uncommon distinction. It is round and has Etruscan wall paintings by *Rebecca*, very delicately done.

On the lawn in front of the house is a FOUNTAIN which was formerly in Albert Square, hexagonal with two basins, the smaller above the larger and a dolphin on top. It was designed

* In this room is the famous seated Theseus by *Thorwaldsen*.

by *T. Worthington & Son*, and the dolphin is by *Cassidy*, 1897. Immediately E of the house and attached to it is the former ORANGERY, probably of *c*.1820, with a canted centre and end pavilions with two-column loggias. The STABLES are NW of the house. On a hill near by is the TEMPLE, a small rotunda of Tuscan columns with dome and lantern. Less fitting is the recent newcomer to the garden furnishings of Heaton Park, the POST OFFICE TOWER, with its concrete shaft and its shovel-like contraptions all round the top. It looks admittedly exactly like sculpture of the 1960s, but it does not look like architecture of the Georgian Age. By the NE entrance is the SMITHY LODGE, an octagon with eight Tuscan columns only just detached. The GRAND LODGE at the SW entrance consists of a monumental archway with large paired Tuscan columns and no pediment and two low square lodges.

At the W end of the LAKE, made by the Corporation in 1912, is a re-erected fragment of the façade of the TOWN HALL in King Street. The building was by *Francis Goodwin* and was built in 1819–34. It was nine bays long, and only the centre was put up in Heaton Park. This imaginative action was taken in 1912, and *Edgar Wood* was one of those pleading for it to be done. It makes indeed a splendid foil to the lake. Four giant unfluted Ionic columns and at each end a closed bay with a niche. Heavy entablature.

HOUGH END *see* CHORLTON-CUM-HARDY

HULME

The boundary is on the N side the Centre, on the E side (not including) Cambridge Street, Lower Cambridge Street, Higher Cambridge Street, Lloyd Street North, on the S side (not including) Moss Lane East and West, on the W side the boundary to Stretford.

ST GABRIEL, Erskine Street. 1866–9 by *Medland Taylor*. A large, blunt church. Red and vitrified blue brick. Short crossing tower and semicircular apse. Lancets and plate tracery. The clerestory has triplets, the middle one being nothing but a plate tracery window-head.

ST GEORGE, Chester Road. By *Francis Goodwin*, 1826–8. A Commissioners' church in fact, not only in appearance. It cost as much as £15,000. Ornate, decidedly pre-archeological W tower with diminishing pinnacles but big pinnacles on top.

porches set diagonally at the NW and SW angles, high three-light Perp windows separated by buttresses, two big E pinnacles, and a high polygonal apse. Only the latter is an unexpected motif. Inside are the expected galleries. Six bays. The piers are thin and Perp. The tierceron-vault must be from *Crowther*'s restoration of 1884. – MONUMENT. The Hon. George Berkeley Molyneux † 1841. Signed by *Physick*. Soldier mourning by a sarcophagus.

ST MARY, Upper Moss Lane. 1856–8 by *J. S. Crowther*. His earliest mature work. Large, with a SE steeple. Three-light aisle windows, six-light E window. Very high interior with a very high chancel arch. Octagonal piers. Steep open roof. – STAINED GLASS. The S aisle SW window from St John, St John's Square. Signed by *W. Peckitt*, 1769, and in his entirely pictorial style.

ST PHILIP, Chester Street. 1859–60 by *Shellard & Brown*. A large, ambitious church for such a district. Rock-faced, with a well-detailed NW steeple. Three-light windows. Tracery of *c*.1300, very varied. Good, serious interior. – STAINED GLASS. In the N chapel no doubt original.

ST STEPHEN, City Road. 1868 by *J. M. Taylor*. Not orientated. The E (really S) window large, with in the tracery six Stars of David in a circle – a totally original motif. The W rose is very original too. The church is of red and vitrified blue brick and has aisle cross-gables.

ST WILFRID (R.C.), Bedford Street. By *Pugin*, 1842, and memorable as a very early case of the archeologically convincing church – internally certainly, with its six bays of octagonal piers and its double-chamfered arches and the N chancel chapel with its round arcade pier. The S chapel has one bay, not two, to avoid the artificiality of over-symmetrical design. The tower, never completed, is NW, not W. The exterior of the church is red brick, with lancet windows. It all had to be done cheaply – Pugin's bane. But he allowed himself the touch of archeological fun of laying his bricks English bond, not Flemish like the hated Georgians.

SOUTH HULME HIGH SCHOOL, Derry Street. By Mr *Besant Roberts*'s Department, 1965–7. For 1,350 children. Built on the CLASP system.

LIBRARY, Stretford Road. 1964–5 by *S. G. Besant Roberts*, the City Architect. A cheerful and entirely up-to-date job. The motifs are all sixties, but they are not overdone.

BRIDGEWATER CANAL. N of Chester Road and E of Egerton

Street are the canal wharves. There are also early WARE-
HOUSES, and the CANAL OFFICES in Chester Road have a
handsome front with two three-bay pediments. They were
originally part of the MILITIA BARRACKS (D. Buttress). Also
in CHESTER ROAD SW of St George's are two houses of *c.*1800
left with the usual doorways.

Hulme is so far the largest development area of Manchester,
many say of England, and some of Europe. At the time of
writing whole blocks lie waste, streets are blocked, and new
streets are made. The whole area involved in the rebuilding
programme is 350 acres. A roundabout by St George's connects
with the MANCUNIAN WAY, designed in 1959. It is about a
mile long, *c.*1,000 yards of it a flyover. This is on twin tapering
supports (designers *G. H. Maunsell & Partners* and *J. Hayes,*
the City Engineer).

LEVENSHULME

The boundary is on the N side (not including) Dickinson Road
and Stanley Grove, on the E side (not including) Mount Row,
Melland Road, Hunsworth Road, Wayland Road, and the Manchester boundary, on the S side the Manchester boundary and
then a straight line from the NE corner of Cringle Fields Park to
Burnage Hall Road and Kingswood Road, and on the W side
Birchfields Road.

ST AGNES, Slade Lane. 1884–5 by *Medland & Henry Taylor.**
The N aisle of 1895. An amazingly wilful design, patently
inspired by E. B. Lamb's work of a generation before. The W
front is perversely lopsided, with an apse on the l., and a
baptistery like a high polygonal apse. The chancel ends in an
apse too, and inside there is more of wondrous detail than one
can describe. The church is aisleless and dominated by the
tricky timbers of the roof and the arch springers. To the r. of
the chancel is a two-bay chapel, one bay W, one E of the chancel
arch. The arcade from the chancel to the chapel has two brick-
built E.E. columns with shafts set two deep. It is all without
any doubt deliberately confusing.

ST ANDREW, Stockport Road. 1908 by *R. B. Preston.* White
brick with red brick and red terracotta, Perp style. Thin S
entrance tower.

ST MARK, Barlow Road. 1908 by *C. T. Taylor.‡* Red brick and

* *Builder*, 2 August 1884; so Mr Spain tells me.
‡ So Mr Buttress tells me.

much stone, with much patterning of the two. Obviously inspired by Stokes. Lively w group of a short tower and the polygonally projecting baptistery. Memorable interior, of exposed brick, low and wide, with a spreading chancel arch starting on strange convex, not concave, curves before turning depressed-pointed. Wide aisles. Pretty, freely-Flamboyant SEDILIA. – STAINED GLASS. Modestly Arts & Crafts.

ST MARY OF THE ANGELS (R.C.), Clare Road. By *H. J. Tijou*, 1882–3. Addition 1914.

ST PETER, Stockport Road. 1860 by *Alfred G. Fisher*, enlarged 1872 and 1896. The church has a s w steeple with broach spire and window tracery of *c*.1300.

TOWN HALL, Stockport Road. 1898–9 by *James Jepson*. Red brick. Not detached. Seven bays with arched upper windows and a cupola. Portal with big brackets.

SLADE HALL. A timber-framed house dated 1585. Two storeys with two gables. Most of the timbering is herringbone-wise, but the smaller of the two gables has lozenges cusped to appear quatrefoiled. The back is early C19 brick. Inside, one upper room has a frieze of extremely naïve plasterwork including hunting scenes.

LONGSIGHT *see* GORTON

MILES PLATTING *see* ANCOATS

MOSSIDE AND WHALLEY RANGE

The boundary is on the N side (including) Moss Lane East and Moss Lane West, on the E side (including) Parkfield Street, Claremont Road, Yew Tree Road, on the s side (not including) Wilbraham Road, on the w side (not including) Egerton Road North, and the Manchester boundary.

ST CLEMENT, Denmark Road, Mosside. 1881 by *Henry R. Price*.

ST EDMUND, Alexandra Road South, Whalley Range. 1881–2 by *H. R. Price*. Geometrical tracery. Polygonal apse. Incomplete NE tower.

ENGLISH MARTYRS (R.C.), Alexandra Road South, Whalley Range. Geometrical tracery and a quite extraordinary NW spire. 1895–6 by *F. H. Oldham*.

ST JAMES, Princess Road, Mosside. 1887–8 by *John Lowe*. Red brick, with a polygonal s w turret; Perp.

ST MARGARET, Whalley Road, Whalley Range. 1848–9 by *J. Harrison*. Dec, with a w tower with broach spire. Arcades with octagonal piers, two-light clerestory windows above the spandrels not the apexes of the arcade arches. Two-bay chancel chapels – i.e. all in the new attitude of archeological faithfulness.

METHODIST CHURCH, Platt Lane. By *Brocklebank & Co.*, completed in 1932.

NEW CHURCH (Swedenborgian), Raby Street, Mosside. 1888 by *A. Banks*. Large, with a SW steeple and geometrical tracery, entirely like a building of the Church of England.

ALEXANDRA PARK. 1869–70. The NW gatepiers are excessively massive and stop-chamfered. The undisciplinedly picturesque LODGE is by *A. Darbyshire*, 1869.

Whalley Range is an area of theological colleges and schools.

LANCASHIRE INDEPENDENT COLLEGE (Congregational), College Road. A long, very impressive, ashlar-faced Gothic front, impressive in particular if one considers the date: 1840–3. The date of course excludes the accuracy of motifs which one would expect of a Waterhouse or a Worthington. The architects were *Irwin & Chester*. Nine bays plus slightly projecting one-bay wings. In the middle a tall, fanciful tower, its top, above the openwork parapet and pinnacles, octagonal and transparent. The recessed lengths of the façade have a ground-floor arcade of arches with four-centred heads. Mullioned and transomed windows above, but a two-storeyed Gothic oriel in the tower. The motifs of the tower are all a little tight, but the rest has much breadth and self-assurance. The entrance hall and assembly hall are disappointing after this display. The back parts of the colleges are brick exposed.

ST BEDE'S COLLEGE (R.C.), Alexandra Road South. Incomplete, but even so of eleven bays. The style is Italian, with Late Quattrocento motifs. Red brick and terracotta. Three-bay porch with coloured majolica reliefs. 1877–80 by *Dunn & Hansom*. The CHAPEL is of 1898. Several later additions.

HARTLEY VICTORIA COLLEGE (Methodist), Alexandra Road South. 1879, the clock tower 1896, the r. block and chapel 1903–6. The earlier parts are stock brick, the later good red brick and ample stone dressings. The CHAPEL is Perp, the block of 1903–6 generally Elizabethan.

WILLIAM HULME GRAMMAR SCHOOL, Spring Bridge Road, Whalley Range. 1886–7 by *A. H. Davies-Colley*. Big and high, of very red brick with a little yellow terracotta. The hall of 1910 continues the same style. Both buildings are symmetrically composed, the school with a central shaped gable and dormers.

(ST GEORGE'S SECONDARY SCHOOL (R.C.), Woodgate Road. 1964–6 by *Mather & Nutter*. Of load-bearing brick construction. For 600 children.)

(MANLEY PARK PRIMARY SCHOOL, College Road. 1962–4 by *S.G. Besant Roberts*'s Department. For 320 children.)

The expansion of Manchester is marked by occasional terraces or houses of *c.*1840–50, e.g. WHITWORTH PARK MANSIONS, Moss Lane East, corner of Lloyd Street. Four stuccoed houses with doorways with pilasters and wreaths in the friezes. Also a pair of houses a little further E facing Whitworth Park. Similarly at Whalley Range in Withington Road are Tudor-style terraces, stuccoed, and ALBERT TERRACE is Italianate and stuccoed.

MOSTON AND NEWTON HEATH

The boundary is on the N and E sides the Manchester boundary from Moston Station to Clayton Bridge Station, on the s side the railway to Miles Platting Station, on the w side the railway from Miles Platting Station, Thorp Road, Church Lane, Norman Road, Ashley Road, Moston Lane.

ALL SAINTS, Old Church Street, Newton Heath. Built in 1814–15, enlarged in 1844, the chancel of 1880. The church replaces one existing in 1573. Of 1814–15 the ashlar-faced exterior, except for the two E bays. Short w tower with polygonal buttresses. The sides with two tiers of windows, smaller and with four-centred arches below, larger and pointed above.

ST ANNE, Oldham Road, Newton Heath. 1881–3 by *A. Wellington Smith*.

ST DUNSTAN (R.C.), Moston Lane, opposite Kenyon Lane. Romanesque, large, of brick, with a s w tower and a low octagonal Italian crossing tower. By *E. B. Norris & F. M. Reynolds*, 1937.

ST LUKE, Kenyon Lane, Moston. 1909–10 by *E. Lingen Barker*.

ST MARTIN, Oldham Road, Newton Heath. Red brick with blue-brick decoration. Crude plate tracery. Bell turret. All the details unorthodox and bad. By *Price & Linklater*, 1871–3.

ST MARY, Nuthurst Road, Moston. 1869 by *Horton & Bridgeford*. Small, with a bellcote. Red brick, with thin brick and stone lancet windows.

ST WILFRID, Oldham Road, opposite Shears Street, Newton Heath. 1909–10 by *Austin & Paley*. Nothing left here of the past glories of Paley & Austin. Red brick, with an asymmetrical front, the w window treated as a canted bay. NW turret. Arcade of piers without capitals and arches dying into them.

DOB LANE CHAPEL (Unitarian), Oldham Road, Newton Heath, on the border to Failsworth. Founded in 1698. Plain, small rectangle. Six bays of lancets provided with minimum plate tracery in 1879.

ST JOSEPH'S CEMETERY, Moston Lane. Opened in 1875. Odd, large, arcaded building, called the Campo Santo. It was erected in 1904. Red brick, three sides of a rectangle. The ends of the wings are gabled and have big sloping buttresses to the l. and r. Big pointed-arched opening. In the re-entrant angles pavilions placed diagonally, also with big arched openings. Centre with three such openings. In between is arcading of cast iron with vividly ornamented spandrels. The CHAPEL and REGISTRAR'S HOUSE are one group, asymmetrical, with a tower.

HOUGH HALL, Hough Hall Road, off Moston Lane. Fragment of a timber-framed house of c.1600, disgracefully treated by the Corporation.

SHACKCLIFFE GREEN SECONDARY SCHOOL, Croft Hill Road, Moston.* By C. B. Pearson & Partners. Good, with all motifs heavier than usual in the English schools of the highest quality, i.e. those of Hertfordshire, Nottinghamshire, Coventry, etc.

NEWALL GREEN see WYTHENSHAWE

NEWTON HEATH see MOSTON

NORTHENDEN see WYTHENSHAWE

OPENSHAW AND CLAYTON

The boundary is on the N side the railway from Clayton Bridge to Clayton Street, on the E side the Manchester boundary to Clayton Street, on the S side the railway from Clayton Lane South to the Audenshaw boundary.

ST ANNE (R.C.), Ashton Old Road. 1884–8 by Simpson. The high bellcote with a Crucifixus below shows influence from St Francis Gorton.

ST CLEMENT, Ashton Old Road. 1879–81 by Enticknap & Booth. The church has no tower. A sober design, looking rather later than it is.

* Just N of the Moston boundary as here defined.

HOLY CROSS, Ashton New Road. 1863–6 by *Butterfield*, and unmistakable inside. Outside it is a very high dark brick building, as overbearing when seen in conjunction with Clayton Hall as are the chimneys and cooling towers of the power station to the w when seen with the church. The brick is striped with blue-brick and stone bands. There is a SW tower with pyramid roof, deliberately made excessive in height. The clerestory is very high too. The features are Middle Pointed, i.e. *c*.1300. The piers are quatrefoil in section, and above them all is red brick with blue diapers. The aisles have blue-brick bands instead. The chancel arch is very high, and behind it there are Butterfield's favourite two-light openings into chapels under one big blank arch. The chancel has blank trefoil-headed arcading and a five-light E window remarkably high up for 1863–6.

ST WILLIBRAND (R.C.), North Road. 1938 by *Reynolds & Scott*. Brick, Byzantine, with a low octagonal central tower not expressed internally. Internally there are instead three sail-domes with transverse arches on wall-piers pierced for aisle passages. The domes are continued to N and S by short tunnel-vaults, and to these correspond hipped gables outside. Lower chancel and apse. It is an interesting plan, inspired very probably by Tapper's Our Lady, Mount Road, Gorton (*see* p. 327).

MUNICIPAL BUILDINGS, Ashton New Road. 1894. Red brick and red terracotta. A symmetrical gabled building with an extension for the baths on the l.

CLAYTON HALL, Ashton New Road, E of Holy Cross. Very little is preserved of this moated manor house which was the home of Humphrey Chetham. The original part is timber-framed with plain panels except for the small gable to the w. On that side the lower floor is brick-faced. The N wing is C18.

STRANGEWAYS AND CHEETHAM

The boundary is on the N and E sides (including) Crescent Road, Greenhill Road, Woodlands Road, Smedley Road, and the river Irk to the boundary of the Centre, on the S side New Bridge Street, on the W side the boundary to Salford.

ST ALBAN, Waterloo Road. 1857–64 by *J. S. Crowther*. An excellent building with a strong SE tower, a high polygonal apse, and a high clerestory. This and the aisles have three-light windows. Impressive interior with four-bay arcades and a very high chancel arch. Two-bay N chapel (the pier of Chartres–Reims–Amiens type; cf. St Benedict, p. 302), one-bay opening into the tower. The apse has prominent blank arcading below the window. Crowther was a learned architect, fully in command of English as well as French motifs.

ST CHAD (R.C.), Cheetham Hill Road, close to the town hall. 1846–7 by *Weightman & Hadfield*. Perp in style. SW tower with higher stair-turret and two three-light bell-openings. Nave and aisles, thin timber roof. Five-light E window. On the way to archeological accuracy. – STAINED GLASS. The E window of *c.* 1847–8 is by *Barnett & Son* of York.

ST JOHN EVANGELIST, Waterloo Road. 1869–71 by *Paley & Austin*. Built at the expense of Lewis Loyd. Massive SW tower with pyramid roof and pinnacles also with pyramid roofs. The windows are mainly lancets, which leaves much sheer wall. Three-bay nave, two-bay chancel chapels. Round apse with two tiers of blank arcading. The W windows are placed unusually high up. Not one of Paley & Austin's best, but, as theirs nearly always are, a serious, thoughtful design.

ST LUKE, Cheetham Hill Road. 1836–9 by *T. W. Atkinson*. A remarkable design, still pre-archeological, but more responsible than most Gothic churches of the thirties. Slim W tower with a fine crocketed spire and tall windows. Nave and aisles, the aisles with slim two-light Perp windows, the clerestory with two small two-light ones per bay. Short chancel and low E vestry. The W entrance hall has a pretty tracery-stuccoed ceiling. The church has piers with capitals trying to be Perp. The galleries are preserved. The E wall is panelled all over with tracery and also has some niches with canopies. – Big, contemporary, much-canopied ORGAN on the W gallery. – Gothic BOX PEWS. – PULPIT. The foot must be brought in from Flanders. Rocks and rising plants, and between them three seated saints, typical of the C18 in proportions, attitudes, and 22 draperies. – PAINTING. Flight into Egypt, Spanish, C17, trimmed.

To the w of the church is a terrace of houses also clearly of c.1840, and to the N are a three-bay somewhat earlier house with a pretty doorway and a seven-bay house with a three-bay pediment.

ST MARK, Cheetham Hill Road. Built in 1794. The chancel lengthened and remodelled in 1855. The tower by *R. Knill Freeman*, 1894. That leaves the body of the church, a straightforward brick parallelepiped of five by five bays with two tiers of arched windows and a barn-type roof. Three galleries, their panelled parapet very good.

Cheetham was the centre of Manchester's Jewry, and I cannot flatter myself that I have solved the problem of the architects and the dates and of the location of those synagogues mentioned in the journals of the C19.*

CENTRAL SYNAGOGUE, Heywood Street. Built in 1927–8 by *J. Knight*. Brick and white stone; neo-Grec detail, Liverpool-looking.

SYNAGOGUE (former), Cheetham Hill Road, at the corner of Park Street. Built as a Methodist chapel. An excellent Late Classical design. Ashlar, with a three-bay front with slender arched windows, a big portal, and a one-bay pediment. The side has giant pilasters. It is five bays long and has windows in two tiers. The end bays are blank, with banded rustication.

GREAT SYNAGOGUE, Cheetham Hill Road, opposite the town hall. Brick, but with a stone façade. Two closed bays with low cupolas and between a loggia with two giant Corinthian columns. By *T. Bird*, 1857. (The interior, so Mr R. R. Emanuel tells me, is based on that of Great St Helen's Synagogue, London, of 1838.)

NEW SYNAGOGUE (former) Cheetham Hill Road, s of No. 124. Built in 1889. Brick, a symmetrical front with round-arched windows. No tower.

UNITED SYNAGOGUE (former), Cheetham Hill Road, originally a Catholic church. w tower with octagonal top, transept, dormer windows. All crudely done.

TOWN HALL, Cheetham Hill Road. 1853–5 by *T. Bird*. Brick and stone dressings. Seven bays with a three-bay centre. Iron

* However, I have received much help on the synagogues from Mr R. R. Emanuel of the Bath School of Architecture.

porte-cochère. The upper hall has a semicircular end wall. The town hall forms or formed part of a little linear group.

Former FREE LIBRARY, opposite. 1877–8 by *Barber & Ellis*. Yellow brick and stone dressings. The centre is one portal and above it a five-bay arcading.

N of the town hall is an OFFICES appendix. Built in 1861–2. Three bays with a porch, decidedly more florid than the town hall. On the N of this were the ASSEMBLY ROOMS, pulled down unnecessarily in 1966, although they were by *Mills & Murgatroyd*, decorated by *John Gregory Crace*, one of the best decorators in the country, and although they were quite exceptionally lavish.

PUBLIC HALL, Cheetham Hill Road. 1892–4 by *Booth & Chadwick*.

LIBRARY, Cheetham Hill Road. 1909–11 by *Henry Price*, the City Architect. With two symmetrical gables and a semi-domed porch. Red brick and stone bands.

STRANGEWAYS PRISON. 1866–8 by *Waterhouse*. The high minaret-chimney is a landmark. Of the rest one does not see much. The architectural motifs are Romanesque, with an octagonal raised centre like a North Italian cathedral or a British workhouse. The gatehouse of the prison is not specially conspicuous.

See p. 480

KENNET HOUSE, Smedley Road, at the E end of Smedley Lane. A vast elliptical block of flats with an inner courtyard, built by the Corporation about 1935 (Corporation Architect at the time *G. Noel Hill*) and the Manchester equivalent to Quarry Hill at Leeds, i.e. with sweeping bands of plastered brick and sweeping bands of windows.

VICTORIA PARK *see* FALLOWFIELD

WHALLEY RANGE *see* MOSSIDE

WITHINGTON *see* DIDSBURY

WYTHENSHAWE AND NORTHENDEN

The boundaries are the river Mersey on the N, the Manchester boundaries on the other sides.

Wythenshawe is famous chiefly as the garden suburb of Manchester. It was laid out by *Barry Parker* in 1931 and is owned by the Corporation, not by a company or an industrial enterprise. The planning technique is that developed by Parker & Raymond Unwin for Letchworth and the Hampstead Garden Suburb, but the style is now neo-Georgian and no longer neo-Tudor. The greatest objection to Wythenshawe has always been the lack of a centre able to satisfy a considerable population. Parker & Unwin, who had not provided any shop or pub or cinema in the Hampstead Garden Suburb, did not wish to make the same mistake here. They had planned a centre; only unfortunately nothing of the sort was in the end provided. So, although Manchester spoke of a satellite town, they did not build one. Now that deficiency is at last being removed at the moment of writing by the building of a TOWN CENTRE. The area to be covered is the triangle between Simonsway, Poundswick Lane, and Brownley Road. The first buildings completed are two blocks of shops and offices facing one another across a pedestrian mall. More shops and offices and multi-storey car parks l. and r. of a circular retail market will be built to the s and civic buildings to the w, i.e. in the apex of the triangle. N of the shopping two high blocks of flats are ready, and two more are following to their E. Also, E of the s end of the present shopping, on the other side of Rowlandsway, the one N–S artery across the site, is a Bowling Centre, essentially windowless. s of this, and also in course of erection, is the Methodist Church, for which see below. The area of new development is to extend E of Brownley Road with new housing. But there is a good deal more to Wythenshawe than shopping and housing, and the items must be taken in their usual order.

ST FRANCIS, Greenbrow. By *Sir Basil Spence*, 1959–61. One of the small suburban churches of which Sir Basil Spence did some equally excellent ones at Coventry. 250 seats only. Triangular brick tower, at some distance from the church. The side of the tower to the street is entirely open, and in it a concrete pier rises and ends in a cross. The church front is composed of cubic shapes. It is brick, but with wood slatting to allow a view in and a side chapel faced with Portland stone, tucked under and kept independent of the rest. The chapel is for weekday services. The interior is a plain oblong, except that the side walls of the chancel project triangularly so as to allow light to fall on to the altar. The ceiling is flat. There are no pretensions, which is a blessing in a church of the sixties.

ST JOHN THE DIVINE, Brooklands Road. By *Waterhouse*, 1864–8. A large church, full of character, honest, and of a certain sternness indicated at once by the use everywhere of

bare, unfoiled circles in the window tracery. There is also no
tower nor a turret, nor are there aisles. So the space is undivided
except for two-bay extensions to N and S under cross gables.
The piers are round and have capitals of the French Early
Gothic type. The interior is faced in yellow brick with some
polychromatic patterning. The steep open roof achieves the
effect of a grandeur just a little gaunt. – Iron ROOD SCREEN. –
STAINED GLASS. N transept by *Kempe*, 1891. – One S aisle
window by *Morris & Co.*, 1897.

ST LUKE, Benchill Road, Wythenshawe. 1938–9 by *Taylor &
Young*. Brick, with a very broad W tower with recessed hipped
roof. Long, narrow paired windows.

ST MARTIN, Blackcarr Road. By *H. S. Fairhurst & Sons*,
1963–4. Nothing to recommend in its architecture.

ST MICHAEL, Orton Road, Northenden. 1937 by *Cachemaille
Day & Lander*. A sensational church for its country and its day.
The plan is a star consisting of two interlocked squares. The
material is brick, bare in four of the corners, with large brick
windows in the other four. The intersecting arches of the
windows are the only period allusion. The interior has very
thin exposed concrete piers and a flat ceiling. The architect had
wanted the altar to be right in the centre – *à la* Liturgical Movement – but the bishop refused permission, and the altar is now
in the triangle facing the entrance. – STAINED GLASS. E window
by *Geoffrey Webb*. – To the r. of the church low PARSONAGE.
The church makes it clear that the architect had studied Continental experiments. The parsonage points to Germany and
Mendelsohn.

ST WILFRED, the parish church of Northenden. In Ford Lane.
1873–6 by *Crowther*, who kept closely to the style of the genuine
Perp building on the site. High five-bay arcades, castellated
capitals. Two-bay chancel chapels. W tower. – FONT. A baluster
stem, with a minute bowl; C18. – SCREEN. Close-set mullions
and a transom high up. Nice thin tracery and a leaf frieze at the
top. The date reported is 1527. – STAINED GLASS. Two S
chapel S windows apparently early *Kempe*. – MONUMENTS.
Tablets to Robert Tatton † 1689 with two uncouth putti; to
Mrs Egerton † 1784 with an urn wreathed by an excellently
carved flower garland; to William Egerton † 1806, son of
William Tatton, with a woman lying right on a sarcophagus
(by *J. Bacon Jun.*); and to Thomas Worthington † 1856 and his
parents, with a mourning woman bent over three sarcophagi,
a weeping willow above (by *M. W. Johnson* of London).

WILLIAM TEMPLE MEMORIAL CHURCH, Simonsway. By *G. G. Pace*, 1964–5. All praise to the clients who were willing to accept so daring a design. Much praise to the architect who had the daring to submit so uncompromisingly 1960s a design. And apologies from the author of this volume who cannot appreciate for worship so aggressive a building, as he cannot appreciate much recent abstract sculpture. This must be said in advance. And now purely a description. The building is oblong, nearly square, but the internal axis runs across diagonally. The pitched roof has one long and one short pitch and moreover two funnel-shapes of La Tourette derivation. Also, in the E wall there is a narrow projection with a very steeply pitched extra roof. Two of the side walls have arbitrary slits with arbitrary concrete lintels, short or long, here or there. The entrance is in the wall opposite the projection, i.e. not on the road. Inside it seems all crowded girders and beams of standard rolled-steel section. 99 That makes the high font canopy the centre of the attack. It is not really a canopy, but three steel supports for the roof. Towards one corner from here is the altar, with pulpit and lectern l. and r. and a semicircular bench behind. Towards the opposite corner a service core of rude concrete and the organ. The materials are brick and concrete, and inside much wall facing with insulating blocks.

MORMON TEMPLE, Altrincham Road, Northenden. By *Sir T. P. Bennett*, completed in 1964. Much more spiky and angular than the previously accepted model for Mormon temples.

WYTHENSHAWE HOSPITAL, Clay Lane. *Powell & Moya* have recently done some work here, and it is good, as all their work is. The Maternity Unit is of 1962–5, the Nurses' and Doctors' Quarters yet more recent.

Several pre-Georgian houses are preserved at Wythenshawe, and they can be taken together.

WYTHENSHAWE HALL, Wythenshawe Park. The house was presented to the City by Lord Simon of Wythenshawe in 1925. He had bought it from the Tatton family. The centre is timber-framed and assigned to the time of Henry VIII. It consists of 16 the hall with symmetrically placed porch and dais bays and two projecting wings. The wings have large gables, porch and bay small gables with well-preserved carved bargeboards and bressumers. The windows are of three to six lights. The timbering is either closely spaced uprights or herringbone struts. On the r. of the house is an addition of *c*.1830 with a long,

shallow canted bay and roughcast walls. Behind on the l. is a
Georgian brick block. The STABLES are Georgian and of brick
too. Inside the old part the hall, which must always have been
confined to the ground floor, has moulded beams and carved
bosses. The very handsome staircase with alternately twisted
balusters is early C18. The room above the hall has a Jacobean
plaster ceiling, mostly imitation, but in order in the bay above
the porch. The chimneypiece has tapering stone pillars and a
beautifully panelled overmantel, looking 1650 rather than
earlier. The walls are panelled too, and the panels have a large
variety of fret patterns inlaid. The LODGE at the N entrance is
dated 1878, and of course in half-timbering more splendid than
that of the house.

BAGULEY HALL, Hall Lane. The way Manchester Corporation
has treated Baguley Hall is a scandal. Here is the best medieval
secular building within the boundaries of the city, and a
building of considerable national interest. At the time of
writing it looked too far gone for restoration, and Manchester
seemed unwilling – though emphatically not unable – to pay
for it.* The building consists of a timber-framed C14 hall and
two brick wings, the N wing medieval and re-faced in brick,
the S apparently late C17. The hall has tall mullioned windows
of later date. However, the doorway inside the gabled late C16
porch is original, and so are the three doorways from the
screens passage formerly to the kitchen, buttery, and pantry.
Two of them are blocked. The timbering of the hall is very
heavy and consists of broad uprights and horizontals and
bracing in the form of heavy cusped St Andrew's crosses. The
12   N wall of the hall, i.e. the wall inside the screens passage above
the doorways, is especially impressive. The screen has a spere
truss, the roof is essentially single-framed. Messrs J. T. Smith
and C. F. Stell, who have recently written on Baguley Hall,‡
have more to say about the roof. They also emphasize that the
uprights and horizontals are not posts and beams, i.e. roughly
of the same width and depth, but planks, i.e. only 7 in. deep.
This, Messrs Smith and Stell say, is Scandinavian rather than
English and can be connected with the Norwegian stave
churches and also the famous boat-shaped houses of Trelleborg,
datable to c.1000 and known by excavation only. Now, as it
happens, Baguley has also at least partially a boat shape. The

* Baguley Hall is now being taken over by the Ministry of Public Building
and Works; so its future happily seems assured.
‡ *Antiquaries' Journal*, XL, 1960.

outer walls converge a little towards the screen. This would be a connexion not only across the North Sea (which, considering the extensive Viking settlements in this part of England, would be nothing surprising), but also across 350 years. The plank argument on the other hand is fully convincing, and sets Baguley apart.* All the more disgraceful is the treatment of the building.

PEEL HALL. The house lies in a moat and is reached by a medieval two-arch stone bridge. The house itself is of brick, c 17, belongs to the Corporation, and is derelict.

NEWALL GREEN FARMHOUSE, Newall Road. A c 17 brick house with two projecting wings and a middle porch. The angles are quoined, and the porch has a semicircular top instead of a pediment.

In this context the only noteworthy house of Northenden must be mentioned: SHARSTON HALL, Altrincham Road. Kelly gives a date 1701, which suits the style. This is the best house of the date in Manchester. Red brick, with small quoins. Three storeys. Lovely doorway with open scrolly pediment and a shield in it. Lovely staircase with twisted balusters and carved tread-ends. The house belongs to the Corporation, and consequently the interior, at the time of writing, is neglected. Wings project at the back. Also a big Victorian addition.

By Northenden church, in FORD LANE, is one pretty three-bay house of the c 18, and the RECTORY, E of the church, is Georgian too.

MARTINSCROFT see WOOLSTON

MAULDETH HALL see HEATON MERSEY

MEDLOCK HALL see FAILSWORTH

MELLING

3000

ST THOMAS. 1834 by J. W. Casson. The chancel enlarged 1873. Red stone; of Commissioners' type. Lancet windows and w tower. – STAINED GLASS. Three-light window with angels by Holiday. – (MONUMENT. Tablet to Margaret Hoskins † 1838 by W. Spence. Gunnis)

ROCK HOUSE, S of the church. 1744. Three bays, brick and red

* The hall of Radcliffe Tower, South Lancashire, which no longer exists, had planks also (see p. 369).

stone dressings. Odd string-courses. The general impression is more c.1700 than 1744.

VICARAGE, E of the church. Probably 1831–2 (MHLG). Tudor, stone, with spacious mullioned windows and low-pitched roofs. The major part of the front is symmetrical. The r. hand addition called 1849 by the MHLG.

BARNES FARMHOUSE, No. 166 Tythe Barn Lane. 1654. Low and humble, with low mullioned windows. The doorway still has a depressed pointed arch.

MICKLEHURST see MOSSLEY

8000

MIDDLETON

Middleton has not the gloom of so many South Lancashire towns of its size. It benefits from its position close to the hills, but it has also the advantage of a large medieval church on a hill and of a number of buildings by one of England's most original architects of the interesting period about 1900.

ST LEONARD. The commanding position of the church has already been referred to. It also has external features to be remembered: the long, relatively low body with the even horizontals of battlements on aisles and clerestory, and the crowning feature of the big W tower, more curious than beautiful. It is a weatherboarded top stage with four decidedly domestic gables. This is of c.1667, a most improbable date. But Thoresby describes it as 'almost like a dovecote' in 1682; so the date is incontestable. The tower is the earliest part, though not the earliest motif, of the church. That is the tower arch, which is a re-set Norman chancel arch of three orders with multi-scalloped capitals and two orders of zigzag in the arch. The arch is pointed and has a big unchamfered order as well. Is that an alteration of the time of re-setting? It is not likely, as the tower is not C13, but belongs to the church consecrated by Bishop Langley of Durham in 1412. Middleton was his native parish. Of the Norman church another fragment is the billet frieze in one N arcade arch. Next in date is the priest's doorway, probably of the late C13. Of Langley's building, apart from the tower, only the S porch remains. This is a very ornate piece, with niches l. and r. of the entrance. Possible re-used Langley material is the parapet of the SE vestry. The rest of the church is latest Perp and later. The nave has octagonal piers and double-chamfered arches. The aisles have windows with cusped lights but no tracery, and the clerestory has uncusped, i.e. the latest, lights. There is no chancel arch. The chancel E window is of 1847, and only the N window is original. The N and S chapels, the latter the Assheton family chapel, are not bonded in with the chancel. Their windows may indicate a post-medieval date, but need not. The date we have for the reconstruction of Langley's church is in fact latest Perp: 1524. The work was undertaken by Richard Assheton. The date is recorded on a stone in the middle of the S aisle parapet. This and the chapel parapet are the only ones distinguished by decorative carving. The SE vestry is yet later than the Assheton Chapel – see the way it blocks part of the chapel E windows. It is probably of after 1660. The original stonework is beautifully weathered; so the authorities may well be worried by it. The NORTH VESTRIES were added by *G. G. Pace* in 1958, in a fitting, square, free Gothic, tactful and not strictly imitative.

FURNISHINGS. The ROOD SCREEN does not retain its original coving and loft; the rest is original. The dado has large heraldic panels, including the Assheton arms. – The STALLS stand against the screen. They have eight simple foliage MISERICORDS and traceried stall ends, with poppyheads including small, not very accomplished animals. – In the S aisle the HOPWOOD PEW, late C17, with twisted balusters in its upper part. – LECTERN. A massive wooden piece of 1843. – STAINED GLASS. In the chancel S window are fragments of glass with kneeling donors (cf. the Assheton church of Ashton-under-Lyne). The window commemorated the victory of Flodden Field in 1513. The people have their names attached, and that includes those of seventeen archers. – PLATE. Set of 1843. – MONUMENTS. In the N aisle a tomb recess. – In the chancel brasses to Sir Richard Assheton and wife, *c.* 1510, to Edmund Assheton, rector of Middleton, † 1522, a 23 in. figure, to Alice Lawrence † 1531 and husbands, 18 in. figures, and also Richard and wife † 1618 and Ralph and wife † 1650. – Rev. James Archer † 1832 (N wall chancel), by *William Spence*, with a large standing female figure.

ALL SAINTS, Wood Street. By *Leach, Rhodes & Walker*, 1963–4. Red brick with jabbing roofs and a flèche. – Inside, massive, nearly abstract cross SCULPTURE by *Geoffrey Clarke*. It is easy to be irritated by the use over and over again of the architectural clichés of the 1960s, but go across the street and look at OUR LADY OF THE ASSUMPTION (R.C.), 1961–2, pale brick, still Romanesque, still with the campanile-like tower, and make your choice. Do you prefer the clichés of the day before yesterday or of today? The one is drained of all blood, the other is at least lustily alive.

ST MICHAEL, Townley Street. 1902 by *Austin & Paley*.[*] With a big NW tower placed W of the N aisle and projecting from it. With its diagonal buttresses it is the dominating and the best feature of the church, a fine, strong job. The doorway into it dies into its imposts. The clerestory tracery is original, more so than that of the W and E windows. The clerestory window arches are round. The interior calls for less comment.

ST STEPHEN, High Street. Built for the Countess of Huntingdon's Connexion in 1824, but now no longer telling of its date.

HOLY TRINITY, Parkfield. 1861–2 by *G. Shaw*.[‡] Details of c.1300, and a pretty bell-turret.

METHODIST CHURCH, Long Street. Here, in this account of Middleton, the name of *Edgar Wood* appears for the first time. More on him is to be found in the Introduction on p. 48. The church was designed in 1897 and built in 1899–1901. It is of stone below, of stock brick above, and it is Gothic, even if the tracery of the main windows is not imitative and the aisle windows have simply two mullions running into the arch. The piers are octagonal, and above them is again exposed stock brick. – The most remarkable piece of furnishing is the stone PULPIT and the low attached stone SCREEN. The pulpit has basic Romanesque columns attached to the body in a frieze of carved roses, leaf, and blooms. – The STALLS also are typical Arts and Crafts work, with the forceful directness of Wood. – The finest thing about the exterior is the grouping with the ancillary buildings on the S. The buildings themselves are comparatively weak, but the gateway, the canted stone oriel between it and the church, and the porch at the r. end of the church accessible by an outer staircase make an impressive picture.

CONGREGATIONAL CHURCH, Market Place. 1859–60. Brick, of four bays, with a big pediment; Italianate. The PROVIDENCE SCHOOL, adjoining it, is of 1879 and consequently livelier and fussier.

CIVIC BUILDINGS, Manchester Old Road. By *Lyons, Israel, Ellis & Partners*, 1965–6. This is only the first instalment. The council suite and assembly hall are still to come, N of the old town hall. The present block of offices is of white concrete with

---

[*] Mr Buttress's information.
[‡] Information given by Mr Buttress.

shuttering marks partly by *in situ* casting, but partly also applied to pre-cast panels. The wall surface is broken up by horizontal chamfering forward above the window bands and by projecting posts between the individual windows.

GRAMMAR SCHOOL, Boarshaw Road. Founded in 1572 and built in 1586. It cost £135. It is a simple one-storeyed house with two-storeyed ends for domestic purposes. The school-room has mullioned-and-transomed windows of five lights, the end parts smaller mullioned windows.

ELM STREET SCHOOL. By *Edgar Wood* and *J. Henry Sellers*, 1908–10, and probably designed by Sellers – see the style of his office building for Dronsfield's at Oldham.* It is a brick building with stone trim, very formally composed, and it has as its principal accent two short turrets with the un-period and anti-period details of blocks and horizontal slabs which Sellers liked. The centre of the composition is a garden. L. and r. are vaulted, arcaded passages reached by cubic archways and leading to the boys' and girls' entrances. L. and r. of the passages are play-yards behind high walls and classrooms. At the end of the formal garden is the hall, nine bays with arched windows and the two memorable towers. And in front of the hall towards the garden is a series of small rooms making up a concave front below the hall windows. The roofs are of concrete.

DURNFORD STREET SCHOOL. 1908–10 by *Edgar Wood* and 91 *J. H. Sellers*, and again most probably by Sellers. This is a larger building, but the elements are much the same. A centre block with two low towers, the centre here housing two super-imposed halls and being of three three-light, three-transomed windows, flanked by two stone bays with canted bay windows with four-transomed three-light windows. Below these main windows a set of ground-floor windows only a little smaller. But that is not all. The one-storey block projecting from the middle is unfortunate. It looks almost like an afterthought. L. and r. of the centre range are three perfectly harmless Georgian bays and one more stone bay with a canted bay window, and then the towers close the group. Like the Elm Street School, this is of brick with stone dressings and a flat concrete roof. Mr Archer, biographer of Wood, adds: 'The west elevation is as stark as a cotton mill.'

TONGE HALL, William Street. Timber-framed, with two gables of different size and with quatrefoil decoration all over. Baines reports the date 1553 on a beam.

* Wood and Sellers went into partnership in 1901.

BOAR'S HEAD INN, Long Street. Elizabethan or Jacobean, timber-framed. The decoration of the gables is not ancient.

The rest of the secular buildings worth recording are all by *Edgar Wood*.

In the MARKET PLACE he did two banks, the DISTRICT BANK in 1889, WILLIAMS DEACON'S BANK in 1892, neither of them very remarkable, the former stone, the latter rendered, the former with a demonstratively asymmetrical skyline, the latter with odd windows with depressed arched lights under a segmental arch and three gabled dormers.

Of HOUSES the following are a (not complete) record. In ROCHDALE ROAD at the corner of Cleworth Road is a pair of 1891–5, the l. Wood's own. It is a consciously uneven pair so as to avoid all memories of the semi-detached. The l. house has a broad gable, the r. house only a dormer, but the r. house has a more substantial canted bay window. This bay window with its totally unmoulded mullions and transoms is close to Voysey. So is the low mullioned five-light window in the middle of the composition. Two larger houses are in the Parkfield neighbourhood: WESTDEANE in Sefton Road and DUNARDEN in Sunny Bank Road. The former is of 1889, the latter of 1898. Westdeane one would hardly notice as anything out of the ordinary. It is again elaborately asymmetrical, with rendering, half-timber, and tile-hanging; Dunarden has a front with two canted bay windows of five sides of a decagon, very tightly set glazing bars, and a hipped roof. Close to this incidentally is Wood's father's house, 1864 by *Mills & Murgatroyd*, typically High Victorian, with Gothic and Elizabethan motifs. The house by Wood at 36 MELLALIEU ROAD is of 1910 and has, according to Mr Archer, Wood's first flat reinforced concrete roof.

Finally in JUBILEE PARK, N of the library and W of the church, is an EXEDRA, reached up a flight of steps and adorned by an inscription in Arts and Crafts lettering. This is by *Edgar Wood* too, but its centre feature, a fountain, does not survive. It dates from 1906.

(BAY TREE MILL and LAUREL MILL, Middleton Junction. Built by *Stott & Sons* of Manchester in 1903. The two mills form a single unit with a single engine house and chimney. Accrington brick and terracotta – a very imposing group. J. B. Howcroft)

ALKRINGTON HALL, ¾ m. SW. 1735–6 by *Giacomo Leoni*.* A nine-bay brick house with stone quoins and giant angle pilasters

* The authorship was found by Mrs Eileen Harris.

for the three-bay centre. The ground floor of this centre is stone too, and rusticated. The mid-window has a pediment. Later low three-bay windows. The house was built by Darcy Lever, descendant of merchants, but himself a graduate of Oxford and an LL.D. His son, Sir Ashton Lever, High Sheriff of Lancashire and F.R.S., had a museum of curiosities in Alkrington Hall.

MILES PLATTING see MANCHESTER, p. 298

MILNROW   9010

ST JAMES. The church was medieval and rebuilt in 1798 and 1815. What we now see is by *Street* and was built in 1868–9 at the expense of the Schofield family. James Schofield, flannel manufacturer who died in 1863, left £3,000 for a future church. In the end his mother and her grandson James gave £3,000 each. James Senior, so the Rev. J. S. Leatherbarrow tells us in his admirable book on Swinton, wished the church to be 'regarded as a thank offering to Almighty God for my worldly prosperity'. The church is solid and serious, but not more, and the interior would hardly make one anxious to inquire for the name of the architect. The octagonal piers have elaborate naturalistic foliage capitals carved by *T. Earp*. The exterior has Dec windows and is dominated by the w tower with its recessed pyramid roof.

In BRIDGE STREET is a row of three cottages which was the Milnrow CHAPEL. The naïve doorway with its Ionic columns and pediment is re-set; it was originally on the upper floor, approached by steps.

CLEGG HALL, 1 m. NW. Derelict, which is much to be regretted. It is a dignified and powerful piece, of basement and two storeys and one attic in the three even gables. The windows are mullioned-and-transomed, and the centre is a two-storeyed porch. The fantastic baluster columns in pairs below show that a date before 1660 is not likely. The single columns above are of fanciful details too. The lower columns are very similar to those of West Riding houses such as The Folly at Settle of 1679.

In addition to Clegg Hall the MHLG lists a number of farmhouses and grades them II, although they have hardly more of remarkable details than mullioned windows. The most interesting is BIRCHINLEY FARM, with mullioned angle windows, and BIRCHINLEY HALL immediately next to it. Both are in WILD HOUSE LANE. Others are MOORGATE EAST FARMHOUSE of 1693 in BROAD LANE, ROUGHBANK FARMHOUSE of 1607 in HUDDERSFIELD ROAD, LOWER CROW NEST FARM of 1669 in KILN LANE, and LADY HOUSE FARMHOUSE of 1631 in LADY HOUSE LANE.)

MONTON

₇₀₉₀

ST PAUL, Egerton Road. 1911 by *R. B. Preston*.* Stock brick and red brick, lancet windows, no tower.

UNITARIAN CHURCH, Monton Green. The dominating building of Monton. It stands in its own graveyard. By *Worthington*, 1875. SW steeple placed outside the S aisle. Transepts and a polygonal apse. Geometrical tracery.

MOORSIDE *see* OLDHAM, p. 360

MOSLEY COMMON *see* BOOTHTOWN

MOSS BANK *see* ST HELENS, p. 385

MOSSIDE *see* MANCHESTER, p. 333

MOSSLEY

₉₀₀₀

A dramatic site, with steep banks and views into the hills.

ALL SAINTS, Micklehurst, itself up a bank. 1891–3 by *Potts, Son & Pickup*. The N tower is odd, with big pinnacles closely framing the octagonal top stage.

(ST GEORGE, Fox Platt, the Mossley parish church. First built in 1755–7. The present church 1879–82 by *A. H. Davies-Colley*. The NE porch tower of 1887.)

ST JOHN BAPTIST, Roughtown. 1878–9 by *Wild & Collins*. With a SW broach spire.

TOWN HALL, by the station, but again up a steep bank. Built as the mansion of George Mayall about 1862. Italianate, asymmetrical, of five bays. Big porch.

MECHANICS' INSTITUTE, Stamford Road, by the old centre. 1858. Of three bays, classical and dignified.

In ROUGHTOWN, which is a street, is a terrace of the early C18, consisting of a two-gabled house with a pedimented doorway and a row of cottages. All windows are mullioned, and most are of four lights. The bigger house has symmetrical fenestration.

But the real monuments around here (*see* Oldham, Introduction) are the cotton-spinning MILLS, large, of four storeys or more.

---

* So Mr Buttress informs me.

mostly of brick and later always with an asymmetrical erection for the tank. A specially old one is in WATERSON LANE. This is dated 1825 (MHLG) and is of stone, four storeys high and nineteen bays long.

MOSSLEY HILL see LIVERPOOL, p. 230

MOSTON see MANCHESTER, p. 335

MYDDLETON HALL see WINWICK

NETHERTON   3000

T OSWALD, St Oswald's Lane, really in Liverpool. By *Quiggin & Gee*, 1960–1. With a detached campanile of the type which is just a concrete frame. The rest is brick.

T BENET (R.C.), Chapel Lane. The mission was founded in 1742 (MHLG), the church built in 1793 (VCH). The only indication of a possible two dates is the fact that the priest's house is brick in Flemish bond, the church brick in English bond. Otherwise the two are exceptionally well integrated. To the street one sees just the house, a neat three-bay house with a pretty doorway. Behind, but on the N side at least flush with it, is the church, with round-arched windows. The altar wall has inside paired Corinthian pilasters and a pediment.

NEWALL GREEN see WYTHENSHAWE, MANCHESTER, p. 345

NEWBOLD see ROCHDALE, p. 380

NEW BURY see FARNWORTH

NEWCHURCH see CULCHETH

NEW HEY   9010

T THOMAS. 1876–7 by *H. Lloyd*. On the hillside, in a spectacular position. The architect was aware of it, and made the most of his dark stone and white stone and his SW steeple. The style he chose was Dec.

NEWTON HEATH see MANCHESTER, p. 335

NEWTON-LE-WILLOWS   5090

T PETER. 1892–1901 by *Demaine & Brierley* of York. Large, of red sandstone, with a sturdy W tower. The style is a free Perp, the details of the tracery with their Arts and Crafts curves

interestingly early for their date. The interior is more con
ventional. – COMMUNION RAIL. Of wrought iron; Georgian
– MONUMENT. By the porch gravestone to Peers Naylor † 1842
with a locomotive in relief. The inscription reads:

> My engine now is cold and still,
> No water does my boiler fill;
> My coke affords its flame no more,
> My days of usefulness are o'er.
> My wheels deny their noted speed,
> No more my guiding hand they heed.
> My whistle, too, has lost its tone,
> Its shrill and thrilling sounds are gone.
> My valves are now thrown open wide,
> My flanges all refuse to guide.
> My clacks, also, though once so strong,
> Refuse to aid the busy throng.
> No more I feel each urging breath,
> My steam is now condensed in death.
> Life's railway's o'er, each station past,
> In death I'm stopped, and rest at last.
> Farewell, dear Friends, and cease to weep,
> In Christ I'm safe; in Him I sleep.

ALL SAINTS, Crow Lane. Minor c20 Gothic; no tower.

ST JOHN BAPTIST, Market Street, Earlestown. 1878 by *C. T
Whitley & Fry* (GR).

ST MARY AND ST JOHN (R.C.), Crow Lane. 1864 by *Edward
Blount*. C13 in style, with an ambitious NE steeple and a poly
gonal apse. The W window is a large convex-sided triangle with
three foiled circles. – The TRIPTYCH over the altar and some
other details modernistic in the English 1930 way, yet by
*Velarde, c.*1958. – (SCULPTURE. Stations of the Cross by *David
John*.)

CONGREGATIONAL CHURCH AND HALL, Crow Lane. Richard
Evans † 1864 left enough money to build a proud Congrega
tional church at Newton. Now they are pulling it down.* The
granite obelisk commemorating him remains, but *si monu
mentum requiris*, other than this, *circumspicere* is no good. What
does however also remain is the preceding church, red brick
with plain lancet windows and a façade with rose-window and
two porches. It probably dates from *c.*1840.

TOWN HALL, Market Street, Earlestown. 1892 by *Thomas
Beesley*. Red brick, in a style ranging happily from plate

---

* At the time of writing.

tracery to shaped gables. The building is placed just off the MARKET PLACE, which is a pity; for that asphalted area is, in spite of an C18 OBELISK, desperately drab.

Earlestown altogether has nothing to recommend it, except perhaps the STATION with a waiting room, Gothic and monumental *en miniature*. It is on the platform, of stone, and has carved beams and a large chimneypiece and an oriel.

Visible from Earlestown is the SANKEY VIADUCT, built by *George* and *Robert Stephenson* for the Liverpool–Manchester Railway to carry it across the Sankey Valley and the Sankey Navigation Canal. So here the county's first railway met the first canal.

For Newton proper the following few buildings have to be added:

TECHNICAL SCHOOL. 1910–11 by *Harry Littler*, the County Architect. Red brick and stone, symmetrical, mildly Baroque

ARCHWAY from Haydock Lodge, now in the High Street. An arch flanked by Tuscan columns which carry a pediment. L. and r. low wings with attached columns and lunette windows. The beginning of the C19 is the most probable date.

DEAN SCHOOL (former), Rob Lane, under the Motorway bridge and l. into the trees. A very humble two-bay cottage with dormers; symmetrical. Built as a school in 1677.

NEWTON PARK, Mill Lane. 1770. Brick, three storeys and five bays. Three-bay pediment. The doorway and the window above it have arched heads.

WOODHEAD, NW of the Winwick access to the Motorway. Probably late C17. Brick, three bays, symmetrical, with mullioned-and-transomed windows – three, two, three lights.

ST OSWALD'S WELL, s of Woodhead. Sunk, and partly stone-lined. The inscription IHS marks it as pre-Reformation.

PARKSIDE COLLIERY. One of the best of the new mines of after the Second World War. 1954–9 by *J. H. Bourne* (National Coal Board). The design is the same as that of the Agecroft Colliery, Pendlebury.

NORDEN *see* ROCHDALE, p. 382

NORRIS GREEN *see* LIVERPOOL, p. 232

NORTH ASHTON *see* ASHTON-IN-MAKERFIELD

NORTHENDEN *see* MANCHESTER, p. 340

OAKENROD *see* ROCHDALE, p. 381

OLDHAM

9000

Mr Kenyon, in his thesis on the mills of Oldham, calls Oldham 'the greatest cotton spinning town in the world'. Before the Industrial Revolution it was no more than a hamlet – as against e.g. Rochdale, which was a market town – and it was water-power driving machines that made Oldham. Mr Kenyon states that the first cotton mill dated from *c*.1778, that by 1780 there were six, three of them still working with horse power, and that the first steam engine went into operation in 1794. By 1800 seven mills used steam. Baines shows the development in these figures: 1794: 12 mills, population 10,000. 1831: 62 mills, population 32,000. 1866: 120 mills, population *c*.80,000. 1888: 265 mills, population *c*.130,000. That the climax is long past hardly needs saying. According to Dr Kenyon it was the time of the cotton famine, i.e. the American Civil War. The greatest building activity belonged to the decade between 1870 and 1880. Closure and demolition characterize the 1930s. Mills before 1850, so Mr Kenyon writes, are near the centre, mostly of stone, and rarely more than four storeys high. Structurally they are essentially of timber. The picture of Oldham is of course entirely dominated by the later mills, long, high, and even, except for a short tower on one end. Nobody can deny that they are impressive. Their bulk dwarfs everything else, and their chimneys make the church spires appear negligible – and, alas, most of the churches architecturally are.

THE CENTRE

From King Street (w) to Mumps (E), and from the railway (s) to the new developments (N).

ST MARY, Church Street, opposite the town hall. The site gives a feeling of spaciousness. The building replaces one which existed in 1448. It was designed by *Richard Lane* and built in 1823–7. The w tower with its polygonal buttresses dominates. The pinnacles here and in the rest of the church are prominent. The bell-openings have intersecting tracery, as have the aisle windows. The chancel is of course short. The aisles seem to embrace the tower. The staircases to the galleries are in these bays; for the church has of course three galleries. The arcade piers are thin and of a Perp type, but with fancy capitals. Octopartite plaster vaults in nave and aisles. One wonders whether the ground stage of the tower can be so early. Porta as well as window look Victorian. – STAINED GLASS. The E window has glass that looks pre-1850. – In the N aisle two windows by *Capronnier* of Brussels, 1866 and 1885. – PLATE. Chalice by *H. N.*, 1663; Chalice of 1678 by *Peter Pemberton*; Flagon by *E. F. Crump*, 1770; Flagon by *T. W.*, 1788; Paten 1790.

T MARY (R.C.), Shaw Street. *See* Outer Oldham.

'or NONCONFORMIST CHAPELS *see* Perambulation.

'OWN HALL, opposite St Mary's. 1841, the architect not recorded. Could it not be *Lane* ? Seven bays, two storeys, ashlar-faced. Four-column portico of unfluted Ionic columns with pediment. In 1879–80 large additions were made and finished with grander façades to Firth Street and Greaves Street, with giant pilasters and giant columns, progressive and impressive work. The architects were *George Woodhouse* of Bolton and *Edward Potts* of Oldham.

;OUNTY COURT, Church Lane. Not at all of the ashlar solidity and taciturn dignity of mid-C19 county courts. This is of 1894 by *Sir Henry Tanner* and decidedly gay. Red brick and yellow terracotta, with plenty of Louis XII and Francis I motifs.

;LUECOAT SCHOOL, Horsedge Street. 1829–34 by *Lane*. Long ashlar front of seventeen bays. The articulation is 3–4–3–4–3. The centre has a steep gable flanked by pinnacles. Pinnacles on other angles as well.

'or other PUBLIC BUILDINGS *see* Perambulation.

;REAVES STREET, already mentioned for the town hall extension, has an interesting small office building by *Edgar Wood*, built in 1901 for solicitors. It is not on a town-centre scale and has decidedly villagey features. Above the doorway a large Art Nouveau panel.

JNION STREET, the main street of Oldham, is wide and has sufficient buildings of some prominence to be remembered. Starting from the station, and indeed still in the street called MUMPS, is the astonishing DISTRICT BANK, with a Baroque corner tower and windows in two storeys separated by paired columns which start naughtily on brackets halfway up the ground-floor windows. The architects were *Mills & Murgatroyd*, and the date is 1902–3. Then, in Union Street, on the S side, the LIBRARY and ART GALLERY of 1883 in a sort of vague Gothic, and on the N side the CONGREGATIONAL CHURCH, 1855 by *R. M. Smith*, with a niche for the portal, a six-light window over with geometrical tracery, and a short, broad, embattled W eminence. On the same side the UNION

CLUB, of six bays with an asymmetrically placed Greek Dori
porch. Opposite the POST OFFICE of 1877. Then, again o
the N side, the SCHOOL OF ART and the LYCEUM, a dignifie
long front, Italianate, with arched upper windows. The buildir
is by *N. G. Pennington*, 1855–6. Opposite are the BATHS o
1854 and 1880 with a French pavilion roof. Here CLEGG
STREET turns N to the town hall, the church, the new develop
ments, and Yorkshire Street, the other main street of the tow
In Clegg Street a number of Late Georgian houses wit
decorated doorcases survive. Then in Union Street the PRU
DENTIAL ASSURANCE, by *A. Waterhouse & Son*, 1901, re
brick of course, with polygonal angle turrets, round-heade
doorways, and mullioned-and-transomed windows. Opposite
the SALVATION ARMY CITADEL of 1886, brick, with tw
turrets. Again on the N side, a white faience CINEMA with
Baroque corner turret (1920, by *G. E. Tonge*). The METHO
DIST CHAPEL on the S side is of 1875, brick with stone dress
ings, Italianate, of five bays with a five-bay pediment, but n
showy. Its neighbour is the TEMPERANCE HALL of 190
low and cheerful, with two segmental tops and diverse motifs o
the late C19.* Turn l. into KING STREET for Messrs DRON
92 FIELD'S offices (opposite Wellington Street) by *J. H. Seller*
1906–7, historically much more remarkable than it is visuall
startling. Just seven bays and two storeys, but the window an
door surrounds of stone cut into such anti-period angul
shapes that the building must be accepted as valid pione
work for a C20 style. The materials are remarkable too: glaze
green brick, Cornish granite, and glass.

In the last few years Oldham and its Borough Architect *T. Car.
lidge* have shown themselves uncommonly enterprising in ne
buildings and large development schemes. They deserve hig
praise. The best building to date is the COLLEGE OF FURTHE
EDUCATION, N of the E end of Middleton Road, not so muc
the long three-storeyed block of brick and glass bands of 1950–
by *Sir Percy Thomas* and *E. Prestwich* as the crisp new building
by *Sir Percy Thomas & Son* of 1965–7.

A new CIVIC CENTRE is growing N of West Street. The ne
HEALTH DEPARTMENT is not up to much, nor is the C. & A
STORE. More is planned, including an assembly hall and
concert hall.

To the E of the N end of GEORGE STREET a new SHOPPIN
CENTRE is being built by *R. Seifert & Partners*, in collaboratio

* Recently changed out of recognition.

with *T. Cartlidge*. One six-storey slab, the rest lower. (The site has a 40 ft fall, and so there are three access-levels from Market Place and Peter Street to a pedestrian deck, from Peter Street to a mid-deck, also pedestrian, and from Silver Street to the service road area.)

Opposite, in George Street, an office building by *Leach, Rhodes & Walker*. In addition very impressive new HOUSING has gone up w of HORSEDGE STREET. This is by the *Ministry of Housing Development Group* in collaboration with *Max Lock & Partners* and *T. Cartlidge*. It is no more yet than ten per cent of the total envisaged, and yet consists already of over 500 dwellings. The scheme has flats as well as terrace houses, in very long ranges, nothing higher than five floors, the higher ranges connected by timber-boarded bridges. There is strict separation of pedestrians from vehicles. The construction is on the 12 M-Jespersen system of precast concrete parts.

OUTER OLDHAM

For churches and public buildings the directions are indicated in brackets.

ALL SAINTS, Chadderton Road (NNW). 1888–91 by *Winder & Taylor*. Very red brick, with a N W tower and mostly lancets. A type characteristic of the date. Normal interior with short columns.

ST ANDREW, Middleton Road (W). 1873 by *Lowe*.

CHRIST CHURCH, Glodwick, E of Mumps Station. 1844 by *A. D. Cuffley*. Only the tower with its fancy battlements and big pinnacles remains. The rest is demolished. The church was built by the Commissioners for c.£2,500.

ST JAMES, Huddersfield Road (NE). 1825–8 by *Goodwin*. A Commissioners' church. It cost £9,652. Grotesquely thin w tower with very thin pinnacles. Three-light Perp windows, the tracery of cast iron. Perp piers of four chamfered projections. Three galleries. The chancel is of 1883.

ST JOHN, Featherstall Road South, Werneth (W). 1844–5 by *E. H. Shellard*. A Commissioners' church (cost £3,026). Perp with a w tower to convince the antiquarian and with transepts. Octagonal piers and capitals with fleurons – again archeologically informed.

OUR LADY OF MOUNT CARMEL (R.C.), Union Street West. 1869–70 by *Mitchell* of Oldham, but mostly now 1907.

ST MARGARET, Chapel Road, Hollinwood (SW). First built i
1766–9, now 1880 by *R. Knill Freeman*. The best feature is th
NW tower outside the N aisle, and that is of 1906.

ST MARK, Glodwick Road (SE). 1876 by *John Wild* of Oldham

ST MARY (R.C.), Shaw Street, just N of the centre. 1838 b
Weightman & Hadfield. With a stuccoed W tower.

ST MATTHEW, Roundthorn Road (SE). 1932–3 by *Taylor &
Young*, and remarkable as a faithful reproduction of a Georgia
chapel. Round-arched windows, entries in the first and las
bays. Small lantern. Only the portal betrays the true date.

ST PAUL, Ashton Road (S). 1880 by *Wild & Collins*.

ST STEPHEN, Lower Moor (N of Mumps). 1873 by *Mitchel*
Tracery of *c*.1300. SW tower with pyramid roof.

ST THOMAS, St Thomas' Circus (SW). 1853–5 by *A. Trimen*,
late Commissioners' church (cost £3,600). NW steeple wit
broach spire. Very flowing tracery in the N transept window.

ST THOMAS, Moorside, off Ripponden Road (2 m. NE). 1872 b
H. Cockburn.

HOLY TRINITY, Bardsley (1¾ m. S). 1844 by *Starkey & Cuffley*
The sides still with long lancets and the W tower very naïve
No aisles, but the transepts as usual about 1840. No gallerie
The parapet is of a kind of Elizabethan openwork. But th
main external feature is the oversized and overhanging pinnacl
pyramids.

HOLY TRINITY, Godson Street (N). 1847–8 by *Shellard*. Nav
with bellcote and chancel.

HOLY TRINITY, Church Street, Waterhead (ENE). 1847 b
Shellard. Built with aid from the Commissioners. Total cos
£2,900. The sides with the Commissioners'-type pairs of lan
cets, but the W tower with a broach spire and the chancel wit
three stepped lancets.

HULME GRAMMAR SCHOOL, Frederick Street (SW). 1893–5 b
J. W. Frith. Red brick, gabled. Central hall with a flèche
Behind it five low classrooms each with its own gable.

Individual buildings need little attention. In WERNETH HAL
ROAD is WERNETH OLD HALL (SW). Its only notable featur
is the gable-end with one five-light window with a transom. A
the S end of ROUNDTHORN ROAD (SE) is the MANOR HOUS
with powerful gatepiers. The house is of five bays, and th
doorway has a pediment.

Recent and interesting are the offices of DEWS & CO. i
FEATHERSTALL ROAD SOUTH (WSW), 1964 by *Leach, Rhode
& Walker*, a quiet, crisp job, and the more exciting and varie

large HOUSING developments by CRETE STREET (SW) and by
PRIMROSE BANK (SW). They are by *Peter Dunham, Widdup
& Harrison* 1963–5 and 1965–7 respectively.
(SPINNING MILLS. Mr J. B. Hawcroft suggests the following,
all early C20, as worthy of special mention:
MAPLE MILLS, off Ashton Road, i.e. S of King Street. By *Sidney
Stott* of Oldham, 1903 and 1914. Accrington brick; not
designed as a group.
ROYD MILL, Hollinwood, near the new Primrose Bank housing.
1906 by *A. J. Howcroft*. Accrington and buff brick.
See also Lees, p. 135, and Royton, p. 383.)

OLD SWAN *see* LIVERPOOL, p. 248

OLD TRAFFORD *see* STRETFORD

OPENSHAW *see* MANCHESTER, p. 336

ORDSALL *see* SALFORD, p. 397

ORFORD *see* WARRINGTON, p. 416

ORRELL   5000

ST LUKE. By *Austin & Paley*, 1927, but the E and W ends as late
as 1938. Polygonal apse. The W tower even now not yet built.
ST JAMES (R.C.), the principal church of Orrell. 1805, lengthened
in 1841, the W tower 1882. The original building must have
been a plain, decently built stone box with arched windows.
The tower is grander, with its ogee cap. The doorway with
pilasters and pediment looks re-used, but is supposed to be
original and *in situ*.
ROMAN CATHOLIC SCHOOL, by the church. By *L. A. G.
Prichard & Partners*. Good.
GREAT MOSS HOSPITAL. An outstandingly good high block
with teak windows and white sill panels and brick entrance etc.
Designed by *A. Brocklehurst* of Chester, 1964–7.
(ABRAHAM GUEST SECONDARY SCHOOL. By *Lyons, Israel,
Ellis & Partners*, 1960–2. Good, with projecting concrete beam
ends.)
ACKHURST HALL, 2 m. NNE. Dated 1686, with two gables, not

of identical size. The smaller belongs to the porch. Round-headed doorway. The recessed centre still has a window much larger than the other (three plus four lights) to mark the hall.

Nos 385–9 GATHURST ROAD, just s of Gathurst Station. This was originally one house. It is dated 1708 and yet still entirely in the Jacobean tradition. Recessed centre and projecting gabled wings. Five-light mullioned windows, asymmetrically set doorway.

BISPHAM HALL, 1 m. SSW. 1573. A symmetrical façade very similar to those of Birchley Hall and Winstanley Hall. Recessed centre and projecting wings. In the re-entrant angles square projections, the r. one the porch with round-arched doorway, the l. one the hall bay. Five gables. Most of the windows with transoms: five lights in the fronts of the projections and in the middle of the hall, four lights in the sides of the wings facing inward and in the hall bay. Round the l. corner is the big chimneybreast of the parlour, and then a large bay window of five sides of an octagon.

An OBELISK with a ball on top, Georgian presumably, faces the front of the Hall.

6090 ## PADGATE

CHRIST CHURCH. 1838, but the chancel by *W. Owen*, 1882. The church has lancet windows and a little modest decoration round the w portal. No galleries inside.

STATION. The type with gables and a variety of Gothic bargeboard patterns.

BRUCHE HALL, Bruche Avenue. Three-bay Georgian house with one-bay pediment. Doorway with thin columns. The front is unfortunately roughcast.

PARKSIDE COLLIERY *see* NEWTON-LE-WILLOWS

PARR *see* ST HELENS, p. 386

PARRS WOOD *see* DIDSBURY, MANCHESTER, p. 320

7090 ## PATRICROFT

Really the w part of Eccles.

CHRIST CHURCH. 1868 by *John Lowe*.

w of the church a three-bay brick house with a decorated doorway and its own stables.

CONGREGATIONAL CHURCH, Franklin Street. Large, of brick, with a stone front. The front has a porch of two pillars and four columns and a big portico all along. Six-bay sides. 1870 by *Woodhouse & Potts*.

The s end of WORSLEY ROAD runs right along the Bridgewater Canal, with the mills across on the other side. The BRIDGEWATER MILL was James Nasmyth's, the famous ironmaster's and inventor's. The works were established in 1836, and a large original building with a plaque 1837 remains among more recent ones. The buildings are now a Royal Ordnance Factory, and a pair of iron GATES from the Woolwich Arsenal will shortly be re-erected. They are supposed to be early C19 and stood in front of the old Shell Foundry.

PEEL *see* WALKDEN

PEEL HALL *see* WYTHENSHAWE, MANCHESTER,
p. 345

PEMBERTON *see* WIGAN, pp. 428, 429

PENDLEBURY 7000

ST AUGUSTINE. By *Bodley*, 1871–4, and one of the most moving of all Victorian churches. Built at the expense of Edward Stanley Heywood, Manchester banker of Heywood Brothers, son of Sir Benjamin Heywood and brother of the Rev. H. R. Heywood, vicar of Swinton, for whom Street built Swinton church in 1869. St Augustine is said to have cost about £33,000. The group including the gatehouse, school, and parsonage, was by Bodley too. The parsonage has been destroyed and the rest is sadly neglected. The whole group is of brick, to deny any sense of luxury. The GATEHOUSE separates the precinct from the road. It has a pointed arch and a LODGE. To the l. is the SCHOOL with two end-gables and mullioned-and-transomed windows. If only someone in building the new school on the opposite side of the precinct had taken care to do something a little better than run-of-the-mill stuff. The church faces you with its E wall. It is a high wall, and the window is placed high up (above the reredos inside). It has flowing tracery, as has the whole chancel. There is blank panelling around, and two flanking pinnacles terminate this part of the composition. The sides of the church appear yet higher. The roof runs through without any break from W to E, penetrated only by the tops of the buttresses, and the side windows are of four lights in the chancel, of three in the nave. The chancel E bay is canted. In the nave the detail is Perp, as if the chancel had been built first. The E bay of the chancel sides cants in a little to meet the E wall. High up, above the top of each window, is a blank arch, so that the window arch is slightly recessed against the top part, a motif Bodley got from Albi and Toulouse, the places which also inspired the interior. On the N side N of the chancel is a two-storeyed vestry. On the S side is a two-storeyed porch, just a little more conventional. The W front has a doorway with statues over and a five-light window, bricked in below the transom. The interior, 159 ft long and 80 ft high, is of breathtaking majesty and purity. Internal buttresses (or what the Germans call wall-piers) pierced only right at the bottom by aisle-like passages, and arches high up from pier to pier with short transverse vaults to the window-tops. This scheme goes through to the very end and is patently derived from Albi. – The commanding REREDOS with tiers of figure painting in the Dürer style was no doubt designed by *Bodley* too. It appears doubly commanding as the sanctuary is raised by eight steps. – The ORGAN CASE is known to be by *Bodley*. – The SEDILIA and the ROOD SCREEN must be his too. – STAINED GLASS. Very individual, especially at the E end. It is all by *Burlison & Grylls*, but apparently designed or supervised by Bodley himself. In a letter to E. J. Heywood he wrote: 'We kept them [the windows] broad in colour, each window having its leading colour. . . . It is about the first time it has been tried in modern times, most new windows having so many colours in them. I think the less variety of colour is more artistic.'* – PAINTINGS. The painted figures in tabernacles high up against the E faces of the niches formed by the wall-piers are by the same hand as the reredos. And whose hand was that?

ST JOHN EVANGELIST, Bolton Road. 1842. Neo-Norman, with a big W tower and side windows of the Commissioners' type. The tower has a row of five round-arched bell-openings and a shallow, rather Italian pyramid roof. The W baptistery is of 1882.

PUBLIC HALL, Bolton Road. Brick, minimum Gothic, 1870 by *W. Williamson*.

ROYAL MANCHESTER CHILDREN'S HOSPITAL. By *Pennington & Brigden*, 1872. With later additions.

* I owe the references to the stained glass to Miss Jean Stevens, and am most grateful to her for this valuable information.

AGECROFT HALL, a timber-framed house, partly of *c.*1500, partly of *c.*1600, was transported in 1926 to New Richmond, Virginia.

The new AGECROFT COLLIERY buildings are among the best of their kind in England. They were designed by *J. H. Bourne* (National Coal Board) and built in 1953–60 (cf. Newton-le-Willows, p. 355).

PENDLETON see SALFORD, p. 394

PENKETH

5080

FRIENDS' MEETING HOUSE, Meeting Lane. Founded 1681, rebuilt 1736. A plain brick parallelepiped with segment-headed windows.

PENNINGTON see LEIGH

PLATT BRIDGE see ABRAM

PLATT HALL see FALLOWFIELD, MANCHESTER, p. 325

POOLSTOCK see WIGAN, p. 428

PRESCOT

4090

ST MARY. The impression of the church is of a classical C18 W tower, aisles with battlements and windows of intersecting tracery, and some bits of masonry (chancel S, N vestry) that indicate an earlier date. The tower is indeed of 1729, with a late C18 spire. The bell-stage has pilasters. And the aisles are of 1819–20. But inside they have plaques with the date 1610, and to that date the five-bay arcade with thin octagonal piers and single-chamfered arches may well belong. But what were the windows of 1610 like? The nave roof is very character-istic work of 1610. It is dated. The wind-bracing is quite different from that of medieval roofs. The date of the Perp stucco panelling of the nave W wall seems unrecorded. – The STALLS with their poppyheads are dated 1636. They are unmistakably C17, but continue the Gothic tradition. – The COMMUNION RAIL, partly projecting W to allow more com-municants to kneel, is a Laudian speciality. – (FONT. 1755. A very pretty piece with a foot with concave sides and leaves and shells. Shallow basin. In the vestry.) – REREDOS. By *Kempe*. – STAINED GLASS. The glass in the E window with its large figures and strong and sombre colours is typical of its date, which is 1840. – S aisle E by *Morris*, date commemorated 1879. It is unusual in that most of the window is filled by light, dainty flower quarries, and there are only three smallish figures: Christ ascending and two angels. – PLATE. Two Cups and two Flagons 1663; two Patens of 1723 and 1738. – MONUMENTS. Sir John Ogle † 1612. Effigy in hose and with hat. Has it always been upright? It may have been. – Thomas Barron † 1751. By *D. Sephton* of Manchester. Tablet with a Rococo cartouche against an obelisk. – Sir William Atherton † 1803. By *Sir Richard Westmacott*. Tablet with a standing angel comforting a kneeling female figure, her hair down.

OUR LADY IMMACULATE, Vicarage Place. 1856–7 by *Joseph A. Hansom*. Wide, aisleless nave, very shallow transepts, divided from the nave by stepped tripartite arcading. Narrow chancel. It is very Hansom.

The terracing E of the parish church is all very fine, but to have pulled down for it the best Georgian buildings of the town remains both stupid and philistine. They were the COURT HOUSE or Town Hall of 1755 and Nos 36–8 Market Place of about the same time.

The mid-passage of the two houses has been re-erected in the garden of FAZAKERLEY HOUSE, Park Road, where at the same time a GAZEBO, also of the same period, has been allowed to collapse.

What remains of Georgian architecture is very small fry: a terrace of cottages in VICARAGE PLACE overlooking the churchyard and one separate house with nice curly brick lintels to the windows, a pair in DERBY ROAD, Nos 52–54, with adjoining doorways, and another, Nos 49–51, with adjoining bow windows, No. 11 HIGH STREET, of five bays, with a pedimented doorcase (and Nos 21–3 SCOTCH BARN LANE, a pair with Gothic details; MHLG).

PRESTOLEE

7000

HOLY TRINITY. By *G. Shaw*, 1863.* A very odd building with very long transepts and a big tower in the angle between nave and S transept. It has an outer staircase rising up two sides of the tower to an upper entrance. The steep set-offs of the diagonal buttresses are as personal. The tower carries a broach spire. Dec tracery. – Bumptious neo-Norman FONT (DB).

(PACKHORSE BRIDGE. Across the Irwell. Built *c.*1790–1800 and 53 yards long but only 5 ft wide. J. D. U. Ward)

* Mr Buttress found the name of the architect.

IRWELL PARK MILLS, Stoneclough. (The MHLG reports that the Riverside Works date in their nucleus from 1823. The chimney, perhaps of 1834, is 180 ft high.) The present mill is enormous, two long seven-storey ranges with identical short towers. Across Market Street is KEARSLEY VALE, the house of the Fletchers (*see* Ringley church) who owned the mill.* It is a three-bay brick house with a porch of pairs of unfluted Ionic columns.

(SEDDON'S FOLD, ¼ m. NW of the church. The farm has a BARN of three pairs of crucks. MHLG)

PRESTWICH

ST MARY. A major church, and one in its medieval parts hard to understand and not as yet fully explained. The E parts are splendid with their height, their two-storey vestry, and their NE turret, but they are by *Paley & Austin*, 1888–9, and offer no problem. The two earlier C19 s chapels are without problems too, one of 1872 the other of 1874. The N chapel poses one *8000* question. Is it original Paley & Austin or a rebuilding of what had been there before? The uncusped tracery is almost convincing Henry VIII, but not quite. The main problems are all round the nave. The tower is normal C15 work. But the aisles have cusped tracery-less windows and a second tier above, of three-light mullioned windows. The clerestory windows are the same. Now the VCH calls that first half of the C16. But they don't seem to mean 1550, and even that surely is too early. The evidence points to an Elizabethan or Jacobean date, and as the only reason for an upper row of aisle windows can be a heightening of the arcades, and as the octagonal arcade piers are very high indeed, must that not indicate that they also are so late? The arches die into them – usually a Dec motif. Re-use? The N aisle w window is indeed Dec of two lights. There is another difficulty inside. The fourth piers from the w include a piece of plain walling and so does the (rebuilt) third pier on the s side. The VCH suggests that the chancel arch corresponded to the latter and that the former is surviving wall of the aisleless chancel of the preceding church. The s porch is dated 1756. – CHANDELIER. Of brass, C18. – MAUSOLEUM. John Brooks † 1849 and his wife † 1851. In the Italian Renaissance style, with figures by *John Thomas* in niches.

---

* The mills were for paper-making, and the Fletchers have nothing to do with the Fletchers of Lever Bridge Bolton (*see* p. 90), who owned collieries.

St Gabriel, Bishop's Road. 1933–4 by *Taylor & Young*. Light brick with a low, broad w tower, broader than it is deep.

St Hilda, Whittaker Lane. 1903–4 by *F. P. Oakley*. Stock brick and red terracotta. Mostly Dec. nw turret.

St Margaret, Rooden Lane, close to Heaton Park, Manchester. A Commissioners' church (£2,000). By *Travis & Mangnall*, 1851–3.

Congregational Church, Newton Street. 1864 by *Alfred Waterhouse*, an early building of his. The school is by him also and followed in 1865.

Wesleyan Chapel, Bury Old Road and Bury New Road. 1865. Red brick with yellow and black brick trim.

Nazareth House, Scholes Lane. The centre, formerly High Bank, is a Georgian five-bay brick house with a three-bay pediment and a porch of two pairs of columns.

In Sedgley Park are still a few manufacturers' mansions left, notably the steep-gabled house now of the Salford Catholic Training College in Queen's Drive.

The Prestwich Hospital started as the County Lunatic Asylum in 1851. In 1862 *Charles Holt* designed additions which were to cost £13,529 (gs). This part of the hospital is immediately w of the Bury New Road. Further sw, in Clifton Road, by the s end of Philips Park, is a second large group, an elongated octagon. This is of 1883–4.

Philips Park survives as a well-tended park, but the house of the Philips family was pulled down in 1950. It was in the Italian villa style. J. & N. Philips & Co. were merchants at Manchester. Mark Philips was one of the first M.P.s for Manchester at the time of the Reform Bill. He later built Welcombe outside Stratford-on-Avon. To this house his brother, who had been M.P. for Bury, later retired too. The London house of the Philips family was in Berkeley Square. The garden furnishings of Philips Park are not of a high order. The prettiest is the thatched cottage close to the Park Lane Lodge, which deserves fully to be restored. The conservatory and the temple near it at the top of the Grass Walk are Early Victorian, the latter with an arch flanked by columns. There is also an icehouse, but at the time of writing its site has been forgotten.

7000

RADCLIFFE

St Mary, Church Green, i.e. about ¾ m. e of the main street. The oldest part of the church is the chancel arch. The details are clearly Dec. The nave arcades of two bays are equally clearly Perp, and probably Late Perp. They are of the type with four broad shafts and four broad diagonal hollows. The big bosses of the (renewed) roof go with such a date, and so do the clerestory windows (uncusped arches to the lights), if they can be trusted. Most of the exterior is Victorian, especially the whole s aisle (1870–3 by *J. M. & H. Taylor*). Its width is that of a former s transept to respond to the N transept, which has some medieval masonry still. But the tower is dated 1665, and the chancel was rebuilt in 1817 (typical tooling). Does the date 1665 also apply to the diagonal buttresses with their many set-offs, or is it only a repairing date? The tower arch anyway looks C15 rather than C17. – SEATS, at the W end of the nave. With panels from the pulpit (date 1606) and some with inscription and date 1665. – STAINED GLASS. In the s aisle a *Kempe* window of 1906. – PLATE. Chalice and Flagon of 1754 by *T. W.* – (MONUMENT. Alabaster slab with the effigies of James de Radcliffe and wife, early C16. Under the altar, says the VCH.)

W of the church is what remains of RADCLIFFE TOWER, a pele tower or tower house, i.e. a tower tunnel-vaulted in the basement. Doorway with a two-centred arch and continuous chamfers. The great hall, which was an eminently interesting timber-framed structure, does not exist any more.

MESOLITHIC SITE. In the gravels just to the s of Radcliffe Tower has been found evidence of a flint industry including flakes and the flake from a transversely sharpened core axe.

ST THOMAS. In the middle of the town, and at first no doubt mistaken by everyone for the parish church of Radcliffe. It is of 1864–9 by *W. Walker* of Manchester, and the estimate was for £7,294 (GS). It is a large Perp church, high and broad, with a commanding W tower, nave and aisles, and chancel. The only unexpected motif is the W windows of the aisles, which make it clear that they house staircases.

ST JOHN EVANGELIST, Stand Lane. 1866 by *J. M. & H. Taylor*. With one of the octagonal crossing towers Taylor was so partial to. s transept rose-window of odd details. W porch and two flying buttresses up the W front, another Taylor favourite. Polygonal apse.

ST ANDREW, Black Lane, 1½ m. NW. 1875–7 by *J. Lowe*.

RADCLIFFE CLOSE METHODIST CHURCH, Bury Street. 1838–9 (enlarged 1898). A typical lancet front of the thirties, with equally typical big pinnacles.

RADCLIFFE BRIDGE METHODIST CHURCH, Milltown Street.

1881–3. Stone, Italianate, with a pedimented portico of two Corinthian columns *in antis*.

TOWN HALL, Spring Lane. 1911 by *W. M. Gillow* and *R. Holt*. Red brick and much stone decoration. Symmetrical, the centre with two giant columns and a segmental pediment. Angle turrets.

MUNICIPAL OFFICES, N of the church in Dumers Lane. Formerly a private villa. The building probably dates from *c.*1830. Brick, five bays, central projection, porch with unfluted Ionic columns *in antis*.

RAINFORD

4000

ALL SAINTS. 1878 by *Aldridge & Deacon*, near the site of a church established in 1577. The NE tower is an addition of 1903 (by Deacon?) and is the best part of the church. Lively top and a charming oriel-like upper ending of the round staircase turret. The interior is not of special interest. – MONU-MENT. Dulcibella Brownbill † 1813. With a small allegorical figure. By *S. & T. Franceys* of Liverpool.

GUILDHALL FARMHOUSE, 2 m. E, close to Billinge. Dated 1688. Brick with a stone porch. Asymmetrical. Gables with ball finials. Mullioned windows.

(SCYTHE STONE DELPH FARMHOUSE, Maggot's Nook Road. 1682. Three bays with central entrance projection. Mullioned windows. MHLG)

RAINHILL

4090

ST ANNE. 1837 by *William Young*. Of that date no doubt the W front with the rather starved Norman tower, and also the aisle-less interior of the nave and its thin-timbered roof. Enlarge-ment of 1843. Is this the S transept and perhaps the W start of a N aisle? All the rest is of 1869 and 1893, Gothic, and of no interest. The CHURCH SCHOOL, W of the churchyard, is dated 1840. It has a nice symmetrical façade with round-arched windows.

49 ST BARTHOLOMEW (R.C.), Rainhill Stoops. Built in 1840. Though not at all large, this is the noblest Catholic church in South Lancashire. The façade is a hexastyle portico of fluted Ionic columns. The S side and the apse have giant pilasters and no windows at all. Attached on the N side is a slightly less severe campanile with the low-pitched roof characteristic of 48 1840. The interior has aisles separated from the nave by giant Corinthian scagliola columns. There are six bays and the apse.

The nave is tunnel-vaulted, with fenestration from clerestory windows which are hidden from outside by a parapet. The apse arch has two columns. The triple archway from the road looks *c.*1880.

LOYOLA HOUSE, by St Bartholomew. The house was Rainhill House, and is supposed to date from *c.*1824. The porch must be recent. The windows have Regency proportions and Tudor hood-moulds.

Rainhill has two worthwhile farmhouses.

RAINHILL OLD HALL, Blundells Lane, ¾ m. SSW. C17. The ground floor stone, the upper floor brick. Mullioned-and-transomed windows. At the back an attached stone wing. (The NMR registers a BARN with crucks.)

MANOR HOUSE, Mill Lane, near its bottom (E) end. 1662. The lintel of the porch entrance has a few large decorative motifs. Mullioned windows.

Also in MILL LANE are two remarkably sumptuous mansions. They are both in a free, undeniably debased Gothic, with all kinds of unexpected motifs. One is BRIARS HEY (St Joseph College). The roof of the stable range is particularly fanciful. The other, THE TOWER (Tower College), is supposed to have been built in 1880, and has a broad tower with two long oriels and a curiously spindly spirelet on top. The designer may have been *George Harris.** It was built for Henry Baxter of Widnes, who made chemicals.

All along Mill Lane and also VIEW ROAD are surprisingly spacious houses. They were presumably for men of Widnes too.

COUNTY LIBRARY, View Road. By *Roger Booth*, the County Architect, 1965–7.

MENTAL HOSPITAL, almost in St Helens, immediately S of Scholes Lane. The oldest part is by *Elmes*, 1847–51. But the huge red brick parts with rubbed-brick dressings and the two identical towers far apart belong to the extensions done by *G. E. Grayson* in 1886.

RAVENHEAD *see* ST HELENS, p. 387

REDDISH

8090

ST ELISABETH, Leamington Road. By *Waterhouse*, 1882–3. A superb job, big-boned, with nothing mean outside or in. Nave, aisles, and apse, SE tower with short spire between pinnacles. The church is of red brick with stone dressings. The windows

* I have to thank Mr R. Dickinson for an informative letter.

are round-headed, and Waterhouse never decides which of the round-arch styles he wants to commit himself to. In the tower is a Norman doorway with zigzag, the s doorway is Transitional, but the interior is Italian in many motifs. Yet Waterhouse is recognizable everywhere. The nave is amazingly high, with a cradle roof. The brickwork is exposed, except for the marble facing of the chancel and apse. The arcade has short, fat columns of polished granite and very wide single-step arches – so wide that the arcade consists of only four bays. The chancel and apse are rib-vaulted, and so is the s chapel, apsed like the chancel. Typical Waterhouse capitals. – SCREEN. Of marble, entirely Venetian, with four figures on top. – REREDOS. Of low marble columns. – STAINED GLASS. In the clerestory by *Frederick Shields*, in the apse by *Kempe*.

Waterhouse also designed the RECTORY, again with many unmistakable Waterhouse features, the more straightforward SCHOOL N of the rectory, and the WORKING MEN'S CLUB, SE of the church and facing it with a big bow-window.

The church was built at the expense of Sir William Houldsworth,
67   and the Houldsworths' REDDISH MILLS just w of the Waterhouse group are indeed a striking sight too. A range of forty-five windows, four storeys high, of red brick, grouped into a centre of nine bays plus one-bay turrets with deep-eaved pyramid roofs plus the wings. The windows above the arched ground floor are set in giant blank arches. The whole is centred on RUPERT STREET. Standing at the w end of this one sees the middle clock feature, the date 1865, and behind it the high factory chimney.

Moreover, a beginning was made to build E of the mill a MODEL ESTATE. A few terraces, especially the two facing the N wing, were actually built, and the street layout indicates how it was meant to go on.

ST MARY, Reddish Road. 1862–4 by *Shellard & Brown*. No tower. The window details are remarkably incorrect, Dec, with colonnettes as mullions.

REDVALES *see* BURY, p. 100

8000   RHODES

ALL SAINTS. 1854–64.

The textile printing-works of SALIS SCHWABE & CO. have an octagonal chimney of exceptional height. It was erected in 1846. Close to it is the works LIBRARY of 1864.

RINGLEY

Of the church built in 1625 the pathetically thin TOWER stands on its own in the churchyard, overtowered by the cooling towers of the Kearsley Power Station behind, just as RINGLEY OLD BRIDGE, a one-arched narrow C17 (?) stone bridge with cut-waters both sides, is outdone by the concrete bridge next to it.

ST SAVIOUR. The new church in the same churchyard is of 1850–4, by *Sharpe & Paley*, but not as interesting as other Lancashire churches by Sharpe. Nave and chancel; SW turret. The aisle piers round, the Late E.E. windows of the simplest. The best feature is the chancel, all lancets. The church was built with a small grant from the Commissioners (total cost £2,500). – MONUMENTS. Matthew Fletcher, J.P., † 1808. A large standing figure with a sword leans on a high pedestal with the portrait medallion. Also a pair of scales in relief. – Ellis Fletcher † 1834. A large female figure weeps over a pedestal with portrait in profile.*

RISLEY

ATOMIC ENERGY AUTHORITY SITE. A large area with a number of big blocks with curtain walls. 1956 etc. They are by *T. L. Viney* and *R. S. Brocklesby*. Two large, six-storeyed office blocks plus laboratories and a reactor.

ROBY see HUYTON

ROCHDALE

INTRODUCTION

In spite of the C13 evidence inside its parish church and the granting of a market before the end of that century, Rochdale is a town of the C19 and C20. Its fame is entirely connected with liberalism – Cobden was M.P. from 1859 to 1865, John Bright's brother the first mayor – and social progress. For at Rochdale the first Co-operative Society, the Rochdale Pioneers, was created in 1844. The population in 1801 was 29,000, in 1851 80,000; it is now about 86,000.

The visual character of Rochdale is determined by the area of town hall and church. Here all is completely different from other

* For the Fletchers see Prestolee.

Lancashire towns, and indeed English towns. The town hall lies surrounded by public gardens on three sides and the church lies up a steep bank, and the bank is also public garden. So the centre is green and pleasant, and the hurried visitor never knows that a few steps away all is mean shopping streets without character or direction. However, Rochdale has big plans for comprehensive redevelopment. The seven high blocks of flats* facing the town hall may do visual damage to that dramatic building, but as an earnest of intention they must be respected. Moreover they are well and crisply designed. Whether high blocks of flats are the answer to slum clearance is another matter, and one which does not concern *The Buildings of England*.

INNER ROCHDALE

CHURCHES

ST CHAD. This, as we have seen, is a medieval church, but externally nobody would expect that. Inside, however, it is obvious that a church existed in the C13. The arcades of six bays have piers alternating between round and octagonal. The first two from the W on both sides have decorated capitals, stiff-leaf, upright leaves, and heads, the piers further E have broaches at the springing of the arches. All the arches are double-chamfered. The high tower arch is C14. All the rest is C19 and chiefly of the restoration of 1850 etc. by *Joseph Clarke* and the years 1883–5, when *J. S. Crowther*, an architect of higher talents, rebuilt and lengthened the chancel. The six narrow bays inside are a fine contrast to the wide bays of the nave. The N aisle was rebuilt in 1854–5, the S aisle in 1873–5. In the seventies also the tower was heightened and given the large and ornate bell-stage. – STALLS and SCREENS. Some parts are original Perp work, especially the heraldic panels. – COMMUNION RAIL in the S chapel with twisted balusters, probably late C17. – STAINED GLASS. *Morris* glass in the W window, 1872–4. The draperies are rather more agitated than is usual in the work of the Morris firm. – PLATE. Chalice C17 (?); Paten of 1698–9 by *S. H.*; Paten 1702; Almsdish 1722; two Flagons 1724 by *Jonah Clifton*; Flagon 1772–3 by *I. C.*; two Chalices 1807 by *W. Abdy*. – MONUMENTS. In the S (Dearden) chapel. Incised alabaster slab to John Dearden,

* COLLEGE BANK FLATS. By *R. D. Thornley*, succeeding *W. H. G. Mercer*. Four are of twenty storeys, three of sixteen. They are built on the No-Fines system, with posts and beams cast *in situ*.

rector in the C14, and brasses to members of the Dearden family. All these are forgeries arranged for by James Dearden at the time, about 1847, when the S chapel had become the Dearden Chapel. – The monument to Jacob Dearden † 1825 is by *Sievier*. It is a large standing monument with a young female leaning over a pedestal with an urn and a profile medallion. – James Hole † 1712. Standing monument with a fluted urn in an aedicule of pilasters and pediment. No figures. It could not be more up-to-date in a London church. – Many tablets, e.g. Thomas Smith † 1806 with a woman by an urn, John Hopwood † 1813 with a trophy, and John Entwisle † 1827 with a sarcophagus.

The VICARAGE is an early C18 brick house of two storeys with stone quoins, a pedimental gable, and a pretty doorway with a small shell carved inside the hood.

ST ALBAN, Manchester Road. 1855–6 by *Joseph Clarke*.

GOOD SHEPHERD, Entwisle Road. 1900–13 by *E. H. Lingen Barker*.

ST JAMES, Yorkshire Street. 1821. Ashlar. w tower with single-storey attachments. Along the sides three-light Perp windows. Short chancel. No aisles, and no galleries now, though probably originally. The SCHOOL of 1831 behind is derelict.

ST JOHN BAPTIST (R.C.), Dowling Street. 1924 by *Hill, Sandy & Norris*. Quite a surprise, with its concrete dome and the four short and narrower arms of a Greek cross. The dome has small windows at its base like Aia Sophia, and chancel and apse are covered with MOSAICS in Early Christian imitation. For its date all this is of course desperately reactionary, but at Rochdale it impresses all the same.

ST MARY, Toad Lane. Of the church of 1740 *Comper* re-used the N side and parts of the W and E walls when, in 1909–11, he built his church behind. The whole is of brick, Comper's lighter and and sounder than the old brick. The C18 windows are arched on pilasters. Comper lengthened them, and the balustrade is his. He wanted that sense of flatness and cubic simplicity to set off his gables. The old church had nave and aisles and three galleries. What Comper used is the N aisle, but the arcade is his. He connected the Georgian with his Gothic in an adventurous way. He made the nave of his N aisle, the old aisle an outer chapel, and built his nave to the S without a S aisle. The old and the new nave are of about the same width, but the new nave is higher than the old and that of course much higher than the old aisle. So we have two arcades, one low, the other emphatically high. The low one has the Tuscan columns of the c18 building* and new round arches, the new one extremely tall piers, alternately round and concave-sided octagonal. The s wall is high, with seven large three-light Perp windows. But the Perp is simplified, and in the nave w window really nearer c17 than c15 Gothic. The s wall shows no separation of chancel from nave. There is a cupola of Comper's on his part of the building. His interior is stone-faced, though the exterior is brick. – *Comper* also designed the ROOD SCREEN and ROOD, the NORTH SCREEN, and alas the STAINED GLASS in the E, the W, and the N aisle (i.e. former nave) E window. These anaemic figures in a technique alien to work in glass have much to answer for. The w window is of 1923, the E window of the old nave of 1926. – The PULPIT comes from the old building, but of course only its body. – The FONT is of 1866, and the new surroundings make it more interesting.

FRIENDS' MEETING HOUSE, George Street. 1807–8, a plain stone house without any adornment.

HOPE STREET CHAPEL. 1810 and 1848. Brick. Three bays, no pediment. Two tiers of windows tied together by a giant arch. The SCHOOL to the w has arched windows too.

BAILLIE STREET METHODIST CHURCH. 1837 with alterations of 1840, 1881, and 1882. Brick, five by six bays. Two tiers of arched windows. Three doorways with Greek Doric columns, the middle one also with a pediment.

TRINITY PRESBYTERIAN CHURCH, at the N end of Manchester Road. 1868–9. Geometrical tracery, modest s w steeple.

UNITARIAN CHURCH, Blackwater Street. 1856 by *Henry Bowman*. Small, with geometrical tracery. No tower; w porch.

PUBLIC BUILDINGS

70 TOWN HALL. The Rochdale Town Hall is one of the dozen most ambitious High Victorian town halls of England. It has not the genius of Elmes's St George's Hall, Liverpool, nor the concentration of Leeds and Bolton, nor the supreme skill of pulling together a complicated composition of Manchester, but it has panache and it is picturesque, and the citizens have every right to be proud of it. A competition was held in 1864 and won by *W. H. Crossland* of Leeds. Building took from 1866 to 1871. The foundation stone was laid by John Bright. The building is 303 ft long. It is Gothic, but such as no Gothic town hall

* It is not certain whether Comper did not lengthen them.

could ever have been. The tower, as built by Crossland, stood at the l. end, as today, but immediately l. of the stepped gable. Another stepped gable is at the r. end of the façade, but the two and their immediate appendages differ so as to avoid symmetry. The Great Hall on the other hand, with its flèche and its three-bay porte-cochère, is in the middle. So it is a composition of various parts, and it can be blamed for being disjointed. Crossland's tower had a spire higher than that now, but the spire was found to have developed dry rot. It caught fire a little later and *Waterhouse*, fresh from his Manchester glories, was commissioned in 1883 to build the new tower, a supremely confident piece with its entirely free crowning features. It is 190 ft high.

As one enters, one is in a three-naved vaulted hall intended to be used as the wool exchange. It leads to the staircase hall, with high vaults on piers between the flights of the staircase, which starts in one and returns in two. The Great Hall is 90 ft long. It has a hammerbeam roof and a WALL PAINTING of Runnymede by *Henry Holiday*, painted in 1870 and 35 ft long. At the ends of the building, which has little depth, are spiral staircases. On the l. of the entrance hall is the Assembly Room, with stencilled walls, transverse stone arches, and a Gothic chimneypiece. Next in order of lavishness of decoration comes the Mayor's Suite. It includes Council Chamber, Reception Room, and Mayor's Parlour with stone chimneypiece, patterned ceilings, stencilled walls, and pictorial friezes. The Council Chamber has four great stone arches with traceried spandrels. In the Reception Room corbels represent Crossland, the Mayor, and others. The Magistrates' Court is as lavish. Glass, carvings, and paintings provide a lot of symbolism and imagery. Stone carving is by *G. Law* of Rochdale, wood carving by *Earp* of London, stained glass and wall painting by *Heaton, Butler & Bayne*. – In the rising park behind the town hall is a STATUE of John Bright by *Hamo Thornycroft*, 1891.

LIBRARY, Esplanade. 1883–4 by *S. Sydney Platt*, Borough Surveyor, but actually designed by *Jesse Horsfall*. Three bays, stone, free-Elizabethan.

ART GALLERY AND MUSEUM, Esplanade. 1903–12. A pretty recessed link connects it with the library. The diagonal gable and the gable to the Esplanade have large panels of figures connected with the arts.

CENTRAL SCHOOL, Nelson Street. 1892. Red brick with red terracotta. Behind, in Fleece Street, an earlier range with pedimented ground floor.

FIRE STATION, Maclure Road. 1933, with a high tower. Brick and much stone.

PERAMBULATION

The centre of Rochdale by the town hall is confusing. The open spaces seem accidental, and the streets have no axial relation. The swagger Georgian white stone building of WILLIAMS DEACON'S BANK in THE BUTTS with its semicircular porch and Palladian windows is, it seems, of 1913, though based on what had been built in 1803. At the beginning of LORD STREET are two rounded corner buildings, always a good start for a street. One of them is LLOYDS BANK in a house of 1708 with pilasters in two tiers. It is an extremely surprising motif in Lancashire for such a date, but yet supposed to be original. Up TOAD STREET on the w side is the pioneer shop from which, in 1844, the whole Cooperative shopping movement started.

OUTER ROCHDALE

NORTH

CHRIST CHURCH, Healey. 1849–50 by *G. Shaw*. Built for *c.*£2,500 with the help of a Commissioners' grant. sw broach spire, geometrical tracery. Three-gabled E end. Wide nave, the piers differing N from S. The fanciful organ arch in the chancel should not be overlooked, and the elaborate wooden SCREENS of the S chapel.

ST EDMUND, Falinge. 1873 by *J. M. & H. Taylor*. In the middle of a circus. Crossing tower with higher stair-turret. Geometrical and fancy tracery. The w porch indicates externally that steps lead up inside it. The church, so Mr Buttress writes, 'was built lavishly from the pocket of Albert Hudson Royd, a prominent freemason. Almost every fitting and feature has reference to the lore of masonry; so that for example the whole building is raised up on a battered stone plinth; certain dimensions are said to relate to, or be proportional to, those of Solomon's temple. All this is carried through with a conviction that is inescapable as one looks at the building. They let themselves go to the tune of £22,000 at a time when a good church could be provided for half that amount. The grand central lantern leads one to expect an open tower inside; originally this was the case, and since it was closed off the interior has lost both light and scale. Four enormous granite shafts, almost detached, bear the great tower walls. The transepts are visually the same length as the nave (which has an extra bay filled by a gallery) and again about the size of the short chancel. Nave and transepts are covered by massive timber roofs; that over the chancel is much richer in design – a tour de force, faceted, columned, and panelled with bewildering complexity. The roof of the Royd Chapel, the carved corbels, capitals, hammerbeams, and reredos, show Arts and Crafts influence.'

ST PATRICK (R.C.), Elliott Street. By *Desmond Williams & Associates*, 1965–8. Simple plan with somewhat raised centre. Brick facing. Most windows very slender and elongated.

FALINGE PARK. Of the mansion MOUNT FALINGE only the façade and two linked one-bay pavilions remain. It was a stone house of the late C18, of five bays and two storeys, with a three-bay pediment. Doorway with four columns.

OLD FALINGE, Falinge Fold, at the end of the old lane. 1721, yet in William-and-Mary style, i.e. with windows with wooden mullions and transoms.

HEALEY HALL, Shawclough Road. 1774. Seven bays and two storeys; stone. Three-bay pediment with a very elementary cartouche. Doorway with attached columns and pediment.

NORTH-EAST

ALL SAINTS, Foxholes Road. 1865–6 by *J. Medland Taylor*. This must have been an inexpensive job. SW tower with broach spire. Nave and aisles, some capitals with non-archeological decoration. Only a touch of the rogue here and there, e.g. in the S transept doorway.

FOXHOLES, Foxholes Road. 1793. A five-bay stone house. Round the corner a large Venetian window to light the staircase.*

BUCKLEY. At Buckley is still the ensemble of MILLS and mill-owner's house. The main mill was built for James Schofield & Co., is dated 1863, and is a big, four-storeyed red-brick block with yellow-brick giant arches. Behind a lower and smaller stone mill, probably the predecessor. The villa is Italianate with a big Elizabethan bow. It was built shortly after 1860 by W. W. Schofield.‡

EAST

ST ANNE, Milnrow Road, Belfield. 1912–13 by *R. B. Preston*. Stone, with a S tower and windows with ogee-arched lights.

---

* Mr Jeffrey Haworth reports an excellent interior.
‡ The mill has recently been demolished.

Typically early C20 the batter of the tower and of the buttresses. Equally typical the arcade piers with, instead of capitals, just slightly projecting chunks.

ST PETER, St Peter's Street, Newbold. 1868–71 by *J. M. & H. Taylor*. Stone laid crazy-paving-wise and red-brick trim. The SW tower was not built. The bricks in places form weird patterns. Large interior with a polygonal apse. The apse has fanciful panelling. – Much STAINED GLASS by *J. Capronnier*, 1888–90 and *F. Comère & Capronnier*, 1894–1908.

SOUTH-EAST

ST LUKE, Deeplish Road, Deeplish. 1888–98 by *R. Knill Freeman*. Red brick, all under one roof, no tower. The windows are two lancets and a circle all beneath a blank arch. It is quite an impressive, even if a derivative building.

ST MARY, Oldham Road, Balderstone. 1871–2 by *J. M. & H. Taylor*. Large, with a NW steeple. Inside, four-light stone screens between chancel and organ chamber and vestry. The only true Taylor touch is the N transept exterior. (The interior has polished granite columns and a central space with high transeptal arches and a yet higher chancel arch. The chancel roof is braced and cusped and panelled. The other roofs have scissor trusses. Worthwhile carving, especially of the roundels over the arcades. D. Buttress) SCHOOL S of the church. PARSONAGE S of the school.

SOUTH

ST MARTIN, Manchester Road, Castleton. 1860–2 by *Ernest Bates*. With a NW steeple, in the late C13 style.

GEORGE AND DRAGON, Manchester Road. By *Edgar Wood* 1897. Picturesque Tudor, gabled, but still in a style more derivative than that of the Middleton Wesleyan Church of two years later. Windows with very small panes. One-storeyed bow at the the r. angle.

SOUTH-WEST AND WEST

Along the MANCHESTER ROAD are the villas of the Victorian affluent. One stands out among them, *Joseph Clarke*'s DUNSTER HOUSE of 1860, mentioned in Eastlake's *Gothic Revival* and indeed very Gothic. (Good fireplaces etc. Mr Sykes tells m that the date 1854 is on a tile in the hall.)*

* Since this was written the house has been pulled down. It is a great pity

(Off the Manchester Road, in the Bolton Road, is BARCROFT, an early house by *Edgar Wood*: picturesque, with its stone-slab roof, its Tudor bay-window set diagonally at a corner, and its homely, low, mullioned windows.)

ST AIDAN, Manchester Road. 1914 by *Temple Moore*, well placed to be viewed from the N and E. Random-laid stone. Broad W tower, chancel a little higher than the nave, the windows lancets, much as about 1820. But how different is the total effect! The interior is white and cream, plaster and stone. Three-bay nave, square piers, those which carry the W tower even more massive than the others. Unmoulded arches. The chancel chapels of two bays N, three bays S. Above them a triforium, and that has pointed arches N, round arches S. Also the chancel has a clerestory, the nave hasn't. It sounds arbitrary, but the ensemble does not lack unity. In the walls stone-surrounded niches for the central heating. An external PULPIT on the S side.

ST GEORGE, Bury Lane, Oakenrod. 1938–9 by *Robert Martin*. Light brick, with a long roof and no tower. Square attachments and straight-headed windows.

MORMON CHURCH, Manchester Road and Tweedale Street. 1961–4 by *T. P. Bennett*. With too many of the gimmicks of the 1960s.

ROCHDALE CEMETERY, Bury Road. Dated 1855 on the gates. The chapel is very curious indeed – on the principle of Anglo-Saxon Barton-on-Humber. The central tower is the nave. Otherwise only a W porch and a chancel bay. By *Moffatt Smith*.

MARLAND HOSPITAL, Bury Road. The core is the former WORKHOUSE of 1851.

TWEEDALE STREET SCHOOL. 1895, and characteristic of that date with its red brick and yellow terracotta.

BURY ROAD. Here, as in the Manchester Road, were villas of rich Victorians. The largest is BEAUMONDS, in a free Jacobean. (This was erected prior to 1863 and rebuilt in 1900.)

NORTH-WEST

ST CLEMENT, Spotland Bridge. 1835 by *Lewis Vulliamy*. A Commissioners' church (cost £4,000). The E front deliberately designed so as to appear W. On the gable is a square bell-turret, and there are the usual one-storey attachments. The sides have pairs of lancets and buttresses. Three galleries inside.

ST PAUL, Norden. 1860–1 by *G. Shaw*. W tower with broach
spire. The s transept with its fancy tracery and its bellcote
facing s is an odd touch.

FERNHILL, off Rooley Moor Road, is dated 1691, but still ha
mullioned windows. The door lintel has the kind of simple
ornamental treatment typical of the West Riding.

ROUGHTOWN *see* MOSSLEY

9000

ROYTON

ST PAUL. Built originally in 1754. The present building is o
1884–9, by *H. Cockburn*. NW steeple. Five bays of short granit
columns. – STAINED GLASS. The E window of five light
evidently by *Hardman*.

ST AIDAN AND ST OSWALD, Rochdale Road. 1964–5 by *E*
Massey. An *omnium gatherum* of materials and of motifs of th
sixties, but without the new aggressiveness. The church i
reached from the street up an asymmetrically placed, long
broken staircase or at ground level at the E end; so marked is th
fall of the site. Tile likenesses of two saints by the *Pilkingto*
Design Unit. The best feature is the altar surround.

ST ANNE, Broadway. One of *Temple Moore*'s most interestin
churches, done in 1908–10 (tower 1927) and, while lackin
some of the refinements of others, more inventive and radica
than most. In fact the one criticism one can make of the interic
is that too many motifs are introduced. Externally there ca
hardly be criticism. The church is reached from the N pa
two SCHOOLS, the E one by *Temple Moore* himself, 1916, th
other by *Leslie Moore*, his son, 1933–4. They are a perfe
prelude, varied in a very free Tudor way, kept low and hence
not competing. The church itself has a high, unbuttressed, i.
sheer and square-topped, s tower. It stands out from the s wa
of the church and is balanced on the N side by a shallow transe
for the organ. The E end has a somewhat lower attachme
housing the Lady Chapel. And whereas nave and chancel ru
on unbroken under one large steep roof, the Lady Chapel
square at the top. Also, whereas most of the windows ha
flowing tracery, there are here plain small Elizabethan or c
mullioned windows. The baptistery is yet lower and has
lean-to roof against the W wall. The interior is hard to describ
The nave is short, of only two wide bays, and has a ceil
wagon roof on wall-piers, to use the translation of the Germ
Wandpfeiler, i.e. really buttresses placed inside (as well

outside) and connected on top by broad, plain pointed arches. They are pierced by low, round-arched aisle passages, and their windows have to the inside a wall-passage with stepped tripartite arcading. The same details are taken up again for the chancel, after the interruption of transept and tower, and the wagon roof runs through without any interruption. But the chancel is raised by four steps. Then, however, the Lady Chapel is separated from the chancel by a triple arcade of pointed arches, and this motif is echoed in the triple arcade between nave and baptistery. Here, in terms of the years before Western countries shed historic precedent entirely, is an architectural polyphony which transforms precedent into something unprecedented.

(ELK MILL. 1926 by *Arthur Tadner*. A late example of the early C 20 type: cf. Oldham, p. 361. J. B. Hawcroft.)

RUSHOLME *see* MANCHESTER, p. 320

ST HELENS

5090

INTRODUCTION

St Helens is a centre of the South Lancashire coal industry. It is also a centre of the British glass industry. Pilkington's employ over 13,500, United Glass nearly 4,000. The technique of casting plate glass had been developed in France in the 1680s. The centre was St Gobain. When in 1773 the British Cast Plate Glass Company was founded at Ravenhead, now part of St Helens, the manager was a Frenchman, Jean-Baptiste François Graux de la Bruyère. The company did not do well at first, and it was only after 1800 that it began to flourish. But other companies at St Helens and in other places cast plate glass too, and yet others on the Continent and in America. The industry had a bad time in the later C 19, and the British Plate Glass Company was finally taken over by Pilkington's of Cowley Hill. It does not do cast plate glass at St Helens now, but pressed glass. Coal, however, had preceded glass at St Helens. Coal pits at Sutton Heath are recorded in 1588, and the Sankey Navigation Works, completed in 1762, i.e. preceding the Bridgewater Canal, were carried out to help the transport of coal. It ran to Warrington and later to Widnes. But even so St Helens was still very small when the C 19 began. There were only c.7,500 inhabitants in 1801. The railway came in 1833. Inhabitants in 1851 were c.25,000. Now there are about 105,000.

Architecturally there is nothing to be said for St Helens. The centre is one of the least acceptable in Lancashire. The best buildings by far are the recent ones for Pilkington's.

THE CENTRE

ST HELEN, Church Street. 1926 by *Caröe*. Large, of red brick, with a high, freely-Gothic NE tower, impressively detailed, and a W porch. The style is developed from Dec and Perp but no longer historicist. The piers inside are of free shapes too. The arcade piers carry arches, but the shafts towards the nave are continued in blank arches framing the clerestory windows and of a shape different from that of the arcade arches. The N transept does not project; the chancel E wall is slightly canted.

HOLY CROSS (R.C.), Corporation Street. 1860–2 by *J. J. Scoles*. Brown and red stone; no tower, Dec style. Thin octagonal piers. A frilly, lacy wooden chancel arch.

ST MARK, City Road. 1883 by *James Gandy* of St Helens. Red brick, with lancet windows and a SW steeple. Apse at the E end. The brickwork is exposed inside. It is a serious, competent building, and the W front is very good.

ST MARY (R.C.), North Road, Lowe House. 1924–30 by *Charles B. Powell*. Large and very ambitious with its high W tower and its copper dome over the crossing. It is unfortunate that the two never agree. The building is mainly Gothic, see the flying buttresses and the quite impressive shape and details of the tower. The octagonal crossing tower is Gothic too and castellated. It would be better if the dome had never been put on. But the windows are all round-headed, and the transepts and apse are semicircular, and inside the impression is even more Mediterranean, in spite of the Gothic rib-vaulting of nave and aisles. The four-bay arcade has pink granite columns with capitals in no way period.

ST THOMAS, Westfield Street. Red brick and large, with a prominent NW tower. The chancel is by *Aldridge & Deacon*, 1890–1, with an E wall and internal details typical of them. The nave was by *James Barry*, 1910, but was burnt in 1960 and rebuilt in a fiery red. Successfully free Gothic tower top. Nave with tall paired lancets. Rather a spindly arcade.

CONGREGATIONAL CHURCH, Ormskirk Street. Brick, large, in an indefinable style. The windows segment-headed, but the major ones with Gothic overtones. The façade is of 1883, by *Picton, Chambers & Bradley*.

METHODIST CHURCH, Corporation Street. 1869. Big, Italianate, of brick.

FRIENDS' MEETING HOUSE, Church Street. 1679–92, rebuilt in 1763 (not 1753, as the sundial says). The rebuilding cannot have amounted to much. The architecture cannot be later than *c*.1700. Low, two-storeyed, of stone, asymmetrical, with low five-light and three-light windows. The E window alone is higher and has a transom. It is of seven lights. The meeting house is the oldest still in use in Lancashire.

TOWN HALL, Victoria Square. 1873–9 by *H. Sumners* of Liverpool. Not a masterpiece. Gothic, of brick with much stone, with an asymmetrically placed tower. The details and those of the whole building, e.g. the canopy over the entrance, are very odd.

GAMBLE INSTITUTE, Victoria Square. 1894, of brick, and of no value.

THEATRE ROYAL, Corporation Street. Reconstructed in 1962–3 under the patronage of Pilkington's by *B. & N. Westwood, Piet & Partners*.

MARKET HALL, Naylor Street North. 1851, of brick, low, with pedimented entrances N and S.

SHAW STREET STATION. Rebuilt nicely in 1960–1 (*W. R. Headley*, architect of the Midland Region).

There is no PERAMBULATION, as there is not a single remarkable private building in St Helens, except perhaps Messrs BEECHAM'S in Westfield Street, because of its high tower. The building is of 1886, by *H. V. Krowlaw & H. May*.

OUTER ST HELENS

NORTH-WEST, NORTH, NORTH-EAST

ST DAVID (R.C.), Eskdale Avenue, Moss Bank. 1956–7 by *J. M. Wilson*. A well-balanced front with a square campanile on the l., low arcades in front of it, and a bare façade wall on the r. with a pitched roof and one large arched window. The church is grouped round a courtyard with presbytery and hall.

ST PATRICK (R.C.), Loughrigg Avenue, Clinkham Wood. By the *F. X. Velarde Partnership*, 1963–4. A group culminating in the impressive church with two monopitch roofs rising towards one another, one of low pitch, the other extremely steep. The vertical wall up to the ridge of the latter is all grass, which results in a dramatic light effect inside.

13—S.L.

ST THOMAS (R.C.), Dentons Green Lane. 1892–3 by *Pugin & Pugin*.

CREMATORIUM, Rainford Road, Dentons Green. 1959–62 by *H. Bannister*. Brick and stone, square and dignified. The small, separate CHAPEL OF REMEMBRANCE is ashlar-faced and windowless.

WINDLESHAW R.C. CEMETERY. In it the W tower of the CHAPEL OF ST THOMAS OF CANTERBURY, founded as a chantry by Sir Thomas Gerard *c.*1435. Plain tower with the arch towards the former nave and the roof-line. Low courses of masonry, largely re-erected, indicate the nave and chancel walls. – E of the tower the tomb-chest of J. B. F. Graux de la Bruyère † 1787.

WINDLESHAW CEMETERY. 1858 with three Chapels and Lodges. The architect was *John Middlehurst*, a local builder.

In VICTORIA PARK the stately Italianate villa of Mr Ansdell, an attorney. The style is typical of *c.*1850. Asymmetrical tower with the low pitched roof of 1840–50. All façades are asymmetrical.

In RAINFORD ROAD No. 57* has a very handsome shell-hood over the door, dated 1742. Carved brackets. One would guess 1710–20 as the date.

EAST

ST MARY IMMACULATE (R.C.), Blackbrook Road, Broad Oak. 1844–5 by *Weightman & Hadfield*. Aisleless and towerless; Dec. Bellcote on the nave E gable.

ST PETER, Broad Oak Road, Parr. 1864–5 by *J. Medland Taylor*. Walling in three different colours, ironstone, red stone, buff stone. SW broach spire; plate tracery. The double S transept leads to odd timber quirks inside. Exterior and interior typical of Medland Taylor's crotchetty performances.

HOLY TRINITY, Traverse Street. 1857 by *W. & J. Hay*. They were the last to hold out for aisleless naves and long, wide transepts, i.e. the pre-ecclesiological theme. Crazy-paved walls. No tower. Style of *c.*1300. The apse is a later alteration (1883–4 by *J. Gandy*).

SOUTH-EAST AND SOUTH

ALL SAINTS, Ellamsbridge Road, Sutton. 1893 by *Austin & Paley*. Sizeable, and in the best Austin tradition. A central

* Just outside St Helens.

tower was unfortunately not built. Red stone, the details and especially the tracery already free of archeological correctness. The preference is for rounded arches inside the Perp windows. The porch at the w end of the s aisle open to the w. Dignified interior.

ST NICHOLAS, New Street, Sutton. 1848–9 by *Sharpe & Paley*. The squat w tower is of 1897. The church has early C14 detail. Typical small clerestory windows with three foiled circles and similar motifs. Typical also the angel corbels and hefty shafts for the roof. – STAINED GLASS. The E window (date commemorated 1879) must be by *Holiday* and *Powell*'s.

ST THERESA (R.C.), Canon Street, Clock Face. Begun 1930 by *Peter Howe*, a stonemason and carver who had worked as such on the Catholic church at Ashton-in-Makerfield. He worked on St Theresa as his own architect and mason. Round-arched, free-Norman. The church was completed by a professional architect.

BOLD HALL, 1 m. SE of Clock Face. The house by *Leoni* has been pulled down. It dated from *c.*1732. Only a bridge and a pair of massive GATEPIERS remain, rusticated with boldly projecting cornice.*

PITHEAD BATHS of the CLOCK FACE COLLIERY and the LEAGREEN COLLIERY, both by *C. G. Kemp*, and both in the Dutch brick style of Dudok. Built *c.*1939.

SHERDLEY HALL by *Thomas Harrison* of Chester, 1805–6, has been demolished. It was the best house in St Helens.

SHERDLEY FARMHOUSE, off Sherdley Road. Dated 1671 (MHLG). With a gabled cross wing and a gabled porch. Low mullioned windows.

SOUTH-WEST (RAVENHEAD)

ST JOHN EVANGELIST, Crossley Road. 1869–70 by *J. M. & H. Taylor*. Stone of three colours and brick. Odd Taylorian difference between the clerestoreyed w bays of the nave and the roofs running down to low outer windows in the rest of the nave. Also, these low windows and a break in the roof slope imply aisles, but there are none.

SACRED HEART (R.C.), Borough Road. 1878 by *Pugin & Pugin*.

PILKINGTON GLASS WORKS, Prescot Road. The new buildings are by *Fry, Drew & Partners*. Designing started in 1956; full completion was in 1965. The buildings are approached by a

---

* Mr J. Haworth told Mr Hubbard that a STABLE BLOCK also survives.

winding drive which allows them to be seen all the time at varying angles. The group consists of two parts, the flagged courtyard with buildings on three sides and on the access side a bridge across, and the pool with the canteen at its N end and a bridge near its formal S end. The Museum of Glass links the two parts S of the bridge. The courtyard area, which is the area of the offices, is dominated by a twelve-storey tower, 170 ft high. It stands with its short side to the courtyard and subtly out of axis so that to its E the courtyard remains open to reach the bridge and the low museum. The buildings on the l. and r. of the courtyard are four-storeyed. The module of the concrete framework chosen is generous. The framework itself is clad with black slate. All sill panels are of opaque glass. Windowless wall surfaces have deep blue glass facing. The bridge across the access to the courtyard alone has its sill panels white. The entrance under the tower has a large abstract glass panel of thick relief and many colours. This is by *Avinash Chandra*. As one enters one sees it reflected in a mirror. The Board Room Suite is on the twelfth floor. The pergola above it hides services, but the two identical tanks stand up above it as an integral part of the tower composition. The N side of the pool has the long low canteen, this also with all sill panels in white. The canteen serves about 1,600 employees. Inside is an abstract panel by *Victor Pasmore*, 72 ft long. The museum is low and long and runs through to below the S end of the tower range. The parts of the group are outstandingly well interlocked and grouped. There has been far more subtlety at work here than the casual visitor may observe, and there is not a single gimmick in the detailing. On the old Ravenhead site is the surviving fragment of the OLD CASTING HALL, built in 1773–6. It was originally 340 ft long and 150 ft wide. Now there are only six bays. The remaining part has a semicircular porch with columns, a pediment, and a cupola. Impressive interior with square pillars and pointed arches. Can they really be of 1773 ?

THE SCHOLES, Scholes Lane, just outside St Helens. The core of this red stone house is probably of the C15. It is the hall rectangle behind the two S porches and extending a little further W. The porches themselves are Elizabethan, and it remains a mystery why there should be two. At the same time the house received two cross-wings to give it an H-shape. The W wing has been demolished, but evidence for its former existence remains in the W wall. Elizabethan also are the staircase projection on the N side and two doorways on the upper floor. The only piece of decorative value of that time is the entrance to the sw porch with its fine mouldings and its four-centred arch. To the sw of the house stands a pillar with an image niche at the top. This is now, very probably correctly, assigned to the early c18, i.e. the time after the year 1704 when the seventh Viscount Molyneux of Croxteth had rented The Scholes and was made Rector of the Lancashire District of the Society of Jesus.

SALFORD

INTRODUCTION

In the vast expanse of Manchester the river Irwell is hardly noticeable. Yet it has ever since the Middle Ages formed the boundary between the town of Manchester and the town of Salford, and it does so still between the two county boroughs. It is an administrative folly, but Salford is as proud of itself as is Manchester. It was a separate manor already in Domesday Book. In 1228 it received the grant of a market and in 1230 its charter. The area of the town then was Greengate and the bottom end of Chapel Street, and the streets in between as far w as Gravel Lane. Blackfriars Road should refer to a Dominican house, but there is no reference to it in Knowles and Hadcock. The medieval parish church, Holy Trinity, was founded only after the Reformation, in 1635, and the present building is entirely c18. Ordsall Hall, at the extreme s end of Salford close to the Docks, was of course a house in the country and without physical connexion with Salford. It is externally mostly post-Reformation too, though its interior is excellent c15 work. Kersal Cell is a minor timber-framed house of the c16 with some Elizabethan decoration. That Manchester was to be bigger than Salford was already decided by the end of the c18. Against Manchester's 70,000 in 1801 stood Salford's c.18,000. The w boundary of the town was about where St Stephen's Street now is. Late Georgian brick houses with pretty doorways survive as few as at Manchester, but at least one long uninterrupted terrace in The Crescent. The Crescent is the w continuation of Chapel Street, and nearly all that mattered architecturally at Salford took place along that long street. The development of church building also resembles that of Manchester: St Stephen off Chapel Street was built in 1794 (and is demolished), the Independent Chapel in Chapel Street in 1819, St Philip by *Smirke* off Chapel Street in 1825–7, Christ Church off The Crescent in 1830–1 (demolished). In the twenties Salford got its severely Grecian Town Hall, almost identical with that of Chorlton-on-Medlock in Manchester. From the thirties the rate of growth increased: Pendleton got a parish church in 1829–31, Broughton in 1836, Ordsall in 1842 (and incidentally Stretford in 1842 too). The population stood at 70,000 in 1841, and reached 102,500 in 1861 and 176,000 in 1881. Incorporation took place in 1844, the establishment of the Catholic see in 1850. The cathedral was begun in 1844 (in Chapel Street) and is ambitious indeed. Of the other Victorian churches none are of the first quality. Manufacturers built themselves large villas. Some survive near the Buile Hill Museum, and some in Broughton Park, laid out *c.*1840–5.

INNER SALFORD

CATHOLIC CATHEDRAL, Chapel Street. 1855 by *Weightman & Hadfield* of Sheffield. The s transept is an addition of 1884. It is a high building with a stately steeple over the crossing. The style chosen was that of *c.*1300 and somewhat later. Cecil Stewart has pointed out that inspiration for the steeple came from Newark, for the nave from Howden, for the choir from Selby. The choir vault is of the tierceron type. The E window has the splendid flowing tracery of Selby. The nave is four bays long, and the chancel also has four bays.

ST MATTHIAS (disused), Blackfriars Road. 1842 by *Weightman & Hadfield*. Red brick, Norman, without a tower. Not a sensitive piece of work.

ST PETER (R.C.), Greengate. 1863 (VCH: 1874). By *E. W. Pugin*. Brick, humble, with an E apse. The E window of the apse goes up into a dormer. Nave and aisles, round columns with typical E. W. Pugin capitals. Clerestory. The motifs are *c.*1300.

ST PHILIP, St Philip's Place. By *Sir Robert Smirke*, 1825. The steeple stands s, but the church is orientated. *Parti* and details are almost exactly as at Smirke's St Mary Wyndham Place, London. Semicircular porch with unfluted Ionic columns, round tower with domed cap. The body of the church has high arched windows. To the w is a three-bay pediment, to the E a pedimented tripartite window. The interior has its three galleries, the frieze with wreaths, the upper order absurdly slender Greek Doric. Flat ceiling. The church cost over £14,500 and all of it was paid by the Commissioners. – Many TABLETS.

SACRED TRINITY, Chapel Street. Founded in 1635. The tower

may be of that date or early c18, the rest is of 1752. The w window of course belongs to the Victorian restoration by *Holden* in 1871–4. So do the bell-openings. But the triglyph frieze above them is c18. The sides are in the state of 1752. Two tiers of arched windows, with blocky capitals, the doorways with alternating rustication. Inside three galleries, and Tuscan columns between them and the ceiling. Victorian timber roof. Short chancel. – PLATE. Flagon 1697.

INDEPENDENT CHAPEL, Chapel Street. 1819. Single-storey five-bay side to the street with arched windows and two arched doorways. Brick.

GRAVEL LANE WESLEYAN CHAPEL. As late as 1891, but of a type more of 1860. Red brick, seven bays wide, with two tiers of façade windows. The style can probably be called a free Italianate.

TOWN HALL, Bexley Square. 1825–7 by *Richard Lane*, and almost identical with the Chorlton-on-Medlock town hall, Manchester. Ashlar, five bays with a three-bay centre. The pedimented portico has two end pilasters and two Greek Doric demi-columns. Wreaths in the frieze. The entrance hall has four Greek Doric columns too.

EDUCATION OFFICES, Chapel Street, E of the cathedral. 1895 by *Woodhouse & Willoughby*. A high and large building, faced with yellow terracotta. The façade is in the French Renaissance style, not quite symmetrical.

GAS BOARD, Bloom Street. 1880, brick, symmetrical, with a tower, the style generally round-arched Gothic.

LIBRARY AND ART GALLERY, *see* below.

LIBRARY (former), Greengate. Brick, small, Gothic. 1870 by *Royle & Burnett*.

COURT HOUSE, Encombe Place, N of St Philip. Probably of c.1860–5. A dignified seven-bay front with alternatingly pedimented first-floor windows. The ground floor is stone-faced, the upper floors are brick.

CITY HEALTH DEPARTMENT, The Crescent. By *G. A. McWilliam*, the city engineer, 1962–3. A satisfactory modern job.

CITY POLICE HEADQUARTERS, The Crescent. By *Bradshaw, Gass & Hope*. Brick, in a proud municipal neo-Georgian. Opened in 1957.

UNIVERSITY OF SALFORD, The Crescent. Opened in 1896 as the Royal Technical College. The original building is by *Henry Lord*, a long, three-storeyed red range with a big central gable. The first new building, by the then county architect *G. Noel Hill*, is large but restless. Between the two, recessed and facing the street, is the LIBRARY AND ART GALLERY, not part of the college. This is a handsome low range of brick in the Italian Renaissance style, symmetrical and with two entrances. It looks the original style of the South Kensington institutions and has a complicated history. It started as Lark Hill, Col. Acker's and later William Garnett's mansion, which was converted and received, at the hands of *Travis & Mangnall*, N and S wings in 1852 and 1857. A further wing came in 1878, the mansion was demolished, and in 1936–8 an extension was built to make the whole symmetrical. Between it and the old building stands a new straightforward tower block (Chemistry), designed by *Courtauld*'s *Architectural Department*. In the forecourt statues of Victoria and Albert by *Noble*, 1854 and 1864. They come from Peel Park (*see* below).

HALLS OF RESIDENCE, Vine Street. 1961–4. By *Tom Mellor & Partners*. Large and brick-faced, on a steeply sloping site.

PEEL PARK. Opened 1846. The Victoria Arch has been demolished, the C18 iron gates from Strangeways Hall removed, and three statues by *Noble* packed away.

PERAMBULATION. There is not much walking to be done. Salford has no centre. Of the medieval centre nothing is left, and today's centre is one long street, shattered by traffic. Against the Manchester side it is screened by numbers of railway bridges, and behind the E part of the street to the N is much derelict land, to be used no doubt for more of the high-rise blocks which crop up in many places without visible system.

Starting from Exchange Station there is due W, in GREENGATE, a handsome building of *c.*1900 with the carved name Motor Garage. It has a round corner turret and is of brick with much stone. In QUEEN STREET is a group of four rows of WORKING CLASS COTTAGES, humane-looking for their date: 1893. They are by *Walter Sharp*.

Then the one and only major street, starting as CHAPEL STREET. Here are the churches and public buildings. In addition, in BLOOM STREET is a big building of 1894, called MODEL LODGING HOUSE, brick and terracotta, mostly with segment-headed windows, but also some Gothic motifs. At the corner of Chapel and Irwell Streets is WILLIAMS DEACON'S BANK, ashlar-faced and Gothic much à la Manchester. Then N of St Philip's church in ENCOMBE PLACE a terrace of four Late Georgian houses with doorways with unfluted Ionic columns and no pediments. Only when THE CRESCENT is reached does one begin to breathe more freely. A loop of the river below is open to sight on the N, and on the S Georgian Salford comes at last into its own. There is a whole long curved terrace of houses with enjoyable doorways, starting with one detached, stuccoed one, with giant pilasters. Then an eleven-bay block with end pediments, built, it appears, in the early forties. After that C20 public buildings, and only two more of the Georgian houses. From them the street becomes Broad Street, i.e. Outer Salford.

OUTER SALFORD

BROUGHTON

GREEK CHURCH OF THE ANNUNCIATION, Bury New Road. 1860–1 by *Clegg & Knowles*. Strictly classical, with a Corinthian portico and Corinthian pilasters along the sides. The carving is uncommonly carefully done. Inside, the piers and the roof are recent. The original polygonal apse appears oddly behind. The size and elaboration of the architecture testifies to the wealth of the Greek colony.

ASCENSION, Church Road. 1869 by *J. M. Taylor*. Big, but towerless, of brick with brick tracery and some brick patterns. Mostly lancet windows; E apse. The W has a porch flanked by two big flying buttresses.

ST BONIFACE, Gerald Road. By *Mather & Nutter*, 1960–1.

ST JAMES, Great Cheetham Street. 1879 by *Paley & Austin*. Of light brick, with a bellcote at the E end of the nave. Brick window tracery. Impressively sheer gables. Octagonal piers, brick arches and brick-faced walls. It is a good building, but not outstanding, as Paley & Austin's can be.

ST JOHN EVANGELIST, Murray Street. 1836–9 by *Lane*; the chancel 1846 by *Gregan*. Between the two lies the conversion to archeological conformity. Ashlar. The nave has long windows with thin minimum-Perp details, and the W front a tower and to its l. and r. porch bays. They, the body of the church, and the tower have battlements. The way the pitch of the nave roof and the pitch of the porch-bay roofs coincide is unusual. Thin octagonal piers inside and only two galleries. – STAINED GLASS. The E window and the chancel side windows have glass by *A. W. N. Pugin*, a naïve affair of no great beauty. – MONUMENT. Rev. John Clowes † 1846. Tomb recess in the chancel. For more on him, *see* below.

ST THOMAS (R.C.), Great Cheetham Street. 1901. Large, red brick, no tower.

CONGREGATIONAL CHURCH, Upper Park Road. 1874–5 by *S. W. Dawkes*. Very large, with an exceptionally high sw steeple. Aisles, transepts, chancel chapels, the s one with an apse. The style is late C13.

SALEM METHODIST CHURCH, Wellington Street. By *T. D. Howcroft* (of *Young & Purves*), 1966. White brick, very introvert, with only slit windows. On the pavement a close group of three crosses. It is an uncommonly excellent design.

BRENTNAL COUNTY PRIMARY SCHOOL, Bury New Road. By *Cruickshank & Seward*, completed in 1966. The core is a former Greek Consul's villa. Buildings were added, and the most recent ones are pavilions of weird, entertaining shape.

ALBERT PARK. Round Albert Park and especially in GREAT CLOWES STREET are many houses of about 1840–50, both classical and stuccoed Tudor. The park itself was only laid out in 1877.

BURY NEW ROAD. This is the continuation of Bury New Road, Manchester. Immediately past the boundary, by Camp Street, there is, on the E side, No. 266, an extremely fanciful black and white house. The story is that in 1822 William Yates moved a house from Market Street in Manchester out here and dressed it up. The oriels are of 1822, the arched panels are of 1822, and of course the brick and stone addition with its cresting is. But some of the concave lozenge patterns are original. In this neighbourhood are also some Late Georgian doorways (268, 297, 299). Further up new housing, a Tudor terrace on the E, a classical terrace on the W, both stuccoed. Just under a mile up from the boundary on the W is the GATEHOUSE to BISHOP'S COURT, by *Ewan Christian*.

Opposite is BROUGHTON PARK, a villa estate probably laid out by the Rev. John Clowes *c.*1840–5. The Clowes family came into possession of the estate by marriage with a Chetham in 1769. John Clowes was a noted gardener and botanist. He died in 1846. Broughton Park has winding streets, and of the large mansions a few are left. One of them was built for himself by *Alfred Darbyshire*. It is called ROOKSWOOD.

NORTH-WEST AND WEST, INCLUDING PENDLETON

ST ANNE, Sharp Street, Brindle Heath. By *F. P. Oakley*, 1914. A very remarkable little church, the sloping buttresses, the little SE turret, the lively details – it is all highly personal.

HOLY ANGELS, Sumner Road. 1926–8 by *Bradshaw, Gass & Hope*. Large, of brick, with a heavy, square SW tower. In the Romanesque so much favoured in those years by architects who wanted to get away from Gothic without risking the contemporary.

ST BARNABAS, Frederick Road, Pendleton. 1887 by *W. H. Booth*.

ST GEORGE, Whit Lane, Charlestown. 1858 by *Shellard*. Dec style. With one of Shellard's broach spires.

ST JAMES, Eccles Old Road. 1860–1 by *W. Scott* of Liverpool. Late C13 style. With a NW broach spire.

ST LUKE, Liverpool Street, Seedley. By *Sir George Gilbert Scott*, 1865, the chancel chapel 1875. Slim, embraced W tower with broach spire. Nearly all the windows lancets. But the clerestory windows are foiled circles. Apse; quatrefoil piers. – STAINED GLASS. The E window looks *Hardman*. – Otherwise much early *Kempe* glass.

ST PAUL, Ellor Street. 1855–6 by *Shellard*. A Commissioners' church (£4,856).

ST PAUL, Moor Lane, Kersal Moor. 1851–2 by *A. Trimen*. Large. W tower with recessed spire, and the stair-turret crowned by a spirelet. Perp style. The interior disappointing.

ST SEBASTIAN, Gerald Road, Pendleton. By *Sinnott, Sinnott & Powell*, 1898–1901. A large brick church, with a SW turret and lancets. Serious and almost forbidding. Inside, low aisle passages with low round arches and a gallery above, i.e. inner buttresses or wall-piers doing the division into bays. Apse with four detached high slim granite columns forming the narrowest of ambulatories.

STOWELL MEMORIAL CHURCH, at the W end of Eccles New Road. 1869 by *J. M. Taylor*. Large, with a SW steeple and geometrical tracery with personal variants. Not an original interior.

ST THOMAS, Broad Street, the parish church of Pendleton. A Commissioners' church built for £7,673 in 1829–31 to the design of *Francis Goodwin* and *Richard Lane*. The type of its date, with a W tower, tall windows of three lights and cusped intersecting tracery, battlements, and a short chancel with a six-light E window. Perp piers, three galleries, octopartite plaster vaults.

ST JOHN METHODIST CHURCH, Longworthy Road. 1891–2. Red brick and yellow terracotta. Perp.

UNITARIAN CHURCH, Cross Lane and Windsor. 1874. Red

brick with lancets. The Rev. A. Vallance points out that there are good reasons for an attribution to *Thomas Worthington*.

WEASTE CEMETERY. 1856–7. The chapels with their little spires are by *Pritchett & Sons*.

PENDLETON TOWN HALL, Broad Street, by St Thomas's church. By *Alfred Darbyshire*, 1865–7. The front only five bays wide, main window with Venetian tracery, the roofs of the French pavilion type. Porch of paired columns.

BUILE HILL MUSEUM. *See* below.

SALFORD COLLEGE OF TECHNOLOGY. The large new building is by *Holliday & Meacham*. Leaf Square, listed by the MHLG and graded II, was razed to the ground for it.

LADYWELL HOSPITAL, Eccles New Road, the former WORK-HOUSE. 1851–2 by *Pennington & Jervis*. Stock brick and red brick, large, with some shaped gables.

No perambulation. In BROAD STREET there are just three Late Georgian houses with ornamented doorways left.

ECCLES OLD ROAD used to have rich Manchester-men's mansions. Many have gone, some recently (e.g. Claremont and Hope Hall, the former the principal Heywood house, the latter of the Armitages). The following are left: BUILE HILL, now a Salford Museum, built for the Potters by *Sir Charles Barry*, 1825–7, unfortunately with a top storey and a big porte-cochère added in the 1860s by *Walters*. The porte-cochère has Greek Doric columns to be in keeping. Barry's villa is restrained and refined. Victorian iron staircase. N of this is SUMMER HILL (Girls' High School), c.1820–30, Tudor, of five bays, with a raised centre and battlements. A little further N in Claremont Road is RIVINGTON, a High Victorian specimen, with steep roofs and gables, very substantial. It was built for the Pilkingtons of St Helens for about £30,000. The date is surprisingly late: 1890.*

In the extreme N of Salford is KERSAL CELL, a timber-framed house of no special merit. It stands on the site of a cell of Lenton Priory, a Cluniac house, and has inside in one room some fragments of Elizabethan wall painting, in another part of a coarse plaster frieze. Handsome late C17 staircase with twisted balusters of two separate strands.

LOWER KERSAL has a group of tower blocks by *Cruickshank & Seward*.

In the very centre of Victorian low-standard housing, S of Broad Street, a large new development is taking shape around ELLOR

* The house has been pulled down.

STREET. It is by the *Architecture Research Unit of the University of Edinburgh* and consists of high blocks, seventeen storeys high. The upper sixteen floors of each block took twelve weeks to erect (Fram Russell Construction Co.). There are also gratifyingly direct lower ranges around them. The church of ST PAUL (*see* above) is being preserved and will assume a new significance in these surroundings. A pity it happens to be a church of little intrinsic interest.

ORDSALL

Ordsall is s of the centre. The area comprised is between Cross Lane on the w and Oldfield Road and Ordsall Lane on the E.

ST BARTHOLOMEW, Oldfield Road. 1842 by *Cuffley & Starkey*. Norman. w tower with big pinnacles, the body of the church with round-arched windows in two tiers under one giant arch. Interior with three galleries on iron columns. Chancel 1887.

ST CLEMENT, Hulton Street. 1877–8 by *Paley & Austin*. Stock brick, with a flèche on the E end of the nave. Three-light windows in the aisles, sexfoiled circular windows in the clerestory. The w front has a complex composition with two segment-headed portals and above three stepped windows under one blank arch. The tracery is all of *c.*1300. High and spacious interior, impressive round piers, and brick all exposed above. The chancel is brick-vaulted.

ST CYPRIAN, Taylorson Road. Immediately next to Ordsall Hall and disgracefully encroaching on it. Stock brick and red terracotta, the clerestory of wood with a black and white gable. Flèche. The church was designed by *Darbyshire* in 1899.*

ST IGNATIUS, Oxford Street. 1900 by *Darbyshire & Smith*. Stock brick and red terracotta. Norman. The church has a big sw tower with pyramid roof.

ST JOSEPH (R.C.), Ellesmere Street. 1871.

OUR LADY OF MOUNT CARMEL (R.C.). 1879–80 by *Samuel Harrison*. Brick with lancet windows.

CUSTOM HOUSE, Trafford Road. 1903. Brick, and decidedly jolly. Asymmetrical, with gables and a doorway with a semi-circular hood starting with little concave curves. Mullioned and transomed windows.

STELLA MARIS, Oldfield Road. A seamen's hostel and club, 1965–6 by *Desmond Williams & Associates*; good.

* I have to thank Mr Buttress for this information.

In ORDSALL LANE Messrs Haworth & Co. are going to re-erect the Marble Arch entrances to Hyde Park: gatepiers and iron railings. They date from 1910.*

ORDSALL HALL is the most important remaining timber-framed building not only of Salford but, now that Manchester is so disgracefully neglecting Baguley Hall, of Manchester as well It consists of a timber-framed s range built in the C15 and richly decorated in the Elizabethan Age and a brick w range of 1639. There was an E range as well and probably a N range Where the E range was is now the church of St Cyprian. The s range is the hall range. Its s wall is all Victorian, with windows with red terracotta details. But the N side and the interior are original. The N side is decorated all over with quatrefoil panels probably of the late C16 or early C17. The hall has a broad high-table bay window on a stone base and with a little ornament on the transom. Above it is a square gable containing a small room. The hall itself has its spere truss complete with large tracery over and the three doorways from the screens passage to the original service rooms. The high-table end has also two spere posts, and there are traces of the coved canopy over the table. The wall above the service doorways has again all quatrefoils, and the roof has wind-braces also composed in quatrefoils. Looking at the hall range from the N there is a second canted bay window w of the hall doorway. This dates from c.1600, a time when the functions of these rooms must have changed. In one of the upper rooms E of the hall is a simple plaster ceiling with the usual thin-ribbed star etc. formation The w range has mullioned windows and a square porch bay to the courtyard. The porch is stop-chamfered, and the stops are sawtooth-wise projecting brick courses. The chimneystacks have zigzag patterns of brick to connect one stack with another.

SANKEY VIADUCT *see* NEWTON-LE-WILLOWS

SCHOLES *see* WIGAN, pp. 428, 429

SEAFORTH

The two main churches make an entertaining contrast.

ST THOMAS, Church Road. 1815. Painted all white and of lovable naïvety in all its features. w tower with octagonal top

* Other parts of the railings are at Greenwich (Maritime Museum and Observatory terrace).

Nave of only two bays with two tiers of Gothic windows, and then what seems a shallow transept coming out full blast with the semblance of aisles and centres of three lancets. The interior does not bear out any of this. It is plain, with three galleries. The church was built at the expense of John Gladstone of Seaforth Hall, a house which has disappeared. The brick chancel is by *Charles Aldridge*, 1893. – STAINED GLASS. The E window is by *Kempe*. – MONUMENT. John Bibby † 1811. Portrait medallion at the foot. Standing figure of Hope above.

OUR LADY STAR OF THE SEA (R.C.), Church Road. By *Sinnott, Sinnott & Powell*, opened in 1901. The Catholic faces the Anglican church broadside, as it is not orientated. It is very deliberately large and serious-looking, and of course exposes red stone instead of white paint. The interior, after the display of a W front with two porches and two high three-light windows and a SW tower (unfinished), is disappointing. It is exceedingly reactionary with its granite columns and naturalistic capitals.

SEAFIELD HOUSE, Waterloo Road. Built in 1880 by the International Marine Hydropathic Society as a Hydro. Debased-Italianate villa with later additions.

SEEDLEY *see* SALFORD, p. 395

SEFTON

3000

ST HELEN. A large church, mostly Perp and with a marvellous 6 wealth of fitments. The oldest part is the N chancel chapel, with Dec windows and a Dec PISCINA, and the W tower, with Dec windows as well. Except for the chapel E window they are of the simplest. One N window is straight-headed. The spire and especially the pinnacles are a problem. The pinnacles are reminiscent of polygonal bollards more than anything. They can't be C14, nor can they be early C16. The C17 seems most likely, but no work is recorded. Could they be very primitive work of 1802, when the spire was damaged by a gale ? The rest of the church is late C15 to *c.*1540, except for the chancel E window, which dates from *c.*1870. The N aisle comes first, with plain three-light windows and a plain double-chamfered doorway. In the W wall traces of the C14 N aisle, much narrower than now. In the tower E wall traces of the C14 roof, much lower than now. Otherwise all is early C16, the large four-light S windows with uncusped lights, the two-storeyed S porch with the leaf spandrels of its entrance and its plain mullioned upper windows (or are they a later Tudor alteration ?), the clerestory,

the two-transomed chancel N and S windows, and the low E
vestry. Molyneux arms appear on the porch, and a Molyneux
was rector from 1535 to 1537. Another Molyneux had been
7 rector in 1489–1509. Inside, the six-bay arcades are also of that
time. They are perfectly even on both sides and have piers with
a section of four demi-shafts and four hollows in the diagonals.
There is no chancel arch. The tower arch is C14, triple-
chamfered and dying into the imposts. SEDILIA, PISCINA, and
AUMBRY in the chancel go with the date of the rest.

  FURNISHINGS. The great glory of the church is the
SCREENS, all early to mid C16, more and of greater variety than
in any other in the county. The rood screen is of noble height
and has a ribbed coving, a splendid broad cresting to the nave,
and a canted tester to the chancel with carved bosses. To the
nave along the top of the dado runs a frieze, already with
9 Renaissance putti. The screens between chancel and N and S
chapels have exquisitely fine Late Gothic tracery. The screen
between N chapel and N aisle is simpler. The S chapel W screen
is quite different, with much broader dado motifs. There are
in addition the screens round the Sefton Pew, again highly
ornate. The pew is not *in situ.* – The chancel has its STALLS
complete. The fronts have shallow recesses with seats for the
choirboys. The ends have poppyheads and much carving,
including the initials of James Molyneux, the rector about
1500. – The BENCH ENDS have poppyheads too, and carved
motifs including the letters of the alphabet. – At the W end of
the N aisle is a plain PEW of the later C18. – REREDOS and
chancel panelling given by Anne Molyneux *c.*1760. – COM-
MUNION RAIL and TOWER RAIL. With twisted balusters,
*c.*1690–1700. The tower rail and the communion rail may have
belonged to one three-sided communion rail. – COMMUNION
RAIL in the S chapel. Jacobean, with closely set balusters. –
FONT. Plain, octagonal, Perp, with quatrefoils. – The FONT
COVER is dated 1688 but still Jacobean in type. – PULPIT.
Dated 1635. Complete with back plate and sounding-board.
Very fine, close arabesque decoration. – CHANDELIERS. Two
large ones, of brass, given in 1773. – STAINED GLASS. Fragments of the original glass in the chancel N and S and the S aisle
E windows. – PLATE. Chalice 1695; Flagon 1715; Chalice of
1729 by *Benjamin Branker*; undated cylindrical Cup with
handle and undated Paten.

  MONUMENTS. In the N chapel early C14 tomb recess and in
it effigy of a Knight, wearing chain mail and with his legs

crossed; late C13. – Another Knight, c.1330, also cross-legged, but bearded and placing his feet against a crouching figure. – Between chancel and chapels two plain tomb-chests with coarse quatrefoils and shields. On one of them now the brasses of Sir Richard Molyneux † 1568 and two wives and children (22–23 in. figures). – In the S chapel brass of Margaret Bulcley † 1528; daughter of Sir Richard Molyneux (30½ in. figure). – In the chancel Sir Richard Molyneux † 1548 and two wives (2 ft figures). – Henry Blundell † 1810. By *S. & T. Franceys* of Liverpool, but designed and made by their apprentice *John Gibson*. Seated figure with allegorical groups, quite small, but as if it were the model for a major monument in Westminster Abbey. – Richard Rothwell, 1844. Wide sarcophagus with inscriptions. Urn on the top. By *Franceys & Spence* of Liverpool.

RECTORY, S of the church. Of c.1700 and rather forbidding. Five bays, two and a half storeys, whitewashed and absolutely plain except for a Late Georgian porch of paired attenuated shafts.

Further S, near Bulkley Hill, is ORCHARD FARMHOUSE with some mullioned windows.

SEFTON PARK see LIVERPOOL, p. 233

SHARSTON HALL see WYTHENSHAWE, MANCHESTER, p. 345

SHAW

Really Crompton Urban District.

HOLY TRINITY, Shaw. Existing in 1515. Rebuilt in 1739. Rebuilt again in 1800, and again in 1870–1 by *J. Drew*. A sizeable building with a crossing tower which has a pyramid roof instead of the intended spire. Chancel lower than the nave, and attachments to the chancel yet lower. Externally this attachment of vestry, etc., partly one-, partly two-storeyed, is picturesque. The interior calls for no comment.

ST JAMES, East Crompton. 1847 by *J. Clarke*. SW broach spire, lancets and plate tracery. This is a Commissioners' church. It cost £3,196.

ST MARY, High Crompton. 1878 by *Wild & Collins* (according to Mr Buttress). With a SE turret.

METHODIST CHAPEL, Rochdale Road, East Crompton. Italianate with a big pediment all across.

TOWN HALL. 1894 by *Harold Cheetham*. Very red brick, asymmetrical, with gables and mullioned and transomed windows.

SHERDLEY HALL *see* ST HELENS, p. 387

SHORE *see* LITTLEBOROUGH

SIMONSWOOD HALL *see* KIRKBY

9010 SMALLBRIDGE

ST JOHN BAPTIST. 1834 by *Lewis Vulliamy*. A small church with the usual lancets and buttresses. The front has a square bell-turret. The church was built by the Commissioners for £3,253.

By the church is the SCHOOL, of seven bays with a steep middle gable – evidently part of the same job. It has a date 1838, but was enlarged in 1867.

WEAVERS' COTTAGES are conspicuous. They are recognizable by the long, many-mullioned upper window.

SMITHILLS HALL *see* BOLTON, p. 89

SPEKE *see* LIVERPOOL, p. 240

SPOTLAND *see* ROCHDALE, p. 381

7000 STAND

40 ALL SAINTS, Church Lane, more Whitefield than Stand. A Commissioners' church. It cost £13,729, and all of this was paid by the Commissioners. This was *Charles Barry*'s first building. Soane had recommended him, and he was certainly amply justified, even if all the merits of Stand are in total contradiction to the Gothic work of Barry some ten years later. Then he prided himself on accuracy of Perp reproduction. In 1822, when he began Stand, he could do accurate Grecian – see the Manchester Art Gallery, designed in 1824 – but his Gothic was highly fanciful. This is precisely what makes Stand so enjoyable. One may well find the w front a little ludicrous, but its mood is catching. The tower rises out of an excessively high ground stage which is a porch. The w entry is an arch as steep as the arches inside Fonthill (at least in Rutter's illustrations), and the lancets l. and r. must be the longest and thinnest ever. The upper part of the tower has polygonal buttresses. The sides have the long windows of the Commissioners' type, and there are pinnacles wherever pos-

sible. But Barry shows future reasonableness already in intro-
ducing a stone band across his side windows to declare that
this is where the galleries are inside. The E end is a canted apse.
A specially charming touch is that the slender Perp piers of the
four-bay nave carry two tierceron-star vaults (of plaster of
course), one for each two bays. The spreading ribs of the apse
vault are repeated above the w gallery, a touch more than any
other proving how blissfully uncommitted Barry still felt to
what real Gothic buildings had and had not done. – STAINED
GLASS. The E window with its strident colours looks c.1830–50.
– MONUMENTS. James Ramsbotham † 1835. With his bust. –
James Clegg † 1836. Bust on a high base with the relief figures
of Faith, Charity, and Hope. Unsigned.

STAND GRAMMAR SCHOOL, Church Lane, opposite the church.
1913 by *Henry Littler*, the then County Architect. Red brick
and stone dressings, good for its date.

STAND HOUSE, Ringley Road, corner of Stand Lane. Georgian,
of brick. Seven bays, two storeys, three-bay pediment, pedimented doorway.

UNITARIAN CHURCH, Ringley Road, ½ m. sw of All Saints.
Founded in 1693. Rebuilt in 1818 and again in 1952, by *Young
& Purves*. Pure Georgian revived, as they did so often in the
United States and so rarely in England.

(A Manchester HOUSING ESTATE is being built by THATCH
LEACH LANE, Whitefield. It is called the Hillock Estate and
consists of 1,299 dwellings. Director of Housing: *J. A. Bent*.)

STANLEY *see* LIVERPOOL, p. 248

STONECLOUGH *see* PRESTOLEE

STONEYCROFT *see* LIVERPOOL, p. 248

STRANGEWAYS *see* MANCHESTER, p. 338

STRETFORD

8090

Stretford is of course part of Manchester and the boundary is
nowhere noticeable. Besides, the Docks are at Stretford. They
were built in connexion with the Manchester Ship Canal, which
in its turn was built in 1885–94.

ST ALPHONSO (R.C.), Agnes Road. 1936 by *Hill, Sandy &
Norris*. The interior has wall-piers with low round-headed
aisle passages.

St Anne (R.C.), Chester Road. 1862–7 by *E. W. Pugin*. Tall NW steeple with a short spire and plain pinnacles. In its w face low down a small medallion with the kneeling donors holding a model of the church. They are Sir Humphrey and Lady Annette de Trafford, who paid for the church. Fancy w rose-window with a carved Crucifixus. Narrow aisles, polygonal apse. The arcade capitals have naturalistic foliage. – *Pugin* also did the Presbytery.

St Bride, Shrewsbury Road. 1878–84 by *Pennington & Brigden*. Large, with a two-bay w porch and two w windows. Octagonal crossing tower with short spire. Polygonal apse.

St John, Agnes Road. 1904–8 by *Preston*. Red brick with red terracotta tracery and a sw tower.

St Matthew, Chester Road and Leslie Street. 1842 by *W. Hayley*. A Commissioners' church. It cost £2,700. Stock brick. w tower and the usual lancets and thin buttresses. The chancel is of 1906. Three galleries, flat ceiling on prettily Gothic shallowly arched braces. – To the s very near the twenty-three-storey block of FLATS which Stretford is building at the time of writing. What justification can there be at Stretford for that height?

St Peter, Portland Road. 1910–16 by *Woodhouse & Howard*. Last-gasp Gothic.

Martin Luther Church. 1963 by *T. D. Howcroft* (of *Young & Purves*). A square main block of white slabs and with narrow windows. Dark brown brick parsonage and church hall. Exceptionally good.

Wesleyan Chapel, City Road. 1860 by *Hayley & Son*.

Cemetery. The chapel is by *Bellamy & Hardy*, with a slender s spire, its lowest stage steeply gabled to w, s, and e – a wilful touch.

The old municipal centre was by the junction of Chester Road and Edge Lane. Here John Rylands gave the Town Hall (1879 by *Lofthouse*, five bays, debased mixed Gothic with a mid-tower), the Baths behind, and a coffee-house, now Midland Bank (corner of Chester Road and Market Street). John Rylands, the Manchester manufacturer, lived at Longford Hall, Stretford (*see* below) between 1857 and his death in 1888. The new Town Hall is in Talbot Road. It is of 1931–3, by *Bradshaw, Gass & Hope*. Large, symmetrical, of brick, with vaguely Adamish detail. High central tower. In a row with the town hall are the Police Headquarters and the Technical College, the former by the then County Architect,

G. Noel Hill, 1954, the latter by *Stephen Wilkinson*, 1940, with extensions by the County Architect *Roger Booth*, 1963.

HENSHAW'S INSTITUTION is in Chester Road, Old Trafford. It was founded for the care of the deaf and the blind in 1823. The oldest building is of 1836–7 by *Lane*. Unfortunately it has been mutilated recently. The centre of the fine ashlar range was the chapel, and that has been ripped out. Only the wings are left, of nine bays with a tight one-bay centre ending in a steep gable and high pinnacles. Behind are large brick additions of 1860 by *James Redford*. Another addition, in Boyer Street, is of 1892.

The GREYHOUND TRACK adjoining is entered by the screen which was once the entrance to the BOTANIC GARDENS. It dates from 1828 and is of stone, with pairs of unfluted Ionic columns under a heavy parapet and two-storeyed lodges each with two attached columns *in antis*. A new STAND has recently been done by *Mather & Nutter*, concrete, boldly cantilevered.

Nothing else of note, except perhaps the shamelessly showy 'modernism' of 1936 of the ESSOLDO opposite the old town hall (by *Henry Elder*) and an uncommonly stately office building for Messrs Duckworth in CHESTER ROAD, opposite Northumberland Road, 1896 by *Briggs & Wolstenholme*, red brick, gabled, and symmetrical. 'Note the fine Neo-Victorian style', says a booklet brought out when the building was new.

LONGFORD HALL, Longford Park, Edge Lane, 1½ m. s of the town hall, was John Rylands's house. It was built in 1857 in an indifferent Italianate style. It is quite large, but without any great pretensions.

That leaves TRAFFORD PARK. The mansion of the de Trafford family was built in 1762. In the grounds in 1857 the celebrated MANCHESTER EXHIBITION OF ART TREASURES was held, the first British exhibition ever of works of ancient art on such a scale. The building was 656 by 200 ft, of corrugated iron and glass, the architecture applied by *Salomons*, the interior decoration by *J. G. Crace*. In 1896 the estate was sold for industrial development, and the result was the TRAFFORD PARK TRADING ESTATE, the earliest of its kind in England. The area is very large; the architecture, however, calls for no comments, except for the new buildings for GEIGY LTD by *Scherrer & Hicks*, an uncommonly satisfactory square block with a concrete frame and projecting concrete sill bands. The building is in ASHBURTON ROAD at the corner of Tenax Road.

STUBLEY OLD HALL *see* LITTLEBOROUGH

SUTTON *see* ST HELENS, pp. 386, 387

SWINLEY *see* WIGAN, p. 429

SWINTON

7000

ST PETER. St Peter replaces a chapel of 1791, a quite substantial, but a very plain building. The new church, of 1869, and the choice of *G. E. Street* as its architect was due certainly to the Rev. H. R. Heywood, son of Sir Benjamin Heywood and brother of Sir Percival Heywood and also of Edward Stanley Heywood, who paid for Pendlebury church. The Heywoods were a Manchester banking family of Nonconformist descent. But Sir Benjamin joined the Church of England, and both Swinton and Pendlebury are the expressions of the Tractarian convictions of his sons. The church, with nearly all the plate, bells, and organ, cost £18,000. Of this the contract with the architect was for £12,233. The architect's fee was £718. Of the money the incumbent gave £4,650, Sir Benjamin £1,100, and yet another brother £1,061.*

The E view of the church is of three gables, chancel and chapels, and the higher aisle gables appearing behind. The W side has a robust tower and the aisle W gables l. and r. of it. The tower has a stair-turret projecting at the NW corner and rising higher than the tower. The vestry on the N side contributes two cross-gables. That is enough variety. The tracery is of the conventional 1300 kind. The interior is robust too: four wide bays, Dec piers, naturalistic capitals (carved by *Earp*), an ample chancel arch, and the two-bay chapels. The chancel has a wagon roof, the nave is of the deliberately elementary single-frame type. The anomaly that there are five windows to four arcade arches is explained as an afterthought of Street's, who felt so strongly about five windows as an improvement over four that he paid for the change himself. One looks at Swinton with respect. It has more body than Scott's Worsley, but it lacks the elating quality of Bodley's Pendlebury. Be that as it may; we ought to be grateful for three such Victorian churches distant from each other by only a few miles. – STAINED GLASS. N aisle

---

* All these facts come from the Rev. J. S. Leatherbarrow's *Victorian Period-Piece*, 1954, an unfortunate title for a serious and indeed exemplary book.

E by *Kempe*; c.1872 and still pre-Kempe in style, but not the worse for that. – In the S aisle *Morris* glass, but late. (The Calling of St Peter is by *J. H. Dearle* of Morris & Co., 1902.*)

MUNICIPAL BUILDINGS, Chorley Road. The church is no longer seen as it should be, owing to the large clearing made for this anaemic neo-classical building. It is of light brick, two-storeyed, with a giant portal arch and a slender middle tower. The architects were *Sir Percy Thomas* and *Ernest Prestwich*. The date is 1937. In few other countries would such a design have been possible as late as 1937. One is specially painfully aware of this tiredness if one remembers that seventy years earlier, at the time of Street's church, England was stronger and more powerful in its Gothic churches than any other country. Pendlebury and Swinton stand out above any contemporary Gothic buildings in France or Germany.

N of the Municipal Buildings and facing on Station Road a new LIBRARY and CIVIC HALL are being built. They are by *Leach, Rhodes & Walker*, of concrete, and gimmicky. Few of the projections and recessions represent functional necessities. Later on new shopping will be added.

THORNHAM   *8000*

ST JOHN. 1907 by *R. Bennett Preston*. Large, with a SW tower. Some of the tracery with its ogee details tells of the date of the church. (The interior‡ is spacious, with low aisles, simple timber roofs, and a squat W baptistery – all characteristic of the period. The walls are of coursed rubble, the piers and dressings of smooth sandstone.)

TONGE FOLD *see* BOLTON, p. 90

TONGE MOOR *see* BOLTON, p. 91

TOXTETH *see* LIVERPOOL, p. 242

TRAFFORD PARK *see* STRETFORD

TUE BROOK *see* LIVERPOOL, p. 249

---

* This piece of information comes from Mr Sewter's yet unpublished catalogue of Morris glass.
   ‡ Described by Mr Buttress.

TYLDESLEY

Tyldesley being a small town, mills seem to dominate more than in the bigger towns.

St George. 1821–4 by *Sir Robert Smirke*. A Commissioners' church. Built for £9,646. A very interesting building; for, though it nowhere abandoned the Commissioners' principles, it is yet archeologically much more careful than most. The W tower e.g. has a recessed spire connected by flying buttresses with the pinnacles – à la Louth. Also the piers are octagonal and the arches double-chamfered, even if the chamfers are too slight for the Perp period, and the capitals are wrong. The chancel was extended in 1887; that accounts for the geometrical tracery of the E window. – Monument. James Mort † 1855. By *Garner* of Manchester.

The School is dated 1829. Flat, two-storeyed front, the windows with Y-tracery.

Tyldesley Chapel. In the main square. The chapel was built in 1789 for the Countess of Huntingdon's Connexion. It is of brick with two entrances from the square and between and above them two very elementary Venetian windows, one on top of the other. The side windows must originally have been Venetian too.

UNSWORTH *see* BURY, p. 100

URMSTON

St Clement, Stretford Road. 1868 by *J. Medland Taylor*, the N aisle by Messrs *Taylor* too, 1873–5. Lengthened to the W in 1887–8 by *Whittenby & Mather*. The tower dates from 1899–1903. The church is in the early C14 style. It has some of the odd touches one expects of its architect. The N arcade has columns with rings, and at its E end there are strange things happening round the pulpit. The chancel arch is cusped, and the aisle E window is circular yet has mullions like a normal window with a pointed arch.

Methodist Church, Stretford Road. Red brick, with a NW tower and Perp tracery.

Police Station, Church Road and Station Road. 1904. Brick with much stone. Uncommonly pretty.

Grammar School, Bradfield Road. 1962–6 by *Lyons, Israel & Ellis*. Central hall and four wings arranged like windmill sails. One has the gymnasium, one classrooms, the other two laboratories, etc. Concrete frame and much glass.

N of Flixton Road and w of Crofts Bank Road a new SHOPPING CENTRE is under construction. The architects are *Leach, Rhodes & Walker*.

VICTORIA PARK *see* MANCHESTER, p. 320

VULCAN VILLAGE *see* WARGRAVE

WALKDEN AND LITTLE HULTON   *7000*

ST PAUL, Walkden. 1848, by *William Young*, says GR.* S tower, nave and aisles and lower chancel. Round and octagonal piers, quatrefoil clerestory windows, lancets otherwise. The point about this is that the architect of 1848 was entirely on the Pugin–Scott side, with no left-overs of the early C19 Gothic in details or plan.

ST PAUL, Peel. 1874–6 by *J. Medland & Henry Taylor*. w tower with broach spire. Dec details.

ST JOHN, Hill Top, Little Hulton. 1876 by the *Taylors*.‡ Polygonal crossing tower. Note the funny (typically Taylorian) way in which the stair-turret links up with the tower. Round apse; no aisles. Really rather a mean interior. The chancel arch responds, one broad respond each side, are caught up each on two corbels.

ELLESMERE MEMORIAL, in the centre of Walkden. 1868 by *T. G. Jackson*, then only thirty-three years old. He won the competition assessed by *Street*. A tabernacle with a very high pinnacle. One would expect a statue in the tabernacle, but there is only a short and fat column. At the corners figures of a cotton-worker, a collier, and two factory girls. Above, figures of Piety, Chastity, Munificence, and Prudence. The monument records the widow of Francis Egerton, first Earl of Ellesmere.

Immediately N of the centre in the Tyldesley Road are the former Duke of Bridgewater's Offices (NATIONAL COAL BOARD), built in 1867, a rather mean, large utilitarian building of red brick with blue-brick trim and an asymmetrically placed tower. Odd window details of blue brick.

PEEL HALL (now a hospital). Attributed by the VCH to Sir Charles Barry and 1840. Neither can be correct. Can *Charles*

---

* Or was it the London *William Young*, and did he do the restorations recorded for 1881–9 or 1904?

‡ I have to thank Mr Buttress for the name.

Barry Jun., the son, be meant ? It is not likely, and the date i
that case would have to be *c*.1850–60. Brick and stone dressing
Wildly picturesque, with an asymmetrical entrance tower an
gables. Gothic and Jacobean mixed, and a wholly Italiana
tower over the gateway to the stables. The entrance hall
fussily decorated with the mixture of motifs one finds in th
fifties. The staircase has a larger scale and more discipline.

URBAN DISTRICT OFFICES, Walkden Road. By *John T. Proffit*
1910–11. Not large, but very Baroque.

COLLEGE OF FURTHER EDUCATION, next door to the former.
Brick and stone, symmetrical, with a recent addition.

ST ANDREW'S SCHOOL, Manchester Road, Little Hulton.
handsome building of 1906. Red brick and yellow terracott
A symmetrical composition. The centre has a Baroque Venetia
window under a gable. The architects were *Bradshaw & Gas*

WORSLEY CIVIC HALL and SHOPPING HALL, Bolton Roa
and Manchester Road. By *Shingler Risdon Associates*, 1963–

WALMERSLEY *see* BURY, p. 100

WALSHAW *see* BURY, p. 101

WALTON *see* LIVERPOOL, p. 251

WARDLEY HALL *see* WORSLEY

090   WARGRAVE

Wargrave is visually just part of Newton-le-Willows.

EMMANUEL. 1840–1. Funny w steeple, the bell-openings
three stepped lancets with lively Somerset tracery. Recesse
spire. The body of the church has the usual lancet window
Unfinished later chancel.

VULCAN VILLAGE. Housing of *c*.1840 provided by the Vulca
Foundry, which had been established in 1830 by Charl
Tayleur, a director of the Liverpool and Manchester Railwa
They began making locomotives in 1832, and Robert Stephe
son later joined the company. The cottages are in terrace
rendered and totally drab. There is a triangular green in th
middle with the school on it.

* And actually in Worsley.

WARRINGTON

INTRODUCTION

Warrington is old. It is mentioned in Domesday, it was granted a market in 1255, and a bridge across the Mersey is first referred to in 1305. The Austin Friars started a settlement about 1280 (always a sign of a flourishing town),* the parish church comes into Domesday too, and fragments of the C12 and C14 are preserved. In the centuries after the Reformation Warrington developed copper-smelting and weaving. The Sankey Canal, to carry coal, actually precedes the Bridgewater Canal (begun 1755; engineer *Henry Berry*), and the first steam engine in the Lancashire cotton industry was erected at Warrington in 1787. By that time the town already had about 9,000 inhabitants. As the Industrial Revolution climbed to its summit, the population grew to 13,600 (1821), 24,000 (1861), 64,700 (1901). Between 1941 (c.76,000) and now there has been no further increase.

CHURCHES

ST ELPHIN. This is a very rare dedication, and no-one knows who St Elphin was. The church is large and lies at the far E end of the old town. It is a medieval building, though its general appearance and the splendid climax of the high spire over the crossing tower are due to *Frederick & Horace Francis* and the work of restoration and rebuilding they did in 1859–67. It is one of their best, if not their best work. There is evidence of a late C12 predecessor church (fragments in the museum). Of the present building the only old parts are the crypt below the E bay of the chancel – the head corbels of its vault seem mid-C14, but the vault itself is C19 – the projecting spiral staircase to the crypt from the chancel (cf. Upholland, North Lancashire), the N transept E wall and N wall (see the C14 corbel heads of the two tomb recesses), and the chancel itself, though the SEDILIA e.g. are a wood and plaster copy of the C14 work. The chancel side windows have interesting tracery, an ingeniously twisted variety of reticulation. The Francises' interior is impressive too, with wide nave and wide aisles and

---

* The AUSTIN FRIARS was immediately S of Friars Gate. The plan of the church was found in 1886. It is very odd, consisting of a narrow nave and chancel and a broad aisled N transept of four wide bays. There was an oblong tower over the W bay of the chancel.

quite splendid neo-c13 crossing piers. The Francises had however been preceded by other post-medieval restorers. Thus the masonry of the crossing tower dates from 1696, and the s aisle fenestration in two tiers presupposes galleries and dates indeed from 1835. – ORGAN SCREEN. A gorgeous Gothic tour-de-force of *William & Segar Owen*, as late as 1908. – STAINED GLASS. The chancel E window designed by *Pugin*,* shattered in the war and partly re-assembled. – Are not other chancel windows by him too? – PLATE. Silver-gilt Hanap, 1615, by *R.N.*; two Chalices and a Paten Cover 1627; Salver 1694 by *H.B.*; Flagon 1699 by *Will. Andrewes*; Flagon 1720 by *John Bathe*; Paten 1722 by *B.N.*; Paten 1731 by *F.S.*; Silver-gilt Flagon 1746. – MONUMENTS. Effigy of a Lady, early c14, defaced, N transept. – Sir John Boteler † 1463 and wife. Alabaster effigies on a tomb-chest with fine alabaster statuettes of angels, saints, etc., also a Crucifixion and an Assumption. N transept, i.e. Boteler Chapel. – The Patten Chapel was w of the s transept (see the irregular window), but the Patten monuments are now in the s transept. Thomas Patten † 1772, restrained, Adamish tablet. It is by *J. F. Moore*. – Dorothea Patten † 1799. By *Thomas King* of Bath, with a standing allegorical figure in the Bacon style. – Anna Maria Wilson-Patten † 1846. Large tomb-chest, but on it *H. H. Armstead*'s recumbent effigy of John Wilson-Patten, Lord Winmarleigh, † 1892. – Thomas Wilson-Patten † 1819. Exceptionally fine, very Roman relief of four figures. – Many more tablets, also in the chancel, e.g. Thomas Lyon † 1818. – More monuments in the churchyard, best among them William Hesketh † 1773 and John Hesketh † 1793. Small sarcophagus and four detached volutes leading from the pedestal up to it. – At the entrance to the churchyard a fine pair of c18 GATEPIERS and a pair of COTTAGES of *c.*1850, of the same red sandstone as the church.

HOLY TRINITY, Sankey Street. 1760, with a w tower of 1862 (by *W. P. Coron*). Red stone in smooth rustication. Two tiers of windows, the upper keyed-in and flanked by pilasters, the lower with Gibbs surrounds. The whole job is in the Gibbs style. Inside three galleries. They are carried on pillars encased in wood, and above them the flat ceilings are carried by Corinthian columns. The E window is larger and of the Venetian type, with pillars decorated with garlands. – WEST GALLERY. Approached in an uncommonly monumental way by a staircase starting in one flight and returning in two. – BOX PEWS. –

* A. W. N. Pugin – a discovery of Mr E. Hubbard.

CHANDELIER of brass. Two tiers of arms, the body of a usual Baroque shape. The chandelier came from the House of Commons and was given to the church in 1801. – PLATE. Paten 1693 by *J.A.*; Chalice and Cover 1709 by *John Eastt*; Flagon 1719 by *David Williams*; Flagon 1764 by *Jacob Marshe*.

T MARY (R.C.), Buttermarket. By *Pugin & Pugin*, 1877, and one of their best works. The slender SW tower is in its top parts with the saddleback roof by *Peter Paul Pugin*, 1906. The side of the church towards the street has very personal clerestory windows and a fine transept front. The style is *c.*1300. Wide nave. Round piers with ornate floral capitals.

RIENDS' MEETING HOUSE, behind the S side of Buttermarket. 1829–30. A clear, clean brick block with a tripartite, segment-headed 'E' window and the original bench arrangement.

OLD STREET METHODIST CHURCH. 1850 by *James Simpson* of Leeds. Big brick building, four by four bays. Late Classical style. No pediment. Broad twin stone doorways. 'Magnificent interior' (P. Fleetwood-Hesketh).

NITARIAN CHAPEL, Cairo Street. 1744–5. A rectangle in plan. Brick, four bays. Two tiers of arched windows. The Perp tracery is of course Victorian. Two pedimented doorways on the entrance side.

EMETERY. Consecrated 1857. The three chapels are by *T. D. Barry*. They are, as usual, as different from each other as possible and tend to be quirky – see especially the one steeple.

PUBLIC BUILDINGS

OWN HALL, Sankey Street. This was built in 1750 by *Gibbs* as 29 Thomas Patten's country house immediately outside the town, or rather on its fringe. It was called Bank Hall. It is the finest house of its date in South Lancashire. The S façade is of nine bays, the outer three and three of exposed brick, the middle three rendered and in ashlar-like rustication. In the middle also an open two-arm staircase with a fine wrought-iron balustrade leading up to the *piano nobile*. For there are a ground floor treated as a basement, and then two and a half storeys. The centre has giant attached Composite columns and a pediment and *piano nobile* windows with arches with the typical Gibbs surrounds. In the side parts this floor has pediments of alternating shape to the windows. The N side is all brick and altogether simpler. The block is flanked by long detached service wings, each of thirteen bays, projecting N as well as S beyond the main block. The service blocks have a rusticated three-bay centre, two and a half storeys high, and with a pediment and lower brick side-parts. The outer staircase leads to a spacious but not at all monumental entrance hall with a fine stone chimneypiece. Altogether the internal scale of the house is nowhere monumental. Towards the back are two three-bay rooms with stucco ceilings. The most interesting feature is the planning with two staircases of identical size in the middle of the short sides of the block. Both have wrought-iron handrails, that on the W side also ample stucco decoration. – Towards the street are gorgeously heavy GATES, with four angels on top. They were exhibited at the London Exhibition of 1862.

COUNTY COURT, Palmyra Square. 1897 by *Henry Turner* of London. Red brick and yellow terracotta. Quite large and varied, in a Frenchy Gothic.

POLICE, Arpley Street. 1900–1 by *R. Burns Dick*. Long, low symmetrical building with a steeply gabled centre with cupola and dormers with big semicircular pediments.

LIBRARY AND MUSEUM, Bold Street. 1855–7 by *John Dobson* of Newcastle. With later additions. An uncommonly dignified building with an unbroken cornice, tripartite ground-floor windows, and on the upper floor blank panels instead of windows. Simple pedimented doorway.

SCHOOL OF ART, Museum Street. By *William Owen*, 1883. Symmetrical; red brick. Two very long upper windows, their arches reaching into the dormers.

TECHNICAL SCHOOL, Palmyra Street. 1900–1 by *William & Segar Owen*. Symmetrical, of eleven bays, the centre with a big semicircular pediment. Doorway hood on huge brackets.

PARR HALL, next to the former. Very plain. 1895 by *W. Owen*.

MARKET, Market Square. 1855–6 by *James Stevens* of Manchester. The façade with an over-large Venetian window and a big pediment. The S entrance in a wild French later C16 or some such style.

CENTRAL STATION. Of stone, low, with a central pediment. N of it an impressive WAREHOUSE. This and the station date from 1873.

PERAMBULATION

Warrington is not at all bad. The main E–W streets wind nicely, the river plays at least some part, and quite close to the main

reets are pleasant two-storeyed houses and cottages still lived
᷉. This scale helps a lot. Also, for those interested in older
uildings, there are still quite a number of Georgian brick houses
ft.

et the walk start by the parish church. In CHURCH STREET is
one timber-framed C17 house with overhang and brick infilling, much restored, and the former NATIONAL SCHOOL,
rather fortress-like, with two canted bays and a mid-gable –
l. for boys, r. for girls. In the BUTTERMARKET, w of the
Catholic church, one Georgian house with a pleasant doorway.
Then turn into ACADEMY STREET, named after the Warrington Academy, an institution to provide education of university
standard for dissenters, who were debarred from universities. It
was founded in 1757 and came to an end in 1783. But in these
less than thirty years it had done remarkably good work.
Joseph Priestley e.g. was a tutor from 1761 to 1767. Marat
incidentally quite probably taught French for a while. The
academy started with three students. Among later students
were Josiah Wedgwood's eldest son and also Malthus. The
original premises in Bridge Street survive (*see* below). By 1762
they were too small and new premises were provided. They were
flanked by two tutors' houses, and it is these which still exist in
Academy Street: No. 11, of five bays, and No. 8, also of five
bays, but with a blatantly incongruous doorway.

t the end of the Buttermarket turn N, along Horsemarket to
WINWICK STREET, where No. 3 is of five bays and three
storeys and has a pedimented doorway, and No. 31a (N of the
station, and facing into a court) is of five bays with a three-bay
pediment. Doorway with attached columns and pediment.
Then, also on the E side, a former CHAPEL, Italianate with
Venetian tracery in the windows. This started Presbyterian in
1808 and went to the Countess of Huntingdon's Connexion in
1854. Maybe the new front was put on then. s of the end of the
Buttermarket down BRIDGE STREET. Here, on the w side, a
series of Edwardian office buildings and at the bridge end the
building of the ACADEMY, built before 1757. Five bays with a
one-bay attachment. Three storeys. Humble porch. (For the
Academy *see* above.) Off the s end of Bridge Street in WHARF
STREET the MERSEY MILLS, 1862 by *Norman* of Glasgow.
Off Bridge Street to the w, a little further N, is FRIARS GATE,
commemorating the house of the Austin Friars, founded before
1308.

rom here s by Barbauld Street to STANLEY STREET, at the end

of which Nos 25–29 are a pleasant Georgian group. No. 25 of four bays is the best.

Back to the top of Bridge Street and along SANKEY STREET. Turn N into the MARKET PLACE. One red-brick house with a pediment, and otherwise only the BARLEY MOW, which is late C16, but has made far too many efforts to look it. From the Market Place W along Mill Street one has as the *point-de-vue* a house in KING STREET, of five bays with a three-bay pediment and a pedimented doorway. In Sankey Street itself is WOOLWORTH'S, an exceptionally refined Gothic office building of 1864.* Next to it the DISTRICT BANK, by *Walters* of Manchester, 1847, a very odd façade with upper column standing decidedly awkwardly on ground-floor Venetian pilasters. But Walters no doubt knew what he was doing. Turn S into BOLD STREET for two comfortable Latest Classical three-bay houses, especially No. 21. Back in Sankey Street W. H. SMITH'S premises, Edwardian, but still daintily Norman Shavian with its stuccoed gable and its oriel windows. By *Wright, Garnett & Wright*. Then, connecting with the town hall, a group of good Georgian houses. No. 84 and No. 86 are almost a pair. Both are detached, of five bays and two and a half storeys, with pretty doorways. No. 86 has a three-bay pediment as well. After that, more informal, another pair, one with a bow, the other with a canted bay window. All this is later C18.

OUTER WARRINGTON

NORTH AND NORTH-EAST

ST ANNE, Winwick Road. 1866–8 by *John Douglas* of Chester. An impressively forceful High Victorian piece, blunt and uncompromising. Dark brick. Lancets and plate tracery. From the street one sees the tower with steep hipped roof and round apse. The tower has a round stair-turret reaching up into the roof zone.

ST PETER, Birchall Street. By *Medland Taylor*, 1890–1, but little left of that firm's former antics. Except for the bell-turret quite a sober job. Brick, with lancets.

ORFORD HALL (Chetham House), School Road, Orford. Five-bay Georgian house of two and a half storeys. Brick with quoins. Pedimented doorway.

* Mr P. Howell and Mr E. Hubbard have recently discovered that this is an early work of *John Douglas*.

SOUTH-EAST AND SOUTH

CHRIST CHURCH, Wash Lane. 1861 by *Kennedy & Rogers*. Rock-faced, early C14 style, with a SW steeple attached to the church only by a link.

Opposite used to stand the timber-framed PLAGUE HOUSE of 1656. The plague of development has spirited it away.

ST JAMES, Wilderspool Causeway. 1829–30 by *Samuel Rowland*. Ashlar. The side walls with high lancets. The intersecting tracery is of wood. Short, narrow chancel. Handsome W front with polygonal buttresses at the angles and the angles of the somewhat projecting tower. If there were galleries, they have been taken out.

OUR LADY OF THE ASSUMPTION (R.C.), St Mary's Street. 1901–3 by *Robert Curran*.

(THE OLD WARPS, Victoria Park. Early C19, seven bays, rendered. Slight central projection with pediment, pilasters at the angles and those of the centre. MHLG)

WEST AND NORTH-WEST

ST ALBAN (R.C.), Bewsey Street. No tower. Front with round arches and Venetian tracery. The church was built in 1808, and the sanctuary enlarged by *P. P. Pugin* in 1893. The front looks later than 1808 and earlier than 1893.

In this neighbourhood are also still a few Georgian houses, e.g. No. 93 BEWSEY STREET.

ST BARNABAS, Lovely Lane. 1879 by *William Owen*. Simple, of brick, incomplete.

SACRED HEART, Liverpool Road. 1894–5 by *Sinnott & Powell*. A remarkably strong, straightforward design, inspired no doubt by Bodley. Brick, W tower, broader than it is deep, with steep saddleback roof and lancet windows in pairs and triplets. Low S attachment with a hipped roof. W porch with passages to the entrances l. and r. Short chancel. Uninteresting interior, but curious arcade capitals.

ST LUKE, Liverpool Road. By *Bodley & Garner*, 1892–3. The church is two-naved like e.g. Hannington in Northants (late C13), with nobly slender piers in the Dec style. There are five bays, and as Bodley provided only one chancel, the E arch goes down only a little and then stops where it meets the apex of the chancel arch. There is the figure of an angel there, but the

14+s.l.

junction remains problematic. Equally problematic is the roof arrangement, with not two roofs, but one, its ridge above the arcade. Moreover, there is a N aisle which looks a later addition, but is not. It is all oddly experimental for Bodley and not a success. Goodhart-Rendel is very scathing: 'like some monstrosity crushed into a barn for storage'. The church has no tower, just a bellcote with ogee-headed opening on the nave E gable.

St Paul, Bewsey Road. 1829–30 by *Blore*, a Commissioners' church which cost £4,239. Ashlar, the w doorway with a nice surround, the sides with stepped lancet triplets under one arch. Short canted chancel and an E entrance to its l. Galleries on iron columns. Flat ceiling. Four-centred chancel arch.

Wyclif Congregational Church, Bewsey Road. 1873 by *George Woodhouse* of Bolton. Big, of brick, with round-arched windows and a square NW tower with pyramid roof. Does the sw corner indicate the intention of another tower? One hopes not.

Bewsey Old Hall, at the far end of Lodge Lane, beyond the river Sankey, just outside Warrington. This was the house of the Botelers, lords of the manor of Warrington, but of their time nothing survives. What one sees now is only the s wing of a house projecting to the E beyond a centre or former centre with great hall etc. Only the s stump of this latter stands, with an entrance made from the N. The remaining range is of brick and has large mullioned and transomed windows, of three or four lights, and that to the s of eight. In the s gable is a stepped three-light window, a type more frequent in Yorkshire. The upper floor evidently had the principal accommodation.

WATERHEAD *see* OLDHAM, p. 360

³⁰⁹⁰

WATERLOO

Christ Church, Waterloo Road. By *Paley & Austin*, 1891–4.* An outstanding design. Red stone, with a mighty N tower with strongly displayed higher stair-turret. The features of the church not all Perp, but with free tracery details. The interior has round arcade piers with four fillets, arches dying into the imposts, and big springers intended no doubt for a stone vault, not for the timber vault we now see. The chancel has a seven-light window and is flanked by two chapels, completely differing

* But the competition was won by *Birkett & Langham*.

one from the other. The r. one is normal, but the l. one is developed as part of a complex composition with a transept and the base of the tower used for the organ. The most surprising and prominent member is a tremendous inner buttress for the tower treated in a way Lutyens would have done later.

ST FAITH, Crosby Road North. The Great Crosby parish church. Built at the expense of Douglas Horsfall (*see* St Agnes Sefton Park, Liverpool, p. 234). It was designed by *Grayson & Ould* and built in 1900. It is a large edifice of red brick with a polygonal SE turret. Free geometrical tracery. Effective interior of brick with simple sandstone dressings. Broad nave with narrow passage aisles, clerestory, and hammerbeam roof. Transepts. The chancel is partially aisled and is narrower than the nave. – PULPIT. Large, with Early Renaissance tendencies. – CHANCEL SCREEN. A later insertion, in memory of Douglas Horsfall's son, killed in the First World War. It is not an improvement.

ST JOHN, St John's Road. 1864–5 by *Culshaw*.

ST MARY, Waterloo Park. The area evidently has a deliberately picturesque layout. The church is of 1877–86 by *W. G. Habershon*. E.E., cruciform, with a very squat tower. The main windows are emphasized by shafting.

ST THOMAS (R.C.). 1877 by *E. Kirby*. E.E.; no tower. The w front with some peculiar details.

BAPTIST CHURCH, Crosby Road North. 1891 etc. by *George Baines & Sons*. Brick with stone dressings. Small, in the Arts and Crafts Gothic.

ST ANDREW'S PRESBYTERIAN CHURCH, Crosby Road North and Great George's Road. 1876 by *Barker*. Stock brick and red brick polychrome effects. Plate tracery. The w end has a semicircular projection and above it a rose window. The transepts are additions of 1888 and 1892. A SW tower was begun but has never been continued. The church is coarse but strong. The HALL matches the church and was built in 1892.

TOWN HALL (i.e. the Crosby Town Hall), Great George's Road. 1862. Three-bay front, but a higher addition of 1893 behind. By *F. S. Spencer Yates*, a surveyor.

LIBRARY, Crosby Road North. By *G. Ronald Mason*, begun in 1964. Brick with a round angle feature carrying a beacon.

Waterloo has a sea-front, the sea-front nearest to Liverpool. It consists of individual terraces and starts from the ROYAL HOTEL, formerly Waterloo Hotel, at the corner of Great George's Road and Marine Terrace. This was built in 1815 and is of nine bays and quite plain. Nor is anything to be said about

Marine Terrace or the following MARINE CRESCENT, begun in 1826, which is not a crescent. A few of the houses here have iron verandas, one of a decided Cragg–Rickman character. In ADELAIDE TERRACE (Adelaide married in 1818 and died in 1849) the houses have giant Doric pilasters. Then in BEACH LAWN they go all gay and gabled, mostly with Italianate features, but also (e.g. No. 1) Gothic. The last house, at the corner of Harbord Road, is High Victorian Gothic and wild in the details. It belonged to Dr Drysdale and was built to certain standards of heating and ventilation which Dr Drysdale and his friend Dr Hayward pleaded for. The house has still got its technical equipment. It must date from 1867.

WAVERTREE see LIVERPOOL, p. 254

WERNETH see OLDHAM, pp. 359, 360

WEST DERBY see LIVERPOOL, p. 259

6000

WESTHOUGHTON

ST BARTHOLOMEW. Medieval origin. Rebuilt in 1731. Again rebuilt by the generosity of Mr Seddon* in 1869–70. The architects were *Cunliffe & Freeman*.‡ It is an ambitious church, but not one which architecturally comes off. Very wide nave with short round piers to divide the nave from the narrowest of aisle passages. The piers carry segmental arches, and above are three-light windows with clumsy plate tracery. SE tower with higher stair-turret.

ST JOHN EVANGELIST, Wingates. By *George Shaw* of Saddleworth. 1858–9.

WESTLEIGH see LEIGH

WHALLEY RANGE see MANCHESTER, p. 333

WHELLEY see WIGAN, p. 429

4090

WHISTON

ST NICHOLAS, Windy Arbor Road. 1864–8 by *Street*. An earnest work of architecture with nothing done just to please. Yellow and red stone. The porch tower stands S of the S aisle and is

---

* His villa, MORTONS, is still standing, just S of the railway station.
‡ This was discovered by Mr Buttress.

unfortunately incomplete. Lancets, stepped lancet lights, and some plate tracery. Inside, rock-faced stone is exposed. The piers are round. To the s chancel chapel, which externally has its own roof, there are two openings filled with large-scale tracery of *c.*1300. – STAINED GLASS. The w windows and the s chapel s windows by *Morris & Co.*, 1897–8, the former with angels and a youthful Christ high up in the centre of a small rose window. – E window no doubt *Clayton & Bell*.

EMMANUEL. Congregational. 1891. In a fancy Gothic with a NW steeple.

WHITEFIELD HOUSE *see* KIRKBY

WIDNES

5080

INTRODUCTION

Widnes had only 2,209 inhabitants in 1841. In 1847 John Hutchinson established alkali works, and since then Widnes has become a centre of chemical industries. By 1891 it had 30,000 inhabitants, in 1901 it was about 52,000. It is not more today. The town falls into two parts, West Bank at the bridge-head of the Mersey bridges, and the town proper a little to the N, with a very uneventful centre, but with a few more ambitious buildings of the last few years.

WEST BANK

The planned grid layout dates from *c.*1860–70. Until then West Bank was rural. Industry arrived about 1850. The uniform streets look dreary now, but it has the redeeming feature of the riverside VICTORIA PROMENADE. Facing the Promenade is St Mary.

ST MARY. 1908–10 by *Austin & Paley*, a splendid building of red stone, big, majestic, and full of imagination in the interior. It has a substantial w tower, embraced by the aisles, high transepts differing in details, Perp windows, and inscription friezes in various places. The NW porch is set diagonally. The interior has exposed rock-faced stone. The tower rests to the inside on mighty E piers. It has a vault too. The chancel arch responds to the tower piers by equally huge round panelled piers. The chancel is flanked by two totally different appendices opening from the transepts. The N organ chamber is high, with a one-bay arch to the chancel, the s Lady Chapel is low and of three bays. – Outside is a stone WAYSIDE PULPIT.

ST PATRICK (R.C.), Church Street. 1887–8 by *J. & B. Sinnott*.
THE BRIDGES. The approach to the railway bridge is by a long,
curved, very effective arched VIADUCT. The RAILWAY
BRIDGE itself is of 1864–8, of iron, with fortress-like stone
pylons. The TRANSPORTER BRIDGE (really *transbordeur*) of
1901–5 has been replaced by a new road bridge. To see the
spectacular sight of a transporter bridge, one has to go to
3 Middlesbrough. The ROAD BRIDGE of 1956–61 is by *Mott,
Hay & Anderson*. It is a single steel arch rising elegantly into
the air and carrying hanging from it the roadway. The span
is 1,082 ft, the total length 1,628 ft. It was the largest steel arch
in Europe when it was built, and the third largest in the world.
The structure consists of two arches connected by zigzag lattice
work. The outer arch starts in a double curve, slightly concave
before it becomes convex.

WIDNES PROPER

The centre is VICTORIA SQUARE.
ST PAUL. 1883–4 by *H. Shelmerdine*, the SE tower only 1907.
Stock brick and red brick. Big, with geometrical tracery, and
handled without much sensitivity. Inside spacious, with
exposed brick. – PULPIT of terracotta. – The VICARAGE, with
mullioned and transomed windows, looks contemporary.
TOWN HALL. 1887 by *F. & G. Holme*. Symmetrical, brick and
terracotta, in a free Frenchy Renaissance. Or is the source
another style? A tower was planned but not built.
LIBRARY AND TECHNICAL SCHOOL. 1895–6; enlarged 1910.
Red brick and red terracotta; free Elizabethan.
The surrounding streets are mean and dreary.
ST MARIE (R.C.), Lugsdale Road. 1864–5 by *E. W. Pugin*. With
a pretty bellcote and a polygonal apse. Thin red sandstone
columns inside. The capitals are typical of E. W. Pugin.
Immediately N of the centre are four promising new buildings:
MUNICIPAL BUILDINGS, completed 1967, and COLLEGE OF
FURTHER EDUCATION, completed 1961, both by *M. Nevile
Player*. The new block is excellent, a block of six storeys on a
podium. White glass sill bands.
SWIMMING BATHS, Vicarage Place and Kingsway. Completed
1961, by *M. Nevile Player* too, with its big hogback roof also
an architectural asset.
MAGISTRATES' COURT AND POLICE. 1966–7 by *Roger Booth*,
the County Architect. The police has a curtain-wall slab as

often seen for offices, but the magistrates' court is low, the walls faced with reconstructed marble and a zigzag roof, rather gay for its purpose.

OUTER WIDNES

Only two churches and two public buildings.

ST AMBROSE, Halton View. By *Doyle*, 1879–83. Stock brick and red-brick trim. Also red terracotta. No tower, though apparently a NE tower was planned. The windows are mostly lancets, but the first and last bays of the clerestory are singled out by more elaborate plate tracery. Why? Polygonal apse of the same height as the nave. Brick is exposed inside. A clean-cut, spacious interior. – PULPIT. Of terracotta. – The VICARAGE is of 1900 and may well be by the same architect.

ST BEDE (R.C.), Appleton Road. 1847 by *Weightman & Hadfield*. Sizeable, with a W tower and the tripartite E end frequent in Catholic churches of that time. – Mrs Stanton has found evidence of an ALTAR supplied in 1850 to *A. W. N. Pugin*'s design, and the STAINED GLASS of a window also designed by him.

WADE DEACON GRAMMAR SCHOOL. 1930–1 by *Stephen Wilkinson*, in the typical scholastic Georgian of between the wars.

WIDNES NORTH STATION. One of a type frequent on this line. They have gables with a variety of bargeboard patterns.

WIGAN

5000

INTRODUCTION

Wigan is not a *parvenu* of the Industrial Revolution.* The parish church is first mentioned in 1199, the town received a charter in 1246 and the grant of a market in 1258, and there are minimal features of the C13 in the parish church. Leland mentions seacoule at Wigan in 1538, and by 1784 a cloth hall was opened, i.e. the town manufactured textiles. But the population in 1801 was only 11,000. Today it is 78,000. Wigan has been much maligned as the *nec plus ultra* of Lancashire gloom. That is untrue, but it is true that the town in the prosperous Victorian decades has shown little of architectural enterprise. No great Victorian town hall must be expected. What there is of large-scale public buildings belongs to this century.

* The site of the Roman settlement of COCCIUM is thought to underlie Wigan, but its siting is uncertain.

INNER WIGAN

CHURCHES

ALL SAINTS. The church is by *Sharpe & Paley* and was built in 1845–50. In style it is much more like Paley than like Sharpe. However, it is in fact a rebuilding, and a faithful one, so Paley said, of the pre-existing building. This must already in the Middle Ages have been about as large as it is now, for the N tower, the two rood-turrets, and the N chapel (Walmesley Chapel) are original. The tower dates from the later C13 in its lower parts (see the W window of three stepped lancet lights and the arch towards the S). It was remodelled in the later Middle Ages and heightened in 1861 by Paley with pairs of three-light windows. The N chapel was rebuilt *c.*1620. It has windows of five stepped lights with uncusped round heads. The two-bay arcade to the nave, however, is Perp in its details. Is this C15 work or also of the early C17? The rebuilding of 1845–50 was largely inspired by the Hon. Colin Lindsay, a son of the 24th Earl of Crawford, and churchwarden at the time. The whole work cost a little over £15,000. It is more impressive outside than inside. The clerestory is of sixteen windows either side. The arcades have six bays with piers of a familiar Perp section. The shafts and corbels for the roof are typical 1840s stuff, but the roof itself and also those of the aisles are largely of old timbers. – STALLS for Mayor and Corporation. At the W end, in rising tiers. They are of *c.*1850 and heavily carved. – (SCULPTURE. A Roman altar is built into the church.) – TILES. Good *Minton* tiling in the chancel and baptistery. – STAINED GLASS. Some old figures and fragments in the N chapel. – The E window (1847), W window (1849), and the window W of the font (1845) are by *Wailes*. The E window still has entirely pictorial scenes, whereas the W window is of twelve upright saints. – Three S aisle windows by *Hardman*, 1855–66, four N aisle windows by *Clayton & Bell*, 1872–99. – In the S aisle also a beautiful *Morris* window: St Christopher, 1868. – DORSAL. A genuine Laudian tapestry dorsal, a great rarity. It is 18½ by 5⅔ ft and is a Mortlake copy of Raphael's Death of Ananias. – PLATE. Mostly of 1706, but remade *c.*1850 by *Keith & Co.* – Two Almsdishes 1724. – MONUMENTS. The monuments said to represent Sir William de Bradshaigh and Lady Mab, his wife, who founded a chantry in the church in

1338, are in a sad state. The female effigy was entirely re-cut
and the male effigy copied by *John Gibson*. The original, totally
defaced male effigy is next to the couple. – (Priest. Only the
head visible. On the sill of a tower window.) – James Bankes
† 1689 and John Baldwin † 1726, both s aisle and both good. –
On the E wall of the s chapel are two large Gothic marble
monuments to the 23rd Earl of Crawford † 1825 and his wife
and to the wife of the 24th Earl † 1850. They are by *Felicie* and
Hippolyte de Fauveau, made in Florence.

s of the church is the WAR MEMORIAL. It is by *Sir Giles Gilbert
Scott* and was erected in 1925. It is high and impressive, in a
Gothic similar to that of late works of Voysey.

ST GEORGE, Church Street. 1781. Brick. The sides have four
bays of arched windows in two tiers, the front a doorway with
broken pediment on columns and a big shaped gable. Inside,
the short chancel is separated from the nave by an opening
with two giant columns. Flat ceiling; w gallery. – FONT. Of
the baluster type, *c*.1710. It comes from All Saints.

ST JOHN (R.C.), Standishgate. 1819. Ashlar front with a porch
of six unfluted Ionic columns. Three arched windows above.
A cupola on the SE corner. Inside, the ample apse comes into 37
its own with attached giant Corinthian columns. The w gallery
is on Corinthian columns too. – CROSS, in front of the church.
1852. By *Pugin*, according to GR. On the base are shields and
the Symbols of the four Evangelists. At the top are the Virgin
and St John, free-standing figures keeping close to the Crucifixus. Above the cross a crocketed gable.

ST JOSEPH (R.C.), Caroline Street. 1878 by *Goldie & Child*.

ST MARY (R.C.), Standishgate. 1818. A large Perp ashlar front
of three bays with battlements and pinnacles and a middle
gable with bellcote. Thin piers and a short chancel. The front
is surprising for its date, but it is said to be original.

ST THOMAS, Caroline Street. 1849–51 by Messrs *Hay*, and
interesting in the light of their work at Liverpool, which keeps
more ties to the Commissioners' past. Here the archeological
approach is evident. SE steeple with broach spire. Alternating
round and octagonal piers. What remains a feature of the past
is the absence of a chancel arch, i.e. a proper chancel.

KING STREET BAPTIST CHAPEL. 1903. Red brick and red
terracotta. Arched windows and giant pilasters, but playful
Gothic details.

ST PAUL'S CONGREGATIONAL CHURCH, Standishgate. B
F. W. Dixon, 1902–3. Gothic.

14*

STANDISHGATE METHODIST CHURCH. Gothic. 1844–5, by *Jabez Hanson*.

(QUEEN'S HALL METHODIST MISSION, Market Street. By *Bradshaw & Gass*, 1907–8.)

PUBLIC BUILDINGS

TOWN HALL. 1866–7 and not worth a line. – INSIGNIA. The Greater Mace is of 1657 and silver-gilt. – The Lesser Mace is of about the same date. – C17 State Sword.

POLICE AND MAGISTRATES' COURTS, Crawford Street. 1888. Large range of brick with mullioned-and-transomed windows.

LIBRARY, Rodney Street. By *Waterhouse*, 1878. Gothic of course.

TECHNICAL COLLEGE and LINACRE SCHOOL, Parson's Walk. By *Howard Lobb* and *Grenfell Baines & Hargreaves*, 1950–4. Of no architectural interest.

The old building in Library Street is much better. It is of 1901–3 by *Briggs & Wolstenholme*, high and gabled, of red brick and red terracotta with Edwardian motifs such as alternately blocked columns.

BLUECOAT SCHOOL. Founded in 1773. The original building, just NW of the church, is no more than a stone cottage, and it still has mullioned windows. It has fallen on evil days, being now a garage for the police. The new building is in Hallgate. It dates from 1823 and is of brick, five bays and two storeys – quite plain.

GRAMMAR SCHOOL, Parson's Walk. Large, neo-Georgian. 1937 by *A. E. Munby*.

CHURCH SCHOOL, New Market, opposite Wigan Hall. By *Street*, 1867, but not worthy of him. An oblong building with a Perp end window and small windows along the flat front.

SWIMMING BATHS, Rodney Street. 1965–6. Not of architectural interest, but all credit to Wigan. It was the fifth in all Britain to go in for Olympic dimensions.

MESNES PARK. Opened in 1878. The area was on the small side, yet there is a serpentine lake. In the centre of the park is a PAVILION of yellow and red brick with iron porches and a glazed lantern. There is also some stone terracing. – STATUE of Sir Francis Sharp Powell, 1910 by *E. G. Gillick*.

PERAMBULATION

Commercial buildings are best seen in King Street and Standishgate. In KING STREET are a rather spreading E.E. front leading into an arcade, built, it appears, c.1870–5, opposite a five-bay Late Georgian brick house with a pedimented doorway on columns, then the PLAYHOUSE of 1916 with a faience front with classical motifs and the COURT THEATRE, red brick and red terracotta with Renaissance motifs on the first floor. The WIGAN EXAMINER presents a most curious façade with a giant arched window in the middle of the first floor framed by a giant rusticated arch and one tripartite pedimented window l. and one r. Continue into CHAPEL LANE to see the highly rewarding fragment of the GAS WORKS of 1822. Of the street range with lodges only a part is preserved, but the range behind with its pairs of short, powerful Tuscan columns and its lion on top will linger in one's memory.

N of Chapel Lane is on the NE the new SCHOLES DEVELOPMENT of housing, not architecturally valuable, but of substantial dimensions, and on the NW in MILLGATE (No. 48) a five-bay Late Georgian house. Millgate leads to Market Street and the Market Place and also to Standishgate.

(In MARKET STREET No. 40 was a branch of W. H. Lever's grocery business, built in 1881 by *Jonathan Simpson* for the future Lord Leverhulme. In 1881 soap-making had not started yet. The name Lever & Co. remains carved beside the shop fascia. E. Hubbard)

In the MARKET PLACE is the MAKINSON ARCADE of 1898 (by *R. Ablett*) with a front of brick and red terracotta in a style of French and English C16 elements and a poor glass arcade behind. STANDISHGATE starts with the WESTMINSTER BANK, built, it appears, before 1875, and yet in a spirited Loire style. Off Standishgate in CHURCH STREET just NW of St George's church is a front with eight Norman-Shaw-like oriels. More Late Georgian terrace houses with enriched doorways in DICCONSON TERRACE and UPPER DICCONSON STREET. Turn SW along NEW MARKET for WIGAN HALL, the rectory and in the Middle Ages the manor house as well, as the rectors were lords of the manor of Wigan. It is by *Street* and dates from 1875. Gatehouse of stone below, half-timbering above. The house itself is also stone below, but the timbers have brick infilling. It is far more fanciful than one expects Street to be. (In the CHAPEL a Flemish ALTARPIECE with carved saints in two tiers and paintings on the outsides.* In the garden a Perp FONT, octagonal with quatrefoil decoration.)

---

* From photographs it seems possible that it might be English – in which case it would of course be an extreme rarity.

OUTER WIGAN

ST ANDREW, Woodhouse Lane, Beech Hill (NNW). 1882 by
F. W. Hunt of London.*

ST CATHERINE, Lorne Street, Scholes (E). By E. Sharpe, 1840–1.
A restless w tower with four gables to mediate to an octagonal
top part which has eight gables to mediate to a spire, a typical
example of the undisciplined inventiveness of church architects
of the C19 before Pugin. One would have expected Sharpe to
do better, considering that he was an expert on the Decorated
style. The sides have the usual pairs of lancets. Short chancel,
three galleries. The church was built for the Commissioners
and cost £3,180.

ST JAMES, Poolstock (SW). 1866 by E. G. Paley. The estimate
was for over £15,000 (GS). Large, with a w tower, nave and
aisles, clerestory of pairs of two-light windows, a lower chancel,
and a s appendix with rose window with, in its tracery, the Star
of David. The period motifs are Dec. Five-bay arcades. – The
chancel decoration and the ornate REREDOS with two tiers of
Ghibertesque figures l. and r. of the E window are of 1877. The
chancel decoration is no longer in its complete form. – COOLING
TOWERS to the S.

ST JOHN, Ormskirk Road, Lamberhead Green (WSW; far out).
1830–2 by Rickman & Hutchinson, and a poor effort. Brick. w
front with a triplet of lancets and square pinnacles. The sides
with lancets. Three stepped E lancets. Three galleries on iron
columns. Flat ceiling. The church is a Commissioners' church.
They spent £4,913 on it.

ST JOHN'S SCHOOL is dated 1828. It is of brick, five bays,
with pointed windows on two tiers.

ST JUDE, St Paul's Avenue, Worsley Mesnes (SW). 1963–4 by
L. A. G. Prichard & Son. Overloaded with the pet motifs of
the sixties to a pitch which cannot do good to a contemplative
state of mind.

ST MARK, Victoria Street, Pemberton (SW). 1891–2 by Heaton
& Ralph. Architects of no fame, yet a good workmanlike job.
s transept and a SE tower.

83 ST MATTHEW, Billinge Road, Highfield (SW). 1894 by Austin &
Paley, and one of their first flight. Red sandstone, with a
crossing tower with recessed spire and beautifully placed

---

* Goodhart-Rendel writes: Design made and published 1878, Bowes A.
Paice.

lucarnes at its foot. The nave with a few lancets placed up high. There is a s aisle of five bays, but a N aisle of only two bays W of the transept. The chancel N side has richly shafted windows, the s side has none, but the group of the SEDILIA instead. The church was built at the expense of Col. Henry Blundell, who owned the Pemberton Colliery, in memory of his wife. He gave about £10,000.

ST MICHAEL, Swinley Road, Swinley (N). 1875–8 by *Street*. Nave and chancel, bellcote between them. E.E.

Just NE of the church, in the main road, is the TYLDESLEY MONUMENT to commemorate the spot where Sir Thomas Tyldesley was killed in the Civil War. It was erected in 1679 and later rebuilt. It is a square pillar with a ball on top.

ST PATRICK (R.C.), Hardybutts, Scholes (E). 1880 by *James O'Byrne* of Liverpool. Brick with small lancets and no tower.

ST PAUL, St Paul's Avenue, Worsley Mesnes. 1913–15 by *W. Chasen Ralph & Son*. Red sandstone, with a W tower and a good interior.

ST STEPHEN, Avenue Road, off Whelley (NE). 1930–8 by *Austin & Paley*. So the firm kept up the Paley & Austin style that long. Brown and red stone. An excellent E view with vestry and bell-cote facing E on the l. of the chancel E window. Inside, arcade piers with arches dying into them. But the 1930s are an odd time calmly to do this 1880s work.

TRINITY METHODIST CHURCH, Ormskirk Road (far W). 1851. Debased Gothic, brick, the façade asymmetrical with a NW tower wearing a funny hat.

MORMON CHURCH, Wigan Lane (N). 1963–8. By the American architects who designed a large number of Mormon churches in other countries as well.

PARK LANE UNITARIAN CHAPEL, Land Gate (3 m. SSW). 1697, but all features victorianized. What remains is just a small oblong and the PULPIT with square panels.

ROYAL ALBERT EDWARD INFIRMARY, Wigan Lane (N). The oldest parts by *Thomas Worthington*, opened in 1873. Red brick, with blue brick trim, symmetrical, the front range not large, but with a tower. Gothic of course. Wards behind, and a Gothic lodge. The Outpatients' Department is of 1913 and more attractive (by *W. Chasen Ralph & Son*).

LIBRARY, Ellesmere Road, Pemberton (SW). 1906–7 by *J. B. & W. Thornely*. Brick and stone, in a conspicuous position. Symmetrical with a gable and mullioned-and-transomed windows, but Baroque motifs as well.

H. J. HEINZ & CO. FACTORY, ½ m. N of Kitt Green (far W, N of Lamberhead Green). 1954–9 by *J. Douglass Mathews & Partners* in association with *Skidmore, Owings & Merrill*. It depends on how one looks at it. If this is an English design, one has nothing but praise; if it is S.O.M., one of the best architectural firms in America and indeed anywhere, and if one compares with their American work, the brickwork is up to their standard of perfection, a joy to gaze at, but the rest lacks just that perfection – which may be a matter of materials used or of finishes insisted on. It is a very large building all on one floor – 26,000 square yards – and it is planned with great ingenuity.

HAWKLEY HALL FARMHOUSE, Carr's Lane, off Poolstock Lane (far SW). A fine C17 front with two slightly projecting wings and a centre not quite symmetrical because the doorway is off centre, with a four-light window l., a six-light window r. The wings have a five-light window each. There are two floors and all the windows have transoms.

WINSTANLEY HALL. Elizabethan. Bought in 1596 by James Bankes, and still in the possession of the same family. The original façade is much like those of Birchley Hall and Bispham Hall, both very near. Two projecting wings and a recessed centre with square projections in the re-entrant angles, one obviously the hall bay, the other originally probably the porch (cf. Bispham). The gables were replaced in the early C19 by a parapet. *Lewis Wyatt* worked at Winstanley in 1818–19. The ground-floor windows have transoms. Most of the others are mullioned only. Round the corner is the present main entrance side. This with its columned doorway and cross-windows is by Lewis Wyatt. So is the canted bay round the l. corner. The STABLES are extensive and of the early C19, with a canted, raised centre. The lower windows are of three lights with canted tops, and the upper windows are circular.*

WINGATES *see* WESTHOUGHTON

WINSTANLEY HALL *see* WIGAN, p. 430

WINTON

7090

Winton, though 1¼ m. from the centre of Eccles, is just part of the W suburbs of Eccles.

---

* Mr Bankes tells me that the NEPTUNE FOUNTAIN is by *William Spence*.

St Mary Magdalene, Westbourne Road. 1913 by *R. T. Beckett*, and a church that makes one want to see more of this architect's work. It is a church big in conception, as one can recognize, even though tower and nave are both unfinished. The large windows have simplified Perp tracery, the smaller just Elizabethan mullions. (The interior* on the other hand is a late attempt at vernacular Gothic. Three bays only. A thin effect altogether, saved only by the massiveness of the piers for the central tower.)

WINWICK   *6090*

St Oswald. Evidently a medieval church, though only the w tower is now convincingly medieval. The details make the early C14 certain. Pretty niches l. and r. of the w window. The N aisle E wall and the s aisle w wall and sw turret are also medieval. On the w wall is an inscription commemorating King Oswald of Northumbria, according to one tradition killed here in 642, and the date 1530 for the *renovatio* of this wall by the then priest Henry Johnson. The interior is puzzling. The s arcade is evidently early C14 in style but was rebuilt in 1836, when the s aisle was rebuilt too. The N arcade has clumsy big piers not fitting their arches. The arches are C14, but are the 4 piers Perp or, as the VCH suggests, of *c*.1600? For the chancel we are on safe ground. *Pugin* rebuilt it in 1847–8 – an Anglican 50 task for this arch-Catholic. However, there was full understanding between Pugin, aged thirty-five, and the Rev. J. J. Hornby, aged sixty-nine. The style is Dec, with three-light side windows and a four-light E window. The SEDILIA are of course Pugin's too. The roof is steep-pitched and higher than that of the nave. Also the vestry is characteristically Pugin, with its castellated chimneystack. Inside the vestry a Pugin fireplace. An interesting feature is the aisle windows with the small plaques with IHS in the intersections of verticals and transoms in the tracery. The windows are Victorian, but supposedly an accurate copy. Of what date? The VCH proposes *c*.1530–50, which could apply to the N piers as well. The clerestory is Late Perp, as the former nave roof-line inside against the tower shows. The E bays of the aisles are the Legh Chapel (s), with a handsome panelled roof, and the Gerard Chapel (N). – FONT. In the N chapel fragment of a big Perp font. – SCREENS. In the vestry one decorated beam from the rood loft of the medieval

* So Mr Buttress writes.

church. – The present screen and STALLS are by *Pugin*. Pugin fervently believed in screens. – IRON SCREENS to the two chapels. They are of 1848. – CROSS. In the N chapel the cross-bar of the head of an amazingly large cross – the bar 5 ft in length. It is Anglo-Saxon and has on the front divers interlace patterns, on the back large blobs and animals and on the short sides a standing man and two men with a third upside down. – SCULPTURE. The Winwick Pig. Small panel in the W front. It is the pig of St Anthony, and the date is hard to guess. There are such panels in Norman sculpture, but this is likely to be later and just primitive. – STAINED GLASS. The chancel windows are to *Pugin*'s designs and made by *Hardman*. They have mostly individual large figures. – CHANDELIER. Of brass, probably C18. – PLATE. Set of 1786; Set of 1795; gilded brass-Almsdish and two Plates, designed by *Pugin*. – MONUMENTS. In the N chapel brass to Piers Gerard † 1495. A 4 ft 9 in. figure, badly rubbed off. He wears broad-toed shoes, an early case. There are fragments of a triple canopy. – The rest in the S chapel: brass to Sir Peter Legh † 1527 and wife. 30 in. figures. He wears the vestments of a priest under his armour, as he was ordained after the death of his wife. – Richard Legh † 1687. Two free-standing busts against baldacchino drapery, not a very refined piece. – Master Benet Legh † 1755, aged eight. Allegorical female figure leaning over a medallion. – Mrs Ellen

44 Legh † 1831. By *R. J. Wyatt*, made in Rome. Relief scene. An angel is ready to take her away. Husband and baby are left behind. – Many more tablets.

MYDDLETON HALL, 1m. E. Dated 1658, but the gables evidently C19. Brick. The front is symmetrical, with one recessed bay between two projecting bays. Mullioned-and-transomed windows.

MYDDLETON HALL FARMHOUSE (or Delph House). Dated 1657. Not symmetrical, with a little raised brick decoration.

WITHINGTON *see* MANCHESTER, p. 317

WOOLFOLD *see* BURY, p. 101

6080   WOOLSTON

ST PETER (R.C.), at Martinscroft. 1831. Oblong brick building with lancet windows and a shallow apse.

WOOLTON *see* LIVERPOOL, p. 260

WORSLEY

What matters in the centre of Worsley is all connected with Francis Egerton, third Duke of Bridgewater, and Lord Francis Leveson-Gower, son of the third Duke's nephew, the Duke of Sutherland. On inheriting from the Duke of Bridgewater he changed his name to Egerton and in 1846 became the first Earl of Ellesmere. Due to the third Duke is the Canal, due to the first Earl of Ellesmere the church and much else.

WORSLEY HALL, built by *Blore* in 1840–6 for Francis Egerton, has been pulled down.* However, the church opposite the gates has survived, and the BRIDGEWATER CANAL, built in 1759–61 by *Brindley* for the third Duke to carry coal from the Worsley mine to Manchester. At Worsley close to the church and the new traffic roundabout are the CANAL BASIN and the LANDING STEPS, and N of Worsley Road one can see the TUNNEL ENTRANCE to the Walkden Level of the mines. Moreover there is along the WORSLEY ROAD much ESTATE HOUSING, the oldest a long terrace with windows with very close glazing bars, the newest along THE GREEN bigger and half-timbered. One unit is a symmetrical group of four. The oldest of the housing appears on a map of 1764, The Green was built in 1907. Also by the roundabout is the very fancifully half-timbered COURT HOUSE. This is of 1849, an early date for such a black and white revival.

ST MARK. 1846 by *Sir George Gilbert Scott*. In a leafy position, as Worsley altogether still is. The W tower shows young Gilbert Scott more playful than he later chose to be. The spire bristles with crockets and gargoyles. The style of the church is Geometrical to Decorated, i.e. Scott's favourite Middle Pointed. Four-bay nave, Dec piers with bossy leaf capitals, the family chapel of three bays on the S side. – PULPIT and ORGAN SCREENS have brought-in panels of various kinds, Flemish C16 and Flemish C17 scenes, French (or North English) Flamboyant tracery, etc. – Iron chapel SCREEN. – STAINED GLASS. E window and S chapel windows with glass of *c.* 1850 in strident colours.‡ – MONUMENT. Francis Egerton, first Earl of Ellesmere, † 1857, tomb-chest with recumbent effigy, designed by

* But the lodge and gates remain, the Ellesmere Memorial in the park remains, a Gothic pillar, by *Driver & Webber*, 1858, and some of the garden layout also remains.

‡ Mrs Stanton has come across evidence of *Pugin* doing glass for Worsley in 1851.

Scott and made by *Philip*, but the effigy by *M. Noble*. – Outside the w entrance cast-iron LAMPS and LIONS.

WORSLEY OLD HALL, N of Leigh Road and the Worsley Hall park. Almost entirely C 19, but at the SE corner is still a fragment of the original timber-framed house. *Brindley* was given quarters here while he built the canal.

WARDLEY HALL, 1 m. NE. Wardley Hall was originally a timber-framed house with an inner courtyard and a moat. 'Originally' means probably c.1500 or a little later. Of that time, however, there is externally only a certain amount of the timbers of the courtyard sides, with closely set uprights and diagonal braces, and internally much of the great hall. This is in the s range. The N range contains the gatehouse and is of brick. It was formerly dated 1625. Externally the other ranges, except for the centre of the s side, are of brick too. This also refers to the hall fireplace. They are much restored and not reliable. All external windows are Victorian or later. The stone chimney of the w wing however is part of the original work. The great hall was open to the roof, but 'relatively early' (VCH) it was divided both by a cross wall and by a floor. For the latter reason the fine arched braces of the hall roof must now be looked for up in the upper storey. In the w range on the upper floor are also arched braces. The range was the family quarters, the E range was offices etc. The inserted ceilings have good moulded beams. But the best beams are in the upper parlour. There are here also moulded wall-posts. The high-table end of the hall had to the s a spacious oblong bay window, now part of a room created later. There was probably also such a bay window to the N, but that, about 1630, was filled in by a staircase. The E range was drastically remodelled in 1903.

In GREENLEACH LANE, ½ m. N, is KEMPNOUGH HALL, C17, timber-framed with two cross gables.

WORSLEY MESNES *see* WIGAN, pp. 428, 429

WYTHENSHAWE *see* MANCHESTER, p. 340

GLOSSARY

ABACUS: flat slab on the top of a capital (q.v.).

ABUTMENT: solid masonry placed to resist the lateral pressure of a vault.

ACANTHUS: plant with thick fleshy and scalloped leaves used as part of the decoration of a Corinthian capital (q.v.) and in some types of leaf carving.

ACHIEVEMENT OF ARMS: in heraldry, a complete display of armorial bearings.

ACROTERION: foliage-carved block on the end or top of a classical pediment (q.v.).

ADDORSED: two human figures, animals, or birds, etc., placed symmetrically so that they turn their backs to each other.

AEDICULE, AEDICULA: framing of a window or door by columns and a pediment (q.v.).

AFFRONTED: two human figures, animals, or birds, etc., placed symmetrically so that they face each other.

AGGER: Latin term for the built-up foundations of Roman roads; also sometimes applied to the banks of hill-forts or other earthworks.

AMBULATORY: semicircular or polygonal aisle enclosing an apse (q.v.).

ANNULET: see Shaft-ring.

ANSE DE PANIER: see Arch, Basket.

ANTEPENDIUM: covering of the front of an altar, usually by textiles or metalwork.

ANTIS, IN: see Portico.

APSE: vaulted semicircular or polygonal end of a chancel or a chapel.

ARABESQUE: light and fanciful surface decoration using combinations of flowing lines, tendrils, etc., interspersed with vases, animals, etc.

ARCADE: range of arches supported on piers or columns, free-standing: or, BLIND ARCADE, the same attached to a wall.

ARCH: round-headed, i.e. semicircular; pointed, i.e. consisting of two curves, each drawn from one centre, and meeting in a point at the top; segmental, i.e. in the form of a segment; pointed; four-centred (a late medieval form), see Fig. 1(a);

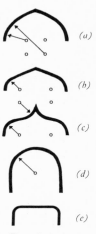

Fig. 1. Arches

Tudor (also a late medieval form), *see* Fig. 1(*b*); Ogee (introduced *c.* 1300 and specially popular in the C14), *see* Fig. 1(*c*); Stilted, *see* Fig. 1(*d*); Basket, with lintel connected to the jambs by concave quadrant curves, *see* Fig. 1(*e*) for one example; Diaphragm, a transverse arch with solid spandrels carrying not a vault but a principal beam of a timber roof. *See also* Strainer Arch.

ARCHITRAVE: lowest of the three main parts of the entablature (q.v.) of an order (q.v.) (*see* Fig. 12).

ARCHIVOLT: a continuous moulding on the face of an arch and following its contour.

ARRIS: sharp edge at the meeting of two surfaces.

ASHLAR: masonry of large blocks wrought to even faces and square edges.

ATLANTES: male counterparts of caryatids (q.v.).

ATRIUM: inner court of a Roman house, also open court in front of a church.

ATTACHED: *see* Engaged.

ATTIC: topmost storey of a house, if distance from floor to ceiling is less than in the others.

AUMBRY: recess or cupboard to hold sacred vessels for Mass and Communion.

Bailey: open space or court of a stone-built castle; *see also* Motte-and-Bailey.

BALDACCHINO: canopy supported on columns.

BALLFLOWER: globular flower of three petals enclosing a small ball. A decoration used in the first quarter of the C14.

BALUSTER: small pillar or column of fanciful outline.

BALUSTRADE: series of balusters supporting a handrail or coping (q.v.).

BARBICAN: outwork defending the entrance to a castle.

BARGEBOARDS: projecting decorated boards placed against the incline of the gable of a building and hiding the horizontal roof timbers.

BARREL-VAULT: *see* Vault.

BARROW: *see* Bell, Bowl, Disc, Long, *and* Pond Barrow.

BASILICA: in medieval architecture an aisled church with a clerestory.

BASKET ARCH: *see* Arch (Fig. 1e).

BASTION: projection at the angle of a fortification.

BATTER: inclined face of a wall.

BATTLEMENT: parapet with a series of indentations or embrasures with raised portions or merlons between. Also called Crenellation.

BAYS: internal compartments of a building; each divided from the other not by solid walls but by divisions only marked in the side walls (columns, pilasters, etc.) or the ceiling (beams, etc.). Also external divisions of a building by fenestration.

BAY-WINDOW: angular or curved projection of a house front with ample fenestration. If curved, also called bow-window: if on an upper floor only, also called oriel or oriel window.

BEAKER FOLK: Late New Stone Age warrior invaders from the Continent who buried their dead in round barrows and introduced the first metal tools and weapons to Britain.

BEAKHEAD: Norman ornamental motif consisting of a row of bird or beast heads with beaks biting usually into a roll moulding (q.v.).

BELFRY: turret on a roof to hang bells in.

BELGAE: aristocratic warrior bands who settled in Britain in two main waves in the CI B.C. In Britain their culture is termed Iron Age C.

BELL BARROW: Early Bronze Age round barrow in which the mound is separated from its encircling ditch by a flat platform or berm (q.v.).

BELLCOTE: framework on a roof to hang bells from.

BERM: level area separating ditch from bank on a hill-fort or barrow.

BILLET FRIEZE: Norman ornamental motif made up of short raised rectangles placed at regular intervals.

BIVALLATE: of a hill-fort: defended by two concentric banks and ditches.

BLIND ARCADE: see Arcade.

BLOCK CAPITAL: Romanesque capital cut from a cube by having the lower angles rounded off to the circular shaft below. Also called Cushion Capital (Fig. 2).

Fig. 2. Block capital

BOND, ENGLISH or FLEMISH: see Brickwork.

BOSS: knob or projection usually placed to cover the intersection of ribs in a vault.

BOWL BARROW: round barrow surrounded by a quarry ditch. Introduced in Late Neolithic times, the form continued until the Saxon period.

BOW-WINDOW: see Bay-Window.

BOX: small country house, e.g. a shooting box. A convenient term to describe a compact minor dwelling, e.g. a rectory.

BOX PEW: pew with a high wooden enclosure.

BRACES: see Roof.

BRACKET: small supporting piece of stone, etc., to carry a projecting horizontal.

BRESSUMER: beam in a timber-framed building to support the, usually projecting, superstructure.

BRICKWORK: *Header:* brick laid so that the end only appears on the face of the wall. *Stretcher:* brick laid so that the side only appears on the face of the wall. *English Bond:* method of laying bricks so that alternate courses or layers on the face of the wall are composed of headers or stretchers only (Fig. 3a). *Flemish Bond:* method of laying bricks so that alternate headers and

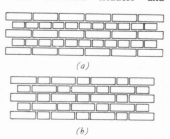

(a)

(b)

Fig. 3. Brickwork

stretchers appear in each course on the face of the wall (Fig. 3*b*). *See also* Herringbone Work, Oversailing Courses.

BROACH: *see* Spire.

BROKEN PEDIMENT: *see* Pediment.

BRONZE AGE: in Britain, the period from *c.* 1600 to 600 B.C.

BUCRANIUM: ox skull.

BUTTRESS: mass of brickwork or masonry projecting from or built against a wall to give additional strength. *Angle Buttresses:* two meeting at an angle of 90° at the angle of a building (Fig. 4*a*). *Clasping Buttress:* one which encases the angle (Fig. 4*d*). *Diagonal Buttress:* one placed against the right angle formed by two walls, and more or less equiangular with both (Fig. 4*b*). *Flying Buttress:* arch or half arch transmitting the thrust of a vault or roof from the upper part of a wall to an outer support or buttress. *Setback Buttress:* angle buttress set slightly back from the angle (Fig. 4*c*).

CABLE MOULDING: Norman moulding imitating a twisted cord.

CAIRN: a mound of stones usually covering a burial.

CAMBER: slight rise or upward curve of an otherwise horizontal structure.

CAMPANILE: isolated bell tower.

CANOPY: projection or hood over

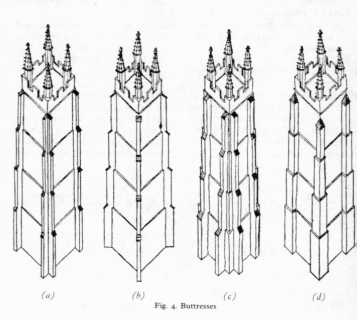

(a)   *(b)*   *(c)*   *(d)*

Fig. 4. Buttresses

an altar, pulpit, niche, statue, etc.

CAP: in a windmill the crowning feature.

CAPITAL: head or top part of a column. *See also* Block Capital, Crocket Capital, Order, Scalloped Capital, Stiff-leaf, *and* Waterleaf.

CARTOUCHE: tablet with an ornate frame, usually enclosing an inscription.

CARYATID: whole female figure supporting an entablature or other similar member. *Termini Caryatids:* female busts or demi-figures or three-quarter figures supporting an entablature or other similar member and placed at the top of termini pilasters (q.v.). Cf. Atlantes.

CASTELLATED: decorated with battlements (q.v.).

CELURE: panelled and adorned part of a wagon roof above the rood or the altar.

CENSER: vessel for the burning of incense.

CENTERING: wooden framework used in arch and vault construction and removed when the mortar has set.

CHALICE: cup used in the Communion service or at Mass. *See also* Recusant Chalice.

CHAMBERED TOMB: burial mound of the New Stone Age having a stone-built chamber and entrance passage covered by an earthen barrow or stone cairn. The form was introduced to Britain from the Mediterranean.

CHAMFER: surface made by cutting across the square angle of a stone block, piece of wood, etc., usually at an angle of 45 to the other two surfaces.

CHANCEL: that part of the E end

of a church in which the altar is placed, usually applied to the whole continuation of the nave E of the crossing.

CHANCEL ARCH: arch at the W end of the chancel.

CHANTRY CHAPEL: chapel attached to, or inside, a church, endowed for the saying of Masses for the soul of the founder or some other individual.

CHEVET: French term for the E end of a church (chancel, ambulatory, and radiating chapels).

CHEVRON: Norman moulding forming a zigzag.

CHOIR: that part of the church where divine service is sung.

CIBORIUM: a baldacchino (q.v.).

CINQUEFOIL: *see* Foil.

CIST: stone-lined or slab-built grave. First appears in Late Neolithic times. It continued to be used in the Early Christian period.

CLAPPER BRIDGE: bridge made of large slabs of stone, some built up to make rough piers and other longer ones laid on top to make the roadway.

CLASSIC: here used to mean the moment of highest achievement of a style.

CLASSICAL: here used as the term for Greek and Roman architecture and any subsequent styles inspired by it.

CLERESTORY: upper storey of the nave walls of a church, pierced by windows.

COADE STONE: artificial (cast) stone made in the late C18 and the early C19 by Coade and Sealy in London.

COB: walling material made of mixed clay and straw.

COFFERING: decorating a ceiling

with sunk square or polygonal ornamental panels.

COLLAR-BEAM: *see* Roof.

COLONNADE: range of columns.

COLONNETTE: small column.

COLUMNA ROSTRATA: column decorated with carved prows of ships to celebrate a naval victory.

COMPOSITE: *see* Order.

CONSOLE: bracket (q.v.) with a compound curved outline.

COPING: capping or covering to a wall.

CORBEL: block of stone projecting from a wall, supporting some feature on its horizontal top surface.

CORBEL TABLE: series of corbels, occurring just below the roof eaves externally or internally, often seen in Norman buildings.

CORINTHIAN: *see* Order.

CORNICE: in classical architecture the top section of the entablature (q.v.). Also the term for a projecting decorative feature along the top of a wall, arch, etc.

CORRIDOR VILLA: *see* Villa.

COUNTERSCARP BANK: small bank on the down-hill or outer side of a hill-fort ditch.

COURTYARD VILLA: *see* Villa.

COVE, COVING: concave under-surface in the nature of a hollow moulding but on a larger scale.

COVER PATEN: cover to a Communion cup, suitable for use as a paten or plate for the consecrated bread.

CRADLE ROOF: *see* Wagon Roof.

CRENELLATION: *see* Battlement.

CREST, CRESTING: ornamental finish along the top of a screen, etc.

CRINKLE-CRANKLE WALL: undulating wall.

CROCKET, CROCKETING: decorative features placed on the sloping sides of spires, pinnacles, gables, etc., in Gothic architecture, carved in various leaf shapes and placed at regular intervals.

CROCKET CAPITAL: *see* Fig. 5. An Early Gothic form.

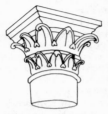

Fig. 5. Crocket capital

CROMLECH: word of Celtic origin still occasionally used of single free-standing stones ascribed to the Neolithic or Bronze Age periods.

CROSSING: space at the intersection of nave, chancel, and transepts.

CROSS-VAULT: *see* Vault.

CROSS-WINDOWS: windows with one mullion and one transom.

CROWN-POST: *see* Roof (Fig. 15).

CRUCK: cruck construction is a method of timber framing by which the ridge beam is supported by pairs of curved timbers extending from floor to ridge.

CRYPT: underground room usually below the E end of a church.

CUPOLA: small polygonal or circular domed turret crowning a roof.

CURTAIN WALL: connecting wall between the towers of a castle. In C20 architecture, a non-load-bearing wall which can be applied in front of a framed structure to keep out the weather; sections may include windows and the spans between.

CUSHION CAPITAL: *see* Block Capital.

CUSP: projecting point between the foils (q.v.) in a foiled Gothic arch.

DADO: decorative covering of the lower part of a wall.

DAGGER: tracery motif of the Dec style. It is a lancet shape rounded or pointed at the head, pointed at the foot, and cusped inside (Fig. 6).

Fig. 6. Dagger

DAIS: raised platform at one end of a room.

DEC ('DECORATED'): historical division of English Gothic architecture covering the period from *c.* 1290 to *c.* 1350.

DEMI-COLUMNS: columns half sunk into a wall.

DIAPER WORK: surface decoration composed of square or lozenge shapes.

DIAPHRAGM ARCH: *see* Arch.

DIOCLETIAN WINDOW: semi-circular, with two mullions.

DISC BARROW: Bronze Age round barrow with inconspicuous central mound surrounded by bank and ditch.

DOGTOOTH: typical E.E. ornament consisting of a series of four-cornered stars placed diagonally and raised pyramidally (Fig. 7).

DOMICAL VAULT: *see* Vault.

DONJON: *see* Keep.

Fig. 7. Dogtooth

DORIC: *see* Order.

DORMER (WINDOW): window placed vertically in the sloping plane of a roof.

DRIPSTONE: *see* Hoodmould.

DRUM: circular or polygonal vertical wall of a dome or cupola.

DUTCH GABLE: *see* Gable.

E.E. ('EARLY ENGLISH'): historical division of English Gothic architecture roughly covering the C13.

EASTER SEPULCHRE: recess with tomb-chest (q.v.), usually in the wall of a chancel, the tomb-chest to receive an effigy of Christ for Easter celebrations.

EAVES: overhanging edge of a roof.

EAVES CORNICE: cornice below the eaves of a roof.

ECHINUS: convex or projecting moulding supporting the abacus of a Greek Doric capital, sometimes bearing an egg and dart pattern.

EMBATTLED: *see* Battlement.

EMBRASURE: small opening in the wall or parapet of a fortified building, usually splayed on the inside.

ENCAUSTIC TILES: earthenware glazed and decorated tiles used for paving.

ENGAGED COLUMNS: columns attached to, or partly sunk into, a wall.

ENGLISH BOND: *see* Brickwork.

ENTABLATURE: in classical architecture the whole of the horizontal members above a column (that is architrave, frieze, and cornice) (*see* Fig. 12).

ENTASIS: very slight convex deviation from a straight line; used on Greek columns and sometimes on spires to prevent an optical illusion of concavity.

ENTRESOL: *see* Mezzanine.

ESCUTCHEON: shield for armorial bearings.

EXEDRA: the apsidal end of a room. *See* Apse.

F AN-VAULT: *see* Vault.

FERETORY: place behind the high altar where the chief shrine of a church is kept.

FESTOON: carved garland of flowers and fruit suspended at both ends. *See also* Swag.

FILLET: narrow flat band running down a shaft or along a roll moulding.

FINIAL: top of a canopy, gable, pinnacle.

FIRRED: *see* Roof.

FLAGON: vessel for the wine used in the Communion service.

FLAMBOYANT: properly the latest phase of French Gothic architecture where the window tracery takes on wavy undulating lines.

FLÈCHE: slender spire on the centre of a roof. Also called Spirelet.

FLEMISH BOND: *see* Brickwork.

FLEURON: decorative carved flower or leaf.

FLUSHWORK: decorative use of flint in conjunction with dressed stone so as to form patterns: tracery, initials, etc.

FLUTING: vertical channelling in the shaft of a column.

FLYING BUTTRESS: *see* Buttress.

FOIL: lobe formed by the cusping

(q.v.) of a circle or an arch. Trefoil, quatrefoil, cinquefoil, multifoil, express the number of leaf shapes to be seen.

FOLIATED: carved with leaf shapes.

FOSSE: ditch.

FOUR-CENTRED ARCH: *see* Arch (Fig. 1*a*).

FRATER: refectory or dining hall of a monastery.

FRESCO: wall painting on wet plaster.

FRIEZE: middle division of a classical entablature (q.v.) (*see* Fig. 12).

FRONTAL: covering for the front of an altar.

G ABLE: *Dutch gable:* a gable with curved sides crowned by a pediment, characteristic of *c.* 1630–50 (Fig. 8*a*). *Shaped gable:* a gable with multi-curved sides characteristic of *c.* 1600–50 (Fig. 8*b*).

GADROONED: enriched with a series of convex ridges, the opposite of fluting (q.v.).

GALILEE: chapel or vestibule usually at the w end of a church

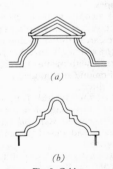

(a)

(b)

Fig. 8. Gables

enclosing the porch. Also called Narthex (q.v.).

GALLERY: in church architecture upper storey above an aisle, opened in arches to the nave. Also called Tribune and often erroneously Triforium (q.v.).

GALLERY GRAVE: chambered tomb (q.v.) in which there is little or no differentiation between the entrance passage and the actual burial chamber(s).

GARDEROBE: lavatory or privy in a medieval building.

GARGOYLE: water spout projecting from the parapet of a wall or tower; carved into a human or animal shape.

GAZEBO: lookout tower or raised summer house in a picturesque garden.

'GEOMETRICAL': see Tracery.

'GIBBS SURROUND': of a doorway or window. An c18 motif consisting of a surround with alternating larger and smaller blocks of stone, quoin-wise, or intermittent large blocks, sometimes with a narrow raised band connecting them up the verticals and along the face of the arch (Fig. 9).

GROIN: sharp edge at the meeting of two cells of a cross-vault.

GROIN-VAULT: see Vault.

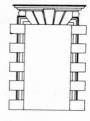

Fig. 9. 'Gibbs surround'

GROTESQUE: fanciful ornamental decoration: see also Arabesque.

HAGIOSCOPE: see Squint.

HALF-TIMBERING: see Timber-Framing.

HALL CHURCH: church in which nave and aisles are of equal height or approximately so.

HAMMERBEAM: see Roof (Fig. 18).

HANAP: large metal cup, generally made for domestic use, standing on an elaborate base and stem; with a very ornate cover frequently crowned with a little steeple.

HEADER: see Brickwork.

HERRINGBONE WORK: brick, stone, or tile construction where the component blocks are laid diagonally instead of flat. Alternate courses lie in opposing directions to make a zigzag pattern up the face of the wall.

HEXASTYLE: having six detached columns.

HILL-FORT: Iron Age earthwork enclosed by a ditch and bank system; in the later part of the period the defences multiplied in size and complexity. They vary from about an acre to over 30 acres in area, and are usually built with careful regard to natural elevations or promontories.

HIPPED ROOF: see Roof.

HOODMOULD: projecting moulding above an arch or a lintel to throw off water. Also called Dripstone or Label.

ICONOGRAPHY: the science of the subject matter of works of the visual arts.

IMPOST: bracket (q.v.) in a wall, usually formed of mouldings, on which the ends of an arch rest.

INDENT: shape chiselled out in a stone slab to receive a brass.

INGLENOOK: bench or seat built in beside a fireplace, sometimes covered by the chimneybreast, occasionally lit by small windows on each side of the fire.

INTERCOLUMNIATION: the space between columns.

IONIC: see Order (Fig. 12).

IRON AGE: in Britain the period from c. 600 B.C. to the coming of the Romans. The term is also used for those un-Romanized native communities which survived until the Saxon incursions.

J AMB: straight side of an archway, doorway, or window.

K EEL MOULDING: moulding whose outline is in section like that of the keel of a ship.

KEEP: massive tower of a Norman castle. Also called Donjon.

KEYSTONE: middle stone in an arch or a rib-vault.

KINGPOST: see Roof (Fig. 14).

KNEELER: horizontal decorative projection at the base of a gable.

KNOP: a knob-like thickening in the stem of a chalice.

L ABEL: see Hoodmould.

LABEL STOP: ornamental boss at the end of a hoodmould (q.v.).

LACED WINDOWS: windows pulled visually together by strips, usually in brick of a different colour, which continue vertically the lines of the vertical parts of the window surrounds. The motif is typical of c. 1720.

LANCET WINDOW: slender pointed-arched window.

LANTERN: in architecture, a small circular or polygonal turret with windows all round crowning a roof (see Cupola) or a dome.

LANTERN CROSS: churchyard cross with lantern-shaped top usually with sculptured representations on the sides of the top.

LEAN-TO ROOF: roof with one slope only, built against a higher wall.

LESENE or PILASTER STRIP: pilaster (q.v.) without base or capital.

LIERNE: see Vault (Fig. 23).

LINENFOLD: Tudor panelling ornamented with a conventional representation of a piece of linen laid in vertical folds. The piece is repeated in each panel.

LINTEL: horizontal beam or stone bridging an opening.

LOGGIA: recessed colonnade (q.v.).

LONG AND SHORT WORK: Saxon quoins (q.v.) consisting of stones placed with the long sides alternately upright and horizontal.

LONG BARROW: unchambered Neolithic communal burial mound, wedge-shaped in plan, with the burial and occasional other structures massed at the broader end, from which the mound itself tapers in height; quarry ditches flank the mound.

LOUVRE: opening, often with lantern (q.v.) over, in the roof of a room to let the smoke from a central hearth escape.

LOWER PALAEOLITHIC: see Palaeolithic.

LOZENGE: diamond shape.

LUCARNE: small opening to let light in.

LUNETTE: tympanum (q.v.) or semicircular opening.

LYCH GATE: wooden gate structure with a roof and open sides placed at the entrance to a churchyard to provide space for the reception of a coffin. The word *lych* is Saxon and means a corpse.

LYNCHET: long terraced strip of soil accumulating on the downward side of prehistoric and medieval fields due to soil creep from continuous ploughing along the contours.

MACHICOLATION: projecting gallery on brackets (q.v.) constructed on the outside of castle towers or walls. The gallery has holes in the floor to drop missiles through.

MAJOLICA: ornamented glazed earthenware.

MANSARD: *see* Roof.

MATHEMATICAL TILES: small facing tiles the size of brick headers, most often applied to timber-framed walls to make them appear brick-built.

MEGALITHIC TOMB: stone-built burial chamber of the New Stone Age covered by an earth or stone mound. The form was introduced to Britain from the Mediterranean area.

MERLON: *see* Battlement.

MESOLITHIC: 'Middle Stone' Age; the post-glacial period of hunting and fishing communities dating in Britain from *c.* 8000 B.C. to the arrival of Neolithic communities, with which they must have considerably overlapped.

METOPE: in classical architecture of the Doric order (q.v.) the space in the frieze between the triglyphs (Fig. 12).

MEZZANINE: low storey placed between two higher ones. Also called Entresol.

MISERERE: *see* Misericord.

MISERICORD: bracket placed on the underside of a hinged choir stall seat which, when turned up, provided the occupant of the seat with a support during long periods of standing. Also called Miserere.

MODILLION: small bracket of which large numbers (modillion frieze) are often placed below a cornice (q.v.) in classical architecture.

MOTTE: steep mound forming the main feature of C11 and C12 castles.

MOTTE-AND-BAILEY: post-Roman and Norman defence system consisting of an earthen mound (the motte) topped with a wooden tower eccentrically placed within a bailey (q.v.), with enclosure ditch and palisade, and with the rare addition of an internal bank.

MOUCHETTE: tracery motif in curvilinear tracery, a curved dagger (q.v.), specially popular in the early C14 (Fig. 10).

Fig. 10. Mouchette

MOURNERS: *see* Weepers.

MULLIONS: vertical posts or uprights dividing a window into 'lights'.

MULTIVALLATE: of a hill-fort: defended by three or more concentric banks and ditches.

MUNTIN: post as a rule moulded and part of a screen.

NAIL-HEAD: E.E. ornamental motif, consisting of small pyramids regularly repeated (Fig. 11).

Fig. 11. Nail-head

NARTHEX: enclosed vestibule or covered porch at the main entrance to a church (see Galilee).

NEOLITHIC: 'New Stone' Age, dating in Britain from the appearance from the Continent of the first settled farming communities c. 3500 B.C. until the introduction of the Bronze Age.

NEWEL: central post in a circular or winding staircase; also the principal post when a flight of stairs meets a landing.

NOOK-SHAFT: shaft set in the angle of a pier or respond or wall, or the angle of the jamb of a window or doorway.

NUTMEG MOULDING: consisting of a chain of tiny triangles placed obliquely.

OBELISK: lofty pillar of square section tapering at the top and ending pyramidally.

OGEE: see Arch (Fig. 1c).

OPEN PEDIMENT: see Pediment.

ORATORY: small private chapel in a house.

ORDER: see Fig. 12. (1) of a doorway or window: series of concentric steps receding towards the opening; (2) in classical architecture: column with base, shaft, capital and entablature (q.v.) according to one of the following styles: Greek Doric, Roman Doric, Tuscan Doric, Ionic, Corinthian,

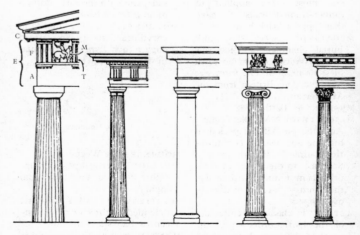

Fig. 12. Orders of columns (Greek Doric, Roman Doric, Tuscan Doric, Ionic, Corinthian)
E, Entablature; C, Cornice; F, Frieze; A, Architrave; M, Metope; T, Triglyph

Composite. The established details are very elaborate, and some specialist architectural work should be consulted for further guidance.

ORIEL: *see* Bay-Window.

OVERHANG: projection of the upper storey of a house.

OVERSAILING COURSES: series of stone or brick courses, each one projecting beyond the one below it.

OVOLO: convex moulding.

PALAEOLITHIC: 'Old Stone' Age; the first period of human culture, commencing in the Ice Age and immediately prior to the Mesolithic; the Lower Palaeolithic is the older phase, the Upper Palaeolithic the later.

PALIMPSEST: (1) *of a brass:* where a metal plate has been re-used by turning over and engraving on the back; (2) *of a wall painting:* where one overlaps and partly obscures an earlier one.

PALLADIAN: architecture following the ideas and principles of Andrea Palladio, 1508–80.

PANTILE: tile of curved S-shaped section.

PARAPET: low wall placed to protect any spot where there is a sudden drop, for example on a bridge, quay, hillside, housetop, etc.

PARCLOSE SCREEN: *see* Screen.

PARGETTING: plaster work with patterns and ornaments either in relief or engraved on it.

PARVIS: term wrongly applied to a room over a church porch. These rooms were often used as a schoolroom or as a store room.

PASSING-BRACE: *see* Roof (Fig. 16).

PATEN: plate to hold the bread at Communion or Mass.

PATERA: small flat circular or oval ornament in classical architecture.

PEDIMENT: low-pitched gable used in classical, Renaissance, and neo-classical architecture above a portico and above doors, windows, etc. It may be straight-sided or curved segmentally. *Broken Pediment:* one where the centre portion of the base is left open. *Open Pediment:* one where the centre portion of the sloping sides is left out.

PENDANT: boss (q.v.) elongated so that it seems to hang down.

PENDENTIVE: concave triangular spandrel used to lead from the angle of two walls to the base of a circular dome. It is constructed as part of the hemisphere over a diameter the size of the diagonal of the basic square (Fig. 13).

PERP(PERPENDICULAR): historical division of English Gothic architecture covering the period from *c.* 1335–50 to *c.* 1530.

PIANO NOBILE: principal storey of a house with the reception rooms; usually the first floor.

PIAZZA: open space surrounded by

Fig. 13. Pendentive

buildings; in C17 and C18 England sometimes used to mean a long colonnade or loggia.

PIER: strong, solid support, frequently square in section or of composite section (compound pier).

PIETRA DURA: ornamental or scenic inlay by means of thin slabs of stone.

PILASTER: shallow pier attached to a wall. *Pilaster Strip: see* Lesene. *Termini Pilasters:* pilasters with sides tapering downwards.

PILLAR PISCINA: free-standing piscina (q.v.) on a pillar.

PINNACLE: ornamental form crowning a spire, tower, buttress, etc., usually of steep pyramidal, conical, or some similar shape.

PISCINA: basin for washing the Communion or Mass vessels, provided with a drain. Generally set in or against the wall to the S of an altar.

PLAISANCE: summer house, pleasure house near a mansion.

PLATE TRACERY: *see* Tracery.

PLINTH: projecting base of a wall or column, generally chamfered (q.v.) or moulded at the top.

POND BARROW: rare type of Bronze Age barrow consisting of a circular depression, usually paved, and containing a number of cremation burials.

POPPYHEAD: ornament of leaf and flower type used to decorate the tops of bench- or stall-ends.

PORTCULLIS: gate constructed to rise and fall in vertical grooves; used in gateways of castles.

PORTE COCHÈRE: porch large enough to admit wheeled vehicles.

PORTICO: centrepiece of a house or of a church, with classical detached or attached columns and a pediment. A portico is called *prostyle* or *in antis* according to whether it projects from or recedes into a building. In a portico *in antis* the columns range with the side walls.

POSTERN: small gateway at the back of a building.

PREDELLA: in an altarpiece the horizontal strip below the main representation, often used for a number of subsidiary representations in a row.

PRESBYTERY: the part of the church lying E of the choir. It is the part where the altar is placed.

PRINCIPAL: *see* Roof (Figs. 14, 17).

PRIORY: monastic house whose head is a prior or prioress, not an abbot or abbess.

PROSTYLE: with free-standing columns in a row.

PULPITUM: stone screen in a major church provided to shut off the choir from the nave and also as a backing for the return choir stalls.

PULVINATED FRIEZE: frieze (q.v.) with a bold convex moulding.

PURLINS: *see* Roof (Figs. 14–17).

PUTHOLE or PUTLOCK HOLE: putlocks are the short horizontal timbers on which during construction the boards of scaffolding rest. Putholes or putlock holes are the holes in the wall for putlocks, which often are not filled in after construction is complete.

PUTTO: small naked boy.

QUADRANGLE: inner courtyard in a large building.

QUARRY: in stained-glass work, a small diamond- or square-shaped piece of glass set diagonally.

QUATREFOIL: *see* Foil.

QUEENPOSTS: *see* Roof (Fig. 16).

QUEEN-STRUTS: *see* Roof (Fig. 17).

QUOINS: dressed stones at the angles of a building. Sometimes all the stones are of the same size; more often they are alternately large and small.

R ADIATING CHAPELS: chapels projecting radially from an ambulatory or an apse.

RAFTER: *see* Roof.

RAMPART: stone wall or wall of earth surrounding a castle, fortress, or fortified city.

RAMPART-WALK: path along the inner face of a rampart.

REBATE: continuous rectangular notch cut on an edge.

REBUS: pun, a play on words. The literal translation and illustration of a name for artistic and heraldic purposes (Belton = bell, tun).

RECUSANT CHALICE: chalice made after the Reformation and before Catholic Emancipation for Roman Catholic use.

REEDING: decoration with parallel convex mouldings touching one another.

REFECTORY: dining hall; *see also* Frater.

RENDERING: plastering of an outer wall.

REPOUSSÉ: decoration of metal work by relief designs, formed by beating the metal from the back.

REREDOS: structure behind and above an altar.

RESPOND: half-pier bonded into a wall and carrying one end of an arch.

RETABLE: altarpiece, a picture or piece of carving, standing behind and attached to an altar.

RETICULATION: *see* Tracery (Fig. 22e).

REVEAL: that part of a jamb (q.v.) which lies between the glass or door and the outer surface of the wall.

RIB-VAULT: *see* Vault.

ROCOCO: latest phase of the Baroque style, current in most Continental countries between *c.* 1720 and *c.* 1760.

ROLL MOULDING: moulding of semicircular or more than semicircular section.

ROMANESQUE: that style in architecture which was current in the C11 and C12 and preceded the Gothic style (in England often called Norman). (Some scholars extend the use of the term Romanesque back to the C10 or C9.)

ROMANO-BRITISH: a somewhat vague term applied to the period and cultural features of Britain affected by the Roman occupation of the C1–5 A.D.

ROOD: cross or crucifix.

ROOD LOFT: singing gallery on the top of the rood screen, often supported by a coving (q.v.).

ROOD SCREEN: *see* Screen.

ROOD STAIRS: stairs to give access to the rood loft.

ROOF: *see* Figs. 14–18. *Single-framed:* if consisting entirely of transverse members (such as rafters with or without braces, collars, tie-beams, etc.) not tied together longitudinally. *Double-framed:* if longitudinal members (such as a ridge beam and purlins) are employed. As a rule in such cases the rafters are divided into stronger principals and weaker subsidiary rafters. *Hipped:* roof with sloped instead of vertical ends *Mansard:* roof with a double slope, the lower slope being larger and steeper than the upper. *Saddleback:* tower roof shaped like an ordinary gabled timber roof. The following members have special names: *Rafter:* roof-timber sloping up from the wall-plate to the ridge. *Principal:* principal rafter, usually corresponding to the main bay divisions of the nave or chancel below. *Wall-plate:* timber laid longitudinally on the top of a wall. *Purlins:* longitudinal members laid parallel with wall-plate and apex some way up the slope of the roof. These are side purlins and may be *tenoned* into the principal rafter, or they may be *through purlins,* i.e. resting in slots cut into the back of the principals. *Clasped purlins:* purlins held between collar-beam and principal rafter. *Collar purlin:* a lengthwise beam supporting the collar-beams, found in the context of crown-post roofs, which do not have a ridge-piece. *Tie-beam:* beam connecting the two slopes of a roof at the height of the wall-plate, to prevent the roof from spreading. *Cambered tie-beam roof:* one in which the ridge and purlins are laid directly on a cambered tie-beam; in a *firred tie-beam roof* a solid blocking piece (firring piece) is interposed between the cambere ! tie-beam and the purlins. *Collar-beam:* tie-beam applied higher up the slope of the roof. *Strut:* an upright or sloping timber supporting a transverse member, e.g. connecting tie-beam with rafter. *Post:* an upright timber supporting a lengthwise beam. *Kingpost:* an upright timber carried on a tie-beam and supporting the ridge-beam (*see* Fig. 14). *Crown-post:* an upright timber carried on a tie-beam and supporting a collar purlin, and usually braced to it and the collar-beam with four-way struts (*see* Fig. 15). *Queenposts:* two upright timbers placed symmetrically on a tie-beam and supporting purlins (*see* Fig. 16); if such timbers support a collar-beam or rafters they are *queen-struts* (*see* Fig. 17). *Braces:* inclined timbers inserted to strengthen others. Usually

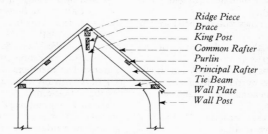

Ridge Piece
Brace
King Post
Common Rafter
Purlin
Principal Rafter
Tie Beam
Wall Plate
Wall Post

Fig. 14. Kingpost roof

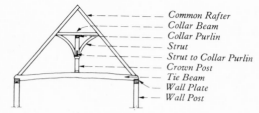

Common Rafter
Collar Beam
Collar Purlin
Strut
Strut to Collar Purlin
Crown Post
Tie Beam
Wall Plate
Wall Post

Fig. 15. Crown-post roof

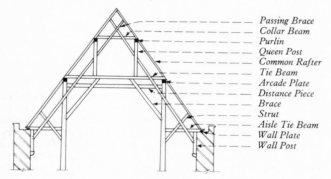

Passing Brace
Collar Beam
Purlin
Queen Post
Common Rafter
Tie Beam
Arcade Plate
Distance Piece
Brace
Strut
Aisle Tie Beam
Wall Plate
Wall Post

Fig. 16. Queen post roof

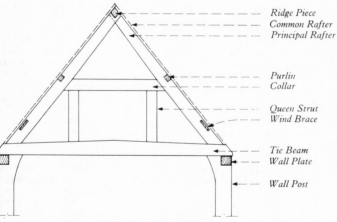

Ridge Piece
Common Rafter
Principal Rafter

Purlin
Collar

Queen Strut
Wind Brace

Tie Beam
Wall Plate

Wall Post

Fig. 17. Queen-strut roof

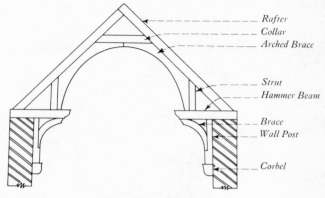

Fig. 18. Hammerbeam roof

braces connect a collar-beam with the rafters below or a tie-beam with the wall below. Braces can be straight or curved (also called arched). *Passing-brace:* a brace, usually of the same scantling as the common rafters and parallel to them, which stiffens a roof laterally by being halved across one or more intermediate timbers within its length (*see* Fig. 16). *Hammer-beam:* beam projecting at right angles, usually from the top of a wall, to carry arched braces or struts and arched braces (*see* Fig. 18). *See also* Wagon Roof.

ROSE WINDOW (or WHEEL WINDOW): circular window with patterned tracery arranged to radiate from the centre.

ROTUNDA: building circular in plan.

RUBBLE: building stones, not square or hewn, nor laid in regular courses.

RUSTICATION: *rock-faced* if the surfaces of large blocks of ashlar stone are left rough like rock;

smooth if the ashlar blocks are smooth and separated by V-joints; *banded* if the separation by V-joints applies only to the horizontals; *vermiculated,* with a texture like worm-holes.

S
ADDLEBACK: *see* Roof.

SALTIRE CROSS: equal-limbed cross placed diagonally.

SANCTUARY: (1) area around the main altar of a church (*see* Presbytery); (2) sacred site consisting of wood or stone uprights enclosed by a circular bank and ditch. Beginning in the Neolithic, they were elaborated in the succeeding Bronze Age. The best known examples are Stonehenge and Avebury.

SARCOPHAGUS: elaborately carved coffin.

SCAGLIOLA: material composed of cement and colouring matter to imitate marble.

SCALLOPED CAPITAL: development of the block capital (q.v.) in which the single semicircular

Fig. 19. Scalloped capital

surface is elaborated into a series of truncated cones (Fig. 19).

SCARP: artificial cutting away of the ground to form a steep slope.

SCREEN: *Parclose screen:* screen separating a chapel from the rest of a church. *Rood screen:* screen below the rood (q.v.), usually at the W end of a chancel.

SCREENS PASSAGE: passage between the entrances to kitchen, buttery, etc., and the screen behind which lies the hall of a medieval house.

SEDILIA: seats for the priests (usually three) on the S side of the chancel of a church.

SEGMENTAL ARCH: *see* Arch.

SET-OFF: *see* Weathering.

SEXPARTITE: *see* Vault.

SGRAFFITO: pattern incised into plaster so as to expose a dark surface underneath.

SHAFT-RING: motif of the C12 and C13 consisting of a ring round a circular pier or a shaft attached to a pier. Also called Annulet.

SHAPED GABLE: *see* Gable.

SHEILA-NA-GIG: fertility figure, usually with legs wide open.

SILL: lower horizontal part of the frame of a window.

SLATEHANGING: the covering of walls by overlapping rows of slates, on a timber substructure. Tilehanging is similar.

SOFFIT: underside of an arch, lintel, etc. Also called Archivolt.

SOLAR: upper living-room of a medieval house.

SOPRAPORTA: painting above the door of a room, usual in the C17 and C18.

SOUNDING BOARD: horizontal board or canopy over a pulpit. Also called Tester.

SPANDREL: triangular surface between one side of an arch, the horizontal drawn from its apex, and the vertical drawn from its springer; also the surface between two arches.

SPERE-TRUSS: roof truss on two free-standing posts to mask the division between screens passage and hall. The screen itself, where a spere-truss exists, was originally movable.

SPIRE: tall pyramidal or conical pointed erection often built on top of a tower, turret, etc. *Broach Spire:* a broach is a sloping half-pyramid of masonry or wood introduced at the base of each of the four oblique faces of a tapering octagonal spire with the object of effecting the transition from the square to the octagon. The *splayed foot spire* is a variation of the broach form found principally in the south-eastern counties. In this form the four cardinal faces are splayed out near their base, to cover the corners, while oblique (or intermediate) faces taper away to a point. *Needle Spire:* thin spire rising from the centre of a tower roof, well inside the parapet.

SPIRELET: *see* Flèche.

SPLAY: chamfer, usually of the jamb of a window.

SPRINGING: level at which an arch rises from its supports.

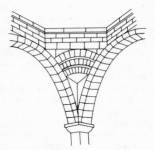

Fig. 20. Squinch

SQUINCH: arch or system of concentric arches thrown across the angle between two walls to support a superstructure, for example a dome (Fig. 20).

SQUINT: a hole cut in a wall or through a pier to allow a view of the main altar of a church from places whence it could not otherwise be seen. Also called Hagioscope.

STALL: carved seat, one of a row, made of wood or stone.

STAUNCHION: upright iron or steel member.

STEEPLE: the tower of a church together with a spire.

STIFF-LEAF: E.E. type of foliage of many-lobed shapes (Fig. 21).

Fig. 21. Stiff-leaf capital

STILTED: see Arch (Fig. 1d).

STOREY-POSTS: the principal posts of a timber-framed wall.

STOUP: vessel for the reception of holy water, usually placed near a door.

STRAINER ARCH: arch inserted across a room to prevent the walls from leaning.

STRAPWORK: C16 decoration consisting of interlaced bands, and forms similar to fretwork or cut and bent leather.

STRETCHER: see Brickwork.

STRING COURSE: projecting horizontal band or moulding set in the surface of a wall.

STRUT: see Roof.

STUCCO: plaster work.

STUDS: the subsidiary vertical timber members of a timber-framed wall.

SWAG: festoon (q.v.) formed by a carved piece of cloth suspended from both ends.

TABERNACLE: richly ornamented niche or free-standing canopy. Usually contains the Holy Sacrament.

TARSIA: inlay in various woods.

TAZZA: shallow bowl on a foot.

TERMINAL FIGURES (TERMS, TERMINI): upper part of a human figure growing out of a pier, pilaster, etc., which tapers towards the base. See also Atlantes, Caryatid, Pilaster.

TERRACOTTA: burnt clay, unglazed.

TESSELLATED PAVEMENT: mosaic flooring, particularly Roman, consisting of small 'tesserae' or cubes of glass, stone, or brick.

TESSERAE: see Tessellated Pavement.

TESTER: see Sounding Board.

TETRASTYLE: having four detached columns.

THREE-DECKER PULPIT: pulpit with clerk's stall below and reading desk below the clerk's stall.

TIE-BEAM: see Roof (Figs. 14–17).

TIERCERON: see Vault (Fig. 23).

TILEHANGING: see Slatehanging.

TIMBER-FRAMING: method of construction where walls are built of timber framework with the spaces filled in by plaster or brickwork. Sometimes the timber is covered over with plaster or boarding laid horizontally.

TOMB-CHEST: a chest-shaped stone coffin, the most usual medieval form of funeral monument.

TOUCH: soft black marble quarried near Tournai.

TOURELLE: turret corbelled out from the wall.

TRACERY: intersecting ribwork in the upper part of a window, or used decoratively in blank arches, on vaults, etc. *Plate tracery: see* Fig. 22(*a*). Early form of tracery where decoratively shaped openings are cut through the solid stone infilling in a window head. *Bar tracery:* a form introduced into England *c.* 1250. Intersecting ribwork made up of slender shafts, continuing the lines of the mullions of windows up to a decorative mesh in the head of the window. *Geometrical tracery: see* Fig. 22(*b*). Tracery characteristic of *c.* 1250–1310 consisting chiefly of circles or foiled circles. *Y-tracery: see* Fig. 22(*c*). Tracery consisting of a mullion which branches into two forming a Y shape; typical of *c.* 1300. *Intersecting tracery: see* Fig. 22(*d*). Tracery in which each mullion of a window branches out into two curved bars in such a way that every one of them is drawn with the same radius from a different centre. The result is that every light of the window is a lancet and every two, three, four, etc., lights together form a pointed arch. This treatment also is typical of *c.* 1300. *Reticulated tracery: see* Fig. 22(*e*). Tracery typical of the early C14 consisting entirely of circles drawn at top and bottom into ogee shapes so that a net-like appearance results. *Panel tracery: see* Fig. 22(*f*) and (*g*). Perp tracery, which is formed of upright straight-sided panels above lights of a window.

TRANSEPT: transverse portion of a cross-shaped church.

TRANSOM: horizontal bar across the openings of a window.

TRANSVERSE ARCH: see Vault.

TREFOIL: see Foil.

TRIBUNE: see Gallery.

TRICIPUT, SIGNUM TRICIPUT: sign of the Trinity expressed by

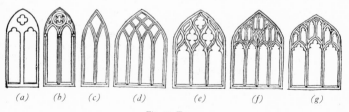

(*a*)   (*b*)   (*c*)   (*d*)   (*e*)   (*f*)   (*g*)

Fig. 22. Tracery

three faces belonging to one head.

TRIFORIUM: arcaded wall passage or blank arcading facing the nave at the height of the aisle roof and below the clerestory (q.v.) windows. (*See also* Gallery.)

TRIGLYPHS: blocks with vertical grooves separating the metopes (q.v.) in the Doric frieze (Fig. 12).

TROPHY: sculptured group of arms or armour, used as a memorial of victory.

TRUMEAU: stone mullion (q.v.) supporting the tympanum (q.v.) of a wide doorway.

TUMULUS: *see* Barrow.

TURRET: very small tower, round or polygonal in plan.

TUSCAN: *see* Order.

TYMPANUM: space between the lintel of a doorway and the arch above it.

UNDERCROFT: vaulted room, sometimes underground, below a church or chapel.

UNIVALLATE: of a hill-fort: defended by a single bank and ditch.

UPPER PALAEOLITHIC: *see* Palaeolithic.

VAULT: *see* Fig. 23. *Barrel-vault: see* Tunnel-vault. *Cross-vault: see* Groin-vault. *Domical vault:* square or polygonal dome rising direct on a square or polygonal bay, the curved surfaces separated by groins (q.v.). *Fan-vault:* late medieval vault where all ribs springing from one springer are of the same length, the same distance from the next, and the same curvature. *Groin-*

vault or *Cross-vault:* vault of two tunnel-vaults of identical shape intersecting each other at r. angles. Chiefly Norman and Renaissance. *Lierne:* tertiary rib, that is, rib which does not spring either from one of the main springers or from the central boss. Introduced in the C14, continues to the C16. *Quadripartite vault:* one wherein one bay of vaulting is divided into four parts. *Rib-vault:* vault with diagonal ribs projecting along the groins. *Ridge-rib:* rib along the longitudinal or transverse ridge of a vault. Introduced in the early C13. *Sexpartite vault:* one wherein one bay of quadripartite vaulting is divided into two parts transversely so that each bay of vaulting has six parts. *Tierceron:* secondary rib, that is, rib which issues from one of the main springers or the central boss and leads to a place on a ridge-rib. Introduced in the early C13. *Transverse arch:* arch separating one bay of a vault from the next. *Tunnel-vault* or *Barrel-vault:* vault of semicircular or pointed section. Chiefly Norman and Renaissance.

VAULTING SHAFT: vertical member leading to the springer of a vault.

VENETIAN WINDOW: window with three openings, the central one arched and wider than the outside ones. Current in England chiefly in the C17–18.

VERANDA: open gallery or balcony with a roof on light, usually metal, supports.

VESICA: oval with pointed head and foot.

VESTIBULE: anteroom or entrance hall.

VILLA: (1) according to Gwilt (1842) 'a country house for the residence of opulent persons'; (2) Romano-British country houses cum farms, to which the description given in (1) more or less applies. They developed with the growth of urbanization. The basic type is the simple corridor pattern with rooms opening off a single passage; the next stage is the addition of wings. The courtyard villa fills a square plan with subsidiary buildings and an enclosure wall with a gate facing the main corridor block.

VITRIFIED: made similar to glass.

VITRUVIAN OPENING: a door or window which diminishes towards the top, as advocated by Vitruvius, bk. IV, chapter VI.

VOLUTE: spiral scroll, one of the component parts of an Ionic column (see Order).

VOUSSOIR: wedge-shaped stone used in arch construction.

WAGON ROOF: roof in which by closely set rafters with arched braces the appearance of the inside of a canvas tilt over a wagon is achieved. Wagon roofs can be panelled or plastered (ceiled) or left uncovered. Also called Cradle Roof.

WAINSCOT: timber lining to walls.

WALL-PLATE: see Roof.

WATERLEAF: leaf shape used in later C12 capitals. The waterleaf is a broad, unribbed, tapering leaf curving up towards the angle of the abacus and turned in at the top (Fig. 24).

WEALDEN HOUSE: timber-framed house with the hall in the centre and wings projecting only slightly and only on the jutting upper floor. The roof, however, runs through without a break between wings and hall, and the eaves of the hall part are therefore exceptionally deep. They are supported by diagonal, usu-

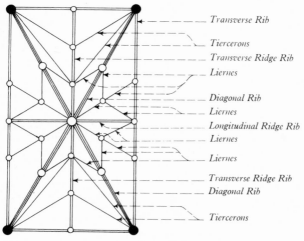

Transverse Rib

Tiercerons

Transverse Ridge Rib

Liernes

Diagonal Rib

Liernes

Longitudinal Ridge Rib

Liernes

Liernes

Transverse Ridge Rib

Diagonal Rib

Tiercerons

Fig. 23. Vault

ally curved, braces starting from the short inner sides of the overhanging wings and rising parallel with the front wall of the

Fig. 24. Waterleaf capital

hall towards the centre of the eaves.

WEATHERBOARDING: overlapping horizontal boards, covering a timber-framed wall.

WEATHERING: sloped horizontal surface on sills, buttresses, etc., to throw off water. Also called Set-off.

WEEPERS: small figures placed in niches along the sides of some medieval tombs. Also called Mourners.

WHEEL WINDOW: *see* Rose Window.

INDEX OF PLATES

INDEX OF ARTISTS

INDEX OF PLACES

ADDENDA

p. 29 [Introduction.] This sentence is as it stands ambiguous, because as a rule contributions under the second grant represent only a subsidy of about 10 per cent.

p. 40 [Introduction.] Here are some telling figures taken too late from G. Kitson-Clark: *The Making of Victorian England*, London 1962, p. 173. At Manchester, Salford, Liverpool, Bolton, Rochdale, Oldham, St Helens, Warrington, increase in accommodation in churches, 1851–80:

C. of E.	39%
Wesleyan	85%
Baptist	106%
Catholic	90%

The absolute figures, however, were still:

C. of E.	185,630 sittings
Wesleyan	64,488
Baptist	29,080
Catholic	48,798

and as for the proportion of sittings as compared with population

1851	32.8%
1880	32.2%

in spite of all the increase.

p. 121 [Heaton Norris, Lancashire Hill.] A large development for Stockport Corporation is under construction, with a twenty-two-storey block and lower buildings. Architect *J. S. Rank*, the Stockport Borough Architect.

p. 163 [Liverpool, Playhouse.] These extensions are now complete. They consist of three cylindrical elements. The largest is two storeys high and fully glazed. It is cantilevered from a central column, and partly overhangs the pavement. To the l. is a smaller cylinder, also cantilevered from a central column and also partly overhanging. It interlocks with the larger cylinder but has little glazing. The third cylinder is to the r. This is entirely enclosed and incorporates the staircase. The accommodation provided is foyer, restaurant, etc.

p. 181 [Liverpool, The Cathedrals, University, and Georgian area.] THIRD CHURCH OF CHRIST SCIENTIST, Upper Parliament Street. 1914 by *W. H. Ansell* as a Temple of Humanity.

p. 229 [Liverpool Suburbs, Kirkdale.] Some Georgian houses in GREAT MERSEY STREET.

p. 232 [Liverpool Suburbs, Mossley Hill.] DALE HALL. Another university hostel, 1958–9 by *Rolf Hellberg*.

p. 253 [Liverpool Suburbs, Walton.] STABLES FOR LIVERPOOL CORPORATION. Near the junction of Queen's Drive and Rice Lane. 1906 by *Brodie*. Much altered but still showing Brodie's remarkable pre-cast concrete construction (E. Hubbard).

p. 289 [Manchester.] BROWN STREET. No. 56, at the corner of Booth Street, was built by *Waterhouse* in 1867. It is of brick with stone dressings and has windows straight-headed or with shouldered arches. The building was pointed out to me by Mr Stuart Smith.

p. 340 [Manchester Suburbs: Strangeways Prison.] Mr Stuart Smith, in his unpublished thesis on Alfred Waterhouse, also mentions as by *Waterhouse* the Magistates' Court (now County Police Court), built in 1867.